British Interventions in Early Modern Ireland

This book offers a new perspective on Irish history from the late sixteenth to the end of the seventeenth century. Many of the chapters address, from national, regional and individual perspectives, the key events, institutions and processes that transformed the history of early modern Ireland. Others probe the nature of Anglo-Irish relations, Ireland's ambiguous constitutional position during these years and the problems inherent in running a multiple monarchy. Where appropriate, the volume adopts a wider comparative approach and casts fresh light on a range of historiographical debates, including the 'New British Histories', the nature of the 'General Crisis' and the question of Irish exceptionalism. Collectively, these essays challenge and complicate traditional paradigms of conquest and colonisation. By examining the inconclusive and contradictory manner in which English and Scottish colonists established themselves in the island, it casts further light on all of its inhabitants during the early modern period.

CIARAN BRADY is Senior Lecturer in History at Trinity College, Dublin. His previous publications include *The Chief Governors: The Rise and Fall of Reform Government in Tudor Ireland, 1536–1588* (1994).

JANE OHLMEYER is Erasmus Smith Professor of Modern History at Trinity College, Dublin. Her previous publications include *Civil War and Restoration in the Three Stuart Kingdoms* (1993), *Ireland from Independence to Occupation, 1641–1660* (1995), *Political Thought in Seventeenth-Century Ireland* (2000).

British Interventions in Early Modern Ireland

Edited by

Ciaran Brady and Jane Ohlmeyer

CAMBRIDGE
UNIVERSITY PRESS

CAMBRIDGE UNIVERSITY PRESS
Cambridge, New York, Melbourne, Madrid, Cape Town, Singapore,
São Paulo, Delhi, Dubai, Tokyo, Mexico City

Cambridge University Press
The Edinburgh Building, Cambridge CB2 8RU, UK

Published in the United States of America by Cambridge University Press, New York

www.cambridge.org
Information on this title: www.cambridge.org/9780521154604

© Cambridge University Press 2005

First published 2005
First paperback printing 2010

A catalogue record for this publication is available from the British Library

Library of Congress Cataloguing in Publication data
British interventions in early modern Ireland / edited by Ciaran Brady and
Jane Ohlmeyer.
    p. cm.
Includes bibliographical references and index.
ISBN 0 521 83530 5
1. Ireland – History – 16th century. 2. British – Ireland – History – 16th
century. 3. Ireland – History – 17th century. 4. British – Ireland – History –
17th century. I. Brady, Ciaran. II. Ohlmeyer, Jane H.
DA935.B74   2004
941.505 – dc22   2004048197

ISBN 978-0-521-83530-5 Hardback
ISBN 978-0-521-15460-4 Paperback

Contents

Contributors

ROBERT ARMSTRONG is a Lecturer in Modern History at Trinity College, Dublin. A former graduate student of Aidan Clarke's, he is currently completing a book on Protestant Ireland and the War of the Three Kingdoms.

SARAH BARBER is a Senior Lecturer, Department of History, Lancaster University. She edited (with S. G. Ellis) *Conquest and Union: Fashioning a British State, 1485–1725* (London, 1995) and authored *Regicide and Republicanism: Politics and Ethics in the English Revolution, 1646–1659* (Edinburgh, 1998) and *A Revolutionary Rogue: Henry Marten and the English Republic* (Sutton, 2000). The chapter in this volume marks a shift in the emphasis of her research from British political theory to a study of comparative European and American colonial research into prejudice in the early modern world.

TOBY BARNARD's publications include *Cromwellian Ireland* (Oxford, 1975, reprinted 2000); *The English Republic* (London, 1982, reprinted 1997); *A New Anatomy of Ireland: The Irish Protestants, 1649–1770* (New Haven, 2003); *Irish Protestant Ascents and Descents, 1641–1770* (Dublin, 2004); *The Grand Figure: Living in Protestant Ireland, 1641–1780* (New Haven, 2004). He has edited (with Jane Clark) *Lord Burlington: Arhitecture, Art and Life* (London, 1995); (with Jane Fenlon), *The Dukes of Ormonde, 1610–1745* (Woodbridge, 2000) and (with Bridget McCormack), *The Records of the Dublin Tholsel Court*. He has been fellow and tutor in modern history at Hertford College, Oxford, since 1976, and is an honorary member of the Royal Irish Academy.

CIARAN BRADY is Senior Lecturer in Modern History and a Fellow of Trinity College, Dublin. He is the author of *The Chief Governors: The Rise and Fall of Reform Government in Tudor Ireland, 1536–1588* (Cambridge, 1994) and *Shane O'Neill* (Dundalk, 1996) and the editor of a variety of works on early modern Irish history and Irish historiography.

He is currently engaged on a study of the nineteenth-century historian, James Anthony Froude.

ALAN FORD is Professor of Theology and Head of the School of Humanities at the University of Nottingham. His most recent publications are 'James Ussher and the godly prince in early seventeenth-century Ireland' in Hiram Morgan (ed.), *Political Ideology in Ireland, 1541–1641* (Dublin, 1999); '"Firm Catholics" or "loyal subjects"? Religious and political allegiance in early seventeenth-century Ireland' in D. G. Boyce, Robert Eccleshall and Vincent Geoghegan (eds.), *Political Discourse in Seventeenth- and Eighteenth-century Ireland* (London, 2001) and 'Martyrdom, history and memory in early modern Ireland' in Ian McBride (ed.), *History and Memory in Modern Ireland* (Cambridge, 2001).

RAYMOND GILLESPIE teaches in the Department of Modern History at the National University of Ireland, Maynooth, and is a member of the Royal Irish Academy. He is the author of numerous works on early modern Ireland. His books include *Colonial Ulster: The Settlement of East Ulster, 1600–1641* (Cork, 1985) and *Devoted People: Religion and Belief in Early Modern Ireland* (Manchester, 1997). He is currently working on the experience of reading and writing in early modern Ireland.

HELGA ROBINSON-HAMMERSTEIN is Senior Lecturer in Modern History at Trinity College, Dublin. She is a specialist on the early Reformation and the history of universities in the early modern period. She has translated into English and edited many Reformation pamphlets and published many papers on the history of early modern universities, university ceremonies and rituals. For the past nine years she has been the General Secretary of the International Commission for the History of Universities.

R. J. HUNTER, formerly a Lecturer in History in the University of Ulster, has written extensively on the plantation in Ulster and on its immediate Gaelic background. His recent publications include 'County Armagh: a map of plantation, c.1610' in A. J. Hughes and William Nolan (eds.), *Armagh: History and Society* (Dublin, 2001) and 'Londonderry and Coleraine: walled towns or epitome' in Gerard O'Brien (ed.), *Derry and Londonderry: History and Society* (Dublin, 1999).

PATRICK KELLY is a Senior Lecturer in Modern History at Trinity College, Dublin. He has edited *Locke on Money* (2 vols. Oxford, 1991), and has published articles on Locke and various topics in Irish political and intellectual history of the seventeenth and eighteenth centuries. He is currently preparing an edition of William Molyneux's *The Case of Ireland . . . Stated.*

BRIAN JACKSON is managing director of the Abbey Theatre, the Irish National Theatre. He is a former of student of Aidan Clarke.

BRÍD MCGRATH is an information consultant, based in Dublin. Her Ph.D. was entitled 'A biographical dictionary of the membership of the Irish House of Commons, 1640–1641'. She has published a number of articles and papers on seventeenth-century Ireland and is currently editing the Clonmel Corporation Book for the Irish Manuscripts Commission.

JANE OHLMEYER is Erasmus Smith Professor of Modern History at Trinity College, Dublin. Her books include *Civil War and Restoration in the Three Stuart Kingdoms. The Career of Randal MacDonnell, Marquis of Antrim, 1609–1683* (Cambridge, 1993; reprint Dublin, 2001); *Ireland from Independence to Occupation, 1641–1660* (ed., Cambridge, 1995); and *Political Thought in Seventeenth-Century Ireland* (ed., Cambridge, 2000). She has also co-edited *The Civil Wars. A Military History of England, Scotland and Ireland, 1638–1660* (with the late John Kenyon, Oxford, 1998), *The Irish Statute Staple Books, 1596–1687* (with Éamonn Ó Ciardha, Dublin, 1998) and *The Stuart Kingdoms in the Seventeenth Century: Awkward Neighbours* (with Allan Macinnes, Dublin, 2002). She is currently writing a book on the Irish peerage in the seventeenth century.

MICHEÁL Ó SIOCHRÚ is a Leverhulme Research Fellow (2002–4) and lectures in History at the University of Aberdeen. His doctoral thesis was supervised by Aidan Clarke at Trinity College, Dublin, and published under the title *Confederate Ireland, 1642–9: A Constitutional and Political Analysis* (Dublin, 1999). He edited *Kingdoms in Crisis: Ireland in the Seventeenth Century* (Dublin, 2001), and is currently writing a book on Oliver Cromwell and Ireland, which will be published in 2005.

HAROLD O'SULLIVAN is a local historian, who has published or contributed to several books dealing with the history of the borderlands of south-east Ulster. In addition, he has written numerous articles for local historical journals. His M.Litt. thesis was 'The Trevors of Rosetrevor a British colonial family in 17th century Ireland' (Trinity College, Dublin, 1985), while his doctoral thesis was 'Landownership changes in the County of Louth in the seventeenth century'.

GEOFFREY PARKER is Andreas Dorpalen Professor of History at Ohio State University and a Fellow of the British Academy. He is author or editor of thirty-one books, including *The Military Revolution: Military Innovation and the Rise of the West, 1500–1800* (Cambridge, 1988; rev. edn, 1996), *Empire, War and Faith in Early Modern Europe* (London, 2002) and *The Grand Strategy of Philip II* (New Haven, 1998). He is currently writing a book on the global crisis of the seventeenth century.

Acknowledgements

This collection of essays originates from a conference – 'Constituting Ireland: Relationships between Argument and Power in Early Modern Ireland' – held in Trinity College, Dublin (24–25 March 2000) in honour of Aidan Clarke. We are indebted to the participants, many of them Aidan's doctoral students, who provided intellectual stimulation in the form of papers or as informal commentators. The conference was made possible thanks to funding generously provided by the Provost of Trinity College and the Dean of the Faculty of Arts (Humanities). Michael Adams and James McGuire helped to make the proceedings particularly convivial, while Christopher Finlay and Michael Brown worked efficiently behind the scenes.

We have also incurred numerous debts as we edited this volume. The photograph of Aidan Clarke, taken during his tenure as President of the Royal Irish Academy, is reproduced with the permission of the Academy and with the assistance of Siobhán Fitzpatrick. Muriel McCarthy of Marsh's Library kindly supplied us with the image used on the front cover. We would like to acknowledge the support of our colleagues in the Department of Modern History at Trinity College, Dublin, and in the History Department at the University of Aberdeen, especially Barbara McGillvray for her secretarial assistance. We are grateful to the anonymous referees who read an early version of this typescript for Cambridge University Press and offered invaluable suggestions for improvement. Bob Hunter, Geoffrey Parker and the late Gerald Aylmer were exceptionally generous with their support. We are particularly indebted to Colm Croker, John Morrill and Micheál Ó Siochrú, who in their different ways, helped to shape this volume. Colm Croker and Sheila Kane served as model copy-editors. Bill Davies and Michael Watson from Cambridge University Press – together with our fellow contributors, Alex Green and Aoife Nic Réamoinn – can only be lauded for their patience. A word of thanks must go to the Clarke family – Oisín, Caoimhe, Subhanora and the late Ceasán – and, above all, Mary, whose generosity of spirit has captivated us all. Finally, we all owe an enormous debt of gratitude to Aidan Clarke himself. For many of us he acted as teacher and thesis supervisor; for all of us he has become a mentor and a friend. This book is for Aidan, but it is also dedicated to the memory of Ceasán.

CIARAN BRADY
JANE OHLMEYER

Aidan Clarke

Aidan Clarke: an appreciation

'What is the point of doing history?' This was the question, in equal parts liberating and unsettling, with which Aidan Clarke would regularly provoke students in his undergraduate seminar on historiography. As was so often the case with Clarke's teaching, the intent of the question was multiple. On one level it referred simply to J. H. Hexter's stimulating essay 'Doing History' which Clarke frequently recommended as among the best and the wittiest examples of the 'nuts and bolts' school of historiography, still dominant in the 1960s and 1970s. This 'practice of history' school eschewed lofty philosophical questions of meaning, purpose, correspondence and coherence as irresolvable, and recommended instead the healthy medicine of getting down to the work.

As a teacher Aidan believed that, from the outset, undergraduates should be made aware that history was not merely a receptive or an acquisitive affair, conducted through the accumulation of large bodies of fact and argument. It was to be an intensely energetic, even restless, activity, requiring more the stamina and vigour of the athlete (in his youth Clarke was no mean sportsman) than the talents of the collector and the taxonomist. Thus it has always been important to Aidan that young minds should be introduced early to the attitudes and perspectives of those who were actually engaged in the business of researching and writing history before they began on the enterprise itself.

But whether they represented their case in the no-nonsense manner espoused by G. R. Elton, or the cheerful adventuresomeness celebrated by Hexter, the practical men of affairs have never been sufficient to Clarke's understanding of history. The philosophical problems – logical, epistemological, ethical and aesthetic – were not to be so easily discounted; and for those who wished – whether undergraduates, postgraduates or colleagues or friends – Aidan was ever willing to engage in serious, but never dogmatic, argument about the best means of coping with them. It was in circumstances like these that many of those who debated with him would have noted his surprising coolness towards the viewpoint of one of the few practising historians – between R. G. Collingwood and the onset of postmodernism – to take a genuinely reflective attitude towards the writing of history, E. H. Carr. Though all of the issues raised in Carr's *What Is History?* were regarded by Clarke as central to the historian's concerns, and though there would be no argument either with the sincerity of Carr's intentions or the sophistication of his approach, what remained troubling to Clarke was Carr's ultimate surrender to relativism. Regarded by Carr as an inescapable consequence of history's insurmountable epistemological and ethical problems, this acceptance of the absence of any standard means of discrimination and validation seemed to Clarke to be an uncalled-for capitulation. It gave away too much, helplessly conceding that a serious form of discourse and dialogue might at any time degenerate into an arena for untrammelled opinion and prejudice. And worse, it surrendered powerful intellectual techniques which with sufficient care, discipline and stamina could be maintained and applied by all practitioners of historical study against all forms of assault, dogmatic or relativist. For Clarke, the acknowledged problems of history as a form of knowledge were not a warning that its claims to significance should be abandoned. Instead they offered corroboration to the far more important claim that history – imperfect as everything else in life – offered, after all, a true reflection of our universal experience of being alive in a world which we can never fully comprehend or ever hope to control. And it was this mirroring of the life of every man and woman that for all its imperfections gave to history its unique importance not merely as an intellectual pursuit, but as a moral inquiry as well.

It is this intellectual vitality, this robust confidence in history's distinctive potential to enable us to get some grasp on the most fundamental conditions of our existence, that has characterised Aidan Clarke's career as an historian in all its aspects. It is reflected first and foremost in his teaching; in the generosity of mind, spirit and (not least) time with which he entertains ideas, interpretations and temperaments which often seem less than congenial to his own personal taste. Though conversely (and fortunately rarely) it may be seen also in the promptness with which all forms of laziness and pretentiousness – intellectual and otherwise – receive dispatch. But the rule has always been simple. To all of his students, gifted or average, whose work displayed a genuine encounter with the problems and possibilities of historical work, Aidan's mind and his door are always open.

Clarke's passionate commitment to the highest standards of historical thinking is evident in his published body of work, the consistent achievement of which has been a source of wonder – and of envy – to all who have worked in his field. The characteristic features of Clarke's historical style – the meticulousness of his research methods, the sophistication of his conceptualisation, and the precision of his expression – will be familiar to all his readers. And whether they are looked for in the original and groundbreaking monographs that have enframed his career thus far, or in the commanding syntheses of early modern political, social and economic history which he contributed to the *New History of Ireland* or in his corpus of profoundly influential essays and articles, they appear with such unfailing frequency as to require no further comment.*

But two related features underlying his whole approach to writing history are particularly revealing. The first is his scrupulous concern with sequence, an insistence that the order of events as they unfolded to contemporaries should be reconstructed and followed by the historian, over the vague associations and broad-spanned generalisations which so often supply historical narratives with an account of affairs deeply deceptive in its simplicity. Underlying this resolve that the perception of the world constructed by historical figures should always be privileged above the self-justifying hindsight of the historian is no pedantic preoccupation with chronology, but rather Clarke's understanding of the distinctive importance of historical study as a whole. That is, its repeated demonstration of the imperfect and confused perceptions and motivations that have driven human beings to undertake historical change. It is this understanding of history's promise that also underlies the second characteristic of Clarke's work. This is his frequently demonstrated ability to re-conceptualise traditional historical problems, to discover and analyse within them underlying ambiguities and tensions, which were often hidden or poorly recognised not only by historians, but by history's agents themselves. Once again, however, the point of Clarke's work has not been to elevate the later historical commentator above the confusions of generations past. Rather his concern has been to show how internal conflicts, left unresolved because they were only half perceived, have yet given rise to fundamental changes which were no less inexorable because they were unintended. Clarke's is a history, then, in which contingency, ignorance and self-deception have their role to play, just as they do in our everyday life. But it is also one in which the effort to understand the manner in which such imperfections displayed by human actors at any one time functioned irreversibly to reshape their world is likewise a necessary obligation.

Clarke's conviction that history has a crucial function to play in understanding our world has gone beyond his roles as teacher, scholar and writer. It has also underpinned the immensely active – and often

* See principal publications of Aidan Clarke, pp. 357–8 below.

onerous – positions which he has assumed in the life of his university and in public life in Ireland. Whether as College tutor, or College Registrar, as Vice-Provost of Trinity College, or as head of its Department of Modern History, Aidan Clarke has played a decisive role in shaping the development of his university over several decades of enormous expansion and change. But, in addition, as a long-serving President of the Irish Historical Society, as Secretary and then President of the Royal Irish Academy, and an active contributing member to several cultural and educational bodies he has made an even larger contribution to the propagation of history as a central feature in Ireland's public culture as a whole. Such are the services that might normally be expected from a distinguished scholar and teacher. But of no less importance to Aidan in maintaining a world where the study of history is valued has been his quiet but indefatigable readiness to lecture to colleges, schools and local historical societies – to make his advice, wisdom and experience accessible to all bodies interested in historical matters in a manner that has placed so many of his contemporaries in his debt.

The selflessness and cheerfulness with which Aidan has constantly responded to the multiple demands of being an historian in Ireland are doubtless rooted in psychological recesses into which it would be presumptuous further to inquire. Yet somewhere at the back of this tireless commitment to maintain history as a pivotal element in our contemporary culture lie a particular set of forces which acted upon his age and generation. Coming to maturity in the 1950s in an era where many of the gods – national, international and religious – had lost the power to attract allegiance and belief, his was a generation that found itself faced with stark choices. There were those who elected in these circumstances for the consolations of self-indulgence, cynicism and affected existentialist despair, about whom much has already been written. But there were others who made the alternative decision to counter this ideological and ethical challenge by assuming an active address to their circumstances, by taking the risk, against the apparent odds, of resuming belief in the possibility of making the world better. Aidan Clarke was of this party. Though it was tempered by a modest recognition of the fragility of the entire undertaking, it was this resolve which attracted so many young minds to reengage critically with traditional forms of knowledge not with the aim of overthrowing them but of releasing their hitherto untapped intellectual potential. It was in these circumstances that Aidan Clarke embarked upon a career in making history relevant in Ireland, neither as a weapon for ideological argument nor a refuge for cultural despair, but as a keen intellectual tool for discovering how much and how little we can know about ourselves in time, and what sense we can derive from that knowledge. And in this he discovered his own answer to the question as to why we should be doing history for which all of us who have known him either as mentor or as exemplar are in his debt. Given the inescapable conditions under which we forsaken, contradictory and confounded creatures must serve, 'doing history' is one of the best means we have of doing life.

Conventions

Unless indicated otherwise dates throughout are given according to the Old (Julian) Calendar, which was used in Scotland, Ireland and England but not in most of continental Europe. The beginning of the year is taken, however, as 1 January rather than 25 March.

Unless otherwise stated all monetary values are sterling.

Spellings from contemporary sources have been modernised, and with proper names (especially people and places) the modern spellings have been preferred.

Abbreviations

BL	British Library, London
BL, Add. MS	Additional Manuscript
Bodl.	Bodleian Library, Oxford
Commons' Jnl, Ire	*Journals of the House of Commons of the Kingdom of Ireland* (28 vols., Dublin, 1753–91)
CRO	County Record Office
CSPI	*Calendar of State Papers relating to Ireland* (24 vols., London, 1860–1911)
CSPD	*Calendars of State Papers, Domestic Series*, 2nd Series (23 vols., London, 1858–97)
DNB	*Dictionary of National Biography*, ed. Leslie Stephen and Sir Sidney Lee (66 vols., London, 1885–1901; reprinted with corrections, 22 vols., London, 1908–9)
EHR	*English Historical Review*
HMC	Historical Manuscripts Commission
HMC, *Ormonde*	*Calendar of the Manuscripts of the Marquess of Ormonde, preserved at Kilkenny Castle* (old and new series, 11 vols., London, 1895–1920)
IHS	*Irish Historical Studies*
IMC	Irish Manuscripts Commission
JBS	*Journal of British Studies*
Lords Jnl, Ire, I	*Journal of the House of Lords of the Kingdom of Ireland* (8 vols., Dublin, 1779–1800), I (1634–98)
MS/MSS	Manuscript(s)
NAI	National Archives, Dublin, Ireland
NHI, III	T. W. Moody, F. X. Martin and F. J. Byrne (eds.), *A New History of Ireland. III Early Modern Ireland 1534–1691* (Oxford, 1976, reprinted, 1978)
NLI	National Library of Ireland
NS	New series; or, in dating, New Style
OS	Old series; or, in dating, Old Style

PRO	Public Record Office, London
PRO, E	Exchequer
PRO, SP	State Papers
PRONI	Public Record Office of Northern Ireland
RCB	Representative Church Body, Dublin
RIA	Royal Irish Academy
Sheffield, WWM	Sheffield City Library, Wentworth Woodhouse Muniments
TCD	Trinity College, Dublin

1 Making good: new perspectives on the English in early modern Ireland

Ciaran Brady and Jane Ohlmeyer

Cromwell came over, and like a lightning passed through the land.[1]

Bishop Nicholas French's dramatic, though retrospective, summary of the violent rupturing of Irish history which occurred in the middle years of the seventeenth century is so striking, so synoptic of the fundamental changes wrought during that epoch, that it has proved irresistible to writers seeking an appropriate expression to indicate a decisive terminal point signalling the end of one era and the beginning of another. Both as *terminus ad quem* and *terminus a quo* the years immediately surrounding Cromwell's campaign in Ireland have served historians remarkably well. They mark the final and well-nigh indisputable eclipse of the two great social and cultural groups whose complex interactions had determined the fundamental patterns of Irish history over the previous five centuries. As an internal political force in the land, the Gaelic Irish were now utterly destroyed, the few pockets of survival in Ulster, the midlands and in Munster which had been the *loci* of their final resistance now suppressed and their lands given over to English occupiers. The 'Old English' – as the descendants of the Anglo-Norman colonial community had for some time chosen to identify themselves – had likewise been brought low. The common fate of disempowerment, dispossession and dislocation which they were now to share with the native Irish served as an appropriate nemesis to the ambivalent and disingenuous relationship which they had deliberately maintained with their Gaelic neighbours over the previous centuries.[2]

Geoffrey Parker and, particularly, Micheál Ó Siochrú both read an early draft of this Introduction and made numerous helpful and insightful suggestions for improvement.

[1] Nicholas French, *The Unkinde Desertor of Loyall Men and True Frinds* ([Paris], 1676) reprinted in S. H. Bindon (ed.), *The Historical Works of . . . now for the first time collected* (Dublin, 1846), p. 13.

[2] Aidan Clarke, *The Old English in Ireland 1625–1642* (London and Ithaca, 1966; reprint Dublin, 2000) and 'Colonial identity in early seventeenth-century Ireland' in T. W. Moody (ed.), *Historical Studies XI. Nationality and the pursuit of national independence* (Belfast, 1978); Nicholas Canny, *From Reformation to Restoration: Ireland 1534–1660* (Dublin, 1987) and *Making Ireland British, 1580–1650* (Oxford, 2001).

At the same time, the 'old religion', the common bond of allegiance to the pope and to Roman Catholicism which had provided the strongest sinews of association between the two groups, was itself broken as a political force, its own internal divisions making it all the more vulnerable to policies of intolerance and outright persecution. The disagreements of the 1640s, which reached a head in 1648 with the papal nuncio's censure of those Catholic Confederates who supported a truce with their Protestant opponent Lord Inchiquin, painfully exposed these splits. After the Restoration the acrimony became embroiled in the 'Remonstrance Controversy', which instead of clarifying the nature of allegiance between a Protestant king and his Catholic subjects, exacerbated these divisions.[3] Only the accession of a Catholic monarch in 1685 briefly resolved the dilemma. However, by supporting James II with such enthusiasm Irish Catholics further alienated their Protestant compatriots, the English parliament and the new sovereigns who succeeded James. The Catholic strategy for survival which had centred on kingship, and the willingness of the monarch to protect them was no longer a viable option.[4]

From another perspective, however, this was an era of 'new foundations', or, more precisely, of the consolidation of other political and social groups whose grasp on power had hitherto been both uncertain and intermittent. It was in these years that the 'New English', the members of the administrative, military, legal, planting and commercial subgroups, whose common sense of identity had first been fused by the hostility and then by the vulnerability of the older communities of the island, now established their ascendancy. Redefining themselves as the 'Old Protestants' of Ireland, they were now in the process of exploiting the ambitious aspirations and practical ignorance of the Cromwellian victors, in the manner that they had once exploited the weaknesses and divisions of their Old English rivals, to establish their dominance both as landholders and as controllers of the island's institutions of local and

---

[3] Alan Ford, ' "Firm Catholics" or "loyal subjects"? Religious and political allegiance in early seventeenth-century Ireland' in George Boyce, Robert Eccleshall and Vincent Geoghegan (eds.), *Political Discourse in Seventeenth- and Eighteenth-century Ireland* (London, 2001), pp. 1–31; Micheál Ó Siochrú, *Confederate Ireland, 1642–1649: A constitutional and political analysis* (Dublin, 1999); Tadhg Ó hAnnracháin, *Catholic Reformation in Ireland: the mission of Rinuccini 1645–1649* (Oxford, 2002), especially chapters 6 and 7; James Brennan, 'A Gallican interlude in Ireland', *Irish Theological Quarterly*, 24 (1957), pp. 219–37.

[4] Aidan Clarke, 'Alternative allegiances in early modern Ireland', *Journal of Historical Sociology*, 5:3 (1992), pp. 253–66; Anne Creighton, 'The Catholic interest in Irish politics in the reign of Charles II' (Ph.D. thesis, Queen's University, Belfast, 2002).

regional administration.[5] Another more recent group whose position in Ireland at the beginning of the seventeenth century had been uncertain, the migrant Lowland Scots, now asserted their hegemony over Ulster. They consolidated their hold on extensive territories east of the Bann and deepened their penetration into the settlements established under the official plantation of central and west Ulster.[6]

The collective result of each of these developments amounted to little short of a political and social revolution: the total displacement of two hitherto dominant groups and their replacement by two new and quite different forces. Through such means and in a far more radical way than its original proponents had ever envisaged, the objective of establishing comprehensive English rule over the whole of the island which had been fought for over the previous century and a half had at last been accomplished. The political and administrative institutions of the island, its legal structures and procedures, and, most importantly of all, its means of acquiring, managing and disposing of property through sale, conveyance, mortgage, lease and inheritance, were all now established in ways that were recognisably English.[7] The aspiration of making a little England in Ireland promoted in so many ways by reformers, propagandists

---

[5] David Dickson, *New Foundations: Ireland 1660–1800* (Dublin, 1987; new revised edn, 2000); Thomas Bartlett, *The Fall and Rise of the Irish Nation. The Catholic question 1690–1830* (Dublin, 1992); T. C. Barnard, *Cromwellian Ireland. English government and reform in Ireland 1649–1660* (Oxford, 1975), 'Planters and policies in Cromwellian Ireland', *Past and Present*, 61 (1973), pp. 31–68, 'Crises of identity among Irish Protestants 1641–1685', *Past and Present*, 127 (1990), pp. 39–83 and 'The Protestant interest, 1641–1660' and 'Settling and unsettling Ireland: the Cromwellian and Williamite revolutions' in Jane Ohlmeyer (ed.), *Ireland from Independence to Occupation, 1641–1660* (Cambridge, 1995), pp. 218–40, 265–91; Karl Bottigheimer, *English Money and Irish Land. The 'Adventurers' in the Cromwellian settlement of Ireland* (Oxford, 1971), 'English money and Irish land. The "Adventurers" in the Cromwellian settlement of Ireland', *Journal of British Studies*, 7 (1967), pp. 12–27 and 'The Restoration land settlement: a structural view', *IHS*, 68 (1972), pp. 1–21; Robert Armstrong, 'Protestant Ireland and the English parliament, 1641–1647' (Ph.D. thesis, Trinity College, Dublin, 1995); L. J. Arnold, 'The Irish Court of Claims of 1663', *IHS*, 24 (1985), pp. 417–30, *The Restoration Land Settlement in County Dublin, 1660–1688* (Dublin, 1993), and 'The Cromwellian settlement of County Dublin 1652–1660', *Journal of the Royal Society of Antiquaries of Ireland*, 101 (1971), pp. 146–53.

[6] Raymond Gillespie, 'The Presbyterian revolution in Ulster, 1660–1690' in W. D. Sheils and Diana Wood (eds.), *The Churches, Ireland and the Irish*. Studies in Church History, XXV (Oxford, 1989), pp. 159–70; Philip Robinson, 'Urbanisation in north-west Ulster, 1609–1670', *Irish Geography*, 15 (1982), pp. 35–50.

[7] Nicholas Canny (ed.), *The Oxford History of the British Empire*, vol. I *Origins of Empire* (Oxford, 1998), especially the chapters by T. C. Barnard and Jane Ohlmeyer; Jane Ohlmeyer, 'Early modern Ireland and the English empire?' in Kevin Kenny (ed.), *Ireland and the British Empire* (Oxford, 2004).

and adventurers since the beginning of the sixteenth century had at last been brought to pass.[8]

For these reasons the unity and coherence of the century and a half or so stretching back from the 1650s to the earliest indications of revived English interest in Ireland under the early Tudors has seemed both obvious and unquestionable. And as long as the themes of political domination and territorial conquest remain central in the main historical narrative of the period, it is not surprising that such a periodising framework should have remained unchallenged. Yet there have always been problems underlying this neat schematisation which have occasionally given rise to some interpretative discomfort, often from quite different perspectives. Historians of the latter half of the seventeenth century, for instance, have always found little profit in attempting to seal off the central political, social and religious issues with which they must grapple from trends which were becoming quite apparent in the earlier part of the century and before.[9] And the more research advances into that most neglected segment of Irish history, the more striking its continuities with earlier periods appear.

I

The phenomenon of Catholic 'survivalism' after 1660 is particularly significant in this regard. Though apparently nullified as a major political force in the island, Catholicism remained the religion of the majority of the population and prospered despite the rabid anti-Catholicism that

---

[8] Richard Beacon, *Solon his Follie, or a Politique Discourse touching the Reformation of Commonweales . . .*, ed. Clare Carroll and Vincent Carey (New York, 1996); Andrew Hadfield and John McVeagh (eds.), *Strangers to that Land: British perceptions of Ireland from the Reformation to the Famine* (Gerrards Cross, 1994); Brendan Bradshaw, Andrew Hadfield and Willy Maley (eds.), *Representing Ireland: literature and the origins of conflict, 1534–1660* (Cambridge, 1993); Hiram Morgan (ed.), *Political Ideology in Ireland 1541–1641* (Dublin, 2000), especially the chapters by Vincent Carey, Nicholas Canny, David Edwards and Eugene Flanagan.

[9] For example, see J. C. Beckett, *Protestant Dissent in Ireland, 1687–1780* (London, 1948; reprinted, 1979), 'The Irish vice-royalty in the Restoration period', *Transactions of the Royal Historical Society*, 5th series, 20 (1970), pp. 53–73, *Confrontations in Irish History* (London, 1972) and 'The Irish armed forces, 1660–85' in John Bossy and Peter Jupp (eds.), *Essays Presented to Michael Roberts*, pp. 41–53; S. J. Connolly, *Religion, Law and Power. The making of Protestant Ireland 1660–1760* (Oxford, 1992) and S. J. Connolly (ed.), *Political Ideas in Eighteenth-century Ireland* (Dublin, 2000); James Kelly, 'The politics of the "Protestant ascendancy": County Galway 1650–1832' in Gerard Moran and Raymond Gillespie (eds.), *Galway. History and society* (Dublin, 1996), pp. 229–70 and 'Public and political opinion in Ireland and the idea of an Anglo-Irish Union, 1650–1800' in Boyce, Eccleshall and Geoghegan (eds.), *Political Discourse*, pp. 110–41.

characterised both the early 1670s and the early 1680s. Gaelic literature and culture, as the recent scholarship of Joep Leersson, Breandán Ó
Buachalla and Éamonn Ó Ciardha highlights, also flourished during the
later decades of the seventeenth century.[10] Despite the plantations and
tenurial upheavals of the early and mid-seventeenth century, a sizeable
number of Catholics, especially members of the social and economic elite,
clung on to their landed estates. Denied a political voice in the Restoration
House of Commons, Catholic lords nevertheless maintained a presence in
the upper chamber and a vocal group represented the 'Catholic interest' at
the royal court in Whitehall.[11] After 1660 recusant students flocked back
to the Inns of Court in London, where they trained as lawyers, returning to Ireland to practise alongside Patrick Darcy and Nicholas Plunkett,
themselves distinguished ex-Confederates who had trained at the Inns in
the prewar years. As in the earlier period, these lawyers continued to act as
particularly effective mediators negotiating local settlements that, at the
very least, protected Catholic interests and, where possible, exploited the
English legal system to the advantage of their native clients. Little wonder that the earl of Anglesey, writing in 1681, wanted to legislate against
'the continuance of such dangerous instruments as the popish lawyers'
whom he maintained made 'use of their learning and skill for subversion
of government and good order. So that Ireland is never like to be quiet if
they be tolerated.'[12] Equally, Old English Catholic mercantile networks,
which often dated back to the Middle Ages, became increasingly sophisticated, criss-crossing continental Europe and feeding directly into the

[10] Breandán Ó Buachalla, 'James Our True King: the ideology of Irish royalism in the
seventeenth century' in George Boyce, Robert Eccleshall and Vincent Geoghegan (eds.),
Political Thought in Ireland since the Seventeenth Century (London, 1993), pp. 1–35 and
the magisterial *Aisling Ghéar na Stíobhartaigh agus an t-aos léinn* (Dublin, 1996); Joseph
Leersson, *Mere Irish and Fíor-Ghael. Studies in the idea of Irish Nationality, its development
and literary expression prior to the nineteenth century* (Cork, 1996); Éamonn Ó Ciardha,
'Gaelic poetry and the Jacobite tradition 1688–1719', *Celtic History Review*, 2:2 (1996),
pp. 17–22; 'The Stuarts and deliverance in Irish and Scots-Gaelic literature' in S. J.
Connolly (ed.), *Kingdoms United? Great Britain and Ireland since 1500* (Dublin, 1999),
pp. 78–94; 'The unkinde deserter and the bright duke: the dukes of Ormond in the Irish
royalist tradition' in T. C. Barnard and Jane Fenlon (eds.), *The Dukes of Ormond, 1610–
1745* (London, 2000) and *Ireland and the Jacobite Cause, 1685–1766. 'A fatal attachment'*
(Dublin, 2002).
[11] Creighton, 'The Catholic interest'.
[12] [Arthur Annesley,] *A Letter from a Person of Honour in the Country* (London, 1681)
reprinted as part of James Tuchet, earl of Castlehaven, *The Earl of Castlehaven's Review*
(New York, 1974), p. 56. For the prewar years see Donal Cregan, 'Irish recusant lawyers
in politics in the reign of James I', *Irish Jurist*, 5 (winter, 1970), pp. 306–20 and Jane
Ohlmeyer, 'Irish recusant lawyers during the reign of Charles I' in Micheál Ó Siochrú
(ed.), *Kingdoms in Crisis: Ireland in the 1640s* (Dublin, 2001), pp. 63–89. Hazel Maynard's
forthcoming doctoral thesis will highlight the dynamism and tenacity of the Catholic
lawyers after 1660.

expansion of the English, French, Habsburg and even Portuguese global empires. Likewise, Catholic migrants, many of whom had been forced from their homes during the 1650s, prospered and, over time, became effective colonists, especially in the West Indies.[13]

On the earlier side of the mid-seventeenth-century divide, other sources of disquiet have also begun to emerge. In terms simply of the master narrative of conflict and dispossession alone, scholars have uncovered significant interruptions, disjunctions and contradictions which, even if they do not override it, substantially complicate the traditional account of conquest. Thus examinations of the thinking behind the reform initiative of the 1540s, or the 'composition' policies of the 1570s and 1580s, or even of the Commission for Defective Titles of the early seventeenth century, all tend to suggest a more complex approach to the aims and manner of anglicisation on the part of English political strategists than the simple account of confrontation and exploitation which the dominant narrative of conquest has allowed.[14] The effect of such work has not, of course, been to deny the reality of what actually occurred. Its principal effect, rather, has been to open up interesting and hitherto unaddressed questions as to why the complex processes involved in the attempt to make Ireland English should have been reduced to such a simple formulation.

Disjunctions and divisions among English agents in Ireland of a rather less lofty nature have also been discovered by historians. Concerns about career, factional loyalties and rivalries and private entrepreneurial opportunism coloured the policy-making process at all stages, something that

[13] Donald Harman Akenson, *If the Irish Ran the World. Montserrat, 1630–1730* (Liverpool, 1997); Martin J. Blake (ed.), *Blake Family Records 1600 to 1700* (London, 1905), pp. 106–13; Thomas M. Truxes, *Irish–American Trade 1660–1783* (Cambridge, 1988); Mary Anne Lyons, 'The emergence of an Irish community in Saint-Malo, 1550–1710' in Thomas O'Connor (ed.), *The Irish in Europe 1580–1815* (Dublin, 2001), pp. 107–26; Louis Cullen, 'Merchant communities overseas' in Louis Cullen and Christopher Smout (eds.), *Comparative Aspects of Scottish and Irish Social History* (Edinburgh, 1977), pp. 165–76. Jan Parmentier's research on the Irish merchant community in Ostend and Bruges in the late seventeenth and eighteenth centuries highlights how merchants, dispossessed during the 1640s, relocated to the southern Netherlands and enjoyed very close links with the Ostend East India Company.

[14] Ciaran Brady, *The Chief Governors. The rise and fall of reform government in Tudor Ireland*: 1536–1588 (Cambridge, 1994); S. G. Ellis, *Ireland in the Age of the Tudors 1447–1603. English expansion and the end of Gaelic rule* (London, 1998), *Reform and Revival. English government in Ireland 1470–1534* (London, 1986) and *Tudor Frontiers and Noble power: the making of the British state* (Oxford, 1995); Bernadette Cunningham, 'Political and social change in the lordships of Clanricard and Thomond, 1596–1641' (MA thesis, National University of Ireland, University College, Galway, 1979) and 'From warlords to landlords: political and social change in Galway 1540–1640' in Moran and Gillespie (eds.), *Galway. History and society*, pp. 97–130; J. G. Crawford, *Anglicizing the Government of Ireland. The Irish Privy Council and the expansion of Tudor rule, 1556–1578* (Dublin, 1993).

many of the chapters in this volume highlight.[15] The manner in which the personal ambitions or needs of principal figures in English politics, such as Robert Dudley, first earl of Leicester, influenced the conduct and shaped the outcome of policy in Ireland has been demonstrated on several key occasions.[16] Similarly, the duke of Buckingham's reckless exploitation of the machinery of Irish government in the early seventeenth century for his own aggrandisement has been revealed through the superb detective work of Victor Treadwell.[17] Such major interventions in Irish policy represented, however, only the most egregious examples of a much broader and chronic practice which shaped the operation of diplomacy, of war-making, of plantation and land settlement, and of routine administrative practices at all levels of the governing system. It need not be suggested that the sum of such private interventions was sufficient in itself to divert the main flow of English policy in Ireland, any more than it need be claimed that more sophisticated arguments as to what anglicisation implied wholly impeded the imperative that it must be proceeded with. Yet, taken together, they amount to a demonstration that the outcome of political actions was in most cases rather different from what had been originally envisaged. Consequently, the character and effects of what was actually done have been revealed to be more complex and untidy than more simple narratives based upon patterns being established and agendas being set have been inclined to concede. The history of an institution such as the Court of Wards provides a revealing instance of this process. During the early decades of the seventeenth century it became a particularly effective instrument for enriching royal coffers, and yet the Court of Wards totally failed in its original purpose as a vehicle of anglicisation and conversion. As Roger Boyle, earl of Orrery, writing in justification of its abolition, bluntly observed in 1661:

The main objection against taking down the Court of Wards is that thereby a hopeful means of converting the Irish is suppressed; but . . . there is no arguing against experiment, and we cannot find six instances in the memory of man of any converted to the Protestant religion by the education of the Court of Wards; and an English education and an Irish religion is much more dangerous than if both were Irish.[18]

---

[15] For examples, see chapters 2, 8, 9 and 14.
[16] Brady, *The Chief Governors*; Brady, 'Conservative subversives: the community of the Pale and the Dublin administration' in P. J. Corish (ed.), *Radicals, Rebels and Establishments. Historical Studies XV* (Belfast, 1985), pp. 11–32 and 'Faction and the origins of the Desmond rebellion of 1579', *IHS*, 22 (1981), pp. 289–312.
[17] Victor Treadwell, *Buckingham and Ireland 1616–1628. A study in Anglo-Irish politics* (Dublin, 1998).
[18] *CSPI, 1660–62*, p. 415; H. F. Kearney, 'The Court of Wards and Liveries in Ireland, 1622–1641', *Proceedings of the Royal Irish Academy*, 57, section C (1955–6), pp. 29–68.

Reservations that have arisen in such a relatively subtle manner in regard to the major political arguments and actions of the period become altogether more obvious in the areas of religious and social history. The salient fact in the history of religion in early modern Ireland – that the Reformation failed even as the process of political conquest triumphed – has long been familiar.[19] Yet beyond reinforcing the comforting traditional view that the hearts and minds of the native Irish were never won over though their bodies were subjugated (expressed in its most modern form in the conclusion that the project of 'making Ireland British' was in this sense a total failure) the implications of this truism have never been adequately addressed. That the Reformation's failure was due, in part, to the inherent strength and pull of traditional Catholicism throughout the island and, in part, also to the weak and half-hearted nature of initial attempts to impose it are traditional explanations that have generally received assent. Yet less attention has been given to the distinctive character of the form of religious practice and belief whose introduction into Ireland was being essayed by English administrators and ecclesiastics.[20]

A church which depended for its authority and legitimacy on the recovery and re-presentation of a distinct national tradition of Christian practice had either to work to uncover such continuities in the actual historical record of the country over which it sought authority, or else to create them artificially, whether through consensus or by force. The construction of such an Hibernian tradition to parallel the Anglican one on which the Church of England rested was from the outset, however, fraught with difficulty.[21] It possessed, in the first instance, little appeal to the

---

[19] For excellent reviews of the pre-1993 literature see 'The Church of Ireland: a critical bibliography' 'Part I: 1536–1603' by James Murray, 'Part II: 1603–41' by Alan Ford, and 'Part III: 1641–90' by James McGuire in *IHS*, 27 (1993), pp. 345–52, 352–8 and 358–62. More recent publications on the Reformation in Ireland include Samantha Meigs, *The Reformations in Ireland. Tradition and confessionalism, 1400–1690* (Basingstoke, 1997); Thomas Connors, 'Religion and the laity in early modern Galway' in Moran and Gillespie (eds.), *Galway. History and society*, pp. 131–148; and numerous works by Raymond Gillespie (see notes 23 and 24 below). Also see Helga Robinson-Hammerstein's review of Ute Lotz-Heumann's monograph on the Reformation in Ireland in *IHS*, 32 (2001), pp. 567–78.

[20] See particularly, Aidan Clarke, 'Varieties of uniformity: the first century of the Church of Ireland' in Sheils and Wood (eds.), *The Churches, Ireland and the Irish*, pp. 105–22.

[21] Alan Ford, James McGuire and Kenneth Milne (eds.), *As by Law Established. The Church of Ireland since the Reformation* (Dublin, 1995); John McCafferty, 'God bless your free Church of Ireland: Wentworth, Laud, Bramhall and the Irish convocation of 1634' in J. F. Merritt (ed.), *Power and Policy: the political world of Thomas Wentworth, earl of Strafford, 1621–1641* (Cambridge, 1996), pp. 187–208 and 'When Reformations collide' in Allan Macinnes and Jane Ohlmeyer (eds.), *The Stuart Kingdoms in the Seventeenth Century: awkward neighbours* (Dublin, 2002), pp. 186–203; Ciaran Brady and James Murray, 'Sir Henry Sidney and the Reformation in Ireland' in E. A. Boran (ed.), *Enforcing Reformation: Ireland and Scotland, 1560–1690* (forthcoming).

majority of the native Irish for whom, given the distinctive origins, character and practices of the Celtic church, it was a cultural impossibility. But, even more seriously, its implicit challenge to the old colonial community, whose claim to legitimacy in Ireland was based precisely upon the assertion of the superiority of their English religious and cultural practices over the degenerate ways of the pre-conquest Celtic church, threatened to rob it of the support of the group on whom English government in Ireland most depended. The inherent contradictions of Hibernicanism – or, in other words, of an Irish Anglicanism – created from the outset most fertile ground for the flourishing of resistance and dissent and, as several of the chapters below illustrate, were the source of the nervous and often contradictory reactions of the Reformation's proponents to the challenge presented to them by the island's indigenous Catholic majority.[22]

The flowering of dissent of a different kind, imported in the main from Scotland, has by contrast long been familiar to scholars, fuelling interpretative doubts about the assumption that the most important sources of religious conflict that had developed since 1536 had been drastically simplified along confessional lines in the century thereafter.[23] But one of the most exciting and fruitful results of recent research has been the uncovering of a more pervasive form of religious dissent arising from a growing dissatisfaction with the spiritual and pastoral defects of the churches, both Catholic and Protestant. Discovering forces of conflict and division within groups where none had been supposed to exist, and revealing similarities and associations across confessional divides, the new approach to the history of popular religion has wonderfully complicated and enriched our understanding of both the political and cultural history of the early modern period.[24]

But, above all, what this critical review of the causes of the Reformation's difficulties in Ireland has highlighted is a contradiction that lay at

---

[22] See especially chapters 4 and 5 below.

[23] J. C. Beckett, *Protestant Dissent in Ireland, 1687–1780* (London, 1948); Kevin Herlihy (ed.), *The Irish Dissenting Tradition 1650–1750* (Dublin, 1995), *The Religion of Irish Dissent 1650–1800* (Dublin, 1996), *The Politics of Irish Dissent 1650–1800* (Dublin, 1997) and *Propagating the Word of Irish Dissent 1650–1800* (Dublin, 1998); Phil Kilroy, *Protestant Dissent and Controversy in Ireland 1660–1714* (Cork, 1994); Michael Perceval-Maxwell, 'Strafford, the Ulster Scots and the Covenanters', *IHS*, 18 (1973), pp. 524–51; Raymond Gillespie, 'The reformed preacher: Irish Protestant preaching, 1660–1700' in Alan J. Fletcher and Raymond Gillespie (eds.), *Irish Preaching 700–1700* (Dublin, 2001), pp. 127–43.

[24] Raymond Gillespie, *Devoted People. Belief and religion in early modern Ireland* (Manchester, 1997) and 'Differing devotions: patterns of religious practice in the British Isles, 1500–1700' in S. J. Connolly (ed.), *Kingdoms United? Great Britain and Ireland since 1500* (Dublin, 1999), pp. 67–77; Clodagh Tait, *Death, Burial and Commemoration in Ireland, 1550–1650* (London, 2002).

the heart of the entire project of engineering social and cultural change in the island. Confident at first of the feasibility of constructing an institutional framework for the reform and propagation of faith in Ireland similar to that in England, the reformers had simultaneously recognised the necessity of ensuring that their endeavours marked no radical historical caesura, but were in strict continuity with the underlying patterns of history. Not for propagandist purposes only, but genuinely to vouchsafe the legitimacy of their mission, they were required to show that their apparent assault on an existing set of institutions was not merely destructive, but an essential part of a programme of reconstruction which, when finally completed, would recover from obscurity the true continuities persisting within. In order to justify their mission of doing good, they were charged with the responsibility of making good. The reformers' dilemma, caught between the desire to change some malign prevailing practices and the need to preserve others in a manner which would validate and legitimate their efforts, was paralleled by the experience of those whose desire both to institute and to control social change was inspired by motives rather less noble: the men on the make.

II

Of all the interpretative challenges presented to it, the paradigm of conquest and expropriation has best been able to explain the motivations and actions of the parvenu. The planters who gained possession of attainted native lands, the soldiers who made their fortunes exploiting their office, using martial law or sheer terror to extort the unfortunates under their rule, the lawyers and administrators who used the knowledge and privileges of the law to secure extensive estates for themselves, collectively embodied the most powerful force of aggressive social change in Ireland in the later sixteenth and seventeenth centuries.[25] Research into their

---

[25] Hugh Kearney, *Strafford in Ireland 1633–41. A study in absolutism* (Manchester, 1959; Cambridge, 1989); Terence Ranger, 'Richard Boyle and the making of an Irish fortune', *IHS*, 10 (1957), pp. 257–97 and 'Strafford in Ireland: a revaluation' in Trevor Aston (ed.), *Crisis in Europe 1560–1660. Essays from Past and Present* (London, 1965), pp. 271–93; Karl Bottigheimer, 'Kingdom and colony: Ireland in the Westward Enterprise 1536–1660' in K. R. Andrews, N. P. Canny and P. E. H. Hair (eds.), *The Westward Enterprise. English activities in Ireland, the Atlantic and America 1480–1650* (Liverpool, 1978), pp. 45–65; Nicholas Canny, 'Dominant minorities: English settlers in Ireland and Virginia, 1550–1650' in A. C. Hepburn (ed.), *Minorities in History. Historical Studies XII* (Belfast, 1978), pp. 17–44, 'The permissive frontier: social control in English settlements in Ireland and Virginia, 1550–1650' in Andrews *et al.* (eds.), *The Westward Enterprise*, pp. 17–44; Nicholas Canny, *The Upstart Earl: a study of the social and mental world of Richard Boyle, first earl of Cork, 1566–1643* (Cambridge, 1982) and *Kingdom and Colony. Ireland in the Atlantic world 1560–1800* (Baltimore, 1988); Rolf Loeber, *The Geography and Practice of English*

operations has been extensive, imaginative, and often ingenious. It has conclusively demonstrated just how powerful this group became, how deeply they penetrated into every aspect of Irish social and economic life, and how extraordinary was their influence in shaping the course of Anglo-Scottish relations, Anglo-Irish relations, and even English political developments over the course of the seventeenth century.

Yet the very extent and apparent conclusiveness of the success of this group – denominated severally and somewhat nervously by historians as the 'New English', the 'Old Protestants' and the 'Anglo-Irish' – has helped obscure the manner in which it was achieved. The seriousness and complexity of the obstacles that they faced in pursuing their ambitions has often been underestimated. Likewise, the manner in which they were required to adapt their strategies, the compromises they made and the extent to which, even as they succeeded, they were compelled to accept defeat on certain key issues have received insufficient attention. Historians of the eighteenth century have long been conscious of the external challenges and internal contradictions that shaped the character of the so-called 'Protestant nation'.[26] But it has not always been recognised that the same forces were at work upon the forebears of this community, even at the time of their greatest advances. At one level, Richard Boyle, the 'upstart' earl of Cork, represents a classic example of a 'man on the make' who combined public service with private gain. Arriving virtually penniless in Ireland in the late 1580s, he was to become, through a variety of entrepreneurial activities, sharp practices and dubious land deals, one of the richest men in Ireland, enjoying by 1641 an annual income of £18,000.[27] Yet his spectacular successes can, at least in part, be attributed to his willingness to make a series of compromises as he negotiated and then renegotiated his position at the local, provincial and national levels. His children and grandchildren married into ancient local families; Catholic legal advisers helped him to manage his vast territorial and business empires; and his political allies included powerbrokers from across the religious divide. He even recognised the need to acquire a genuine interest in Irish culture, language and history, if only to adapt them to suit his own ends.[28]

Colonisation in Ireland 1534 to 1609 (Athlone, 1991), *A Biographical Dictionary of Architects in Ireland 1600–1720* (London, 1981), and 'Settlers' utilisation of the natural resources' in Ken Hannigan and William Nolan (eds.), *Wicklow. History and society* (Dublin, 1994), pp. 267–304.

[26] Tony Claydon and Ian McBride (eds.), *Protestantism and National Identity. Britain and Ireland c.1650–c.1850* (Cambridge, 1998).

[27] A. B. Grosart (ed.), *The Lismore Papers*, 2nd series (5 vols., 1888) and Canny, *The Upstart Earl*.

[28] Canny, *The Upstart Earl*, pp. 126–8.

Certain failures, to be sure, have always been obvious. The difficulties encountered by the royal plantation in mid-Ulster in securing settlers, in developing holdings and in dealing with the displaced and dispossessed native population have been the subject of detailed investigations.[29] But assessments of the degree and significance of this failure have frequently been moderated both by demonstrations of the manner in which this botched official project was overtaken by successful Scottish, English and Irish entrepreneurs, and by awareness of the final defeat and elimination of the native Irish inhabitants as an independent political force in the years after mid-century.[30] It was, of course, the manifest weakness of the native Irish, not only in Ulster but everywhere else in the island, in face of the New English assault from the late sixteenth century onwards that, more than any other factor, seemed to underpin the notion of an unrelenting colonial conquest. The successful exploitation by New English adventurers of the Gaelic lordships' internecine rivalries, military weakness and fragile tenurial status either through overt attack and plantation or piecemeal expropriation has long featured as a central theme in the political and social history of the period. And the effect of much recent richly documented work on Gaelic lordships in Leinster, Connacht and,

---

[29] T. W. Moody, *The Londonderry Plantation 1609–1641. The city of London and the plantation in Ulster* (Belfast, 1939); Jane Ohlmeyer, 'Strafford, the "Londonderry Business" and the "New British History"' in Merritt (ed.), *The Political World of Thomas Wentworth*, pp. 209–29; Raymond Gillespie, *Colonial Ulster. The settlement of East Ulster 1600–41* (Cork, 1985); Michael Perceval-Maxwell, *The Scottish Migration to Ulster in the Reign of James I* (London, 1973); Philip Robinson, *The Plantation of Ulster* (Dublin, 1984), *East Ulster, 1600–1641* (Cork, 1985), and 'The Ulster plantation and its impact on the settlement pattern of County Tyrone' in Charles Dillon and Henry Jefferies (eds.), *Tyrone. History and society* (Dublin, 2000), pp. 233–66; A. J. Sheehan, 'Official reaction to native land claims', *IHS*, 92 (1983), pp. 297–318; R. J. Hunter, 'Plantation in Donegal' in William Nolan, Liam Ronayne and Mairead Dunlevy (eds.), *Donegal. History and society* (Dublin, 1995), pp. 283–324, 'County Armagh: a map of plantation, c.1610' in A. J. Hughes and William Nolan (eds.), *Armagh. History and society* (Dublin, 2001), pp. 265–94, 'Londonderry and Coleraine: walled towns or epitome' in Gerard O'Brien (ed.), *Derry and Londonderry. History and society* (Dublin, 1999), pp. 259–78 and 'Ulster plantation towns 1609–1641' in David Harkness and Mary O'Dowd (eds.), *The Town in Ireland* (Belfast, 1991), pp. 55–80; William Roulston, 'The Ulster Plantation in the manor of Dunnalong, 1610–70' in Dillon and Jefferies (eds.), *Tyrone*, pp. 267–90. See also chapter 6.

[30] Nicholas Canny, 'Hugh O'Neill, earl of Tyrone, and the changing face of Gaelic Ulster', *Studia Hibernica*, 10 (1970), pp. 7–35, 'The treaty of Mellifont and the reorganisation of Ulster, 1603', *Irish Sword* (1970), pp. 249–62, 'The flight of the earls', *IHS*, 17 (1971), pp. 380–99; Hiram Morgan, 'The end of Gaelic Ulster: a thematic interpretation of events between 1534 and 1610', *IHS*, 26 (1988), pp. 8–32 and 'Extradition and treason-trial of a Gaelic lord: the case of Brian O'Rourke', *Irish Jurist*, 22 (1987), pp. 285–301; Ciaran Brady, 'Sixteenth-century Ulster and the failure of Tudor reform' in Ciaran Brady, Mary O'Dowd and Brian Walker (eds.), *Ulster. An illustrated history* (London, 1989), pp. 77–103 and *Brady, Shane O'Neill* (Dundalk, 1996).

above all, in Ulster has been to confirm this traditional account of the way in which the great Gaelic lordships were brought to ruin.[31]

From among the descendants of the original Anglo-Norman colonials, represented by the great provincial feudal dynasties, the *arrivistes* encountered stiffer opposition. Modern historians have sometimes noted that it was against these older colonisers rather than the Gaelic Irish that the principal hostility of the newcomers was directed.[32] Thus by the middle of the 1580s the great Fitzgerald lordship of Desmond in Munster was destroyed and its lands distributed to English investors.[33] Two decades later the once invulnerable house of Ormond was under serious attack made possible by the family's own internal squabbles and the fact that the tenth earl outlived his sons. But, it is important to recall, the house of Ormond survived its dynastic crisis and James, twelfth earl and later first duke, went on to dominate Irish affairs from the 1640s until the mid-1680s.[34] It is worth noting also that the Fitzgerald house of Kildare, itself afflicted by a similar and more chronic set of succession crises in the late sixteenth and early seventeenth centuries, likewise survived, in part thanks to the earl of Cork's determination in the 1630s to 'employ all my best endeavours, to reduce [the Kildare lineage] to its former lustre'.[35]

Elsewhere other representatives of the old colonial families, such as the Burkes of Clanricard and the Barrys and Roches of Munster, not only survived, but recovered from the parlous state they had endured in the

---

[31] Rolf Loeber, 'The changing borders of Ely O'Carroll lordship' in William Nolan and Timothy P. O'Neill (eds.), *Offaly. History and society* (Dublin, 1998), pp. 287–318; Patrick Duffy, David Edwards and Elizabeth Fitzpatrick (eds.), *Gaelic Ireland. Land, lordship and settlement c.1250–c.1650* (Dublin, 2001); K. W. Nicholls, *Gaelic and Gaelicised Ireland in the Later Middle Ages* (Dublin, 1972) and *Land, Law and Society in Sixteenth-century Ireland* (Dublin, 1976); Mary O'Dowd, *Power, Politics and Land. Early Modern Sligo 1568–1688* (Belfast, 1991); Bernadette Cunningham, 'The composition of Connacht in the lordships of Clanricard and Thomond, 1577–1641', *IHS*, 24 (1984), pp. 1–14 and 'Native culture and political change in Ireland, 1580–1640' in Ciaran Brady and Raymond Gillespie (eds.), *Natives and Newcomers. The making of Irish colonial society 1534–1641* (Dublin, 1986), pp. 148–70.

[32] Clarke, *Old English in Ireland* and *The Graces, 1625–41* (Dundalk, 1968).

[33] Michael MacCarthy-Morrogh, *The Munster Plantation: English migration to southern Ireland, 1583–1641* (Oxford, 1986).

[34] David Edwards, 'The Ormond lordship in County Kilkenny, 1515–1642' (Ph.D. thesis, Trinity College, Dublin, 1998) and 'The poisoned chalice: the Ormond inheritance, sectarian division and the emergence of James Butler, 1614–1642' in Toby Barnard and Jane Fenlon (eds.), *The Dukes of Ormond, 1610–1745* (London, 2000), pp. 55–82; William Neely, 'The Ormond Butlers of County Kilkenny' in William Nolan and Kevin Whelan (eds.), *Kilkenny. History and society* (Dublin, 1990), pp. 107–26.

[35] PRONI, Kildare Letter Book, D3078/3/1/5, p. 3. Vincent Carey, *Surviving the Tudors: The 'wizard' earl of Kildare and English rule in Ireland, 1537–1586* (Dublin, 2002) and Patrick Little, 'The Geraldine ambitions of the first earl of Cork', *IHS*, 23 (2002), pp. 151–68.

sixteenth century to enjoy by 1640 positions of genuine influence.[36] Several of the lesser Old English noble families of the Pale, such as the Nugents, the Dillons, the Barnewalls and the Flemings, had established positions of wealth and regional influence by that date far greater than they had held a century before.[37] More interesting still, despite the tenurial upheavals and warfare of the mid-seventeenth century, many of these families re-emerged in the 1670s with their lands and local power relatively intact. For example, the active involvement of the Barnewalls of Trimleston in the Confederation of Kilkenny did not preclude their involvement in post-Restoration County Meath politics or prevent them from increasing their landed holdings (roughly 4,000 acres in Counties Meath, Dublin and Galway). Writing in 1686, Robert, ninth baron, explained to his son how he had 'taken a great deal of pains to acquire the most part of this estate for you', adding 'I have also made some considerable improvements thereon.'[38] In the instances of other lesser Old English aristocratic families, a connection with Ormond often proved the key to their economic and political survival after 1660. Ormond regularly intervened on behalf of his kinsmen, protecting the estates and interests of minor Butler houses (the Mountgarrets, Dunboynes, Galmoys and Ikerrins), together with other Catholic dynasties with whom he was allied by marriage (especially the Fingals, the Clancarthys and the Clanricards).[39]

Ormond's achievements in the years after 1660 built upon the less well known but equally important restructuring of the old colonial community that took place in the first half of the seventeenth century. This was

---

[36] Bernadette Cunningham, 'Clanricard Letters: letters and papers, 1605–1673, preserved in the National Library of Ireland manuscript 3111', *Journal of the Galway Archaeological and Historical Society*, 48 (1996), pp. 162–208; Patrick Little, 'Family and faction: the Irish nobility and the English court, 1632–42' (M.Litt. thesis, Trinity College, Dublin, 1992) and ' "Blood and friendship": the earl of Essex's protection of the earl of Clanricarde's interests, 1641–6', *EHR*, 112 (1997), pp. 927–41; Thomas Connors, 'The impact of English colonial expansion on Irish culture: the clergy, popular religion, and the transformation of the family in early modern Galway' (Ph.D. thesis, Urbana, Ill., 1997).

[37] John Kingston, 'Catholic families of the Pale', *Reportorium Novum: Dublin Diocesan Historical Record*, 1:2 (1956), pp. 323–50 and 2:2 (1960), pp. 236–56; Gerald Dillon, 'The Dillon peerages', *Irish Genealogist*, 3:3 (1958), pp. 87–100; Stephen B. Barnwell, 'The Barnewell family during the sixteenth and seventeenth centuries', *Irish Genealogist*, 3:8 (1963), pp. 311–21.

[38] Terence O'Donnell, 'Lord Trimleston's advice of his son – a fragment', *Riocht na Midhe*, 3:2 (1964), p. 152. Also see Barnwell, 'The Barnewell family', pp. 311–21.

[39] Eleanor O'Keeffe, 'The family and marriage strategies of James Butler, 1st Duke of Ormonde, 1658–1688' (Ph.D. thesis, Cambridge, 2000); John Prendergast, 'The Butlers, Lords Ikerrin, before the Court of Transplantation at Athlone, AD 1656, and at the second Court of Claims', *Butler Society Journal*, 3 (1987), pp. 72–6; Sean O'Brien, 'The Butlers of Lower Grange, Viscounts Galmoy', *Old Kilkenny Review, Journal of the Kilkenny Archaeological Society*, 16 (1964), pp. 16–23; John Kingston, 'Lord Dunboyne', *Reportorium Novum Dublin Diocesan Historical Record*, 3:1 (1961–2), pp. 62–82.

a major process whose significance – indeed, whose very existence – has been obscured by high-profile catastrophes such as the Kildare rebellion, the fall of the house of Desmond and the attainder of Viscount Baltinglass, and deflected by such equally striking developments such as the rise of Richard Boyle, earl of Cork. The dominant paradigm of conquest and colonisation has also tended to obscure the enlargement and internal development of the Irish nobility which was a broad and complex phenomenon involving Old English, Gaelic Irish and their New English rivals.[40] Of the great attainders mentioned above, only Desmond's proved irreversible, and though the failure of attempts to co-opt the great Gaelic lords into an anglicised nobility was common, notable exceptions could be identified among the O'Briens of Thomond and Inchiquin, the Fitzpatricks of Upper Ossory and the Magennises of Iveagh.[41] Meanwhile, the breadth of the process was indicated by the incorporation into the Irish peerage of the old Scottish enemy from the Western Isles, the MacDonnell, created earl of Antrim in 1620.[42]

In fact, during the first three decades of the seventeenth century, the crown bestowed 258 new Irish knighthoods, 'of which just under a third was awarded to men of Old English or Irish name'.[43] Between 1603 and 1640 the resident Irish aristocracy more than doubled, from twenty-nine peers to sixty-nine. The number of Catholic lords rose, while the number of Protestant peers increased tenfold, from three to over thirty-six. Thus the crown created a 'service nobility', a new generation of ambitious and avaricious peers, who were determined either to consolidate their patrimonies and political influence or to make their fortunes in Ireland and to secure public reward and social recognition.[44] Though it might sometimes be seen simply as part of 'the inflation of honours' of early Stuart Britain, the development of an Irish nobility was a process that had long been under way as part of the series of major policy initiatives introduced under the aegis of the Kingdom of Ireland Act in 1541. To make

[40] G. R. Mayes, 'The early Stuarts and the Irish peerage', *EHR*, 73 (1958), pp. 227–51.

[41] Donough O'Brien, *History of the O'Briens* (London, 1949); Ivar O'Brien, *The O'Briens of Thomond. The O'Briens in Irish history 1500–1865* (Chichester, 1986); John A. Murphy, 'Inchiquin's changes of religion', *Journal of Cork Historical and Archaeological society*, 72 (1967), pp. 58–68; John Ainsworth (ed.), *Inchiquin Manuscripts* (IMC, Dublin, 1961); Harold O'Sullivan, 'The Magennis lordship of Iveagh in the early modern period, 1534 to 1691' in Lindsay Proudfoot (ed.), *Down. History and Society* (Dublin, 1997), pp. 159–202; David Edwards, 'Collaboration without anglicisation: the MacGiollapadraig lordship and Tudor reform' in Duffy, Edwards and Fitzpatrick (eds.), *Gaelic Ireland*, pp. 77–97; Brian Ó Dálaigh, 'A comparative study of the wills of the first and fourth earls of Thomond', *North Munster Antiquarian Journal*, 34 (1992), pp. 48–63.

[42] Jane Ohlmeyer, *Civil War and Restoration in the Three Stuart Kingdoms: the political career of Randal MacDonnell, First Marquis of Antrim (1609–83)* (Cambridge, 1993; paperback reprint Dublin, 2001), p. 21.

[43] Treadwell, *Buckingham and Ireland*, pp. 105–6.   [44] *Ibid.*, p. 299.

a reality out of this constitutional aspiration, the elements of a genuine kingly polity had to be constructed, and the reform and extension of the Irish nobility became from the outset an essential part of this process of political, social and administrative reconstruction.

The very existence of an indigenous Irish nobility, however fragile and heterogeneous, unstable and internally divided, presented newcomers to the kingdom with a challenge that worked on several levels: social, political, governmental and even constitutional. The challenge of social competition was ostensibly the most serious, yet it became the least complex as time wore on. Recent researches on elite family histories have revealed that, while both sides remained ambivalent when presented with the possibility of social integration, and some rejected it, marriage across the religious divide proved remarkably widespread amongst the aristocracy in Ireland and the decision to engage in it was a very conscious and carefully calculated one.[45] Old English and Gaelic spouses brought the newcomers rank and social status. Thus Protestant peers intermarried with insolvent native aristocratic families with a view to consolidating and expanding their territorial empires while, at the same time, creating an ancient and distinguished lineage for their recently ennobled line. The marriages that the first earl of Cork negotiated with the houses of Barrymore, Curraghmore and Kildare are, as Nicholas Canny and Patrick Little have shown, excellent examples of this.[46]

Other members of the Boyle dynasty adopted similar strategies during the later seventeenth century, as did other Protestant powerbrokers. For example, the children of Arthur Annesley, earl of Anglesey, intermarried with prominent, albeit impoverished, Catholic peers. In return for helping the childless marquis of Antrim to secure the restoration of his Ulster estates and to alleviate some of his more pressing debts, Anglesey arranged the marriage of Elizabeth, one of his daughters, to Antrim's heir and brother, Alexander. Since Elizabeth died without producing a male heir, Annesely's return on this investment was a poor one.[47] At least the match in 1654 between his eldest daughter, Dorothy, and Richard Power, fifth Baron Le Power (Annesley had served as guardian to Richard's lunatic

---

[45] Donald Jackson, *Intermarriage in Ireland 1550–1650* (Montreal, 1970). Contemporary commentators repeatedly highlighted the very real links of kinship that united Irish society on the eve of the rebellion. Or, in the words of Sir John Temple, Irish society formed 'one body, knit and compacted together with all those bonds and ligatures of Friendship, Alliance, and Consanguinity as might make up a constant and perpetual union between them', Sir John Temple, *The Irish Rebellion . . .* (London, 1679), pp. 27–8.

[46] Little, 'Geraldine ambitions'; Canny, *The Upstart Earl*, p. 44.

[47] George Hill, *An Historical Account of the MacDonnells of Antrim* (Belfast, 1873), p. 361.

father), provided a male heir. Annesley used his influence initially with the Cromwellians and later with Charles II to safeguard the family's County Waterford estates and to secure first a viscountcy and then the earldom of Tyrone for his Catholic son-in-law who, when he was later implicated in the Popish Plot, protested his Protestantism.[48] Thanks no doubt to his grandfather's influence, Tyrone's son, John Lord Decies, conformed to the established church. To expand even further the family's territorial empire, Annesley also insisted that the eight-year-old John marry his twelve-year-old first cousin (and Annesley's ward), Catherine, heiress to the vast territory of the Decies.

Of course, these intermarriages left the Old Protestants vulnerable to charges of degeneracy, just as unions between the Old English and native Irish had once provoked the scorn of earlier commentators.[49] Distasteful as these unions were to some, they nevertheless helped to forge a real sense of community, especially among the landed elite. Already well established by 1641, these cross-ethnic and interdenominational alliances survived the upheavals of the 1640s and 1650s. In a report to Rome in 1670 the Catholic primate, Oliver Plunkett, illustrated the manner in which intermarriage had served to foster tolerance and social cohesion in his own diocese. Invited to dinner by the countess of Drogheda, he noted that her daughter Penelope had married a Catholic lord in 1665 and that the countess's own husband 'although a Protestant, has not a single Protestant in his whole estate, and he has handed over all the churches to my priests and Mass is said publicly'. And again, the primate noted with pleasure that 'The earl of Charlemont treats me with great respect, so that I am able to appear publicly in every part of my diocese as in Dublin, unmolested. I have already written to you that the Protestant primate [Michael Boyle] gave me permission to have Catholic school teachers in my diocese.'[50] Only the onset of the Popish Plot in the late 1670s soured these harmonious relations.

If an indigenous nobility at times presented a social and economic challenge to the newcomers' ambitions which was not to be met by simple

---

[48] HMC, *Report 11. Appendix 2* (London, 1887), p. 218; *The Information of Hubert Bourk, Gent., touching the popish plot in Ireland, carried on by the conspiracies of the Earl of Tyrone...* (London, 1680).

[49] For example, see Charles Vallancey, *Collectanea de Rebus Hibernicis; or Tracts Relative to the History and Antiquities of Ireland* (4 vols., Dublin, 1786), I, p. 105.

[50] John Hanly (ed.), *The Letters of Saint Oliver Plunkett, 1625–1681, Archbishop of Armagh and Primate of All Ireland* (Dublin, 1979), p. 127. The earl of Charlemont to whom the archbishop refers was William Caulfield, the younger brother of the unfortunate Toby who had been murdered in 1641. William had married a daughter of Charles, second Viscount Moore of Drogheda.

confrontation, it also held out a set of political and administrative obstructions at both local and central levels which required an equally judicious response. To make good on their economic and social gains, New English adventurers found it necessary to gain control of those instruments of local and regional administration which would normally be expected to be under the influence of the provincial nobility. This they had achieved by the early seventeenth century by deft use of the oath of supremacy and their superior influence in the legal and administrative offices of central government. But the real effectiveness of their control was severely tested and shown wanting on several occasions before its full exposure in 1641.[51] Even after the Restoration, given the precarious nature of royal finances and in the absence of an army to coerce the population or of a significant body of bureaucrats to administer them, the Stuart monarchs found it hard to rule the 'dark corners of the land' and depended on securing the goodwill and cooperation of regional powerbrokers, whatever their religion.[52] This compromise that the co-option of the Catholic elite represented might have proved distasteful to some Protestants, but it nevertheless reflects the realities involved in ruling seventeenth-century Ireland.

What was true of regional and local administration was shown to be equally so at central levels when the summoning of a parliament was deemed necessary. Here again the privileged position of the New English officials would appear to have granted them significant political and managerial advantages over the peers and the constituency members. But, once more, closer examination of the history of Irish parliaments from the late sixteenth century to the middle of the seventeenth century reveals a more complex story. James I had created forty parliamentary boroughs out of the newly founded plantation towns with the specific intention of packing the 1613 Irish House of Commons with Protestant MPs and thereby diluting the Old English influences which had predominated in all earlier parliaments. Yet the Old English MPs managed to thwart the government's plans in 1613. Much to the king's disgust and the embarrassment of Lord Deputy Chichester, they disrupted the opening session by disputing the legality of the Protestant majority and becoming involved in an unseemly scuffle to replace the government nominee for speaker with their own candidate, Sir John Everard. When Everard was ejected, the

---

[51] For example, worried by the strategic threat that Catholic Ireland represented after 1624 as the English state mobilised for war against Spain, the government increased the English military presence there. Yet funding these troops proved impossible until the king made a series of significant concessions, known as the 'Graces' (1628), to an Irish delegation, dominated by Old English representatives, Clarke, *The Graces, 1625–41*.

[52] Ohlmeyer, *Civil War and Restoration*, p. 289.

opposition, egged on by the Old English peers, then withdrew, effectively sabotaging proceedings.[53]

Determined not to repeat Chichester's mistakes, Lord Deputy Wentworth adopted very different tactics in the parliament which met in 1634. In the lower house the government secured a clear majority with 142 Protestant MPs, many of them recent planters, together with a high number of office-holders and non-residents. New temporal creations, many of whom were non-resident, gave the government control of the upper house for the first time. To consolidate further his position, Wentworth also forged an alliance with the Old English activists during the early weeks of the parliament, which saw the passage of the subsidy bills and other important legislation. However, the lord deputy's refusal to enshrine the 'Graces' in statute quickly shattered this uneasy coalition, and while Wentworth succeeded in pushing through the government's agenda, he alienated in the process key members of the Old English community. Equally, Wentworth's ruthless pursuit of 'thorough' government, which often excluded New English planters from administrative office or challenged their titles to land, alienated many Protestant power-brokers. Despite the lord deputy's best attempts to repeat this strategy in the parliament which assembled in March 1640, his political enemies now allied against him. Working closely with their patrons in the Dublin upper house and their allies in Westminster, this cross-denominational coalition finally secured the chief governor's downfall.[54] Charles II's Irish parliament (1661–66) proved more biddable, passing eighty-seven bills, including the controversial and lengthy (600 pages) Act of Settlement (31 July 1662), followed by the Act of Explanation (23 December 1665). For the first time Old English influences had been removed from the Commons, which was now an exclusively Protestant body. However, the readmission of Catholic peers to the Lords afforded some political clout to a 'Catholic', rather than an Old English, interest. Equally, despite the trauma of civil war and Cromwellian occupation, intermarriage had

---

[53] S. G. Ellis, 'Parliament and community in Yorkist and Tudor Ireland' in Art Cosgrove and James McGuire (eds.), *Parliament and Community* (Belfast, 1983), pp. 43–68; R. Dudley Edwards, 'The Irish Reformation parliament of Henry VIII, 1536–7' in T. W. Moody (ed.), *Historical Studies VI* (London, 1968), pp. 59–84; John McCavitt, 'An unspeakable parliamentary fracas: the Irish House of Commons, 1613', *Analecta Hibernica*, 37 (1998), pp. 223–35; V. Treadwell, 'The House of Lords in the Irish parliament of 1613–15', *EHR*, 80 (1965), pp. 92–107; Bríd McGrath, 'The membership of the Irish House of Commons, 1613–15' (M.Litt. thesis, Trinity College, Dublin, 1986).

[54] Bríd McGrath, 'A biographical dictionary of the membership of the Irish House of Commons, 1640–1641' (Ph.D. thesis, Trinity College, Dublin, 1997) and 'Parliament men and the confederate association' in Ó Siochrú (ed.), *Kingdoms in Crisis*, pp. 90–105; Aidan Clarke, 'The policies of the "Old English" in parliament, 1640–1' in J. L. McCracken (ed.), *Historical Studies V* (London, 1965), pp. 85–102.

helped to forge a more traditional political elite with common interests that transcended ethnic differences and religious divides. Sitting as the highest judicial authority in Ireland, the peers heard endless petitions from dispossessed and disgruntled landowners and often favoured the 'innocent papists' and prewar planters much to the fury of the Protestant newcomers who had settled in Ireland during the 1650s.

What such complications and unexpected reversals revealed time and again to the New English was the sheer impracticality of any attempt to establish their hegemony over the island by means of force alone. And gradually the inescapable necessity dawned that they must compromise and make accommodation with the circumstances in which they found themselves in Ireland if they were to protect the gains that they were in the process of making. The repeated political and social frustrations of the New English were not, however, fortuitous or merely circumstantial. They were, in fact, systemic, chronic symptoms of a profound structural disjunction which lay inherent in the entire edifice of government within which they operated.

Well entrenched in Dublin and becoming increasingly influential in the planted areas and the provincial and coastal towns of Ireland, New English interests also had their means of exerting considerable influence at the very centre of power, the royal court. But because there was only one court, and because that court was becoming increasingly a forum for the representation and advancement of a broad range of disparate and conflicting interests, the possibility that promoters of an exclusively New English interest could gain an effective monopoly in presenting Irish affairs at court was always problematic given the survival of a signifi-cant Catholic interest. In the prewar years the earls of Clanricard and Antrim enjoyed direct access to Charles I and his Catholic consort and to influential patronage networks in Whitehall. They used these effec-tively both to protect and promote their own Irish interests and those of their Catholic followers. Thanks in part to bonds forged during a decade of continental exile, a select band of Irish Catholics, especially the Talbot brothers and the earls of Carlingford and Clancarthy enjoyed royal favour and the patronage of leading courtiers throughout the later decades of the seventeenth century. While greed, generous bribes and the promise of Irish land explain why after 1660 so many of the mandarins and minions at Whitehall embraced Irish causes, others recognised the importance of securing the support of leading Irish Catholics for the Restoration land settlement. As the earl of Clarendon put it, 'the surest way to preserve that kingdom' was by restoring to their lands handpicked Catholics, both Old English and Gaelic Irish.[55] The accession of the

---

[55] Clarendon to Ormond, 18 July 1663, Bodl., Carte MSS 32, f. 719.

Catholic James II transformed the importance of these favoured few and opened up to them and their clients positions in the Irish army, judicature and administration. This, however, simply alienated even further James's Protestant subjects in all three of his kingdoms.[56]

III

This frustration of the New English interest at court, however, was more than simply the result of structural dysfunction. That there could be no special Irish court, no court other than the one that actually existed, was inherent in the imperfect nature of the polity inaugurated in 1541. Ireland was a kingdom which lacked a separate monarch and yet which made claims of a cultural unity and historical continuity which could not in reality be sustained. But given the formidable obstacles to attempting a new conquest, the persistence of the English monarchs in regarding their Irish kingdom as a separate element within their dominion, and their insistence that their Irish subjects should be viewed within the same structures of hierarchy, order and status as that of their subjects in the other parts of their realm, there was little that the English in Ireland could do about it. Unsatisfactory though the hybrid Irish polity might be, it was the only one available, and so the New English had not only to acquiesce in its existence, but positively to develop its strengths and diminish its weaknesses, to make it work.

The imperative of making good the deficiencies of the Irish kingdom within which they were also to attempt to make their fortunes was commonly among the New English a material one. But it was neither necessarily nor exclusively so. In the earlier stages of its existence, as the first conflicts of reality with theoretical aspirations began to appear, the representatives of English government in Ireland could be seen making strenuous efforts to adapt and manipulate the constitutional structure imposed on them in ways that might genuinely have provided the basis for a common sense of allegiance to and unity under a shared government. Later on, under mounting fear that the group most seriously excluded from the peculiar Irish kingdom, the native Irish, might with foreign support become sufficiently powerful to impose their own vision

---

[56] J. Miller, 'The earl of Tyrconnell and James II's Irish policy, 1685–8', *Historical Journal*, 20 (1977), pp. 803–23; James McGuire, 'Richard Talbot, earl of Tyrconnell (1603–91) and the Catholic Counter-Revolution' in Ciaran Brady (ed.), *Worsted in the Game. Losers in Irish history* (Dublin, 1989), pp. 73–84; Lilian Tate, 'Letter-book of Richard Talbot', *Analecta Hibernica*, 4 (IMC, Dublin, 1932), pp. 99–138; J. I. McGuire, 'The Church of Ireland and the "Glorious Revolution" of 1688' in A. Cosgrove and D. McCartney (eds.), *Studies in Irish History presented to R. Dudley Edwards* (Dublin, 1979), pp. 137–49.

of a united Irish polity upon them, the English in Ireland again found themselves compelled to conceive of ways of affirming and advancing the inclusivist aspirations intrinsic in the idea of the kingdom. And later still, as they became more fully aware of the manner in which they too faced a threat presented by the most English elements within the multiple British monarchies, apologists for the English interest in Ireland again sought for means of defending the autonomy and distinctiveness of a single Irish kingdom. The frustrations suffered by the English in Ireland as a result of their paradoxical cultural and constitutional identity are epitomised in the tortuous history of that first great constitutional instrument of the Tudor reintervention in Ireland, Poynings' Law (1494). Originating as a piece of legislation designed to curb the power of the house of Kildare, Poynings' Law became in the following centuries the focal point of contention between the English crown and its Irish subjects, Old and New English alike. But the fact that their repeated attempts to resolve the anomalies of their position helped forge a distinctive tradition of political and historical thought among the English in Ireland shows that their travails went not entirely for naught.

Thus crossed and undermined by central elements in the political culture from whence they had sprung and which legitimated their very presence in Ireland, successive waves of English colonists in early modern Ireland found themselves on the horns of a dilemma. Regarded as less than the English of England itself, they were compelled, in order to advance their enterprise in Ireland, to accept the reality of that perception, and to construct a distinctive identity for the Irish kingdom even as they had once sought to subvert it. In this, ironically, they were following upon the course set by the previous colonisers. But by the time their fate became apparent, it was clear also that, partly as a result of their defeat of the Gaelic Irish and their manipulation of the Old English, the options once open to that first group of colonisers were no longer available to them. And so, simply to keep the gains they had made, they entered into a series of expediential accommodations and compromises of identity that they were never satisfactorily to resolve.[57]

---

[57] Jacqueline Hill, 'Ireland without Union: Molyneux and his legacy' in John Robertson (ed.), *A Union for Empire: political thought and the British Union of 1707* (Cambridge, 1995); S. J. Connolly, 'The Glorious Revolution in Irish Protestant political thinking' in S. J. Connolly (ed.), *Political Ideas in Eighteenth-Century Ireland* (Dublin, 2000), pp. 27–63; Patrick Kelly, 'Recasting a tradition: William Molyneux and the sources of *The Case of Ireland . . . Stated* (1698)' in Jane Ohlmeyer (ed.), *Political Thought in Seventeenth-Century Ireland* (Cambridge, 2000), pp. 83–106 and 'William Molyneux and the spirit of liberty in eighteenth-century Ireland', *Eighteenth-Century Ireland: Idris an da chultur*, 3 (1988), pp. 133–48; Neil Longley York, *Neither Kingdom nor Nation. The Irish quest for constitutional rights, 1698–1800* (Washington, 1994).

IV

The complexities indicated in the foregoing discussion are, in large part, reflections of the new research and fresh perspectives contained in the chapters that follow. To be sure, the main outlines of the conventional narrative must survive in any reinterpretation, if only because, as the essays by Sarah Barber (chapter 13) and R. J. Hunter (chapter 6) demonstrate, so many of the New English themselves – both in terms of their general conceptualisations and particular local practices – were determined that it should be so. But, as these essays also indicate, such efforts to force actualities to conform to aspirations were suffused with difficulty: the Bible and the bawn did not sit easily together in plantation Ulster; and the tortured efforts of Richard Lawrence to find legitimations for English expropriations in Ireland through mythical history and ethnographic comparison bear eloquent testimony to the difficulty of the task. The artificiality of Lawrence's grand conceptualisations is further revealed in Toby Barnard's close examination in chapter 14 of the manner in which the changing circumstances within which he operated forced him – silently more than overtly – to modify his views in accordance with his experiences and, gradually, to reach a deeper appreciation of the ambiguous nature of the colonist's status in Ireland. Barnard's demonstration of Lawrence's educative experience as a colonist in a particular place and at an especially crucial time offers a timely reminder of the importance of contextualisation – both spatial and temporal – in our attempts to discover the character of the recently arrived English settlers' encounter with Ireland. This same attention to contextualisation is adopted over a longer period and within a larger region in Harold O'Sullivan's survey of south-east Ulster from the late fifteenth to the mid-seventeenth century (chapter 3). This essay provides a valuable case study of the manner in which the English colonial community was divided and reshaped in response to the specific conditions of the region in wholly unexpected ways. Once again, the very sequence of settlement served to alter the possibilities of development in ways diverging far from those originally envisaged.

The desire to reconstruct prevailing problems and conditions within an acceptable conceptual framework was not alone restricted to *arriviste* colonial adventurers. Similar problems confronted those with quite different agendas. Thus in the second chapter Ciaran Brady uncovers the ambitious attempt of Sir Henry Sidney to lay down a common foundation of allegiance for all the inhabitants of Ireland on the basis of a synthetic and mythical historical tradition. In examining the evolving historical perspective of the colonists, Raymond Gillespie's survey of the

readings to which Sir John Temple's *The Irish Rebellion* was submitted
in the later seventeenth century (chapter 15) offers a test case of the
ways in which the now nervously ascendant group sought to establish
and reshape the official memory of their great mid-century crisis. And in
the closing chapter, which takes up several of the themes of conquest and
consent raised by Brady, Patrick Kelly analyses the persistent ambiguities and weaknesses inherent in attempts of the dominant settler group
to establish satisfactory grounds for their brand of English sovereignty in
Ireland.

The intractability of Irish realities in face of the preferred interpretative frameworks of the English was the result neither of the fundamental perversity of the Irish environment, as Lawrence in his darker
Spenserian moments liked to imagine, nor yet to mere contingency or
accident. Between the extremes of necessity and chance lay the intermedi-
ary but powerfully influential force of historical inheritance. The manner
in which a complex history, itself enframed by geography, determined the
political evolution of the distinctive region in Ulster is also the subject of
O'Sullivan's chapter. But a more specific form in which an historical tradition delimited the possible courses of political action is the subject of a set
of related chapters. Of central importance here in linking the discussions
of the pseudo-histories and commentaries noted above with the practical
political activities of the English in Ireland is Micheál Ó Siochrú's con-
tinuation of the venerable history of Poynings' Law (chapter 10). Once
consigned to the closet of constitutional and legal historians, the unan-
ticipated obstacles and opportunities presented at once to supporters of
the crown and its opponents among the English in Ireland by this late
fifteenth-century expedient for almost three centuries is evidence not only
of the highly ambivalent nature of the English presence in Ireland, but of
the continuing centrality of one of the most important inheritances of the
original English enterprise, that is, the establishment of an independent
parliament for Ireland. Too often discounted in the narrative of conquest
and rebellion, the central importance of the Irish parliament in the island's
political and social history is demonstrated and explored in two chapters
below. In chapter 8 Jane Ohlmeyer evaluates the political significance of
the parliamentary peers in the Irish parliament of 1640–41 and particularly the role that they played, along with their counterparts in Whitehall
and Westminster, in securing the downfall of Wentworth. In a companion
piece (chapter 9) Bríd McGrath examines the relationships between the
Lords and the Commons and untangles Wentworth's electoral strategy
in the 1640 parliament. Initially very effective, the lord deputy's political
initiatives quickly began to unravel, allowing members from both houses

to form a formidable opposition that only dissipated with the outbreak of the rebellion in October 1641.

Statutory legislation, parliament and the protocols of common law presented, however, only one aspect of history's fateful bequest to the English in early modern Ireland. Of no less importance was the character of the old colony's church, the *ecclesia inter Anglos*, upon which in the form of religious reformation they were to place even larger burdens. The essays by Alan Ford (chapter 7) and Robert Armstrong (chapter 11) document the struggles of the Church of Ireland's episcopate in seeking to turn this cumbersome instrument into an effective means of enforcing authority and conformity, and they offer striking parallels with the studies of the Irish parliament by Ohlmeyer and McGrath. But from the church even more was required than authority or mere adaptation to change: it was obliged to initiate change itself. In their chapters Ford and Armstrong give prominence to the political pressures suffered by the bishops as they sought to honour this imperative in the crisis decades of the mid seventeenth century. Two further essays focus on the intense internal tensions to which it also gave rise. Brian Jackson's dissection in chapter 5 of the public controversy engaged upon by the Protestant divine John Rider with the Catholic theologian Henry Fitzsimon gives telling evidence of the anxieties of the representatives of the established church to demonstrate their superior hold on faith and truth; while on a broader canvas, Helga Robinson-Hammerstein discusses in chapter 4 the manner in which attempts to apply conventional ideas of university education foundered on the rocks of Irish realities. As with Barber's commentary on Lawrence, Robinson-Hammerstein's essay reveals how limited the application of other European models would be to the English in attempting to make sense of Ireland.

Yet, at another level, these European models remain valuable and offer some basis for further comparative research. Robinson-Hammerstein's chapter facilitates analysis of the similarities and differences between the experiences of Trinity College, Dublin, as a 'civic institution' with universities in Germany, the Dutch Republic and Scotland which were founded during these years in order to train ideologically compliant clergy. A number of the chapters draw attention to the problems, especially the political, constitutional and religious ones, inherent in running a multiple monarchy during the early modern period.[58] Geoffrey Parker (chapter 12) compares and contrasts the revolts and rebellions that erupted throughout the

[58] H. G. Koenigsberger, 'Dominium regale or dominium politicum et regale' reprinted in *Politicians and Virtuosi: essays on early modern history* (London, 1986). Also see Jenny Wormald, 'The creation of British multiple kingdoms or core and colonies?', *Transactions*

Spanish and Stuart kingdoms in the mid-seventeenth century, identifying seventeen denominators common to the majority (including Ireland),
and then deftly situates these insurrections in the 'global general crisis'
of the seventeenth century.[59]

Other chapters shed light on the rather awkwardly termed 'New British
and Irish histories'.[60] Parker highlights the parallels between the 'thorough' policies of Lord Deputy Wentworth and the count-duke of Olivares,
chief minister of the Spanish Habsburg composite state, which are striking, with both men displaying a genius for providing a common focus
for opposition groups that otherwise had none. Parker's chapter also provides a European context for Ó Siochrú's discussion of Poynings' Law
during the 1640s. In this, Ó Siochrú highlights the wider constitutional
struggle within the Stuart kingdoms, with the Catholic Confederates des-
perately trying to reassert the independence of the Irish parliament and
thereby protect themselves against the predatory and imperial ambitions
of the one at Westminster.[61] Thus the Irish Confederates were as much
'constitutional nationalists' as the Covenanting Scots or the insurgents in
Catalonia and Italy rebelling against the Spanish monarchies.[62] Equally
contested throughout the Stuart monarchies was the form and nature of
Anglicanism during the middle decades of the seventeenth century. In
the 1630s Archbishop Laud's religious policies, as Ford argues, enjoyed
a distinctive 'three kingdoms' perspective, and for the archbishop Ireland
represented a testing ground where he could implement his ideological
vision. A decade later, as Armstrong shows, the challenges came from
an aggressive form of Scottish Presbyterianism, which from its base in
Ulster spread south throughout the island. Just as the Scottish Covenanters regarded the imposition of Presbyterianism as a 'British' imperative,
so too Anglicans in Ireland viewed the need to defend the position of the

of the Royal Historical Society, 6th series, 2 (1992), pp. 175–94; Michael Perceval-
Maxwell, 'Ireland and the monarchy in the early Stuart multiple kingdom', *Historical
Journal* 34 (1991) and 'Ireland and Scotland, 1638 to 1648', in John Morrill (ed.), *The
Scottish Covenant in its British Context* (Edinburgh, 1990).

[59] Aidan Clarke, 'Ireland and the General Crisis', *Past and Present*, 48 (1970).

[60] For full discussions of recent works on the interactions within and between the three kingdoms, see the bibliographies in Brendan Bradshaw and John Morrill (eds.), *The British
Problem c.1534–1707. State formation in the Atlantic Archipelago* (London, 1996); Glenn
Burgess (ed.), *The New British History: Founding a modern state 1603–1715* (London,
1999); Jane Ohlmeyer, 'Seventeenth-century Ireland and the new British and Atlantic
histories', *American Historical Review* 104:2 (April, 1999), pp. 446–62; and Allan I.
Macinnes and Jane Ohlmeyer (eds.), *The Stuart Kingdoms in the Seventeenth Century:
awkward neighbours* (Dublin, 2002).

[61] For an alternative perspective, see Patrick Little, 'The English parliament and the Irish
constitution, 1641–1649' in Ó Siochrú (ed.), *Kingdoms in Crisis*, pp. 106–21.

[62] Ó Siochrú, *Confederate Ireland*, pp. 237–9 and Jane Ohlmeyer, 'A failed revolution?' in
Ohlmeyer (ed.), *Ireland from Independence to Occupation*, pp. 1–3.

established church in terms of all three kingdoms. In the eyes of these clerical combatants, national boundaries meant little; the fates of Ireland, Scotland and England were inextricably intertwined.

Of course, the real value of exploring the dilemmas confronted by the English and Scots in Ireland does not lie in a desire to celebrate their successes or to seek sympathy for their disappointments. Rather, it is by examining the inconclusive and contradictory manner in which they established themselves in the island that we can cast further light on all of its inhabitants in the early modern period as a whole, rediscovering in the process some of the ambiguities and disjunctions, continuities and corre-spondences that the dominance of the simple paradigm of conquest has for so long obscured. This alone is the common principle upon which the present collection rests. Arising from a series of papers given at a conference in honour of Aidan Clarke by his friends, students and col-leagues, this volume purports to offer no comprehensive review of early modern Irish history, nor to represent a specific school of thought, nor even to provide a complete study of the New English or any other group-ings in Ireland. It aims merely to offer a collection of new perspectives on the period, moving beyond the old framework of conquest and coloni-sation which, for all its interpretative value and ideological comfort, has excluded so much history from our attention.

Because its aspirations are explorative rather than conclusive, illumi-native rather than definitive, no fixed editorial position has been imposed on contributors in their choice of topics, in their methods or in their interpretations. Though some important interpretative themes and links have been indicated here, it would have been against the spirit of the enterprise to impose yet another overarching interpretative frame. Thus we have elected to present the chapters in largely but not completely chronological order. Taken together, it is hoped that they will offer an accumulating sense of the complexity of political and cultural change in early modern Ireland by revealing the increasing difficulties presented to one particular group which, having initiated so much of that process of change, was also compelled to contain it.

2 The attainder of Shane O'Neill, Sir Henry Sidney and the problems of Tudor state-building in Ireland

Ciaran Brady

Why was Shane O'Neill attainted some two years after his death by means of a statute of attainder passed by the Irish parliament which met in January 1569?[1] The answer would appear to be as simple as the question. Shane was attainted because the crown wished to employ the easiest and most comprehensive way of confiscating all of his lands and rights of lordship and the lands and lordships of those, both among the O'Neills and among the other Ulster dynasties, who had pledged allegiance to him. It was a sly move, it has commonly been observed: for after actively opposing all of Shane's tenurial and feudal claims during his lifetime, now that he was dead the English government chose after all to accept such claims at their fullest in order to extract the greatest possible yield.[2] For those seduced by the pleasures of prosecution this mode of explanation has always been enough: perfidious Albion once again supplementing brute force with subtle legal subterfuge.

Yet however vicious and malign England's intentions towards Ireland may be presumed to have been in general, a moment's reflection will suggest that in this particular case the means chosen for such a design were remarkably clumsy. Not only was it unnecessary, as will be demonstrated below, it was also replete with concessions, implicit and explicit, that rendered it quite subversive of its own supposed purpose. In what follows it will be argued that such apparent redundancies and contradictions were not the product of an overweening vindictiveness, but were rather intrinsic elements of a subtle and highly ambitious strategy by which the Elizabethan viceroy, Sir Henry Sidney, sought to establish a new foundation for English sovereignty and allegiance to the English crown

---

[1] The bill was made statute in the third session which opened on 23 February, 11 Elizabeth I, session 3, chapter i, *The Statutes at Large Passed in the Irish Parliaments Held in Ireland, 1310–1800* (20 vols., Dublin, 1786–1801), I, pp. 322–38.

[2] For a representative statement of this standard interpretation, see G. A. Hayes-McCoy's comments in *NHI*, III, p. 93.

in Ireland which would overcome all of the problems similar attempts had hitherto encountered.

I

Declarations of attainder by parliamentary bill and statute, as distinct from attainder procedures based upon verdict or outlawry or that were consequent upon the death of individuals previously proclaimed to be guilty of treason or felony, were a relatively unusual weapon in the Tudor legal armory in either kingdom.[3] A practice which had been established at least by the middle of the fifteenth century, when both sides in the great dynastic struggle between the houses of York and Lancaster employed it against each other with some frequency, the use of parliamentary bill and statute as a means of attainder had remained common during the reign of Henry VII.[4] Under Henry VIII it was so regularly employed that it was once confidently declared by historians to be 'the characteristic instrument of Tudor policy'.[5] Cardinal Wolsey, Thomas More, Thomas Cromwell, Catherine Howard, the duke of Buckingham, the duke of Norfolk and the earl of Surrey all fell victim to the procedure, along with a good many lesser-known figures.[6] But the historical importance of these individual instances has tended to obscure the fact, revealed by cooler analysis, that under Henry attainders were in fact in decline, that there were no attainders by statute before 1523, that only one took place – that of the duke of Norfolk – after 1542, that far and away the bulk of the attainders were passed during the ascendancy of Thomas Cromwell, and, most importantly, that thereafter the procedure fell into rapid decline.[7] Only two legislative attainders apiece were enacted in the reigns of Edward VI and Mary I. Only one was to pass in England in the reign of Elizabeth I, and none had yet been enacted at the time that the bill for Shane O'Neill was presented to the Irish parliament.[8]

---

[3] J. G. Bellamy, *The Tudor Law of Treason: an introduction* (London, 1979), pp. 23–9, 41–4, 210–14; Stanford E. Lehmberg, 'Parliamentary attainder in the reign of Henry VIII', *Historical Journal*, 18 (1975), pp. 675–702; for some qualifications of this view see also William R. Stacy, 'Richard Roose and the use of parliamentary attainder in the reign of Henry VIII', *Historical Journal*, 29 (1985), pp. 1–15.

[4] J. R. Lander, 'Attainder and forfeiture, 1453 – 1509', *Historical Journal*, 4 (1961), pp. 119–51; J. G. Bellamy, *The Law of Treason in England in the Later Middle Ages* (Cambridge, 1970), pp. 177–205.

[5] A. F. Pollard, *Henry VIII* (London, 1905), p. 29.

[6] G. R. Elton, *Policy and Police* (Cambridge, 1972); Bellamy, *Tudor Law of Treason*.

[7] Lehmberg, 'Parliamentary attainder', pp. 701–2.

[8] These were the attainders of Sir William Sharington and Sir Thomas Seymour under Edward and the duke of Northumberland and the earl of Suffolk under Mary; the first Elizabethan attainders of the earls of Northumberland, Westmorland and Cumberland were passed, after judicial process, in 1571.

In Ireland in the Tudor period legislative attainder had previously been used even more sparingly. In 1536 under the Cromwellian regime a bill for the attainder of Thomas Fitzgerald, tenth earl of Kildare, and his uncles had been introduced in the Irish parliament partially to avoid potentially troublesome treason trials when the presumed traitors were still living, and partially to secure rapid access to the lucrative properties of the house of Kildare and its adherents.[9] And in the same parliament that the bill concerning Shane was introduced three other attainders were to be presented, the first relating to Thomas Fitzgerald, 'the Knight of the Valley' (i.e., the knight of Glin), an ally of James Fitzmaurice Fitzgerald, the second concerning Thomas Comerford of Ballymacka, and the third concerning John Fitzgerald, the White Knight, all of whom had died while in actual rebellion but before any proclamation had been made against them.[10] In regard to Shane, however, none of these conditions applied. Unlike Kildare and his uncles, he had not surrendered and had died in rebellion. Unlike the knight of Glin and the others, he had been formally proclaimed a traitor no less than three times, in June 1561, in March 1563 and in August 1566. None of these proclamations had been remitted by an official pardon, though the first two had arguably been superseded by subsequent peace negotiations. But the third and most recent, which contained damning evidence that he had conspired with foreign princes, was fully in force at the time of his death in June 1567.[11]

This under the Tudor law of treason was, strictly speaking, sufficient. But in the case of O'Neill, a further avenue of approach was also available. For Shane was an Irish 'O', a figure whose status as a subject had never received any formal recognition. Condemned by proclamation, he might have been regarded in English law, in the manner of so many Gaelic figures who had fallen while technically in rebellion against the crown, simply as an outlaw, without any sense of legal impropriety and had his lands and goods declared forfeit by judicial decree. It is true that the seriousness of the challenge he had posed and the magnitude of the possessions now forfeited might have advised a more public and more ceremonial action than a decree in chancery. But here too there was precedent enough in the seizure by statute of the lands occupied by such unrecognised natives

---

[9] R. D. Edwards, 'The Irish Reformation parliament of Henry VIII, 1536–7' in T. W. Moody (ed.), *Historical Studies VI* (Dublin, 1968), pp. 59–84.

[10] 11 Eliz. I, sess. 3, ch. iii; 12 Eliz. I, sess. 2, ch. i; 13 Eliz. I, sess. 1, ch. iii, *Statutes of Ireland*, I, pp. 340–1, 374, 387–8; the parliament also passed a bill declaring the retrospective attainder of Christopher Eustace and others executed for treason after the Kildare rebellion in the 1530s, and the reversal of the Kildare attainder passed at that time.

[11] The texts of the proclamations can be found in PRO, SP 63/4/13 enclosure i, 23 June 1561; SP 63/8/19, 15 March 1563; HMC, *Fifteenth Report* (London, 1893), appendix III, 'Haliday Mss', pp. 172–5, 2 August 1566.

in the act establishing the plantation of Laois–Offaly, which, without making any reference to attainder, simply asserted the crown's ownership of the territories as 'of right' and, denying all title to the O'Mores and the O'Connors, regarded them simply as squatters.[12] The treatment of the midlands Irish might have been regarded as both politically unwise and morally unjust; but as native Irish, who had not completed any surrender settlements under the kingship act of 1541, they were still 'the king's Irish enemies', without any constitutional rights under English law at the time of their defeat, and were treated accordingly. That there was no ambiguity in law perceived here is clearly illustrated by the fact that in the same parliament the statute authorising the midlands plantation was, without any sense of incongruity, followed by another re-establishing with papal sanction the kingdom of Ireland.

In regard to the territory occupied by the O'Neills, moreover, the Tudors enjoyed even stronger claims than those asserted by the crown in the midlands. For the medieval earldom of Ulster, established at the beginning of the thirteenth century, could be claimed to have been directly inherited by them through the house of York.[13] Henry VIII had emphatically reasserted such a right in the 1530s and the 1540s, and in the early 1570s Elizabeth was to resort to it in part justification of the grant issued to the earl of Essex.[14] On such grounds alone it could readily have been asserted that, as a rebel both to the crown and the earl of Ulster, Shane had long ago forfeited all possible rights as a subject and could so be accounted a constitutional nonentity. The Tudor right over the whole of Ulster and all its occupiers could then be simply reasserted under the title of the earldom alone, without recourse to the cumbersome mechanism of attainting O'Neill.

It might be argued, however, that one extenuating consideration applied in Shane's case that might have moved the crown to caution. In September 1563 a peace negotiated with Shane by Sir Thomas Cusack on behalf of the crown at Drumcree had made some major concessions, in particular one granting Shane 'the leading and service of so many lords and captains as shall be proved to have of ancient custom appertained to such as have been and held the place of O'Neill', and another agreeing that all disputes outstanding between Shane and the Pale be settled by representatives of both sides and not by the crown alone.[15]

---

[12] 3 & 4 Philip and Mary, sess. i, ch. i, *Statutes of Ireland*, I, pp. 240–1.

[13] The line of descent to the Tudors ran from the Mortimer earls of March through the house of York to Henry Tudor by marriage to Elizabeth daughter of Edward IV grandmother of Elizabeth I.

[14] 'Memorandum of the covenants between Her Majesty and the earl of Essex', 9 July 1573, PRO, SP 63/41/72.

[15] On the course of the negotiations see Ciaran Brady, *Shane O'Neill* (Dundalk, 1996), pp. 48–58.

Such concessions went beyond any acknowledgement previously granted to Shane; it seemed to allow the O'Neill a regional political authority that went beyond his status as a Gaelic dynastic lord and suggested that he be regarded almost as a foreign power. In the circumstances arising after Shane's death, the embarrassment to which such generosity now gave rise might be seen to have required serious retrospective modification in the form of a declaration affirming O'Neill's perennial subjection to the English crown. But the move was hardly necessary. It is important to recall that, though concluded in Ireland, the peace of Drumcree never received formal ratification by the queen in Whitehall. Instead, the letters patent which were finally drafted at Whitehall almost a year after the negotiations had taken place omitted crucial clauses from the treaty including one relating to Shane's outstanding disputes with the Pale.[16] The revisions marked a clear withdrawal from the status accorded to Shane in Cusack's peace. Shane held out for the original terms, and the negotiations stalled until he was finally proclaimed a traitor again in 1566. Thus, however embarrassing they may have been in 1564, the concessions proffered in 1563 had no legal standing in 1569 and required therefore no awkward readjustment.

On several grounds, then, there appears to have been no pressing case why the crown should have thought it necessary to attaint Shane O'Neill by statute: he died a proclaimed rebel; no constitutional status had ever formally been accorded to him; and he was a usurper of the territories claimed by the Tudors as the rightful heirs of the earldom of Ulster. Superfluous to the purpose, the decision to proceed by bill of attainder is even more remarkable when the less happy implications of the procedure, theoretical and practical, are considered. For, of itself, the attainder implied that there had in fact been a lineage of O'Neill enjoying political and tenurial rights under the law of England which, having been disgraced by the unnatural conduct of its most recent representative, Shane, was now to be extinguished forever. This seems decisive, but it is also more generous than it might appear: for in explicitly recognising a lineage of O'Neill, subjects of the English crown, the act seemed to concede that there had, after all, been something fundamentally valid in Shane's claim for recognition as earl of Tyrone, something repeatedly denied to him in his lifetime. This implicit concession is made more overt by a second explicit qualification which appeared to be even more subversive of the act's ostensibly punitive and exploitative intentions. This was the clause identifying by name several of Shane's allies and supporters in rebellion which, on the grounds that they had been terrorised by him, that they

[16] *Ibid.*, pp. 53–4.

had opposed him when the opportunity arose, and that they were now living peacefully and suing for mercy, declared that they should be pardoned and restored to their livings at the discretion of the viceroy.[17] Had the mere desire to capitalise upon Shane's fall been, as the story goes, the principal intention of the Tudor administration in Ireland, this was a curiously generous dispensation, opening up by statute broad avenues of exculpation, exoneration and bargaining which might better have been entered into in private negotiations. Redundant in law, and apparently subversive of its ostensible purposes, the act of attainder of Shane O'Neill seems on the surface to have been a particularly eccentric instrument of Tudor policy in Ireland. But the eccentricity of this particular statute as a weapon of royal power appears even more strikingly when, moving from form to substance, the actual content of the statute is viewed and in particular when the long preamble in which the attainder itself is couched is examined in detail.

II

Even among this rare species of legislation, the attainder of O'Neill was an extraordinary composition. It was among the Irish attainders by far the longest and the most ambitious in scope. Bills of attainder presented to both the English and Irish parliaments tended to follow a common pattern: the crucial enacting clause was typically preceded by a preamble detailing to a greater or lesser extent the villainous, treacherous, unnatural and unpardonable actions of the subject of the attainder in a manner that purported to be definitive.[18] The O'Neill attainder followed this pattern up to a point. Thus the enacting clause was preceded by a preamble which opened with the expected recitation of all of Shane's evil doings from his usurpation of the place of Matthew, baron of Dungannon, as his father's chosen successor in the late 1550s to his suitably ignoble death, amidst drink, pride and anger at the hands of the Scots. Accounting for close on 3,500 words, this was a respectable and conventional indictment. But it was succeeded within the preamble by a second and even longer part which, moving far beyond the case of Shane O'Neill, offered nothing short of a general and wholly original constitutional history of Ireland. Reciting the various titles by which the English crown claimed sovereignty over Ireland in general and Ulster in particular, this statutorily sanctioned history of Ireland embodied a number of remarkable and somewhat inconsistent assertions, locating the roots of English sovereignty in

---

[17] *Statutes of Ireland*, I, pp. 335–7.
[18] See, for example, the preamble to the Kildare attainder, 28 Henry VIII, sess. 3, ch. i, *ibid.*, I, pp. 166–70.

Ireland in the mists of time, announcing the final completion of the process of conquest in the very recent past, reserving a special place to the current viceroy in this grand historical process, and declaring that it was only against this larger historical context that the peculiar iniquities of Shane were properly to be judged.

This official history begins not, as might be expected, with the twelfth-century conquest, but with the legendary King Gurmundus, son of Belan, king of Great Britain, and lord of Bayon in the Spanish province of Biscan, whose claim to have been the first sovereign of Irishmen rested on two counts. First, as lord of Bayon, he was overlord of the early Irish even before they left Spain to settle in the north; and second, because it was he who gave explicit permission to the leaders of these proto-Irishmen, Hiberus and Hermon, to settle in Ireland 'and assigned unto them guides for the sea to bring them thither'.[19] Thus, as descendants of the figure who first gave the right of inhabiting Ireland to the Irish, the monarchs of England inherited the first and most ancient title of sovereignty over the island. In this particular origin legend the act departed significantly from the accepted authority of the English title to Ireland, the canonical *Expugnatio Hibernica* of Giraldus Cambrensis, which had asserted that the ancestors of the native Irish had occupied Ireland long before the lifetime of Gurmundus, and allotted to him merely the role of an early anticipator of the conquest of Ireland, an event which was not really to be completed until the coming of the Normans.[20]

Largely left implicit in the statute of attainder, the significance of the divergence between Giraldus and this new account was elaborated upon in another closely contemporaneous text whose relationship to the act itself is of central importance. This was Edmund Campion's quasi-official 'Two Bokes of the Histories of Ireland' (1571), which, having been effectively commissioned by Lord Deputy Sidney as an accompaniment to his parliament's proceedings, was compiled by Campion while staying in Dublin under Sidney's protection in the house of the Speaker of the Irish Commons, James Stanihurst.[21] According to Campion's 'Histories', the island of Ireland, before the coming of Gurmundus's Biscan clients, was in a state of chronic disorder with no one people holding sway. It was only when Hiberus and Hermon and their followers (with the blessing of

---

[19] *Ibid.*, I, pp. 328–9.

[20] Giraldus Cambrensis, *Expugnatio Hibernica: The Conquest of Ireland*, ed. A. B. Scott and F. X. Martin (Dublin, 1978), book II, chapter 6.

[21] A. F. Vossen (ed.), *Two Bokes of the Histories of Ireland, compiled by Edmund Campion* (Assen, 1963); for the circumstances surrounding Campion's stay in Ireland and the composition of the *Histories* there, see Colm Lennon, 'Edmund Campion's *Histories of Ireland* and reform in Tudor Ireland' in Thomas M. McCoog, SJ (ed.), *The Reckoned Expense: Edmund Campion and the early English Jesuits* (Woodbridge, 1996), pp. 67–84.

the British king) had imposed their rule upon it that anyone could claim to have established control in the place and that a line of sovereignty could be traced.[22] For this argument from history Campion and the parliamentary draftsmen drew not on Giraldus but on the earlier and considerably more mythical *History of the Kings of Britain* by Geoffrey of Monmouth, composed around 1138.[23] Respect for antiquity was hardly the source of Campion's preference in this instance. By the time he wrote Geoffrey's authority had long been questioned by scholars, and that the resort to Geoffrey was motivated by expediency is confirmed by its very selectivity.[24] For having used him in preference to Giraldus in this critical instance, both Campion and the composers of the bill of attainder altogether ignored Geoffrey's far more extensive account of the forceful conquest of Ireland by King Arthur for reasons which will presently be considered.[25]

Both in Campion, then, and in the bill of attainder, the twelfth-century conquest of Ireland is presented not as the primary act of conquest, as in the *Expugnatio*, but as the second, even the third, of England's claims to sovereignty over Ireland.[26] And even in this reduced status the authority of Giraldus is qualified. The claim based upon the bull *Laudabiliter* which had featured centrally for Giraldus is, naturally enough, suppressed, and likewise the retrospective ratification of the conquest given by the synod of Cashel. But, significantly, the far more shadowy clerical assembly which had taken place at Armagh regarding which Giraldus had been extremely sketchy (and for whose occurrence he was in fact the only authority) is given prominence in the act, being invoked to confirm native assent to the Anglo-Norman enterprise before the conquest had actually been completed. In marked contrast to Giraldus, moreover, for whom they were the heroes of his epic, the role of the adventurers Strongbow, FitzStephen and FitzGerald is subordinated in the act to that of Henry II, who alone is credited with securing the submission of all the great Irish lords 'of their own good will'. And in case the point was not made sufficiently by this, the preamble went on to explain: 'For that the chronicles make no mention of any war or chivalry done by the king.'[27] This emphasis upon voluntary submission is continued in the next and final title recited in this section of the act – the tour of Richard II, who in 1395 again gracefully

[22] Campion, *Histories*, pp. 17–19, 42–9, 81.
[23] The Penguin edition, edited and translated by Lewis Thorpe (Harmondsworth, 1980) has been consulted here; the relevant passages are at pp. 99–101.
[24] On the standing of Geoffrey among sixteenth-century scholars, see T. D. Kendrick, *British Antiquity* (London, 1950), chapter 3.
[25] *History of the Kings of Britain*, pp. 220–2.   [26] *Statutes of Ireland*, I, p. 329.
[27] *Ibid.*, p. 330.

received the petition 'of all the Irish of Ireland, who became his liege men'.[28]

For commentators attracted by 'the hermeneutics of suspicion' this sustained attempt to diminish the role of conquest in Irish history – and here the point of excising Geoffrey of Monmouth's King Arthur from the sequence becomes clear – and the repeated desire to emphasise the theme of consent can be interpreted merely as a matter of deception: 'to mask an original act of violent conquest'.[29] Perhaps it was; but if so, the question as to why such occlusion would have been deemed necessary in a bill presented before a parliament of the English colonial community in Dublin, who traditionally rejoiced in its heritage of conquest would seem to require further explanation than has yet been supplied. But, in any case, elsewhere in its text the preamble's history displayed little embarrassment about the reality of violent conquest. In a directly following section it traced the various titles enjoyed by the crown in Ulster, in particular from the alleged establishment of the earldom of Ulster through military force under John de Courcy[30] through its various revivals in the later Middle Ages, during which times, said the act, 'the O'Neills were of no estimation nor durst bear up head in Ulster'.[31] Yet even this claim by right of conquest was interpolated with contrasting observations concerning the long obeisance paid by the O'Neills not only as vassals of the earls of Ulster, but 'as vassals and obedient people to the crown of England'.[32] Moreover, while the decline of the earldom and the general weakness 'of the commonwealth' gave opportunity to the O'Neills 'to withdraw from their duty of allegiance and so to do all that appertained to rebellious and undutiful subjects', they had in the reign of Henry VIII 'with all humility, free consent and goodwill submitted themselves unto his Grace' in a further reinforcement of the voluntary submission they had shown since the first appearance of the English in Ireland so many centuries before.[33] And now under Elizabeth the crown's title was finally being confirmed in the act itself with the affirmation that the conquest now completed had been achieved without 'any great effusion of blood but was a Godly conquest in the winning of people, who, now being fatigued of war, begin to ask first for your mercy and next for your justice'.[34]

This ambivalent interweaving of apparently contrasting themes of conquest and consent may seem unsettling. But such unease is in large

---

[28] *Ibid.*, p. 331.

[29] Andrew Hadfield, 'Briton and Scythian: Tudor representations of Irish origins', *IHS*, 28 (1993), pp. 390–408, especially p. 400.

[30] The claim within the act that de Courcy, rather than his enemy Hugh de Lacy, was the founder of the earldom of Ulster is, of course, erroneous, but is made, presumably, to establish the earliest possible title.

[31] *Statutes of Ireland*, I, p. 330.   [32] *Ibid.*, p. 331.   [33] *Ibid.*, p. 332.   [34] *Ibid.*, p. 334.

part anachronistic, arising from a premature application of certain familiar polarities in English constitutional thought, between, for instance, the ancient constitution and the feudal law, time immemorial and the initiating conquest of 1066, which, while they were to become of central importance in the constitutional thought and arguments of the early seventeenth century, had not yet developed in the high sixteenth century the sharp definition and mutual opposition which they were later to acquire.[35] Instead, for most of the Tudor period a more complex, if less intellectually coherent constitutional view prevailed, within which the organic development of English law through custom, cases and legislation was seen occasionally to be accompanied and sustained by instances of conflict and resolution without any great sense of incongruity.[36] From this perspective, the theory of constitutional development implicitly deployed in the act – from consent to conquest and back again – would have seemed far less disjointed than it appeared from the perspectives of the seventeenth century and beyond.[37] But, once more, the argument left implicit in the statute is explicitly stated in Campion's semi-official commentary. Summarising exactly as in the statute England's various claims to sovereignty, he concluded: 'Thus when their own free consent, the dedition [donation] of their princes, lawful conquest and prescription is adjoined it forces an invincible title to Ireland.'[38] The effect of this summary is twofold: it serves at once to clarify the nature of the claim to sovereignty recited in the act, but also to reposition the emphasis from the largely chronological way it had been outlined within it. The claim, that is to say, is not simply originative in character, giving Gurmundus pride of place. But neither is it simply cumulative, adding one event in sequence upon another. It is in fact organic, fusing claims of different orders arising and recurring at different times into one coherent title.

It is in this context that Campion's final term 'prescription' is of crucial summary importance. A legal concept of reasonably clear definition, prescription conferred a title from time out of mind, presuming but

---

[35] See J. G. A. Pocock, *The Ancient Constitution and the Feudal Law* (2nd edn, revised and enlarged, Cambridge, 1987); J. P. Sommerville, *Politics and Ideology in England, 1603–40* (London, 1986).

[36] See, *inter alia*, P. A. Fiedler and T. F. Mayer (eds.), *Political Thought and the Tudor Commonweal: deep structure, discourse and disguise* (London, 1992); see also the important debate on 'History, English law and the Renaissance' conducted between Donald R. Kelley on the one side and Christopher Brooks and Kevin Sharpe on the other in *Past and Present*, 65 (1974), pp. 24–51 and 72 (1976), pp. 133–42. For a discussion of the way the reign of an unmarried female monarch reshaped conventional constitutional thinking, see A. N. McLaren, *Political Culture in the Reign of Elizabeth I: queen and commonwealth* (Cambridge, 1999).

[37] See chapter 16 below.   [38] Campion, *Histories*, pp. 34–5.

without depending upon or referring to any specific originating grant, but resting upon evidence of long actual use.[39] In this way it rendered redundant debate as to whether conquest or consent was of primary or original importance by affirming that both were inextricably fused in a cumulative claim based on immemorial usage.

The thinking underlying the act (and Campion's commentary) was therefore by no means as contradictory as it subsequently appeared. Yet at the same time it must be conceded that this was an argument of remarkable, indeed unprecedented, subtlety and originality. In England itself arguments from prescription, though common enough in cases of property, had rarely been pressed to the fore in constitutional thought. In Ireland, however, where the twelfth-century conquest was fundamental to the identity of the old colonial community, this interpretative shift signalled a subtle but hugely significant strategic move on the part of Sidney, Campion and individuals such as James Stanihurst, nominated Speaker in the Irish House of Commons, and Lucas Dillon, a senior figure in Sidney's administration who helped frame the statute.[40] The redefinition which it implied for the political identity and constitutional status of the English in Ireland was, in short, no less radical, and a good deal more disturbing, than that which it seemed to envisage for the O'Neills and the native Irish in general. Viewed in this perspective, then, the original question as to why the statute's devisers chose to proceed at all with the attainder against Shane, when a range of other expedients was on offer, re-emerges in an entirely different light. It suggests that in their strategic thinking they were not primarily concerned with Shane or the O'Neills or with the broad acres of Ulster, but that they were intent, under cover of these means, upon nothing less than a fundamental reconstruction of the Irish polity and of the place and the interrelationship of each of its constituent elements. Concerning the origins and the purpose of this revolutionary strategy no candid explanation is to be found, naturally enough, either in Campion or in the act itself. To have made declarations of an intent that was still far from being attained to parties who were bound to be suspicious and hostile would have been deeply unwise. Yet some indications as to what was actually being attempted and as to why such an attempt had been deemed necessary can be discerned through investigation in two related contexts. The first, and most immediate, relates to the general nature and purpose of the parliament in which the bill was to be introduced; the second, and slightly more distant, bears directly on

---

[39] Roger Bird, *Osborn's Concise Law Dictionary*, 7th edn (London, 1983), p. 261.

[40] Evidence for preparations leading up to the parliament is sparse: it is fully considered in Victor Treadwell, 'The Irish parliament of 1569–71', *Proceedings of the Royal Irish Academy*, 65, section C (1966–7), pp. 55–89.

Shane and the problems he had presented to the government of Ireland long before he met his death in rebellion.

III

When the parliament summoned by Sir Henry Sidney eventually ended after two years of frustrating and tumultuous sittings, its statute roll retained few surviving marks of a coherent government strategy.[41] But in the earliest drafts of bills prepared by Sidney and his advisers, Lucas Dillon and James Stanihurst, in the spring of 1568 a very clear plan of action can be seen to emerge from two clusters of bills which accounted for the bulk of what was supposed to be the parliament's total legislative schedule.[42] The first of these groups concerned that set of arbitrary, semi-feudal exactions known collectively as 'coyne and livery'. Accompanying a bill once more condemning and outlawing the evil was a set of supplementary bills regulating the keeping of retinues, suppressing captainries, enforcing the registration of 'idle men', abolishing fosterage, initiating the shiring of unshired regions and determining their boundaries, and empowering the governor to issue patents fixing the tenurial and feudal status of all freeholders within the Irish lordships.[43] In addition, several other bills claimed association with the same objective: thus the subsidy bill claimed justification on the grounds that 'coyne and livery' was now to be abolished, while the attainder of the knight of Glin emphasised his use of the evil of coyne.[44] But the O'Neill attainder went further: concluding that the list of English titles to Ireland from Gurmundus to Henry VIII had confirmed the right of the English monarchy in Ireland, it declared:

Yet is there of late, to the great glory of God, your immortal fame and good encouragement, a *greater* conquest than this wrought in this your land of Ireland, which is the abolition and extirpation of that horrible and most detestable coyne and livery which was the very nurse and teat that gave suck and nutrient to all disobediences, enormities, vices and iniquities of this realm . . . By the extermination whereof, there is, in so short a time, such an alteration of this estate happened that, where before there was everywhere but howling, crying, cursing,

---

[41] For a detailed account of the parliament's proceedings, see Treadwell, 'Irish parliament'.

[42] PRO, SP 63/27/12–15: the lists are dated provisionally as January 1569 in *CSPI, 1509–73*, pp. 400–1; but it is clear that they were produced for consideration by the privy council before Sidney left for Ireland in the previous autumn; the lists should also be compared with the section of proposed legislation included in an early draft of Sidney's viceregal instructions in July 1568, PRO, SP 63/25/50; on the immediate preparations for the parliament, see Treadwell, 'Irish parliament', pp. 62–3.

[43] PRO, SP 63/27/14, nos. 3, 4, 7, 10, 17, 19.

[44] As expressed in the printed statutes, *Statutes of Ireland*, I, pp. 333–4.

penury and famine, now there is instead thereof mirth, joy, jollity, and blessing of
Your Majesty, with such plentifulness of grain and victuals among the people of
this realm, as the like hath not been seen nor heard within the memory of man;
all parts of the same realm so quieted and the people, as it were, of themselves, so
inclined to justice as we dare say Your Majesty's commissioners and justices and
commandments may have at this day free concourse throughout this your realm
of Ireland.[45]

Overblown rhetoric, to be sure, at once factually inaccurate – for at
the time that the great peace was being celebrated, rebellion was in reality raging throughout Munster – and somewhat stale into the bargain.
Long before 1569 coyne and livery had been universally regarded as
a sin among the English in Ireland and all right-thinking people were
against it. Centuries of legislation, decades of political tracts and successive royal instructions to viceroys had all declared it to be so.[46] Yet
Sidney's renewed attack on coyne was different. Whereas previous enact-
ments had been simply proscriptive, outlawing coyne and livery as felony
and treason,[47] and earlier proclamations had been aspirational, calling
for a steady abandonment of the practice by those who employed it,[48]
the new legislation was intended to be more than merely declaratory.
Instead, it aimed to be instrumental. For, in addition to a standard con-
demnation, the new legislation was made up of a set of separate proposals
which collectively provided a variety of means by which the old evil would
be qualified, transformed and even tolerated, all at the discretion of the
viceroy and his commissioners. Thus the bills concerning the suppression
of captainries and the registration of idle men each contained qualifications concerning the circumstances in which, and the extent to which,
the government might still allow the continuance of the old practices
to be permitted.[49] The bills concerning the regranting of Irish titles by
letters patent and those establishing and bounding the new shires did
likewise.[50] A separate bill excluded the governor from the provisions of

[45] *Ibid.*, pp. 33–4. Italics added.
[46] Prohibitions of the arbitrary exactions later known collectively as 'coyne and livery' can
be traced back as far as the Statutes of Kilkenny, but the term itself became current in the
early fifteenth century; parliamentary proscriptions were frequent during the fifteenth
century, but the problem continued to grow and was a central preoccupation of the
reform literature of the early sixteenth century; for representative statements see 'Report
on the state of Ireland, *c.*1515' in *State Papers, Henry VIII* (11 vols., London, 1830–52),
II, part ii, pp. 1–31, 'Instructions to John Alen, 1533' and 'Report on Ireland, *c.* March
1534', *ibid.*, pp. 162–6, 182–92, and Patrick Finglas's influential 'Book of the getting of
Ireland and of the decay of the same', *c.*1534, PRO, SP 60/2/7.
[47] See, for example, 10 Henry VII, ch. 18, *Statutes of Ireland*, I, p. 54.
[48] See, for example, King Henry VIII's 'Commands' to the Irish Council, 24 September
1546, PRO, SP 60/12/48.
[49] *Statutes of Ireland*, I, pp. 319, 345.   [50] *Ibid.*, pp. 367–75.

earlier restrictions, explicitly entitling him and those authorised by him to undertake the hiring and maintenance of Scots mercenaries.[51] And, of course, the saving clause of the attainder bill itself, in pleading for the cases of those who had been forced into rebellion by Shane, reserved to the governor the right of determining just what livings should be allotted to them. Negotiations on the terms of the individual items in this set of bills from their first introduction in parliament to their transmission and final certification at Whitehall confirmed this underlying intent to empower the executive. Thus Sidney was prepared to make several concessions in particular instances and to safeguard individual interests, such as those of the earl of Ormond whose opposition he was most anxious to forestall. But throughout he was determined to hold out for the discretion of the viceroy, or see the bill fall.[52]

What this approach indicated was an important shift in the manner in which the English government in Ireland looked upon the practice of coyne and livery. No longer to be seen as a deplorable evil or a challenge to royal authority, it was now to be looked upon as a complex but opportune instrument of political intervention, the manipulation of which would supply the governor with sufficient leverage to conduct finely calculated negotiations between the crown and the great lords, their vassals and tenants as to how each group's status might be recognised under English law with the minimum of dispute. And at the centre of each of these local negotiations, mandated and supported by a clutch of statutes empowering him to determine the manner in which they were to be conducted and concluded, and sanctioned, above all, by the constitutional framework laid down in the act of attainder of Shane O'Neill, would be the uniquely powerful figure of the Irish chief governor, Sir Henry Sidney.

From this perspective, it now becomes clear that the constitutional restructuring being enacted in the O'Neill attainder was intent on effecting not merely an elevation of the status of the native Irish as subjects, and a corresponding diminution of the special status of the English in Ireland as descendants of the Norman conquerors, but also the subordination of both to the authority of the notional Irish monarch in the person of a real Irish viceroy. And, moreover, in a manner that was here made more explicit than in the case of its other implications, the act itself underlined the point in regard to the viceroy. For in the passage immediately succeeding that celebrating Queen Elizabeth's completion of the English title to Ireland, it left no doubt as to whose achievement it really was:

---

[51] *Ibid.*, pp. 359–60.
[52] Much material was generated concerning the earl of Ormond's case to be exempted from the prohibition on coyne, PRO, SP 63/ 26/ 68–75; in face of opposition the bill on the regulation of retinues was withdrawn.

This is the diligent and painful industry of your good servant Sir Henry Sidney, whose part we may not leave unreported without breach of conscience; who, laying God for his foundation, hath proceeded by the direct line of justice, according to your Highness's instruction, without corruption or respect of persons to bring these great things to pass.[53]

It is in relation to this bold elevation of a single individual – the Irish viceroy – that the second cluster of official legislative proposals prepared in advance of the parliament acquires its particular significance. For together, the renewal of the subsidy, the new import duty on wines, and the proposal that each nominee in a pardon should pay 50 per cent of the entire costs of the process, constituted a general programme for raising a revenue sufficient to allow for increased executive action without recourse to additional subvention from England.[54] Equally significant, however, was a further supplementary group of bills of more indirect fiscal importance. These were the bills empowering the viceroy to resume all waste lands, rebel lands and monastic lands, and to appropriate certain lands of the bishops of Lismore and Ferns to be used at his discretion.[55]

According to taste, such measures, in company with the unashamed self-promotion indulged in the attainder's preamble, may be seen to provide evidence of Sidney's personal ambition and colonialist greed. Alternatively, however, it can be interpreted as a conservative or even a defensive reflex. For the attempt to re-found his administration on the basis of a great constitutional declaration, backed up by the acquisition of a large tranche of crown lands and revenues which could be used as a means of developing sources of patronage and dependence as well as generating a revenue, carried powerful echoes of one of the earliest and most original attempts at Tudor state-building in Ireland: the policies introduced and the strategies deployed by Sir Anthony St Leger in the 1540s.[56] In this light it can be argued that in the desperate times of the late 1560s Sidney was merely intent on recreating and improving upon the conditions that had underpinned the most successful viceroyalty of the century. As ever, Sidney cannot be confined within such simple polarities; and for those intent on finding it, he will supply evidence of both. But the central point, transcending inconclusive speculations about his personal motivations, is his determination to secure for the English viceroy in Ireland an additional set of tools which would extend his capacity to initiate and conclude settlements in the localities in a manner that had evaded all of his predecessors. These bills were intended, then, to complement the

---

[53] *Statutes of Ireland*, I, p. 334.   [54] PRO, SP 63/27/14, nos. 5, 18, 19, 20.
[55] *Ibid.*, nos. 9, 11, 15, 16.
[56] Ciaran Brady, *The Chief Governors: the rise and fall of reform government in Tudor Ireland, 1536–1588* (Cambridge, 1994), chapter 1.

enabling legislation concerning coyne, supplying a sustaining external force to its own internal momentum.

IV

Such was Sidney's strategy outlined in the official schedule of legislation drafted in advance of the parliament of 1569. But the question which remains is why at this stage he had deemed it appropriate to undertake such a bold manner of proceeding. That Sidney was an innovator has often enough been claimed, though the nature of his innovations and the motives underlying them have just as frequently been the subject of dispute.[57] But, leaving aside the venerable debate concerning Sidney the militant Protestant or Sidney the representative of a new colonialist ideology, one demonstrable motivation arising from political and diplomatic developments in Ireland itself in recent decades can be discerned. This was a factor which bore not only upon the general problems of constitution-making confronted by the English government in the island in general, but, suitably enough, on the particular challenge that had been presented to it in the person of Shane O'Neill himself.

In 1564–5, as we have seen, negotiations between Shane and the English crown over his claim to be recognised as heir to the earldom of Tyrone had been stalled by his insistence that, before his claims to the earldom had been granted, he should, in arbitrations with the borderers of the Pale, be accorded the status not of a subject but of an independent power. Such a presumption, of course, was unacceptable to the crown, yet it merely represented Shane's mischievous but plausible inference drawn from a compelling constitutional argument which had been advanced by him during his embassy to the court of Queen Elizabeth in 1562.[58] The argument then deployed claimed that, since the original 1542 treaty recognising Conn Bacach O'Neill as earl of Tyrone had been rendered invalid through the undisputed illegitimacy of his nominated heir Matthew, it was now necessary to start again with the one who indisputably occupied the place held by Conn at the time of that treaty, that is, the current O'Neill, Shane.[59] For a variety of people, and for a variety of reasons this was considered an unpalatable option at Whitehall,

---

[57] Nicholas Canny, *The Elizabethan Conquest of Ireland: a pattern established* (Hassocks, 1976*)*; Brendan Bradshaw, 'The Elizabethans and the Irish', *Studies: An Irish Quarterly*, 65 (1977), pp. 38–50; Ciaran Brady (ed.), *A Viceroy's Vindication? Sir Henry Sidney's memoir of service in Ireland, 1556–78* (Cork, 2002), pp. 1–37.

[58] James Hogan, 'Shane O'Neill comes to the court of Elizabeth' in Séamus Pender (ed.), *Féilscríbhinn Tórna* (Cork, 1947), pp. 154–70.

[59] Brady, *Shane O'Neill*, pp. 38–47.

and so the negotiations were allowed to peter out.[60] But among the few substantial arguments raised against Shane was the simple riposte of his main adversary, the earl of Sussex. Sussex's position was constituted by two related points: first, that the original agreement was a simple one between a defeated and repentant rebel, Conn O'Neill, and his sovereign lord, the monarch of England and Ireland, who out of grace and mercy decided in a completely independent action to confer on him the status and power of an English earl; and secondly, Sussex went on, since this was an entirely new creation, made out of grace and favour, the elevation of Matthew to the peerage as baron of Dungannon and the contemporaneous declaration that he was to be heir to the earldom of Tyrone was, his illegitimacy notwithstanding, entirely within the power of the sovereign. The crown of Ireland, in short, could do as it pleased.[61]

Useful enough as a bargaining ploy, Sussex's hardline rebuttal, however, placed the crown in an unexpectedly vulnerable position. It was, in the immediate term, quite impracticable, as Shane's killing of Matthew's son and heir soon showed. But it was also historically inaccurate. Though Conn O'Neill had indeed surrendered as a rebel and been received by the mercy of the king on 24 September 1542, the charter creating him earl of Tyrone drawn up seven days later had confirmed to him not only all his lands and castles but also all his rights of lordship and dominion which he had held 'time out of mind' – that crucial phrase – without specification or inquisition.[62] In doing so, it had, perhaps inadvertently, returned to him not only those attributes he enjoyed as an individual but those also which he had acquired as the O'Neill. For several of these 'regalities and seigneuralities' had been, as Shane and his lawyers claimed to be able to demonstrate, derived from a series of obligations to give protection and service which the O'Neill had entered into with the people of Tír Eoghain over many centuries.[63] The obligations were antecedent to the privileges, and in regranting the privileges, the crown was, whether it knew it or not,

---

[60] Ciaran Brady, 'Shane O'Neill departs from the court of Elizabeth: Irish, English, Scottish perspectives and the paralysis of policy, July 1559 to April 1562' in S. J. Connolly (ed.), *Kingdoms United? Great Britain and Ireland since 1500* (Dublin, 1999), pp. 13–28.

[61] Sussex's 'Reply' and 'Confutation' of Shane, 14 February 1562, PRO, SP 63/5/30–1.

[62] Conn O'Neill's 'surrender' was made on 24 September 1542, *Letters and Papers Henry VIII*, XVII, nos. 831–3; his creation as earl of Tyrone occurred on 1 October; the only full text of the creation with all its concessions is to be found in Thomas Rymer, *Foedera: conventions, literae et . . . acta publica inter reges Anglie et alios* (10 vols., London, 1741), VI, part iii, pp. 101–2.

[63] 'Articles' presented to O'Neill and his 'Answers, 7 February 1562, PRO, SP 63/5/21–3; further 'responses', *Calendar of Carew Mss, 1515–74*, ed. J. S. Brewer and William Bullen (London, 1867), pp. 305–6; though dated 1560, these documents clearly arise from the negotiations conducted in February 1562.

reconstituting the obligations of O'Neill as the 'officer of his people'.[64] Back in the 1540s this had been a classic Henrician fudge, necessary to get the process started, and it is clear from a series of negotiations entered into over the decade with O'Neill and the other Ulster lords that the crown had intended strictly to limit the extent of O'Neill's claims in Tír Eoghain and in Ulster in general.[65] But the very assumption that such a round of negotiations would be required itself implied a recognition that some residual rights remained in the O'Neillship and an acknowledgement that something other than the creation of a new peer had taken place. These tensions inherent between the 'surrender' phase of the process and the consequent 'regrant' were further deepened by a number of concessions made explicitly but inadvertently in subsequent government arbitrations between O'Neill and other parties in Ulster. One, for instance, was the recognition implied in the crown's demand that Conn O'Neill should see to the enforcement of the Act of Supremacy 'in his dominions'.[66] Another was the point (granted even by Sussex) that Matthew had been nominated as heir because he was recognised as O'Neill's tanist.[67] And finally there remained the damaging concessions given to Shane at Drumcree concerning his claims over other Ulster lords which, even though the treaty had finally not been ratified, seemed to allow that the arguments raised by Sussex in 1562 were no longer held to by the crown.[68]

All of this suggested that the processes initiated in the 1540s were a good deal more complex than Sussex's retrospective interpretation had taken account of. But Sussex's position was not only historically imprecise; its assertion, and Shane's rebuttal, raised even more fundamental diplomatic problems for all of the parties who had already entered, or were now considering entering, into surrender negotiations with the crown. For the great lords who regarded their position as comparable to that of O'Neill, the claim that they were mere rebels who could be treated on whatever terms the crown pleased was hardly reassuring. Yet, conversely, the implication that whatever settlement had originally been negotiated by the crown was final and beyond revision, except at the desire of the monarch, was equally disturbing to other parties within the lordships who may have contested or resisted their lords' initial claims. Finally, for the agents of crown policy, faced with the actual collapse of some of the early arrangements, the claim that they would enforce original settlements without regard to the case of the interested parties was, as sorry experience had shown among the O'Briens of Thomond, the

---

[64] *Calendar of Carew MSS, 1515–74*, p. 306.   [65] *Ibid.*, pp. 203–7, 215–22.
[66] Rymer, *Foedera*, p. 102.   [67] Sussex's 'Confutation', PRO, SP 63/5/31.
[68] *Calendar of Carew Mss, 1515–74*, pp. 352–4; 'Articles' and 'Petitions', 18 November 1563, PRO, SP 63/9/60, ff. 62–5.

O'Byrnes, the O'Tooles and the Kavanaghs in Leinster, and, of course, among the O'Neills themselves, manifestly impracticable.

The moral high ground seized by Sussex in 1562 had therefore been strategically self-destructive. Yet it had nonetheless exposed the ambiguities and weaknesses inherent in the hastily initiated processes of the 1540s. By 1569 those weaknesses had long been made plain not only in regard to the O'Neills, the O'Briens, and other major Gaelic dynasties such as the O'Donnells and the O'Reillys, but in fact in all of the territories where the formula had been applied. It was in relation to the O'Neills, however, that the central issue concerning the status of the great native dynasties had most pointedly been raised and that the crown's difficulties in effecting political transformation had most dramatically been exposed. Thus it was this signally representative problem that Sidney set out to address in the act of attainder by means of erecting an entirely new (and quite fictitious) historical framework which offered an escape both from the impossible inflexibilities of Sussex's position in the early 1560s and more importantly from the deeper obfuscations which had preceded them twenty years earlier.

In conceding that Shane was, after all, the scion of a once legitimate lineage, but in rooting this concession in a history that founded the lineage of O'Neill, along with that of every other Irish dynasty, upon a claim that they were from time immemorial the obedient subjects of the English crown, the act appeared to have resolved at a stroke two of the most serious problems facing English government in Ireland. First, it denied the right of any one dynasty to claim a superior status as defenders of their inferiors; and secondly, it established simultaneously the broadest possible foundations upon which the crown could commence the renegotiation and reconstruction of tenurial and feudal relations within the lordships in terms recognisable under English law. In tandem with the enabling legislation concerning coyne and the bills extending the executive freedom of the governor, this revisionist new history of 1569 was conceived to supply the basis of a second 'constitutional revolution of the sixteenth century' which would overcome all of the conceptual and practical difficulties that had afflicted the first in the 1540s. Clear grounds for establishing the basis of allegiance among the freeholding subjects of the Irish lordships had been laid down. The claims which the Gaelic chieftains asserted over other principal families in their lordships as rights distinctive to their office as chief were now abrogated in principle, to be referred in practice to detailed local negotiation. And the ability of the Irish viceroy to intervene in the politics of the Irish lordships in a deeper and more persistent manner than had ever before been possible was now confirmed.

Like the first revolution of the 1540s, however, Sidney's bold experiment in constitution-making also proved abortive, and its failure, moreover, took place a good deal more rapidly than that of its predecessor. The parliament which was supposed to be brief, compliant and enthusiastic, turned out to be protracted, suspicious and turbulent.[69] Resisted and mistrusted from the beginning, Sidney's legislative programme was mauled. Almost all of the official bills were challenged on some ground; many, including the O'Neill attainder itself, were delayed, and several were amended. At the outset Sidney had drawn up a legislative schedule of forty-six acts for presentation to a parliament which was intended to last no more than a matter of weeks; when the parliament was finally prorogued over two years later, only twenty-nine statutes had been passed, several of which had not formed part of the original scheme. Several of Sidney's most important measures, including bills on the resumption of waste land in towns and boroughs, for the restoration of parish churches, the regulation of retinues, and the raising of revenue from pardons, were lost altogether.[70]

Sidney accounted for much of the hostility he had encountered in terms of the short-sightedness of the members and the intrigues of his enemy the earl of Ormond. But in view of the far-reaching implication of the official legislative programme analysed above, it is clear also that the parliament's suspicion was aroused by more than local intrigues, and the ambitions of the adventurer Sir Peter Carew and the tactlessness of John Hooker. Though detailed evidence of the character of the debate has been lost, there are indications to be detected in the closing speeches made to the parliament by both Sidney and Speaker Stanihurst, in the bitter wranglings over the suspension of Poynings's Law, as well as in some of the ancillary material produced by Sidney in explanation of his plans, that at least some of Sidney's opponents were reacting not only against the attempted aggrandisement of viceregal power implied in many of the proposed bills,[71] but also against the equalisation of native Irish and English Irish which so much of the legislation also entailed.[72] Once more in order to strengthen the claims of the English crown over the country as a whole, the English colonial community was being asked to accept

---

[69] Treadwell, 'Irish parliament'.

[70] The extent of the losses can be measured from a comparison of the bills listed in PRO, SP 63/27/12–15; with the printed statutes, *Statutes of Ireland*, I, pp. 313–90.

[71] Of particular importance here was the resistance to the suspension of Poynings's Law: Treadwell, 'Irish parliament', pp. 65–70.

[72] Such sentiments may be reflected indirectly in the speeches made at the closing of the parliament by Speaker Stanihurst and Sidney himself; a more direct statement of the view is contained in the anonymous 'Discourse against the abolition of coyne and livery', PRO, SP 63/26/68.

and support a set of innovations which challenged their very identity as a distinctive historical entity in the island. And as was the case in regard to the religious reformation which the Tudors had sought to introduce among them, the English of Ireland chose to reject it.

The refusal of the Irish parliament to become the engine of political and social reform in Ireland proved a deep disappointment to Sidney, something he remembered to the close of his career. But the more immediate lesson which he was to draw from the débâcle was the disturbingly radical idea that the new political and social structures he sought to establish might be achieved by means other than parliamentary legislation. In the years immediately following the failure of his parliament, acting under the advice of his sometime counsellor, Edmund Tremayne, Sidney was to devise an alternative and even more radical strategy for the refoundation of political legitimacy and tenurial stability in Ireland which he denominated simply as 'composition'.[73] A policy which aimed at linking the political, social and legal status of the island's inhabitants to their ability to yield a graduated annual revenue without recourse to parliamentary consent, 'composition' was, as Sidney's own lord chancellor and eventually Queen Elizabeth herself were to confirm, an even more un-English way of seeking to establish government in Ireland than the statutory programme of 1569, and in the later 1570s the English of Ireland combined once again to destroy it. But this confirmation of their victory over a viceroy who would have radically reshaped their constitutional and historical status in Ireland served only to obscure for an interval the persistence of two related challenges to this cherished sense of identity, both of them profound and both unresolved. One was the haunting menace that the interests of the crown and those of its English subjects in Ireland would not always coincide and might often be directly in conflict. But arising from this was a second, even more disturbing, prospect: that the distinctive status upon which Ireland's English had insisted in regard both to their sovereign and to the other inhabitants of the island was an anachronism which history was unlikely to sustain.

[73] On the origins and development of 'composition', see Brady, *The Chief Governors*, chapter 4.

3 Dynamics of regional development: processes of assimilation and division in the marchland of south-east Ulster in late medieval and early modern Ireland

Harold O'Sullivan

Our understanding of the political and social history of provincial Ireland in the early modern period has been retarded by a conspiracy – more passive than active, more assumed than asserted – between two contrasting and divergent historiographies. The first, the dominant partner in this unintended conspiracy, has been the great master-narrative of Irish history, which, regardless of local variations and accommodations, has given overwhelming prominence to the principal themes of conflict, conquest and confiscation. The second, and less noticed, one has been the work of the local historian, engaged in the more modest pursuits of antiquarian and genealogical research, usually without reference to the assertions of the great national narrative, rarely daring to register a disagreement with it, never overtly challenging it, and often suppressing its own genuine discoveries under the weight of the dominant tradition. The losses arising from this tactful arrangement have been several, perpetuating a misunderstanding of events, of individuals, and of social and cultural practices. But one of its most serious costs has been the disregard of an important alternative framework of analysis which, intervening between the larger level of nation or country and the lower level of locality and the individual, has elsewhere provided a most fertile soil for the growth of a better appreciation of historical change. By this I mean the *region*.

For long a source of interpretative renovation in other historiographies, notably in France, in Italy and latterly in England, the region as a framework of analysis has come late to early modern Ireland.[1] Studies of

---

[1] The development of local and regional history in France is especially associated with the Annales school: see among several classic contributions, Lucien Febvre, *A Geographical Introduction to History*, trans. E. G. Mountfor and J. H. Paxton (London, 1925) and Emmanuel Le Roy Ladurie, *The Peasants of Languedoc*, trans. John Day (Urbana, Ill., 1974). Italy by virtue of its history has always encouraged a regionalist approach to historical study and interpretation: for historical and theoretical perspectives, see Carl Levy (ed.), *Italian Regionalism: history, identity, politics* (Oxford, 1996). There are numerous

inescapably distinct cultural areas such as Ulster east of the Bann have, understandably, led the way.[2] More generally, the development of a comparative approach to Irish history by scholars such as Robin Frame, Rhys Davies and Steven Ellis has, in identifying the similarity of frontier lands and marcher lands in England, Wales and Ireland, helped to highlight individual examples of such regions as subjects for special analysis.[3] This chapter is an attempt to build upon such work. Whereas the perspective of these recent scholars has largely been comparative, indicating similar and dissimilar characteristics with the purpose of diluting a national or general norm which has so often been simply presumed by historians, the approach adopted here is primarily dynamic. The intent of this approach is not to supersede such important comparative and structural analyses, but rather to supplement them by devoting particular attention to the ways in which the sequence and interaction of political events were not only influenced by, but themselves served to shape, the distinctive characteristics of a region.

I

The marchland of south-east Ulster, consisting of east Monaghan, south Armagh, south Down and north Louth, like marches elsewhere, was throughout most of the late medieval and early modern periods a place of chronic lawlessness, political instability and violence.[4] In seeking to understand this persistent and identifying feature, it is doubtless best to begin with geography; for the territory possessed unique geographical

studies for early modern England, especially during the civil wars of the 1640s, see for a few examples, Alan Everitt, *The Community of Kent and the Great Rebellion, 1640–1660* (Leicester, 1966), John Morrill, *Cheshire 1630–60: a county government during the English revolution* (Oxford, 1974), B. G. Blackwood, *The Lancashire Gentry and Great Rebellion, 1640–1660* (Manchester, 1978) and Ann Hughes, *Politics, Society and Civil War in Warwickshire, 1620–1660* (Cambridge, 1987).

2 Raymond Gillespie, *Colonial Ulster: the settlement of east Ulster 1600–1641* (Cork, 1985); Michael Perceval-Maxwell, *Scottish Migration to Ulster in the Reign of James I* (London, 1973); Philip Robinson, *The Plantation of Ulster. British settlement in an Irish landscape* (Dublin, 1984).

3 Robin Frame, 'Two kings in Leinster: the crown and the Mic Murchadha in the fourteenth century' in T. Barry, R. Frame and K. Simms (eds.), *Colony and Frontier in Medieval Ireland. Essays presented to J. F. Lydon* (Dublin, 1995), pp. 155–76 and 'Military service in the lordship of Ireland, 1290–1360: institutions and society on the Anglo-Gaelic frontier' in Robert Bartlett and Angus MacKay (eds.), *Medieval Frontier Societies* (Oxford, 1989), pp. 127–50; Steven G. Ellis, *Tudor Frontiers and Noble Power: the making of the British state* (Oxford, 1995). Also see Robert Bartlett, *The Making of Europe. Conquest, colonisation and cultural change 950–1350* (London, 1993).

4 For religion and society in the march in the fourteenth century, see Katherine Walsh, *A Fourteenth-Century Scholar and Primate, Richard FitzRalph in Oxford, Avignon and Armagh* (Oxford, 1981), pp. 318–48 and Henry A. Jefferies, *Priests and Prelates of Armagh, in the Age of Reformations, 1518–1558* (Dublin, 1997).

qualities. Bordering and in part encompassing the great south-east Ulster drumlin belt, its northern and western segments formed something like a natural frontier. However, unlike other clearly demarcated borderlands, the frontier here was distinctly 'soft': that is, it was an area where natural obstacles were influential enough to help shape settlement, travel and communication but yet were never sufficiently obstructive to determine them altogether. To the south and the east, moreover, ready access to the coast and a generous endowment of navigable rivers and protected inlets set up a countervailing force to simple frontier formation which was often powerful enough to attract trade, commerce and even settlement from deep in the heart of Ulster. Such centrifugal forces might seem on the face of it to have militated against any recognisable pattern of regional formation; but the matter is more complex. Natural features did not combine to create a territory which was clearly defined, substantially uniform or internally stable. What they did help shape, however, was an area which was at once heterogeneous in its features, but also permeable in its external boundaries and internal frameworks, and was thus intrinsically dynamic, sensitive to and supportive of alterations in social settlement and economic activity, and to the political competition that arose from such changes. Thus it was that in the years between 1450 and 1650, as in previous centuries, the evolution of south-east Ulster as a distinctive region was to be as much shaped by the actions recorded in human history as by the characteristics bequeathed by physical geography.

II

Following the collapse of the de Burgo earldom of Ulster in the early fourteenth century, the strength of the Ulster Irish ensured that extensive territories in the eastern parts of the province, conquered in the earlier period, were recovered, while the intended colonisation of the south-eastern kingdom of the O'Carrolls of Airghialla ended in a partition.[5] Only that part along the coastline from Dundalk Bay to the Drogheda estuary remained under the control of the colonial settlement to become known variously as Uriel/Oriel (Airghialla) or Louth. Of the rest of Airghialla, the western portion came under the control of the MacMahons, in what is now County Monaghan, while the northern

---

[5] For the Anglo-Norman settlements in Ulster, including the kingdom of Airghialla and English Uriel, see T. D. McNeill, *Anglo-Norman Ulster. The history and archaeology of an Irish barony* (Edinburgh, 1980); Brendan Smith, *Colonisation and Conquest in Medieval Ireland. The English in Louth 1170–1330* (Cambridge, 1999); A. J. Otway-Ruthven, *A History of Medieval Ireland* (London, 1968); Edmund Curtis, *A History of Medieval Ireland* (London, 1938).

section, now County Armagh, came under the domination of the O'Neills of Tyrone.

Throughout the fifteenth century, the Englishry of Uriel made some recoveries of territories lost earlier to the Irishry.[6] These included the Fews area bordering with Armagh, where the Bellews of Roche engaged in a chronic state of warfare with the O'Neills of Tyrone in the 1440s and 1450s. While the O'Neills succeeded in retaining the greater part of the Fews, the Bellews recovered an area now in County Louth known as 'the five townlands of the Fews'. Recoveries were also made in territories bounding with the MacMahon lordship. These included the extensive manors of Louth, Castlering and Ash, which were reclaimed by the Talbots of Malahide in 1465. Other English families to settle cadet branches in the western march at this period were the Bellews of Roche, who settled at Lisrenny and Thomastown; the Plunketts of Beaulieu at Tallonstown; the Flemings of Slane at Laggan and Bellahoe; and the Clintons of Stabannon at Nizelerath. By the end of the fifteenth century the only lands held by the Irishry in Uriel were in the Faughart area north of Dundalk and extending eastwards to include Omeath in the Cooley peninsula. The O'Hanlons possessed these lands until the early sixteenth century, when they ceded them to the earls of Kildare.

The Irishry of the march were a disparate group of lordships which emerged in the period following the Anglo-Norman settlement, apparently in feudal affiliation with the earldom of Ulster, in some cases as a stratagem to avoid the domination of the O'Neills of Tyrone. If the king of England was generally accepted as lord of Ireland, the denial to the Irishry of the full benefits of that lordship, which was applied only to the English colonists, ensured a continuance of political instability and periodic violence. In 1449 the lord lieutenant, Richard, duke of York, made an attempt to establish a new relationship between the crown lordship and the Irishry of Ulster. In a treaty signed at Drogheda in that year it was agreed that the Tyrone O'Neill would become the feudal tenant of the earl of Kildare, paying the military service traditionally associated with such tenancy, and that O'Neill should have precedence over all the other Irish lordships as the mesne or intermediate lord between them and the earldom.[7] However agreeable this may have been to the earl and to O'Neill, it was not one consented to by the marcher lords,

---

[6] For details of these recoveries, see Harold O'Sullivan, 'The march of south-east Ulster in the fifteenth and sixteenth centuries, a period of change' in Raymond Gillespie and Harold O'Sullivan (eds.), *The Borderlands: Essays on the history of the Ulster–Leinster border* (Belfast, 1989), pp. 55–74.

[7] Katharine Simms, '"The King's friend": O'Neill, the crown and the earldom of Ulster' in James Lydon (ed.), *England and Ireland in the Late Middle Ages* (Dublin, 1981), p. 214; see also Otway-Ruthven, *A History of Medieval Ireland*, chapter 12 and Curtis, *A History of Medieval Ireland*, pp. 315–19.

whose resistance to the O'Neill overlordship predated in many cases the Norman invasion. Throughout the next century and a half, as the O'Neills struggled to make their overlordship a reality in the face of a consistent opposition by the Irish lords themselves, they were to experience a less than consistent support for their policy by the English crown itself. It was this very ambivalence on the part of the crown and its representatives in Ireland regarding the role which the O'Neill was to be allowed play in its affairs that was to be central to the evolution of the region in the late fifteenth and early sixteenth centuries.

Apart from their perceived common ethnicity the Irish lords of the region had little in common with each other.[8] To the west lay the MacMahon lordship of Airghialla.[9] The original Norman plan for the conquest of Airghialla having failed, only in the lordship of Farney, bordering with English Uriel, or Louth, was any foothold retained. Even there it was a compromise, the MacMahons holding the lordship from the crown in return for an annual rent.[10] A Cenél Eoghain family, the MacMurphys of Muintir Bearn in County Tyrone, had settled the territory of the Fews, which bordered with the MacMahons to the east, in the earlier period. This connection with the Cenél Eoghain may have been the justification later used by the O'Neills for their intrusion into the Fews. By the mid-sixteenth century the O'Neills of the Fews had become a separate lordship outside the overlordship of the O'Neills of Tyrone.[11] Their neighbours to the east were the O'Hanlons, who had been driven southwards by the O'Neills from their ancestral lands of Oneilland in north Armagh in the late twelfth and early thirteenth centuries. Their close association with the English town of Dundalk is evidenced by the inclusion of their heraldic emblem, the boar ermine, as a supporter in the early fourteenth-century coat of arms of the town corporation.[12]

---

[8] See Katharine Simms, 'The Gaelic lordships of Ulster in the later Middle Ages' (Ph.D. thesis, Trinity College, Dublin, 1976), and 'The O'Hanlons, the O'Neills and the Anglo-Normans in thirteenth century Armagh', Seanchas Ardmhacha, 9:1 (1978), pp. 70–94.

[9] For the pre-Norman Irish kingdom of Airghialla, see Tomás Ó Fiaich, 'The kingdom of Airghialla and its sub-kingdoms' (M.A. thesis, National University of Ireland, 1950).

[10] For the MacMahon lordship, see E. P. Shirley, The History of the County of Monaghan (London, 1879), pp. 13–14; Peadar Livingstone, The Monaghan Story (Enniskillen, 1980), chapters 3 to 6; and Phillip Moore, 'The MacMahons of Monaghan 1500–1593', Clogher Record, 1 (1955), pp. 70–94.

[11] For the O'Neills of the Fews see Tomás Ó Fiaich, 'The O'Neills of the Fews', Seanchas Ardmhacha, part I, 7:1 (1973), pp. 1–64, part II, 7:2 (1974), pp. 263–315 and part III, 8:2 (1977), pp. 386–413.

[12] For relations between the O'Hanlons and the English colony in Louth see Smith, Colonisation and Conquest, chapters 3 and 4; for the seal of the corporation of Dundalk see Harold O'Sullivan, Tempest's Annual (1968), pp. 63–5, and Raghnall Ó Floinn, 'Two medieval seals from County Louth', Louth Archaeological and Historical Journal, 22:4 (1992), p. 387.

The Magennises of Iveagh trace their descent from the ancient Uladh and, with their cousins the MacCartans, were the last remnant of the ancient kingdom to survive the Norman invasion of Ulster.[13] Their lordship extended over the areas east of the River Bann, south of Lough Neagh eastwards to Castlewellan and southwards to Carlingford Lough. As the earldom of Ulster contracted the Magennises extended themselves into the adjoining territories of Mourne and Lecale, occupying de Courcy's great castle-keep at Dundrum and the de Lacy castle at Greencastle on Carlingford Lough. By the end of the fifteenth century they were the leading Irish lordship in west and south Down.

The closing decades of the fifteenth century were a period of rapprochement between the Englishry and Irishry of Ulster, largely as a result of the influence of Gerald Fitzgerald, eighth earl of Kildare, who was the king's deputy lieutenant between 1478 and 1492. No small part was played in these developments by the marriage connections established between himself and the O'Neills of Tyrone.[14] The appointment of the English-born Sir Edward Poynings as lord deputy in 1494 brought war to the march.[15] Determined to assert the authority of the English crown against that of Kildare, the former and politically compromised viceroy, Poynings demanded pledges for good behaviour and regarded the Gaelic lords' refusal to yield them as an act of rebellion.[16] O'Hanlon's lordship had been particularly devastated, and, having consulted with the earl, O'Hanlon was advised to sue for peace. This was agreed, O'Hanlon giving his son as a hostage.[17] In a sequel to the affair, Kildare was accused of having connived with O'Hanlon and Magennis and of being guilty of treason. He was arrested and sent for trial in London. His subsequent successful defence was in no small part due to the evidence collected by Octavian de Palatio, the archbishop of Armagh, from both O'Hanlon and Magennis.[18] He was returned to Ireland as the king's deputy and with an English wife, Elizabeth St John. In 1505 O'Hanlon granted away to Kildare an extensive area of land in north Louth extending from Faughart, north of Dundalk, to Ravensdale, and across the Cooley mountains to Omeath in the Carlingford

[13] For the Magennises at this period, see McNeill, *Anglo-Norman Ulster*, p. 5.
[14] Conn More O'Neill father of Conn Bacach was married to Fitzgerald's sister Eleanor.
[15] S. G. Ellis, *Ireland in the Age of the Tudors 1447–1603* (London, 1998), p. 91.
[16] *Ibid.*
[17] Harold O'Sullivan, 'The landed gentry of the County of Louth in the age of the Tudors', *Louth Archaeological and Historical Journal*, 22:1 (1989), pp. 67–8.
[18] For Octavian's examinations of O'Hanlon and Magennis see Sughi Mario Alberto, *Registrum Octaviani alias Liber Niger: The Register of Octavian de Palatio archbishop of Armagh 1478–1513* (IMC, 2 vols., Dublin, 1999), 5:1, pp. 11–12 and 5:2, pp. 40–2.

area.[19] On his return to Ireland, Kildare received the submissions of the marcher lords, all of whom swore fealty to Henry VII.[20] The peace which Kildare had won in Ulster by means of quiet diplomacy survived until his death in 1513. But the tensions within the English interest in Ireland, between the old colonial community as represented by Kildare, and the representatives of royal government as represented by Poynings, in their approaches to the Gaelic lordships of Ulster, were soon to resurface.

In the period after the death of 'the Great Earl' of Kildare in 1513 the march suffered repeated attacks from a succession of English-born lord deputies sent over from Whitehall, most notably the earl of Surrey (1520–22), Sir William Skeffington (1534–35) and Lord Leonard Grey (1536–40).[21] But the occasional punitive raids launched by English viceroys did not automatically secure for them the friendship of the house of Kildare and its Geraldine allies among the Englishry of the march. Gerald Oge, the ninth earl of Kildare, was responsible for one of the most damaging raids launched against the O'Hanlons in 1517, and throughout the 1520s the English of Louth maintained a low-level pattern of raid and reprisal against their Irish neighbours. An even greater threat came from Kildare's chief but not entirely dependable ally, Conn Bacach O'Neill, who was ever attuned to exploit the vulnerabilities of the Gaelic lordships in relation to the English, whether local or foreign. The dilemmas presented to the lesser Irish lordships caught between the interstices of O'Neill–Kildare politics on the one hand, and Kildare and Whitehall politics on the other, account most clearly for their positive response when an altogether different opportunity was presented to them within the context of the so-called 'constitutional revolution' initiated by the representatives of the English crown in 1541.[22]

Of the many constitutional and political initiatives introduced by Lord Deputy Sir Anthony St Leger in the 1540s, that known as 'surrender and regrant' was, for the Irish lords of the march, the most important.[23] The marcher lords recognised that 'surrender and regrant' would not only achieve greater security of tenure for themselves, but would relieve them also of the burdens of the O'Neill overlordship and, should they return, of Geraldine hegemony. It is not surprising, therefore, that when St Leger moved against Conn Bacach O'Neill's initial refusal to accept the

---

[19] Grant by Malachy O'Hanlon, captain of his nation to Gerald Fitzgerald, earl of Kildare, of the lands of Omee [Omeath] near Carlingford, 1508, PRONI, D3078/1/25/1–7.

[20] Ellis, *Ireland in the Age of the Tudors*, p. 98.

[21] *Ibid.*, chapter 6.

[22] Brendan Bradshaw, *The Irish Constitutional Revolution of the Sixteenth Century* (Cambridge, 1979).

[23] For 'surrender and regrant' see *ibid.*, pp. 196–200, and O'Sullivan, *The Borderlands*, pp. 63–6.

reforms, all the marcher lords readily supported St Leger. Their resistance was of crucial importance in O'Neill's decision to yield to St Leger and to sign articles of surrender in Dundalk in December 1541.[24] In the following year Conn travelled to London, where, having accepted terms of surrender and regrant, he was created earl of Tyrone and his heir apparent, Matthew, was created baron of Dungannon.

The Magennises of Iveagh were among the first to come into the scheme of 'surrender and regrant'. Following the murder of Murtagh Magennis, lord of Iveagh, by the Englishry of Louth at the instigation of some of the Magennises, a succession dispute arose between Donal Oge of Rathfriland and Art MacPhelim of Castlewellan. St Leger intervened in the dispute in 1540 by appointing two arbitrators, Art MacGlasny Magennis and Sir Patrick Gernon of Killencoole, County Louth. An agreement was concluded in May 1541 providing that while Donal Oge would succeed to the lordship, Art MacPhelim would be excluded from his jurisdiction, and in the event of Donal Oge predeceasing him, he would then succeed to the lordship.[25] The implications of this agreement were substantial. It was the first time that the king's deputy was involved in the election of a Magennis – an election which also provided for the separation of Art's lands at Castlewellan from the Magennis lordship. Furthermore, it effectively gave Art a form of freehold tenure to his estates under the English common law, the implications of which would not have been lost on the other Magennis families. Thus, for one of the lesser Gaelic lords of the region, the promise of anglicisation had been provided. Yet for others it raised crucial and indeterminate questions: how far would their own internal forces allow them to proceed in this direction? More seriously, how far would their more powerful neighbours amongst the Irish and the English look on in approval and support of this transformation?

These complexities aside, two other important events took place at the time of Conn Bacach O'Neill's ennoblement as earl of Tyrone, the effects of which were to be felt in the march throughout the rest of the sixteenth century. The first was the acknowledgement by Conn Bacach of the assertion that his eldest living son, Matthew, was the product of an adulterous liaison between himself and one Alison Kelly, a blacksmith's widow from Dundalk. It was an admission of his heir's illegitimacy that was laden with risk not only for the stability of the O'Neill lordship but for

[24] O'Sullivan, *The Borderlands*, p. 65.

[25] Harold O'Sullivan, 'The Magennis lordship of Iveagh in the early modern period 1534–1691' in Lindsay Proudfoot (ed.), *Down: history and society* (Dublin, 1997), pp. 160–1.

the whole of Ulster.[26] The second, quite unconnected event, was Conn's request for a pardon to be granted to the fugitive Englishman Nicholas Bagenal, who had served as a mercenary in Conn's forces. Revealing the strong possibility that Bagenal served as a double agent, it was submitted by the Irish council that Bagenal, 'having hither fled','has since done very honest and painful service'.[27] The petition was fatefully successful and on 2 March 1543 Bagenal was granted a 'general pardon of all murders by him committed'.[28]

Following this rehabilitation, Bagenal's advancment within the crown service was spectacular.[29] In 1547 he was appointed marshal of the army, and in 1550 to the Irish council. In 1550 he secured a twenty-one-year lease of the confiscated properties of the Cistercian abbey of Newry. The stated objectives of this settlement were 'to plant a captain with furniture of men for the reduction of those rude and savage quarters to better rule and obedience'.[30] At the same time he also acquired Martin O'Kyrne's interests in the farm of Carlingford on a twenty-one-year lease.[31] Within the next two years Bagenal succeeded in having his leaseholds of Newry and Carlingford converted to one of knight's fee. At the same time he also acquired the lordships of Mourne and Greencastle.[32]

On the surface, these disparate actions of O'Neill – the acknowledgement of Matthew's illegitimacy and the legitimation of Bagenal – may have appeared, even to him, as quite unrelated. However, underlying both must have been an anxiety arising from the implications of his acceptance of the earldom. Conn recognised Matthew not only because he was his eldest son, but also because such recognition gave him an important leverage among the English colonial community of the region. Yet conscious also of the ramifications that his elevation as an earl raised both for his Irish allies and the English of the march, he sought simultaneously to

---

[26] On the implications of this admission see Ciaran Brady, *Shane O'Neill* (Dundalk, 1995), chapter 2; for the O'Neill connection with Alison Kelly and the town of Dundalk, see Harold O'Sullivan, 'Rothe's castle, Dundalk and Hugh O'Neill, a sixteenth-century map', *Louth Archaeological and Historical Journal*, 15:3 (1963), pp. 281–91.

[27] *State Papers, Henry VIII, Foreign Correspondence, 1545–47*, 7 December 1542, pp. 439–40; he had been outlawed for murder in his native Staffordshire, see also P. H. Bagenal, *Vicissitudes of an Anglo-Irish Family 1530–1800* (London, 1935), chapter 4.

[28] *State Papers, Henry VIII* (11 vols., London, 1830–52), III, part iii, p. 442.

[29] For Bagenal's advancement, including his acquisition of landed estate in the Carlingford Lough area, see Harold O'Sullivan, 'A 1575 rent-roll, with contemporaneous maps of the Bagenal estate in the Carlingford Lough district', *Louth Archaeological and Historical Journal*, 21:1 (1985), pp. 31–47.

[30] Bagenal, *Vicissitudes*, p. 33; *Calendar of the Patent and Close Rolls of Chancery in Ireland*, ed. James Morrin (3 vols., Dublin, 1861–63), I, p. 228 (24 November 1550).

[31] *Ibid.* (19 July 1550).

[32] *Calendar of the Patent Rolls Preserved in the Public Record Office, Edward VI to Elizabeth, 1547–75* (16 vols., London, 1924–73), VII, i, pp. 387–90 (20 April 1552).

find a new source of support among the Englishry to sustain his position. This was a perilous strategy, and it soon began to come apart.

By 1551 Conn Bacach's controversial succession plans had provoked deadly internecine war among the O'Neills. The dynasty imploded, and by the end of the decade Conn's youngest son, Shane, had established his supremacy as O'Neill, killing Matthew and his eldest son, Brian, and forcing the youngest son, Hugh, to seek shelter in the Pale. Shane's rule was sustained largely by terror enforced by his dangerous dependence on Scottish allies and the mercenaries hired by them.[33] In the interim Bagenal had exploited the war to establish his own position as an independent force in the region. Through the 1550s and 1560s Bagenal, aided by his son and heir, Henry, steadily consolidated his family's position in the march. Their estates in the Carlingford area extended over an area of 120,000 acres, including the upland and mountainous areas of the Cooley peninsula and the Mournes. A contemporary rent roll shows that while the chief tenants had Welsh surnames, the greatest number of the tenancies were either native Irish or Old English.[34] By the 1570s the large number of O'Morgans and MacMorgans mentioned in the rent roll suggests that by that date the settlement had 'gone native'. An important development by Bagenal was the founding of the town of Newry, the construction of which may have begun shortly after Bagenal's reappointment as marshal in 1568. In 1575 Sidney described it as 'well planted with inhabitants and increased in beauty and buildings'.[35]

The county of Louth had suffered severely from the depredations inflicted by the respective parties in the campaigns conducted by Shane O'Neill. Martial law was enforced at various times, giving power to local martial law commissioners to act in the absence of the lord deputy, to 'raise [i.e. conscript] the inhabitants, to resist and punish enemies and rebels, and to elect one or two of their number to be generals of the forces in the field'.[36] Military men such as a Plunkett of Tallonstown or a Babe of Darver might have been happy collaborators of the lord deputy in the enforcement of martial law. However, the generality of the population felt oppressed by the obligation to pay cess for the maintenance of the army and by the withdrawal of ordinary norms in the administration of justice implied by martial law. Even Shane, the begetter of much of the disorder, was to complain to the queen in 1561, probably with tongue in cheek, of the intolerable burdens endured by the families of the Pale in the payment of 'cess, taxes, and tallages both of corn, beef, muttons,

---

[33] Brady, *Shane O'Neill*, chapter 3.   [34] See O'Sullivan 'A 1575 rent-roll', pp. 34–42.

[35] Bagenal, *Vicissitudes*, pp. 27, 29.

[36] For details of commissions issued during 1561, see *The Fiants of the Tudor Sovereigns, Henry VIII to Elizabeth I* (Dublin, 1994), no. 379–81.

porks and baks', alleging that above 300 farmers had fled from the Pale as refugees into his country.[37]

Shane's defeat and assassination in 1567 created a political vacuum in the Tyrone lordship, but enabled a period of recovery in the south-east, disturbed only by the planned confiscation and plantation of the lands escheated from O'Neill and by the independent enterprise in 1573 of Walter Devereux, earl of Essex. Although Essex's grant pertained largely to Ulster east of the Bann, it also included portions of the MacMahon lordship of Farney, the O'Hanlon lordship of Orier, the MacCartan lordship of Kinelarty, together with lands in the lordship of Iveagh held by the Magennises of Corrocks and Aghnemulragh.[38] Essex died before he could make good his grant of Farney, leaving Ever Mac Con Uladh MacMahon in possession of the farm at an annual rent of £300.[39] The attempted plantations were a failure. Following the return of Sidney as lord deputy in August 1575, a policy of rapprochement towards the marcher lords was initiated, resulting in the revocation of these grants and the reinstatement of the Irish lordships. Upsets of this kind, however, made the Irishry of the march, caught between the pretensions of the O'Neills on the one hand, and the unreliability of English policies and promises on the other, ready to oppose the former when opportunity offered and to treat the blandishments of the latter with cunning dissimulation and prevarication. Even the Englishry of the loyal shire of Louth had become disenchanted by the behaviour of the new rulers out of England. When in 1574 Essex planned an expedition against Shane's successor as O'Neill, Turlough Luineach, and called on the Englishry to give him support, only the Flemings of Slane responded. Essex retorted that the people of Louth would do nothing but complain that they were overtaxed and 'as they think to have greater thanks for denial to come with me than in their forwardness in this service; they do so often and so openly exclaim and complain unto me, and I am not able to address it as I am truly weary of myself'.[40] This was simply a reflection of the growing disenchantment between the New English administrations of the late Tudor period and the Old English elite of the Pale, and which was to reach its crisis in the early seventeenth century.

In October 1575 Hugh Magennis of Rathfriland, lord of Iveagh, petitioned to have his estates formally granted to him by the queen. He

[37] Richard Bagwell, *Ireland under the Tudors* (3 vols., London, 1885–90), II, pp. 269–70.

[38] For Essex's attempted plantation of Farney see Shirley, *History of Monaghan*, chapter 3; see also O'Sullivan 'The march of south-east Ulster in the fifteenth and sixteenth centuries', pp. 68–70, for the attempted plantation of the lands of the Magennises of Corrocks and Aghnemulragh, see *CSPI, 1574–84*, p. 435.

[39] Shirley, *History of Monaghan*, p. 63.   [40] Bagwell, *Tudor Ireland*, II, pp. 269–70.

pointed out that 'ever since his revolt from Shane O'Neill' he had shown 'fidelity to her majesty'. The petition was granted, and in the following year Magennis received a knighthood. In 1584 he further consolidated his position in Iveagh by obtaining a grant *in capite* of the crown 'of the entire country or territory of Iveagh'.[41] This did not include the territories of Kilwarlin, which were in the northern parts of the lordship and held by Ever MacRory Magennis, to whom a separate grant of the lordship and manor of Kilwarlin was made in 1585. These transfers were subsequently confirmed by letters patent and mark a complete break by the Magennises from the old Irish laws of land tenure. There is also some evidence to suggest that some degree of sub-infeudation took place at this period involving subordinate Magennis families who may have acquired fee-farm grants of their ancestral lands, providing for the payment of a rent or chiefry to either Sir Hugh or Ever MacRory Magennis.[42] While the Bagenals were to claim that they were influential in weaning the Magennises and the O'Hanlons away from their Old Irish leanings, neither needed the advice of a Bagenal in evaluating the advantage of surrender and regrant, whether as a protection against arbitrary actions by the crown and its officials or the avoidance of overlordship by the O'Neills.

The developments, which took place in respect of the Magennises of Iveagh between 1575 and 1590, correspond with similar developments in the case of another and more recently established figure in the region, Hugh O'Neill, the surviving son of Matthew, baron of Dungannon.[43] Having largely supported the crown after his reinstatement in Armagh by Sir Henry Sidney in 1568, the young Dungannon steadily expanded his position within the territory of the O'Neills and, having done further service against the rebels in Munster in the early 1580s, he was at length rewarded for his loyalty by elevation to the peerage as second earl of Tyrone in 1585, and by a very favourable division of the Gaelic lordship of Tyrone between himself and Turlough Luineach which Lord Deputy Perrot had brokered around the same time.

With this emplacement of an amenable O'Neill in the Tyrone lordship, the hope that the acculturation processes begun by St Leger in the earlier part of the century might still come to full blossom in this portion of Ulster was clearly still alive. But times had changed. The internal politics of the region had made both the Irish and the English more nervous of each other than ever before. More importantly, there was no St Leger among

---

[41] O'Sullivan, 'Magennis lordship', pp. 162–3.   [42] *Ibid.*

[43] He also occupied a castle at Ballymascanlan, north of Dundalk; it is marked on Robert Lythe's map of the Carlingford Lough area, probably by Cecil as 'Er Tyrone', see O'Sullivan, 'A 1575 rent-roll', p. 43.

the Englishry of the 1580s and 1590s to give effect to such a process. Even if there had been, it is unlikely that he would have been effectual, for, driven by the Bagenals and their adherents, English attitudes towards the native lords had undergone a drastic change over the intervening decades. The new representatives of the crown now looked to government office not as a means of advancing social assimilation and political integration, but rather as an instrument for the acquisition of landed estates and thereby as a means to achieve political hegemony in the region.

In the years between 1589 and 1596 tensions increased between the Englishry and Irishry of the march, provoked in large measure by the growing hostility between O'Neill and Bagenal.[44] In 1587 a proposal that Sir Henry Bagenal be appointed commissioner for Ulster had been suggested but had been vehemently opposed by O'Neill. However, when O'Neill eloped with Bagenal's sister Mabel in 1591 and married her without his consent, the mutual dislike became a deep enmity, which ended only at the defeat and death of Bagenal at the Yellow Ford in 1598. Revealing his feelings at the time of the marriage, Bagenal exclaimed: 'I can but accurse myself and fortune that my blood which in my father and myself hath often been spilled in repressing this rebellious race, should now be mingled with so traitorous a stock and kindred.'[45]

The burgeoning tension between those Irish who sought integration with the English community in Ireland and the New English *arrivistes* was acutely revealed in the crisis arising from the succession dispute of the MacMahons in Monaghan in 1591. After a failed attempt by Lord Deputy Fitzwilliam to install Hugh Roe MacMahon as lord of his territory, a ruse was resorted to which aimed at a partition of the lordship.[46] Fitzwilliam had earlier proposed such a division, but in face of opposition by the MacMahons did not pursue it at the time. With all the appearance of trumped up charges, Hugh Roe was arrested and was tried by a jury in Monaghan in 1592, found guilty of treason, and executed. This affair, which has a distinct appearance of political expediency overcoming the rule of law, had considerable repercussions in Ulster. Suspicions of corruption abounded concerning Fitzwilliam, who was accused of having taken bribes from several parties, but more significantly concerning Nicholas Bagenal, who had already established a significant interest in the lordship through the acquisition of the church lands of Muckno in the barony of Cremorne. Fynes Moryson was later to claim that among

---

[44] For this period, see Hiram Morgan, *Tyrone's Rebellion: the outbreak of the Nine Years War* (Woodbridge, 1993), chapter 3.
[45] Bagwell, *Tudor Ireland*, III, pp. 223–4.
[46] The break-up of the MacMahon lordship and its implications are dealt with in Morgan, *Tyrone's Rebellion*, pp. 61–71.

the Irishry there were 'heart-burnings and loathing of the English govern-ment in the northern lords against the state and they shunned as much as they could to admit any sheriffs or any English to live among them, pretending to fear like practices to overthrow them'.[47]

Similar abuses taking place in the west of the province were shortly to provoke outright rebellion when the Maguires, aided by the O'Donnells of Donegal, resisted the encroachment of English officials into local affairs. There the situation came to a head in 1593 when Maguire and O'Donnell raided into Sligo and Roscommon and thence into Monaghan. Lord Deputy Fitzwilliam, who had done so much to provoke the crisis, then called on Tyrone and Bagenal to counterattack, which they did, defeating Maguire at Belleek in October. Tyrone complained that Bagenal belittled his participation in these events and claimed that Fitzwilliam and Bagenal were conspiring against him.[48] These complaints were a counter to charges of treason alleged by Bagenal against O'Neill. O'Neill rejected the charges and offered to stand trial. The proceedings were conducted in Dundalk in 1594. O'Neill was cleared, but was cautioned 'not to meddle with compounding controversies in Ulster outside Tyrone'.[49] Fitzwilliam and Bagenal, for their part, were cautioned that 'they had used the earl against law and equity' and that the former 'had not been indifferent to the earl'.[50] Later that year Sir William Russell replaced Fitzwilliam, who was instructed to inform Tyrone that Bagenal had been forbidden to act against him.

These peace manoeuvres were shattered in 1595 when O'Neill invested the town of Monaghan. Bagenal succeeded in relieving the town, but on his return journey to Dundalk was attacked at Clontibret and almost over-whelmed by O'Neill.[51] By this time the Magennises of Iveagh had been drawn into the approaching conflict. In the autumn of 1593 Sir Hugh Magennis and others, seeking to be freed from the power of Tyrone, laid charges against him declaring him to be in league with traitors. By March of the following year, the crown having failed to respond to Magen-nis's pleas for support, the latter capitulated to O'Neill's demands and joined in the rebellion.[52] It was reported at the time that 'all the Irishry the O'Hanlons and the Magennises have combined with the earl but not from any love they bear him'.[53] In August, Ever MacRory of Kilwarlin was

[47] Fynes Moryson, *An History of Ireland from the year 1599–1603, with a Short Narration of the State of the Kingdom from the year 1169, to which is added a Description of Ireland* (2 vols., Dublin, 1735), I, pp. 23–6.

[48] For this period, see Morgan, *Tyrone's Rebellion*, chapter 7.

[49] Moryson, *An History*, I, pp. 29–30.   [50] *Ibid.*

[51] G. A. Hayes-McCoy, *Irish Battles* (Dublin, 1980), p. 87.

[52] O'Sullivan, 'Magennis lordship', pp. 164–5.

[53] *CSPI, 1588–92*, p. 499; *CSPI, 1592–96*, pp. 149, 229.

expelled from his lands, and O'Neill took a prey of 1,500 cattle from Sir Hugh Magennis and Sir Nicholas Bagenal, whose mills at Newry were destroyed.[54] In June 1595 O'Neill was proclaimed a traitor and ordered to disclaim all rule over Magennis and O'Hanlon.

Sir Hugh Magennis died in 1596, sparking off a succession dispute between the remainder-man, his son Art Roe, and Glasny MacAholly [Mac Eachmilidh] Magennis of Clanconnell, whose territories lay between the Bann and Lagan rivers, and whose claim to succeed was based upon the Irish law of tanistry.[55] Surprisingly, Hugh O'Neill, who was Art's father-in-law, did not support his claim, which was based on the English law of succession, instead giving his support to Glasny as tanist, which carried the message that in a lordship over which he claimed overlordship only Irish law would apply. Meanwhile, O'Neill negotiated a truce with the Englishry from which a pardon and settlement ensued in May 1596. Art Roe Magennis had made his bid for the succession at Dundalk where he came, 'craving our lawful aid and favour for maintenance of his title and right by her majesty's letters patent'.[56] A commission was established under the lord chancellor to examine the matter, and on 19 July 1596 O'Neill undertook to bring Glasny before them for examination. In the meantime, Art Roe joined in support of O'Neill, who married Art's sister Catherine in August 1597, thereby making him brother-in-law as well as son-in-law of O'Neill. He appears to have been in action with O'Neill against the newly arrived lord deputy, Thomas, Lord Burgh, when the latter captured Armagh in July 1597.

After Burgh's death in October 1597, Thomas Butler, earl of Ormond, was appointed lord lieutenant general. Negotiations having been commenced with O'Neill, a truce was concluded in Dundalk in December 1597. During this period O'Neill called upon Ormond to regularise Art Roe's position. In March 1598 the latter together with Brian MacHugh Oge MacMahon, Ever Mac Con Uladh MacMahon and Oghie O'Hanlon came in to Dundalk and made formal submission. In the same month articles of agreement were concluded with O'Neill on the basis of which a pardon under the great seal was granted to him in April. The peace, however, proved only short-lived. In August his old adversary, Sir Henry Bagenal, set out from Dundalk with a force of 4,000 foot, 320 horse and four artillery pieces to relieve the Blackwater fort, north of Armagh. The

---

[54] *CSPI, 1588–92*, pp. 149, 229, Ever MacRory Magennis murdered by the earl of Tyrone's son-in-law (Art Roe of Rathfriland), pp. 279 and 358, *Calendar of Carew Manuscripts preserved in the Archiepiscopal Library at Lambeth* (6 vols., London, 1867–73), V (1589–1600), p. 93: 'Ever MacRory Magennis of Kilwarlin a man brought under the law and of good obedience to her majesty is now utterly expulsed out of his country.'
[55] O'Sullivan 'Magennis lordship', pp. 165–6.   [56] *CSPI, 1592–96*, p. 457.

outcome was the great battle of the Yellow Ford where Bagenal's forces were defeated and Bagenal himself killed by a shot to the head.[57] Next followed the fruitless Essex expedition of 1599. Art Roe Magennis was one of the six witnesses who attended the conference between O'Neill and Essex at the Lagan ford in August 1599.[58] With the appointment of Mountjoy as lord deputy in January 1600, a new departure in the struggle between the English and O'Neill was begun.

In May 1600 Mountjoy advanced into the Moyry Pass, north of Dundalk and, after a sharp encounter with O'Neill, broke through to Newry.[59] A policy of harassment of the marcher lords followed. Sir Arthur Chichester laid waste all the countryside within 20 miles of Carrickfergus, including the Magennis lands of Kilwarlin, while Sir Samuel Bagenal performed a similar service about Newry. In the early months of 1601 Turlough MacHenry O'Neill of the Fews, Ever Mac Con Uladh MacMahon of Farney and Sir Oghie O'Hanlon of Orier all came in to Dundalk and made their submissions. In May a general 'rising out' of the Old English of the five shires of the Pale was ordered, while the Irish submittees were required to 'attempt something against the arch-traitor O'Neill and to put them in blood against him and his confederates'.[60] In June a force under Sir Richard Moryson was dispatched into County Down, and having marched into Iveagh and thence into Lecale overnight, 'lest the rebels should have leisure to burn the country and carry away the prey', it captured and plundered Downpatrick.[61] Phelim MacEver Magennis of Castlewellan surrendered, and was followed by Ever MacRory Magennis of Kilwarlin. Art Roe and his uncle Edmund Boy offered to surrender, but this was refused until they had performed some service against O'Neill.

The destruction of Downpatrick, coupled with the burning of corn and the preying of cattle by Mountjoy's invading army, would have had a devastating effect. It is clear that Art Roe's anxiety to surrender arose from his fear of such devastation spreading into his own territories. On 30 June 1601 he again sought to surrender and was given protection for nine days conditional on him coming in to Dundalk to sue his pardon. On 3 July Art Roe duly made his submission and was pardoned.[62] Considering Magennis's prominence and his relationship with O'Neill, the

---

[57] Hayes-McCoy, *Irish Battles*, p. 106.

[58] For a contemporary description of this meeting see Shirley, *History of Monaghan*, pp. 102–6 and *Calendar of Carew Manuscripts*, V, pp. 321–2.

[59] For Mountjoy's attack on the Moyry Pass, see Moryson, *An History*, I, pp. 185–9, and *CSPI, 1600*, pp. 524–32.

[60] Moryson, *An History*, I, p. 235.   [61] *Ibid.*, pp. 253–4.

[62] For the surrender of Magennis, see O'Sullivan, 'Magennis lordship', p. 167.

terms granted were not ungenerous and were consistent with Mountjoy's policy of drawing the marcher lords away from O'Neill. In April he entertained them in Dublin 'with solemn pomp' and plied them with 'plenty of wine and all kindness'. In a speech Mountjoy assured them that 'as he had been a scourge to them in rebellion, so now he would be a mediator for them to her majesty in their state of subjects, they standing firm and constant to their obedience'.[63] Mountjoy's policy towards those who had submitted in the Ulster march certainly availed to contain them 'in due obedience'. While O'Neill was to bring pressure to bear on them before his march to Kinsale in November 1601, all held to the compacts made with Mountjoy, including O'Neill's half-brother Turlough MacHenry of the Fews, O'Hanlon of Orier and Art Roe Magennis of Iveagh. After his formal submission on 30 March 1603 at Mellifont, County Louth, O'Neill received a pardon and was restored to his earldom together with his estates in Tyrone and Armagh. His ascendancy in Ulster was, however, at an end. But so too, in a real sense, was the character of the region as it had developed since the late Middle Ages.

The disappearance of the O'Neill influence might have been expected to exert a simplifying effect on the character of the region, removing one element from the complex game of Irish and English–Irish intrigues that had characterised the politics of the region for centuries. But the manner of the collapse of the O'Neill lordship ensured that its effect would be quite opposite. It removed at a stroke one volatile but nonetheless identifiable force whose aim was the exploitation rather than the extinction of the lesser lordships of south-east Ulster, and replaced it with a power vacuum into which a multifarious horde of English adventurers poured. The intent of the latter to fashion existing sources of power and allegiances in the region to suit their own ends was soon apparent. The beginnings of a new gentry class in opposition to the native Irish nobility and gentry was at hand.

III

With the appointment of Sir Arthur Chichester as lord deputy in 1605, the arrangements for the dismantling of the Irish lordships were begun. This involved the surveying of the respective lordships to determine their extent and the nature of the existing land titles. Crown title was then established in proceedings taken in the local assize courts, followed by a division of the lordships into several freehold allotments, each of which was allocated to specific individuals who were usually, though not invariably, leading

---

[63] Moryson, *An History*, I, pp. 227–8.

members of the extended family of the former lordship. The freehold was to be held *in capite* from the crown on the basis of an annual rent payable to the exchequer. Church properties were reserved for allocation to the emerging diocesan administrations of the church establishment, while former monastic properties were seized into the exchequer for subsequent allocation in freehold tenure, usually to planting ex-soldiers. Many of these were ex-officers of the Elizabethan army, such as Edward Trevor in west Down, Edward Blayney in Monaghan, Marmaduke Whitchurch, Toby Caulfield and Francis Roe in Armagh and Tyrone, and Fulke Conway in Antrim. All were later to establish themselves in substantial estates in the march and elsewhere in Ulster to which they had originally come with little more than their officers' pay. They were to provide a cadre of local officials who were to spearhead the replacement of the Irish lordships of the march with colonial English settlement.

In County Monaghan the scheme for the division of the lordship of 1591 had been largely upset by the controversy over the tenancy of Essex's barony of Farney, held by Ever Mac Con Uladh MacMahon, whom Fitzwilliam had intended to replace with John Talbot of Castlering in County Louth. This could not be effected until the arrival of Mountjoy in 1600. In the submissions made by the various MacMahon families, Ever Mac Con Uladh was continued in the tenancy paying the rent, an arrangement which was agreed to by Talbot. The freeholding commission was introduced into County Monaghan by Chichester at the assizes of 1606.[64] Large-scale confiscation and plantation of Irish lands was not yet policy, and it is not surprising that the settlement of 1591 was largely confirmed, with Ever Mac Con Uladh as the leaseholder of Farney from the earl of Essex at an annual rent of £250 for six years. Eight other named freeholders included Sir Edward Blayney, who obtained a grant of two ballybetaghs in Cremorne as well as the monastic lands granted originally to Bagenal. The freeholding of Monaghan effectively confirmed possession by the native Irish of 61 per cent of the lands of the county. With Ever Mac Con Uladh's leasehold of Farney added, this percentage increased to 78 per cent.

In Iveagh, Art Roe Magennis actively promoted the application of the proceedings of the freeholding commission in his lordship.[65] His objectives were twofold: to avoid his land titles being found defective; and to secure new letters patent confirming the entire territory of Iveagh as his demesne lands. Apart from any objections that might have been raised

<hr>

[64] For the freeholding of Monaghan under Chichester, see Livingstone, *The Monaghan Story*, pp. 95–101.

[65] For the freeholding of Iveagh, see O'Sullivan, 'Magennis lordship', pp. 168–72.

by the other Magennises, Chichester would not have countenanced such an expectation. His intentions were to reduce, as he put it, 'overmighty lords' such as Magennis, and to recover church and bishop's lands in Iveagh, which he believed had been alienated by the Magennises, with a view to the provision of a resident Protestant bishop in Dromore. He also expected to recover monastic properties for subsequent distribution in grants to ex-soldiers and others whose relocation to Iveagh would provide a nucleus for a British colonial settlement. In the event, the lordship was divided into fifteen freeholds all of which were allotted to the various Magennis families, including Sir Art Roe Magennis of Rathfriland and Brian Oge MacRory Magennis of Kilwarlin. In addition, fee-farm leases were assigned to several other families, principally Magennises, the chiefries of which were payable to Art Roe Magennis. The Magennises generally must have been reasonably satisfied with the outcome of the freeholding proceedings. The total percentage of the lands granted to Irish families was 84.72 per cent, with the balance passing to the bishop as church lands. Only one non-Irish person, the Welshman Captain Edward Trevor, obtained a freehold grant. He had come into Ireland with Sir Samuel Bagenal in 1599 and subsequently settled in the Newry area.[66]

Turlough MacHenry O'Neill of the Fews, who had not supported O'Neill, succeeded in having 'the country of the Fews' granted to him by letters patent in 1603, which was further confirmed by Chichester in 1611.[67] Sir Oghie O'Hanlon was by 1600 an old man and was not disturbed until after the O'Doherty uprising of 1608. His son Oghie, who was married to O'Doherty's daughter, was implicated in the uprising, and Chichester held Sir Oghie accountable. He escheated his estate, allowing him only a pension of £80 a year in lieu.[68] It formed the barony of Orier and was included in the Ulster plantation. It was allocated to servitors (exsoldiers), Irish, English and Welsh. Thirty-nine Irish (mostly O'Hanlons) got small grants; the most important of these was Art MacBaron O'Neill, half-brother of the earl of Tyrone. Although a servitor who had rendered good service to the English, he was transplanted from his estate in Oneilland to Orier, where he was granted a life interest only, the remainder to pass to Lord Audley; one effect of this was to disinherit Art's son Owen Roe O'Neill, later to distinguish himself as general in the army of the Catholic Confederation of Kilkenny. The only other substantial Irish

[66] For the Trevors, see Harold O'Sullivan, 'The Trevors of Rosetrevor, a British colonial family in 17th century Ireland' (M.Litt. thesis, Trinity College, Dublin, 1985).
[67] For Turlough MacHenry, see Ó Fiaich, 'The O'Neills of the Fews', *Seanchas Ardmhacha*, part I, pp. 25–64.
[68] George Hill, *An Historical Account of the Plantation in Ulster at the Commencement of the Seventeenth Century 1608–1620* (Shannon, 1970), pp. 64–6.

grant was to the servitor Redmond O'Hanlon.[69] The Englishry had their grants principally in the northern and more fertile parts of the barony.

IV

In the early years of the Stuart dynasty, and following the collapse of the O'Neill lordship, came the gradual appearance of a new type of British settler within the native territories, and, most subtly, the movement to convert rights of overlordship and land use among the Gaelic dynasties into terms comprehensible under English law. Cumulatively these changes served to effect a radical reshaping of relations between the crown and the native aristocracy. At the same time, however, an equally serious reorientation was taking place among the English communities in the region through the rapid deterioration of relations between the Old English elite of County Louth and the incoming New English, a process which had begun in the last decades of the sixteenth century. The frequently reiterated assertions by the Old English of fealty to England, which were utterly genuine, no longer held good under a regime which tested political loyalty on the basis of religious belief. In seeking to bring them to heel by the enforcement of the recusancy laws, the new Stuart administration only alienated them still further. Prominent among the protestors in County Louth were men who had demonstrated their loyalty on the battlefield, such as the barons of Louth and of Slane, Thomas Gernon, James Warren, William Plunkett, Peter Taaffe, Walter Babe, William Cashel, Joseph Cashell and Patrick Bellew.[70] The influx of Jesuits and friars of the mendicant orders from the continent in the early Stuart period brought the forces of the Counter-Reformation into Ireland. The failure of the established church to win over any sizeable section of the population had created an organisational vacuum, which was soon filled by the newcomers. In a mission preached by the Franciscans in Dundalk in 1618 it was reported that the 'mass-house' had the capacity for 700 worshippers. As the seventeenth century progressed the organisation of the Catholic church became well established throughout the county, with friaries in all the principal towns and even a convent of nuns in Drogheda.[71] In 1635 Sir William Brereton described the population of Dundalk as being for

---

[69] For this servitor, see Harold O'Sullivan, 'Land confiscations and plantations in County Armagh, 1650–1680' in A. J. Hughes and William Nolan (eds.), *Armagh: History and society* (Dublin, 2001), pp. 340–3.

[70] *CSPI, 1603–6*, p. 362.

[71] For this period in Dundalk, see Harold O'Sullivan, 'The Franciscans in Dundalk', *Seanchas Ardmhacha*, 4:1 (1961), pp. 41–7; for the convent at Drogheda, see Harold O'Sullivan, 'Women in County Louth in the seventeenth century', *Louth Archaeological and Historical Journal*, 23:3 (1995), pp. 344–5.

the greater part 'popishly affected', who had rejected the lord deputy's nominees for election to the 1634 parliament in favour of 'a couple of recusants'. He reported that an 'abundance of Irish, both gentlemen and others, dwell in this town, wherein they dare to take the boldness to go to mass openly'.[72]

Although since the late sixteenth century religion had become a common cause between the Gaelic Irish and the Old English of the region, little else bound them together. The Old English were as ready as the New to exploit their relationships with the newly gentrified Old Irish of the march, who frequently had recourse to the services of local Old English lawyers in helping them to cope with the intricacies of the new system of landownership. In the new world in which they found themselves they also required loans and credits – and these too were provided by the self-same lawyers. These included the Hadsors of Cappoge, the Bellews of Lisrenny and the Chamberlains of Nizelrath.[73] Among the New English *arrivistes* was Carroll Bolton, the younger son of the chancellor Sir Richard Bolton of Knockbridge in County Louth, who established a legal practice in County Armagh, where he also engaged in money-lending by way of mortgage leases.[74] One of his clients was Sir Phelim O'Neill of Kinard, to whom he advanced a loan of £1,000 in 1638.

The market for such services was clear. The new system of land tenure, which had been introduced under the most unfavourable economic circumstances, embodied an inherent flaw. It replaced a system of landholding, which had existed unchanged for centuries, with an alien system whose gradual evolution elsewhere had taken place within an entirely different social and economic setting.[75] It was not to be expected that it would readily translate itself within a space of a few decades, more especially since it was begun at a very low level of economic activity. The after-effects of war and famine made it difficult to secure tenants who could be relied upon to pay their rents in a regular manner.[76] The need to borrow money was constant. In addition to meeting social necessities, ready money had to be found to meet the demands of the crown in

[72] Sir William Brereton, *Travels in Holland, the United Provinces, England, Scotland and Ireland, 1634–5*, ed. Edward Haskins (Chetham Society, London, 1844), I.

[73] For the Hadsors, see Shirley, *History of Monaghan*, pp. 107–8, for John Bellew, see Harold O'Sullivan, *John Bellew, 1605–1679* (Dublin, 2000), for the Chamberlains of Nizelrath and the MacCartans, see O'Sullivan, 'Women', p. 352.

[74] For Bolton, see O'Sullivan, 'Land confiscations and plantations in Armagh', pp. 363–4.

[75] For County Monaghan, see Livingstone, *The Monaghan Story*, pp. 119–26 and for County Down, see O'Sullivan, 'Magennis lordship', pp. 168–79.

[76] For a study of the colonial impacts on early seventeenth-century east Ulster, see Gillespie, *Colonial Ulster*.

regard to feudal incidents, such as the suing out of livery, the payment of fines for pardons of alienation, and the cost of taking out letters patent. Yet another problem was the need to provide for children and close relatives who under the old Irish customs would have held land in common. While few of the newly established freeholders had ready access to funds that could be used to provide for members of the extended family, what may have been readily available at this time was a surplus of land. In many instances lands were assigned or alienated on long-term or mortgage leases, in fee-farm grant, or sold to the Englishry for ready cash. Economic circumstances therefore left many of the Old Irish open to the carpet-bagging activities of their English neighbours. With access to ready cash, men such as Bolton, Hill, Trevor, Whitchurch and the Old Englishman Chamberlain advanced loans on mortgage leases, often under onerous conditions. In the many default proceedings which ensued, changes in landownership were a frequent result.

In the period prior to 1641 the transformation which took place in landownership was remarkable. In Monaghan, apart from Farney, the percentage of Irish-held land fell from 78 to 55 per cent. Significantly, the change was most marked in the northern and western baronies where the acculturation processes had least penetration. In Farney and in Cremorne, adjacent to the Louth borders where the Irish had a greater familiarity with the system, little English penetration occurred. In Iveagh the reduction was equally marked, falling from 85 to 48 per cent by 1641, and much of the latter was encumbered by debt. In Lower Iveagh the Kilwarlin estate, consisting of 28,000 acres, had been acquired before 1640 by Moses Hill and his son Arthur, while the Loughbrickland estate of 1,250 acres in Upper Iveagh had gone to Marmaduke Whitchurch, whose estate had by 1640 amounted to 4,400 acres. Edward Trevor acquired the Milltown Magennises' estates in Clonallan and Kilbroney parishes in the 1620s, and by 1640 he had an estate in Iveagh of over 16,000 acres. Apart from Lower Iveagh, where the Hills and others encouraged Scottish and English Protestant planters, the Irish tenants in the upper, or southern, barony remained undisturbed by the Trevors, the Whitchurches or the Bagenals. By 1641, while Protestant tenants occupied the bulk of the land in Lower Iveagh, Catholics held the majority in the baronies of Upper Iveagh, Newry and Mourne. The pattern of settlement in County Monaghan and south Armagh was the same.

Denied participation in government and with a growing mountain of debt upon their estates, it was inevitable that several of these displaced and declining figures should have become involved in the conspiracy which led to the insurrection of 1641. It is significant that many of the chief participants were drawn from the Dundalk area and its immediate hinterland

and that their leader was Rory O'More, a descendant of the O'Mores of Offaly, who had acquired a lease of the Audley-Castlehaven estate in Orier, which he had managed from his residence in Dundalk.[77] Another Dundalk resident involved in the conspiracy was Thomas MacKiernan, the guardian of the Dundalk Franciscans. From nearby Farney came two MacMahons, Ever, who was the vicar-general of the diocese of Clogher, and Colla MacBrian, the grandson of Ever Mac Con Uladh and lease-holder of Farney from the earl of Essex.[78] Prominent in political affairs and a member of the 1634 parliament, Colla established and maintained contact with other leading Irish sympathetic to the idea of an uprising. His house at Lisaniskey, Carrickmacross, served as one of the venues used by the conspirators as a meeting-place, as did Turlough O'Neill's house at Lough Ross. Turlough was the son of Sir Henry O'Neill, who succeeded as head of the Fews O'Neills in 1640.[79] From the Magennises came Sir Conn, one of the sons of Art Roe, Viscount Iveagh, whose estate in Maghera and Kilcoo was deeply encumbered with debt.[80] Finally, from the O'Neills of Tyrone came Sir Phelim O'Neill, another of the leaders of the 1641 rising, and his brother Turlough Oge, both direct descendants of Shane, whose father, Sir Henry Oge O'Neill of Kinard, had assisted Chichester in quelling the O'Doherty rebellion.[81]

The intensity of their involvement is a reflection of the pressures which living in a region characterised by susceptibility to outside forces, to competing interests, and above all to sudden alterations of influence imposed upon its inhabitants. In 1641 they were compelled, amidst all the confusions, to choose what they perceived as the best means of defending their holdings; this involved following precedents established in the stormy 1590s and in the happier horizons of a century before. Whatever they may have hoped for from the insurrection, they hardly could have foreseen the cataclysm that was to follow.

At the Restoration the Old English succeeded in recovering 47 per cent of the land that they had held in Louth in 1641, but the Irish of the counties of Monaghan and Armagh disappeared as landowners, and in County Down only the Magennises of Castlewellan and Corgary survived.[82]

---

[77] O'Sullivan, 'Land confiscations in Armagh', p. 340.
[78] Livingstone, *The Monaghan Story*, chapter 8.
[79] For Turlough, son of Henry, see Ó Fiaich, 'The O'Neills of the Fews', part II, pp. 272–4.
[80] For Conn Magennis, see O'Sullivan, 'Magennis lordship', pp. 177–84 and George Ernest Hamilton, *The Irish Rebellion of 1641* (London, 1920), chapter 7.
[81] O'Sullivan, 'Land confiscations in Armagh', pp. 337–39.
[82] For Monaghan, see Livingstone, *The Monaghan Story*, pp. 119–26, for Armagh and Louth, see O'Sullivan, 'The Restoration land settlement in the Diocese of Armagh' in *Seanchas Ardmhacha*, 16:1 (1994), for Down, see O'Sullivan, 'Magennis lordship', pp. 189–93.

Their replacements were, in the main, second-generation colonists of the Ulster plantation who had given their loyalty to the English Commonwealth in the divisions of 1648–49. It was the landed gentry who really suffered. For, as Oliver Plunkett, the Catholic archbishop of Armagh, put it in 1671, the Irish Catholic gentlemen are 'completely ruined', while the 'peasantry, those who cultivate the land, are all right'.[83] The descendants of the latter, together with their counterparts in County Louth, most of whom were also native Irish, have constituted the majority of the population of the former march to this day.

[83] John Hanly (ed.), *The Letters of Saint Oliver Plunkett, 1625–1681* (Dublin, 1979), pp. 245–48.

4   The 'common good' and the university in the age of confessional conflict

Helga Robinson-Hammerstein

In 1547, in one of the earliest of what was to be a long sequence of proposals arguing for the establishment of a university in Ireland, Archbishop George Browne suggested that the archbishop and the mayor of Dublin should together contribute to the expense of founding a university for the sake of serving the 'common good'.[1] Generally passed over in accounts of the prehistory of Trinity College, Dublin, in favour of political, administrative or religious themes, Browne's phrase concerning the 'common good' is nonetheless laden with significance.[2] The idea that, beyond its narrow seminarian functions, a university should serve the interests of the broader community was more than cant. In fact, when viewed against the broader canvas of early modern cultural history, it can be shown to have been a sincere and profound commitment in the foundation of universities not only in Ireland but also in early modern Europe as a whole.

The idea that the university should care for the interests of its extramural community surfaces in several of the proposals put forward in Ireland from the 1540s onwards.[3] But it is highlighted in one particular memorandum which itself arose from a particular community, the municipality of Dublin. John Ussher, alderman of Dublin and a decidedly

[1] E. P. Shirley (ed.), *Original Letters and Papers in Illustration of the History of the Church of Ireland* (London, 1851), pp. 5–14.
[2] James Murray, 'St Patrick's Cathedral and the university question in Ireland, *c.*1547–1585' in Helga Robinson-Hammerstein (ed.), *European Universities in the Age of Reformation and Counter Reformation* (Dublin, 1998), pp. 1–33.
[3] W. M. Brady (ed.), *State Papers Concerning the Irish Church in the Time of Queen Elizabeth* (London, 1868). After Archbishop Browne's proposal for the founding of a university (PRO, SP 61/1/10) the most important later ones were 'The Plat' of *c.*1565 in Shirley (ed.), *Original Letters and Papers*, p. 126 and John Ussher's of 1582 (PRO, SP 63/111/73). For an assessment of the failed policy, see Murray, 'St Patrick's Cathedral', Ciaran Brady, *The Chief Governors. The rise and fall of reform government in Tudor Ireland, 1536–1588* (Cambridge, 1994). For an independent proposal developed by Sir William Herbert see Ciaran Brady, 'New English ideology in Ireland and the two Sir William Herberts' in A. J. Piesse (ed.), *Sixteenth-Century Identities* (Manchester, 2000), pp. 75–111.

Protestant member of the civic establishment, was concerned to make the values of his co-religionists the norms for all in the interest of shaping a new society.[4] There was a consensus in an otherwise confessionally divided early modern Europe that ignorance was to blame for all social evils, and this was a recurring theme in the documents relating to the foundation of the University of Dublin in 1592. What looks like an exclusive preoccupation with the religious polarities at the end of the sixteenth century was, however, another way of energising the civic community in Dublin to offer its developed sense of the 'common good' and extend it over the whole country to ensure its stability. The university was the inspiration of the municipality of Dublin.

Archbishop Adam Loftus, the first, albeit nominal, provost of the new college, saw in the communal tradition of Dublin the only basis on which to build a stable Irish society. In his other capacity as a government official, he was well aware that no funds would be forthcoming from Queen Elizabeth I. In his speeches to the mayor and aldermen he referred to the danger of allowing the sons of the patriciate to travel abroad; they would never conform to the norms of society that the Irish authorities were trying to establish.[5] Adam Loftus, a very shrewd tactician with a sharp analytical mind, appealed to the aldermen's mercantile self-interest. He told the patriciate that the new university would serve the *utilitas publica* by bringing profit together with civility to the community. Furthermore, Loftus stressed that the graduates of the Dublin university would eventually assimilate 'the rest' to overcome 'barbarity' throughout Ireland.[6]

All these arguments were clearly already present in the minds of the Dublin establishment *before* Adam Loftus expressed them. Their communal sense of the 'common good' at the end of the sixteenth century was responsible for the idea that a new university would help to ensure the welfare of the state. Dublin had the only new university of the late sixteenth and early seventeenth centuries that was not predominantly financed by the ruling prince.[7] Instead, a significant effort was made to involve the whole country in the university education of its future civil servants and preachers; this appears to have been the principal purpose of the circular letter sent by the lord deputy and council to the chief men of each county recommending them to serve the 'common good'. The

---

[4] H. L. Murphy, *Trinity College, Dublin* (Dublin, 1951), pp. 5–9, 11–12.
[5] John William Stubbs (ed.), *Adam Loftus and the Foundation of Trinity College, Dublin* (Dublin, 1892), pp. 8–13.
[6] *Ibid.*, pp. 3–6.
[7] John Pentland Mahaffy, *An Epoch in Irish History* (London, 1903), pp. 62 ff.

intention of the government had always been to educate an elite of men for service in their own localities, using the university as an instrument to constitute a law-abiding, civilised community. The university scheme was saved by the Dublin patriciate, assisted by some members of the queen's government in Ireland who appreciated this 'Irish problem'.[8]

An influential humanist circle consisting of the members of the Ussher and Stanihurst families and their friends fervently believed in the power of the university to create a well-ordered society. The religious ambivalence of this group in the 1570s had resolved itself by the time of the actual foundation of the university. The Ussher family network consisted of reliable Protestants, while the Stanihursts had moved decidedly into the Catholic camp. This religious dissent among the leading promoters of the university project augured ill for the success of the 'civilising mission' of their university. For families like the Usshers, the enforcement of the legally established state religion was the *raison d'être* of the civilising process initiated by the university. The influence of the Catholic Irish colleges abroad and the educated men they sent back as missionaries finally shattered the Dublin establishment's agreed vision of the *bonum commune* served by their university.[9]

I

Disregard of this important dimension in the thinking about the purposes of a university in Ireland is due in large part to a similar neglect in historical writing about the functions of a university in Europe. Until recently, serious study of the significance of serving the community in the establishment of universities has been blocked by the prevalent assumption that the reference to the 'common good' was no more than a high-sounding term that could be suitably used in association with other pedagogical stereotypes and that conveniently increased propagandistic advantages for the charter-issuing ruler without committing him/her to anything specific. Since the charters were always issued in the name of the illustrious founders, it is natural that historians concentrate on the relationship between the founders and their academic creations. The 'common good'

---

[8] Land grants, John William Stubbs, *The History of the University of Dublin* (Dublin, 1899), app. V–XI, XIII, pp. 357–65, 367–8; a second important support structure was the network that was being built up by intermarriage among the upper bourgeoisie, TCD MS 1065 and TCD, T.1.8, William Reeves, 'A collection of genealogical and historical papers relating principally to Archbishop Adam Loftus' (compiled in the 1880s).

[9] Helga Hammerstein, 'Aspects of the continental education of Irish students in the reign of Queen Elizabeth', *Historical Studies VIII* (Dublin, 1971), pp. 137–53.

appears almost coincidentally as a static term that does not require further examination.[10] The authors see competing dynastic states, each founding its own territorial university and expecting little more than obedience and competence from it. The question *why* the authorities in the age of confessional strife should have encumbered themselves with an institution of dubious value is barely touched upon. This chapter suggests that, far from being such an encumbrance, the university was employed as the crucible with which to realise the political aims of regulating the 'common good' within the territory.

There is no doubt that the *bonum commune* referred to in charters of the later Middle Ages is the 'common' (general) welfare of the as yet undivided Christendom. The 'beneficial role' assigned to the universities in this context was to conserve and defend the received wisdom of the Ancients and of Christian tradition for the good of all Christians.[11] Hence during the Great Schism (1378–1417) the masters and doctors of universities were expected to devise practical means of restoring unity – through true knowledge – to a discordant church. It was in this traditional perception of their duties that university masters like John Wyclif of Oxford and John Hus of Prague were convinced that their status in the university gave them the right to advocate a universal reform of church and society 'for the good of all Christians'.[12]

It is also well known that in the late fifteenth century universities were treated as crucial to the Empire Reform Movement, that is, the attempt – at least in political discourse – to give an overall coherence to the many disparate parts of the Empire and to the measures adopted for its general welfare.[13] In practice, however, the foundation of universities became an indicator of the individual prince's commitment to the stabilisation of his own territory, without explicitly rejecting the Empire:

---

[10] Notker Hammerstein, 'Die Obrigkeiten und die Universitäten: ihr Verhältnis im Heiligen Römischen Reich Deutscher Nation' in Andrea Romano and Jacques Verger (eds.), *I poteri politici e il mondo universitaria (XIII–XX secolo)* (Messina, 1994), pp. 135–48.

[11] Hilde de Ridder-Symoens (ed.), *A History of the University in Europe. I Universities in the Middle Ages* (Cambridge, 1992).

[12] On the universality of the medieval university see Rudolf Stichweh, *Der frühmoderne Staat und die europäische Universität. Zur Interaktion von Politik und Erziehungssystem im Prozess der Ausdifferenzierung (16.–18. Jahrhundert)* (Frankfurt am Main, 1991), pp. 15–23, especially pp. 18–19; see also Heinz-Horst Schrey, 'Gemeinnutz/Gemeinwohl' in *Theologische Realenzyklopädie*, vol. 12 (Berlin and New York, 1984), pp. 339–46 (the assessment of the changing historical basis, pp. 340–1) and Roman Herzog, 'Gemeinwohl' in *Historisches Wörterbuch der Philosophie*, vol. III (Basel and Stuttgart, 1974), columns 248–58.

[13] Roderich Schmidt, *Fundatio et Confirmatio Universitatis. Von den Anfängen Deutscher Universitäten* (Bibliotheca Eruditorum, vol. XIII, Goldbach, 1998); see especially, 'Die Nachrichten über die Aufforderung Maximilians I. an die Kurfürsten, Universitäten einzurichten', *ibid.*, pp. 297–305.

the role of the emperor was, after all, essential in the whole process of creating learned institutions. The university was expected to generate the political and social reforms desired by the princes. Safeguarding territorial common interest was the practical purpose of founding a university. For example, in 1472 Duke Maximilian of Bavaria dedicated his new university of Ingolstadt to the 'common good'. The foundation charter links the act with the founder's desire to 'plant – through the right learning – good manners' in his subjects.[14] Frederick the Wise, the elector of Saxony and future patron of Martin Luther, founded his university of Wittenberg in 1502 as *pater patriae*, for the good of his subjects.[15] Princes, as dynastic lords over a feudal society, founded universities, in the conventional phrase of the foundation charters, 'to the praise of Almighty God, the strengthening of good Christians in their traditional faith and the common good and furtherance of lawful conduct'.[16]

The eighteenth-century princes were interested in promoting a comprehensive range of education and training for the benefit of their territorial states. This more modern notion of the 'common good' considered the *utilitas publica*, emphasising the talents of the individual as crucial to the welfare of the state. Whereas the late fifteenth-century concept was formulated in terms only of the 'preservation' of the existing feudal order, the eighteenth century stressed the need for the 'improvement' of society. In parts of Germany the sense of commitment to the 'common good' had been intensified by the Pietism of men like August Hermann Francke. The whole of society must be coordinated as one of useful interdependence, adapting the practical designs of the *Fruchtbringende Gesellschaft* [fruitbearing association].[17]

The relationship between the 'common good' and the university in the early modern period – when universalism no longer existed and the many later initiatives for the benefit of the common weal had not yet started – has

---

[14] Hammerstein, 'Die Obrigkeiten', pp. 137–8.
[15] W. Friedensburg, *Geschichte der Universität Wittenberg* (Halle, 1917), pp. 7 ff.; W. Friedensburg (ed.), *Urkundenbuch der Universität Wittenberg*, part I (1502–1611) (Magdeburg, 1926), no. 1; Gerd Heinrich, 'Frankfurt und Wittenberg. Zwei Universitätsgründungen im Vorfeld der Reformation' in Peter Baumgart and Notker Hammerstein (eds.), *Beiträge zu Problemen deutscher Universitätsgründungen der frühen Neuzeit* (Nendeln and Liechtenstein, 1978), pp. 119 ff.
[16] Notker Hammerstein, 'Universitäten und Reformation', *Historische Zeitschrift*, 258 (1994), pp. 339–57. I am grateful for Notker Hammerstein's valuable advice.
[17] Wilhelm Kühlmann, 'Pädagogische Konzeptionen' in Notker Hammerstein and August Buck (eds.), *Handbuch der deutschen Bildungsgeschichte. Vol. 1: 15.–17. Jahrhundert* (Munich, 1996), pp. 153–96, especially 168 ff.; Horst Weigelt, 'Pietismus' and Wolfgang Sommer, 'Aufklärung' in Gerhard Müller, Horst Weigelt and Wolfgang Zorn (eds.), *Handbuch der Geschichte der Evangelischen Kirche in Bayern* (St Ottilien, 2002), pp. 511–44 , 545–73; Martin Bircher and Klaus Conermann (eds.), *Fruchtbringende Gesellschaft: Die Deutsche Akademie des 17. Jahrhunderts* (Tübingen, 1992).

remained a topic in need of further study. Here the recent findings of an interdisciplinary project dedicated to the exploration of the 'common good' are particularly enlightening, although they never mention the role of the university.[18] All authors dealing with the later Middle Ages and the early modern period agree that the topos *bonum commune* designated an 'aim' that changed its orientation in the later sixteenth and early seventeenth centuries when communalism and consolidation of the territorial state adapted and extended the 'common good' to define their solidarity and purpose. Peter Blickle has demonstrated that the 'common good' became a value-oriented term used to legitimate the activities of the civic community. His case study is Basle, where the pursuit of the 'common good' simultaneously assisted the formulation and implementation of economic and social policies, including poor relief, basic health care and schooling in good conduct.[19] Eberhard Isenmann, taking up some of the earlier researches of Blickle, concentrates on the 'common good' and individual norms of conduct: the peacekeeping and administrative laws.[20] Thomas Simon agrees that while civic communities and their value-oriented regulations provided the model, the frequent invocation of the 'common good' provided the justification of the *Polizeiordnung* (general policy) of the consolidating state. In addition, he stresses that creating peace, setting norms of economic life and guiding political decisions 'functionalised' the 'common good'.[21] None of the authors indicates *how* this extension and 'functionalising' should be achieved. This chapter suggests that the territorial 'common good' was to be served by a territorial university benefiting from an urban 'common good'.

By adopting three thematic approaches, the argument can be more fully explored. First, it is necessary to assess the political circumstances that determined the founding of a university, testing out to what extent the communal model of the *bonum commune* was used by the state in search of stability and a plausible identity. Second, the didactic content of the syllabus as a consciously adopted means of furthering the common weal,

---

[18] Herfried Münkler and Harald Bluhm (eds.), *Gemeinwohl und Gemeinsinn*. vol. 1 *Historische Semantiken politischer Leitbegriffe* (4 vols., Berlin, 2001).

[19] Peter Blickle, 'Der Gemeine Nutzen. Ein kommunaler Wert und seine politische Karriere' in Münkler and Bluhm (eds.), *Gemeinwohl und Gemeinsinn*, pp. 85–107, here pp. 85–6; and in an earlier version, Peter Blickle, 'Gemeinnutz in Basel. Legitimatorische Funktion und ethische Norm' in M. Erbe, H. Füglister, K. Furrer, A. Staehelin, R. Wecker and C. Windeler (eds.), *Querdenken. Dissens und Toleranz im Wandel der Geschichte* (Mannheim, 1996), pp. 31–40.

[20] Eberhard Isenmann, 'Norms and values in the European city, 1300–1800' in Peter Blickle (ed.), *Resistance, Representation, and Community* (Oxford, 1997), pp. 187–215, especially p. 213.

[21] Thomas Simon, 'Gemeinwohltopik in der mittelalterlichen und frühneuzeitlichen Politiktheorie' in Münkler and Bluhm (eds.), *Gemeinwohl und Gemeinsinn*, pp. 129–46, especially pp. 132, 137, 142–3.

utilitas publica, needs to be examined, especially in the Protestant universities. The Catholic foundations had their teaching largely determined by the Jesuit order, which adapted the established model of the *ratio studiorum*. Finally, an analysis of the universities' ceremonial 'initiation rites' determines whether they amounted to a mnemonic device to implant an image of the *bonum commune*, or, in other words, to stimulate an appreciation of the university in the service of the territorial 'common good'. Such an inquiry is facilitated by three sets of 'dedicated' sources: the foundation documents and their frequent pledges to the *bonum commune*; the university statutes, as well as tracts by distinguished professors giving guidelines for the content and purpose of teaching; and contemporary programmes, designs of festivities and correspondence between leading scholars, including extensive eye-witness reports.

A few case studies have been selected for detailed analysis. These include the Protestant universities of Giessen (1607) in central Germany, and Helmstedt (1575–76) in northern Germany, with a brief look at Catholic new universities like Paderborn (1613) in north-western Germany, and Würzburg (1575–76) in southern Germany.[22] The University of Dublin (1592) is also examined, since it seems to present an intriguing parallel to Giessen. The problem here is not that the University of Dublin was outside the Empire, but that Irish scholars have never perceived it as a tool to assist statecraft, as a cultural bonus *after* the 'country had emerged from barren disorder'.[23] Since the 'common good' is mentioned so often in the foundation charters, it can be assumed that the authorities wished to adopt a more systematic approach to poor relief, to develop a basic health service and to guard the purity of the faith, thereby extending to the territory what had been devised as essential for stable urban civic communities.

II

Giessen, founded in 1607, was not the first university to be established in a territory in need of stabilisation, but the motivation and the steps taken

---

[22] Twenty new German foundations came into being between 1500 and 1650, but the documentary evidence is not as rich as for the universities selected above: see Volker Press, 'Adel, Reich und Reformation' in Wolfgang J. Mommsen, Peter Alter and R. W. Scribner (eds.), *Stadtbürgertum und Adel in der Reformation* (London, 1979), pp. 330–83; see also Anton Schindling, 'Die Universität Giessen als Typus einer Hochschulgründung' in Peter Moraw and Volker Press (eds.), *Academia Gissensis. Beiträge zur älteren Giessener Universitätsgeschichte* (Marburg, 1982), pp. 83–113, especially p. 84.

[23] R. B. McDowell and J. A. Webb, *Trinity College, Dublin, 1592–1952. An academic history* (Cambridge, 1982), p. 1; see generally J. P. Mahaffy, *An Epoch in Irish History. Trinity College, Dublin, its foundation and early fortunes, 1591–1660* (London 1903; repr. Port Washington and London, 1970).

to achieve the aim of the transfer of the communal to the territorial 'common good' emerge more clearly here than elsewhere. The opening of the university was advertised as an act of thanksgiving for the creation of a new Lutheran state in Hesse-Darmstadt, which would be maintained and strengthened by this academic institution. It had started as a *gymnnasium illustre*, a school teaching all subjects, but not awarding generally recognised degrees.[24] In 1607 Emperor Rudolf II issued the imperial charter needed to transform it into a full university.[25]

Giessen was in many ways an unsuitable location from which to start an active application of a communal sense of the 'common good' for the benefit of a new territory. Lacking any notable schooling tradition, it had to imitate that of neighbouring Marburg, which was founded by Philip of Hesse as the first university to consolidate a Lutheran 'common good' in 1527, but which had been forced to adopt the Calvinism of its ruler in 1603.[26] The communalism of Giessen had to be enhanced to act as a commonweal *in nuce* at the very moment its university was established. Fortunately many famous Marburg university professors, unwilling to abandon their Lutheran faith, settled in Giessen. One of the greatest 'catches' was the former Marburg law professor Gottfried Antonii, whose work contributed greatly to the revised interpretation of the 'common good'.[27] The professors from Marburg formed the nucleus of a rapidly growing network of bourgeois university families serving the 'common good'; all the professorial staff intermarried and influenced the development of the Lutheran church as well as the civil service in the territory. The university was organised as a distinct commonweal *in nuce*. Masters and students enjoyed the privileges of a self-regulating guild in academic matters. All members were exempt from taxation on books and also on food and drink. The town of Giessen, looking after the 'common good' of the civic community, appreciated its university from the beginning. The *Actus Restaurationis* (29 March 1650), when the university returned to Giessen after an absence of twenty-five years (necessitated by the Thirty

---

[24] Peter Moraw, *Kleine Geschichte der Universität Giessen, 1607–1982* (Giessen, 1982), pp. 18–19.

[25] Schindling, 'Die Universität Giessen', p. 92; see also H. Wasserschleben (ed.), *Die ältesten Privilegien und Statuten der Ludoviciana, Giessen* (Giessen, 1881), pp. 4–5.

[26] Schindling, 'Die Universität Giessen', p. 93. At Calvinist Marburg, Hermann Kirchner demonstrated the usefulness of the university to the 'common good' in his 'Conservatio Reipublicae per bonam educationem' (1608), see Walter Heinemeyer, Thomas Klein and Helmut Seier (eds.), *Academia Marburgensis* (Marburg, 1977), pp. 207–9.

[27] A letter (19 August 1605) by the theologians Heinrich Leuchter, Johannes Winckelmann, Jeremias Vietor and Balthasar Mentzer to Landgraf Ludwig V makes this clear: cited in Oberhessisches Museum (ed.), *375 Jahre Universität Giessen, 1607–1982. Geschichte und Gegenwart* (Giessen, 1982), p. 15.

Years War), showed how much the citizens had depended on the university in their understanding of the 'common good' of their own and the territorial community.[28]

Giessen University was built according to a purposely planned total design: no old buildings were reutilised, no church property remodelled. The duke himself contributed 58 per cent of the cost in cash and lands, and with this he directly encouraged the economic drive of the town.[29] The town of originally 3,000 not very wealthy inhabitants (around 1500) had grown sufficiently to be able (in 1606) to commit 150 florins annually to sponsor students; the citizens also contributed 2,000 guilder to the acquisition of the imperial privileges.[30] This commonweal *in nuce* developed an innovative social character. Students shared the houses of professors, merchants and other townspeople. The children of the students' landlords were to learn good manners from the lodgers.[31] The university-trained elite was to be an example to the other ranks of the social hierarchy, guaranteeing law and order. A new university and the communal service to the 'common good' were at the centre of a rising state in need of stability. The result was a typical early seventeenth-century *Personenverbandsstaat* (association of people to make up a territorial state), with the unique formation of *Bürgerbeamtentum* (the trained bourgeoisie as civil servants) of Hesse-Darmstadt, a stakeholder society.[32]

Already in 1575–76 the Lutheran Duke Julius of Braunschweig-Wolfenbüttel had established an impressive university in the small town of Helmstedt in northern Germany.[33] It enjoyed its greatest influence from the time of its foundation until 1634, when it suffered from the ravages of the Thirty Years War, and it eventually closed down as a result of the Napoleonic intervention in Germany in 1810. At a time of great confusion and discord within Lutheranism, the duke had opted for the Formula of Concord (only valid in southern Germany).[34] He was convinced that he could stabilise his Lutheran state as an extension of communal traditions

[28] Oberhessisches Museum (ed.), *375 Jahre Universität Giessen*, pp. 42–5.
[29] Wilhelm Bingsohn, 'Zur Wirtschaftsgeschichte der Universität Giessen von der Gründung bis zum Beginn des 18. Jahrhunderts' in Moraw and Press (eds.), *Academia Gissensis*, pp. 137–60, especially pp. 139 and 151; see also Moraw, *Kleine Geschichte*, p. 40.
[30] Moraw, *Kleine Geschichte*, p. 19.
[31] Oberhessisches Museum (ed.), *375 Jahre Universität Giessen*, p. 41.
[32] Schindling, 'Die Universität Giessen', pp. 83–113; Moraw, *Kleine Geschichte*.
[33] Peter Baumgart, 'Die Gründung der Universität Helmstedt' in Dieter Henze (ed.), *Die Gründung der Universität Helmstedt* (Helmstedt, 1977), pp. 217–41 especially, pp. 218 ff.
[34] Helga Robinson-Hammerstein, 'Le luthéranisme allemand (1555–vers 1660)' in John Miller (ed.), *L'Europe Protestante aux XVIe et XVIIe siècles* (Dijon-Quetigny, 1997), pp. 229–49; Gerhard Müller, 'Das Ringen um die Einheit der Kirche. Ein Beitrag aus Helmstedt' in *Academia Julia – Universität Helmstedt* (Helmstedt, 2002), pp. 49–70.

with the help of a university. The duke insisted that civil servants and theologians must be educated for service in his consolidated territory in the institution at Helmstedt, even if this meant 'fabricating' a sense of communal responsibility in an incipient stakeholder society to accommodate the university that would act as a provider.[35] The duke's motives emerge clearly from the instructions to the negotiators sent to Vienna to obtain the necessary charter.[36]

Helmstedt with its underdeveloped sense of the 'common good' did not at first see any advantage in assisting its duke, but within a few years the town reached its full potential as a communal model for territorial extension with the help of its university.[37] The most convincing persuader was the duke's vigorous promotion of economic interests. With renowned professors, attracted to the new institution, Helmstedt University rapidly developed into the envisaged 'common good' *in nuce*. The individual faculties were privileged corporations with their own limited jurisdiction.[38] The professorial families began to dominate the centre of the civic community through their self-confident new buildings. Academic intermarriage and marriage with the local bourgeoisie created a social network that ensured the ready acceptance of the notion of the 'common good' and the benefits to be gained from its extension.[39] Helmstedt grew fast, since it housed the only university in northern Germany. Students with varied social backgrounds, including members of the gentry and nobility, were in theory useful for the transformation of an urban bourgeois 'common good' into a territorial one, but they failed to form a harmonious community with the urban elite. Helmstedt was to become notorious throughout Germany for the unruly conduct of its students.[40] Nevertheless, the small territory made its name as the sponsor of a distinguished scholarly institution.

Not only Lutheran but also Catholic territorial rulers sought to extend an urban model of the 'common good' to their territory by means of a

---

[35] Baumgart, 'Die Gründung der Universität Helmstedt', p. 233.

[36] Vienna H. H.St.A, RHR., Conf. priv. lat. exped., Fasz. 9, cited in Baumgart, 'Die Gründung der Universität Helmstedt', p. 7. See also Uwe Alschner, 'Der historische Zusammenhang' in Alschner, *Universitätsbesuch in Helmstedt, 1576–1810* (Helmstedt, 2000), pp. 49–93, especially pp. 56–61.

[37] Baumgart, 'Die Gründung der Universität Helmstedt', pp. 217–41; Bernd Becker, *Die Privilegien der Universität Helmstedt und ihre Bekämpfung durch die Stadt 1576–1810* (Diss. T.U. Braunschweig, 1939).

[38] Baumgart, 'Die Gründung der Universität Helmstedt', pp. 219 and 230.

[39] My doctoral student Richard Kirwan is currently working on intermarriage, new buildings and the new community of Helmstedt.

[40] Peter Baumgart, 'Die Anfänge der Universität Helmstedt im Spiegel ihrer Matrikel (1576–1600)', *Braunschweigisches Jahrbuch*, 50 (1969), pp. 5–32, especially pp. 10–11, 20–5.

new university. The steps taken by the Lutheran, Julius of Braunschweig-Wolfenbüttel in northern Germany, with Helmstedt as its newly refashioned centre, and by Prince-Bishop Julius Echter von Mespelbrunn in southern Germany, with Würzburg as its strongly developed communal centre, to define the territorial 'common good' were almost identical. In the age of confessional divisions, Catholic and Protestant universities could serve the same purpose. This confirms the validity of Rudolf Stichweh's observation that territorialism and confession were 'defining and therefore confining topoi'. The university – harnessed to these terms – did not develop any such limitations.[41] The privileges for Helmstedt and Würzburg, issued in the same year, 1575, provide the evidence.

The sources of Würzburg's urban development show that it had a long-established sense of communal service to the 'common good'.[42] Julius Echter merely prepared the ground for the transfer of the civic community's sense of the 'common good' to his territory by means of the university. He did so primarily by eliminating the Protestant citizens, who had, however, recently strengthened the values and norms that determined the local 'common good'. Despite the removal of its creators, the prince-bishop managed to restore a useful urban model and brought the resisting regional knights to heel.[43] His purpose in establishing a university at Würzburg on an entirely urban model was to consolidate his diffuse territory as a Tridentine-inspired state with the help of the Jesuit order. The academic enterprise was financed by church property, which had not come into the hands of any Protestant bourgeoisie. The ruler made extensive use of it.[44] The diocesan clergy also contributed financially, although they may have done so to retain some power over the Jesuits. Their nine years' tax (1582–91) yielded more than 117,000 florins.[45]

The prince-bishop, as soon as he was consecrated, sought to ensure the re-enforcement of the intellectual and social connections between the

[41] Rudolf Stichweh, *Der frühmoderne Staat und die europäische Universität. Zur Interaktion von Politik und Erziehungssytem im Prozess ihrer Ausdifferenzierung (16.–18. Jahrhundert)* (Frankfurt, 1991), p. 23; Schmidt, *Fundatio et Confirmatio Universitatis*, p. 23; Peter Baumgart, 'Universitätsgründungen im konfessionellen Zeitalter: Würzburg und Helmstedt' in Baumgart and Hammerstein (eds.), *Beiträge zu Problemen*, pp. 191–215; Bodo Nischan, 'Germany after 1550' in Andrew Pettegree (ed.), *The Reformation World* (London and New York, 2000), pp. 387–409, especially p. 400.

[42] Hermann Hoffmann (ed.), *Würzburgische Polizeisätze. Gelehrte Ordnungen des Mittelalters, 1125–1495. Ausgewählte Texte* (Würzburg, 1955).

[43] Ernst Schubert, 'Julius Echter von Mespelbrunn' in *Fränkische Lebensbilder*, NF, vol. III (Würzburg, 1969), pp. 158–93.

[44] See generally, Peter Baumgart, 'Die Anfänge der Universität Würzburg. Eine Hochschulgründung im konfessionellen Zeitalter', *Mainfränkisches Jahrbuch für Geschichte und Kunst*, 30 (1978), pp. 9–24; see also Schindling, 'Die Universität Giessen', p. 90.

[45] Baumgart, 'Universitätsgründungen im konfessionellen Zeitalter', pp. 202–3.

existing elite and the teaching staff of the university. Where he was not obliged to employ Jesuit staff in the seminary and in some areas of the arts faculty, he forged new ties of communal relations by employing members of the bourgeois laity as professors. He wished the professorial families to intermarry with the local elite.[46] It seems that Catholic lords such as Echter von Mespelbrunn in Würzburg found it easier than Protestant rulers to extend the sense of the 'common good' from the communal to the territorial application. Their success did not depend on religious orientation – as an examination of the content of the teaching at all these universities will show – nor on the strength or weakness of a communal practice of the 'common good', but on the ready availability of ecclesiastical property to promote the university as the crucial instrument of statecraft.

The case of Paderborn in northern Germany, however, shows that a determined lord over a very small territory could entirely dispense with a strong communal experience of the 'common good', when there was enough monastic property. Prince-Bishop Dietrich von Fürstenberg relied on the labours of the Jesuit order to shape his university. When he made his application to Pope Paul V to issue university privileges for Paderborn on 31 October 1613, he stressed his need for theologians and civil servants.[47] The legitimating arguments made no direct reference to the 'common good', neither urban nor territorial; rather, the dominant image was inspired by the notion of state-building as a missionary enterprise. He called Paderborn *his* city, a centre where not only the whole of ancient Saxony but also peoples beyond its borders would be educated to labour in the vineyard of the Lord.[48] Paderborn is the only case where the connection between the university and the 'common good' emerges only incidentally.

III

The European humanist ideal blending intellectual, social and political principles in the active promotion of the 'commonweal of the educated' to ensure the well-being of the rest of the territorial society informed all early modern petitions to promote a university. An educated elite would avoid social chaos by introducing norms that could be 'understood'. Social conduct would be guided by sound knowledge of the classics, by 'speaking

---

[46] *Ibid.*, pp. 200–1.
[47] Karl Hengst, *Jesuiten an den Universitäten und Jesuitenuniversitäten. Zur Geschichte der Universitäten der Oberdeutschen und Rheinischen Provinz der Gesellschaft Jesu im Zeitalter der konfessionellen Auseinandersetzung* (Paderborn, 1981), pp. 190–1.
[48] *Ibid.*, appendix 4, p. 326.

well', and shored up by natural law. It was necessary to teach *more geometrico* to reveal the underlying symmetry in everything that governed the 'common good'.

There is agreement among scholars that the content of teaching at Catholic, especially Jesuit, universities was very similar to that of new Protestant universities.[49] Baumgart has described Johannes Sturm of Strasbourg, assisted by Philip Melanchthon of Wittenberg, as the 'bridge between Protestants and Catholics'. Their aim was *sapiens et eloquens pietas*, to be achieved by providing a good grounding in arts subjects.[50] The more innovative universities of both confessions also followed Justus Lipsius. His writings that defined the 'common good' in theory suited Protestants during his early career, while the same writings also appealed to Catholics, after he had reconverted to Catholicism.[51] The teaching at new Protestant universities was clearly fashioned according to the need to stabilise the state. The Protestant authorities selected their professors to suit this purpose; the Catholic institutions used the Jesuits, asking them to adapt their preformulated programme.

The founder of the University of Giessen ensured that it was well provided with academic posts: the nineteen permanent chairs were increased to twenty-two in 1629. His actions coincided with the wishes of his bourgeois subjects in the town. They believed fervently in a rigorous classical education as the precondition for serving the public good, because it would result in a renewal of manners and ethical conduct.[52] Their republication in 1615 of Luther's tract *To the Councilmen* with its plea to preserve the great learning of the age was just one indication of their commitment.[53] To learn from the German past, all students were expected to study the Augsburg Confession (1530), the Golden Bull (1356) and other documents of imperial law, together with the universal history by Carion and other chronicles, and the works of Melanchthon and Sleidan.[54] To facilitate this learning Giessen bought the huge library of Strasbourg in 1612.[55]

The arts faculty, the basis of all other studies, responded to the demands of the 'common good' by converting the *trivium* into the *humaniora* (grammar, rhetoric, poetics, logic, ethics and history) and the *quadrivium* into the various branches of the natural sciences. There was also a

---

[49] Anton Chroust, *Stufen der Entwicklung unserer Universitäten* (Leipzig, 1939), p. 325.
[50] Baumgart, 'Universitätsgründungen im konfessionellen Zeitalter', p. 203. Jakob Sturm, *De literarum ludis recte aperendis liber* (Strasbourg, 1538); also Schindling, 'Die Universität Giessen', p. 109.
[51] Baumgart, 'Universitätsgründungen im konfessionellen Zeitalter', p. 207.
[52] Schindling, 'Die Universität Giessen', pp. 98–9.   [53] *Ibid.*, p. 83.
[54] Oberhessisches Museum (ed.), *375 Jahre Universität Giessen*, pp. 16, 55–7, 90–4, 116–21.
[55] Moraw, *Kleine Geschichte*, p. 23.

significant innovation with the introduction of modern languages such as French, Italian and Spanish.[56] The acknowledged achievement in 'didactics' – a word frequently used in contemporary documents – was the publication of knowledge in academic works, although the main emphasis was no doubt on the training of memory and formal instruction. History, politics and ethics were treated as practical subjects with a vast treasury of positive (stimulating) or negative (discouraging) examples.

From the scientific courses, formerly the *quadrivium*, the duke demanded 'useful' knowledge. For example, the professor of mathematics must understand the art of fortification in the interest of the whole community. All professors were encouraged to think of the greater 'common good' and ways of improving it. One response was the memorandum submitted by Wolfgang Rathke (1571–1635) at the meeting of the Imperial Diet in 1612 in Frankfurt, discussing the improvement in the learning process for the purpose of preserving the linguistic unity and clear thinking of the leaders of the Empire in its individual territories. Rathke had absorbed insights from Francis Bacon, the Anabaptists and the Rosicrucians, all of whom had reflected on the 'common good'.[57] The 'didactics' serving the 'common good' involved greater openness for 'new things', but these were assimilated to the traditional syllabus.[58] Duke Ludwig V of Hesse-Darmstadt was an eager scientist, especially keen on astronomy. He built the necessary instruments himself and had contact with Tycho Brahe, Johannes Kepler and Galileo. The 2 metre high astronomical globe, improving on that in Copenhagen, embodied his understanding of the 'common good'. Kepler is said to have admired it as the most amazing achievement of the harmonisation of society.[59]

The medical faculty of Giessen was undoubtedly a distinguished promoter of the 'common good', providing the necessary scientific knowledge and furthering the appropriate ethical attitude. Professor Gregor Horstius sought to combine the principles of Hippocratic and Hermetic medicine in the interest of scientific progress. His study of anatomy, *De Natura Humana*, published in Wittenberg in 1612, was the Giessen course

---

[56] Professors listed in Oberhessisches Museum (ed.), *375 Jahre Universität Giessen*, p. 117.

[57] Recorded by Ruth Stummann-Bowert, *ibid.*, pp. 117–20.

[58] On new requirements assimilated to the old syllabus of the *gymnasium illustre*: see Hans Czczech (ed.), 'Die Dietrich'sche Chronik von 1613 veröffentlicht und mit Anmerkungen versehen von Magister Rambach; "Giessener Wochenblatt" 1771', *Mitteilungen des Oberhessischen Geschichtsvereins*, NF, 49:50 (1965), pp. 6–38, especially pp. 31–2.

[59] Wilhelm Diehl, *Landgraf von Hessen-Butzbach* (Darmstadt, 1909), pp. 50 ff. extensively citing Johannes Winckelmann's report; see also Schindling, 'Die Universität Giessen', pp. 105–9; it was considered dynamic, despite the fact that it was created out of an adapted communal 'common good'.

book. From the moment of his appointment in 1608 he conducted public anatomy classes for all 'lovers of knowledge'. Citizens were invited by posters and personal letters to attend his 'dissection demonstrations'. Since some of the advertisements have been preserved, one can gain an insight into the comprehensive purpose of the *Anatomiae Publicae*. It was considered essential for philosophy to understand the interactions of the human body to demonstrate the perfection of God's creation. Anatomy could assist jurisprudence in the form of forensic anatomy and theology to reveal the wisdom and goodness of God. In short, *Anatomiae Publicae* could further social harmony.[60]

The Statutes of Helmstedt reveal that the content of teaching had been arranged on the same assumption in a similar pattern.[61] By the inculcation of knowledge in the arts, superstition and barbarism in conduct could be dealt a fatal blow. As in all other new foundations, 'speaking well' (a reference to being conversant with the selected classical texts) was considered essential for the good care of the community.[62] The aim of the teaching in the arts faculty, in preparation for the higher faculties, was defined by Philip Melanchthon and his understanding of Lutheranism. It is clear from the statutes that in the arts and the various components of the study in these initial training courses that everything would be useful to practical Christianity in the *res publica*.[63] With the appointment of the humanist Johannes Caselius (1533–1613), professor of rhetoric at Rostock, a chair of politics was created to assist this process.[64] Reviewing the statutes, Horst Dreitzel observed that the university was intended not merely for the education of pastors and theologians, but of civil servants, lawyers and doctors, and represented a source of general knowledge of the local habits and customs.[65]

In the law faculty of Helmstedt the *Institutiones Justiniani* became the foundation of the canon of the teaching of Roman law, which was considered 'the epitome and sum of jurisprudence'; it was accepted as the binding interpretation of natural law implanted in all humans by their creation, as Melanchthon had suggested. Lawyers were supposed to be

---

[60] Corpses had to be released by order of the prince. In the later seventeenth century the bodies of executed criminals were used; these also included 'dead witches'. Jost Benedum in Oberhessisches Museum, *375 Jahre Universität Giessen*, pp. 91–2; on Gregor Horstius's *De Natura Humana* of 1612, *ibid.*, p. 109.

[61] Peter Baumgart and Ernst Pietz (eds.), *Die Statuten der Universität Helmstedt* (Göttingen, 1963).

[62] *Ibid.*, section 7; also Horst Dreitzel, 'Die Universität Helmstedt' in Horst Dreitzel, *Protestantischer Aristotelismus und Absoluter Staat. Die 'Poetica' des Henning Arnisaeus (ca. 1575–1636)* (Wiesbaden, 1970), pp. 27–53, especially pp. 33–4.

[63] Baumgart and Pietz (eds.), *Die Statuten der Universität Helmstedt*, section 184.

[64] Dreitzel, 'Die Universität Helmstedt', p. 44.

[65] *Ibid.*, p. 34, Baumgart and Pietz (eds.), *Die Statuten der Universität Helmstedt*, section 9.

guardians of the written law, on the assumption that the survival of the state depended on its correct interpretation.[66] The actual function of the faculty, however, was to serve the implementation of law and order. The detailed guidelines concerned the complexities of devising a practical-systematic method. Didactics sought to direct the exegetical-analytical as well as the historical-antiquarian approaches to a practical end. In 1579 Dethard Horst tried to arrange private law systematically with the help of Peter Ramus's new method.[67] Other faculties also introduced new methods without getting rid of the established syllabus. Helmstedt's theological faculty offered regular instruction in church history and homiletics.[68] Yet the development of theology was hampered by the rigid observance of Lutheran orthodoxy 'to secure peace and concord' in the urban community and in the territory. Consensus could never be established.[69] The personal scientific interests of the prince ensured that the medical faculty had four chairs.[70] The statutes prescribed anatomical exercises every six months; a special building was erected to facilitate these. The prince donated the bodies, initially two and, from 1597, three a year. Botanical excursions were arranged to discover the healing potential of herbs. Visits to the sick were obligatory to serve the 'common good'. This did not, of course, mean that the medical students could ignore the conventional books. What mattered was how they used them. Galen's *Corpus Hippocraticum* and Avicenna's works were commented on in the lectures.[71]

The Würzburg syllabus and the thinking behind its arrangement can be easily reconstructed, since catalogues have been preserved from 1604–5 to 1608–9.[72] The earliest statutes suggest that the *Ratio atque Institutio Studiorum* of 1586 directed the arts faculty. The humanist basis of the teaching was covered by Aristotle's logic, with physics, nichomachean ethics and metaphysics dominating the syllabus. The prince attempted unsuccessfully to give contemporary humanism a better chance by inviting Justus Lipsius to take up a chair, after his reconversion to

[66] Baumgart and Pietz (eds.), *Die Statuten der Universität Helmstedt*, section 91–2.
[67] Dreitzel, 'Die Universität Helmstedt', p. 38.   [68] *Ibid.*, p. 39.
[69] Inge Mager, 'Reformatorische Theologie und Reformationsverständnis an der Universität Helmstedt im 16. und 17. Jahrhundert', *Jahrbuch der Gesellschaft für Niedersächsische Kirchengeschichte*, 74 (1976), pp. 11–33, especially pp. 11–13.
[70] H. Hofmeister, 'Die medizinische Fakultät der Universität Helmstedt in den Jahren 1576–1713', *Jahrbuch des Geschichtsvereins für das Herzogtum Braunschweig*, 9 (1919), pp. 109–48.
[71] Dreitzel, 'Die Universität Helmstedt', p. 37 points out that the empirical exercises were in opposition to the introduction of the statutes that forbade even the slightest deviation from the established authorities and called them 'heresies that insult God'.
[72] I have followed up Baumgart's references, especially in Franz Xaver Wegele, *Geschichte der Universität Würzburg*, 2 parts (part II: *Urkundenbuch*) (Würzburg, 1882 (reprinted Aalen, (1969)), no. 90.

Catholicism in 1591.[73] The teaching remained strongly influenced by Spanish-Portuguese scholasticism, especially that of Petrus Fonseca. This combination was also absorbed into the study of theology. Thomism dominated moral and controversialist theology.[74] The study of law concentrated on the exegesis of the traditional law books as well as canon law, while medicine, a later addition, was anchored in the Graeco-Arabic tradition of the *Corpus Hippocraticus* and Galen, slowly becoming more praxis-oriented to serve the community.[75]

At Paderborn, Prince-Bishop Dietrich von Fürstenberg wrote in 1614 to the Jesuit general Aquaviva suggesting that the two faculties of his new university should teach logic, ethics, mathematics, physics and metaphysics, theology as *scholastica positiva* and Hebrew.[76] The aim, succinctly stated, was to 'overcome the laziness and ignorance of parishioners . . . and to oppose the heretics'.[77] In short, Jesuit didactics were adapted to the welfare of the local and territorial communities.[78]

It is in this light that the planning behind the establishment of Trinity College, Dublin, in the 1590s should be seen. From the outset Trinity was a characteristic institution of the city of Dublin, closely modelled on the traditional city guild. As in Giessen, the masters were encouraged to see their task of teaching as a business (*negotium*). Their teaching was geared especially to the efficient training of a Protestant clergy and laity intended to live as good neighbours in a coherent and interdependent community. There was also an appeal to the gentry and nobility to abandon their prejudice against 'bookish and clerkly learning', since it was useful to the state.[79] The university syllabus relied for this purpose on the Puritan humanism of the universities of Cambridge and Edinburgh, but it hardly differed from that of Lutheran Helmstedt and Giessen. The intellectual link between these types of humanism was Luke Challoner, one of the founders of the library at Trinity College, Dublin. The thoroughly practical systematisation of Aristotelian logic by Peter Ramus gave

---

[73] Baumgart, 'Universitätsgründungen im konfessionellen Zeitalter', pp. 191–215, especially p. 206.

[74] *Ibid.*   [75] *Ibid.*, p. 207.

[76] Hengst, *Jesuiten an Universitäten*, pp. 194–5 and Document no. 5, p. 327.

[77] *Ibid.*, pp. 327–8. The foundation privilege issued by Pope Paul V, 2 April 1615, confirms the position of the Jesuits in the teaching programme. The charter issued by Emperor Matthias II is inspired by the same thinking: *ibid.*, Document no. 7, especially p. 332; no. 8, pp. 335–9.

[78] Hengst, *Jesuiten an den Universitäten*, p. 203.

[79] See Lawrence Stone, 'Social control and intellectual excellence: Oxbridge and Edinburgh, 1560–1983' in Nicholas Philipson (ed.), *University, Society and the Future* (Edinburgh, 1983), pp. 1–29; M. H. Curtis, *Oxford and Cambridge in Transition, 1559–1642* (Oxford, 1959), pp. 75, 183; Helga Robinson-Hammerstein, 'Commencement ceremonies and the public profile of a university: Trinity College, Dublin, the first one hundred years' in Andrea Romano (ed.), *Università in Europa* (Messina, 1995), p. 240.

coherence to the Dublin syllabus.[80] The overall concern – as in all other new foundations – was the efficient training of an intellectual elite 'to speak well', having internalised the classical precepts of 'good manners' so that they could serve the 'common good'.[81]

All in all, the didactics of the newly founded universities, adapting humanism to the purpose of encouraging *eloquens et sapiens pietas*, were worked out to offer the best possible service to the 'common good' in relatively unstable societies. There cannot be any doubt, however, that confessional divisions hindered the realisation of the 'common good' didactics by giving priority to the education of confessionally antagonistic clergy. Giessen and Helmstedt, while seeking to ensure the institution of the 'true faith' as central to the 'common good', explicitly included the setting of relevant norms and inculcated values through legal and scientific studies. These were designed – mostly by the rulers themselves – to allow a better appreciation of the interdependence of all creation.

IV

The ethos of serving the communal and, by extension, the territorial 'common good' was embodied in the new foundations. This is best illustrated in the opening ceremonies. Eye-witness accounts make it clear that they were carefully fashioned to leave a lasting impression of the university as a tool to further the 'common good'. The symbolism was meant to encode this purpose beyond the moment of the actual ceremony. All aspects of the ceremony had to be arranged as the expression of a well-ordered state, with participants appearing in the order of their relative importance. The various acts of dedication underlined harmony by observing the 'correct' sequence. Such ceremonies had – at least since the spread of Burgundian court culture in late medieval Europe – been considered more than mere decoration. The university ceremonials were, in fact, an adaptation of an established part of the power display of the ruler. The church also played its role, often by providing the ceremonial space and allowing the adaptation of its traditional liturgical sequences. Rule by means of symbolic acts was a well-known device to bind ruler and ruled together: the image was believed to stand for reality.[82]

---

[80] Robinson-Hammerstein 'Commencement ceremonies', pp. 247–8.
[81] Elizabethanne Boran, 'Ramism in Trinity College, Dublin, in the early seventeenth century' in Mordechai Feingold, Joseph S. Freedman and Wolfgang Rother (eds.), *The Influence of Petrus Ramus* (Basle, 2001), pp. 177–99, especially p. 179.
[82] Thomas Rahn, 'Grenzsituationen des Zeremoniells in der Frühen Neuzeit' in Markus Bauer and Thomas Rahn (eds.), *Die Grenze. Begriff und Inszenierung* (Berlin, 1997), pp. 177–206.

At the official opening of Giessen University on 7 October 1607 a procession moved through the town to the church of St Pancrace in the well-established sense of the orderly progress of those most prominently serving the 'common good'. It was organised around the insignia of the new institution. The centrepiece of the procession was the gold-embroidered cushion on which the charter, issued by the emperor, was placed. It was carried along with two new sceptres and five seals (one for the whole university and four for the individual faculties). The matriculation book, the keys, the Bible in Luther's translation, Luther's Large Catechism and the German translation of the *Confessio Augustana* came next. These were the significant symbols of the nascent Lutheran society: the books were in the vernacular. The arrangement of the procession not only demonstrated the source of inspiration of the Lutheran notion of the 'common good'; it also specified the main elements of its content.[83] The ceremony itself had at its true core the sermon by Professor Johannes Winkelmann, a scholar of exceptional reputation, who presented a topical exposition of Luke 4:16: the good news of the release of the captives ending with the words 'today this is fulfilled in your hearing'. Applying this to the occasion, the preacher suggested that the university was the means of liberating the people from ignorance and bad manners and of ensuring the 'common good' of the whole community. After the reading of the imperial charter the seals were handed over to the deans as their signs of office in the presence of representatives of town and 'state'.

In the afternoon the shared festive meal (*convivium*), another traditional courtly act adapted to suit the purpose, gained special significance as a form of bonding intended to create a coherent community dedicated to the 'common good'. The celebrations culminated in speeches on political theory interpreting what constituted the 'common good'. The formal public proceedings were followed by the entertainment of the people with the performance of a comedy. To suit the occasion, instead of classical legend, the story of the abduction of the Saxon princes, taken from the local past, was utilised to inculcate good conduct. It was a curious assimilation of old and new.[84]

At the opening of Helmstedt, a whole generation earlier in 1576, the university's 'initiation rites' reveal a clearer emphasis on role of the prince.[85] The duke dominated the preceding two days of festivities with a

---

[83] Hans Grünberger, 'Wege zum Nächsten. Luthers Vorstellung vom Gemeinen Nutzen' in Münkler and Bluhm (eds.), *Gemeinwohl und Gemeinsinn*, pp. 147–68, here pp. 164–6.

[84] The formal ceremony of 7 October 1607 is described in detail in a contemporary chronicle in Czczech (ed.), 'Die Dietrich'sche Chronik', pp. 6–38.

[85] What follows is summarised in Baumgart, 'Die Gründung der Universität Helmstedt', pp. 233–5.

banquet at the castle in Wolfenbüttel. As three contemporary eye-witness accounts relate, on 14 October 500 horsemen accompanied the guests to Helmstedt, where they were received by professors and students at the entrance to the town. In a symbolically significant act, the council and armed citizens admitted the duke into the town and accompanied him from the wall.[86]

The arrangement of the ceremonies on 15 October highlights the duke's intention to extend the 'common good' from Helmstedt to his territory by means of the university.[87] An ordered procession made its way to the church of St Stephan. Music introduced the sermon by Martin Chemnitz on the 'necessity of schools', drawing on Luther's views. Mynsinger von Frundeck, the chancellor and imperial commissioner, read the imperial privilege. He declared the hereditary prince the rector of the university and enrobed him. The new rector then spoke to the assembled 'society' of duties of the university. The *Te Deum*, thanksgiving and prayers of intercession concluded the ceremony in the church. The next part of the programme included the reading of the disciplinary laws and an address thanking the princely founder. The meal which the prince hosted in the town hall was restricted to professors and guests, while the students and townsfolk amused themselves in their own way with 'jollifications'. On the next day, when the prince presented degrees, students from the rank of the nobility were invited to the festive meal. A play by the professor of poetics, summing up the message of the festivities, was an allegorical reworking of the history of the dynasty, lauding especially Duke Julius. The students were encouraged to participate in a fencing display in the marketplace.

The inauguration of the University of Würzburg took place between 2 and 5 January 1576.[88] These ceremonies form the Catholic counterpart to those of Helmstedt, with the prince-bishop, as rector, at the centre. Significantly, the Jesuits kept a low profile. The public display stressed the union of the Catholic town, the cathedral chapter and the university with its students, promising a secure future of the 'true faith'.

The University of Paderborn was opened in 1617. The very small, newly formed state to be served by this university had a distinctly Counter-Reformation orientation. Although, or perhaps because, the

---

[86] *Historica narratio de inauguratione academiae Juliae* (Helmstedt, 1713); an academic advertisement, agreeing with the content of the first report called *Historica narratio de introductione universitatis Juliae* (Helmstedt, 1579) and the account representing possibly personal memories of a participant included in the first biography of Duke Julius by Franz Algermann concluded in 1598, printed in *Feier des Gedächtnisses der vormahligen Hochschule Julia Carolina zu Helmstedt* (Helmstedt, 1882), pp. 171 fol.

[87] Baumgart, 'Die Gründung der Universität Helmstedt', p. 234.

[88] Wegele, *Geschichte der Universität Würzburg*, part II: *Urkundenbuch*, no. 59.

territory lacked any sense of identity and was without any communal experience of the 'common good', ceremonies presided over by the self-confident prince-bishop acted out the pretence of the 'tradition of the common good resurrected'.[89] The public ceremonies implied an impressive visual commitment to the universal Catholic interpretation of what constituted the 'common good' and how it could best be served. The carefully choreographed public act started with a mass celebrated by the aged prince-bishop himself for the first time in his long career. It highlighted the special significance of this public act of dedication of the university.

The remainder of the ceremonial brimmed with classically inspired authenticating references, as seemed to befit a Counter-Reformation university run by the Jesuits.[90] The whole of the future success of the institution appeared to depend on it. The reading of the papal charter was followed by a performance of instrumental music. The subsequent prayers of intercession implored God to allow the small university to play its part in preserving the universal Catholic faith. These prayers united town and territorial community.

The three acts of proclamation, internalisation through music and confirmation through prayers of intercession framed the publication of the imperial mandate that sanctioned the new foundation. The usual insignia were on public display and then ceremoniously handed over to the Society of Jesus. The acceptance of the assignment by the Jesuit provincial was recorded in a homily on a scriptural text (not specified in the report). Harmonised choral singing of the *Te Deum* and prayers of intercession announced to the whole assembly that the public act of dedication of the new university was completed. The *convivium* that followed also served the purpose of securing the support of the leading civic and landed gentry families for the objectives of the university and its interpretation of what constituted the best service of the 'common good' of the territory.

The afternoon's entertainment continued the theme of the university's service to the 'common good'. With didactic purpose the new students performed a Christian humanist play elaborating the wisdom of Solomon. They also gave other demonstrations of useful knowledge available at this Jesuit university, including a presentation of the *theorema mathematica*. There was no social basis for drawing on any *Bürgerbeamtentum* and committing it to the task of working for the state. The elaborate fiction of the *redivivus* theme of the celebrations had to make up for this lack. It was also

---

[89] Hengst, *Jesuiten an den Universitäten*, p. 197, note 172, p. 198; Document 9, eye-witness account.

[90] *Ibid.*

graphically encoded in a monument that the prince-bishop had designed as a memorial to his endeavours. A 17-metre-high column projected his work *sub specie aeternitatis*. Central to the whole edifice was the university. The founder, the prince-bishop, had himself placed exactly at the central point, contemplating the ethereal vision of the new institution, the instrument to revitalise the 'true faith' as the best start of the service of the 'common good' in its local and wider context.[91]

At first sight, Trinity College, Dublin, may appear to be an exception to this rule. There was no festive opening of the University of Dublin in 1592, but by 1614 the very solemnity of commencements conducted in that year illustrates the growing significance of the ceremonial to the university.[92] This first structured conferring of degrees on the Cambridge model, initiating graduates into the company of the elite that supported the 'common good', projected a clear self-image. The ceremonial was the enactment of a deliberate construction combining the traditional civic ritual and the new purpose.[93] The celebrations were spread over two days.[94] There had been commencements before 1614, but they were too improvised to impress with any symbolic significance, although sociability in *convivia* uniting town (with government officials) and gown played a crucial role.[95] In 1614 the government officials were considered important enough to fix the dates – 17 and 18 August – to suit their convenience. The college buildings provided the ceremonial space on the first day, which began with a Latin sermon *ad clerum* in the chapel to demonstrate that the ecclesiastical hierarchy was being prepared well for its crucial task of serving the 'common good' by spreading the 'pure word' in the country. In 1614 and at all future commencements the first sermon was an exposition of an Old or New Testament text that related specific biblical events to the 'common good' served by the college.

---

[91] This statue was built in Paderborn to commemorate the prince-bishop's work.

[92] Helga Robinson-Hammerstein, 'Royal policy and civic pride: founding a university in Dublin' in David Scott (ed.), *Treasures of the Mind* (London, 1992), pp. 1–15.

[93] Robinson-Hammerstein, 'Commencement ceremonies and the public profile of a university' applying the insights of Edwin Muir, 'Images of power: arts and pageantry in Renaissance Venice', *American Historical Review*, 84 (1979), pp. 16–52 and *Civic Ritual in Renaissance Venice* (Princeton and Guildford, 1981).

[94] The programmes of commencements are preserved in the Manuscript Room, Trinity College, Dublin. Of special interest are: *Account of the Commencement held on the 18th of August 1614 as given in the Chronicle of Lord Chichester's Government of Ireland* (reprinted in *The Whole Works of the Most Rev. James Ussher, D.D.*, ed. C. R. Elrington (17 vols., Dublin, 1847–64), I, pp. 17–19); *The University Statutes of 1615* (?, not later than 1617, but after 1614), cap. 11, see TCD, MUN/P/1/201.

[95] Robinson-Hammerstein, 'Commencement ceremonies and the public profile of a university', p. 244.

The ceremonies on the second day were designed to demonstrate the dignity of the college as an integrated space that was able to protect its staff and students by the high walls surrounding it (like Oxford and Cambridge colleges).[96] The high walls had their own inner logic. They communicated the message that the university protected the impressionable youths against the wicked world outside. The college stood at the edge of the city and was not immune to attack from the surrounding countryside. For the purposes of the ceremonial, however, the gate to the city was opened for an 'orderly procession' to St Patrick's Cathedral.[97] The body corporate, headed by the archbishop of Dublin as 'the moderator of the theological acts', walked according to rank as members of the government, the university and the church. The aldermen of Dublin were considered hosts of this event on the second day. They apparently did not play an active part but were merely spectators while the procession, after emerging from the college, made its way through their city.[98]

The commencement ceremonies in 1614 highlighted the role of the divinity graduates in St Patrick's Cathedral as men who had a vital role to play in serving the 'common good' in Ireland. The ceremonial centred on the induction of three doctors of divinity with the standard insignia of office. An anonymous private observer of the acts predicted that the university would produce the kind of learning that would benefit the church and the commonweal (i.e., the 'common good').[99] The role of the university was indeed memorably projected. In intention at least it was the very tool of the extension of the 'common good' notion from the civic community, the city of Dublin, to the state with the active and willing support of the bourgeoisie. Trinity College arose out of 'the bowels of the city's bounty'.[100]

From the foregoing case studies it can be seen that, both in Ireland and in the newly emerging German states, the foundation charters justified the establishment of the new universities by pointing to their service of the 'common good'. Highly determined rulers of new unstable states utilised the communal experiences of the town – even if they had to 'fabricate' them – to legitimate their power by pledging themselves to serving the 'common good' in their territory. Humanism informed the didactics of these 'useful' institutions in the arts faculties. In some universities the higher faculties were anxious to demonstrate their commitment to the

---

[96] Stone, 'Social control and intellectual excellence', p. 6.
[97] *Account of the Commencement . . . 1614.*   [98] *Ibid.*, p. 250.   [99] *Ibid.*
[100] Colm Lennon, '"The bowels of the city's bounty": the municipality of Dublin and the foundation of Trinity College in 1592', *Long Room* 37 (1992), pp. 10–16.

comprehensive service of the 'common good' in their innovative teaching. The universities gave expression and lent power of persuasion to the benefits they conferred upon the whole community in the mnemonic designs of their public celebrations. Each new university was intended to be the crucible to regulate the 'common good' when it was extended over the whole territory.

5 The construction of argument: Henry Fitzsimon, John Rider and religious controversy in Dublin, 1599–1614

Brian Jackson

Disputation and rhetoric were at the core of the Renaissance university curriculum. Formal training in, and fostering of, these skills was a major part of the education of the higher clergy. One consequence of the Reformation and the subsequent schism was that the emphasis of this training shifted from rhetoric to eristic.[1] This development operated in a number of ways. At a political level, Cardinal William Allen[2] and his associates at Douai aimed to replicate the collegiate world of Oxford as religious tests forced them and other recusants out of the English university system. Eristic literature therefore provided an initial manifesto for the alternative value-system of the exiles and their adherents. At a more popular level, this body of writing served to give coherent expression to the novel political, social and religious realities experienced by the laity. And as these realities shifted and developed over time, so too did the form and content of the texts themselves.

This chapter looks at a peculiarly Irish aspect of a major theme in controversial disputation and writing. While the action took place in Ireland and was shaped, to an extent, by very local concerns and conditions, the substantive core of the dispute was at the heart of prevailing theological dispute. All of the significant participants, Catholic and Protestant, shared a common formal education, and the form, content and choreography of the disputation reflects this bond. The subject matter of the dispute, essentially whether or not certain practices were part of the fundamental fabric of the primitive Apostolic church, and therefore valid and legitimate, introduced an element of historical inquiry and a degree of relativism into what had been previously an area of 'timeless absolutes', *saecula saeculorum*. This of itself determined the shape and modulation

---

[1] While rhetoric is essentially an art of constructing a persuasive, well-ordered and stylish argument, eristic is arguing to win.

[2] William Allen (1522–94), quondam fellow of Oriel College, Oxford. Allen left England in 1561. He was the founder of the English College at Douai and he was created cardinal in 1587.

of the arguments marshalled by the parties to the debate and allowed it to develop over time. By this process, the stylistic conventions of argument were applied, were transformed and were ultimately subverted by the process of engagement.

Both parties to the debate, the Irish Jesuit Henry Fitzsimon and John Rider, the dean of St Patrick's Cathedral, Dublin, shared a common education and common assumptions. As they battled for the hearts and minds of a very specific target audience, the aldermen and burghers of Dublin, they thought they were appealing to the very same sets of arguments. And as they conducted this debate there was a great sense of purpose, of tension and of engagement between the combatants and their supporters. They were not simply constructing arguments, they were seeking to make good an intellectual rift that was alienating the state from its traditional supporters among the Old English urban elite. But the moment passed. The gulf had widened, and the sense of tension and of engagement that was present in the accounts of the first debates between Fitzsimon and his opponents had evaporated from his later writings. These later works were not about advancing an argument or making a case. They were about justification.

I

One evening late in November 1599 a group of people sat around a Dublin dinner table. As is often the way, talk turned to issues of the day. There were eight in the party, hosted by a Mr and Mrs Blackney.[3] Three of the guests were identified in subsequent depositions as priests: Charles Rede, Edward Oprey and the Jesuit Henry Fitzsimon. Also present were a Mr George Taylor, a Mr William Tipper and another guest identified only by his trade, a tailor. According to William Tipper's account of events, Fitzsimon introduced a topic of contention, asking Taylor: 'And say, how came we by this kingdom?' According to Tipper, George Taylor's answer was unequivocal:

We conquered it and won it by the sword and after it was confirmed by the pope to the king, but to what king he knows not, but he heard him speak of King John and he thinketh he meant him, and that the people of the kingdom yielded up their lands to the king, and take it of him again, and so we hope we shall hold it forever.[4]

---

[3] George Blackney of Rickenhore is remembered as a special friend and benefactor by H. Fitzsimon in *The Iustification and Exposition of the Diuine Sacrifice of the Masse and of al Rites and Ceremonies thereto Belonging Deuided into Two Bookes* (Douai, 1611), p. 361. A George Blackney and a Fitzsimon represented Swords in the 1613 parliament.

[4] PRO, SP 63/206/101.

Taylor's own account of the exchange is even more direct:

The said Henry having talked of the state of the country uttered that the rebels had won a great part of the country. No, said the said George, I thank God that they have not won any part of the English Pale, though they have wasted a part of it and I hope in God the Queen's Majesty with her force will soon put them down. Said Mr Fitzsimon, how came the English to the possession of this land, the said George answered, by conquest. Fitzsimon answered, every conquest is not lawful, the said George said, that soon upon the conquest it was allowed by the clergy and as I have heard say, confirmed by the pope and with all the lords and chief men of the land did give up their titles and government unto King Henry the Second and to sundry other kings since. Mr Fitzsimon said, well you see how the Irishry prosper notwithstanding, whereunto the said George answered, those questions are not good, nor to be reasoned upon, give them over, for I love them not these discourses. So taking my leave I departed home.[5]

It is more than likely that one of the guests, probably George Taylor, alarmed by this dangerous talk, hurried away to inform the authorities and, shortly afterwards, Fitzsimon was arrested and detained in Dublin Castle. It is clear that the political sensibility of those around the table was firmly rooted in an historical narrative framework, and this was not going to be set aside because someone wanted to make an unhelpful and dubious causal link between success and right.

Fitzsimon determined to make the most of his new circumstances. One of his first acts was to call upon Luke Challoner, a fellow of Trinity College, Dublin – and, coincidentally, his cousin – to engage in a formal disputation. Challoner declined the match, excusing himself on the pretext that any formal acknowledgement of the Jesuit would displease the crown.[6] A second opportunity for dispute presented itself when, as Fitzsimon alleged, Meredith Hanmer, prebendary of St Michan's in Christ Church Cathedral and an Oxford contemporary of Fitzsimon, was briefly confined to the Castle on account of his drunken and disorderly behaviour. In front of a crowd that included an Irish councillor, Sir William Warren, Fitzsimon goaded the unfortunate and presumably very hung-over Hanmer to debate. Hanmer did not rise to the challenge, but was provoked into an ill-tempered outburst against Puritanism.[7] A further disputant presented himself before Fitzsimon when another of his kinsmen came to visit, the precocious James Ussher. The Jesuit sent

---

[5] PRO, SP 63/206/102.
[6] H. Fitzsimon, *Britannomachia Ministrorum in plerisque et fidei fundamentis, et fidei articulis dissidentiu* (Douai, 1614), sig. Av.
[7] *Ibid.* sig. Av-Air.; Edmund Hogan (ed.), *Words of Comfort to Persecuted Catholics* (Dublin, 1881), p. 80.

him away. Fitzsimon had clear ideas as to how any debate should be conducted, and Ussher, an unknown youth, added no cachet to his game.[8]

Some months later, on 29 September 1600, talk around another Dublin dinner-table touched on similar themes of legitimacy, authority and tradition. The host on this occasion was another of Fitzsimon's Oxford contemporaries, John Rider, dean of St Patrick's Cathedral. Among his guests was William Nugent, a prominent Old English recusant and brother of the baron of Delvin, who maintained that there was no diversity of belief or of religion between 'the Catholics of these times and the primitive Catholics of the lives of the Apostles'. Furthermore, maintained Nugent, the Jesuits and Roman priests of the kingdom were able to prove by reference to the Scriptures and to the works of the Fathers that these positions were Apostolic and Catholic.[9] Rider rejected this notion and asserted that the early Christians were Protestant in their belief and practice. Shortly after this exchange a letter dated 21 October 1600, purporting to come from doubtful Catholics and addressed to the priests of Ireland, circulated and set out six propositions: that transubstantiation was never taught by the Fathers nor written of in the first 500 years since the Ascension; that the early church used the vernacular; that purgatory and prayers for the dead were not taught; that images and prayers to saints were not used; that the mass was unknown; and that there was no supreme bishop and that he should not have jurisdiction over the state.[10]

At last Fitzsimon had found the challenge he had been waiting for. Over the course of the next three months he prepared a response which he sent to Michael Taylor, his cousin, who delivered it to Rider. Four days later Rider called upon Fitzsimon in Dublin Castle, complimented him on his answer, and promised a rejoinder. In September 1602 Rider published his response, *A Friendly Caveat to Ireland's Catholickes*. He presented Fitzsimon with a copy.[11]

Fitzsimon's reaction was swift. Within days the Jesuit had written to the lord deputy, Mountjoy, requesting a formal disputation with Rider.

[8] *The Works of James Ussher*, ed. C. R. Elrington (17 vols., Dublin 1847–64), I, pp. 12–14; Edmund Hogan, *Distinguished Irishmen of the Sixteenth Century* (London 1894), pp. 228–30; Bodl., Barlow MSS 13, ff. 80r–82v.

[9] John Rider, *A Friendly Caveat to Ireland's Catholickes concerning the daungerous dreame of Christs corporall (yet invisible) presence in the sacrament of the Lords Supper* (Dublin, 1602), sig. B2r.

[10] *Ibid.*, sig. B1v–B2r. Fitzsimon suggests that Rider was the source of the letter. H. Fitzsimon, *A Catholike Confutation of Mr John Riders clayme of antiquitie and a caulming confort against his caueat* (Roan, 1608), sig. O2r. This work also contains a reply to Rider's 'Rescript'.

[11] Hogan, *Distinguished Irishmen*, p. 242.

Mountjoy sent Henry Knivet, his gentleman usher, to Fitzsimon to suggest that the fellows of Trinity College be appointed as arbiters. Accordingly, Fitzsimon wrote to Luke Challoner on 7 November.[12] Challoner replied that the college was prepared to judge prepared texts only, not a disputation as such. Fitzsimon asked for access to books, a clerk and liberty to correspond, so that he might present a formal response before college or the Irish council. The request for books and a clerk was granted; Fitzsimon was given unlimited access to the college library and the services of his nephew as a clerk.[13] However, permission to correspond freely with other scholars was refused. In spite of this, Fitzsimon produced a response running to 2 quires of paper. Ultimately, however, the Jesuit was refused any opportunity to present his case in a public disputation.

In Fitzsimon's account of the dispute, published three years after his release from Dublin Castle, he concluded that there had never been any intent on the part of the state to allow a formal debate. The tactic was merely to delay, to appease and, finally, to avoid any disputation. Fitzsimon suggested that Rider, in particular, was anxious to avoid a confrontation before the college, and implied that there were tensions between the dean and the fellows.[14] Rider, who felt, not unreasonably in view of the fact that the Challoners and the Usshers were relatives and part of a web of connection around Fitzsimon, that the dice was unfairly weighted against him,[15] insisted that, to borrow Fitzsimon's phrase, 'he would be tried no where, but in Oxford'.[16] It was not until April 1604 that Rider finally consented to arbitration by the college in Dublin. Fitzsimon maintained that when it became clear that he (Fitzsimon) was to be released and deported, Rider hurriedly produced a further account, as if to have the final word.[17] This rather backfired on Rider when the mayor of Dublin, whom Fitzsimon regarded as a timorous church papist, publicly challenged the dean for 'wounding a man bound'.[18] A blustering Rider assured him, before a crowd in the Cornmarket, that he would confound Fitzsimon to his face if the mayor would be good enough to accompany him to the Castle. The mayor agreed, and invited the dean to dine with him first, lest he had cause to change his mind. And so, in the presence of the mayor, Justice Palmer, Captain Godl, Sir Richard Cooke, secretary to the Irish council, and about one hundred others in the Castle courtyard, Fitzsimon accepted Rider's challenge to have a public disputation before the college on the central issue of the authority of tradition in the church.

---

[12] Fitzsimon, *Replye*, pp. 6–7. This work was published as part of the *Catholike Confutation*.
[13] Fitzsimon, *Replye*, p. 4.   [14] *Ibid.*, p. 11.   [15] *Ibid.*, p. 15.   [16] *Ibid.*, p. 16.
[17] Rider's 'Rescript' does not survive as a discrete work in print. However, the text is reproduced in Fitsimon's *Replye*.
[18] Hogan, *Distinguished Irishmen*, p. 247.

Fitzsimon handed Rider a gold ring that he would deliver back to him at the debate. Rider was unwilling to accept the ring. Fitzsimon refused to take back what was in effect a contract publicly entered into. Eventually the mayor obliged by taking the ring into his custody. This apparently trivial incident serves as a measure of Fitzsimon's talent for allusion. He used recognisable business practices to discomfort his opponent before an audience of merchants who would appreciate the significance of Rider's reluctance to accept the ring. But he also nodded in the direction of great events on the European stage, with specific allusion to the personal challenge of the Holy Roman emperor, Charles V, to Francis I, king of France, before an audience of the Sacred College of Cardinals.[19] As far as Fitzsimon was concerned, this was not going to be a trivial, localised dogfight; it was going to be an important debate about big issues, and he had every intention that the audience should remain aware of this fact.

On the following day Rider approached the Irish council to obtain permission for the disputation to go ahead. Later that evening he dined at the Castle, along with Fitzsimon, a number of other prisoners, and the constable of the Castle, Tristram Eccleston. A measured discussion arose over the proper Greek construction of the Ave Maria. This soon degenerated into an unseemly row, and the constable, unable to restore order, left the room. This incident may appear to be something of a curiosity, but it is symptomatic of a wider intellectual division that lay at the heart of the debate over authority and tradition in the church. Essentially the disputants can be divided into two camps: Aristotelians and those who might be characterised as historical relativists. On the one hand, Fitzsimon espoused the Aristotelian termist view, which held that words have absolute and universal meanings. Rider, on the other hand, was a relativist whose preferred mode of argument was to examine the sequential development of a text and the changing meaning attributed to the words used.[20] Such a line of inquiry would ultimately lead to a questioning of the historical validity of practices traditionally accepted as having always been a part of the fabric of the church.

The next morning Rider was summoned to the council board, where he was rebuked by Fullerton, the clerk of the council, and Secretary Cooke,

[19] *Ibid.*, p. 250.
[20] This debate over the Angelic Salutation was a feature of controversial encounters between Protestant and Catholic clergy, E. Hogan (ed.), *Life and Letters of Henry Fitzsimon* (Dublin, 1881), p. 237. Fitzsimon dismissed Rider's mode of argument: 'I told you, Mr. Rider, that you would carry your empty pitcher so oft to the Greek stream that it would come home broken. What! Did Christ speak Greek?', *ibid.*, p. 236.

who criticised his handling of the incident on the previous evening, impugning his talent for logic. It was later alleged by Fitzsimon that Rider's proofs were considered by Fullerton to be inadequate to his own propositions.[21] On 14 May 1604 fellows of Trinity College delivered their verdict on Fitzsimon's dispute with Rider. Predictably, the arbiters found that Fitzsimon had been unable to prove that there had been any conciliar or patristic teaching on transubstantiation within 500 years of the Ascension of Christ, whereas the propositions of Rider had convinced them to the contrary position. Fitzsimon rejected the decision. He cited it as evidence of puritanical treachery and represented it as a public rebuke to the college.[22]

II

This sequence of events was little more than a set piece choreography for religious disputation. The challenge, the circulated propositions, the prison debate were a self-conscious reenactment of the final months of the English Jesuit Edmund Campion. With reckless theatricality, Campion had his challenge to English Protestantism, the *Rationes Decem*, privately printed at Stonor Park and distributed around St Mary's church, Oxford, before the University Act of 27 June 1581. Shortly afterwards he was arrested and imprisoned in the Tower of London. While in custody he participated, along with Ralph Sherwin, in a series of debates. Alexander Nowell, dean of St Paul's, and William Day, dean of Windsor, were their principal opponents. But the authorities, impatient with this course of action, abandoned debate and moved to trial. The Jesuits stood 'accused not of heresy, but of treason'.[23] Campion was determined that even in death he would fulfil his obligation to the expectations of his audience. He chose as the text for his scaffold speech an adaptation of 1 Corinthians 4:9: 'We are made a spectacle, or a sight, unto God, unto his Angels, and unto men.'[24] This Dublin reenactment, however, stopped short of the expected final spectacle that awaited many of the principal actors who feature in this story. The lives of Edmund Campion, Peter Ramus and Giordano Bruno all ended in acts of theatrical cruelty; whereas Fitzsimon was merely bundled out of the country in haste, so anxious were the

---

[21] *Ibid.*, pp. 237–8.   [22] Fitzsimon, *Replye*, p. 20.

[23] T. M. McCoog, 'Playing the champion: the role of disputation in the Jesuit mission' in T. M. McCoog (ed.), *The Reckoned Expense: Edmund Campion and the early English Jesuits* (Woodbridge, 1996), p. 136.

[24] For a detailed eye-witness account see Thomas Alfield, *A True Reporte of the Death and Martyrdome of M Campion Jesuite* (London, 1582).

authorities to see him gone. Dublin would appear to have been a safer place to voice dissent than London, Paris or Rome. Comforted by connection and influence, Fitzsimon could make self-serving allusion and reference to Campion. Indeed, his principal motive for seeking a debate with Hanmer was the role that the latter had played in the refutation of Campion's *Rationes Decem*.[25]

Taken in isolation, this debate between Fitzsimon and Rider might simply be read as part of a diminishing quarrel over ownership of the Irish church. However, Fitzsimon's activities, although conducted with considerable theatricality on the small Dublin stage marked out by the Castle, the deanery and the college, had intellectual and personal roots in another confined space – within the walls of the University of Oxford. Fitzsimon was the son of a well-connected and wealthy Dublin merchant. He matriculated from Hart's Hall, Oxford, on 26 April 1583. Fitzsimon made much of his Protestant education to rhetorical effect in his later writings; however, there is no record of his commencement, and it is likely that he did not proceed to his degree for reasons of conscience.[26] In 1587 he was in Paris under the wing of Thomas Darbyshire, a nephew of Bishop Bonner and former chancellor of the diocese of London, responsible for the examination of those unfortunates suspected of heresy by the Marian regime. From there Fitzsimon went to Pont-à-Mousson, where he graduated MA in 1591. In the following year he was admitted to minor orders and studied theology at Louvain and Douai before returning to Dublin in 1597.

Although similar in form, John Rider's career was more conventional. He originally came from Cheshire, attended Jesus College, Oxford (he was admitted to the BA degree in 1581 and took his MA in July 1583). Meredith Hanmer was another contemporary, whose Oxford career started in the 1560s at Corpus Christi; he was admitted to the BD degree in 1581 and proceeded to a doctoral degree in July 1582.

Fitzsimon, Rider and Hanmer all moved within the same orbit and experienced at first hand the radical changes that transformed Oxford in the wake of Campion's defection. Elizabethan Oxford was an intimate society of halls and colleges. With a total population of around 1,100, the university was about the size of a large school today. The

---

[25] Hanmer penned two works in particular. *The Jesuits' Banner* (London, 1581) attacked the Society of Jesus as a foreign superstitious sect founded by a low-born crippled soldier. *The Great Bragge and Challenge of Mr Champion* (London, 1581) set out to refute Campion's propositions. Robert Parsons's assessment of Hanmer's books was that they only served to further Campion's cause with a wider audience, R. Parsons, *A Brief Censure upon Two Bookes* (Douai, 1581).

[26] Fitzsimon, *Replye*, p. 46.

BA degree, based around a highly literary and rhetorical culture and the study of Aristotle, remained the cornerstone of the curriculum. However, the influence of humanist concerns with philology, biblical language and textual study helped to shift the emphasis away from the termist logic and speculative grammar characteristic of syllogistic argument towards a study of the humanities. Content aside, the significant feature in the development of the Elizabethan university was the transformation of the teaching system, focused around colleges offering intramural tutorial study and the systematic examination of students.[27] At the core of this scheme were formal exercises, where opponents and respondents took part in public disputations without the aid of notes. The MA course also involved the giving of lectures, formal disputations, and formal declamations for and against a given topic. The subject-matter for these disputations comprised those same questions that preoccupied sixteenth-century controversialists: issues of tradition, authority and the national character of the church.[28]

The training afforded Catholic seminary students followed broadly similar lines. They learned Greek and Hebrew in order to read and understand the Scriptures. Scriptural texts were studied and their approved meanings expounded in hall at meal times. Relevant scriptural references for controversial debate were memorised. Disputations were held on set passages twice a week. The skill of preaching in English was taught. Scholastic and pastoral theology and the major patristic controversies were also studied. As Cardinal William Allen explained:

We preach in English in order to acquire greater power and grace in the use of the vulgar tongue, a thing on which the heretics plume themselves exceedingly, and by which they do great injury to simple folk. In this respect the heretics, however ignorant they may be in other points, have the advantage over many of the more learned Catholics, who having been educated in the universities and the schools do not commonly have command of the text of scripture or quote it except in Latin. They [the seminarians] are taught successively Greek and Hebrew, so far as is required to read and understand the scriptures of both testaments in the original and to save them from being entangled in the sophisms which heretics extract from the properties and meanings of words.[29]

The Oxford curriculum of the 1580s was focused on the theory and defence of the national church. The institutions of the university had

---

[27] J. McConica (ed.), *The History of the University of Oxford*, III, *The Collegiate University* (Oxford, 1986), chapters 1 and 10.

[28] J. M. Fletcher, 'The Faculty of Arts' in McConica (ed.), *History of the University of Oxford*, III, *The Collegiate University*, pp. 158–95.

[29] William Allen to Jean de Vendeville, 16 September 1578, T. F. Knox (ed.), *The Letters and Memorials of William Cardinal Allen* (London, 1882), p. 65. T. F. Knox (ed.), *The First and Second Diaries of The English College, Douai* (London, 1878), pp. xxxviii–xliv.

been purged and the curriculum sanitised, first under Leicester and later Hatton. The curriculum of the seminaries, devised by the group of men that had fled Oxford in the first years of Elizabeth's reign, offered a regime that was concentrated on refuting this official position.

It is noteworthy that the evolution of the printed book reflects the development of these formal, parallel, curricula. The earliest printed works closely resembled the great manuscripts, glosses and student adversaria of the university libraries. From this the printed book moved towards a form and structure that is more familiar. It is in this context that the physical structure and layout of the printed materials examined here should be considered. Unlike Harding's response to Jewel's defence of the Anglican church, which replicates in its typographical form and structure the standard layout of a manuscript gloss, the later works of Fitzsimon and, for example, Robert Parsons are instantly recognisable as 'modern' books. The emphasis on narrative style and glosses are confined to footnotes or endnotes and contra positions are corralled into rubrics and notes in the margin.[30]

Development of form is accompanied by a discernible and substantive development of content. William Allen's essential point was that Protestant apologetic was inclined to a philogistic rather than a syllogistic mode of argument. This Protestant sensibility had two aspects to it: first, it was linguistic, teasing out the meanings of words and their evolution in translation; and, second, it was also self-consciously historical in perspective, exploring in the roots of meanings of texts the true origins and intentions of the primitive church. The earliest examples of the controversial genre suggest the distinction is valid. The contrast is apparent in the works of John Jewel, where simplicity, directness of style and an argument focused around an historical narrative abandoned the conventions of rhetorical construction.[31] This contrasts starkly with the formally scholastic response of Jewel's most vociferous opponent, Thomas Harding. From the Catholic perspective, Harding's adherence to a formal traditional style made an overtly political point. The exiled priest was claiming the moral and intellectual high ground of tradition, authority

---

[30] H. J. Jackson, *Marginalia: readers writing in books* (New Haven, 2001), pp. 45–9.
[31] D. K. Wiesner, *The Prose Style of John Jewel: Salzburg Studies in English Literature 9* (Salzburg, 1973). Jewel threw down the gauntlet of controversy in his famous 'challenge' sermon delivered on 26 November 1559, asserting that the communion service established by the Elizabethan church was a restoration of the practice and belief of the primitive church. There followed a public disputation between Protestant and Catholic clergy at Westminster late in the following March. The printed works prompted by this debate were central to the intellectual and political formation of the clergy, whether Catholic or Protestant. Details of the specific works are set out in P. Milward, *Religious Controversies of the Elizabethan Age* (London, 1977), pp. 1–16.

and truth, based on a formal mode of discourse that was essentially timeless.

Like Fitzsimon, Hanmer and Rider, Jewel and Harding shared a common past and their controversial writings were underpinned by a tangible animosity. Harding and Jewel both came from Devon, where they attended the same school in Barnstaple. They were contemporaries at Oxford and, when it was fashionable, were disciples of Peter Martyr. Harding recanted his reformist leanings, and his career prospered under Mary. He was a member of the chapter that elected Jewel bishop of Salisbury. Yet subsequently Jewel sat on the commission that deprived Harding and forced him into exile in Louvain. Here his circle included the Wykehamists John and Nicholas Harpsfield, Nicholas Sanders, Thomas Dorman, John Rastell, Thomas Stapleton and Owen Lewis, all of whom attended New College, Oxford. Like Harding, all were denied preferment under the new dispensation in England. It is little wonder, then, that the responses of Harding and his contemporaries became intensely personal in nature. Jewel and his allies had effectively pushed them off the career ladder and stolen their jobs. And so, they worked to create a counterculture of career preferment around the English and Irish colleges of Europe.

The distinction between a recusant 'sophistication' and a reformist 'simplicity' of style is notable in the case of Edmund Campion and Meredith Hanmer. Campion's *Rationes Decem*, itself a product of the traditional rhetorical schema, distinguished heretical writings by their categories of argument. Prominent among these was 'paralogism', an obsession with the roots of words. His own view, following that of Aquinas, was that 'In words we are to observe not so much from whence they are derived as to what by warrantable custom they are applied.'[32] This 'flaw' in Protestant reasoning is further characterised as 'homonymia', a tendency to strain and distort the meaning of phrases.[33] Campion's point – and it was one echoed by most Catholic controversialists – was that Protestant apologists relied on a philosophical relativism of shifting meaning. This allowed them to develop arguments grounded in a national sense of history. For example, Campion's argument might best be summed up in his famous rallying cry: 'The expense is reckoned, the enterprise is begun, it is of God, it cannot be withstood, so the faith was planted, so it must be restored.'[34] Hanmer's rejoinder appealed to a national sensibility:

---

[32] *Campion Englished, or a Translation of the Ten Reasons* (n.p., 1632), p. 32.
[33] *Ibid.*   [34] Hanmer, *The Great Bragge*, p. 24.

Neither was it the pope that first preferred Christian religion into this land and now the word of God being purely taught here and received, Rome is not to restore hither the rages of your idolatry now for a long time rooted out. Yield yourself, become a good subject that you may know how to esteem of Sion and to prefer her liberty before the captivity of Babylon.[35]

The controversy between Rider and Fitzsimon must be viewed in the context of a tradition of argument between Protestant and Catholic apologists, and it is typical of a canon of published controversial literature. Rider's *A Friendly Caveat* appeared first, in September 1602.[36] Rider set out six propositions at the beginning of the work and immediately shifted the burden of proof in the debate by a process of inversion. Answering the original positions, he recast the issue in such a manner that a Catholic apologist was required to offer an answer with a positive burden of proof — for example, that Scriptures should not be perused by the vulgar, or that the supremacy of the pope was acknowledged. As originally circulated the proposition was that the early church used the vernacular and that there was no supreme bishop. This attention to the nuances and meaning of words is a common and enduring theme of the *Friendly Caveat*. Throughout the work Rider's focus was on the interpretation of texts. His book was, in fact, a detailed philogistic exposition of the canon of the mass. Indeed, Rider was impatient with established scholastic modes of argument and ridiculed the technique of alleging the proving of a proposition with the proposition itself, which he dismissed as a childish sophistry.[37] His own approach was more akin to a critical analysis of texts. Of transubstantiation, for example, he asserted:

The term is new, lately invented and compounded by yourselves, and as your consecration was never found in the New Testament, so transubstantiation was never found in the new or old. No, I do not remember that in all my grammatical travels and studies, that ever I read . . . this word transubstantiare [*sic*], much less of the sense, which is to change substances of several kinds, one substance into another.[38]

The focus throughout the *Friendly Caveat* was on the meaning and origin of words, the nuance of tense, case and voice, and on the mechanics of translation and mistranslation of original sacred Hebrew and Greek texts into base Latin glosses. Rider's interest in language predated his

---

[35] *Ibid.*
[36] The book was printed in Dublin by John Frankton. It was dedicated to Charles Blount, who had a reputation for bookishness and a taste for controversy himself. Hans Pawlisch, *Sir John Davies and the Conquest of Ireland* (Cambridge, 1985), pp. 103–4.
[37] Rider, *Caveat*, p. 27.   [38] *Ibid.*, pp. 57–8.

career as a controversialist. In 1589 he had published his *Bibliotheca Scholastica*, an English–Latin dictionary with a Latin index.[39] This work followed, and relied heavily upon, the models of Baret's *Alvearie* (1573) and Thomas Thomas's *Dictionarium Linguae Latinae* (1587).[40] However, Rider was more than a mere compiler. His dictionary distinguished itself by the wealth of etymological information provided, the use of grammatical categories to order words, and the indication of correct grammatical usage. Rider placed his words in a changing, historical universe of meaning.

In his response to Rider, Fitzsimon ridiculed him as 'the dictionary compiler' and sought to denigrate both his learning and his approach to textual analysis. For, as Fitzsimon put it, Rider 'glories in his grammarian labours, he that made the Latin Dictionary, into which he introduced nothing new but ridiculous words, is he ignorant of Latin? This figurative Latin locution is beyond your capacity. Before you betake yourself to new grammarian labours and dictionary inventions, learn to understand a plain Latin metaphor.'[41] Furthermore, Fitzsimon found it strange that Rider, who could find so many strange words to ornament his dictionary, would omit any definition of transubstantiation: 'Yet he that sought it [the word Transubstantiare] had a veil upon his heart and a mist upon his eyes toward the word.'[42] Here Fitzsimon echoed Campion's view:

To signify an old belief with more efficacy a new term is imposed . . . which words are to be measured according to the propriety of them and the authority whence they proceed rather than according the antiquity of them. St Augustine saith: It is a most contentious part, to contend about the name when the thing is known; and as Cicero saith: Calumniatorum proprium est verba confectari [It is the preserve of those who maliciously misrepresent truth to twist and destroy the meaning of words]. By the definition of transubstantiation, we will be instructed, how sound and ancient it is.[43]

This is an articulation of the traditional semantic web of resemblance that characterised scholastic epistemology. The word used was not itself the issue, but it signified, according to the conventions of convenience, emulation, analogy, or sympathy the true sense or meaning to be understood. There is a disjunction here between a syllogistic, ternary epistemology of known and finite similitudes within a constant universe (essentially the position adopted and articulated by Allen, Harding, Campion

[39] The dictionary was dedicated to Francis Walshingham and to Rider's patrons, the earl of Sussex and William Waad. More than a dozen different editions of the dictionary were published before 1650.
[40] Fitzsimon, *Catholike Confutation*, p. 125.
[41] Hogan (ed.), *Life and Letters of Henry Fitzsimon*, p. 241.
[42] Fitzsimon, *Catholike Confutation*, p. 126.   [43] *Ibid.*, pp. 126–7.

and Fitzsimon) and a religious world-view informed by an historical perspective and a consciousness of living language (as demonstrated by Jewel, Hanmer, Rider and Ussher). It would be easy to attribute this concern for the properties and meanings of words to the influence of Peter Ramus, whose ideas were in vogue among reformist circles at the time.[44]

The career of Ramus was dedicated to the rejection of the inductive syllogism of Aristotelian logic. Rather, he employed disjunctive syllogism[45] as a tool for the nominalistic manipulation of words as a rhetorical technique. For Ramus, truth was not expounded logically; rather, it was grasped intuitively. However, Elizabethan Oxford, where our disputants received their formal training, was a bastion of Aristotelian orthodoxy. It was Cambridge, not Oxford, where the ideas of Ramus enjoyed a currency, a point made succinctly by Robert Parsons, who described Meredith Hanmer in the following terms: 'Quietly, plainly and good fellow like, excepting a fowl lie or two, joined familiarly with Campion, his fellow student at Oxford.'[46] Parsons then contrasted Hanmer with the brash and brazen William Charke, whose overtly Ramist argument focused on structure and variance within original biblical texts. Parsons ridiculed Charke's approach:

I pray you, let me know how you came by this knowledge, not by Aristotles demonstrations which yet are the only means of certain science properly. How then, by faith, but you know that faith can assure nothing which is not revealed by the word of God. What part of God's word then teacheth us that William Charke in particular serveth the Lord aright.[47]

Witheringly, Parsons asked, 'What boy in Cambridge would ever have reasoned thus.'[48] It is interesting that it is Robert Parsons, with his direct, combative, energetic style, who departed from the distinctive traditional schema adopted by Campion and the Catholic exiles and engaged with the historical philological argument on its own relativist terms.

It is tempting, if unlikely, to attribute some influence to Giordano Bruno, who made two visits to Oxford during the spring and early summer of 1583 when both Rider and Fitzsimon were at the university. Bruno was a man who left an impression wherever he went and, like

---

[44] For an assessment of the importance of Ramus, see N. E. Nelson, 'Peter Ramus and the confusion of logic, rhetoric and poetry' in *Contributions in Modern Philology* (Ann Arbor, 1947) and W. Ong, *Ramus, Method and the Decay of Dialogue: from the art of discourse to the art of reason* (Cambridge, MA, 1958).

[45] The deliberate introduction of a converse proposition.

[46] R. Parsons *A Defence of the Censure given upon two bookes of William Charke and Meredith Hanmer* (n.p., 1582), p. 7.

[47] *Ibid.*, p. 112.   [48] *Ibid.*

Parsons, ridiculed the Calvanist and Ramist notions of revealed truth.[49]
He dismissed Ramus as the 'Archpedant of France'.[50] His denunciation
of the University of Oxford was equally robust, asserting that 'a doctor's
degree is to be had there as cheaply as sardines'[51] and dismissing the
fellows as 'grammarian pedants'.[52] Bruno's controversial career reached
its violent conclusion when he was executed in Rome at around the same
time as our two combatants were squaring up to debate in Dublin. The
nature of Bruno's death serves to underline the essentially mannered and
civilised rules of engagement of this particular disputation in Dublin.
Nobody went to the stake.

One distinctive trait in Fitzsimon's writing was his studied conser-
vatism, including a stated distaste for writing in the vernacular – an
affectation, for example, eschewed by the more polemical and engaging Parsons. Another feature that cannot be overlooked was the strong
current of personal animosity towards Rider. Despite Fitzsimon's earlier
encounter with Hanmer, the two men remained on good terms. Hanmer
continued to visit him in prison and supplied him with food and beer.
Fitzsimon had a soft spot for Hanmer, whom he indulgently refers to as
a 'dear droll jolly soul, entirely given to eating, drinking, scoffing and
jesting'.[53] As for Challoner and Ussher, they were his own kinsmen, and
Fitzsimon accorded them respect. This makes the invective heaped upon
Rider even more startling and suggests a very personal dimension to
the controversy, on a par with the resentment and animosity Harding
felt towards Jewel. Fitzsimon used every opportunity to undermine his
opponent's standing in the eyes of the reader. He questioned Rider's
knowledge of Irish, of Latin and of Greek and highlighted his readiness
to cite sources he could not have either read or understood. Throughout
his writings Fitzsimon sought to create an impression of his opponent's
stupidity and intellectual dishonesty. He quoted a letter from his fellow Jesuit, Sabine Chamber, whom he styled Rider's master at Oxford.
Chamber alleged that his own aunt paid for Rider's education, but that
her charity was repaid with impudence, laziness and stupidity. Chamber
added a charge of perjury, stating that Rider proceeded from BA to MA
in the same year in spite of regulations.[54]

[49] H. Gatti, *The Renaissance Drama of Knowledge. Giordano Bruno in England* (London, 1989), pp. 27–8.
[50] F. A. Yates, *The Art of Memory* (London, 1966), p. 242.
[51] R. McNulty, 'Bruno at Oxford', *Rennaisance News*, 13 (1960), p. 304.
[52] F. A. Yates, *Giordano Bruno and the Hermetic Tradition* (London, 1964), pp. 205–11.
[53] E. Hogan (ed.), *Ibernia Ignatiana* (Dublin, 1880), p. 126.
[54] Fitzsimon, *Replye*, p. 10. This allegation is most certainly false. Chamber was Rider's contemporary at Oxford where he was a student at Broadgates Hall. Both of them commenced to the BA degree in 1580 and were admitted MA in 1583.

There is also a heavy undercurrent of snobbery throughout Fitzsimon's work. He presented Rider as an upstart and a poor scholarship boy. Fitzsimon used every opportunity to underline this social distinction. In one instance he quoted Rider as asserting that he ' "has sifted my answer and proved it to be bran". This saying is part borrowed and part natural. It is borrowed from Martin Mar-Prelate. It is natural, as Rider's father was a miller and himself a baker.'[55] These attacks were not confined to Rider, but reached out to his son and his servants. The copy of Fitzsimon's *Catholike Confutation* held by Trinity College, Dublin, bears heavy marginal annotation by Rider.[56] The volume was cropped and rebound in the nineteenth century; at which point a significant proportion of the marginal notations were unfortunately excised. However, sufficient remains to allow us to read along with Rider and react as he would have done as he encountered each insult and allegation. This is one of the rare instances where the status of marginalia can rise above that of anonymous graffiti to inform and enrich our understanding of the dynamics of the debate and of the particular reader's engagement with the text.[57] Rider's comments on textual points were generally neat, precise and closely written. Annotations accompanying personal slights or Fitzsimon's more scurrilous allegations were heavy, urgent and angry.[58]

Fitzsimon developed the thesis that Rider had distinct Puritan and iconoclastic leanings.[59] Fitzsimon maintained that Puritans undermined the social order and contrasted their seditious plotting with the respect and loyalty shown by Catholics towards King James, 'our forsayed sovereign and sacred king'.[60] Indeed, as if to prove his own loyal credentials, he quoted the royal warrant for his own release, which cited his 'good demonstration of his loyalty and dutiful affection to his majesty and the state'.[61]

---

[55] Hogan (ed.), *Life and Letters of Henry Fitzsimon*, p. 241.

[56] TCD, press mark DD 10 8.

[57] Jackson, *Marginalia* explores the phenomenon of marginalia and the motivations of the marginal annotator.

[58] For example, annotations at pp. 20, 21, 62 and 210. For an example of textual annotation see p. 53.

[59] Fitzsimon asserted that Rider's son was killed by a falling statue in the cathedral while attempting to pull down an image in May 1604. Rider rejects the suggestion in the margin. Incidentally, accidents of the kind were common enough. They quickly became common tropes in the mythology of iconoclasm. For example, workmen who attempted to remove images from the rood screen in St Paul's in London were crushed in the act, to the grim satisfaction of conservative commentators, D. MacCulloch, *Tudor Church Militant: Edward VI and the Protestant Reformation* (London, 1999), p. 71.

[60] Fitzsimon, *Replye*, p. 225.   [61] *Ibid.*

Given Fitzsimon's firmly stated position at the time of his arrest, this line of argument is interesting and suggests that his position on royal legitimacy and authority had moved on in the intervening decade. His stance, and indeed his style, continued to develop, to mature and to adapt in the years following the publication of the *Catholike Confutation*. He returned to the theme of authority and legitimacy some years later in the *Britannomachia* (Douai 1614), which is a sustained critique of the Hampton Court Conference of 1604. But it was also a rigorous investigation of the basis of Protestant claims for the purity of their peculiarly 'British' strand of Apostolic Catholicity. Fitzsimon engaged with this argument on its own terms, moving into the realm of historical inquiry. In many ways this work was a precursor to subsequent expressions of interest in the historical roots of the Irish church and, specifically, the lives and missionary endeavours of the early Irish and Scottish saints.[62] In it Fitzsimon looked at the historical development of Protestantism in England, Scotland and Ireland and ridiculed the notion of any uniformity of belief in the face of Puritan diversity. He made an interesting political and linguistic point that the newly adopted royal style and title *Rex Magnae Britanniae* was itself a conceit, masking the reality of religious heterodoxy in the polity.[63] This marked a departure for Fitzsimon as he engaged with issues of language within an historical framework. The mode of argument had shifted substantially as he teased out linguistic modulation to religious texts in different versions of the Bible. From this point he moved on to consider the issue of the selection of texts for inclusion in the Authorised Version (1611). Here, he alleged, texts are excluded, not because they are of dubious provenance but because they simply do not square with reformed notions. As an example, he looked at the Book of Tobit, consigned to the apocryphal works by the Hampton Court divines. This text, Fitzsimon affirmed, had running through it themes of pilgrimage, angelic intercession, and the benefits of charitable works and neighbourliness, all of which were antithetical to Protestant sensibilities. Throughout the work Fitzsimon invoked historical fact and anecdote to build what is an empirical case, rather than an argument based on logical categories.

The literary forms employed by apologists inadvertently converged within the framework of an historical narrative. Where Fitzsimon invokes Richard Creagh, archbishop of Armagh, who refused to consecrate

---

[62] H. Fitzsimon, *Catalogus Praecipuorum Sanctorum Hiberniae* (Liège, 1619).

[63] H. Fitzsimon, *Britannomachia* (Douai, 1614), p. 139 and book 3, *De Ministrorum in Sacramentis, et in plerisque doctrinae capitibus, confusione, ac paradoxis.*

Anglican bishops when a captive in the Tower, so Rider and Hanmer invoked Richard FitzRalph, archbishop of Armagh, the scourge of the friars and, in the eyes of the reformers, a proto-Lollard. Violently they disagreed upon outcomes, but upon the manner in which they reached their conclusions there was no longer any dispute.

III

From this a few points emerge. First, it would appear that Allen's essential argument on discourse is accepted. The ground rules of controversy were established. Even though opponents would repeatedly reposition themselves within the established framework, the form and the substance of religious discourse had been set. And within this a form embryonic within the English language had been developed. Second, it is clear that interest and participation in controversy and disputation was not confined to the clergy. The laity had a keen interest in, derived entertainment from, and often initiated and influenced such debates. William Nugent, Rider's dinner guest, was not an isolated case. Piers Crosbie raised the very same issue of Apostolic purity with the Jesuit William Malone, and he even suggested the appropriate opponent with whom the issue should be debated.[64] This suggests a rather touching, old-fashioned view that intellectual rigour and truth would win out in open debate. But it may also point to a much cruder and more basic instinct for competitive sport or baiting, whether of bears or priests. This instinct rather than the former may account for much of the excitement surrounding Fitzsimon's encounters with Rider.[65]

Even more significant is the extent to which the laity took issue with views or actions that were unpalatable to them. It is important to remember how and why Fitzsimon found himself in prison, and to discern the modulation of his views on the legitimacy of the monarch's position. The fact that the person of the monarch had changed, that he was the legitimate male heir of a recognised Catholic sovereign, rather than a female, an excommunicate and, in the eyes of the church, a bastard, may have made the process more palatable.

Fitzsimon's tacit acceptance of the monarch's temporal authority falls short of William Malone's enthusiastic endorsements.[66] The zeal of both men caused difficulties for those assiduous guardians of the Irish church's image, Luke Wadding and David Rothe, who effectively managed and

---

[64] William Malone, *A Reply to Mr James Usher his Answere* (n.p., 1627), sig. e2v–e3.

[65] Fitzsimon's public encounters took place before large groups of excited onlookers, Hogan, *Distinguished Irishmen*, p. 248.

[66] Malone, *Reply*, sig. a4v.

silenced the ominous rumblings of internal controversy. To a very great extent, our received view of the Irish Counter-Reformation as heroic national struggle, led and directed as a uniform clerical initiative, is a narrative of their construction.[67]

[67] Brendan Jennings (ed.), *Wadding Papers* (IMC, Dublin, 1963), pp. 265–6, 274. Fitzsimon's book on the mass created a flurry of controversy within the church, giving offence to Francis Nugent, who delated Fitzsimon and the book to the Roman Inquisition, F. X. Martin, *Friar Nugent* (Rome, 1962), pp. 169–171. Aquaviva to John Henry, 3 October 1612, Archivium Romanum Societatis Iesu, Gallo Belg 1 f. 19.

6 The Bible and the bawn: an Ulster planter inventorised

R. J. Hunter

The most enduring changes brought about in early seventeenth-century Ulster were the introduction of Protestantism and the decision to carry out a plantation there. In origin neither coincided exactly with the other, but they soon came to interlink. The final plan of plantation in 1610 produced on the whole a regional scheme for the allocation of the confiscated lay land in the six forfeited counties there – Cavan, Fermanagh, Donegal, Londonderry, Tyrone and Armagh – whereby, using the barony as a unit, English grantees were allocated to some areas, Scots to others, and those Irish who were restored, placed alongside servitors or former military men, to yet other areas.[1] A crucial agent in the extension of the structures of Protestantism into much of Ulster was George Montgomery (d. 1621), who had already, in 1605, been appointed bishop of Derry, Raphoe and Clogher.[2] A Lowland Scot who had obtained preferments in England both before and with the union of the crowns in 1603, and more an ecclesiastical administrator than one who had sought solely to organise a mission (now anyhow of uncertain success) to the Gaelic Irish, his achievement, from one perspective, was to establish the Church of Ireland in his northern dioceses on a sound economic basis. Having been appointed a commissioner for planning the plantation, he secured, before his own removal to the diocese of Meath, with which he was allowed to retain Clogher, in 1610, a significant endowment of lands for the episcopate within the plantation dioceses, some of which, albeit formerly of an ecclesiastical character, might otherwise have gone to lay settlers, as well as of glebe land for the parish clergy. His proposal that a university be established at Derry, on the other hand, came to naught, but the

---

This chapter is offered in less than adequate tribute to Aidan Clarke, to remind him of his years in Northern Ireland, though with the hope that his memory is not too acute in points of detail.

[1] The exception was the Londonderry plantation.

[2] Henry A. Jefferies, 'George Montgomery, first Protestant bishop of Derry, Raphoe and Clogher (1605–10)' in Henry A. Jefferies and Ciaran Devlin (eds.), *History of the Diocese of Derry from Earliest Times* (Dublin, 2000), pp. 140–66.

endowing of grammar schools, one in each county, may have derived from his suggestion. Also, in order to begin the establishment of Protestantism at parochial level in his dioceses, he got permission to bring over nineteen 'painful preachers', English and Scottish, to be employed 'for planting the churches in those northern parts'.[3] One of these, the subject of this chapter, was the Reverend Edward Hatton. In his case, not an entirely typical one, both Protestantism and plantation – the Bible and the bawn – came to overlap, since he became the owner of a plantation estate. Some of them became an administrative elite amongst the new Protestant clergy in Ulster. One, John Tanner, was to be made bishop of Derry in 1613 and died there in 1615. Another, James Heygate, a Scot, was made archdeacon of Clogher diocese and lived at Clones, County Monaghan.[4]

I

Edward Hatton was admitted as a sizar to Pembroke College, Cambridge, in 1585 and took his MA from St Catherine's in 1597.[5] He would have been born, therefore, about 1568 or a little later; his place of birth cannot readily be established. He bore in his coat of arms core armorial elements used by the larger Hatton family, which had originated in Cheshire and moved downwards in England in the course of time.[6] Origins for him in Cheshire could be quite plausible, though a possible identification with an Edward Hatton of Gravesend in Kent – which would make him a nephew of Lord Chancellor Sir Christopher Hatton – can be no more than a possibility.[7] He was ordained for the diocese of Norwich in August 1591 and instituted as rector of Brampton (which he surrendered in 1601) in August 1592, and he became vicar of Westhall in February 1597, both being contiguous parishes in north-east Suffolk.[8] Three of his children, Edward (who may have died young), James and Susanna, in that order, were baptised in Westhall between December 1595 and

---

[3] *CSPI, 1615–25*, p. 253.
[4] J. B. Leslie, *Derry Clergy and Parishes* (Enniskillen, 1937), pp. 6–7, 274; *CSPI, 1606–8*, p. 427; Leslie, *Clogher Clergy and Parishes* (Enniskillen, 1929), p. 42; *Irish Patent Rolls of James I: facsimile of the Irish Record Commissioners' calendar prepared prior to 1830*, with foreword by M. C. Griffith (IMC, Dublin, 1966), p. 326; Armagh Public Library, Visitation Book, 1622, pp. 172–3.
[5] John Venn and J. A. Venn, *Alumni Cantabrigienses*, part I (4 vols., Cambridge, 1922–27), II, p. 331.
[6] Bernard Burke, *The General Armory of England, Scotland, Ireland and Wales* (London, 1884), p. 467; BL, Add. MS 19,646.
[7] J. P. Rylands (ed.), *The Visitation of Cheshire in the year 1580* (Harleian Society, 18, London, 1882), pp. 114–15.
[8] Norfolk Record Office, Norwich, MS DN/Reg. 14, book 20, ff. 210, 248v, 295v.

December 1602.[9] His first wife, Anne Beaumont, was probably of a Suffolk family.[10] The fact that the patron of the vicarage was the dean of Norwich gave him a link to the deans, and so to George Montgomery, who held the deanship of Norwich from 1603 by royal nomination, in addition to a rectory in Somerset where he forged West Country links.[11] Hatton was himself also made a prebendary of Norwich cathedral in 1604, but in the following year relinquished it, in exchange for one of Southwell, in favour of Thomas Jegon, master of Corpus Christi College, Cambridge, and brother of the then bishop.[12] Another factor drawing Hatton towards Ireland might well have been contact with his successor in Brampton, William Flowerdew. Not only was another Flowerdew to be a Virginia planter, but Thomas Flowerdew, from Hethersett near Norwich, was to be a grantee of a plantation estate in Ulster in 1610.[13]

In Ireland in the 1620s he was be to called 'a master of arts of ancient standing' and 'a grave preacher', and – a little earlier – a minister who was 'a good teacher of the Word of God'.[14] Being at Cambridge in the period of theological controversies of the 1580s, he must surely have come under the influence of Lancelot Andrewes, whose lectures on the Ten Commandments at Pembroke embraced recommendations on a proper preaching style. That he may have tended towards moderation, however, may account for him taking his MA in 1597 from St Catherine's, Cambridge, whose master then, Edmund Hound, was a man of moderate view.[15] As against that, it was said of him (in common with about a third of the clergy in Suffolk at that time) in Bishop Redman's diocesan visitation, also in 1597, that 'he weareth not the surples'. Here too it was noted that while 'he preacheth' – unlike many – he did not 'catechise the youth'.[16] Later, in 1604, he was to be listed among the graduate clergy of

[9] Suffolk Record Office, Lowestoft, MS 163/D1/1 (unfoliated).

[10] NLI, G[enealogical] O[ffice] MS 68, p. 180, MS 69, p. 109.

[11] Ian Atherton, Eric Fernie, Christopher Harper–Bill and Hassell Smith (eds.), *Norwich Cathedral: church, city and diocese, 1096–1996* (London and Rio Grande, 1996), pp. 513–14; W. C. Trevelyan and C. E. Trevelyan (eds.), *Trevelyan Papers*, III (Camden Society, 1st series, 105, London, 1872), pp. 35–6, 44–72.

[12] John Le Neve, *Fasti Ecclesiae Anglicanae*, corrected and continued by T. Duffus Hardy, II (Oxford, 1854), p. 498.

[13] Norfolk Record Office, Norwich, MS DN/Reg. 14, book 20, f. 295v; *Cal. pat. rolls Ire., Jas I*, p. 167.

[14] Armagh Public Library, Visitation Book, 1622, p. 178; George Hill, *An historical account of the plantation in Ulster at the commencement of the seventeenth century, 1608–20* (Belfast, 1877), p. 483.

[15] H. C. Porter, *Reformation and Reaction in Tudor Cambridge* (Cambridge, 1958), pp. 209, 346, 391–8. I am indebted to Professor D. MacCulloch for this reference.

[16] *Diocese of Norwich, Bishop Redman's Visitation 1597: presentments in the archdeaconries of Norwich, Norfolk and Suffolk*, ed. J. F. Williams (Norfolk Record Society, XVIII, Norwich, 1946), pp. 19, 127, 152. Hatton was formally licensed to preach in 1604–5.

the diocese who were 'of honest life' and 'able to catechise' and did not appear in any list of those who were subject to criticisms, though it was noted of him, under Westhall, that he had conducted one marriage there 'without license or banes asking'.[17] While he was certainly no outright nonconformist opposed to episcopacy, Hatton's own precise theological reasoning on any subject is not known since none of his sermons was reproduced in print. That at any rate he aspired to some continuing learning can be seen when, on a return journey from England to Ireland in July 1620, the commodities he brought with him included 'books for his study'.[18] Although the precise nature of these books is unknown, they symbolise a process of cultural transfer into an Ulster whose growing number of English residents now shared a common culture with England itself.

Hatton's Ulster appointments were to be in Montgomery's diocese of Clogher, but he was also favoured, perhaps as security to fall back on in the event of any new Ulster crisis, with two parishes (one a vicarage) in the diocese of Meath.[19] Monaghan became his base, where, to stiffen control over a county whose land ownership had been remodelled among local lords and freeholders in the settlement of 1591, an English seneschal had been put in place, to hold also by lease the lands nearby which had formerly pertained to the lordship's MacMahon ruler, which function was now abolished.[20] In the aftermath of the failure of the Nine Years War, that settlement had been restored, though with modifications which increased the share of New English ownership, with Sir Edward Blayney, commander of the forces there, receiving a lease of Monaghan and this associated land in January 1607, which (except for the castle or fort), with additional lands, was granted to him outright in June 1611.[21] There a small colonising outpost was now in the process of growing up, building houses in the emerging town and erecting a new parish church. It was in the town of Monaghan that Hatton was placed, and where he was to be 'most commonly resident'. He also held the parishes of Tyholland and Galloon, the latter including part of plantation County Fermanagh within its bounds.[22] This alone illustrates the problem of extending Protestantism into Ulster at this time: a lack of clergy in sufficient supply. England, even with Scotland now, did not have a sufficient or willing pool to draw

---

[17] Norfolk Record Office, Norwich, MS DN/VIS 3/3, ff. 68, 101v.
[18] PRO, E190/1332/1, ff. 25rv.   [19] Leslie, *Clogher clergy*, p. 59.
[20] For the settlement of Monaghan see 'Fiants of the reign of Queen Elizabeth', nos. 5621–80 in *The Sixteenth Report of the Deputy Keeper of the Public Records in Ireland* (Dublin, 1884), appendix IX, pp. 184–94.
[21] *Cal. pat. rolls Ire., Jas I*, pp. 95, 103, 199.
[22] Armagh Public Library, Visitation Book, 1622, pp. 178–9.

from; Trinity College, Dublin, was only at an infant stage. To have sought alternatively to employ the pre-existing Irish clergy in numbers (though some few did adjust) in an Ulster where recent rebellion had had profound linkages to religion would have presented mutual incompatibilities. From now, in fact, two churches were to emerge in Ulster, with the Catholic one retaining religiopolitical connections with continental Catholicism and with the former Ulster lords and their descendants in Europe in the aftermath of the flight of the earls. Hatton officiated and lived in his Meath diocese parishes from time to time as well as having a curate there. But the curate was his nephew Bartholemew Hatton, a 'reading minister', and he also had a parish of his own. In Ulster in 1622 he was 'of late without a sufficient curate'. Curates too were in short supply. A further problem concerned the church fabric. While on the eve of his appointment the church in Monaghan was in good order and that of Tyholland, a parish in which in any case much land still continued in Catholic occupation, was then 'repaired', that of Galloon was, like many others, 'in decay'.[23] What was to happen in regard to church buildings in this area in the longer term is of some interest. In fact by 1622 a new church was to have been built under the aegis of James Heygate at Clones, itself the nub of a substantial monastic estate granted in lease at its dissolution in 1587 to Henry Duke, and now coming to be actively colonised under his successors.[24] Also, as Newtownbutler developed as a centre of settler population, a new church was built there by the 1630s.[25] For the same reason, the pre-existing chapel at Magheraveely, location, as will be seen, of a small plantation village, may also have been put to Protestant use. Where new churches could best be built to suit the emerging pattern of plantation had been made a matter for investigation in the later 1620s. Thus although the proposal at the time of plantation that a new church should be built for each plantation estate was on the whole not acted on at the time, a process of rationalisation in church location was beginning to receive some attention.[26] These churches were also very much an element in the town planning of the time.

When Hatton first came to Ireland is not clear; some initial hesitancy about being placed in Ulster may well have affected him, given residual uncertainties about Spanish intentions in the aftermath of the flight of

---

[23] HMC, *Report on the Manuscripts of the late Reginald Rawdon Hastings* (4 vols., London, 1928–47), IV, pp. 154–56; NAI, Book of Survey and Distribution, County Monaghan, pp. 112, 129–32, 156–8.

[24] 'Fiants Ire., Eliz.', no. 5042; Armagh Public Library, Visitation Book, 1622, pp. 172–3.

[25] TCD, MS 835, ff. 36rv, 176rv.

[26] T. W. Moody (ed.), 'Ulster plantation papers', *Analecta Hibernica*, 8 (1938), p. 286; *Inquisitionum in Officio Rotulorum Cancellariae Hiberniae . . . Repertorium* (Dublin, 1829), II, Fermanagh (11) Chas I.

the earls. Only when the new Jacobean Ireland seemed of more certain creation, and with plantation in Ulster coming into being too, did he fully commit his future to it. In November 1614 he returned from a visit to England (via Chester to Dublin) bearing goods including books for the bishop of Meath, and having surrendered his Suffolk living.[27] He was replaced in Westhall in July 1614.[28] Thereafter he immersed himself in settler society in Ireland. His son and heir James was sent to Trinity College, Dublin, where he graduated in 1619, and was eventually to succeed him in the church, though as rector of Galloon solely. A glimpse of him can be obtained in 1627, when, a curate and 'a man of reasonable good gift in pulpit' and then employed as schoolmaster to the children of Sir William Stewart in County Tyrone, he was expected to preach an assize sermon before the judges in Enniskillen, in what must have been the new church there, then nearing completion.[29] A daughter, Martha, was to marry another clergyman of the diocese, the Reverend James Slack, while another daughter married Nicholas Willoughby, who became tenant of some of the Clogher episcopal land. When a second wife was required, she also came from settler society: Anne Piggot of Kilmainham, County Dublin, was probably a relative of an Elizabethan captain of that surname.[30] As a figure in church administration, Hatton appears as chancellor of the diocese of Clogher in January 1614, and when he died in 1632 he was archdeacon of Ardagh. Also since the late Elizabethan creation of counties in Ulster had now been made effective, it emerges that he had been a justice of the peace of both Counties Monaghan and Fermanagh.[31] Somewhat materialistic in outlook, or ambitious as a married clergyman with children to provide for, and committed to the English view that a radical new beginning in Ulster through plantation should be made, he had also become owner of a Fermanagh plantation estate.

Under the plan for plantation in Ulster, the forfeited secular land in the barony of Clankelly, County Fermanagh, previously owned in gavelkind under Maguire rulership principally by the MacMulrooneys, MacDonaghs and MacDonnells, was allocated both to English undertakers (five in all) and, as part of a larger educational endowment, to Trinity College, Dublin, and also – unusually, since those Irish who were restored to land under the plantation were normally gathered together in other baronies alongside army officer grantees (themselves not formally required to plant their estates with settler tenantry) – to one Irish grantee,

[27] PRO, E 190/1330/11, f. 37.

[28] Norfolk Record Office, Norwich, MS DN/Reg. 16, book 22, f. 49v.

[29] G. D. Burtchaell and T. U. Sadleir, *Alumni Dublinenses* (2nd edn, Dublin, 1935), p. 380; *The Spottiswoode Miscellany*, I (Edinburgh, 1844), pp. 121–2.

[30] NLI, GO MS 68, p. 180.   [31] *Cal. pat. rolls Ire., Jas I*, p. 519; NLI, GO MS 68, p. 180.

Brian MacMulrooney, presumably head of his sept.[32] The grantee of one of these undertakers' estates, one of a group from East Anglia, Robert Bogas, had been slow to take out his patent, and indeed by 1613 his allotment of land had 'neither tenants, cattle nor building', nor had he himself arrived.[33] A neighbouring estate had been granted to Thomas Flowerdew. Hatton acquired Bogas's estate, much of it in Clones parish. Bogas came from the Stour valley in south Suffolk, a pasture region, commercialised through the cloth trade and prone to advanced Protestantism.[34] The earliest contact between them can be traced to 1614, on Hatton's return to England. On 24 May Hatton purchased the estate from Bogas for probably quite a small sum and under an arrangement which may have left Bogas with some residual interest.[35] They may have recruited jointly some tenantry for it from Suffolk at the same time. The estate in question was, by the assessed measurement of the time, a 1,000 acre one – a 'small proportion' in the plantation scheme of things – made up of great and little tates (Ir.? táití), the ancestors of the modern townlands, which had been grouped together, for the purposes of issuing the patents, on the appropriate barony map in the series prepared during the survey of the plantation counties in 1609. Its modern statute acreage was some 2,867 acres, or 4.5 square miles. However, by established convention the occupants of many townlands had rights of use over hilly and other land, their 'barrs [Ir. barra, tops] and mountains', to the north.[36]

The land granted to Brian MacMulrooney, adjoining the Bogas estate – just under 400 statute acres (granted as 240) but with 'barrs' also – came to Hatton by another route and reveals other linkages. Acquired by Hugh Culme, originally from Devon, who had been a captain in the English army in Ireland since the later stages of the Nine Years War and who had been granted an estate, not far distant, in County Cavan, it was bought for £120 from him by Hatton who mortgaged it to raise money in February 1621[-/2?] to Nicholas Willoughby (b. 1586), another Devonian, for £160 stg 'of pure silver coin'.[37] Willoughby, who at this time lived in County Meath, was not only a Montgomery connection (arising from the latter's West Country days), being related to his wife, but his mother had been a Culme. In Ireland under Montgomery's

---

[32] Cal. pat. rolls Ire., Jas I, p. 186.   [33] HMC, Hastings MSS, IV, p. 166.

[34] D. MacCulloch, Suffolk and the Tudors: Politics and religion in an English county, 1500–1600 (Oxford, 1986), pp. 7–52, 179–80.

[35] Inq. cancell. Hib. repert., II, Fermanagh (5) Chas I.

[36] Cal. pat. rolls Ire., Jas I, p. 167; Inq. cancell. Hib. repert., ii, Fermanagh (5) Chas I. The modern acreage has been calculated from the Ordnance Survey.

[37] NAI, RC 5/28, pp. 44–8.

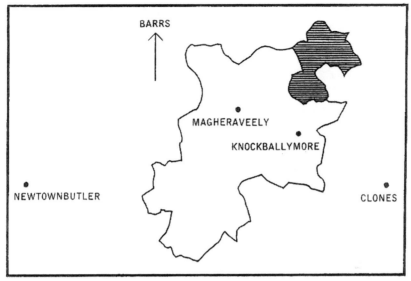

D.McC

Map 1 The Hatton Lands, County Fermanagh; lands granted to Brian
    McMulrooney are hatched

aegis, he was already since 1614 tenant of some of the episcopal land
in Fermanagh, on which he later came to live at Gortnacarrow, and, as
has been seen, he was to marry Hatton's daughter and remain closely
intertwined in his affairs.[38]

Under Hatton's ownership, plantation proceeded on the main estate.
As one of the undertaker category, he was required under the regulations
to plant settler tenantry there (in a defined social structure) who should
replace the Irish, who had to be removed. Since it was a small proportion,
the newcomers should consist of a minimum of ten families including his
own. He was also bound by regulation to build for himself, and to 'draw'
his tenants to build nearby 'as well for their mutual defence and strength
as for the making of villages and townships'.[39] Investigations some years
after he became owner reveal that by then, although it is not possible to
pin person to place, all or most of the land had been let to British – English
and Lowland Scottish – tenants, with Hatton himself retaining an area in
demesne. An inquiry in 1618–19 found two freeholders, five lessees and
eight cottagers 'of British birth' (mainly English, as will be seen) planted

[38] *Trevelyan papers*, III, pp. 78, 89–90, 101–4; *Cal. pat. rolls Ire., Jas I*, p. 519.
[39] T. W. Moody (ed.), 'The revised articles of the Ulster plantation, 1610', *Bulletin of the
Institute of Historical Research*, 12 (1934–35), pp. 178–83.

there, or fifteen families, with amongst them 'not above twenty men in all'. This had increased to twenty-one families (which included Hatton's), with some thirty men, including servants, by 1622.[40] The site of his own stronghold, at Knockballymore, strategically located beside a pre-existing 'thoroughfare' and at a river to power his 'water-mill for corn', had been chosen to be as close to Clones (1½ miles away) as possible. Here he had built an 'excellent strong house and bawn' of stone and lime construction: the bawn (a defensive courtyard), with three flanker towers, measured in 1622 as 70 ft square and 14 ft high, with the house within 70 ft long and, in an apparent error in transcription, described as five storeys high. A later description had the bawn as 68 ft square, and the house – 60 ft long by 28 ft wide – 31 ft high, i.e., to the ridge.[41] In essence, therefore, it must have been a two-storey house with a pitched roof, with a floor area of about 1,700 square feet. By the standards of Ulster plantation architecture, house and bawn were of about average size, conforming well to the plan laid down. The house can be taken to have followed recent English styles in that it was storeyed and chimneyed, while the entity as a whole – called, as was usual, a castle – was, above all, a small privately constructed fort, flankered for protection, with the residence, at once a castle (on its side) and a house, built lengthwise within a taller outer wall and domesticated with windows, probably mullioned and square-headed, on its inner side. Neither building cost nor artisan/contractor's identity can be recovered.

In the matter of his estate village, the plan was less adhered to. Here beginnings were made, not at Knockballymore but at a more centrally located spot about a mile further inwards along the same 'thoroughfare' at Magheraveely, the site of a small church which was a chapel of Clones parish. Here too Hatton was empowered in April 1618, for a yearly fee of £1 stg (in addition to his quit-rent of £5 6s 8d on the estate and £2 11s 4d on the MacMulrooney lands), to hold a Saturday market and two annual fairs. Here he had also built, but this time timber houses, with a village of eight 'cottagers' now in existence. Although the occupations of these – the skilled poor of the plantation – are not to be found, this was primarily a settlement for artificers of various kinds, each with a house, a 'garden plot' or 'backside' and 'four acres of land'. It also became an administrative centre. Not only was the court leet of the manor held at Magheraveely, but inquisitions ordered by the central administration

---

[40] Hill, *An Historical Account of the Plantation in Ulster*, pp. 483–4; BL, Add. MS 4756, f. 105.
[41] *Inq. cancell. Hib. repert.*, II, Fermanagh (5) Chas I.

were occasionally taken there also, with the chapel probably used as their location.[42]

The tenants on the estate, despite the requirement that all should live in villages for security, as well as in the interests of ordered planning and social regulation, came to live on the whole in dispersed settlement on their holdings, their housing generally unremarked on. Some, with a number of townlands, held more land than others, and were thus becoming, with their fellows on other estates, a gentry (below the ranks of the actual landowners) in the settler society. One such was Clinton Maund. A man with some money to invest located in the northern portion of the estate and having for a time some interest in the MacMulrooney lands nearby, he had erected a substantial stone-built house specially noted in 1622, and indeed to have its dimensions recorded, so striking was it – long but low – at the end of the decade.[43] By implication, the houses of the tenantry at large were not substantial structures, and so initially they may not have been people of any great wealth.

When these settlers were mustered for training in the use of arms in about 1630, forty-four males attended, mostly with swords and pikes, though with eighteen unarmed.[44] If, to take account of some few absentees or because some families (if they had children old enough) might have been represented by only one member, some increase should be made, then fifty to sixty might be the truer figure. This, mainly due to the fact that the estate village had remained small (since, overshadowed by close proximity to Clones and given the much greater growth of Newtownbutler, each equidistant from it by some 3 miles, it had not developed as a trading and processing centre), indicates rather low-intensity plantation, with about one adult male settler per 50 acres. The economy of the estate was largely pastoral, though (despite rainfall levels) with considerable tillage and haymaking taking place as well.[45] Two possible sources of recruitment for some of these tenants already suggest themselves: East Anglia and indeed Hatton's own personal connection, and the English West Country. A smaller group, Armstrongs among them, had Lowland Scottish names; some others may have been from the north of England. A few, Thomas Seaton, Sebastian Cottingham and John Slack, were,

---

[42] *Cal. pat. rolls Ire., Jas I*, p. 367; TCD, MS 835, f. 265; BL, Add. MS 4756, f. 105; *Inq. cancell. Hib. repert.*, II, Fermanagh (5) Jas I (1623), (5) and (10) Chas I (1629–30). A piece of land here was technically claimable by the bishop, but Hatton was allowed to use it.

[43] *Inq. cancell. Hib. repert.*, II, Fermanagh (5) Chas I. It was 86 ft long by 20 ft wide and 16 ft high.

[44] BL, Add. MS 4770, f. 59v.   [45] This impression is based on the 1641 depositions.

perhaps not surprisingly, in view of the ownership of the estate, relatives of other clergy.

While for the Irish the implications of plantation could not but be profound, their position on this estate is by no means fully clear. For them also there was to be some divergence from prescription. All were not just simply removed, though some – perhaps even a fairly considerable number – might well have moved to the nearby college lands which were much less planted. Some had grazing let to them by the settler tenantry (probably on annual subtenancies), but were seemingly fewer in number than on neighbouring estates where there were fewer settlers.[46] At another level, apart from these grazing farmers interspersed with the settlers on some townlands, Irish workmen may well have been employed in the varied labours on the land, not least in whatever new improvements were being carried out by way of enclosure – hedging and ditching – for tillage or meadow fields or of outward bounds of farms.

Edward Hatton was recorded as having died in the town of Monaghan in 1632 with his plantation at this stage.[47] Three at least of his children survived him: James, now his heir, who may have supervised the estate as well as being a curate, Martha Slack, and Willoughby's wife, probably either Susanna or Mary. He had also added further to his possessions by obtaining the lands of one of the County Monaghan freeholders, Edmund Oge MacMahon, who died in 1621. Acquired to advance his daughter, these lands were held by her husband Willoughby in 1641.[48]

If the son (in particular) had clearly benefited from his father's decision to come to Ireland, the father also left problems to his successor. Bogas's widow, Anne, made claims for her 'thirds and right of dower', which came to litigation in 1638 after James Hatton had died. At the time of probate of his father's will James was immediately confronted by proceedings in the prerogative court, by his father's widow, Anne, concerning her rights, which resulted in a chancery suit between them. By the time of James's death she was receiving a jointure of £40 stg out of the estate. Controversy between himself and Willoughby over his mortgage of the MacMulrooney lands was eventually resolved by arbitrators, but only after his death.[49]

James Hatton died prematurely in May 1637. What emerges about him is that he had been an improver. In his will he stated that he 'would have' his executors – Willoughby, John Heygate (son of the Reverend

---

[46] BL, Add. MS 4756, f. 105. An indication of who some of these Irish were can be gleaned from TCD, MS 835, ff. 142, 179, 210.

[47] NLI, GO MS 68, p. 180.

[48] 'Fiants Ire., Eliz.', no. 5644; *Inq. cancell. Hib. repert.*, II, Monaghan (17) Chas I, and Fermanagh (5) Chas I; NAI, Book of survey and distribution, County Monaghan, p. 71.

[49] *Inq. cancell. Hib. repert.*, ii, Fermanagh (43) Jas I; NA, CP/S25.

James, now bishop of Kilfenora, who had himself also purchased an estate in Clankelly, and who died in 1638), and his own son Edward, then aged six – 'go forward with the building [a new house apparently] I have begun on Knockballymore'. To link himself with the new urban development at Armagh (as a potential regional capital) promoted by Archbishop James Ussher, he had already in 1634, following an initiative by his father, acquired a lease for a house there, adjoining 'the new sessions house', and 20 acres allotted to it.[50] He had also held new houses by lease in Monaghan, probably acquired by his father. His will was a revealing document in many respects.[51] He was to be buried within the church in Clones close to his wife, who had predeceased him. Something of his theological position may be found in its introductory phrasing, albeit a familiar formula: he bequeathed his soul 'unto almighty God, assuring myself through the merits, death and passion of Jesus Christ his only Son and my only Saviour to obtain remission of all my sins and life everlasting'.

He disposed of the manor of Knockballymore to his eldest son, Edward, while the MacMulrooney lands were to go to his younger son, James. His leases of houses in Monaghan and Armagh, some of which had been applied by his father to the benefit of Martha Slack, should pass to his daughter Jane. She should gain possession from his executors when fourteen, while the sons, whose tuition should lie with the executors, should succeed at eighteen. Members of his immediate family also received bequests: his 'sister Slack' should get £20 stg and two of her daughters, one now married to a settler in County Cavan, £10 each, to be paid out of ensuing rents. His cousin Edward Hatton was to receive £5. The sum of £4 a year should be expended on a young boy called Webster to 'bring him up to writing and reading' until he was fifteen, when £10 should be paid to apprentice him to 'some good trade'.

Through James's will, two important figures also come to light. One was agent of the estate, a native Irishman: James left £10 to his 'old servant' (a witness to the will, competent and literate in English) Patrick O'Brien, 'who hath spent his youth with me and done me faithful service'. Since James had succeeded his father as rector of Galloon, the other may well have been his curate there and was certainly his successor: to Edward Howe he left all his books. Howe, one of a second generation of clergy now coming to the fore, was at this precise time, in an orientation towards Scotland followed later by Edward Slack (son of two English-born parents

---

[50] On the development of Armagh at this time see R. J. Hunter, 'Towns in the Ulster plantation', *Studia Hibernica*, 11 (1971), pp. 57–66.
[51] NA, RC 5/28, pp. 49–54. His funeral entry is in NLI, GO MS 70, p. 179.

and also from Fermanagh), in the final stages of his studies at Glasgow University, *alma mater* alike of both Heygate and Montgomery, where he was defined as 'Anglo-Hibernus'.[52] Hatton left the adjudication of the dispute between himself and Willoughby over the MacMulrooney lands to Edward Aldrich and Nicholas Sympson, two prominent settlers in this region and 'especial friends unto us both', under the umpirage, if necessary, of George Baker or Barker of Dublin, probably a lawyer. The names of witnesses to his will, as well as those mentioned in it, show something of the circle of which he was part in the settler society of Fermanagh, Monaghan and Cavan, just as the earlier mortgage between his father and Willoughby (then in the Pale) had revealed, interestingly for its time, some Old English links: an Edward and a John Dowdall were witnesses to it.

Since new patents now had to be taken out under Wentworth's administration, Aldrich and Sympson proceeded fairly swiftly to their adjudication in April 1638. Willoughby stated that he had lived in the castle, or part of it, for eleven years, and although Edward Hatton and his family came there from Monaghan from time to time and had kept servants there, he had never demanded any rent, nor had he redeemed the mortgage. He had dealt with millers there and had spent £80 on 'building, repairing and fencing of the said castle, outhouses and lands', and had received no portion from Hatton with his wife in marriage. The decision arrived at by Aldrich and Sympson, whereby Willoughby should retain the tenancy of two of MacMulrooney's four great tates and be paid £50, reveals also who then occupied them: one was in the hands of Willoughby and Patrick O'Brien; the other was held by an Irishman, Redmond Maguire, a typical Irish grazier.[53] Two further developments in the colonisation of the estate may also have taken place during James Hatton's ownership. William Bignall, millwright, living on the more over-crowded Newtownbutler estate nearby in 1630, had moved – in a still fluid situation – to another of these MacMulrooney townlands in the 1630s, from which he was to be dislodged in 1641.[54] Another newcomer to the estate at large, ejected also in 1641, exemplifies the East Anglian connection. Simon Crane – of a surname with a Bogas link – who was registrar of Clogher diocese as well, may be taken to have been a relative of the Reverend Felix Crane, another clergyman who now lived at Castleblayney (where a new church was also built, the old one being put

[52] *Munimenta alme universitatis Glasguensis: records of the university of Glasgow from its foundation till 1727*, ed. C. Innes (4 vols., Maitland Club, Glasgow, 1854), III, pp. 90, 92; TCD, MS 835, ff. 29rv, 120rv. Howe was dislodged from Galloon in 1641.

[53] NAI, RC 5/28, pp. 55–63.

[54] BL, Add. MS 4770, f. 63v; TCD, MS 835, ff. 47v–8.

to Catholic use) and who had been curate of Brampton in 1603.[55] For his part, Willoughby (the younger single-function man of affairs who may have somewhat dominated Edward Hatton), may in fact only have moved to his new house at 'the Carrow', some miles away, at about the time that James Hatton succeeded.

James Hatton had died, however, at a fateful time, as the countdown to the War of the Three Kingdoms was beginning. The settlers on the estate were apparently mostly 'put out' of houses and lands in the terror which accompanied the easily understandable attempt at repossession in 1641. Those from it who were killed then included (as far as certainty can allow) Maximilian Tibbs, high constable of the barony; Miles Acres, possibly born in Westminster, where there were Hattons, in 1599;[56] Peter Maddison, a witness, by mark, to James Hatton's will; Thomas Ashton; Thomas Seaton (a Scot); and Sebastian Cottingham.[57] The churches at Clones, Newtownbutler and Monaghan were burnt and various clerical libraries destroyed.[58]

Willoughby and O'Brien, together at the outbreak of the rising, were among those who fled to Dublin. It fell to the latter, occupying a crucial role since James Hatton's death, to leave the only account of what the income from the estate – some £200 per annum – had been at this time. To Edward Hatton was owing rents of £198 10s 4d per annum and other debts of £176 18s 6d and to his sister, Jane, small sums.[59] O'Brien, an Irish Protestant, went on to die as an army lieutenant. He too, it emerged, had acquired some Irish freeholder land in Clones parish, County Monaghan, which Willoughby survived to claim as his 'executor or heir'.[60] By then the Irish attempt at counter-revolution in all its aspects had been defeated and plantation in Ulster was restored. Hatton ownership in direct male line did not, however, prove enduring. Hatton's son Edward had not survived; his son James had died young. They had not in the best of times been a strong family; the first Edward, despite his energy, had been unwell in 1622. By the Restoration, the estate had passed to the ownership of William Davies by right of marriage to James Hatton's daughter Jane, who himself died in 1662.[61] The Hattons had been in at the start of a major transformation in Ulster, but they did not survive to found a dynasty there. Their story, however, serves as a case study in the

---

[55] TCD, MS 835, ff. 198rv; Armagh Public Library, Visitation Book, 1622, pp. 178–9; Norfolk Record Office, Norwich, MS DN/VIS 3/3, f. 66.
[56] A. M. Burke (ed.), *Memorials of St Margaret's Church, Westminster: the parish registers, 1539–1660* (London, 1914), p. 62.
[57] TCD, MS 835, ff. 35, 82v, 174, 265–6.   [58] *Ibid.*, f. 198v.   [59] *Ibid.*, ff. 82rv, 203.
[60] NAI, Book of Survey and Distribution, County Monaghan, p. 158.
[61] NLI, GO MS 70, p. 339; Aidan Clarke, *Prelude to Restoration in Ireland: the end of the Commonwealth, 1659–60* (Cambridge, 1999), p. 183.

exercise of power on one estate in plantation Ulster. It also indicates in microcosm not only the difficulties of implementing both plantation and Protestantism in Ulster, but also the degree of success being achieved in both areas. Whatever interrelationships between settlers and native Irish as may have been developing were mostly shattered by the outbreak of the rising of 1641.

II

The value of the document which accompanies this account of the Hattons as planters lies in its virtually unique character. It derives from the litigation between James Hatton and his father's widow in the Court of Chancery in Dublin, forming part of his answer to her bill.[62] However, its actual production arose from a commission out of the prerogative court, to appraisers nominated by both parties, to establish the value of the estate at the time of Edward Hatton's death. The document bears heavily the marks of the damage it sustained in 1922 and is also incomplete. In full, it would have given a list of all the tenants on the estate. The importance of what remains of it lies in the fact that whereas the sizes of plantation land-lord houses in Ulster are well known, the number of rooms within them is not, while a systematic recording of the contents is very rare indeed, owing to the very limited survival in Ireland, unlike England, of probate inventories. An added bonus lies in the record of the mixed agriculture practised on the land directly farmed in the neighbourhood of the 'castle', as well as in the hints it gives both to linen and woollen industries and to the presence of English and Irish cattle. There were a lot of horses. The values given for all items are extremely useful. The inventory might also be used to assess the 'civility' of an Ulster rural landowner's residence, though with the precaution that it had not in this case been lived in con-tinuously by one family. It is a very English document both in the words used for some of the rooms – parlour, chamber – and in the fact that the values are given in sterling and not in Irish currency. In the following transcription illegible words and characters are denoted by empty square brackets; in some instances putative readings are given in angle brackets.

A scedule inventory and particular of all the goods chattles and cattles leases debts sperate and desperate which were the said Edward Hatton's at the day of his death and belonging to him which any ways came unto this defendants hands or to his knowledge being truly [ ] prized and valued as be herein set forth by commission out of the prerogative court by such apprizors as were nominated by the parties, plaintiff and defendant, as followeth:

[62] NAI, CP/S25.

	£	s.	d.
Imprimis, *in the parlour*			
2 long tables vizt one being a drawing table	1	10	0
1 great cubbord and a liv'y cubbord	1	0	0
2 chairs, two dozen of joyne stooles	1	2	[ ]
[ ] cushens		2	0
2 old carpets and a brekar		[ ]	0
2 pistols		15	0
5 pikes one without [ ]			6
1 long fowling piece		10	0
22 pounds of course yarn		7	0
1 pestel and mortar		3	4
In the room at the stayres head			
3 flock beds and bowlsters		15	0
4 old caddows		10	0
1 feather bed and bowlster	1	0	0
1 old bedsted		2	0
In the old chamber over the hall			
2 feather beds, 2 bowlsters and pillows	3	0	0
2 bedsteds and hangings	1	0	0
3 caddows, 1 blanket	1	0	0
1 flock bed		5	0
1 truckle bedsted		2	0
1 livery cubbord		7	0
1 small table and 2 chairs		3	0
1 carpet		3	0
1 chest and 1 old trunk		6	0
1 warming pan		3	0
1 old cushion stool and a pair of bellows, fire shovel and thongues and 1 iron grate	5		0
1 old watch out of temper		10	0
Silver plate in the said room:			
1 great double salt weighing 31 oz. at 4s. the ounce	6	4	0
4 brass candles weighing 45 oz. at 4s. the ounce	9	0	0
4 small bowls, whereof 3 wine bowls weighing 31 oz. at 4s. the ounce	6	4	0
15 spoons weighing 24 oz. at 4s. the ounce	3	16	0
1 little gilt salt without a cover weighing 9 oz. at 4s. the ounce	1	16	0
1 gilt sugar dish weighing 15 oz. at 4s. the ounce	3	0	0
1 small aquavite cupp weighing 2 oz.		8	0
In the chamber over the kitchen			
2 feather beds and 6 feather pillows	2	0	0
2 old coverlets		6	0
2 old caddows and 1 blanket		8	0
1 old bedsted and old curtens		2	6
3 trunks and 4 chairs		10	0

In the chamber over the brewhouse

2 truckle bedsteds and 1 old bedsted	4	0
1 old spinning wheel	1	6
1 old rotten trunk	1	0

In the chief chamber
[the document is badly damaged at this point]

1 pair of iron racks		6	8
2 spitts		2	0
2 dozen and a half of pewter dishes	1	10	0
1 pewter bason and yewer		5	0
6 sawcers 6 pottingers 6 old chamber pots, 2 [ ] candlesticks		11	6
2 flaggon pots of pewter		10	0
2 pewter basons and a cullendar		4	0
4 brass candlesticks		10	0
2 old brass pots and chefing dish		17	6
2 small brass pans		6	8
1 dripping pan		3	6
2 little iron pots		5	0
1 chopping knife, a basting ladle, a grater, a frying pan and a grid iron		4	6
9 pitch forks, 8 wooden hay rakes		2	6
1 churn, 5 milk tubbs and a basket		5	0
1 old trunk 1 old c[ ]		2	0
1 scimmer 1 marking iron, a cleever and a beef fork		3	6
[ ]		10	0
2 cheeves full of course wool		3	0
some hops and an old bag		10	0
1 close stool and pan, 1 other close stool and pan		7	0
2 stone jugs		8	0
1 pail and a small firkin		1	0
9 flat milk cheeses		4	0
8 small c[ ]s of rendered tallow		12	0

Lyning [linen] praysed:

10 pair and 1 sheets Irish cloth old and new	3	3	0
1 white English cloth for sheets		10	0
1 diaper table cloth, cubbord cloth and tweel and diaper for another small table cloth	1	1	0
7 Irish cloth towels		7	0
2 dozen and 8 napkins Irish cloth		10	0
8 old piltcheeres		12	0
2 old cubbord clothes		2	0
5 old table cloths for a small round table		5	0

In the studdy

1 chair and 1 old cushion	<5>	6
1 desk	3	4

40 books great and small	3	0	0
1 <piece> of old gold waight		2	0
In the buttery			
5 hogsheads		7	6
2 barrels and 1 firkin		7	0
2 <powdring tubs>		2	0
1 brass pan		13	4
2 small pails		1	0
In the kitchen			
1 old washing tub, 1 pair of pothooks 2 hangers		2	6
In the deary			
A boulting tub, a churn, 4 small tubbs with other implements as milk bowls and old barrels		5	0
In the brewhouse			
1 old furnace	1	6	8
2 kevers		6	8
1 open hogshead, a coole <pip> measure and a pail		[ ]	0
Plowe implements:			
6 iron chaynes with coulters, 2 socks, 2 plow implements			
		16	0
2 spades			6
Corn praysed and hay			
Corn in the haggard	30	0	0
Hay in the haggard	10	0	0
Barley in the barn	1	0	0
4 barrels of wheat threshed in the house	1	6	8
6½ barrels of oats		<13>	0
Corn in ground			
5½ barrels of wheat sown	2	15	0
6½ barrels of bear		12	0
Hay in blackwater meadow		15	0
Cattle praysed			
16 oxen praysed	27	0	0
17 cows	24	0	0
12 heifers and a bullock	8	5	0
2 bulls	2	0	0
6 calves	1	10	0
6 Irish cows	4	10	0
Another cow	1	0	0
Horses mares and colts			
1 dune colt 3 years old	1	0	0
1 small gray mare colt 3 years old		15	0
1 bay mare colt 3 years old		15	0
2 black yearling colts	1	0	0

6 old working mares	6	0	0
1 old hipt mare and 2 yearling colts	1	0	0
1 bald gelding with 4 white feet	4	0	0
1 old grey gelding	2	10	0
1 chesnot horse and a rawe horse	<4>	0	0
4 hogs	1	0	0
1 bore, 1 sow and 2 pigs		15	0

7   'That Bugbear Arminianism': Archbishop Laud and Trinity College, Dublin

Alan Ford

Archbishop Laud's ecclesiastical and political energy has left historians gasping behind him. This is not simply a result of his passion for detail and singleminded capacity for hard work; it is also a product of his geographical and administrative range. With remarkable prescience, he anticipated current concern with the broader 'British' dimension of early modern history and viewed religious policy not in a narrowly English sense, or confined only to church matters, but in terms of all three royal dominions, and extending to education as well. The result is a standing challenge, not merely to historians' stamina, but also to the instinctive compartmentalisation of their approach to the 1630s which has sought to confine Laud within national boundaries and see him solely as an ecclesiastical leader.

To understand Laud's policies and those of his royal master thus requires historians to expand their horizons beyond the southern province of England, to the more marginal regions of England and Wales, and even to the remote fastnesses of Scotland and Ireland.[1] Recent studies of Laud's involvement in Ireland, for example, have demonstrated how the change in context and freedom of action can help to reveal some of his inner motives and ideological concerns. In England it is possible to argue about whether Laud in fact exercised any direct power, even to claim that he was merely an obedient servant of the real driving force, King Charles I, thus replacing 'Laudianism' by 'Carolinism'.[2] But, in Ireland, Laud's close alliance with the all-powerful lord deputy, Thomas Wentworth, and his loyal ecclesiastical henchman, Bishop John Bramhall of Derry, gave him a far greater freedom of manoeuvre which he used to put his favoured policies into effect. As a result, Ireland can be viewed as a testing ground

---

[1] Conrad Russell, *The Causes of the English Civil War* (Oxford, 1990); Conrad Russell, *The Fall of the British Monarchies 1637–1642* (Oxford, 1991); Julian Davies, *The Caroline Captivity of the Church. Charles I and the remoulding of Anglicanism 1625–1641* (Oxford, 1992); Kevin Sharpe, *The Personal Rule of Charles I* (New Haven, 1992); J. S. Morrill, 'A British patriarchy? Ecclesiastical imperialism under the early Stuarts' in Anthony Fletcher and Peter Roberts (eds.), *Religion, Culture, and Society in Early Modern Britain* (Cambridge, 1994), pp. 209–37.

[2] Davies, *Caroline Captivity*.

where the true thrust of Laudian religious policies can be identified and investigated.[3]

Nor did Laud limit himself solely to directing church affairs. He also played a highly significant role in driving official policy towards universities. In 1630 he was elected chancellor of Oxford where he took a direct, indeed detailed, interest in university affairs, overseeing discipline, securing manuscripts for the library, endowing chairs and, most notably, taking in hand the complete revision of the university statutes.[4] In 1636 he gained royal confirmation of his right to visit Cambridge and Oxford as metropolitan, thus extending his powers to include the other English university. But here too there is an Irish dimension to Laud's activities. In 1633 he was made chancellor of Trinity College, Dublin, where he also rewrote the statutes and took an active interest in the imposition of order. Moreover, given the fact that he never actually exercised his right to visit Oxford and Cambridge, his Irish involvement again takes on an added significance, for Laud not only reformed the Irish university's constitution, he also decisively reshaped its religious outlook away from Calvinism to a committed Arminianism. The purpose of this investigation, therefore, is to provide an additional dimension to two aspects of Laud's activities – his involvement in Ireland and his interest in universities – by investigating a hitherto neglected episode, his involvement in the reform of Trinity College, Dublin, and by exploring what this intervention tells us about Laud's wider motivations and religious outlook.

Laud's interest in the reform of Trinity College, Dublin, in the 1630s marked a decisive period in the history of the only early modern Irish university. He played a leading role in both devising and implementing an extensive programme of change. As chancellor from 1633, he personally rewrote the statutes, secured a new charter, replaced the provost with his own nominee, and subjected the college firmly to the control of the state. He thus established the constitutional framework which would govern the college well into the nineteenth century. Yet

---

[3] Amanda Capern, 'The Caroline church: James Ussher and the Irish dimension', *Historical Journal*, 29 (1996), pp. 57–85; John McCafferty, '"God bless your free Church of Ireland": Wentworth, Laud, Bramhall and the Irish convocation of 1634' in J. F. Merritt (ed.), *The Political World of Thomas Wentworth, Earl of Strafford, 1621–1641* (Cambridge, 1996), pp. 187–208; John McCafferty, 'John Bramhall and the reconstruction of the Church of Ireland, 1633–1641' (University of Cambridge, Ph.D. thesis, 1996); A. Ford, 'Dependent or independent: the Church of Ireland and its colonial context, 1536–1647', *The Seventeenth Century*, 10 (1995), pp. 163–87.

[4] K. Fincham, 'Oxford and the early Stuart polity' in Nicholas Tyacke (ed.), *The History of the University of Oxford: seventeenth century Oxford*, IV (Oxford, 1997), pp. 198–210; K. Sharpe, 'Archbishop Laud and the University of Oxford' in H. Lloyd Jones, V. Pearl and B. Worden (eds.), *History and Imagination. Essays in honour of H. R. Trevor-Roper* (London, 1981), pp. 156–62.

despite its evident importance, his role in Trinity history has received little critical analysis. For his biographers, it has been overshadowed by his similar role in relation to Oxford.[5] For those interested in Irish history, Laud's involvement has generally been seen as subsidiary to that of Lord Deputy Wentworth, the true driving force behind Irish policy in the 1630s.[6] Only from earnest Trinity historians has Laud received more than cursory treatment, and even here insult has generally replaced analysis, with Laud's appointment as chancellor being followed, according to one writer, by the 'enthralment and degradation of Trinity College'.[7] Such neglect has enabled two mistaken impressions to develop: first, that Laud was concerned in his university reform with little else than the imposition of order and discipline; and second, that he was a subsidiary figure in the development of official policy towards Ireland in the 1630s.

Any attempt to redress the imbalance requires first a careful examination of Laud's involvement with Trinity, concentrating in particular upon the motivation of his reforms and the way in which they changed the college. We begin, therefore, with an examination of what kind of a university Trinity was, and how Laud came to play an increasingly influential role in its affairs, then explore how in the period after 1633 Laud and his allies set about reforming Trinity. The penultimate section analyses the nature of changes that Laud introduced in the statutes. The conclusion links Laud's reforms of Trinity to the wider historiographical debate over his motivation and ideology.

I

Founded in 1592, Trinity College, the only college of Dublin University, had by the 1620s developed a distinctive character. It was Calvinist, it was riven by faction, and it was determined to preserve its self-government from outside interference. Its Calvinism had a distinctly Puritan tinge:

---

[5] H. R. Trevor-Roper, *Archbishop Laud 1573–1645* (2nd edn, London, 1965), pp. 242, 271–92; C. Carlton, *Archbishop William Laud* (London, 1987), pp. 92 fol., 132–43.

[6] H. F. Kearney, *Strafford in Ireland* (2nd edn, Cambridge, 1989), pp. 31, chapter 10, though cf. pp. xxvii–xxviii; T. O. Ranger, 'Strafford in Ireland: a revaluation' in Trevor Aston (ed.), *Crisis in Europe 1560–1660* (London, 1965); *NHI*, III, chapter 9.

[7] W. Urwick, *The Early History of Trinity College, Dublin 1591–1660* (London, 1891), p. 37. See also C. R. Elrington (ed.), *The Works of James Ussher* (17 vols., Dublin 1847–64), I, pp. 191–201; J. W. Stubbs, *The History of the University of Dublin from its Foundation to the end of the Eighteenth Century* (Dublin, 1889), pp. 62–78; J. P. Mahaffy, *An Epoch in Irish History. Trinity College, Dublin, its foundation and early fortunes 1591–1660* (London, 1903), chapter 6; C. Maxwell, *A History of Trinity College Dublin, 1591–1892* (Dublin, 1946), pp. 38–43; H. L. Murphy, *A History of Trinity College, Dublin* (Dublin, 1951), chapter 7; R. B. McDowell and D. A. Webb, *Trinity College Dublin 1592–1952. An academic history* (Cambridge, 1982), pp. 13–16.

the provostship offered sanctuary to a succession of English Protestants who found the rigorous enforcement of conformity in England too burdensome: Walter Travers (1595–98), Henry Alvey (1601–9) and William Temple (1609–27).[8] Though far from being a *wholly* Puritan institution, Trinity extended the limits of comprehension in a similar way to English colleges such as Emmanuel or Sidney Sussex.[9] The results surface regularly in Trinity's early seventeenth-century history, in the reluctance to don the surplice, the neglect of Holy Communion, in the title of the divinity chair – the Professor of Theological Controversies – and in the fact that even Archbishop Abbot of Canterbury, as chancellor of the university, felt constrained to try to repress Trinity's Puritan leanings.[10] In its second characteristic – fractiousness – it was hardly unique amongst universities then or now. What turned the normal tensions between provost, fellows and students into serious rifts was the nature of the college's constitution.[11] This established three competing *loci* of power – the provost, the senior fellows and the junior fellows – without providing any adequate mechanism for settling disputes between or within them.[12] Even the archbishop of Armagh, James Ussher, one of the first students of Trinity, later its vice-chancellor, and an invariable defender of his *alma mater*, had to admit that Trinity's constitution was seriously flawed.[13]

What enabled Trinity to preserve its distinctive character despite its internal disputes was its independence from outside control. By its foundation charter Trinity's fellows had secured the vital rights to elect the provost and to draw up statutes.[14] Such freedoms were under almost continuous attack in universities in England in the early modern period as

---

[8] A. Ford, 'The Church of Ireland 1558–1641: a puritan church?' in A. Ford, J. McGuire and K. Milne (eds.), *As by Law Established. The Church of Ireland since the Reformation* (Dublin, 1995), pp. 52–60.

[9] S. Bendall, C. Brooke and P. Collinson (eds.), *A History of Emmanuel College, Cambridge* (Woodbridge, 2000).

[10] Trinity College Dublin Muniments (hereafter TCD Mun.), P/1/72, 99, 129, 168; J. P. Mahaffy (ed.), *The Particular Book of Trinity College, Dublin* (London, 1904), p. 97b; E. S. Shuckburgh (ed.), *Two Biographies of William Bedell* (Cambridge, 1902), p. 271; Elrington (ed.), *Ussher*, XV, p. 72, XVI, p. 458.

[11] For examples of internal disputes, see Elrington (ed.), *Ussher*, XV, pp. 389, 574 fol. (this letter is dated in Bodl., Sancroft MSS 18, p. 14), XVI, pp. 330, 335; Shuckburgh (ed.), *William Bedell*, p. 274; TCD Mun. P/1/110; Stubbs, *History of the University of Dublin*, p. 390; TCD, MS 543/2/1.

[12] Elrington (ed.), *Ussher*, XV, p. 375; the statutes entrusted the government of the college to the provost and the majority of the seven senior fellows. Beneath them were nine junior fellows: Bedell's statutes, c.4, c.6, c.20, Mahaffy, *Epoch*, pp. 335, 337, 363 fol.

[13] Elrington (ed.), *Ussher*, XV, 574 fol.

[14] H. H. G. MacDonnell, *Chartae et Statuta Collegii Sacrosanctae et Individuae Trinitatis Reginae Elizabethae, juxta Dublin* (Dublin, 1844), pp. 4, 7.

the king and his ministers sought to impose their will.[15] The Dublin college was acutely aware of this, but the judicious use of delaying tactics, and skilful exploitation of its distance from the centre, secured its privileges from attack for most of James's reign.[16] But at the end of James's reign the English privy council warned the fellows of Trinity that they were not to appoint to the provostship when it fell vacant without the king's approval.[17] And, indeed, under Charles, royal involvement in Irish patronage became even more marked.[18] Moreover, shifts in attitudes at court meant that such royal appointments could threaten not merely the college's independence, but also its distinctive religious position, by imposing a candidate out of sympathy with Trinity's tradition.[19] The interplay of these forces was of direct relevance to Trinity because, between 1627 and 1634, three vacancies occurred in the provostship, leaving the College exposed to the shifts in patronage and influence. The result was a decided change in theological and constitutional direction.

Even before his death in January 1627, Provost Temple's failing health had made the succession a sensitive issue. A similar problem had arisen at the equally Calvinist Emmanuel in 1622, when the fellows had secured the resignation of the ageing master, Laurence Chaderton, and the immediate election of a safe successor, John Preston, in order to avoid the appointment becoming a bone of contention at court.[20] A similar procedure was attempted at Trinity. In 1626 an anonymous letter was written to an influential courtier exhorting him to secure a letter from the king – preferably, it was urged, when no Arminian bishop was present – granting the next vacancy to the Cambridge graduate and preacher at Gray's Inn, Richard Sibbes.[21] Otherwise, the writer warned, someone will be imposed 'who will be as pricks and thorns in our side'. The motivation was made plain in the writer's praise of Sibbes as a 'sound good anti-Arminian', and his view of his nomination as 'a means under God to preserve the

---

[15] J. McConica (ed.), *The History of the University of Oxford*, III (Oxford, 1986), pp. 434–40.

[16] Bodl., Carte MSS 30, ff. 73r, 80r, 84r; TCD Mun. P/1/76, 77, 78, 80, 84; printed (with some inaccuracies) in Stubbs, *History of the University of Dublin*, pp. 379–88; and see Ussher's revealing *'dictum sapienti'* in 1613, Elrington (ed.), *Ussher*, XV, p. 73.

[17] TCD Mun., P/1/156; printed in Stubbs, *History of the University of Dublin*, p. 389.

[18] In James's reign many Church of Ireland clergy were appointed to Irish sees; under Charles I there was a far greater reliance upon Church of England clergy personally known to the king, Carlton, *Laud*, pp. 76, 92, 107.

[19] P. A. Welsby, *George Abbot: The unwanted archbishop* (London, 1962), pp. 120–2; K. Fincham, 'Prelacy and politics: Archbishop Abbot's defence of protestant orthodoxy', *Historical Research*, 61 (1988), pp. 53 fol.

[20] Irvonwy Morgan, *Prince Charles's Puritan Chaplain* (London, 1957), pp. 112–15.

[21] For Sibbes, see M. E. Dever, 'Moderation and deprivation: a reappraisal of Richard Sibbes', *Journal of Ecclesiastical History*, 43 (1992), pp. 396–413, and M. E. Dever, *Richard Sibbes. Puritanism and Calvinism in late Elizabethan and early Stuart England* (Macon, 2000).

wholesome seed of a sound ministry' in Ireland 'free from Popery and Arminianism'.[22] Archbishop Abbot was reportedly already aware of the importance of the succession in 1625.[23] By early 1627 he and Ussher had agreed on Sibbes as Temple's successor and had persuaded the latter to step down, but their plans were foiled by the death of Temple and the refusal of Sibbes to go to Ireland.[24]

In the end Abbot and Ussher settled for the appointment of William Bedell, whose Calvinist credentials would have been reassuring to the anonymous letter-writer.[25] But, from the fellows' point of view, the battle was won at the expense of the war, for Bedell was only 'freely elected' by the fellows after the king had directed them to choose him.[26] The college was, as a result, no longer insulated from court patronage and central direction. The transfer of the *de facto* power to choose the provost to London was all the more important since by the time of the next vacancy Laud had replaced Abbot as the power behind the throne.[27] In 1628 Laud had been appointed bishop of London and was soon in correspondence with Archbishop Ussher.[28] Proof of Laud's role in Irish patronage came in the following year. It was Laud who secured the bishopric of Kilmore and Ardagh for Bedell, it was Laud to whom the Trinity fellows appealed to preserve their freedom to elect a successor, and it was Laud who played the key role in advising the king on how the vacancy should be filled.[29] Ussher's agent in London warned him of the danger which this shift in power posed: Trinity might have imposed on it a provost 'who

[22] PRO, SP 63/268/29 (*CSPI, 1647–60*, p. 83).

[23] PRO, SP 63/241/124 (*CSPI, 1625–32*, p. 39).

[24] Elrington (ed.), *Ussher*, XV, pp. 361 fol., 375, XVI, pp. 440 fol.

[25] Shuckburgh (ed.), *William Bedell*, p. 24; Elrington (ed.), *Ussher*, XVI, p. 457; TCD Mun., P/1/181; printed in Stubbs, *History of the University of Dublin*, p. 392. Ironically Bedell's reluctance to embrace the fierce anti-Catholicism of the Irish Protestants led Joshua Hoyle, the Professor of Theological Controversies at Trinity, to accuse him of Arminianism, Elrington (ed.), *Ussher*, XVI, pp. 474 fol.; Shuckburgh (ed.), *William Bedell*, pp. 26 fol.; Charles McNeill (ed.), *The Tanner Letters* (IMC, Dublin 1943), pp. 99 fol.

[26] TCD Mun. P/1/178, 179, 181, 183; Stubbs, *History of the University of Dublin*, p. 392.

[27] Welsby, *George Abbot*, pp. 120–2; H. R. Trevor-Roper, *Catholics, Anglicans and Puritans* (London, 1989), p. 67; Carlton, *Laud*, pp. 74–6.

[28] W. Scott and J. Bliss (eds.), *The Works of the Most Reverend Father in God, William Laud, D. D. sometime Lord Archbishop of Canterbury* (7 vols., Oxford, 1847–60), VI, p. 258 is the first letter that survives, but refers to earlier correspondence, see A. Ford (ed.), 'Correspondence between Archbishops Ussher and Laud', *Archivium Hibernicum*, 46 (1992).

[29] Elrington (ed.), *Ussher*, XV, pp. 433, 443, 445 fol.; Scott and Bliss (eds.), *Laud*, VI, p. 261; Shuckburgh (ed.), *William Bedell*, pp. 94, 299, 326; PRO, SP 63/248/78 (*CSPI, 1625–32*, p. 452); PRO, SP 63/252/55 (*CSPI, 1625–32*, p. 609); for further evidence of Laud's role in Irish ecclesiastical appointments see the Falkland Letter Book, NA, MS M2445, pp. 2, 54.

will not, it may be, so truly aim at the religious education of the students; for some one deeply tainted with the Arminian tenets, putteth in close to be recommended thither by his Majesty'.[30] Laud was indeed pushing precisely such a candidate: he wanted William Chappell, a fellow of Christ's College, Cambridge, who had lived down his early reputation for Puritanism to become one of Laud's *protégés*.[31] But Chappell, who had already spent a brief period as catechist in Trinity, was unwilling to leave his fellowship in Cambridge to go back to Ireland.[32] Hence Laud was able to claim to Ussher 'I am engaged for none', and, even more disingenuously, 'I heartily love freedoms granted by charter, and would have them maintained.'[33] In default of an external candidate, the choice settled on one of the fellows, Robert Ussher, who, with the approval of his uncle the primate, was nominated by the king and duly elected by the fellows.[34]

Despite his growing influence with the king, Laud's capacity to act in Irish matters was limited by his lack of direct powers over the Irish church. The latter, though under the same supreme governor, was, of course, not only jurisdictionally separate from the Church of England, but also jealous of its independence.[35] Two decisive events in 1633, however, significantly changed the nature of Laud's influence in Ireland. First, on 3 July Thomas Wentworth was appointed as lord deputy of Ireland. Wentworth was already close to Laud, and even became that rare commodity, one of the archbishop's friends. He shared with Laud a common vision of a 'thorough' policy of strict discipline, and also possessed a steely determination in enforcing it. He relied upon Laud both for advice and direction about ecclesiastical affairs in Ireland, and to protect him from political intrigue in England.[36] *De jure*, of course, religious affairs in Ireland were still, after Wentworth's appointment, the preserve of the independent Irish church, its primate, James Ussher, and its supreme governor, the king. *De facto*, however, Charles gave his directions not

---

[30] Elrington (ed.), *Ussher*, XV, p. 433.
[31] J. Peile, *Biographical Register of Christ's College, Cambridge* (2 vols., Cambridge, 1910), I, p. 232; Andrew Kippis (ed.), *Biographia Britannica* (5 vols., 2nd edn, London, 1778–93), pp. 339–43; J. Morgan, *Godly Learning: puritan attitudes towards reason, learning, and education, 1560–1640* (Cambridge, 1986), p. 258.
[32] Mahaffy (ed.), *Particular Book*, p. 205b; Scott and Bliss (eds.), *Laud*, VI, pp. 355 fol.
[33] Scott and Bliss (eds.), *Laud*, VI, p. 261.
[34] Elrington (ed.), *Ussher*, XV, pp. 445 fol., 449 fol., 456; Shuckburgh (ed.), *William Bedell*, 300; Elrington (ed.), *Ussher*, I, pp. 100 fol.; Scott and Bliss (eds.), *Laud*, VI, p. 267.
[35] Ford, 'Dependent or independent', pp. 163–87.
[36] Trevor-Roper, *Archbishop Laud*, p. 242; Kearney, *Strafford in Ireland*, pp. 29–31, 217; the standard biography of Wentworth remains C. V. Wedgwood, *Thomas Wentworth first Earl of Strafford 1593–1641. A revaluation* (London, 1961). Cf. Lord Deputy Falkland's comments, on the Wentworth's good fortune in having an archbishop of Canterbury who was both a friend and 'withall a person of especiall power', NA, MS 2445, Falkland Letter Book, MS 2445, p. 328.

to Ussher, but to Laud, and it was therefore through Laud in England, and through Laud's allies in Ireland, Wentworth and Bishop Bramhall of Derry, that ecclesiastical policy was effectively decided and implemented, while Ussher became an increasingly marginalised figure.[37] The second event which increased Laud's capacity for direct action in Ireland was the death in August 1633 of George Abbot. Laud succeeded not merely to the archbishopric, but also, at the insistence of James Ussher, to the chancellorship of Trinity.[38] He was, at last, in a position to direct the affairs of Trinity College.

II

Laud and Wentworth were not slow in exercising their new capacity for direct action. They quickly identified Trinity as one of their priorities: 'religion and civility in that kingdom will much depend upon the reformation of that place'.[39] Reformation meant two things: the total revision of the college's constitution, and the replacement of troublesome and unorthodox members by 'half a dozen good scholars' from the English universities.[40] The twin tasks were begun in 1634. In March, Laud asked for a copy of the statutes, and over the next three years he worked on a thorough revision of the Trinity code. The first personnel problem was Provost Ussher, seen as weak and ineffectual, even by his uncle.[41] Wentworth tempted him to resign by the offer of an alternative position.[42] Laud, meanwhile, had his chosen successor waiting. In 1633 he had persuaded William Chappell to go to Ireland as dean of Cashel.[43] In the following year, following an audience with Laud, Chappell reluctantly agreed to take up the challenge of reforming Trinity.[44] Wentworth then confronted the equally reluctant fellows and 'persuaded' them on 21 August to elect Chappell as provost.[45]

---

[37] F. R. Bolton, *The Caroline Tradition of the Church of Ireland with Particular Reference to Bishop Jeremy Taylor* (London, 1958), pp. 10–19; R. B. Knox, *James Ussher: Archbishop of Armagh* (Cardiff, 1967), pp. 44–53.

[38] TCD Mun. V/5/1, p. 4; Elrington (ed.), *Ussher*, XV, pp. 572, 574; PRO, SP 63/254/119 (*CSPI, 1633–47*, p. 48).

[39] Scott and Bliss (eds.), *Laud*, VII, p. 248.

[40] *Ibid.*, VI, pp. 355 fol. 399; HMC, *Report on the Manuscripts of the late Reginald Rawdon Hastings* (4 vols., London, 1928–47), IV, p. 64; Sheffield, WWM, vol. VI, pp. 45, 179, 271, 296.

[41] Elrington (ed.), *Ussher*, XV, 574 fol.   [42] Sheffield, WWM, vol. VI, pp. 45 fol., 77.

[43] F. Peck, *Desiderata Curiosa* (2 vols., London, 1732–5), II, book XI, p. 3; Kippis (ed.), *Biographia Britannica*, III, p. 440.

[44] Scott and Bliss (eds.), *Laud*, VI, p. 385; Peck, *Desiderata Curiosa*, II, book XI, p. 4.

[45] TCD Mun. V/5/1, p. 5; Sheffield, WWM, vol. VI, pp. 77, 126.

If Chappell was to push through Laud's reform programme, he needed to strengthen his position within the college. This he did by the simple expedient of importing fellows and students from his old college in Cambridge.[46] He paid particular attention to elections to senior fellowships, since, under the existing constitution, the seniors could effectively block change. His first attempt to secure his support among the fellows was successful when in June 1635 Alexander Hatfield, a graduate from Christ's, was elected senior fellow.[47] But when Chappell tried to fill further vacancies in the following year he sparked off a major dispute in the college. What began in January 1636 as an argument over precedence in the election of fellows, soon became the focus for an ever-widening series of personal, constitutional, political and theological battles. The story of the conflict is an immensely complex one, only half-told in the surviving sources.[48] Briefly, it derived from Chappell's attempt to promote one of his *protégés*, Arthur Ware, over the heads of three of the junior fellows, Nathaniel Hoyle, Thomas Feasant and Charles Cullen, whose failure to attend chapel and, in Hoyle's case, refusal to wear the surplice suggested at the least religious laxity, but, more likely, Puritan principles.[49] Chappell's attempt split the senior fellows, who were unable to agree on a candidate, and caused the juniors to broaden the dispute by appealing to the seven college visitors.[50]

The visitors, closely identified with the Trinity *status quo*, were prominent Dublin officials and churchmen, including among their number two of the leading Protestant bishops and former fellows of the college, James

---

[46] *Commons' Jnl, Ire*, I, 197. John Garthwaite, admitted sizar, Christ's College, under Mr Chappell, 1633, can be confidently identified with the Trinity scholar (c.1635), bachelor (by 1637) and fellow (1637); Robert Cook, admitted pensioner, Christ's College, under Mr Chappell 1631 can be tentatively identified with the bachelor and fellow of the same name at Trinity: Peile, *Biographical Register*, I, pp. 407, 427; TCD Mun. V/5/1, pp. 55, 59; and see also p. 146 below.

[47] TCD Mun. V/5/1, p. 48; Peile, *Biographical Register*, I, p. 232.

[48] The main sources for the dispute are the letters of Wentworth and Laud, and the accounts of the proceedings and petitions in the PRO, SP 63/256/6, ff. 10r–31v (*CSPI, 1633–47*, pp. 145 fol., but inadequately transcribed), some of which is duplicated in TCD Mun. V/5/1, pp. 51–3. It should be noted that the narrative account at the conclusion of PRO, SP 63/256/6, ff. 27r–30v, though written in the third person, is in fact based very largely upon an account of the dispute written by Chappell, *ibid.*, ff. 24v–26r. What the sources lack is an account of the affair from the perspective of Ussher and the visitors – Ussher's 'three sides of a paper in his small, close hand' detailing the affair to Laud have not survived, Scott and Bliss (eds.), *Laud*, VI, p. 464. The most thorough secondary treatments of the dispute are by Elrington in Elrington (ed.), *Ussher*, I, pp. 191–8, and Mahaffy, *Epoch*, pp. 239–47.

[49] PRO, SP 63/256/6, ff. 10r–11r, 24v, 27r; TCD Mun. V/5/1, p. 53.

[50] PRO, SP 63/256/6, ff. 11r, 24v, 27r.

Ussher and Anthony Martin of Meath.[51] On 18 May 1636 a visitation was held. After an acrimonious hearing the visitors decided the issue of precedence in favour of the three petitioners, and ordered that they be admitted in order of seniority.[52] There followed a lengthy impasse. The provost simply denied the visitors' right to act, first because it conflicted with the the privilege of the provost and fellows to elect to fellowships; and second because the three fellows had no right to appeal to the visitors anyway. The statutes, Chappell rather dubiously and pedantically argued, prescribed that all domestic disputes were to be settled within the college, and anyone who sought to appeal outside the college (which he inter- preted to include the visitors) without the consent of the provost and fellows, could be expelled.[53] Moreover, he argued, the visitors should seek to support the authority of the lord deputy rather than give credence to the 'groundless and untrue' complaints of 'heady and refractory young men'.[54]

Chappell made it quite clear that he had no intention of accepting the visitors' decision, while the visitors were equally adamant that their ruling must be enforced. Ussher threatened to have Chappell removed from his position. Chappell pointedly warned that he would appeal to the chancel- lor.[55] In their attempts to resolve the impasse, fellows, visitors and provost alike appealed to progressively higher authorities. First the junior fellows, with, Chappell claimed, Ussher's connivance, brought their grievance to the Irish council, of which Ussher and Martin were members. When, in the absence of Wentworth, and in the presence of Ussher, the case came before the council in June and July 1636, Chappell, not surpris- ingly, failed to receive a sympathetic hearing, though he continued to refuse to accept the visitors' decision.[56] On 20 July the visitors returned to Trinity and attempted once again to impose their will.[57] In response, the provost and his supporters among the fellows appealed to the lords justices, who referred the case to the lord deputy on his return, and to the king.[58] The latter, as Chappell well realised, meant Laud, for when the

---

[51] PRO, SP 63/256/6, f. 13r. The visitors were: the chancellor or vice chancellor of the university, the archbishop of Dublin, the bishop of Meath, the vice-treasurer, the trea- surer at wars, the lord chief justice and the mayor of Dublin, MacDonnell, *Chartae et Statuta*, p. 8.

[52] PRO, SP 63/256/6, ff. 11v–14r, 24v, 27r.   [53] *Ibid.*, ff. 14v–15r.

[54] *Ibid.*, ff. 15r, 14v.   [55] *Ibid.*, ff. 12r–15v, 24v–27v.

[56] *Ibid.*, ff. 17r–19v, 22r–23r, 25rv, 28rv. Though Wentworth formally handed over power to the lords justices on 3 July, he was already in London by 30 June, F. M. Powicke and E. B. Fryde (eds.), *Handbook of British Chronology* (2nd edn, London, 1961), p. 159; W. Knowler, *The Earle of Strafforde's Letters and Despatches* (2 vols., London, 1739), II, p. 8.

[57] PRO, SP 63/256/6, ff. 23r–24r.

[58] *Ibid.*, ff. 22r–24r; Scott and Bliss (eds.), *Laud*, VI, p. 465.

archbishop talked to his royal master about the matter, Charles delegated the settlement of the dispute to him.[59]

Throughout August Laud reviewed the official papers and petitions concerning the dispute. Ussher sent him a lengthy letter (carried by, significantly, Thomas Feasant). Following this, Laud wrote to Wentworth that, if Ussher's account were true, the provost 'is much to blame'.[60] Chappell's faith in his patron, however, was justified. By the end of August, having received representations from Chappell, Laud was convinced that the business was no more than an attempt to discredit the provost.[61] To help him sort the matter out he drew up a brief account of the dispute, circulating it to the various parties.[62] He was faced with a very difficult decision. Privately his preference was to preserve the authority of the provost rather than 'give . . . encouragement to such young heads'.[63] The difficulty was that passions were so high that to vindicate one side would seriously alienate the other, and Laud and Wentworth could afford to do neither: Chappell was his carefully chosen agent for the reform of Trinity, whose authority he was determined to preserve; but, equally, Ussher was the widely respected primate of the Church of Ireland. Ussher's acquiescence – at the very least – was essential if Laud and Wentworth were to put into effect their policy in Ireland. Rather than risk a decision, Laud asked Wentworth to look again at the matter on his return to Ireland and see if he could effect a compromise.[64]

His task did not prove easy. The hostility between the visitors and the provost and fellows had become personal. Chappell claimed that Ussher labelled him wilful and his writings childish, and, on another occasion, was aroused to 'a great passion' when Chappell appeared before him at the council table.[65] Laud thought it a 'grievous and a violent business' which had generated such passion that it had 'fallen into a fever', and was convinced that Ussher had taken a strong personal dislike to Chappell.[66] Wentworth, always a defender of a primate he regarded as saintly figure, suggested that the violence came less from Ussher than from his fellow visitor Anthony Martin, and was even (though only after the dispute was over) willing to concede privately the problem of Chappell's 'severity and stiffness of self-opinion'.[67] As a result, it was not until April 1637 that Laud was finally informed that the differences within the college,

---

[59] Scott and Bliss (eds.), *Laud*, VI, p. 468.   [60] *Ibid.*, VI, p. 464.   [61] *Ibid.*, VII, p. 275.
[62] *Ibid.*, VI, p. 468; Laud to Ussher, 18 October 1636, Scott and Bliss (eds.), *Laud*, VI, pp. 469 fol.
[63] *Ibid.*, VI, p. 467.   [64] *Ibid.*, VII, pp. 279–81, VI, p. 468.
[65] PRO, SP 63/256/6, ff. 23v, 18r.   [66] Scott and Bliss (eds.), *Laud*, VII, pp. 279 fol.
[67] Knowler (ed.), *The Letters and Despatches*, II, pp. 15, 26; Laud still blamed Ussher, Scott and Bliss (eds.), *Laud*, VII, p. 275; Sheffield, WWM, vol. VII, f. 169v.

and between the provost and the primate, had been settled by the lord deputy.

Each side could claim victory. Cullen, one of the original petitioners, was to be made a senior fellow, and the provost promised not to question the decisions of the visitors. On the other hand, Chappell's *protégé*, Ware, was admitted senior to Cullen, Feasant was expelled, and the provost was left free to take action against refractory fellows.[68] Though apparently a compromise, in fact the balance of power had shifted firmly towards Chappell, as the twin thrusts of the reform programme, replacement of personnel and statutory revision, made progress. Despite the appointment of Cullen (who in any case soon absented himself from the college), Chappell, with the help of Wentworth, was continuing to replace both staff and students with more candidates of their choosing.[69] Thus in April 1637 the lord deputy took the unusual step of ordering Trinity to elect John Harding as a senior fellow, an order that was repeated the following month, this time in favour of Thomas Marshall.[70] Both were graduates from Christ's College, Cambridge.[71] On 5 June 1637 two new senior and six new junior fellows were elected.[72] Of the latter, half were from Christ's.[73] On the following day, less than two months after their election as fellows, Harding was made vice-provost, and Marshall bursar.[74] By 1639 three out of the seven senior fellows were from Christ's.[75]

As the weeding out of troublesome members progressed, so too did the revising of the statutes. Throughout the dispute over precedence Laud had been working on a new draft. Laud thoroughly rewrote the existing code, which had been drawn up by Bedell in 1627.[76] Though he retained the basic structure of Bedell's statutes, he subjected each clause to a

---

[68] HMC, *Hastings Manuscripts*, IV, p. 73; Sheffield, WWM, vol. VII, f. 35r.

[69] TCD Mun. V/5/1, p. 62.   [70] TCD Mun. V/5/1, pp. 56 fol., 60, 62.

[71] Peile, *Biographical Register*, I, pp. 232, 253, 395 fol.

[72] TCD Mun. V/5/1, p. 58; for the text of the Laudian statutes see TCD Mun. V/2, printed in MacDonnell, *Chartae et Statuta*, pp. 29 fol.

[73] William Clopton, Robert Cock, John Garthwaite, TCD Mun. V/5/1, pp. 58 fol; Peile, *Biographical Register*, I, pp. 389 fol., 407, 427.

[74] TCD Mun. V/5/1, p. 60.

[75] Harding, Clopton, Hatfield, Mahaffy, *Epoch*, p. 252; Peile, *Biographical Register*, I, pp. 232, 389 fol., 395 fol.; Peile's identification of another fellow as a Christ's man is based on Mahaffy's erroneous transcription of the name of Gilbert Pepper as Christopher Pepper.

[76] Printed in Mahaffy, *Epoch*, pp. 327 fol. Though for convenience called here 'Bedell's statutes', Bedell's main role was in fact that of collator, bringing together the scattered originals, probably dating from the time of Temple, Shuckburgh (ed.), *William Bedell*, p. 272; Elrington (ed.), *Ussher*, XVI, p. 458; for the earliest references to statutes in Trinity see Mahaffy (ed.), *The Particular Book*, pp. 214b, 220b, TCD Mun. P/1/58. Temple's statutes were in their turn in partly derived from those of Cambridge (in particular Trinity College) as suggested by the charter, J. Morrin, *Calendar of the Patent Rolls and Close Rolls*

minute revision, extending even to punctuation. Unlike at Oxford, where Laud at the beginning had had a university committee to assist him, this first draft was his own work.[77] It was not until it was completed in October 1635 that he asked for comments from Chappell, Wentworth, Ussher and the archbishop of Dublin, Lancelot Bulkeley.[78] Though some amendments were suggested at this stage, there is little doubt that the final version of the statutes, which was approved and signed by the king and sent over to Ireland in March 1637, was primarily Laud's work; they are, rightly, called 'Laud's statutes'.[79] So extensive were the changes that Laud was proposing to the constitution of the college, that he had also to draft a new charter.[80] The new statutes and charter were formally accepted by the college on 5 June 1637.[81]

III

One way of exploring the underlying concerns which lay behind Laud's reform of Trinity is by identifying and analysing the changes that he made to the statutes. The themes which dominate are indeed the archetypal Laudian ones of order, hierarchy, discipline and detail. The new statutes seek to end the endemic feuds and quarrels by concentrating power in the hands of the sovereign, the chancellor and the provost.[82] The selection of the provost was entrusted entirely to the sovereign – the new charter removed the right of the fellows even to a 'free election' following royal nomination.[83] The power of the chancellor was greatly reinforced at the expense of the visitors – clearly reflecting the problems caused by the recent dispute. The number of visitors was reduced from seven to two – the archbishops of Dublin and Armagh – with the chancellor being placed over the visitors as primary visitor, to whom the two archbishops were to refer all important matters.[84] Within Trinity, Laud did all that he could

of Chancery in Ireland (2 vols., Dublin 1861–63), II, pp. 345 fol.; MacDonnell, Chartae et Statuta, p. 7; Laud had already been lent a copy of the College statutes by Bedell in 1628, Elrington (ed.), Ussher, XV, p. 396.

[77] Fincham, 'Early Stuart polity', p. 201; Scott and Bliss (eds.), Laud, VII, pp. 107, 116, 183.

[78] HMC, Hastings, IV, p. 62; Scott and Bliss (eds.), Laud, VII, pp. 183 fol., 212, 235, 248; Sheffield, WWM, vol. VI, pp. 271, 296.

[79] TCD Mun. V/5/1, p. 60; Scott and Bliss (eds.), Laud, VI, 487; Sheffield, WWM, vol. XX/165.

[80] Scott and Bliss (eds.), Laud, VI, 487, VII, 310; Sheffield, WWM, vol. VII, p. 19.

[81] TCD Mun. V/5/1, p. 58. For the text of the Laudian statutes see TCD Mun. V/2, printed in MacDonnell, Chartae et Statuta, pp. 29 fol.

[82] Cf. the similar thrust of his Oxford statutes, which sought to transfer power from congregation and convocation to the chancellor, Fincham, 'Early Stuart polity', p. 202.

[83] MacDonnell, Chartae et Statuta, p. 18.   [84] Ibid., pp. 26 fol.

to strengthen the position of the provost. Where Bedell had envisaged the provost and the senior fellows as governing the college together as an aristocracy, Laud was emphatic that 'in every well constituted society a parity of members is to be totally avoided, as tending to anarchy and universal confusion'.[85] Typical of Laud's revisions is the punishment for students who committed grave crimes and misdemeanours: where Bedell ordered them to be deprived by the provost with the consent of the majority of the senior fellows, Laud gave the power to expel them to the provost alone.[86]

Closely linked to his reinforcement of the authority of the provost was Laud's general tightening up of discipline, rules and procedures. He increased the number of deans to two, proscribed extravagant clothing, prescribed how the students were to conduct themselves towards the provost and fellows, and described more clearly how offending students were to be punished.[87] Some of the changes were relatively minor,[88] but others were of greater import, reflecting the hard-won lessons of the recent dispute. For example, the procedures for election to fellowship were revised to take account of the all-too-pertinent problem of what to do in the event of a stalemate – Laud simply gave the power of nomination to the chancellor.[89] Similarly, Laud tackled the laxity of the statutes over attendance at chapel, doubling Bedell's fine of one penny, and prescribing an exemplary punishment for recidivists: after a warning, continued failure to attend would result in their being expelled by the provost.[90] Equally pertinently, he eliminated a loophole in Bedell's statutes by insisting that the provost and all others of whatever rank were to be present

---

[85] Bedell's statutes, c.4, Mahaffy, *Epoch*, p. 335; Laud's statutes, c.4, MacDonnell, *Chartae et Statuta*, p. 35.

[86] Bedell's statutes, c.22, Mahaffy, *Epoch*, pp. 368 fol.; Laud's statutes, *c*. 23, MacDonnell, *Chartae et Statuta*, p. 92. See also the new powers given to the Provost to assign pupils to tutors, to veto the election of the vice-provost, to choose the examiners (along with the chief lecturer), and to decide on the allocation of rooms, Bedell's statutes, c.8, c.10, c.18, c.20, Mahaffy, *Epoch*, pp. 341, 346, 356, 364; Laud's statutes, c.10, c.12, c.19, c.21, MacDonnell, *Chartae et Statuta*, pp. 51, 58 fol., 73, 87.

[87] Bedell's statutes, c.11, c.9, Mahaffy, *Epoch*, pp. 343–9; Laud's statutes, c.13, c.11, MacDonnell, *Chartae et Statuta*, pp. 53–60.

[88] The new statutes lengthened the time which the provost was permitted to be absent from college on business, changed the dates and names of terms, fixed precise times for the election of college officers, and altered the hours during which the librarian had to be present in the library, Bedell's statutes, c.3, 10, 16, 18, 19, Mahaffy, *Epoch*, pp. 334, 346, 356, 360, 362; Laud's statutes, c.2, 10, 14, 17, 19, 20, MacDonnell, *Chartae et Statuta*, pp. 34, 58 fol., 63, 72 fol., 80, 82.

[89] Bedell's statutes, c.25, Mahaffy, *Epoch*, pp. 372–4; Laud's statutes, c.25, MacDonnell, *Chartae et Statuta*, p. 98.

[90] Bedell's statutes, c.11, Mahaffy, *Epoch*, pp. 347 fol.; Laud's statutes, c.13, MacDonnell, *Chartae et Statuta*, pp. 60–2.

for prayers on all festivals in clean surplices and (where appropriate) hoods.[91]

Laud also regulated the college's academic life. In an effort to ensure that Trinity extended its graduate studies beyond divinity, the new statutes insisted that one of the fellows should study law and one medicine.[92] Like the Oxford statutes, the Trinity ones paid particular attention to the performance of academic exercises.[93] Laud also reformed the curriculum, specifying precise textbooks for the students and revising the subjects each of the four undergraduate classes were to study, reasserting the primacy of Aristotle in what had previously been a Ramist institution.[94]

Finally, Laud also turned his attention to the religious life of the college, and here in particular some of his underlying theological and religious concerns are apparent. His revisions demonstrate a particular interest in the due observance of liturgy and ceremony, including requiring the use of the English rather than the Irish prayer book.[95] In the statute De Cultu Divine he sought to ensure that services were performed regularly and with due respect, paying particular attention to the Eucharist and the duty of frequent public prayer.[96] He also sought to downplay the importance of preaching and the Word. Bedell's provision for the recitation by students of parts of the Bible from memory during lunch or dinner, and his acceptance that this might usefully give rise to pious discourse, was omitted by Laud.[97] In Bedell's version a fellow on election swore to serve the church of God 'by engaging in the ministry of the Word'. Laud dropped this phrase.[98] A parallel elision occurred in the provost's oath, where Bedell had affirmed the Protestant primacy of the Word over

---

[91] Bedell's statutes, c.1, Mahaffy, *Epoch*, pp. 329 fol.; Laud's statutes, c.9 MacDonnell, *Chartae et Statuta*, p. 45; it should be noted that Provost Temple, who may well have drafted the original version of Bedell's statutes, strongly resisted the wearing of the surplice, TCD Mun., P/1/69, 70.

[92] If none wanted to do so, a fellow was to be nominated, and if he refused, expelled: Laud's statutes, c.18, MacDonnell, *Chartae et Statuta*, pp. 74 fol.

[93] Bedell's statutes, c.14, Mahaffy, *Epoch*, p. 354; Laud's statutes, c.16, MacDonnell, *Chartae et Statuta*, pp. 68–72.

[94] Bedell's statutes, c.13, Mahaffy, *Epoch*, pp. 351 fol.; Laud's statutes, c.15, MacDonnell, *Chartae et Statuta*, pp. 66 fol.

[95] Bedell's statutes, c.1, Mahaffy, *Epoch*, pp. 329, 331; Laud's statutes, c.9 MacDonnell, *Chartae et Statuta*, pp. 45, 47. The insistence on the English prayer book is curious, since the Irish one conformed to its English counterpart.

[96] Bedell's statutes, c.1, Mahaffy, *Epoch*, pp. 329, 331, 348; Laud's statutes, c.9, MacDonnell, *Chartae et Statuta*, pp. 44 fol., 49, 60 fol.

[97] Bedell's statutes, c.1, Mahaffy, *Epoch*, p. 331; Laud's statutes, c.9 MacDonnell, *Chartae et Statuta*, p. 48; Shuckburgh (ed.), *William Bedell*, p. 25.

[98] Bedell's statutes, c.7, Mahaffy, *Epoch*, p. 340; Laud's statutes, c.8 MacDonnell, *Chartae et Statuta*, p. 44.

tradition.[99] A similar change was made in the statute 'De Baccalaure-
orum et Magistrorum Exercitiis', which in Bedell's version included a
ringing attestation of the sole purpose of preaching being to convey and
consolidate faith. In Laud's revision the reference was toned down considerably, adding 'good manners' to faith as the edifying purpose of the
masters' exercises.[100]

The statutes also contained a faint but clear echo of the debate over
Sunday observance. In *De Cultu Divino* Laud eliminated the godly ideal
of 'keeping Sunday holy' and replaced it with the more neutral and unsab-
batarian 'observing', adding to this the anti-Puritan requirement that 'all
other feast-days' also be kept.[101] Indeed, Laud already thought the Irish
church particularly lax in this latter regard, and in the statutes repeatedly
had to add references to feast-days.[102]

Further evidence of underlying theological concerns in the rewriting of
the Trinity statutes can be seen in their approach to the Roman Catholic
church. The Church of Ireland was deeply hostile to Catholicism,
as evident in its 1615 confession, which declared that the pope was
Antichrist.[103] Bedell's statutes match this hostility in defining the purpose of the university as being to help free 'the Irish people oppressed
by the tyranny of antichristian religion', and enjoining the provost and
senior fellows to ensure that 'no papal or any other heretical religious
opinion' flourished in the college – a formula also found in the statutes of
those other two Puritan foundations, Emmanuel and Sidney Sussex.[104]

---

[99] Bedell's statutes, c.3, Mahaffy, *Epoch*, pp. 333 fol.; Laud's statutes, c.3, MacDonnell,
Chartae et Statuta, pp. 33 fol.

[100] Bedell's statutes, c.14, Mahaffy, *Epoch*, p. 353; Laud's statutes, c.16, MacDonnell,
Chartae et Statuta, p. 69.

[101] Bedell's statutes, c.1, Mahaffy, *Epoch*, p. 331; Laud's statutes, c.9, MacDonnell, *Chartae
et Statuta*, p. 49.

[102] Scott and Bliss (eds.), *Laud*, VII, pp. 299, 305, 309; Laud's statutes, c.9, 13,
MacDonnell, *Chartae et Statuta*, pp. 49, 60; Bedell's statutes had in fact gone to some
length to remove references to feast days. Compare Bedell's c.11 with its model, from the
statutes of Trinity College, Cambridge, from which it is copied. Cambridge: 'ut omnes
socii, discipuli . . . diebus festis et Dominicis precibus matutinis ac vespertinis, diebus
autem profestis saltem matutinis intersint', *Documents Relating to the University and Colleges of Cambridge* (3 vols., London, 1852), III, pp. 419 fol. Bedell: 'ut omnes socii, discipuli . . . diebus Dominicis precibus, sacrae communioni, et concionibus, diebus autem
profestis, precibus matutinis et vespertinis ad horam constitutam intersint': Bedell's
statutes, c.11, Mahaffy, *Epoch*, p. 347.

[103] *Articles of religion agreed upon by the archbishops and bishops, and the rest of the cleargie of
Ireland in the convocation holden at Dublin in the yeare of our Lord God 1615: for the avoidance
of diversities of opinions: and the establishing of consent touching true religion* (Dublin, 1615),
article 80.

[104] Bedell's statutes, c.1, Mahaffy, *Epoch*, p. 332; *Documents Relating to the University and
Colleges of Cambridge*, III, pp. 503, 556, the Sidney Sussex phrase was abrogated by
James II.

Laud's revision had a markedly different ecclesiological perspective. The reference to antichristian religion was removed entirely, and the 'any other' from 'papal or any other heretical religious opinion' was simply deleted, suggesting a much more moderate approach towards the status of the Roman Catholic church.[105]

Finally, the new statutes also demonstrate a Laudian concern to stress the distinctiveness of the clerical state. References are added distinguishing those students or staff who were ordained from those who were not, and prescribing that students or fellows should be ordained. For example, to Bedell's requirement that all masters perform the solemn duty of public prayers, Laud added the caveat that they must be ordained priests or deacons.[106]

IV

Although he consulted with the king on several occasions over the reform of Trinity College, it is amply apparent from his correspondence with Wentworth that the implementation and even the formulation of policy on this issue, as in other matters relating to religious affairs in Ireland, was left up to Laud.[107] Assessment of the Laudian changes in the statutes can therefore be related directly to Laud's personal convictions and motivation. Particularly in the area of religious life, the statutes repeatedly, if sometimes quietly, echo familiar concerns in Laud's personal theology: order and decency in the conduct of religious ceremonies, with a particular emphasis upon the Eucharist and prayer and a consequent tendency to diminish the significance of preaching and the Word; anti-sabbatarianism and a desire to ensure the due observance of feast-days; a more moderate approach to the Church of Rome; and lastly, a heightened awareness of the distinctiveness and importance of the clerical state.[108]

---

[105] Laud's statutes, c.9, MacDonnell, *Chartae et Statuta*, p. 50.

[106] Bedell's statutes, c.1, 9, 14, 17, Mahaffy, *Epoch*, pp. 330, 354; Laud's statutes, c.9, 11, 16, 18, MacDonnell, *Chartae et Statuta*, pp. 47, 57, 70, 75.

[107] Scott and Bliss (eds.), *Laud*, VI, p. 468, VII, pp. 116, 122, 275, 281. Some have argued that the king played a much greater role than has been imagined in the formulation of religious policy, J. E. Davies, 'The growth and implementation of "Laudianism" with special reference to the southern province' (Oxford D.Phil. thesis, 1987); Kevin Sharpe, 'Archbishop Laud', *History Today*, 33 (1983).

[108] Ann Hughes, *The Causes of the English Civil War* (London, 1991), p. 98; Kenneth Fincham, *Prelate as Pastor. The episcopate of James I* (Oxford, 1990), pp. 235 fol., 279 fol.; K. L. Parker, *The English Sabbath: A study of doctrine and discipline from the Reformation to the Civil War* (Cambridge, 1988), pp. 50 fol., 112 fol., 189, 208–13; Anthony Milton, 'The Laudians and the Church of Rome c.1625–1640' (Ph.D. thesis, Cambridge University, 1989).

However, what these various elements add up to theologically is a matter of vigorous historical and historiographical dispute. To some contemporaries and to some recent historians, they show that Laud was an Arminian. For William Prynne, the organiser of the prosecution of Laud before the House of Lords in 1643, the archbishop was the leader of a conspiracy which sought to eliminate Calvinism and the principles of the Protestant reformation from the English church and replace them with an Arminian theology which led directly to Rome.[109] More modern interpretations have played down the conspiracy and firmly denied the Romanising tendencies, but nevertheless maintained that Laud was an Arminian in one or both of two meanings of the term: first, in the narrow theological sense, of believing in universal grace and questioning the Calvinist approach to double predestination; second, in a broader English meaning of the word, which brings together the various theological and ceremonial emphases of Laud and his allies, many of which flowed from their different concept of grace.[110] As an Arminian in either of these two senses, it is argued, Laud enthusiastically oversaw the implementation of changes in ceremonies and theology in the 1630s, while at the same time denouncing those who adhered to Calvinism as Puritans. The proclamation of June 1626 forbidding theological discussion of 'new opinions', though theoretically even-handed, was in fact used to suppress the public expression of Calvinist theology.[111] Moreover, this Arminian theology went hand in hand with a political philosophy which stressed order, hierarchy and obedience, and deeply feared the populist aspects of Calvinism. The result of these policies of Charles and Laud in the late 1620s and 1630s was 'a clear break with both the Jacobean and Elizabethan past'.[112]

There is, however, an alternative view of Laud's ideological motivation, which can be traced back to his defence at his trial. This is that he was simply fulfilling the normal responsibility of the primate of the Church of England – that of ensuring decency, order and conformity within the church, in accord with the wishes of its supreme governor. As

[109] William Prynne, *A Breviate of the Life of William Laud* (London, 1644); Prynne, *Canterburies Doome* (London, 1646).
[110] N. R. N. Tyacke, 'Puritanism, Arminianism and counter-revolution' in Conrad Russell (ed.), *The Origins of the English Civil War* (London, 1973); Tyacke, *Anti-Calvinists: The rise of English Arminianism c.1590–1640* (Oxford, 1990), appendix II; H. R. Trevor-Roper, *Catholics, Anglicans and Puritans* (London, 1987), p. 79; Fincham, *Prelate as Pastor*, pp. 5, 276–88; Andrew Foster, 'Church policies of the 1630s' in Richard Cust and Ann Hughes, *Conflict in Early Stuart England. Studies in religion and politics, 1603–1642* (London, 1989); P. Lake, 'Calvinism and the English church, 1570–1635', *Past and Present*, 114 (1987).
[111] D. R. Como, 'Predestination and political conflict in Laud's London', *Historical Journal*, 56 (2003).
[112] Tyacke, *Anti-Calvinists*, p. 245.

Laud himself put it, all he had engaged in was 'the maintenance of the doctrine and discipline of this Church established by law'.[113] Laud was thus the natural heir of archbishops such as Whitgift and Bancroft, who had also vigorously sought to impose their authority where they saw due order and decency threatened.[114] Far from himself being Arminian, in the strict sense of the term, Laud, it is claimed, felt that such issues were too complex to explore, and even-handedly sought to end public debate on the issue by Calvinists and Arminians alike. His broader theological concerns, rather than being the product of his theology of grace, came from a number of different intellectual sources, such as his interest in patristics. Laud was, it is true, hostile to Puritanism and promoted many clergy who were similarly inclined. But to see Arminianism as the driving force behind his policies is to allow oneself to be duped by Prynne's conspiracy theory.[115]

One example which has been cited in order to prove that the Laudian concern for order and discipline was divorced from any Arminian theological subtext is his chancellorship at Oxford. Kevin Sharpe, examining the 'ideals and objectives' behind Laud's policy in Oxford, points out that Laud's statutes were notable for the '*absence* of detailed injunctions on religious matters' and their '*silence* on questions of theological controversy'.[116] This is true, but not quite so significant as Sharpe claims. The silence is, in fact, less a product of Laud's theological disinterestedness, than of the nature of the statutes on which he was working. The Oxford statutes are *university* statutes, which one would in any case expect to focus primarily upon the efficient running and academic regulation of the institution. The Trinity statutes are, on the other hand, *college* statutes, a much more appropriate context to look at for the detailed regulation of religious observance and for evidence of the expression of Laud's theological concerns.

Was Laud, then, engaged in the elimination of Calvinism as the dominant theology in Trinity and its replacement by Arminianism? If so, what kind of Arminianism are we dealing with? The Laudian statutes certainly went beyond the tightening up of regulations to eliminate Puritanism and hinted at an alternative theological subtext. But by themselves they could not accomplish any such *renversement*. More significant in assessing the

---

[113] Scott and Bliss (eds.), *Laud*, IV, p. 373.

[114] G. W. Bernard, 'The Church of England *c.*1529–*c.*1642', *History*, 75 (1990), p. 201.

[115] P. O. G. White, 'The rise of Arminianism reconsidered', *Past and Present*, 101 (1983); White, *Predestination, Policy and Polemic: conflict and consensus in the English church from the Reformation to the Civil War* (Cambridge, 1992), chapters 14 and 15; Davies, 'The growth and implementation of "Laudianism"'; Sharpe, 'Archbishop Laud'.

[116] Sharpe, 'Archbishop Laud and the University of Oxford', pp. 56–62.

shift in the theological outlook of the college is the impact of the changes in personnel which went with the statutory revision. Much depended upon the religious and theological tenor of the provost, fellows and students, who would, after all, give life to the new statutes. In particular, to what extent did Chappell and the English students and fellows whom he imported represent an Arminian influx?

Some contemporaries clearly thought in such terms. As has been noted, defenders of Trinity in the 1620s sought to ensure the Calvinist succession against the threat of an Arminian provost. Laud's choice of Chappell in 1629 and 1634 merely confirmed their worst fears. Chappell's theological development has been the subject of varying interpretations. When he was appointed to the post of catechist in Trinity in 1612, he would have come with the double recommendation of being a Ramist, like the provost, and also a product of a good Calvinist, even Puritan, college.[117] By the 1620s, however, both his college's and Chappell's Calvinist credentials were more dubious. Christ's was no longer the godly stronghold of Perkins's day.[118] As for Chappell, as early as 1619 Ussher had been warned of his possible Arminianism by John Preston.[119] By 1634 Ussher and his friend Samuel Ward, the theology professor at Cambridge, had no doubts that Chappell, about to take up his post as provost, was an exponent of Arminianism, that Pelagian heresy which, Ward lamented, 'is much promoted underhand, both here and, as it seemeth, with you'.[120] Within two months of Chappell's appointment, the bishop of Dromore, Theophilus Buckworth (Archbishop Ussher's brother-in-law) was reported to Laud as having in private linked the new chancellor's determination to overthrow the college statutes and 'spoil the College' with Laud's encouragement of Arminianism in Ireland.[121]

Chappell further aroused suspicion by his replacement of the existing fellows and students by fellow Christ's men from England. In 1641, after the departure of his protector Wentworth, Chappell was accused in the Irish parliament of having 'subverted the ancient foundation' of Trinity, 'fetched in strangers' from among his pupils at Cambridge, and so discouraged 'the natives of this kingdom' that there was only one native senior fellow left.[122] Prynne added the sweeping allegation against Chappell that 'all his scholars were Arminians'.[123] In fact, however, little

[117] Morgan, *Godly Learning*, p. 258; H. C. Porter, *Reformation and Reaction in Tudor Cambridge* (Cambridge, 1958), pp. 236–8.

[118] Porter, *Reformation and Reaction in Tudor Cambridge*, pp. 417 fol., 420; Trevor-Roper, *Catholics, Anglicans and Puritans*, p. 49.

[119] Elrington (ed.), *Ussher*, XVI, p. 371.

[120] *Ibid.*, XV, pp. 578 fol., 581; XVI, p. 520.

[121] Scott and Bliss (eds.), *Laud*, VII, pp. 94 fol.   [122] *Commons' Jnl, Ire*, I, p. 197.

[123] Prynne, *Canterburies Doome*, pp. 178, 359; Masson, *Life of Milton*, I, p. 129.

evidence survives of the religious attitudes of the fellows or students he
brought over to Trinity. What is left is Chappell's own religious orientation. Here there are three key questions: first, was he an Arminian?;
second, if so, was Laud aware of this, and, more precisely, when did it
first come to his attention?; and, third, what did Laud then do?

Of Chappell's Arminianism, both in the narrow and the broad senses
of the term, there can be little doubt. Soon after his arrival in Ireland
Chappell made plain his dislike of the Calvinist theology of the Church
of Ireland (and deeply offended Ussher) by arguing in Irish Convocation
for the repeal of the Irish Articles of 1615 and their replacement by the
Thirty-Nine Articles.[124] Within Trinity, his approach to worship was a
cause of contention, particularly his habit of bowing to the altar upon
entering the chapel, a practice which was denounced by his opponents
as idolatry.[125] Chappell himself, in his verse autobiography, explained
the bitterness and misery of his time in Trinity in theological terms as a
continual struggle with the turbulent forces of Geneva.[126] Not surprisingly, one of the charges against Laud at his trial was his preferring the
Arminian Chappell, described by Prynne as 'the most notorious seducing
Arminian in the whole university of Cambridge', to the provostship.[127]
Ussher's successor as Professor of Theological Controversies at Trinity,
Joshua Hoyle, who had (mistakenly) accused Bedell of Arminianism and
later became a member of the Westminster Assembly, was to give evidence at Laud's trial that Chappell was 'a great Arminian', had preached
justification by works in Christ Church cathedral in Dublin, and had
declared that priests ought not to be subject to the secular power.[128]

The question remains, of course, of whether Laud was aware of
Chappell's Arminianism. Laud's defence, here as elsewhere when the
views of his *protégés* were thrown in his face, was to deny that Arminianism had anything to do with the person's preferment.[129] At his trial he
claimed that Chappell had been 'a Cambridge man, altogether unknown
to me save that I received from thence great testimony of his abilities, and

---

[124] Sheffield, WWM, vol. VI, p. 356; Scott and Bliss (eds.), *Laud*, VII, p. 287. On the
Irish Articles, see A. Ford, *The Protestant Reformation in Ireland, 1590–1641* (Frankfurt,
1987), pp. 194–204.
[125] Scott and Bliss (eds.), *Laud*, VII, p. 280; Sheffield, WWM, vol. VII, fol. 129v.
[126] Peck, *Desiderata Curiosa*, II, Book XI, p. 4.   [127] Prynne, *Canterburies Doome*, p. 178.
[128] See note 25 above; Scott and Bliss (eds.), *Laud*, IV, pp. 298 fol.; HMC, *House of Lords
Manuscripts*, XI (London, 1962), p. 440; on Hoyle see, A. à Wood, *Athenae Oxoniensis*,
ed. P. Bliss (4 vols., Oxford, 1813–20), II, cols. 382–3; J. Ware, *The Whole Works of Sir
James Ware concerning Ireland*, ed. W. Harris (2nd edn, 2 vols., Dublin, 1764), II, p. 341.
[129] Kenneth Fincham, 'William Laud and the exercise of Caroline ecclesiastical patronage',
Journal of Ecclesiastical History, 51 (2000), pp. 87–91, is sceptical of Laud's claims that
he promoted Calvinists as well as Arminians.

fitness for government, which that college then extremely wanted.'[130] At
the same time, he accepted that Chappell subsequently 'studied so long
the 5 pointes of Arminianism that he came round himselfe at last'.[131] But
Laud's knowledge of this came with the benefit of hindsight: 'No man ever
complained to me, that he favoured Arminianism.' If he had truly broken
the royal injunction banning public discussion of such controverted
points, then Archbishop Ussher should have punished him.[132] Chappell
is therefore an interesting case, since, first, Laud subsequently admitted
that he was, in the strict theological definition of the term, Arminian, and,
second, it is possible to trace Laud's and Wentworth's discovery of, and
attitude towards, Chappell's Arminianism at the time through their private (and presumably truthful) correspondence, and assess the honesty
of Laud's assertion that his Arminianism was immaterial to his choice for
Trinity.

To a certain extent, Laud's defence at his trial is confirmed by the
correspondence. He first refers to the possibility that Chappell might
be Arminian in a letter to Wentworth of 22 August 1636, indicating
his opinion that at the bottom of the dispute lay not merely a quarrel
between fellows and provost, but a major theological disagreement over
Arminianism. Laud made quite clear his longstanding opinion that

> Truth, whate'er it be, is not determinable by any human reason in this life. And
> therefore it were far better (had men that moderation) to be referred up to the next
> general known truth in which men might rest, than to distract their consciences
> and the peace of the church by descending into interminable particulars.[133]

By early September Laud had had confirmation that one of the causes
of Ussher's hostility to Chappell was 'that the provost inclines to
Arminianism'. Writing to Wentworth, Laud claimed, echoing his statement at his trial, that he had first encountered Chappell simply as someone who had been recommended to him as 'a sober man and a good
governor', but that if indeed he was Arminian, he would have no protection from Laud:

> If he have not in all things obeyed his Majesty's declaration concerning these
> points in difference, let him be punished, on God's name, as a man that attempts
> to break the peace of the church.[134]

Taken at face value, then, Laud was simply unfortunate to be associated with a client who turned out to have Arminian views. There are,
though, at least three grounds for suspicion about his own account of

---

[130] Scott and Bliss (eds.), *Laud*, IV, p. 299.
[131] HMC, *House of Lords Manuscripts*, XI, p. 440.   [132] *Ibid.*, IV, p. 299.
[133] *Ibid.*, VII, p. 275.   [134] *Ibid.*, p. 280 fol.

his relations with Chappell. First, Chappell was certainly not 'altogether unknown' to Laud at the time of his appointment as provost: by 1634 Laud had already been his patron for a significant period, having proposed him for the vacancy in 1629, and persuaded him to accept the deanery of Cashel in 1633.[135] Second, as his correspondence with Wentworth shows, it was misleading to imply that he was unaware of complaints about Chappell's theological leanings. Finally, his reference to punishment of Arminians being Ussher's responsibility, though strictly true, was disingenuous. The prime movers in ecclesiastical matters in Ireland were the king, Wentworth, Laud and Bramhall. When an Irish Calvinist bishop published a predestinarian treatise, it was Laud who conveyed to Ussher the royal order that the work be suppressed.[136] It was for Wentworth and Laud, not the timid Ussher, to initiate action against known Arminians who infringed the royal prohibition on debate over predestination. However, they had no intention of taking any such action against Chappell. Wentworth defended Chappell from the charge of idolatry – what Chappell did was no more than Wentworth had seen Bishop Andrewes do hundreds of times in the king's chapel – and with regard to Arminianism, ever pragmatic, he confessed: 'Sure I am the provost is an excellent preacher, but whether an Arminian I can neither tell nor am able to judge because I understand not the points.' As for punishment, Wentworth casually disregarded Laud's stern words: 'Your grace saith he never declared himself to you, and by my troth he shall never be asked the question by me.'[137] Laud accepted that Chappell was an Arminian, but, conniving in Wentworth's laxity, dismissed the matter lightly, saying that he would be accounted guilty of whatever Wentworth wished.[138] Unsurprisingly, Chappell escaped unpunished.

The difficulty for Laud and Wentworth was that Chappell was indispensable in carrying through their self-imposed task of reforming Trinity. Searches for a replacement proved fruitless.[139] Even when he was rewarded with the sees of Cork and Ross in 1638, despite the clear injunction in the new Laudian statutes against such pluralism, Wentworth and Laud allowed Chappell to remain as provost, ignoring in the process righteous protests from Archbishop Ussher.[140] It was not until 20 July 1640, some three months after Wentworth (now earl of Strafford)

---

[135] Scott and Bliss (eds.), *Laud*, VI, pp. 355 fol. Chappell refers to Laud as 'patronum meum', Peck, *Desiderata Curiosa*, II, bk. XI, p. 4; cf. Wentworth's comments in Sheffield, WWM, vol. VI, p. 356.

[136] As in the case of George Downham, *The Covenant of Grace* (Dublin, 1631): Scott and Bliss (eds.), *Laud*, VI, p. 375.

[137] Sheffield, WWM, vol. VI, pp. 356 fol.

[138] Scott and Bliss (eds.), *Laud*, VII, pp. 287 fol.   [139] *Ibid.*, VI, p. 535, VII, p. 464.

[140] *Ibid.*, VI, p. 535, VII, pp. 447, 463, Sheffield, WWM, vol. VII, f. 128v.

had finally left Ireland, that Chappell politicly decided to resign the provostship and retire to his bishopric.[141] With Strafford's departure, and the political crisis in England, the Laudian attempt to reform Trinity collapsed. In February 1641 the Irish House of Commons established a committee to consider the affairs of the College, with a wide remit to visit Trinity, and examine its charters and statutes, investigate 'innovations of . . . government', and consider all grievances.[142] The names of those who came forward were not unfamiliar: Charles Cullen and Thomas Feasant.[143] Chappell was ordered to remain in Dublin while articles of impeachment were drawn up against him, only escaping to England after the rebellion of October 1641 provided more urgent matters for consideration.[144]

V

The Laudian reform of Trinity can be viewed in several ways. On the surface it was about discipline and order. Archbishop Abbot struggled to reform Trinity in the second decade of the seventeenth century. Laud continued these efforts. With the statutes weighted in favour of democracy, Chappell had considerable difficulty both in asserting his authority and in imposing much-needed reforms upon what even Archbishop Ussher, his sternest opponent, conceded was an ill-governed society. Seen in this light, Chappell provided the firm hand that was necessary to rescue Trinity from anarchy, while Laud's revision of the statutes provided the essential constitutional support. Whatever the immediate fate of the reforms, in the long term the model constitution which he and Laud established governed the college from the Restoration until well into the nineteenth century.

But the dispute was more than an attempt to impose order on chaos. As Laud and Wentworth were well aware, it also aroused deeper ideological tensions – they accepted that while they could restore outward unanimity, private antipathy would continue.[145] Essentially, the reform policy aroused opposition for much the same reasons that Wentworth's other Irish policies did, because they attempted to subject Irish institutions to more direct English control, threatening the distinctive *modus vivendi* which the New English ruling class had arrived at in both church and state. Thus in Trinity selection of the provost passed from the fellows in Ireland to the king in England; the power previously held by the Irish

[141] TCD Mun. V/5/1, p. 5.   [142] *Commons' Jnl, Ire*, I, pp. 180, 186, 194 fol.
[143] *Ibid.*, pp. 204, 218, 232.
[144] *Ibid.*, pp. 204 fol., 221 fol., 228, 243 fol.; Kippis (ed.), *Biographia Britannica*, III, p. 441.
[145] Scott and Bliss (eds.), *Laud*, VI, pp. 499, 551 fol.

visitors was placed effectively in the hands of the English chancellor; the Irish prayer book was ditched for its English counterpart; Calvinism was replaced by Arminianism; and, most importantly, English fellows supplanted 'Irish' (i.e., New English) ones. The complaints in the Irish parliament in 1641–42 about the way in which the 'native' interest had been driven out of Trinity by Chappell's *protégés* were therefore symptomatic of much wider New English resentment and unease at their exclusion from power and influence under Wentworth.[146]

In addition to this political dimension, however, the problems encountered by Laud and Chappell in Ireland also had a distinctive theological context. Scholars may debate over the extent to which a Calvinist consensus existed in the Church of England. No such debate is likely in relation to the Church of Ireland in the early seventeenth century. It was firmly Calvinist, committed to double-predestination by its articles of faith, and therefore instinctively hostile to the reforms that Laud and Chappell attempted to introduce in the 1630s.[147] The appointment of Chappell challenged this consensus, not merely in Trinity, but also, as has been noted, in Convocation, and further exacerbated the situation by linking his reforms to the Arminian critique of Calvinism. To someone such as Bishop Buckworth, the appointment of Chappell to Trinity and his subsequent policies as provost would have fully justified his equation of Laudianism and Arminianism, whatever Laud's private disavowals. It is difficult to believe that Laud was himself unaware of Chappell's Arminianism.

What, then, of Laud's motives in reforming Trinity? Three overlapping elements have been identified. First, generally, there is his familiar interest in order, discipline and detail, so evident in his chancellorship at Oxford. Second, there is his particular involvement in religious issues, which is in marked contrast to his work on the Oxford code. Laud's Oxford statutes may be characterised as a practical exercise, demonstrating no theological or religious undercurrents. Trinity's can not. They betray *both* a concern with order *and* implicit theological subtexts which hint at markedly different intellectual emphases. They might be labelled, depending upon one's historiographical prejudices, Laudian or, in its broader sense, Arminian, or even *avant garde* conformist. Whatever the label, Laud's theological concerns were markedly different from those of his predecessors. Finally, there is complicated story of Laud's patronage of Chappell. Chappell was the firm provost that Laud so desired for Trinity. He was also an Arminian. Privately Laud distinguished his own predestinarian agnosticism from Chappell's conscious Arminianism and bewailed his opponents' obsession with 'that bugbear Arminianism', but publicly he continued to support him as the only possible provost.[148]

Trinity, like Ireland as a whole, offered Laud a rare and, for later historians, a revealing opportunity to implement his dearest ideological concerns. There is clearly much more to the battles and arguments of the 1630s than either a simple determination to establish firm government or a straightforward confrontation between Calvinism and Arminianism. At the same time, however, to discount entirely the role of theological principle and to portray the struggles solely in terms of an attempt by a detached chancellor to impose discipline upon a disordered society, as has been done in relation to Oxford, would be to neglect the 'other motives' which even Laud recognised as being present. It would also ignore the differing theological and ecclesiological emphases that can be discerned in Chappell's religious outlook and in Laud's revision of the statutes, and overlook the way in which these emphases furthered the broader ideals of 'Arminian' (as their opponents labelled them) or Laudian ministers, committed to creating a clericalist, sacramentally based, liturgically rich, non-Calvinist, visible church, half-way, as Chappell put it in his autobiography, between Rome and Geneva.[149]

[148] Scott and Bliss (eds.), *Laud*, VII, p. 275.
[149] See note 128 above.

8   The Irish peers, political power and parliament, 1640–1641

Jane Ohlmeyer

The contempt in which Thomas Wentworth, later earl of Strafford, held the Irish peerage is well known. Shortly after he arrived in Ireland in 1634 he noted how 'they would have nothing shew more great or magnificent than themselves so they might . . . lord it the more bravely and uncontrollably at home, take from the poor churl what, and as they pleased'.[1] The need to declaw and harness the power of these overmighty lords – Catholic and Protestant alike – quickly become a feature of Wentworth's lord deputyship. He rewarded and nurtured the select few, such as the earl of Ormond, and castigated and humiliated the vast majority.[2] The earls of Antrim, Clanricard, Cork, Fingal, Kildare, Meath and Westmeath; Viscounts Dillon of Costello-Gallen, Loftus of Ely, Roche of Fermoy, Sarsfield of Kilmallock, Valentia and Wilmot of Athlone; Lords Balfour of Glenawley, Esmond, Lambert, Mountnorris – to name just a few – all fell foul of Wentworth's waspish pen and heavy hand.[3]

Late in February 1641 the Irish peers struck back. A petition to the king articulated their collective position: 'That, of late years, the nobility of this your realm have been [held] in so little esteem, and so much undervalued by the powerfulness and misgovernment of Thomas, earl of Strafford.' Their appeal continued 'that by his untrue representations and misinformations unto your majesty' and his employment of 'sundry persons of mean condition' he had not only performed a great disservice to the king but had dishonoured the nobility.[4] This chapter analyses how the peers attempted to reverse this judgement and how they

I am grateful to the Leverhulme Trust for funding a Fellowship, which facilitated the research for this chapter, and to Micheál Ó Siochrú for commenting on an earlier draft of it.

[1] W. Knowler (ed.), *The Letters and Despatches . . .* (2 vols., London, 1739), I, p. 348.
[2] William P. Kelly, 'The early career of James Butler, twelfth earl, and first duke of Ormond (1610–1688), 1610–1643' (Ph.D. thesis, University of Cambridge, 1994), especially chapters 2 and 3.
[3] James Balfour, baron of Glenawley, died in the spring of 1639. He was succeeded by his brother, Alexander, who died shortly after his brother. The title then became extinct and has not been included in the Appendix.
[4] *Lords Jnl, Ire*, I, p. 164.

orchestrated their own onslaught against Wentworth, his acolytes and his policies in three distinct but interconnected arenas: the Irish parliament in Dublin, the English parliament at Westminster, and the royal court at Whitehall.[5]

I

By 1640 the Irish temporal peerage numbered 99 individuals: 30 were absentees, and of the 69 resident peers 29 were barons, 27 viscounts and 13 earls. In terms of religious persuasion, 33 were Catholic and 36 were Protestant (seven of whom were fairly recent converts from Catholicism). However, as contemporary commentators repeatedly pointed out, these religious divisions should not obscure the very real links of kinship, friendship and mutual indebtedness that united the parliamentary peers on the eve of the rebellion.[6] Given that most of these connections had been forged during the early decades of the seventeenth century, the nature of interrelationships in the 1640–41 House of Lords proved markedly different from those in the earlier Irish parliaments of 1613–15 and 1634–35. Twelve Catholic and four Protestant peers had attended the Lords in 1613, leaving the government embarrassingly dependent on the support of 20 bishops. Equally serious from the perspective of the Dublin administration, the 12 Old English peers, led by Lord Gormanston, enjoyed 'a mutual combination and confederacy' with the belligerent recusant MPs in the Commons and fully supported their boycott of proceedings when 11 withdrew from the house.[7] Given the recalcitrance of the recusant

---

[5] Conrad Russell, 'The British background to the Irish Rebellion of 1641' reprinted in *Unrevolutionary England, 1603–1642* (London, 1990), pp. 263–80 and Michael Perceval-Maxwell, 'Ireland and the monarchy in the early Stuart multiple kingdom', *Historical Journal*, 34 (1991), pp. 279–95. The parallels with developments in England, and, particularly, the extent to which the peers and their aristocratic networks shaped the critical opening months of the Long Parliament, are striking. See Sheila Lambert, 'The opening of the Long Parliament', *Historical Journal*, 28 (1984), pp. 265–87; Paul Christianson, 'The peers, the people, and parliamentary management in the first six months of the Long Parliament', *Journal of Modern History*, 49 (1977), pp. 575–99; Conrad Russell, *The Fall of the British Monarchies 1637–1642* (Oxford, 1991), chapters 5–7; and John Adamson, 'The baronial context of the English Civil War' reprinted in Richard Cust and Ann Hughes (eds.), *The English Civil War* (London, 1997), pp. 83–110 and 'Parliamentary management, men-of-business and the House of Lords, 1640–49' in Clyve Jones (ed.), *A Pillar of the Constitution. The House of Lords in British politics, 1640–1784* (London, 1989), pp. 21–50.

[6] For examples see Sir John Temple, *The Irish Rebellion . . .* (London, 1679), pp. 27–8 and [Arthur Annesley, earl of Anglesey], *A Letter from a Person of Honour . . . written to the earl of Castlehaven* (London, 1681), p. 31.

[7] *CSPI, 1611–14*, p. 352. Also see R. Dudley Edwards, 'Letter-book of Sir Arthur Chichester 1612–14', *Analecta Hibernica*, 8 (1938), pp. 70, 95–103; John McCavitt, 'An unspeakable parliamentary fracas: the Irish House of Commons, 1613',

peers in 1613, the king determined to increase the government majority in any future Irish parliament. Thus by 1634 the composition of the upper house had been radically transformed. Membership trebled to 123 – 99 lords temporal and 24 lords spiritual and – two-thirds of whom were Protestant and one third non-resident.[8]

This influx of new peers gave the government a clear majority, for the first time, an advantage that Lord Deputy Wentworth planned to make the most of. In a confidential memo sent to England in the spring of 1634, he outlined his parliamentary strategy:

> I shall endeavour, the lords house be so composed as that neither the Recusants, not [nor] yet the Protestants shall appear considerably more one than the other, and holding them as much as may be, upon equall balance, for they will prove them easier to governe, than if either party were absolute.[9]

For Wentworth's 'divide and rule' agenda to succeed in the Lords, he required the full support of the bishops (which the king agreed to secure for him) and control over the proxies of all of the non-resident peers.[10] In accordance with his wishes, the king encouraged non-residents to absent themselves and to send Wentworth their blank proxies. George Calvert, Lord Baltimore, noted how it had been suggested that he and 'other members of that Parliam[en]t that are here [i.e., in England], to be absent from it [the Irish parliament]', adding: 'I conceive it good manners to accept of it, for it is lit[t]le less of than a com[m]and to do soe.'[11] Thus Wentworth's strategy for managing the Lords revolved around his control over the thirty-six proxies of absent peers, preferring 'their proxies' to 'their company'.[12] As a result, eight peers, each armed with four or five proxies, 'could outvote all the temporal nobility present'.[13]

   Analecta Hibernica, 37 (1998), pp. 223–35 and *Sir Arthur Chichester. Lord Deputy of Ireland 1605–16* (Belfast, 1998), pp. 182–9; V. Treadwell, 'The House of Lords in the Irish parliament of 1613–15', *EHR*, 80 (1965), pp. 92–107.

[8] The bulk of creations dated from between 1617 and 1629 and included thirty-five non-resident peers, G. R. Mayes, 'The early Stuarts and the Irish peerage', *EHR*, 73 (1958), pp. 231–2, 233 and Hugh Kearney, *Strafford in Ireland 1633–41. A study in absolutism* (Cambridge, 1989), pp. 48–52.

[9] Sheffield, WWM, 14 (19), Strafford's 'Humble opinion concerning a Parliament [in Ireland]', annotated by John Coke, 12 April 1634, point no. 24.

[10] Knowler (ed.), *The Letters and Despatches*, II, p. 408; *CSPI, 1633–47*, pp. 237–8.

[11] Sheffield, WWM, XIV (117) for Baltimore. Also see 14 (126) and 14 (169) for Chaworth.

[12] Knowler (ed.), *The Letters and Despatches*, I, p. 246, also p. 240. Also *CSPI, 1633–47*, pp. 55, 59, 82, 93.

[13] *Lords Jnl, Ire*, I, p. 152. As a result, thirty-six proxies were then dished out to eight Protestant lords who could be relied upon to support the government. Protestant 'leaders', who held proxies in 1634 were Loftus of Ely, Baltinglass, Castle Stuart, Conway, Ormond, Moore of Drogheda, Esmond and Clandeboye.

Wentworth had his way in 1634 – but what of his second Irish parliament?[14] How many of the 69 resident temporal peers were politically active in 1640–41? According to the lists printed in the *Journals of the House of Lords*, attendance at this parliament was small, especially when compared with the 1634 parliament (which had attracted 43 temporal lords for the first session, 39 for the second, and 24 for the third). Only 38 (55 per cent) of the resident lords attended at least one of the sessions in 1640; while the opening session of 1641 (26 January – 5 March) attracted only 24 (35 per cent) temporal peers. The reasons for this low turnout in January 1641 are fourfold.[15] First, a number of absences can be easily explained: Le Power was a lunatic; Hamilton of Strabane was a minor; Roche of Fermoy had been banished to London; Cork asked that his two sons be excused 'in regard they were both underage';[16] while ill-health and old age kept Chichester and Athenry at home (though they sent proxies). Second, Castlehaven, Clanricard and Conway, who all held English titles, took their seats in the English Lords, as did Cork in his capacity as an English privy councillor. Cork's eldest son, Dungarvan, and Lord Herbert of Castle Island sat as MPs in the English Commons. Third, a significant number of Irish peers had flocked to London either as members of a delegation from the Lords or as prosecution witnesses at Wentworth's trial which began on 22 March 1641 (frenzied preparations for it dated from mid-November 1640).[17] Finally, a number of Protestant lords who had supported the government with such enthusiasm in 1634 stayed away from the early sessions of 1641.[18] Given a frustrating absence of evidence for the final sessions (the journals from 5 March to 1 August 1642 are not extant), it is likely that attendance for the heated fourth session (11 May until 7 August, when it was adjourned) was much higher and included a significant number of the lords who had been absent in England for the earlier sessions.[19]

[14] The first session of Charles I's second Irish parliament met between 16 March and 17 June 1640; the second session between 1 October and 12 November 1640; the third session between 26 January and 5 March 1641; the fourth session between 11 May and 17 November 1641 (it was adjourned 7 August and reassembled 16 November); and the fifth session, attended by only a handful of Protestant peers, between 11 January 1642 and 9 February 1647.

[15] The house mandated on 11 February 1641 that no lord might be excused 'without any just cause' and fined delinquents accordingly, *Lords Jnl, Ire*, I, p. 149. Bríd McGrath has shown that Wentworth actively encouraged some of these absences to enhance the government's ability to manage the Lords, see chapter 9 below.

[16] A. B. Grosart (ed.), *The Lismore Papers*, NS (10 vols., 1886–8), 2nd series, IV, p. 106.

[17] For details see the Appendix, pp. 180–5.

[18] They included Thomond, Lecale, Esmond and Clandeboye (though Thomond and Esmond reappeared for the fourth session).

[19] *Lords Jnl, Ire*, I, p. 274. Also see Paul Christianson, 'The obliterated portions of the House of Lords Journals dealing with the attainder of Strafford, 1641', *EHR*, 95 (1980), pp. 339–53.

With about a dozen exceptions, the bulk of the peers who attended in 1640–41 had taken their seats in the upper house in 1634, while Muskerry and Sarsfield of Kilmallock had served as MPs in the Irish Commons, and Lambert had gained political experience in the English Commons in 1626 and 1628–29.[20] Twenty-three 'activists' (see the Appendix for details) quickly emerged.[21] Of these 23 lords, 13 were Catholic (only Antrim and Slane lacked previous parliamentary experience) and 10 Protestant (only Baltinglass lacked previous parliamentary experience). As Bríd McGrath's research on the Irish Commons of 1640–41 demonstrates, virtually all of them enjoyed links with members of the lower house.[22]

Perhaps because of the poor turnout, the Lords quickly settled down to business. By the end of March 1640 four subsidies had been voted 'with one voice'.[23] Wentworth, now on the verge of departure from Ireland, was delighted with the proceedings and attributed this to the intervention of key ministers of the state, which ensured that the others dare neither 'to oppose or open their mouths'.[24] While the Lords may have been cowed into compliance during the spring of 1640, at the beginning of the second session on 1 October they adopted a more belligerent stance. As the political climate shifted dramatically in England, they took the offensive, picking as their battleground the government's manipulation of proxies in 1634. Determined that this should not happen again, Gormanston, whose father had led the Old English opposition in 1613, supported by Digby of Geashill, a Protestant newcomer, moved 'that no proxy be received without sight of the proxy, and allowance of this House'.[25] Gormanston and Sarsfield of Kilmallock then asked the

---

[20] Upper Ossory, Trimelston, Dunboyne, Antrim, Fingal, Thomond, Baltinglass, Clanmalier, Montgomery, Muskerry, Sarsfield of Kilmallock, Magennis of Iveagh acceded to their titles after 1634.

[21] The term 'activist' has been used here to describe anyone who attended the Lords regularly, participated in debates, sat on committees (especially the important Committee of Privileges and Grievances) or served as members of delegations to England.

[22] See chapter 9 below and Bríd McGrath, 'A biographical dictionary of the membership of the Irish House of Commons 1640–1641' (Ph.D. thesis, Trinity College, Dublin, 1997). Thus the sons of Mayo, Moore and Fingal sat as MPs; as did the brothers of Baltinglass, Digby of Geashill and Maguire. Kerry, Gormanston, Slane, Netterville, Fingal, Moore of Drogheda, Baltinglass, Trimelston, Slane, Sarsfield of Kilmallock either had a father-in-law, a son-in-law or a brother-in-law who sat in the Commons. While friends, clients or tenants of Ormond, Kerry, Antrim, Netterville, Maguire, Muskerry, Slane, Dunsany, Howth, Lambert, Sarsfield of Kilmallock served as MPs. Also see the Appendix.

[23] *Lords Jnl, Ire*, I, pp. 102, 106–7.

[24] Knowler (ed.), *Letters and Despatches*, II, p. 402.

[25] *Lords Jnl, Ire*, I, p. 138. The proxy reforms of 1626 in the English House of Lords were the result of the concerted effort of the opposition peers, Jess Stoddart Flemion, 'The nature of opposition in the House of Lords in the early seventeenth century: a revaluation' in Clyve Jones and David Lewis Jones (eds.), *Peers, Politics and Power: the House of Lords, 1603–1911* (London, 1986), p. 8.

Committee of Privileges and Grievances to consider whether 'lords as
have titles of honour only in this kingdom, and no lands, may be compelled to purchase lands in a convenient time, or otherwise forfeit their
votes in parliament'.[26]

The issue of proxies and the absentee peers, together with fifteen other
grievances relating to Wentworth's 'unlawful, arbitrary and tyrannical
government', formed the basis of a list of grievances from the Lords
(18 February 1641) and a further petition to the king from Gormanston
and Sarsfield of Kilmallock.[27] Their complaints coalesced around a number of issues that had long concerned the Old English members of both
houses, together with others that related to Wentworth's harsh treatment of the peers: unlawful imprisonment, the use of scornful language,
preventing the peers from hunting on their own land, and placing his
cronies in positions of authority.[28] In February 1641 the Irish Commons
provided further fodder for those determined to topple Wentworth by
compiling a list of twenty-one 'Queries' for the Irish judges, which questioned the legality of his government of Ireland since 1634. As Aidan
Clarke has noted, these Queries 'were not simply a random series of
grievances: they were, rather, the balanced ingredients of a calculated
policy of rendering impossible a repetition of the events of the recent past
by establishing an agreed delimitation of the competence of the executive
government'.[29] Then, at the end of February, impeachment charges were
brought against Wentworth's leading administrators: Richard Bolton, the
lord chancellor; John Bramhall, the bishop of Derry; Gerard Lowther,
the chief justice of the common pleas; and Sir George Radcliffe, Wentworth's private secretary (the latter case was dropped).[30] Ultimately these
impeachment proceedings came to naught, but, in the short term, they
deprived the chief governor of key defence witnesses at his trial.

The anti-Wentworth factions in London immediately seized upon
these collective grievances, and they formed the basis of a number of
charges subsequently brought against the disgraced earl.[31] Wentworth's

---

[26] *Lords Jnl, Ire*, I, p. 142, also p. 147.

[27] *Ibid.*, p. 157; and *CSPI, 1633–47*, pp. 261–2.

[28] *CSPI, 1633–47*, pp. 261–3. With the exception of the spiritual lords these petitions
enjoyed the overwhelming support of the peers, *Lords Jnl, Ire*, I, p. 150.

[29] Aidan Clarke, 'The policies of the "Old English" in parliament, 1640–41' in J. L.
McCracken (ed.), *Historical Studies V* (London, 1965), p. 93. Also see Aidan Clarke,
'Patrick Darcy and the constitutional relationship between Ireland and Britain' in Jane
Ohlmeyer (ed.), *Political Thought in Seventeenth-Century Ireland* (Cambridge, 2000),
pp. 38–46 and chapter 10 below.

[30] *CSPI, 1633–47*, p. 259. This had been in the pipeline since the previous November,
John McCafferty, '"To follow the late precedents of England": the Irish impeachment
proceedings of 1641' in D. S. Greer and N. M. Dawson (eds.), *Mysteries and Solutions
in Irish Legal History* (Dublin, 2001), pp. 51–72.

[31] John Rushworth (ed.), *The Tryal of Thomas, Earl of Strafford* (London, 1680) and Maija
Jansson, *Proceedings of the Long Parliament*, III (Rochester, NY, 2002).

heavy-handed treatment of the Irish peers – especially Clanricard, Cork, Wilmot of Athlone, Loftus of Ely and even Mountnorris – had alarmed many English lords who no doubt felt that a dangerous precedent was being set.[32] In order to raise awareness further among the English political nation about Wentworth's 'powerful acts', the Irish peers bombarded the English Lords and Commons with petitions over the winter of 1640 and spring of 1641.[33] Details of Mountnorris's humiliations since 1635 were also printed and circulated in London. According to one tract, Wentworth's 'arbitrary forme of government' had deprived Mountnorris 'of those honourable imployments', 'his owne private fortunes, and the birthright and liberty of a subject', together with his 'his honour and integrity'.[34] The anti-Wentworth propaganda mill was also fed by reproducing the Queries alongside various speeches made to the Lords by the Speaker of the Irish Commons 'concerning their priviledges, and their exorbitant grievances in that kingdome'.[35] The Irish contribution to Wentworth's downfall was not simply limited to petitions and pamphlets. In all, at least nineteen Irish peers (twelve Protestant and seven Catholic) appeared in London to testify against him.[36] At the trial Wentworth claimed that 'a strong conspiracy against me' had been hatched between the Irish Lords and the English Commons.[37] Even though Wentworth later withdrew this allegation and apologised, there is undoubtedly some truth in it.

[32] Knowler (ed.), *The Letters and Despatches*, I, pp. 479, 508 and II, pp. 2, 6, 131, 152; Edward Hyde, earl of Clarendon, *History of the Rebellion*, ed. W. D. Macray (6 vols., Oxford, 1888; reissued 1992), I, pp. 293, 295.

[33] They included Roche of Fermoy, Kildare, Dillon of Costello-Gallen, Loftus of Ely, Mountnorris, Meath, Westmeath, Valentia and Netterville, Michael Perceval-Maxwell, *The Outbreak of the Irish Rebellion* (Dublin, 1994), pp. 95–6, 101; HMC, *Report 4. Part 1. Report and Appendix* (London, 1874), pp. 44, 51, 58, 61, 68, 101, 102; Rushworth (ed.), *The Tryal of Thomas, Earl of Strafford*, pp. 16, 18; *Journals of the [English] HL*, IV: *1628–42*, pp. 151, 168; *CSPI, 1647–60*, pp. 253–4.

[34] *The Sentence of the Councell of vvarre* . . . [London, 1641], pp. 18, 11–2, 15. Also see *A True Copie of the Sentence of Warre pronounced against Sir Francis Annesley* . . . (London, 1641).

[35] *A Speech Made before the Lords in The Upper House of Parliament in Ireland, by Captain Audley Mervin* . . . (London, 1641). Also see *Captaine Audley Mervin's speech* . . . (London, 1641); *Irelands complaint against Sir George Ratcliffe* . . . (London, 1641) and *Sixteene queres propounded by the Parliament of Ireland* . . . [London, 1641]. Interestingly, a copy of Mervyn's speech to the Irish House of Lords, 4 March 1640/1 is extant in the Bristol archive Public Record Office, PRO 31/8/198 transcripts of the Digby MSS, 1605–1695, p. 565; together with lists of the February grievances from the Irish House of Lords (pp. 537, 543).

[36] See the Appendix for the names. Rushworth (ed.), *The Tryal of Thomas, Earl of Strafford*, pp. 14, 113, 159; *Journals of the [English] HL*, IV: *1628–42*, p. 188.

[37] Rushworth (ed.), *The Tryal of Thomas, Earl of Strafford*, p. 113; Lambert, 'The opening of the Long Parliament', pp. 275–6, 279, 281, suggests that, despite Pym's prominence as spokesman in the impeachment proceedings, 'the commoners were very much junior partners' (p. 276).

Certainly kinship, marriage and clientage links afforded a select coterie of Irish peers, especially Antrim, Cork and Clanricard, direct access to influential, and often overlapping, patronage networks in both the English parliament and at court.[38] Antrim's marriage to the duke of Buckingham's widow brought him the patronage of Charles I himself, together with that of his queen and William Laud, archbishop of Canterbury. The Villiers connection also linked Antrim to the earls of Desmond, Arundel, Suffolk, Northampton, Nithsdale and Pembroke and two of the most powerful men at court – the dukes of Hamilton and Lennox (the latter of whom was in 1641 also created duke of Richmond).[39] As Patrick Little and Michael Perceval-Maxwell have shown, Cork's English contacts were also impressive. Since the early 1630s he had assiduously cultivated members of the queen's court by wedding his children off to influential members of it, including Sir Thomas Stafford, the queen's gentleman usher, Lord Goring, her master of horse, and the earl of Dorset, her lord chamberlain. Cork also enjoyed, again thanks largely to astute marriages, contacts with the opposition earls of Bristol, Salisbury, Northumberland, Warwick and Bedford.[40] Although Clanricard's English contacts may not have been as extensive as Cork's or Antrim's, his prolonged residence at court and his deep ties of kinship ensured that he exercised as much, if not more, influence. He enjoyed access to the opposition peers thanks to the political influence of his stepbrother, the earl of Essex, and his friendship with the earl of Bristol.[41] Clanricard's courtly contacts included the earl of Northampton (his father-in-law), the Catholic marquis of Winchester (his brother-in-law), the earl of Holland, a prominent member of the queen's household, and the duke of Lennox and Richmond, the king's cousin and a great favourite. Presumably it was Clanricard who ensured that members of the Irish delegation, Thomas Bourke and Nicholas Plunkett, enjoyed 'private access' to the king during their negotiations on behalf of the Irish parliament.[42]

---

[38] Carte, *Ormond*, VI, p. 219; Clarendon, *History of the Rebellion*, I, p. 202; Knowler (ed.), *The Letters and Despatches*, I, p. 333.

[39] Jane Ohlmeyer, *Civil War and Restoration in the Three Stuart Kingdoms: the political career of Randal MacDonnell, first marquis of Antrim (1609–83)* (Cambridge, 1993; paperback reprint, Dublin, 2001), pp. 49–55.

[40] Patrick Little, 'The earl of Cork and the fall of the earl of Strafford', *Historical Journal*, 39 (1996), pp. 626–7.

[41] Patrick Little, '"Blood and friendship": the earl of Essex's protection of the earl of Clanricarde's interests, 1641–6', *EHR*, 112 (1997), pp. 927–41. Clarendon, *History of the Rebellion*, I, p. 197.

[42] HMC, *Report on the Manuscripts of the Earl of Egmont*, I, part I (London, 1905), p. 129. Certainly both Clanricard and Cork took a very keen interest in the activities of the Irish Committee 'whose counsel', according to Clarendon, 'was entirely followed in whatsoever concerned' Ireland, Hyde, *History of the Rebellion*, I, p. 370.

The fact that Cork and Clanricard focused their efforts on influencing politics in London (neither returned home until the summer of 1641) should not obscure their political clout in Ireland. While Cork saved his sons for well-connected English heiresses, he married his daughters into some of the great Irish aristocratic families. The earl of Barrymore, who had been his ward, married Alice, and this linked Cork to many of the leading Catholic lords. Another daughter, Sarah, wed as her first husband the younger brother of Viscount Moore of Drogheda, while Robert Digby of Geashill was her second. Joan Boyle married George, earl of Kildare, himself a ward of Lennox before Cork took over his guardianship.[43] Finally, Katherine married Arthur Jones, Viscount Ranelagh's son and heir, who sat as an MP in the Long Parliament. Bonds of indebtedness supplemented these ties of marriage: Kildare and Barrymore quickly became financially dependent on their father-in-law; while Cork lent money to a host of other Irish peers.[44] Patrick Little has suggested that 'Cork's extensive correspondence shows that his ready abdication of parliamentary influence in the Irish House of Lords was matched by an astonishing lack of interest in the elections for the lower house in the spring of 1640.'[45] This may well have been true; but, in the event, many of his kinsmen and clients were nevertheless returned.[46] What then of Clanricard? In the Lords, he was related by marriage to Brittas, Castle Connell, Clanmories (which in turn allied him to Slane and the lords of the Pale) and Mayo. While Clanricard could not muster the same number of supporters in the Irish Commons as Cork, he served as the patron to at least six influential lawyers, who played a critical role in shaping developments in the later sessions of 1641.[47] In addition, he had a number

[43] Patrick Little, 'The Geraldine ambitions of the first earl of Cork', *IHS* (2002), pp. 151–68.

[44] They included Lords Muskerry, Sarsfield of Kilmallock, Fitzwilliam, Dowcra, Valentia, and Roscommon, Grosart (ed.), *The Lismore Papers,* 1st series, V, pp. 9, 17, 171, 184, 210–11, 232–3.

[45] Little, 'The earl of Cork', p. 624 and chapter 9 below.

[46] Ties of debt associated him with Peregrine Bannister (MP for Clonakilty) and Patrick Barnewall of Kilbrew (MP for Trim). He was related to Joshua Boyle (MP for Ardee) and family marriages linked him to a twelve further MPs including Viscount Chichester's second son, John (MP for Dungannon), Simon Digby (MP for Philipstown), and Sir William Parsons, master of the Court of Wards and MP for Wicklow county, McGrath, 'A biographical dictionary', pp. 51, 55, 75, 82, 106, 120, 135, 145, 166, 209, 211, 233–4, 237, 245, 257, 267, 275, 285, 292.

[47] Sir Richard Blake, MP for County Galway in 1640; Sir Valentine Blake, MP for Galway in 1640; Geoffrey Browne, MP for Athenry; Patrick Darcy, MP for [Tyrone?] 1640; Roebuck Lynch, MP for Galway; and Richard Martin, MP for Augher in 1640, McGrath, 'A biographical dictionary', pp. 69, 70, 81, 126, 202, 209. Also see Jane Ohlmeyer, 'Irish recusant lawyers during the reign of Charles I' and Bríd McGrath, 'Parliament men and the Confederate association' in Micheál Ó Siochrú (ed.), *Kingdoms in Crisis: Ireland in the 1640s* (Dublin, 2001), pp. 63–89 and 90–105.

of relatives who sat as MPs, including his nephew Thomas Burke, an active member of the Irish parliamentary delegation to London.[48]

Whether in London or Dublin, what united the Irish peers was their hostility to Wentworth. Having successfully ousted him (he was beheaded on 12 May 1641), they focused their efforts on a reform programme that aimed to dismantle any policies – especially those that related to land tenure and plantation – that threatened to undermine their Irish power bases. However, their stance on other matters demonstrates that this anti-Wentworth coalition was fluid and, at times, fraught with tensions. This meant that membership of various interest groups operating in the Lords fluctuated according to specific issues. However, as the parliamentary opposition increasingly grew in confidence, Ormond's position as the principal and, at times, only influential ally that the government had in the upper house (aside from the spiritual peers) forced him to resort to delaying and obstructionist tactics.[49] For example, in the impeachment proceedings against Wentworth's acolytes, Lord Lambert, with Catholic support, urged the Lords 'to follow the late precedents of England' and to arrest them.[50] Ormond, together with Kerry and Mayo (all three of whom were converts from Catholicism and had been favoured by Wentworth), retaliated by repeatedly trying to block their initiatives. In particular, Ormond used his chairmanship of various committees in the Lords in an effort to derail the impeachment proceedings and to undermine the competence of the Irish parliament to judge on the Queries, which, he maintained, intruded on the royal prerogative.[51]

But how much influence did Ormond actually wield? Unlike Antrim, Cork and Clanricard, his English contacts were fairly limited, but his close associations with Wentworth and his extensive kinship links, especially with the lesser Butler houses and Muskerry, gave him considerable clout in both houses.[52] Thanks to Ormond's influence, six (of the twelve)

---

[48] Burke was later described by the Protestant council in Dublin as 'a rigid papist, a man suspected for a fomenter of the rebellion'. This is doubtful but he certainly was involved in the controversial 'Antrim Plot' and he served as one of Clanricard's envoys to the king and parliament in the early months of the rebellion, Little, ' "Blood and friendship" ', p. 934 and Jane Ohlmeyer, 'The "Antrim Plot" of 1641 – a myth?', *Historical Journal*, 35 (1992), pp. 905–19 and 'The "Antrim Plot" of 1641: a rejoinder', *Historical Journal*, 37 (1994), pp. 431–7.

[49] While Ormond attended parliament regularly from October 1640, he was largely absent from the first session owing to his military command and his wife's difficult pregnancy.

[50] McCafferty, ' "To follow the late precedents of England" ', pp. 56, 60, 68.

[51] Kelly, 'The early career of James Butler', pp. 143, 146–60. They eventually agreed on a compromise whereby Lowther and Bramhall were committed; and Bolton given bail, *Lords Jnl, Ire*, I, pp. 166, 167, 170, 175, 176, 177, also pp. 309–10.

[52] McGrath, 'A biographical dictionary', pp. 63, 93, 126, 146, 150, 211 and Kelly, 'The early career of James Butler', pp. 93–6.

MPs returned for the Kilkenny constituencies were government men. Elsewhere some of Ormond's Old English 'clients' and a number of his Butler kinsmen also sat as MPs. In the upper house Ormond's ties of kinship perhaps secured the effective neutrality of at least Dunboyne, Ikerrin and Upper Ossory, who appear to have absented themselves from the Lords for much of the proceedings. However, his brother-in-law, Muskerry, was politically active and chastised Ormond for his delaying tactics. According to an anonymous account, Muskerry visited Ormond at home in the spring of 1641 and 'told him yt [that] he smelt him out, and was convinced yt his carping . . . [was] but out of a design to keep ye House in heats to delay by yt means ye impeachm[en]t ag[ainst]t ye E[arl] of Strafford, and therefore in plain dealing told him he must no longer depend upon his friendship to be dissuaded from being call'd to ye bar and sent to castle chambers'.[53] Ultimately Ormond's Protestant allies in the Lords proved more biddable. Bonds of indebtedness linked him to leading government men and a number of others, especially Viscount Moore of Drogheda.[54] Drogheda had been the other government 'manager' in the 1634 Parliament.[55] However, Moore of Drogheda's family connections with Cork, Ranelagh, Wilmot of Athlone and Loftus of Ely forced him to adopt a more ambiguous stance in 1640–41.[56] With Wentworth out of the way, he clearly favoured a reform agenda and supported Digby of Geashill in the debate over the legitimacy of the fourth session (11 May – 17 November). Yet in the discussions over the Queries, Moore of Drogheda rallied behind Ormond, as did his son-in-law Blayney, Inchiquin, Thomond, Esmond and the aged Valentia.[57]

What then of the opposition? The tactics of the dissident activists centred on the removal of the person of Wentworth. Once this had been achieved, they aimed to restrict the power of the executive by having the judges respond to the Queries, and, following English precedents, to exercise the parliamentary right of impeachment. During the 1640 sessions the opposition peers included the Catholic lords of the Pale, led by Gormanston, together with Sarsfield of Kilmallock and Muskerry, and at least four Protestants: Digby of Geashill (himself a nephew of the earl of Bristol and Cork's son-in-law), Baltinglass, Dillon of Costello-Gallen and Lambert. When the bulk of these men shifted their sphere of political operations to London in the spring of 1641, Netterville, Slane and

---

[53] James Graves, 'Anonymous account of the early life and marriage of James, first duke of Ormond', *Journal of the Royal Society of Antiquaries of Ireland,* 7 (1862–63), pp. 289–90.
[54] HMC, *Egmont,* vol. 1, part I, pp. 130, 140.
[55] Knowler (ed.), *The Letters and Despatches,* I, pp. 97, 352.   [56] *Ibid.,* II, pp. 257, 360.
[57] Perceval-Maxwell, *The Outbreak of the Irish Rebellion,* pp. 123–4; J. T. Gilbert (ed.), *History of the Irish Confederation and War in Ireland* (7 vols., Dublin, 1882–91), I, p. 219.

Maguire joined Lambert to form the core of the opposition.[58] Lambert's position is particularly interesting. Raised by his mother in Cornwall, he married in 1625 a sister of the earl of Radnor, later one of the opposition lords in the Long Parliament.[59] He returned to Ireland in 1634, with a letter of support from Lennox, and almost immediately crossed swords with Wentworth over the plantation of Connacht.[60] He also alienated Cork by disputing the title to property held by the earl in Roscommon, with Cork maintaining, quite plausibly, that Lambert intended to use parliament to regain these lands.[61] Self-interest explains, at least in part, why Lambert embraced the opposition with such enthusiasm and, according to one waspish observer, 'carryes yt here with a great rage, havinge by sidinge with the papist partie gained strength'.[62]

However, the Protestant members of the 'papist partie' did not form a homogeneous body. By the middle of June one government supporter maintained that 'Protestant party [was] much disgusted with the course held by the other party, in their retrenchment of His Majesty's due profits, and pressing too near upon the honour and power of the government'.[63] Yet, despite rumours throughout June and July of a split 'between the Papists and Protestants', the dissident lords appear to have maintained a remarkably united front and in July sent a further petition directly to the king complaining about the subsidies.[64] By August the lords justices found 'the Popish party in both Houses of Parliament to be grown to so great a height, as was scarcely compatible with the present government'. In an attempt to counter this and to secure the support of the leading Protestant 'reformers', Lambert, Dillon of Costello-Gallen and Digby of Geashill, were admitted as members of the Dublin government.[65]

The confidence of the opposition stemmed in large part from the apparent success of their commissioners in London. In July the king and his council had agreed to a further raft of concessions and promised to enact

---

[58] By the end of April one of the lords justices noted how 'All the Lords of the Pale came to press them, and with one voice spake against plantations in general, which is now the main work of the papists', *CSPI, 1633–47*, p. 279.

[59] Lambert had gained parliamentary experience in the English House of Commons (he had sat as the MP for Bossiney) during the later 1620s and had witnessed the various impeachment proceedings there.

[60] Knowler (ed.), *The Letters and Despatches*, I, p. 334; Grosart (ed.), *The Lismore Papers*, 2nd series, IV, p. 106.

[61] *Lords Jnl, Ire*, I, pp. 169, 179. Darcy and Martin acted for Lambert, providing an interesting possible link with Clanricard.

[62] Grosart (ed.), *The Lismore Papers*, 2nd series, IV, p. 208.

[63] *CSPI, 1633–47*, p. 302.   [64] *Ibid.*, pp. 315–16.

[65] *Ibid.*, p. 330; HMC, *Ormonde*, NS, II, p. 19. In February 1641 Charles had tried to placate the leading English dissident peers by making them privy councillors, Russell, *Fall*, pp. 263–4.

the 1628 Graces.[66] Having achieved most of their objectives, the parliamentary delegation prepared, in the words of Arthur Annesley, later earl of Anglesey, to return home 'fully satisfied and loaden with all the Graces and Bounties, good subjects could hope to receive'.[67] All that remained was for the Irish parliament to enshrine 'these bounties' in legislation. To celebrate their victory, Cork hosted in August a slap-up dinner at the Nag's Head in Cheapside for the members of 'the comyttees of bothe howses' and lent Sarsfield of Kilmallock £600 to finance his trip home.[68]

Despite enjoying the support of Ormond and a handful of other Protestant peers, together with the bishops, who early on distanced themselves from the dissidents, the Irish government had clearly been outmanoeuvred in both London and in Dublin.[69] Why? First, the English connections, especially of Cork and Clanricard, provided essential human links with the English parliament. More importantly, these facilitated meaningful interaction with the king, who, after all, remained – in the words of Aidan Clarke – the source of 'supreme political authority in Ireland'.[70] Little wonder, then, that the Irish lords paraded their loyalty to Charles I. They supported him both militarily and financially during the Bishops' Wars (May–June 1639 and August–October 1640) and involved themselves in a myriad of royalist intrigues, particularly the Army and the Antrim Plots (spring of 1641).[71] Second, with the removal of Wentworth, the government lacked effective leadership, which in turn seriously impacted on its ability to manage the Lords and to prevent the peers working closely with the lower house. The 'divide and rule' strategy that had proved so successful in 1634 failed miserably, especially in the sessions of 1641. One example highlights the government's abysmal performance. The admission to the Commons in February 1641 of John Fitzgerald, who had been returned as MP for Inistiogue the previous November despite being involved in litigation with Lord Kerry, a government supporter, created uproar among the peers, who believed that Fitzgerald's admission impugned their privilege and honour.[72] The Commons responded by beseeching the Lords to drop their protest and to 'keep the bond of unity' between the two houses. Despite Ormond's best

---

[66] *CSPI, 1633–47*, pp. 317–20, 326.
[67] [Annesley], *A Letter from a Person of Honour*, p. 30.
[68] *CSPI, 1633–47*, p. 269; Grosart (ed.), *The Lismore Papers*, 1st series, V, p. 184.
[69] *Lords Jnl, Ire*, I, p. 150.
[70] Aidan Clarke, *The Old English in Ireland, 1625–42* (London and Ithaca, 1966; reprinted Dublin, 2000), p. 151.
[71] Cork's son-in-law, Goring, and eldest son, Dungarvan, were involved in the former, Little, 'The earl of Cork', pp. 621–9; Russell, *Unrevolutionary England*, chapter 16 and Ohlmeyer, 'The "Antrim Plot" of 1641 – a myth?', pp. 905–19.
[72] *Lords Jnl, Ire*, I, pp. 146, 154, 156, 158, 168, 174; *CSPI, 1633–47*, p. 268; Kelly, 'The early career of James Butler', pp. 148–55.

attempts to manipulate this issue of privilege to derail the Queries and to stir up animosities, the matter was quietly dropped. The two houses continued to work very closely together, and the frequency of their meetings increased until these occurred on an almost daily basis by July.

Finally, effective management of the peers rested on the government's ability to control proxies, and the Lords repeatedly frustrated their attempts to do this by disallowing the proxies of non-residents.[73] By May the lords justices had become desperate and begged the English privy council to intervene and to support them over this critical issue.[74] A list of proxies was dispatched to London with a request that 'The most to [do] come [to] Ormond, Kerry, Thomond and [Montgomery of the] Ards.'[75] Matters deteriorated further over the early summer and reached crisis point early in August. On 3 August, Lord Justice William Parsons reported that the Queries, which the Commons had approved, were now with the Lords and 'by plurality of votes of the Papist party and much urgency of some of the Commons are . . . like to pass'.[76] To prevent this, the lords justices adjourned parliament on 7 August until November on the grounds that 'Great mischiefs will follow if this parliament is allowed to have its way.'[77]

II

As it turned out, 'great mischief' did follow when rebellion erupted in Ulster a few months later.[78] The reaction of the peers, who had returned to their estates after the adjournment, is well known. On 24 October, Gormanston, Netterville, Fitzwilliam, Howth, Dunsany and Slane, together with the earls of Kildare and Fingal – 'all noblemen of the English Pale' – professed their loyalty and asked for arms to defend their homes.[79] The Dublin government responded by issuing a proclamation, which, according to one Catholic lawyer, was 'stufft with bitter invectives against the papists'.[80] Equally significant, the executive demanded that parliament be prorogued.[81] When parliament finally reconvened, under an

---

[73] *CSPI, 1633–47*, pp. 256, 288, 298.   [74] *Ibid.*, p. 285.
[75] Mary Hickson (ed.), *Ireland in the Seventeenth Century* (2 vols., London, 1884), I, p. 333.
[76] *Ibid.*, I, p. 340.   [77] *CSPI, 1633–47*, p. 339.
[78] Temple, *The Irish Rebellion*, pp. 135–6.
[79] *Ibid.*, p. 58; HMC, *Ormonde*, NS, II, pp. 4, 11.
[80] Gilbert (ed.), *History of the Irish Confederation*, I, p. 18, also see pp. 20–1, 228; HMC *Report on the Manuscripts of the earl of Egmont* vol. 1, part I (London, 1905), p. 143.
[81] Contemporaries later debated the wisdom of this decision. Castlehaven argued that it proved disastrous and only served to irritate 'the whole nation', [James Tuchet, earl of Castlehaven], *The Earl of Castlehaven's Review, or, his memoirs of his engagement and carriage in the Irish Wars* (London, 1684), p. 34. Temple maintained that national security depended upon it, *The Irish Rebellion*, p. 244.

armed guard, in mid-November, a committee from both houses implored the lords justices to reconsider their decision to abandon the session.[82] They refused 'to the great surprise of both houses, and the general dislike of all honest and knowing men'.[83] Despite this, both houses drew up a further protestation condemning the insurrection and appointed a delegation to meet with the insurgents.[84] Finally, in a last-ditch attempt to regain control over events, the Lords instructed Dillon of Costello-Gallen to travel to Scotland to persuade the king to continue parliament 'at least till the rebels (then few in number) were reduced'.[85] After sitting for two days parliament was prorogued, an act that the earl of Castlehaven later claimed was the 'greatest discontent' of all. Parliament had become 'the only way the nation had to express their loyalty and prevent their being misrepresented to their sovereign; which had it been permitted to sit for any reasonable time, would in all likelihood without any great charge or trouble, have brought the rebels to justice'.[86]

Whether this might have been the case remained a matter of debate among contemporaries. While conspiracies, especially the Antrim Plot, may have in some way inadvertently fostered the plans for an uprising hatched by Lord Maguire and his co-conspirators, there is no clear evidence to suggest that the Catholic peers supported Maguire. Their initial reaction to the insurrection and their determination to find a political solution to solve it highlights this. However, the abortive parliamentary session of November, combined with the bungling and hyperbole of the lords justices, Sir Charles Coote's military excesses, and the deteriorating political climate in England, effectively undermined any negotiated settlement to the crisis.

As the rising gathered momentum and the 'common sorts' seized the initiative, the Catholic lords of the Pale had no alternative but to rally behind the insurgents if they were to regain control over their followers and to secure their estates. Having done so, these peers – in order to

---

[82] Gilbert (ed.), *History of the Irish Confederation*, I, pp. 20, 24, 26, 28, 31.

[83] *The Earl of Castlehaven's Review*, p. 35.

[84] According to the lords justices, 'the Popish party in the house' laboured 'earnestly to express the actions of the rebels in a language far below the heinousness of their crimes, standing earnestly not to have them called rebels or traitors or using terms of aggravation against them under pretence of danger to themselves and their estates', HMC, *Ormonde*, NS, II, p. 25.

[85] *The Earl of Castlehaven's Review*, p. 35. This infuriated the lords justices who claimed that Dillon of Costello-Gallen had left without their consent and carried letters of loyalty 'signed by many Papists of the nobility and gentry of this kingdom' together with offers to repress the rebellion without English aid. If this was indeed the case, they continued, the consequences would be dire and result in the extirpation of the English interest in Ireland, HMC, *Ormonde*, NS, II, p. 25; Perceval-Maxwell, *The Outbreak of the Irish Rebellion*, pp. 198–9 and Clarke, *Old English*, pp. 165–8, 174.

[86] *The Earl of Castlehaven's Review*, p. 40.

ensure their own survival – pressured, cajoled and threatened their fellow Catholic lords to join them, together with those who had recently converted to Protestantism. Many, including Castlehaven, Antrim and Clanricard, initially refused. Others joined unwillingly and only when the spread of unrest to their respective localities gave them no realistic alternative. For instance, news of the outbreak of the rebellion of October 1641 reached Muskerry, after a dinner party attended by Cork, his sons 'and some other men of quality of the Irish nation, with whom they lived in an easy and familiar way'.[87] According to a later account, 'My lord Muskerry, who was a facetious man, and an excellent companion, employ'd all the wit he was master of to turn the whole story into ridicule.'[88] Of course, the insurrection proved to be no laughing matter. In March 1642 Muskerry reluctantly threw in his lot with the insurgents on the grounds that the rebellion had become the only means of preserving Catholicism, the king's prerogative and the 'antient privileges of the poore kingdome of Ireland established and allowed by the Common Law of England'.[89] Thus from the outset Catholic aristocratic commitment to an armed rising as the best means of securing their political, tenurial and constitutional objectives was fraught with contradictions.

III

What is clear from the activities of the temporal peers in 1640–41 is that, despite the very real religious differences which civil war so painfully exposed, they enjoyed a common political and constitutional agenda, albeit one tempered by individual landed and family interests and by political intrigue in Dublin and in London. With few exceptions, Wentworth's policies had seriously challenged personal aristocratic power bases, and so the determination of the peers to oust him comes as no surprise. United by bonds of kinship and mutual indebtedness, the peers created powerful webs of intersecting interest groups within both houses that cooperated, however loosely, in order to render obsolete the men and mechanisms that Wentworth had devised in order to control them. While it would be unwise to downplay the significance of individual MPs and the sheer complexity of events during these months, at certain key moments the peers, like their counterparts in England, shaped the Irish parliamentary agenda.[90] They may well have been obsessed with matters

---

[87] Eustace Budgell, *Memoirs of the Lives and Characters of the Illustrious Family of the Boyles: particularly of the late eminently learned Charles, earl of Orrery* (London, 1737), p. 38.
[88] *Ibid.*, p. 39.   [89] BL, Add. MSS 25277, f. 58.
[90] Lambert, 'The opening of the Long Parliament', pp. 265–87.

of protocol, precedence and procedure, but the need to protect their position in the social and political hierarchy ensured that this grouping had became politicised across ethnic and sectarian divides.

Thus the parliament of 1640–41 marked an important departure in a number of respects. The parliamentary reform strategy, formulated by the opposition peers, which incorporated many issues that had traditionally been the preserve of the Old English, represented a wider basis for cooperation than hitherto thought possible. This aimed to turn the clock back to the 1620s 'when a weak, irresolute, and financially dependent administration was constantly vulnerable to organised pressure and had been forced to govern through concession and compromise'.[91] It also sought to clarify Anglo-Irish constitutional relationships by stressing the primacy of the Irish parliament as a legislative body and its importance as the principal point of contact between the king and his Irish subjects. While many of these issues continued to be debated throughout the 1640s and, again, after the Restoration, the onset of civil war shattered the pre-war political groupings. A small Protestant rump lingered on in Dublin while the bulk of the Catholic peers took their seats in the Confederate General Assembly at Kilkenny.[92]

That the dissident lords failed to achieve all of their objectives in 1640–41 should not disguise the significance of their attempts, and when set in the wider context of seventeenth-century Irish history, these pre-war parliamentary sessions proved unique. The assembly which met in 1661 was a very different body. The Commons was now exclusively Protestant, severely curtailing the ability of the Catholic peers, but not the Protestant ones, to dominate proceedings. The composition of the upper house remained largely unchanged, with a significant minority of peers having attended the 1640–41 parliament. A dozen or so Catholics took their seats, and Old English lords accounted for roughly half of the members who sat on parliamentary committees between 1661 and 1666.[93] This continuity of membership ensured that, despite the radically different political context in Ireland and the growing pre-eminence of the Westminster parliament, matters which had dominated proceedings two decades earlier resurfaced. Disquiet over the non-residency of Irish peers and debates over the vexed issue of control over proxies (now limited to two per lord) echoed earlier discussions.[94] Equally, the extent to which

---

[91] Clarke, 'The policies of the "Old English"', p. 92.   [92] See chapter 10 below.

[93] Francis G. James, *The Lords of the Ascendancy. The Irish House of Lords and its members 1600–1800* (Dublin, 1995), p. 35 and F. M. O'Donoghue, 'Parliament in Ireland under Charles II' (M.A. thesis, University College, Dublin, 1970), p. 139. Also see the Appendix.

[94] Coleman A. Dennehy, 'Parliament in Ireland, 1661–6' (M. Litt. thesis, University College, Dublin, 2002), p. 59.

bonds, largely forged in the pre-war years, had survived a decade of civil war and a further decade of Cromwellian rule is striking. 'The resident Irish peerage', according to one recent historian, 'had begun to meld into aristocratic elite whose sense of identity transcended diverse ethnic and even different religious affiliations.'[95] Increasingly, Catholic peers became dependent on their Protestant counterparts to temper the extremes of the Cromwellian and Restoration land settlements. In July 1662 members of the upper house asked that Catholic peers – Westmeath, Mayo, Galmoy, Athenry, Brittas and Sarsfield of Kilmallock – who regularly attended be immediately restored to their estates for 'their better encouragement and the support of the dignity'.[96] In the aftermath of the Act of Settlement (December 1665), the temporal lords rallied behind Lewis O'Dempsey, Viscount Clanmalier, who had lost his estates in King's and Queen's Counties to an avaricious and favoured courtier despite being declared innocent by the Court of Claims. In November 1665 Roscommon, a Protestant of Old English extraction, made an impassioned speech to the upper house on Clanmalier's behalf:

> Only give me leave to tell you that you never had a fairer opportunity to show the care you take of your own members, and that you never will hear a subject more worthy of your concern. You have now before you the case of the only peer that hath the honour to sit in this House and that is not in some manner provided for, and an honourable family reduced to great streights [*sic*] and the prospect of a sadder extremity.[97]

Roscommon invited his colleagues to ask Ormond to intercede with the king, 'who since he has showed so much mercy to the guilty cannot but have reserved some pity for the unfortunate'.[98] He also enlisted the support of his uncle, Orrery, in a sustained attempt to secure adequate provision for a fellow lord who no longer had the means 'to support his dignity'.[99] Yet, despite the best efforts of Roscommon, Orrery and Ormond, Clanmalier was one of the few Catholic lords to lose his estates.[100]

In short, the forces of continuity which linked the pre- and post-war parliaments should not disguise the very real changes that had occurred during the 1640s and 1650s, especially the decisive shift in the balance of power towards the English parliament. Little wonder that after 1666 Irish peers spent ever-increasing amounts of time in London. Irish Protestant lords relocated to England and, if they failed to secure an English title, stood for seats in the English House of Commons. Deprived of a political

---

[95] James, *Lords of the Ascendancy*, p. 36.   [96] *Lords Jnl, Ire*, I, p. 316.
[97] *CSPI, 1663–65*, p. 676.   [98] *Ibid.*, p. 677.   [99] *CSPI, 1666–69*, p. 43.
[100] *CSPI, 1663–65*, pp. 676–7; *CSPI, 1666–69*, pp. 7, 15, 16, 433; *Lords Jnl, Ire*, I, p. 665.

voice at home, Irish Catholics also flocked to London. The focus of their attentions was not, however, Westminster, but the royal court at White-hall, where an influential group of peers promoted the Catholic interest and their own political and landed agendas with the same energy and sophistication as their predecessors had done.[101]

[101] Anne Creighton, 'The Catholic interest in Irish politics in the reign of Charles II' (Ph.D. thesis, Queen's University, Belfast, 2002).

Appendix: The political activity of the resident temporal Irish peers, 1640–41 ('Activists' are indicated in bold)[1]

Key [E]HL – [English] Irish House of Lords [E]HC – [English] Irish House of Commons Rel – religion Cttee – committee membership abs – absent prox – proxy P – Protestant C – Catholic d. – date of death W – involved in proceedings against Wentworth [E]HLC – [English] Irish House of Lords Committee sh – son and heir h – heir gs – grandson bh – brother and heir HC/HL – links between the HL and HC: OK – 1–3 close contacts; G[ood] – 1–9 close contacts; V[ery] G[ood] – 1–5 close contacts; E[xcellent] – 10 and more MP – member of House of Commons.

Surname	Forename	Rank; Title	1634	Cttee	Rel	Age in 1640	1640	Cttee	W	1641	Cttee	HC/HL	HC/HL 1661–6	Cttee
Butler	**James**	**earl: 12th earl of Ormond**	**HL**	**X**	**P**	**30: d.1688**	**HL**	**X**		**HL**		**E**	**X[2]**	**X**
Fitzgerald	George	earl: 16th earl of Kildare	HL		P	37: d.1660	abs		X	abs		VG	sh	sh
Boyle	Richard	earl: 1st earl of Cork	HL	X	P	74: d.1643	prox		X	abs		E	sh[3]	sh
Brabazon	William	earl: 1st earl of Meath	HL		P	60: d.1651	prox			prox			sh	sh
Dillon	James	earl: 1st earl of Roscommon	HL		C	d.1642	prox			abs		G	sh	sh
Nugent	Richard	earl: 1st earl of Westmeath	HL	X	C	57: d.1642	HL			abs		OK	sh	sh
MacDonnell	**Randal**	**earl: 2nd earl of Antrim**	**HL (1636)**	**X**	**C**	**31: d.1683**	**HL**	**X**		**prox**		**VG**	**X**	**X**
Plunkett	**Christopher**	**earl: 2nd earl of Fingal**	**HL (1637)**	**X**	**C**	**d.1649**	**HL**	**X**		**HL**		**OK**	**X**	**X**
Ridgeway	Robert	earl: 2nd earl of Londonderry	abs		P	d.1641	abs			abs			sh/prox	
Tuchet	James	earl: 3rd earl of Castlehaven	prox		C	23: d.1684	E HL		X	abs		VG	X	X
Burke	Ulick	earl: 5th earl of Clanricard	prox		C	36: d.1657	E HL		X	abs		E	h	X
O'Brien	Barnaby	earl: 6th earl of Thomond	HL		P	50: d.1657	HL			abs		OK	sh	sh

Surname	First name	Title											
Barry	David	earl: 1st earl of Barrymore	HL		P	35: d.1642	prox		abs		OK	sh	sh
Boyle	Richard	viscount: 1st viscount Dungarvan			P	28: d.1698	EHC		abs	X		X	X
Conway	Edward	viscount: 1st viscount Conway	HL	X	P	46: d.1655	HL		abs	X	OK	sh	sh
Fitzwilliam	**Thomas**	**viscount: 1st viscount Fitzwilliam**	**HL**		**C**	**59: d.1650**	**HL**		**HL**			**sh**	**sh**
Cromwell	Thomas	viscount: 1st viscount Lecale	HL	X	P	46: d.1653	HL	X	abs	X			
Loftus	Adam	viscount: 1st viscount Loftus of Ely	HL		P	72: d.1643	abs		prox	X	G	sh	?
Netterville	**Nicholas**	**viscount: 1st viscount Netterville**	**HL**		**C**	**59: d.1654**	**HL**		**HL**	X	**OK**		
Wilmot	Charles	viscount: 1st viscount Wilmot of Athlone	prox		P	70: d.1644?	prox		abs	X			
Butler	Pierce	viscount: 1st viscount of Ikerrin	HL		C	d.1661	HL	X	abs				
Jones	Roger	viscount: 1st viscount Ranelagh	HL		P	d.1644	HL	X	abs	X	OK	sh	sh

[1] The principal sources for this Appendix are *Lords Jnl, Ire*, I, and Brid McGrath, 'A Biographical Dictionary of the Membership of the Irish House of Commons 1640–1641' (unpublished, Ph.D. thesis, Trinity College Dublin, 1997).

[2] His sons Ossory and Arran also sat in the parliament of 1661–66.

[3] His son, Shannon, also sat.

(*cont.*)

Appendix (*cont.*)

Surname	Forename	Rank; Title	1634	Cttee	Rel	Age in 1640	1640	Cttee	W	1641	Cttee	HC/HL	1661–6	Cttee
Taaffe	John	viscount: 1st viscount Taaffe	HL		C	d.1642	HL			abs		OK	sh	sh
Roper	**Thomas**	**viscount: 2nd viscount Baltinglass**	**HL** (1638)		**P**	**d.1670**	**HL**		**X**	**HL**		**OK**	**X**	**X**
Burke	Thomas	viscount: 2nd viscount Clanmories	HL		C	d.1650	HL			abs				
O'Dempsey	Lewis	viscount: 2nd viscount Clanmalier	HL (1637)		C	d.1683	prox			abs		OK	prox	
Bourke	**Miles**	**viscount: 2nd viscount Mayo**	abs	**X**	**P**	**d.1649**	**HL**			**HL**	**X**	**OK**	**gs**	**gs**
Montgomery	Hugh	viscount: 2nd viscount Montgomery	HL (1636)		P	d.1642	HL	X		abs		G	sh	sh
Moore	**Charles**	**viscount: 2nd viscount Moore of Drogheda**	**HL**		**P**	37: **d.1643**	**HL**	**X**		**HL**		**OK**	**sh**	
Butler	Richard	viscount: 2nd viscount Mountgarret	HL	X	C	62: d.1651	HL			abs		OK		
MacCarthy	**Donough**	**viscount: 2nd viscount Muskerry**	**MP**		**C**	46: **d.1665**	**HL**		**X**	**HLC**		G	**X**	**X**
Sarsfield	**William**	**viscount: 2nd viscount Sarsfield of Kilmallock**	**MP**		**C**	**d.1648**	**HL**	**X**	**X**	**HLC**		**OK**		

Magennis	Arthur	viscount: 3rd viscount Iveagh	abs		C	d.1683	abs		abs	G	
Dillon	Thomas	viscount: 4th viscount Dillon of Costello-Gallen	HL		P	35: d.1673	prox	X	HLC	VG	prox
Preston	**Nicholas**	**viscount: 6th viscount Gormanston**	**HL**		**C**	**32: d.1643**	**HL**	**X**	**HLC**	**OK**	
Roche	Maurice	viscount: 8th viscount Roche of Fermoy	HL (1635)		C	d.1670	prox	X	abs	VG	
Boyle	Lewis	viscount: 1st viscount Kinalmeaky	HL		P	21: d.1642	abs		abs		
Chichester	Edward	viscount: 1st viscount Chichester	HL	X	P	72: d.1648	prox		abs	G	sh
Hamilton	James	viscount: 1st viscount Clandeboye	HL	X	P	d.1644	abs		abs	OK	sh/prox
Power	**Henry**	**viscount: 1st viscount Valentia**	**prox**	**X**	**P**	**78: d.1642**	**HL**		**HL**		
St Lawrence	**Nicholas**	**baron: 10th baron Howth**	**HL**	**X**	**C?**	**43: d.1644**	**HL**	**X**	**HL**	**OK**	**sh**
Bermingham	Richard	baron: 11th baron Athenry	HL		C	70: d.1645	prox		abs?		sh
de Courcy	Gerald	baron: 14th baron Courcy of Kinsale	HL		C	d.1642	prox		prox	OK	sh

(cont.)

Appendix (cont.)

Surname	Forename	Rank; Title	1634	Cttee	Rel	Age in 1640	1640	Cttee	W	1641	Cttee	HC/HL 1661–6	Cttee
Fleming	**William**	**baron: 14th baron Slane**	**HL**		**C**	**d.1642**	**HL**	**X**		**HL**	**X**	**G**	
Fitzmaurice	**Patrick**	**baron: 18th baron of Kerry**	**HL**	**X**	**P**	**45: d.1661**	**HL**	**X**		**HL**	**X**	**G**	**sh**
Digby	**Robert**	**baron: 1st baron Digby of Geashill**	**HL**	**X**	**P**	**d.1642**	**HL**	**X**	**X**	**HL**	**X**	**OK**	**sh**
Bourke	Theobald	baron: 1st baron of Brittas	prox		C	d.1654	abs			abs			sh
Aungier	Gerald	baron: 2nd baron Aungier of Longford	prox		P	d.1655	abs			abs			sh
Blayney	**Henry**	**baron: 2nd baron Blayney**	**HL**	**X**	**P**	**d.1646**	**HL**			**HL**		**OK**	**sh**
Dockwra	Theodore	baron: 2nd baron Dockwra of Culmore	abs		P	31: d.1647	HL	X		abs			
Maguire	**Connor**	**baron: 2nd lord Maguire**	**HL**	**X**	**C**	**28: d.1645**	**HL**			**HL**	**X**	**OK**	
Butler	Thomas	baron: 3rd baron Caher	HL		C	d.1648	prox			prox			
Stewart	Andrew	baron: 3rd baron Castle Stuart	HL (1639)	X	P	d.1650	HL			abs			sh/prox
Bourke	William	baron: 5th baron of Castle Connell	HL (1638)		C	17: d.1665	HL			abs		OK	
Power	John	baron: 5th baron Le Power	abs		C?	43: d.1662	abs			abs			sh	sh
O'Brien	**Murrough**	**baron: 6th baron Inchiquin**	**HL**		**P**	**26: d.1674**	**HL**			**HL**	**X**	**G**	**X**

Plunkett	**Oliver**	**baron: 6th baron Louth**	**HL**		**C**	**32: d.1679**	**HL**	**X**		**HL**	**X**	**OK**		
Fitzpatrick	Barnaby	baron: 6th baron of Upper Ossory	HL (1638)		C	d.1666	prox			abs		OK		
Barnewall	**Matthias**	**baron: 8th baron Trimleston**	**HL**	**X**	**C**	**26: d.1667**	**HL**	**X**		**HL**	**X**	**OK**		
Plunkett	**Patrick**	**baron: 9th baron Dunsany**	**HL**	**X**	**C**	**45: d.1670**	**HL**	**X**		**HL**	**X**	**OK**		
Herbert	Edward	baron: 1st baron Herbert of Castle Island	prox		P	57: d.1648	EHC		X	abs				sh/prox
Annesley	Francis	baron: 1st baron Mountnorris	HL		P	56: d.1660	prox		X	abs		OK	sh	sh
Boyle	Roger	baron: 1st baron of Broghill	HL	X	P	19: d.1679	abs			abs			X	X
Caulfield	Toby	baron: 3rd baron Caulfield of Charlemont	HL (1640)	X	P	19: d.1642	HL	X		abs		OK	bh	bh
Esmond	Laurence	baron: 1st baron Esmond	HL	X	P	d.1645	abs			abs		OK		
Folliott	Thomas	baron: 1st baron Folliott of Ballyshannon	HL	X	P	27: d.1697	HL			abs		OK	X	X
Hamilton	James	baron: 3rd baron Hamilton of Strabane	HL (1638)		C	7: d.1655	abs			abs			sh	sh
Lambert	**Charles**	**baron: 2nd baron Lambert**	**prox**		**P**	**40: d.1660**	**HL**	**X**		**HL**	**X**	**OK**	**sh**	
Butler	James	baron: 4th baron of Dunboyne	HL (1640)		C	d.1662	prox			abs		VG		

9   The Irish elections of 1640–1641

Brid McGrath

> The Bishop of Rapho tells me your Ma[jes]tie was told all this Kingdom
> was disposed to trouble. It is wonderful how men are inclined nowadays
> to report all wherein I am concerned to ye worst possible source. For . . .
> there hath not been all this while the least appearance or complexion
> to any such thing, nor is there yett, or any likely to be, for any thing I
> can see. Nay Sir, after all their gaping upon me and after me, it will be
> found I have Estimation & Affection in the Places where I serve you.[1]

The Irish parliament which met on 16 March 1640 was one that Thomas
Wentworth, earl of Strafford, wanted, and it acted in a manner that
appeared to support this sanguine view of his happy position in Ireland.
The Commons' 235 members, 161 Protestants and 74 Catholics, gave
him the most comfortable Protestant majority ever, and the Irish council
declared that 'we observe the Persons returned to serve this Parliament
all generally so well affected and disposed to reason'.[2] It held a perfunc-
tory opening session on Monday 16 March at which Sir Maurice Eustace
was unanimously selected as Speaker, and adjourned for two days, awaiting Wentworth's arrival from England. On its first full day's legislative
business on the following Monday it agreed to four subsidies, and on
26 March sat at three o'clock in the afternoon 'for the reading of the act
of four intire subsidies the third time, for expedition of the business of the

---

[1] Wentworth to king, 6 August 1639, Sheffield, WWM, consulted on microfilm in NLI,
P. 2850, p. 89.
[2] W. Knowler (ed.), *The Letters and Despatches* . . . (2 vols., London, 1739), II, p. 394,
19 March 1640; these figures exclude disfranchised boroughs, and double or disputed
returns. The official list is included in the *Commons Journals*, before the account of the proceedings in the house. The figures also differ from those calculated by Michael Perceval-
Maxwell, *The Outbreak of the Irish Rebellion* (Dublin, 1994), p. 70. The list shows a number
of instances of readjustment. For example, William Peisley and Robert Byron were listed
as representing Augher (the result of a second election, which cancelled John Karnes's
return) and Francis Cosbie and Edmond Cossens as replacements for the doubly returned
Walter Loftus and Thomas Harman respectively. Further adjustments, including replacements for the other double returns, remained to be made.

House'.[3] The bill was passed that afternoon, and a committee of three privy councillors and three prominent Catholics was appointed to meet the Lords to frame a declaration to be appended to the Act of Subsidies. The declaration was agreed on 30 March, and two days later parliament was adjourned for two months, having displayed only enthusiastic cooperation with the administration. There was no repetition of the tumult of the opening of the 1613 parliament or the lengthy dispute about the legality of returns in 1634, and Sir Richard Barnewall's request for the scrutiny of the returns was mild, polite and ineffectual.[4] Leaving Ireland after this successful opening, Wentworth informed his private secretary Windebank that, 'I have left that people as fully satisfied and as well affected to his Majesty's person and service, as can possibly be wished for, notwithstanding the Philosophy of some amongst you there in the Court, who must needs have it believed, true or false, that that People are infinitely distasted with the present government, and hating of me.'[5]

The second part of the first session began peacefully, but the administration's control of affairs then deteriorated rapidly. As there were minimal changes in membership between March and June 1640, it is instructive to look at the original returns and their management and to contrast these with the changes that the same house produced only three months later. The original returns show a number of separate groupings of sectional interests. On the Protestant side this included at least nineteen MPs who were part of Wentworth's Yorkshire connections and adherents and fifteen who were privy councillors. The remainder comprised leading members of the administration and their extensive connections, together with men of Scottish ancestry.[6] The seventy-four Catholic MPs fall into distinct categories: Old English gentry, Gaelic families, merchants from old boroughs and lawyers. The gentry included members of families who exercised considerable power within their own localities, such as the Barnewalls, Bellews, Butlers, Dillons and Walshes. The merchants represented the old cities and boroughs which they had traditionally ruled; thus Henry Archer and Pierce Rothe sat for Kilkenny, and Pierce Creagh and Dominic White represented Limerick. The lawyers included Geoffrey Browne, Nicholas Plunkett, Hugh Rochford, John Taylor and John Walsh.

---

[3] *Commons' Jnl, Ire*, I, 26 March 1640.

[4] This dispute extended over three days and included two divisions – a sign of very serious disagreement, *Commons' Jnl, Ire*, I, 16 July, 17 July, 18 July 1634. For Barnewall, see *Commons' Jnl, Ire*, I, 16 March 1640.

[5] Knowler (ed.), *The Letters and Despatches*, II, pp. 403–4.

[6] Bríd McGrath, 'A biographical dictionary of the membership of the Irish House of Commons 1640–1641' (Ph.D. thesis, Trinity College, Dublin, 1998), I, pp. 33–4 for these groupings.

I

The administration's electoral strategy which produced this parliament was based on four different, but coordinated, elements. First, the timescale was a rapid one which offered little opportunity for reaction. Second, Wentworth carefully limited the size of both houses of the parliament. Third, he arranged the return of government supporters upon whom he could depend. Fourth, he curtailed cooperation between the two houses and, thereby, limited parliament's scope. An atmosphere of efficiency and of aggressive hostility to local interest hung over the parliament which grew out of Wentworth's policies of restricting and destroying all power bases but his own. As Wentworth was in England, the management of the election fell to George Radcliffe, his close friend and principal secretary.[7] In a letter dating from February 1640 Wentworth noted how Radcliffe had 'taken all possible care there on that side in making choyse of the knights and burghesses for this issuing parliament'.[8]

The process of electing a parliament required a certain amount of time. Following the issuing in London of a commission for the summoning of parliament, the court of chancery sent out writs for election to the sheriffs in each county. These writs ordered them to hold elections for the knights of the shire and to direct the chief magistrates of the cities and boroughs in their county (mayors, provosts, port-reeves or sovereigns, depending on the boroughs' individual charters) to elect their citizens and burgesses. Returning officers were ineligible for election for their own constituencies.[9] Where seats became vacant during a parliament, the house would order new writs through the chancery for the election of replacement MPs.

There was no single election day.[10] Counties' returns were made at the monthly assizes in the county town; city and borough elections took place as soon as practicable after the receipt of writs, allowing time to notify electors of the election's time and place.[11] The speed of returns

---

[7] Aidan Clarke, *The Old English in Ireland, 1625–42* (London and Ithaca, 1966), p. 126.

[8] T. D. Whitaker (ed.), *The Life and Original Correspondence of Sir G. Radcliffe* (London, 1810), p. 195.

[9] Bramston, Belfast's sovereign was unseated in 1634 for that reason, *Commons' Jnl, Ire*, I, 19 July 1634. A number of MPs in 1613 also served as returning officers, but not for their own constituencies, and they were not unseated although their elections were technically invalid, Bríd McGrath, 'The Membership of the Irish House of Commons, 1613–15' (M.Litt. thesis, Trinity College, Dublin, 1986), p. 30.

[10] In 1613, the administration had used this fact as an element in its electoral strategy, creating new constituencies during the course of the election to ensure a Protestant majority, McGrath, *ibid.*, p. 34.

[11] Some sheriffs or sub-sheriffs specified a timescale within which the writ of return was to be delivered to them. For example, the Youghal return in 1634 allowed twelve days for

depended on the distance from Dublin, the means of dispatch and the location of the sheriff.[12] Although the timescale for the 1640 parliament was not particularly of Wentworth's choosing and the intention of holding an election was well known, the shortness of time for elections had its advantages for the administration, dictating a rapid election, which gave the government the initiative and allowed little opportunity for reaction.[13] The 1640 elections occurred over a period of only six and a half weeks; compared with seven and a half weeks in Wentworth's first Irish parliament of 1634, and ten and a half weeks in 1613 (see below).[14]

Timescale for returns, 1613–40

Year	Commission	Writ	Elections	Meeting	Timescale
1640	29 January	2 February	6 February–13 March	16 March	$6\frac{1}{2}$ weeks
1634	23 May	24 May	June–July	14 July	$7\frac{1}{2}$ weeks
1628[a]	September		?5–7–9 October	[8 November]	$<9\frac{3}{4}$ weeks
1613	6 March		2 April–17 May	18 May	$10\frac{1}{2}$ weeks

[a] Due to a procedural error, the 1628 parliament never actually met.

the return of the writ to the sheriff, R. Caulfield (ed.), *Council Book of the Corporation of Youghal* (Guildford, 1878), p. 181.

[12] McGrath, 'Membership of the Irish House of Commons, 1613–15', pp. 6–25 and McGrath, 'Biographical dictionary', I, pp. 28–30, for electoral practice. For the session beginning October 1640, the clerk of the hanaper prepared writs for the return of burgesses five weeks before parliament was due to meet, *Commons' Jnl, Ire*, I, 6 October 1640. Electing county members would have required more time. It was regarded as suspicious that Inistiogue, 50 miles distant from Dublin, could make a return within five days of the writ's issue. See also the 1613 Trim election, when a second election was held because the first was poorly advertised, *CSPI, 1611–14*, pp. 363, 442. For Inistiogue, see *Commons' Jnl, Ire*, I, 18 February 1641.

[13] The intention to hold a parliament was, however, well known. Dublin Corporation voted an extra £50 to the mayor to cover his anticipated expenses in entertaining visitors for the parliament: 'it is for certain published that there will be a Parliament held in this cittie sometime the next ensuing march, and that the same is thought will prove very chargeable unto Mr. Maior now bein, in Keeping such greate and liberall hospitalitie', J. T. Gilbert (ed.), *Calendar of Ancient Records of Dublin* (18 vols., Dublin, 1889–1922), III, p. 365, 16 January 1640.

[14] In 1628 the writs were sent out before the commission arrived from London, but that parliament was cancelled because of procedural errors. See Clarke, *Old English*, pp. 53–6 for a discussion of the problems of non-compliance with Poynings' Law. The known elections are given in Bríd McGrath, 'Parliament men and the confederate association' in Micheál Ó Siochrú (ed.), *Kingdoms in Crisis: Ireland in the 1640s* (Dublin, 2001), pp. 90–105, although there may also have been an election in Kilkenny, see NLI, MS 11,048(7). For a 1634 writ see Caulfield (ed.), *Council Book of Youghal*, p. 180. According to the official compilation, Londonderry made its return on 25 March, although the parliament met on 16 March.

While the shortness of the time for the 1640 election can be seen as part of a pattern of tightening timescales for returns to parliament in the early seventeenth century, the six and a half weeks hardly allowed for returns, especially for county members. The commission to hold the parliament was issued on 29 January 1640. Assuming that it would have taken at least five days to travel from London to Dublin, and that the clerk of the hanaper would then have to issue writs for elections which would then have to be transmitted to the sheriffs, wherever they might be, it would be reasonable to assume that the writs to the sheriffs could not normally be issued before 4 February at the earliest. In fact the proclamation for the parliament was issued in Dublin on 1 February 1640, before the commission could possibly have arrived, and by 6 February it was known in England that the Irish writs had already been issued, so they must have been sent out on 1 February with the proclamation.[15] The first known election was conducted with exceptional speed in Clonmel on 6 February, an alacrity which left little time for the sheriff of Tipperary to compose the mandate and to issue it to the mayor and corporation.[16] The return was exceptional for Clonmel, as it returned, for the first and only time, placemen rather than burgesses.[17]

[15] Letters from Dublin to London might only take three days but the return journey was longer, because of the prevailing winds; presumably there were greater delays in winter, because of severe weather, M. MacCarthy-Morrogh, 'The English presence in early seventeenth century Munster' in C. Brady and R. Gillespie (eds.), *Natives and Newcomers: essays on the making of Irish colonial society, 1534–1641* (Dublin, 1986), pp. 171–90. Aidan Clarke, *Prelude to Restoration in Ireland: the end of the Commonwealth, 1659–1660* (Cambridge, 1999), pp. 22–3 notes the standard time in the 1660s was six days each way and discusses the problems caused by the delay in transmitting information. The commission is enclosed in the Corporation book of Youghal together with the sheriff's mandate, Caulfield (ed.), *Corporation Book of Youghal*, p. 197. W. Hawkins to the earl of Leicester on 6/16 February 1639–40: 'The writs for the Parliament in Ireland are issued already, but those for England lye ready made by unsealed', G. D. Owen (ed.), *Report on the Manuscripts of the Right Honourable Viscount De L'Isle & Dudley: preserved at Penshurst Place, VI, 1626–1698* (London, 1966–), p. 230; 1 February was a Saturday and a disinclination to conduct business on the Sabbath may have influenced the early issuing of the proclamation and the writs, as leaving them until the Monday would have lost the administration two days.

[16] Dublin to Lismore generally took five days; Clonmel was similar, MacCarthy-Morrogh, 'The English presence', pp. 171–90.

[17] Richard Gethings, secretary to the president of Munster, Sir William St Leger, and William Smyth, Ormond's secretary, had to be admitted as freemen over the following weeks, NLI, MS 19171, pp. 319 fol. For further information on these men, see McGrath, 'Biographical dictionary', I, pp. 166–7, 271–2. The election was immediately succeeded by the appointment of an agent for the town to deal with some common lands under the Commission for the Remedy of Defective Titles. Ormond's growing influence in the town had been underlined by the invitation from the mayor for him to oversee the election of its mayor the previous autumn. Henry White to Ormond, 23 September 1639, NLI, MS 2306, p. 215. The mayor (Richard Wale) was the returning officer for the parliamentary election. Clonmel had been threatened with *quo warranto* proceedings to abolish its right to parliamentary representation, and equally significantly, one of its 1634 burgesses, Geoffrey Baron, had been expelled from that parliament by Wentworth,

At least as significant as the timescale was the confused state of the writs of election: a third of the returns listed had no date, and there are many omissions (especially the by-elections) and other mistakes.[18] Despite these deficiencies, it is possible to reconstruct at least part of the electoral process. Most of the constituencies noted as having returns in February are from parts of Munster furthest from Dublin; four Leinster boroughs which were noted as having held elections were disfranchised, and three of them elected only one MP each.[19] The inference is that all of these proceeded to elections without waiting for a writ; additionally, Ardee was disfranchised for refusing to make a return acceptable to the sheriff.

More curious than the fact that counties so far distant from Dublin made their returns so early is the evidence that the counties close to the capital did not. County Dublin's return was made on 2 March, and that of the capital city on the following day, and Swords two days later; again, the dates of Newcastle Lyons and Trinity College's returns have not survived, but Newcastle, as a disfranchised borough, may, like some of the others, have proceeded without waiting for the mandate. Meath, Athboy and Navan all made their returns on 4 March, but Trim and Kells waited until 13 March for their elections. Lord Robert Dillon, the Protestant eldest son of the earl of Westmeath, a privy councillor who was heavily involved in the organisation and opening of the parliament, may have been hoping for a county seat, and the Trim election was deferred until the last minute, as he was certain of a return for that borough, which he had also represented in 1634.[20] This does not, however, explain the delay in all the Meath seats, especially Kells, and it does not reflect the way

---

Aidan Clarke, '28 November 1634: a detail of Strafford's administration', *Journal of the Royal Society of Antiquaries of Ireland*, 43 (1963), pp. 161–7. Baron remained a significant figure in Clonmel, being chosen as the town's agent to deal with Ormond about some of the corporation's lands (1 July 1639) and successfully petitioning for a lease (October 1639), NLI MS 19171, pp. 307, 315. For Baron, see also McGrath, 'Parliament men' in Ó Siochrú (ed.), *Kingdoms in Crisis*, and W. P. Burke, *History of Clonmel* (Waterford, 1907), pp. 469 fol.

[18] While the writs themselves have not survived, the composite list of returns made by John Lodge has, NA, Lodge MSS 1A/53/56. This list is published in R. Lascelles, *Liber Munerum Publicorum Hiberniae*, Part 1 (London, 1824), with a few errors.

[19] The four Leinster boroughs were Ardee, Fore, Bannow and Taghmon, all of which returned Catholics. These boroughs first made returns in 1634, and while their burgesses were initially accepted as MPs by that parliament, the attorney general later questioned their right to be represented, only, however, after the Catholic MPs had questioned the right of thirty other boroughs incorporated since 1604, all of whom returned Protestants; the Catholics' petition is not noted in the *Commons Journals*, see notes of Philip Ferneley, clerk of the parliament, about the questioned boroughs, made in Trinity Term 1636. TCD, MS 672, f. 239 and *Commons' Jnl, Ire*, I, 24 and 31 July 1634. Athlone was also noted as having made a return in February 1640, but it had a history of returning writs to the sheriffs of both Westmeath and Roscommon.

[20] For Dillon and the other Meath representatives, see Bríd McGrath, 'Meath members of parliament, 1634–1641', *Riocht na Midhe*, 12 (2001), pp. 90–107.

that Meath dealt with elections in 1613. A similar situation obtained in Louth, where the county returns were made on 5 March, with Drogheda on 2 March, and Dundalk four days later.

This is in contrast to Augher, County Tyrone, much further from Dublin, which managed to make two returns in the same space of time (27 February and 7 March, because William Peisly had presumably failed to be returned for another seat).[21] It appears that the Old English community in Meath and Louth was deferring returns, either hoping for local agreement, or waiting, in vain, for the peers to take the lead.[22] Given the level of intimidation, it is understandable that people who had crossed swords with Wentworth (including the leading lawyer Patrick Darcy, who had represented Navan in 1634) declined to seek a seat.[23] Unfortunately, since information on the process for selecting candidates, especially on the Catholic side, has not survived, it is not possible to recreate the local political communities in Ireland as has been done so successfully in England.[24]

Yet, interestingly, more than half of the twenty-four constituencies who returned MPs of different religions were county seats, which were much less open to crown influence (or pressure) than the boroughs.[25] There

---

[21] The local Scot, John Karnes was returned in the first election, only to be replaced by Peisley, a man with close connections to Wentworth. William Parsons seems to have acted as the agent for this change. Tallow may also have held two elections: Lodge lists the borough's return as some time in February, but Sir Piercy Smyth writing on 3 March expected the election in the following week. Either the list is wrong, or, equally possibly, having agreed on a mixed pair of John Ogle and John Barry, pressure was applied to make the burgesses (or someone controlling the return) accept a second Protestant, Smyth himself, who was the nephew of Lord Cork, who controlled the borough, Chatsworth House, Lismore MSS 20, no.152, Sir Piercy Smyth to Cork, 2 March 1640. I am grateful to Mr Peter Day, Keeper of the Collections, for supplying me with a copy of this letter.

[22] An alternative reading is that the administration delayed the issuing of the writs, but this seems less probable.

[23] Darcy was unique among Catholic MPs in 1634 in representing a seat with which he had no connections. His brothers-in-law and fellow lawyers Richard Martin and Robuck Lynch were also returned in 1634, all of whom were closely allied with Clanricard, who had supported their legal education in London. Darcy's return for Navan was apparently due to the influence of his fellow lawyer in London, Christopher Darcy of Plattin, whose family was prominent in the area. Bríd McGrath, 'Parliament men' in Ó Siochrú (ed.), *Kingdoms in Crisis*, and 'Ireland and the third university: Irish men at the Inns of Court, 1603–1649' in D. Edwards (ed.), *Land, Law and Lords: essays commemorating the work of Kenneth Nicholls* (Dublin, forthcoming, 2004).

[24] J. K. Gruenfelder, *Influence in Early Stuart Elections, 1604–1640* (Columbus, 1981) and M. Kishlansky, *Parliamentary Selection: social and political choice in early modern England* (Cambridge, 1986). The sole Irish clues come from Youghal, where four candidates were voted on by the Commons, Caulfield (ed.), *Council Book of Youghal*, p. 146, and Kilkenny, where the aldermen drew up a shortlist of six candidates, all townsmen and including the recorder, for the electorate to choose from, 4 October 1628, NLI, MS 11,048(7).

[25] The boroughs that did have burgesses with different religious allegiances were Kilmallock, Dungarvan and Tallow (the latter two subject to Boyle's influence), Gowran

were fewer double returns than in previous parliaments, and the MPs so returned were less significant crown officials than in 1634 (apart from the chancellor of the exchequer, Richard Meredith, who was also a double return in 1634), indicating that the privy councillors had no difficulty in ensuring their own election, as well as the return of any men they favoured.[26] The state of the returns indicates the administration's contemptuous attitude to the elections and the personnel of the parliament. The shortness of the timescale and the extensive use of blanks may explain the state of the initial returns, but it does not account for the confusion of the returns for the by-elections for this parliament.

II

The parliament, which met on 16 March 1640, was smaller than its seventeenth-century predecessors. This was true as much for the House of Lords as for the Commons, and it is clear that Wentworth was controlling the parliament as much in its size as in its personnel, in both the upper and lower chambers. Unlike 1628, there were no new creations for the 1634 or 1640 parliaments.[27] In 1634 Wentworth considered the possibility of calling Lord Robert Dillon (the eldest son of the earl of Roscommon) as a peer in his own right, and Lord Cork's young sons, Lords Dungarvan, Kinalmeaky and Broghill. Ultimately, Wentworth supported Dillon's advancement but not Dungarvan's (and even less that of his brothers, partly on account of their extreme youth). In the event, Dillon sat in the Commons, as he had in 1634, and there were no new creations.[28]

In 1634 and 1640 Wentworth's influence in the Lords stemmed from his control over the issuing of summonses, and Sarsfield of Kilmallock and Gormanston later objected to Wentworth's use of proxies, claiming that peers had not received summons to attend the parliament.[29] The truth is more complex: peers were made aware that their attendance

and Callan (in which Ormond's influence is clear), Drogheda and Dundalk, Carlow and Old Leighlin and Trim (which returned the Protestant Old English privy councillor, Dillon).

[26] McGrath, 'Biographical dictionary', I, pp. 213–14.

[27] Victor Treadwell, *Buckingham and Ireland 1616–1628. A Study in Anglo-Irish Politics* (Dublin, 1998), p. 292. Three new barons were created, thirteen viscounts and four earls, although three of the earls already held minor titles. Muskerry and Molyneux were created too late for the proposed parliament, G.E.C., *Complete Peerage*, III, Appendix H, p. 642. There had also been other elevations, including Sarsfield of Kilmallock, the previous year.

[28] Knowler (ed.), *The Letters and Despatches*, I, p. 240. However, Dungarvan sat in the English parliament in 1640.

[29] PRO, SP 63/258, p. 163, Gormanston and Kilmallock's petition to the king, February 1641.

was not desired. Some were able to use this opportunity to their own advantage. Cork received early warning that his absence would be welcome, agreeing with Wentworth in December 1639 that Ormond, on whom the viceroy depended for his management of much of the business in the Lords, should receive his proxy. Cork used the opportunity to extract a long-awaited royal warrant for the college in Youghal.[30] By 10 March Clanricard had not received his writ of summons, although he had been notified that his personal attendance was not required. He then sent a message to Wentworth that 'Upon receiving of my writt I will make my owne addresses to him & give my L[ordshi]p a good accompt of the disposing of my proxie.' He went on to raise the question of the issuing of a patent, clearly linking the disposal of his proxy and the granting of the favour.[31] Conway's licence to be absent was dated 11 March and directed him to give his proxy to 'some Nobleman of that Kingdom'.[32]

The calculated tardiness in issuing the writs and licences insulted the lords and stressed their powerlessness, especially since Roche of Fermoy, waiting in London for his summons and licence to be absent, knew that Wentworth had left London very early in the morning of 5 March.[33] Clanricard, Conway and Cork were to sit in the English Lords, but the apparently casual approach to proxies suggests that Wentworth had enough to be able easily to control the upper house, and, at this stage, it was more important to limit the numbers attending.[34] Having an in-built majority provided by bishops and loyal peers (predominantly privy councillors), it suited Wentworth to exclude as many peers as possible, especially those likely to be less than wholehearted in their support for the government, and those who controlled or influenced significant numbers of MPs, as their contributions could delay proceedings and detract from the necessary extravagant display of loyalty to the crown.

---

[30] The concession was clearly linked to his absence from Parliament, A. B. Grosart (ed.), *The Lismore Papers* (10 vols., NS, 1886–8), 1st series, V, p.119; the letters arrived on 18 February 1639–40 (*ibid.*, p. 126). It is possible that Cork was in an even more favourable position, as he may also have controlled his sons' proxies: by 1640, Kinalmeaky was 20 years old and would be 21 by May 1640; Broghill was nearly 19 at the opening of the parliament.

[31] PRO, SP 63/258, p. 27, Clanricard to ?, 10 March 1640.

[32] PRO, SP 63/258, pp. 29–30, warrant to Conway, 11 March 1640.

[33] Grosart (ed.), *The Lismore Papers*, 1st series, V, p. 129. Roche of Fermoy received his writ and licence on the evening of 14 March, 36 hours before the parliament was due to meet. The next day he enclosed his proxy in a letter to Mountgarret. He wrote in the knowledge that he had given his vote to a man with whom he had been on very bad terms for years and also that the proxy could not possibly arrive in time for the beginning of the parliament, PRO, SP 63/258, p. 33.

[34] Henry Leslie, bishop of Down, was also unable to attend the opening of the parliament, due to sickness, Knowler (ed.), *The Letters and Despatches*, II, p. 392.

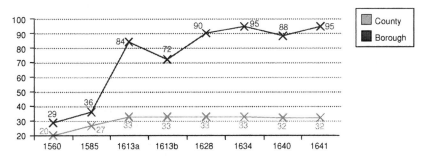

Figure 1 Constituencies, 1561–1641

It would also remove them from ready access to MPs who might work with them in the Commons, as peers with licences to be absent could not remain in Dublin.[35]

The size of the Commons also shrank. While the number of counties was well established by 1613 and, with the exception of the amalgamation in 1637 of the historical church lands (which formed the county of Cross Tipperary) with the secular property in the same county, remained unchanged into the 1990s, the number of boroughs was open to change. Traditionally this had been done only by increasing the number of parliamentary boroughs, most obviously between 1585 and 1613, when the number of urban constituencies more than doubled from thirty-six to eighty-four seats.[36] As Figure 1 illustrates, further constituencies were created for the proposed parliament of 1628 and an additional eleven seats by 1634.

While Wentworth had no difficulty in promoting the incorporation of parliamentary boroughs in England, he may not have incorporated any in Ireland.[37] On the contrary, in 1640 he reversed a trend by cutting the number of constituencies, and would have further reduced them had other constituencies not agreed to return Protestants under threat of having their charters wholly revoked. As parliament met rarely, but trade

<hr/>

[35] Not that it was their usual place of abode. Cork and Clanricard were resident in England at this time, Roche of Fermoy was exiled to England, and Conway was occupied with the army in the Bishops' Wars.

[36] McGrath, 'Membership of the Irish House of Commons', pp. 31–5; 'A biographical dictionary', I, pp. 25–8.

[37] Gruenfelder, *Influence in Early Stuart Elections*, p. 95 notes that 'In the whole of Elizabeth's reign and that of her first two Stuart successors, Hertford's restoration was unique, coming not as the result of local pressures but as the consequences of court intervention' whereas in Ireland, the crown's needs were overwhelmingly more important than local pressures in the creation of parliamentary boroughs. See also A. J. Fletcher, 'Sir Thomas Wentworth and the restoration of Pontefract as a parliamentary borough', *Northern History*, 6 (1971), pp. 89–97.

was conducted daily, this was a potent inducement not merely to the merchant communities, but also to landholders who would need to sell their produce locally. Most boroughs appear to have bowed to the threat of removing charters, apart from Naas and Ardee, which were disfranchised for refusing to return Protestants.[38]

In the county constituencies the sheriffs conducted the return at the assizes, in a place and at a time known to the electorate, usually one of the principal towns of the county. While there were occasional disputes about the location of the assizes, they were generally well known and accepted.[39] Assizes served as the obvious election venue, attracting considerable numbers of county notables who gathered in the town to deal with legal matters and to socialise. Thus any decision to move the election to an alternative venue could produce surprise results. There is some evidence that the location of elections may have been altered in 1640. For instance, the 1640 assizes were held in Belfast, for the first and only time before 1850, with the town hall fitted up for use as a courthouse. The sheriff of Tyrone attempted to hold the by-election for the county seat away from the county town in 1641.[40] This ploy may have been used on other occasions during the Irish elections. Certainly Wentworth also used it in England later in the same year, moving the election for Yorkshire's county members to Pontefract, a borough in which his interest was supposed to be greater.[41]

Despite the lack of clarity about the dates of elections, the identity of the men returned for individual constituencies by 16 March is well

[38] Sarsfield of Kilmallock and Gormanston's petition noted the threat of 'suspending divers ancient boroughs from their liberty of election of burgesses upon pretence of seizure of their liberties uppon surreptitious writte of Quo warranto', PRO, SP 63/258, p. 163. Ardee apparently held an election in February 1640, on an unspecified date, but the sheriff refused to forward the result. Previously, the town had always returned local merchants; when it returned MPs after October 1640, its members were Henry Moore and Joshua Boyle, both of whom were closely linked to Lord Cork.

[39] This stipulation is given in the instructions for sheriffs in the election in 1613, *Commons' Jnl, Ire*, I, p. 3; the location of the election was one of the points at issue in the by-election for Tyrone in 1641, *Commons' Jnl, Ire*, I, 1 March 1641. However, in some cases, there were disputes about the location of the assizes. For example, see MacCarthy-Morrogh, *The Munster Plantation: English migration to Southern Ireland, 1583–1641* (Oxford, 1986), pp. 271–2, that details the quarrel about the location of the Waterford county assizes, between Tallow, a New English settlement, and Waterford. At the mid-summer quarter sessions in Waterford in 1639 the Protestant JPs assembled in Tallow and the Catholics in Waterford City. In this case, a slim majority of the justices were Catholics and if this religious balance was replicated in other counties, the possibility of moving the venue for the assizes to facilitate Protestant and discourage Catholic attendance, could have a significant effect on returns, and help to explain the loss of Catholic county seats between 1634 and 1640, Clarke, *Old English*, p. 126. The quarter sessions were held in Dungarvan in 1619, Grosart (ed.), *The Lismore Papers*, 1st series, I, p. 210.

[40] R. M. Young, The *Town Book of the Corporation of Belfast, 1613–1816* (Belfast, 1892), p. x.

[41] Gruenfelder, *Influence in Early Stuart Elections*, p. 186.

established in virtually all cases. Serious intimidation was involved in
many returns, particularly in Clonmel and Ardee. Sarsfield of Kilmallock
and Gormanston later accused the government of 'overawing & sway-
ing elections by letters, messages and intimations from his lordship
and those of his partie for persons engaged to his will and power'.[42]
Privy councillors came under serious pressure to deliver seats and later
to support the administration's position in parliament. According to
Kilmallock and Gormanston, this was done 'By overpowering of diverse
members of that assemblie, especially those of the privy council, to com-
plie to his lo[rdshi]ps propositions, for feare of loss of their places and
imployment.'[43]

The government's task was eased by the fact that so many important
people, apart from members of the council, opted out of a role in the elections. This was in stark contrast to the elections to the 1634 parliament.[44]
Cork's curious lack of interest in the 1640 elections has already been
noted.[45] Six years earlier he had made a great fuss about the parliament,
ordering his robes for the opening session, sorting out nominations, filling
in blanks for returns, and giving his niece £10 to buy a new dress for the
occasion.[46] Yet in 1640 his correspondence and diaries remained curiously silent on the subject of elections, and he showed little interest in
the entire parliament. He was residing in England during these months,
and the men returned for the boroughs in which he had a special interest
were not of the same quality or as close to him personally as those returned
in 1634 (his nephew Sir Piercy Smith and his brother-in-law William
Fenton).

Other prominent men who had formerly protected their interests
through the return of clients to the Commons, and their own presence
in the Lords, were also noticeably absent, including the disgraced Lord
Treasurer Mountnorris.[47] A large number of MPs in 1634 did not return
to the 1640 parliament, especially for the first session. The most obvious
Catholic absences were the lawyers Patrick Darcy, Richard Martin, Luke
Netterville, Robert Talbot, Geoffrey Baron and Adam Cusack, all of
whom had been prominent in 1634. Given their previous experiences
at Wentworth's hands, they clearly chose not to stand. A number of
significant Protestants were not in the house, notably John Clotworthy and Arthur Jones, later members of the Long Parliament, along
with Mountnorris's clients and several prominent lawyers.[48] The rump

---

[42] PRO, SP 63/258, p. 163.   [43] *Ibid.*
[44] MacCarthy-Morrogh, *Munster Plantation*, pp. 260–9.
[45] *Ibid.*, pp. 265–7.   [46] Grosart (ed.), *The Lismore Papers*, 1st series, IV, pp. 28–9, 35.
[47] See chapter 8 above.
[48] These included Jerome Alexander, MP for Lifford, who had fallen foul of Wentworth,
who described him as a 'scurvy puritan', Clarke, *Prelude to Restoration*, pp. 171–2. There

of Chichester's clients, still obvious in 1634, had also disappeared. A number of prominent soldiers were also absent, but this may be explained by their military duties, given the Scottish situation.

From the administration's point of view, it appeared more important to prevent the return of opponents than to arrange for the return of useful MPs. While the use of blank returns was well established in previous parliaments, the confusion over the returns suggests that this device was more widespread on this occasion.[49] The first business after Speaker Eustace's opening speech on 20 March 1640 was Christopher Wandesford's motion that those doubly returned should be requested to select which constituency they wished to represent and that new elections should be held for their replacements. The Commons agreed to this and also ordered new writs 'in the place of any such of the House as are absent in England, or elsewhere, and of such as are mis-named in any of the returns already made'.[50] The most obvious absent MPs were John Wandesford and George Wentworth, who were also returned to the Short Parliament, although Wentworth retained his Irish seat into 1641. The reference to misnaming may well indicate the level of blanks being used by the administration. There is, for example, no evidence that John Wandesford, who was returned for Inistiogue, ever visited Ireland, and another Wandesford, variously described as Michael and Nicholas, who was returned for Thomastown, cannot be identified.[51] John Wandesford's

---

were more serious reasons to mistrust Alexander, who had been disbarred in England for falsifying legal documents; however, this did not prevent his advancement to the position of second justice of the Common Pleas, *Breviate of a Sentence Given against J. A. . . . in the Court of Star Chamber . . .* (London, 1644). For the community of lawyers, see McGrath, 'Ireland and the third university'.

[49] Writing in 1634, Cork noted that 'Mr. Walley sent me two bl[a]ncks under the officers' hands, and town seales, of Tallagh (Tallow) and Lismore, with power to insert such 4 burgesses names as I should think to serve his Majesty in the next parliament', Grosart (ed.), *The Lismore Papers*, 1st series, IV, p. 33. Lodge's list of returns dates the returns as 17 and 18 June respectively. No writs of return are known to have survived for Ireland. The official compilation of returns gives dates for a number of constituencies, but for very many simply lists the month in which they were made. For the English House of Commons see, *Lists of Members' Returns. Members of Parliament, Part 1, Parliaments of England, 1213–1702, Part 2 Parliaments of Great Britain . . .* (London, 1878). There are many errors in this work cited in W. W. Bean, *The Parliamentary Returns of Members of the House of Commons from 1213 to 1874* (London, 1883), although these do not cover the 1640 Irish parliament in any detail. However, the far greater problem with this compilation from the point of view of this chapter is the omission of most of the by-elections and a number of other inaccuracies in the lists of Irish MPs. As these compilations were made on the basis of transcriptions by Lodge, who had access to the original writs, the strong probability is that this reflects the state of the original writs and requires further explanation.

[50] *Commons' Jnl, Ire,* I, 16 March 1640.

[51] The fact that Inistiogue is the only constituency listed in the official returns as having made its return on 1 March 1640 (a Sunday), lends credence to the notion that blanks were used. John Wandesford had recently returned to England after eleven years as consul

fellow MP, Robert Maude, was also a Yorkshireman, but there is no evidence of his involvement in Ireland before the parliament. He may have been, like John, a Yorkshireman at a loose end in England who might be prevailed upon to come to Ireland as part of the collection of Wentworth-Wandesford-Radcliffe adherents and dependants.

Central to Wentworth's parliamentary strategy in 1640 was the ability of the government to limit cooperation between the houses; this was largely achieved by reducing the numbers and managing the personnel. Peers who had been effectively excluded were not available to work with, defend, support or direct, members of the lower house. It is in this context that the lateness of the writs of summons (and the issue of licences for absence) should also be seen. In the absence of surviving records of returns or mandates to elect, the course of the elections can only be surmised. However, it is interesting to note that the increase in the number of active peers in the upper house coincides with a series of by-elections which reflected their interests. Close cooperation between the houses is obvious from 1641, not from the first session.

As Aidan Clarke has shown, Wentworth's ingenious interpretation of Poynings' Law spancelled the parliament's movement and may have contributed to the lack of interest in the elections to parliament: if parliament was impotent, what interest was served by membership? However, even by the end of the first session, the situation began to change. The Commons established a committee to

consider and advise of what laws have been propounded in the House this session of Parliament, and also of what other laws and ordinances they do conceive are wanting, and not yet thought on, that may be useful, and tend to the better settling of this Commonwealth and the remedying of which abuses and inconveniences, for redress whereof laws have not heretofore been ordained; and that the said Committee show draw and prepare bills for the same to be presented to the Lords and others of the Committee of the Councel-head.[52]

Wentworth's removal from Ireland, and the reversion to a previous interpretation of Poynings' Law, set the scene for a rush of new blood into the parliament, and to an upsurge in discussion about the best means of managing public affairs.

III

Following the dissolution of the Short Parliament in May 1640 and Wentworth's failure to replicate in London his successful dominance of

for the English merchants in Aleppo, and while Maude had Irish connections, they seem to date from the years after 1640. McGrath, 'Biographical dictionary', I, pp. 299–300 and 210–11.

[52] *Commons' Jnl, Ire*, I, 1 April 1640.

politics in Dublin, his control in Ireland also began to slip. When the Irish parliament reassembled in June, the administration under Wandesford found it increasingly difficult to manage political life.[53] The house's membership altered very significantly between March 1640 and November 1641. Apart from the double and disputed returns, at least ten members died;[54] five, all Protestants with close connections to the administration, were expelled;[55] three succeeded to titles of honour;[56] and twenty-one resigned their seats[57] during the first four sessions. A number of by-elections returned replacements, although it is not always clear when these took place, for which constituencies and who was returned as a result of them. The vast majority of those recorded as leaving the Commons were Protestants (thirty-two compared with seven Catholics), and they were often replaced by Catholics (thirty-three Catholics and twenty-two Protestants). While this altered the balance significantly, it did not produce an actual or a working Catholic majority in the house, although the Irish parliamentary system in this period did not generally operate in a majoritarian way or divide along religious lines.[58]

The pattern of replacement of MPs reflected the prevailing political climate. The early by-elections (March–October 1640) favoured the administration, with Protestants replacing Protestants in the double-returned seats. Thus Robert Loftus took Christopher Wandesford's seat, Robert King moved up to a county seat from a borough, and the stalemate over Ardee's returns continued. Even the new MP for Kerry was a son-in-law of the Protestant Lord Kerry. In June 1640 the Commons ordered the issue of writs for returns to the disfranchised boroughs, but the administration stalled for a further four months, although it arranged for

---

[53] Perceval-Maxwell, *Outbreak of the Irish Rebellion*, pp. 76–8 suggests that opposition alliances began to form after knowledge of the failure of the Short Parliament and that the first suggestions of resistance came on 8 June.

[54] Six Protestants – Thomas Madden, Robert Loftus, Thomas Little Sr, Christopher Wandesford, George Nettleton and Simon Thoroughgood – and four Catholics – Valentine Browne, Edward Fitzharris, Thomas Peppard and Oliver Plunkett – died.

[55] They were Joshua Carpenter, Edward Lake, Thomas Little Jr, William Peisley and Thomas Radcliffe.

[56] Two Catholics, James Butler and Donough MacCarthy, and the Protestant Toby Caulfield.

[57] These included twenty Protestants, William Alford, Francis Butler, William Gilbert Jr, Robert King, William Kingsmill, Walter Loftus, Philip Mainwaring, Robert Maude, George and Hugh Montgomery, Henry Osbourne, Dudley Philips, Toby Poyntz, George Radcliffe, William Reading, William St. Leger Jr, John Wandesford, George Wentworth, Maurice Williams and William Wray and a single Catholic, Piers Butler. It may be assumed that others also resigned or ceased to attend, especially those who had been closely associated with Wentworth's administration, particularly the other members of the Wandesford family and Robert Nettleton, although their resignations are not recorded in the *Commons Journals*.

[58] Perceval-Maxwell, *Outbreak of the Irish Rebellion*, p. 69.

by-elections in cases of double returns or deceased members. At least one double return was dealt with, as John Edgeworth was nominated to a committee, although the speed of his return is suspicious. The parliament was prorogued shortly afterwards, amidst increasing friction between the administration and the MPs. Elections for the disfranchised boroughs had not taken place by the opening of the second session, as the lord chancellor refused to issue the writs which had been prepared five weeks before the new session began. This session saw a more militant approach by the Commons. MPs requested that writs for replacement of dead MPs be issued automatically and questioned the deputy clerk of the hanaper and then the lord chancellor about the writs. They suspended all business on 7 October and, on reassembling two days later, dissolved into a grand committee 'to consider of the privileges of this House now in question'.[59] A further order for the issuing of all the writs except that for the borough of Fore was made on 21 October, and on the following day the house ordered the release of the sheriff of Louth, suggesting that agreement had been reached about the returns for Ardee.[60] The death of Sir Robert Loftus, MP for Inistiogue, on 11 October caused a further by-election, and the advocate general was expelled on 9 November, leaving another vacant seat.[61] One day before the session ended on 12 November a by-election took place that marked the end of the administration's control of elections, with the precipitate return for Inistiogue of John Fitzgerald, the knight of Kerry, providentially providing him with privilege from arrest during his dispute with Lord Kerry.

During this second session most committees had Catholic majorities and sizeable numbers of Protestant opposition members who worked together on an agreed agenda, including a substantial reduction in the level of subsidies, the discontinuation of the bill for the plantation of Connacht, the restoration of the disputed boroughs' franchise, and the content of the Remonstrance addressed to the king in England. Wandesford forbade the committee appointed to transmit the Remonstrance to leave Ireland, but two members, John Bellew and Oliver Cashel, travelled to London, and their introduction to the Long Parliament by Clotworthy coincided with the English Commons' attack on Wentworth. The identity of the Protestant opposition leaders in the third session can be seen in this committee, which included Richard Fitzgerald (a Perceval connection, but also linked to Cork and Parsons), Sir Hardress Waller

---

[59] *Commons' Jnl, Ire*, I, 9 October 1640.
[60] References may be found in *Commons' Jnl, Ire*, I.
[61] Loftus was buried on 16 October, *Association for the Preservation of the Memorials of the Dead in Ireland, Some funeral entries of Ireland from a manuscript volume [Add. MS 4820] in the British Museum* (Dublin, 1907). p. 179.

(also linked to Cork), Edward Rowley (brother-in-law of Clotworthy and Audley Mervyn), Simon Digby (a Cork connection and Lord Bristol's cousin), Sir William Cole (formerly imprisoned by Wentworth) and James Montgomery. Other Protestant leaders included two government supporters, Lord Robert Dillon and Sir James Ware. However, prominent administration members, such as Sir Adam Loftus and Charles Coote, had joined in the opposition alongside other New English men such as Cork's cousin Robert Travers and Sir Edward Denny, a major landowner in Kerry.[62]

The ten-week interval between the second and third sessions saw a series of by-elections which the opposition won hands down. By the opening of the third session on 26 January 1641 the disfranchised boroughs returned twelve Catholics and Ardee returned burgesses linked to Lords Cork and Moore of Drogheda. Over the course of the following months a series of returns strengthened the position of the Old English and New English oppositions. It is not always possible to identify the influences behind returns, and in the cases of old boroughs such as Kildare and Drogheda they seem to reflect the restored power of the burgesses to represent themselves. However, in many cases the influence of peers or of other significant local figures is demonstrable. Thus by the end of the third session in March the Trevors of County Down achieved two returns in their interests and Boyle acquired an additional place for a client (through the expulsion of Wentworth's associates Thomas Little and Joshua Carpenter). Virtually the last recorded act of the Commons in the third session was to arrange for the issue of yet more writs, replacements for ten Protestants, including six closely associated with Wentworth.[63] In addition, a place was created for the return of Sir William Stewart, the privy councillor who had failed to win a seat in Tyrone.

By this time there were rumours in London that the Irish parliament was about to be dissolved and a new one elected. The Catholic John Barry of Liscarroll wrote to Viscount Muskerry asking him to persuade his brother-in-law, Ormond, to arrange for his return – an indication of the current trend in nominations.[64] In the event, the parliament was not

---

[62] Denny expressed the disquiet felt generally in Ireland at Wentworth's appointment, 'Ye lord Viscount Wentworth arrived in Ireland to govern ye Kingdom as Deputy. Many men feare', entry in Denny's diary, 23 July 1633, *Journal of the Association for the Preservation of the Memorials of the Dead in Ireland*, 7 (1907–9), p. 371. For Denny see McGrath, 'Biographical dictionary', pp. 132–3.

[63] They were George Radcliffe, Philip Mainwaring, George Wentworth, Maurice Williams, Thomas Little Sr and John Jackson.

[64] BL, Add. MSS 46,925, f. 210r, John Barry of Liscarroll to Philip Perceval, London, 8 March 1641. Barry informed Perceval on 24 November 1640 that the English parliament 'is making an order to chastise all Papists in the army, and among the rest myself;

dissolved, and during the interval between the third and fourth sessions, and throughout that fourth session, there occurred a further series of by-elections, which reflected the influence of those represented in the Long Parliament.[65] They also show an unprecedented level of involvement by peers, as well as an exceptional level of cooperation between Catholic and Protestant interests. Elections in Tyrone resulted in the return of two of Clanricard's clients – the lawyers Patrick Darcy and Richard Martin – as well as Sir Phelim O'Neill. These results, especially O'Neill's, could only have been possible with the cooperation of Audley Mervyn and the Chichesters. Martin's return may even have involved Sir William Parsons. The Chichesters must also have cooperated with Lord Antrim in the return of Philip Wenman for Belfast, as Antrim presumably cooperated with Sir William Parsons in Arthur Hill's election for Carysfort, in Wicklow. The return of Redmond Roche for County Cork served the combined interests of Lords Muskerry, Cork and Roche of Fermoy and Sir Hardress Waller. Sir Philip Perceval gained an additional ally in the lower house with the election of his brother-in-law, William Dobbins, for Askeaton. Ormond and Mountgarret would both have been pleased at the election of Richard Bellings for Callan. The St George–Coote coalition was presumably behind the return of Thomas Johnson for Carrick-on-Shannon, and Lord Taaffe may have secured a return in Sligo. Robert King, although preoccupied with events in England, ensured the election of two of his connections for Boyle and Roscommon in July 1641. Cork, the Moores, Digby and the privy councillor Sir Robert Forth would have welcomed Barnabas Dempsey's return for Ballinakill and Sir Matthew De Renzy's election for an unidentified constituency.

The Commons also maintained its own membership. On 28 June 1641 it ordered that 'the Clerk of this house shall inform this House, tomorrow morning, what Boroughs have not sent burgesses to Parliament' – presumably a prelude to more by-elections.[66] Overall, the by-election returns of these months show a remarkable level of cooperation between

---

they fall out bitterly against us all, and begin to banish us out of town and to remove all from Court . . . I was never a factionary in religion, nor shall ever seek the ruin of any because he is not of my opinion. I have my end in this world if I can satisfy my own conscience', BL, Add. MSS 46924, ff. 144–5r. Barry's comment about his career as a soldier is also significant. Catholics, including men like James Dillon, had received commissions in the new army in 1640 for the first time in many years. Kenneth Nicholls (personal communication) suggests that Barry was the MP for Tallow. For his career, see W. Kelly, 'John Barry a Catholic royalist in the 1640s' in Ó Siochrú (ed.), *Kingdoms in Crisis*, pp. 141–57.

[65] The expulsions of Wentworth's associates, William Peisley and Thomas Radcliffe, created two further vacancies.

[66] *Commons' Jnl, Ire*, I, 28 June 1641.

the Old and New English, including privy councillors, regardless of religion. The number of MPs of Gaelic origin also increased: at least five replacements – Bryan and Phelim O'Neill, Patrick and Robert Casey and Barnabas Dempsey – were Gaelic (two were Protestant). Seats vacated by Scotsmen, generally clients of the Hamiltons and Montgomerys, drew their replacements from the same families and their connections. The administration obviously fought hard for some seats. For instance, in Ennis a servant of Lord Robert Dillon was returned, presumably through the earl of Thomond's influence. By and large, though, the government was outflanked. While the confusion in the returns makes it hard to match many of the seats, the personnel returned show that the administration had completely lost control of the parliament and the peers had regained it.

Between the end of the fourth session on 7 August and the beginning of the next session on 9 November the rebellion broke out. There was a debate about whether or not the parliament would reassemble, which may have lessened interest in by-elections; but if elections were to be held for vacant seats, the writs should have gone out by the end of September, three weeks before the outbreak of the rising. There is no evidence that they did. On the contrary, the writ for Gowran was probably only issued after the decision to allow the parliament to meet.[67] As a result, and presumably through Ormond's agency, Sir Piers Crosbie, readmitted to the council in the summer, and one of those who argued that parliament should meet, was returned for Gowran, a seat which had been vacant since the summer.[68] Perhaps at that stage it seemed that the administration would again resume control of the house.

IV

The administration aggressively controlled elections to the Irish parliament in March 1640 using a combination of tactics: an almost unrealistically tight timescale; a reduction in the number of seats available; and a concerted campaign to return government supporters by placing severe pressure on boroughs to return placemen, forcing at least two boroughs to revise their returns and doubly returned members. Unlike previous parliaments, those doubly returned were generally lobby fodder, rather than significant figures in the administration, indicating that the campaign of

---

[67] Kilkenny City Archives, MX CR/K/56, mandate from Sir Cyprian Horsfall, sheriff of Kilkenny to Pierse Keally, Portreeve of Gowran, 7 November 1641. I am grateful to David Edwards for bringing this reference to my attention.
[68] Clarke, *Old English*, p. 171.

ensuring the election of important officials was more easily achieved in 1640 than previously.

It is equally clear that many people opted out of membership of the 1640 parliament for themselves or for their clients, on the grounds that membership would be of no advantage to them or their communities – either because the parliament was so impotent that membership was pointless, or that opposition could only damage their own positions. This was as true for the House of Lords as for the Commons, and the interaction between the two needs further study. Instead, the members adopted a position of constructive acquiescence to the government's demands. However, from June 1640, when it appeared that effective opposition was possible, there emerged a coalition of interests that altered the composition of the house and the way it was able to work. At first the administration successfully resisted the change, both by winning by-elections and preventing others from taking place. Yet by the middle of October it had lost the initiative; and while the first by-elections were of Catholic gentry and merchants representing their local communities, increasingly the by-elections allowed the peers and those privy councillors who had not been sympathetic to Wentworth or prospered under him, to secure the return of their own clients. The elections also show the return of people with contacts in the opposition in the Long Parliament. These patterns of return are also reflected in the composition of the committees working in the Commons, where New and Old English, Protestant and Catholic, cooperated in the business of the house. This situation continued until the rebellion in October 1641, with the last known by-election of that year resulting in the return to the Commons, apparently at the behest of Ormond, of the improbable establishment figure and recently reinstated privy councillor, Sir Piers Crosby.[69]

The by-elections demonstrate the ease with which political cohesion had been achieved between the New English and the Old English communities and highlight their commitment to parliament as a means of solving political problems. They present a picture of a heterogeneous community coming to terms with considerable social and political change and able, at least in the short term, to show flexibility, imagination, cooperation and sophisticated political thinking. Thus, the later sessions of this parliament were characterised by enlightened mutual support, albeit for limited political ends, making the subsequent deep divisions even more striking.

---

[69] Aidan Clarke, 'Sir Piers Crosby (1590–1646): Wentworth's "tawney ribbon"', *IHS*, 102 (1988), pp. 142–60.

However, with the onset of the insurrection, the Catholic MPs were either expelled for rebellion or voluntarily left the parliament, leaving only a Protestant rump to sit for another seven years. In June 1642 the Catholics established their Confederation in Kilkenny, an alternative representative assembly, which carefully did not call itself a parliament. Yet it was consciously modelled on the Dublin parliament, and its most prominent members were the MPs who had sat in 1634 and 1640. Most importantly, it allowed those who had been rigorously excluded from exercising political power or administrative office in Ireland to adopt those roles and to govern at least part of the country until 1649.[70] The Cromwellian reconquest cut short their political activities and also ushered in a brief period of direct rule from Westminster. With the restoration in 1660 of Charles II, the Irish parliament was also reinstated. However, the Commons proved to be a very different body to the house elected in 1640; the only Catholic returned to the 1661 lower house was the Galway lawyer Geoffrey Browne, who was unable to take his seat in what now had become an exclusively Protestant assembly.

[70] McGrath, 'Parliament men' in Ó Siochrú (ed.), *Kingdoms in Crisis*, pp. 90–105.

10 Catholic Confederates and the constitutional relationship between Ireland and England, 1641–1649

Micheál Ó Siochrú

On Wednesday 17 January 1649, at a lavish ceremony in Kilkenny Castle, the Catholic Confederates signed a peace treaty with the lord lieutenant, James Butler, marquis of Ormond. In an emotional speech, the chairman of the Confederate General Assembly, Sir Richard Blake, hoped the agreement would 'restore this nation in its former lustre'. Ormond responded generously, with a promise of further concessions from the king. In an uncharacteristically dramatic flourish, he announced: 'There are no bounds to your hopes.'[1] The mutually congratulatory nature of these proceedings belied the six years of tortuous and often rancorous negotiations which preceded the agreement. Historians of the mid-seventeenth century have tended to focus on the bitter religious divisions of the period. But attempts by Confederates and royalists to clarify the constitutional relationship between Ireland and England proved equally controversial. The operation of Poynings' Law and increasing interference by the English parliament in Irish affairs emerged as the two key points of contention during peace talks.

In an article on the political thought of Patrick Darcy, Aidan Clarke argues that the Confederate stance on Poynings' Law was an issue of trust rather than constitutional principle. They were only interested in a suspension of the act in order to speed up the ratification of treaty terms by the Irish parliament, without interference from the king.[2] Similarly, Confederate demands for a declaratory act on the independence of the Irish parliament could be interpreted as nothing more than a tactic to

I would like to thank Aidan Clarke, Kevin Whelan, David Ditchburn, Phil Withington and the editors of this volume for reading and commenting on earlier drafts of this chapter. I would also like to thank the Leverhulme Trust for funding a research fellowship, which enabled me to complete work on this article.

[1] *The Marquesse of Ormond's Proclamation Concerning the Peace Concluded with the Irish Rebels . . . with a speech delivered by Sir Richard Blake . . . also a speech delivered by the marquesse of Ormond* (London, 1649).

[2] Aidan Clarke, 'Patrick Darcy and the constitutional relationship between Ireland and Britain' in Jane Ohlmeyer (ed.), *Political Thought in Seventeenth-century Ireland* (Cambridge, 2000), pp. 48–9.

ensure that Westminster would not attempt to overturn the peace settlement. Alongside these immediate short-term considerations, however, there is strong evidence to suggest that the Confederates, following their experiences under Lord Deputy Thomas Wentworth in the 1630s, and the subsequent efforts of the English parliament to claim jurisdiction over Ireland, believed that the constitutional relationship between Ireland and England required urgent clarification.

I

The development of Poynings' Law, from its inception in 1494 until 1641, has been examined in a series of articles in *Irish Historical Studies* by D. B. Quinn, T. W. Moody, R. D. Dudley-Edwards and, of course, Aidan Clarke. Brendan Bradshaw also discusses the act in detail in *The Irish Constitutional Revolution of the Sixteenth Century*.[3] Collectively these studies illustrate the confusion surrounding the implementation of the law throughout this period, the interpretation of which seemed to change with each new chief governor. Poynings' Law, as originally drafted in 1494, required the Irish executive to seek royal licence to hold a parliament. Proposed legislation also had to be certified into England under the Irish great seal in order to receive royal approval. The act, therefore, involved the English monarch directly in the government of Ireland, initially to supervise the activities of the executive in Dublin.

The operation of Poynings' Law initially proved extremely flexible. Acts were enrolled by parliament which had not been formally certified, and amendments added to various bills. The law was modified in 1557, allowing the chief governor and council to transmit bills when parliament was already in session, that is, after the initial certification procedure. This also facilitated the introduction of amendments to proposed legislation. Private bills were usually submitted directly to the lord deputy for transmission to England, but parliament only presented the titles of public bills, which were then drafted by the chief governor and council. Poynings' Law did not define who sat on this 'council', but its core usually consisted of the great officers of state, augmented by leading members of the nobility and gentry. This 'reinforced council' was probably the origin of the claim by Old English Catholics in 1611 and again in 1634 that they had a right to be consulted over proposed legislation.[4]

---

[3] D. B. Quinn, 'The early interpretation of Poynings' Law, 1494–1534', *IHS*, 2:7 (1941), pp. 241–54; T. W. Moody and R. D. Edwards, 'The history of Poynings' Law, Part I, 1494–1615', *IHS*, 2:8 (1941), pp. 415–24; Aidan Clarke, 'The history of Poynings' Law, 1615–1641', *IHS*, 18:70 (1972), pp. 207–22; Brendan Bradshaw, *The Irish Constitutional Revolution of the Sixteenth Century* (Cambridge, 1979).

[4] Prior to the 1613–15 parliament, the lord deputy, Sir Arthur Chichester, dismissed Catholic demands – as part 'of the grand council' – to be consulted over legislation as

Following the Kildare rebellion in 1534–45 and the replacement of local magnates as chief governors by Protestant 'new men' from England, the Old English interest began to assert itself more forcibly in parliament. Catholic members frequently obstructed legislation, particularly on religious matters, through a rigid application of Poynings' Law.[5] Not surprisingly, successive chief governors sought to have the law suspended for the duration of parliament. The last to succeed was Sir Henry Sidney in 1569, though only after agreeing to amend the act to prohibit future suspensions, except by formal resolutions passed first in both the Commons and Lords in Ireland. It would prove impossible, therefore, for the Dublin administration to present parliament with a suspension bill already bearing royal approval.[6] During the parliament of 1585 MPs successively defeated an attempt by the chief governor, Sir John Perrot, to suspend Poynings' Law and introduce various anti-Catholic measures. Until the early seventeenth century, therefore, the Dublin administration continued to regard the act as an obstacle to their legislative programmes, while Catholic representatives valued it as a useful political tool.[7]

All this changed in the 1630s when the new lord deputy, Thomas Wentworth (later earl of Strafford), devised an alternative strategy on Poynings' Law. For the 1634 parliament he rejected a proposal from the English attorney general for a suspension of the act. Confident of his ability to manipulate parliament, and of the king's total support, Wentworth planned to use the provisions of Poynings' Law to maintain rigid control of the legislative programme.[8] He refused the nobility and gentry a role in drafting bills for the initial transmission to England, citing an earlier denial in 1611 by Lord Deputy Chichester as a precedent for his actions. In his typically abrasive manner, Wentworth advised the Catholic earl

---

unprecedented and unwarranted. He suggested that the Catholics send their own legislative proposals to England along with the Irish government's proposals. They declined his offer. According to Moody and Edwards, Chichester was anxious that the Catholic opposition would not know the government's intentions in advance. Moody and Edwards, 'History of Poynings' Law', pp. 423–4; John McCavitt, *Sir Arthur Chichester* (Belfast, 1998), pp. 178–9.

[5] Moody and Edwards, 'History of Poynings' Law', p. 418. By proposing numerous amendments, MPs could delay legislation almost indefinitely.

[6] Hugh Kearney, *Strafford in Ireland, 1633–41: A study in absolutism* (Cambridge, 1989), p. 55.

[7] In December 1612, the lord deputy, Sir Arthur Chichester, sought a suspension of Poynings' Law for the forthcoming parliament, but 'touching private bills only'. He hoped to gain support for government-sponsored legislation by offering selective collaboration for the passage of certain private bills. The English privy council, however, rejected the proposal because it feared that a well-organised grouping in parliament might force through undesirable legislation, McCavitt, *Sir Arthur Chichester*, pp. 177–8.

[8] Clarke describes his intentions as 'revolutionary', Clarke, 'History of Poynings' Law', p. 211. Chichester had set a precedent by refusing to consult with the Catholic elite on proposed legislation, but Wentworth saw the advantage of maintaining Poynings' Law throughout the parliamentary session.

of Fingal 'not to busy his thoughts with matters of this nature'.[9] Therefore, when parliament finally met, the members had no idea what to expect in terms of legislation, and with Poynings' Law firmly in place, any bills proposed by the Lords or Commons would have to be certified by the lord deputy and the Irish council.[10] Wentworth's radical interpretation of Poynings' Law undoubtedly helped convince Ormond, lord lieutenant during the 1640s, of the value of the act. Conversely, the Confederates, many with direct experience of the 1634–35 and 1640–41 parliaments, proved equally determined to have it repealed or, at the very least, suspended.

Wentworth's trial in 1640–41 had a direct impact on the constitutional relationship between Ireland and England. Before 1640 the English parliament did not interfere in Irish affairs. Legal experts, for the most part, accepted that Ireland was a dependency, not of England, but of the English crown. As recently as 1621 James VI and I had confirmed the constitutional separation of the two parliaments, while Sir John Davies, the influential former attorney general of Ireland, advised the English Commons that 'This kingdom here cannot make laws to bind that kingdom [Ireland], for they have there a parliament of their own.'[11] According to Conrad Russell, however, 'it was difficult to impeach Strafford without claiming authority in Irish affairs', as most of the charges against him related to his Irish administration.[12] The trial enabled an aggressively anti-Catholic parliament at Westminster to claim jurisdiction over Ireland, and to declare in April 1641 that Ireland was 'united to England, and the Parliament of England had always the cognizance of the original suits in Ireland'.[13]

These developments were viewed with increasing unease across the Irish Sea. The Irish parliament had initially cooperated with Westminster against Wentworth, and now seized the opportunity to reopen a direct line of communication with the king. In January 1641 the Irish House of Commons sent a committee to England to request, among other things, a clarification of Poynings' Law. The committee sought royal confirmation

[9] Quoted in Aidan Clarke, *Old English in Ireland* (London and Ithaca, 1966, reprinted Dublin, 2001), pp. 76–7.

[10] Kearney's account includes a detailed chapter on Wentworth's political manoeuvrings during the 1634–35 parliament, Kearney, *Strafford in Ireland*, pp. 53–68.

[11] Clarke, 'Patrick Darcy and the constitutional relationship between Ireland and Britain' in Ohlmeyer (ed.), *Political Thought*, p. 40. See also Patrick Little, 'The English parliament and the Irish constitution, 1641–9' in Micheál Ó Siochrú (ed.), *Kingdoms in Crisis: Ireland in the 1640s* (Dublin, 2001), pp. 107–8. Little argues that Sir Edward Coke's view, that the English parliament did have power to legislate for Ireland (arising from his report on Calvin's case), received no significant support at the time.

[12] Conrad Russell, *The Fall of the British Monarchies, 1637–42* (Oxford, 1991), p. 385.

[13] Michael Perceval-Maxwell, *The Outbreak of the Irish Rebellion of 1641* (Dublin, 1994), p. 164.

of the right to prior consultation on the drafting of bills, and an assurance that the transmission of bills from parliament would not be hindered by the executive in Dublin. Both Clarke and Perceval-Maxwell describe these proposed reforms as modest and conservative, as nothing more than an attempt by parliament to regain the initiative lost under Wentworth.[14] But the provisions of Poynings' Law were vague and subject to arbitrary interpretation, as Wentworth had dramatically demonstrated. The Irish parliament now sought to have its own interpretation of the procedures clarified in law. The intent may have been conservative, to avoid the excessive delegation of authority to the executive, but the effect of these reforms would have been radical, with the legislative initiative passing from the executive to parliament.[15]

The campaign against the abuse of power by the Dublin executive sparked a discussion on the issue of legislative independence. According to Clarke, the primary purpose of Patrick Darcy's 'Argument', presented to the Irish House of Lords in June 1641, involved addressing the illegality of various governmental practices. In the course of doing this, however, Darcy claimed that Ireland, 'annexed to the crown of England', enjoyed complete legislative autonomy.[16] The Irish parliament agreed, declaring in July:

> The subjects of this his Majesty's kingdom of Ireland are a free people, and to be governed only according to the common-law of England, and statutes made and established by the parliament in this kingdom of Ireland, and according to the lawful customs used in the same.[17]

This interpretation of the constitutional relationship between Ireland and England received support from Robert Sidney, earl of Leicester, appointed lord lieutenant of Ireland following Wentworth's execution. He commented: 'It seems to me very clear, that an Act of parliament made in England neither is nor ever was of force in Ireland until it be resolved and confirmed by the parliament in Ireland.'[18] The English privy council, however, disagreed, while Charles I had already rejected any

---

[14] Aidan Clarke, 'Colonial constitutional attitudes in Ireland, 1640–1660', Proceedings of the Royal Irish Academy, 90, section C, no. 11 (1990), pp. 367–8; Perceval-Maxwell, *Outbreak of the Irish Rebellion*, p. 166.

[15] Micheál Ó Siochrú, *Confederate Ireland 1642–1649: A constitutional and political analysis* (Dublin, 1999), p. 59.

[16] Patrick Darcy, *An Argument Delivered by Patrick Darcy Esquire by the Express Order of the Commons in the Parliament of Ireland, 9 June 1641* (Waterford, 1643, reprinted 1764). According to Clarke, Darcy made the point 'incidentally', after discovering no evidence of the legal authority of the English parliament in the kingdom of Ireland, Clarke, 'Colonial constitutional attitudes', p. 359.

[17] Quoted in Clarke, 'Colonial constitutional attitudes', p. 359.

[18] Quoted in Perceval-Maxwell, *Outbreak of the Irish Rebellion*, pp. 176–8, 203. In fact Leicester never travelled to Ireland but Perceval-Maxwell speculates that his views on the constitutional issues may well have persuaded many leading Irish Catholics to abandon

reinterpretation (modest or otherwise) of Poynings' Law. Irish Catholics, who favoured the reforms as a means of ensuring the confirmation of royal concessions and of preventing the manipulation of parliament by a powerful lord deputy, were bitterly disappointed. As Clarke has outlined, their fortunes were shown to be totally dependent on whoever controlled political power in England – an increasingly disturbing prospect given recent developments at Westminster.[19]

II

The outbreak of the rebellion in October 1641 radically altered the political landscape in Ireland, as the Dublin administration lost control over most of the country. The pre-emptive strike by the 'deserving Irish' in Ulster sparked a nationwide revolt, motivated by a variety of grievances. Constitutional issues figured prominently in many of the early petitions produced by the insurgents to justify their actions. One group of supplicants blamed the lords justices in Dublin for attempting to make the kingdom of Ireland subordinate to the English parliament, and for closing off traditional passages of redress to the king. Another remonstrance, from 'the Irish of Ulster', rejected attempts by the Westminster parliament to establish power and jurisdiction in Ireland, 'having no dependency of them, or any other, but only of your Majesty'.[20] Henry Jones, the dean of Kilmore, received information of a meeting of lay and clerical leaders in Multyfarnham, County Westmeath, a few weeks before the rebellion began. His informant listed the many demands raised at Multyfarnham, including the repeal of Poynings' Law. Furthermore, while Catholics would continue to recognise Charles I as their sovereign, Ireland was to be declared a kingdom independent of England.[21]

After months of confusion and chaos the Catholic elite began to organise alternative power structures to those in Dublin. The initial impetus came from the province of Connacht, where in early 1642 a number of lawyers, led by Patrick Darcy, prepared a model for government, under the sponsorship of Ulick Burke, earl of Clanricard. The propositions included a 'free parliament, without dependency of the parliament

various plots, formulated during the summer of 1641, to use the Irish army to assert the kingdom's independence from the English parliament.

[19] Clarke, 'History of Poynings' Law', p. 221.
[20] J. T. Gilbert (ed.), *History of the Irish Confederation and War in Ireland* (7 vols., Dublin, 1882–91), I, pp. 246–53; J. T. Gilbert (ed.), *A Contemporary History of Affairs in Ireland from AD 1641 to 1652* (3 vols., Dublin, 1879), I, pp. 450–60.
[21] Dean Jones was hostile to the Catholic interest in Ireland, but as Percevel-Maxwell points out, there is other evidence for the meeting in Multyfarnham, and the dean's account can be compared to what subsequently happened, Perceval-Maxwell, *Outbreak of the Irish Rebellion*, pp. 236–8.

or state of England'.[22] Much of this document was later incorporated into the Confederate 'model for government' and formed the basis for negotiations with the king. Constitutional issues assumed even greater significance when on 19 March 1642 the English parliament passed the Adventurers' Act, specifically designed to finance English military involvement in Ireland through the large-scale confiscations of Catholic estates. The king, unable to raise sufficient military resources on his own to deal with the rebellion in Ireland, reluctantly consented to the act. In the face of Westminster's determination to legislate for Ireland, it became absolutely vital for Catholics to proclaim the independence of the parliament in Dublin and to clarify the exact nature of the constitutional link with England.

During the summer of 1642, following several meetings of the Catholic clergy and laity, an embryonic system of government emerged, centred on the city of Kilkenny. The new structures included an executive supreme council and a general assembly, which functioned to all intents and purposes as an alternative parliament. Anxious not to be seen as challenging the principle of royal authority in Ireland, the Confederates insisted that they did not intend 'this assembly to be a parliament, or to have the power of it'.[23] As Richard Bellings later explained,

For though they endeavoured their assemblies after the model of the most orderly meetings, yet they avoided, so far as was possible for them, all circumstances that might make it thought they had usurped a power of convening a parliament, the calling and dissolving wherof the Supreme Council, by petition sent to the king, after adjournment of this assembly, avowed to be a pre-eminence inseparable from his Imperial Crown.[24]

Although the circumstances of war forced the Confederates to act increasingly in a sovereign manner, they never seriously contemplated a break with the Stuarts and loudly proclaimed their loyalty to Charles I throughout the 1640s.[25] However, they were also determined to preserve the

22 Examination of Edward Dowdall, 13 March 1642, TCD, MS 816, f. 44; Gilbert (ed.), *Irish Confederation*, I, pp. 289–90.
23 Petition of the Confederates to the king and queen, December 1642, Ulick Burke, *Clanricarde Memoirs* (London, 1757), p. 299.
24 Bellings' 'History', Gilbert (ed.), *Irish Confederation*, I, pp. 111–12. The Galway lawyer, Richard Martin, described the assembly as 'a general meeting, to consult of an order for their own affairs until his majesty's wisdom has settled the present troubles'. Martin to Clanricard, 2 December 1642, [Burke,] *Clanricarde Memoirs*, pp. 296–8.
25 The only major work to call for the expulsion of the Stuarts, and all English from Ireland, was a book by an exiled Jesuit, Conor O'Mahony, entitled *Disputatio Apologetica*. O'Mahony's book was roundly condemned by the Confederate leadership, and publicly burnt in Galway, Galway Corporation records, Book A, f. 191b; Peter Walsh, *The History and Vindication of the Loyal Formulary or Irish Remonstrance* ([London and Dublin], 1674), pp. 736–9. The extreme response to this work suggests that O'Mahony's ideas may well have enjoyed considerable support among the lower social orders.

constitutional integrity of the Irish kingdom from the threat posed by Westminster. In the oath of association, administered by Catholic clergy in every parish, the Confederates swore to 'defend, uphold and maintain . . . the power and privileges of the parliament of this realm'.[26] They offered military assistance in return for a series of concessions from the king, including a clarification of the constitutional relationship between the kingdoms of Ireland and England.

In response to these developments, the Dublin administration adopted a flexible attitude towards Poynings' Law. In early 1642 the lords justices discussed the passage of an act of attainder for those involved in the rebellion. Without a suspension of Poynings' Law, however, the proposed bill would have to be amended and retransmitted, perhaps on a number of occasions, as they added further names to the list of rebels. Moreover, the bill would also be subject to a moderating influence from the king in England. The lords justices, therefore, favoured a suspension of Poynings' Law, to give the Dublin parliament the power 'to pass acts for attainting of those who are or shall be in this present rebellion, without transmitting them into England'.[27]

This Dublin parliament, which continued to sit throughout the 1640s, has received relatively little attention from historians. It consisted of a Protestant rump, with no Catholic members after November 1641.[28] In August 1642 a Commons committee prepared the draft of a bill to suspend Poynings' Law for specific measures, including the proposed attainder of the rebels. Unfortunately the texts of the various bills (if they ever existed) do not appear to have survived, so their content is unknown. The Lords also established a committee, which included the earl of Ormond, to consider these drafts. One of the bills contained a reference to the Adventurers' Act, recently passed by Westminster, which the Lords believed 'would be prejudicial to this kingdom, by admitting the parliament of England to be of force, to oblige us here, without being confirmed'.[29] This issue had not been resolved when the parliament adjourned a few days later, but neither the Commons nor the Lords

---

[26] The Stowe collection in the British Library contains numerous examples of the Confederate oath. See, for example, BL, Stowe MSS 82, ff. 66, 92, 303 etc.

[27] HMC, *Ormonde*, NS II, p. 90.

[28] By virtue of numbers alone, the Confederate assembly in Kilkenny might well have claimed to be the legitimate representative body of the kingdom. Sir James Ware recorded how in June 1642 the parliament in Dublin, with only thirty members present (six lords, twenty-four MPs), expelled forty-one Catholic MPs for joining the Confederate association, TCD, MS 6404 (Ware manuscript), f.128.

[29] *Lords Jnl, Ire*, I, p. 183. Throughout the 1640s both Catholics and Protestants proved extremely sensitive on the issue of the independence of the Irish parliament from the *diktats* of Westminster.

appear to have objected in principle to the suspension of Poynings' Law in particular circumstances.

Following the outbreak of the civil war in England in August 1642, both royalists and Confederates proved anxious to start peace negotiations in Ireland. In early 1643 Charles sanctioned the first official contacts between Dublin and Kilkenny. In light of his experiences during the 1641 negotiations, he anticipated that the Confederates might seek a repeal of Poynings' Law and associated acts, 'under the pretence that they were made when a great part of Ireland had none to answer for them in that Parliament there'. The king strenuously opposed any such innovation in a time of rebellion, as 'the whole frame of government of that kingdom would be shaken'. Concerning the claims of Westminster to legislate for Ireland, Charles declared that Ireland was not obliged by statutes made in England. However, in order to avoid a clash with the English parliament, he continued that this should 'be admitted by way of declaration of what is their right, not as granted *de novo*'.[30] Both Charles and his representative in Ireland, Ormond, were initially of one mind as to the strategic and tactical undesirability of any concessions on Poynings' Law or a declaratory act.[31] The king subsequently changed his mind as his military position in England became increasingly desperate, but Ormond never budged, ultimately winning the political battle with the Confederates as the royalists lost the war with the English parliament.

The immediate suspension and ultimate repeal of Poynings' Law, along with an act declaring the independence of the Irish parliament from Westminster, emerged as key Confederate demands in the ensuing peace negotiations. However, the determination with which the Confederates pursued these objectives altered as the talks progressed. The 'peace party', concerned primarily with the endorsement of a settlement, proved more willing to sidetrack constitutional issues than the 'clerical party', whose political and religious aims were more radical. Although eager to come to terms with the king, all shades of Confederate opinion insisted that the terms of any settlement be ratified in a 'free' Irish parliament, in which there would be no impediments on Catholics sitting or voting. Given the

---

[30] Charles to Ormond, 12 January, 1643, Thomas Carte, *History of the Life and Times of James the First Duke of Ormond* (6 vols., Oxford, 1851), V, pp. 1–3. The king's anticipation of Confederate objections to Poynings' Law suggests that the Catholic delegation in 1641 may well have argued that before the Act of Kingly Title in 1541 (or perhaps even later) the entire Irish nation was not represented in the Dublin parliament.

[31] Ormond gradually assumed control of the Dublin administration during the course of 1643. He was appointed lord lieutenant of Ireland by the king in November of that year and raised to the title of marquis.

ncertainty in England, the word of the monarch on its own no
ovided sufficient security for an agreement.

nfederates adopted a twin-track approach with regard to Poynings' Law. In the short term, the suspension of the act would remove the immediate requirement to transmit bills to England, where, in such a hostile environment, legislative proposals were liable to be rejected or altered. In the longer term, they recognised the need to reconsider the whole issue of Poynings' Law as a consequence of Wentworth's interpretation of the act. The Trim Remonstrance, presented to the royalist delegation by the Confederates in March 1643, demanded a suspension of the act for the duration of parliament, at which time the king (with the advice of parliament) would consider whether it should be repealed or retained.[32]

Evidence exists, however, to show that influential figures in Kilkenny believed that a newly elected parliament might make excessive demands and undermine the prospect of a permanent settlement. Clanricard informed Ormond that leading Confederates had expressed fears 'of some tumultuous elections likely to be made of their own side'. He suspected that these individuals would prefer to gain concessions by agents 'until it might be confirmed in a more settled time by act of parliament'.[33] Ormond shared these fears of populist agitation and rejected demands for fresh elections during the truce negotiations in June 1643. He explained to the royalist Colonel John Barry that with the Protestant community driven from most of the kingdom, 'few but themselves [the Catholic Confederates] are like to be of that parliament'.[34] At first the Confederates angrily demanded an explanation for the refusal to summon a new parliament, but shortly afterwards accepted that existing circumstances in the three kingdoms precluded fresh elections. Instead they would 'in due time expect his Majesties pleasure therein'.[35] With the Confederates clearly divided on this issue, this capitulation was hardly surprising. For all subsequent negotiations, therefore, the General Assembly nominated a committee of treaty which, until 1646 at least, was dominated by the peace faction.

Proper negotiations for a peace settlement did not begin until after the cessation agreement between royalists and Confederates in September

---

[32] Remonstrance of grievances (Trim), 17 March 1643, Gilbert (ed.), *Irish Confederation*, II, pp. 226–42.

[33] Carte, *Life of Ormond*, V, pp. 472–4. Clanricard's letter is one of the earliest indications of the divisions which would almost destroy the Confederate association in subsequent years.

[34] 1 June 1643, Ormond to Barry, Gilbert (ed.), *Irish Confederation*, II, pp. 284–5.

[35] Cessation debates, June–August 1643, Gilbert (ed.), *Irish Confederation*, II, pp. 308, 351, quote at p. 353.

1643. A Confederate delegation led by Donough MacCarthy, Viscount Muskerry, Ormond's brother-in-law, travelled to the king's headquarters at Oxford in March 1644. Muskerry restated the position outlined at Trim, seeking a suspension of Poynings' Law 'for the speedy settlement of the present affairs'. He explained that a quick ratification of the peace terms in the Irish parliament would enable Charles to obtain vital military aid from the Confederates. Unconvinced that Wentworth's administration was an aberration, Muskerry also insisted that the repeal of the act 'be further considered of' when circumstances permitted.[36] This position, suspension followed by possible repeal, formed the basis of the Confederate position when negotiations resumed in Dublin later that same year.

The Confederates also demanded that all acts, ordinances and attainders of the 'pretended parliament' in Dublin since November 1641 be declared void, and that the Adventurers' Act be repealed. In light of the manipulation of parliamentary representation by both James VI and I and Wentworth, they sought the introduction of residential and property qualifications for the Lords and Commons, as well as stricter rules on the use of proxy votes.[37] Finally, in an effort to forestall any future attempts by Westminster to legislate for Ireland, the Confederates requested 'that an act be passed in the next parliament, declaratory that the parliament of Ireland is a free parliament of itself, independent of and not subordinate to the parliament of England, and that the subjects of Ireland are immediately subject to your Majesty as in right of your crown'.[38]

Two Irish Protestant delegations also travelled to Oxford in 1644: one from the royalist Irish council, representing Ormond's position; the other authorised by the rump parliament in Dublin. With a peace settlement on the horizon, including a new parliament (possibly controlled by the Catholics), the attitude of Irish Protestants towards Poynings' Law had changed dramatically since 1642. Having earlier contemplated a suspension of the act, both delegations now strenuously opposed any changes. Agents from the Dublin administration described Poynings' Law as 'one

---

[36] Gilbert (ed.), *Irish Confederation*, III, pp. 128–33.   [37] See chapters 8 and 9 above.
[38] Confederate demands, 28 March 1644, Gilbert (ed.), *Irish Confederation*, III, pp. 128–33. In 1643 the Confederates had published Patrick Darcy's 'Argument' of 1641 (see note 17). Although, as already outlined, Darcy was primarily concerned with abuses by the executive, his strong assertion of the independence of the Irish parliament clearly appealed to the Confederates. A tract, dated 1644 and entitled 'A declaration how, and by what means, the laws and statutes of England, from time to time, came to be of force in Ireland', dealt with the issue of legislative independence in more detail. A published version first appeared in Walter Harris (ed.), *Hibernica* (2 vols., London, 1750), II, pp. 1–21. The authorship of this tract is disputed and the person responsible may well not have been a Catholic Confederate, see Clarke, 'Patrick Darcy and the constitutional relationship' in Ohlmeyer (ed.), *Political Thought*, pp. 48–9.

of the wisest acts that was ever made for the establishment and continuance of the English government in Ireland'. They considered suspension or repeal 'a very high demand and of most dangerous consequence'.[39] Moreover, a new parliament would allow Irish Catholics to 'assume all power into their own hands', as they now controlled the machinery of local government through which election writs were issued.[40] Therefore, 'that which they call a free parliament must consist of Papists for there can be very few or no Protestants in it'.[41] The delegation took no position on the issue of the independence of the Irish parliament, reflecting the uncertainty of the Irish council as how best to proceed. 'This proposition concerns the high courts of parliament of both kingdoms and is above our reach, and therefore, we humbly desire to be excused and not to intermeddle therein.'[42]

The Protestant agents from the Dublin parliament generally adopted a harder line on concessions to Irish Catholics. Although not necessarily anti-cessation, they sought to protect Protestant interests in any future peace settlement through the introduction of a number of key military, political and religious safeguards.[43] The agents shared the Dublin administration's fears of a Catholic-controlled parliament. On the issue of Poynings' Law, they urged the king to reject all 'propositions tending to introduce so great a diminution of your royal and necessary power for the confirmation of your royal estate and protection of your good Protestant subjects both there and elsewhere'.[44] Faced with a series of conflicting demands, the king's advisers at Oxford despaired that 'it would be impossible for the king to grant the Protestant agents desires and grant a peace to the Irish [Confederates]'.[45]

In a detailed response to the Confederate delegation, Charles consented to a new parliament, but only on condition that the Confederates agreed not to pass any bills that had not first been transmitted to England, or that would prejudice Irish Protestants. The Dublin legislature was not to be given a free hand by the king, who would 'by no means consent to the suspension of Poynings' Act'. The Confederate position on the independence of the Irish parliament may well have appealed to Charles, by now embroiled in a bitter civil war with the English parliament, but his position as the constitutional head of both the English

---

[39] The submission of the Irish council is contained in HMC, *Report on the Manuscripts of the Earl of Egmont*, I (London, 1905), pp. 212–29, quote at p. 217.

[40] *Ibid.*, p. 219.   [41] *Ibid.*, p. 216.   [42] *Ibid.*, p. 226.

[43] Robert Armstrong, 'Protestant Ireland and the English parliament' (Ph.D. thesis, Trinity College Dublin, 1995), pp. 115–16. The demands of the Protestant agents are listed in John Rushworth, *Historical Collections of Private Passages of State, Weighty Matters of Law, Remarkable Proceedings in Five Parliaments* (7 vols., London, 1680–1701), V, pp. 953–71.

[44] Rushworth, *Historical Collections*, V, p. 957.   [45] *Ibid.*, p. 959.

and Irish kingdoms presented him with a dilemma. He tried, the
to steer a middle course, referring the question 'to the free debate and
expostulation of the two parliaments'. The king declared his neutrality
on the issue, 'being so equally concerned in the privileges of either that
he will take care to the utmost of his power that they shall contain themselves within their proper limits, his Majesty being the head and equally
interested in the rights of both parliaments'.[46] This must have sounded
particularly hollow to the Confederate delegation, in view of the fact that
Charles had already signed the Adventurers' Act into law. Nothing more
was concluded at Oxford, except that negotiations would continue back
in Ireland, with the king represented by his lord lieutenant, Ormond.

III

The Confederate and royalist negotiating teams that assembled in Dublin
later that year knew each other well. The delegation from Kilkenny
included Geoffrey Browne and Nicholas Plunkett, both of whom had
attended the talks in London during the summer of 1641, as well as
Patrick Darcy, one of the foremost constitutional lawyers in Ireland.[47] On
the royalist side, the lord chancellor, Sir Richard Bolton, assisted Ormond
in dealing with constitutional issues raised by the Confederates. These
two men had strong political and personal reasons for opposing changes
to Poynings' Law. Ormond, having witnessed at first hand the actions
of his predecessor and mentor, Wentworth, valued the act as a powerful
political tool for controlling the Irish parliament. Moreover, despite the
peace negotiations, he had no intention of handing the legislative initiative over to a Catholic-dominated assembly. In 1641 the Irish parliament
had attempted to impeach Bolton, in a move, according to the lord chancellor at least, contrary to the provisions of Poynings' Law. Although he
was removed from the chairmanship of the House of Lords, the charges
were eventually dropped following the outbreak of the Ulster rebellion.[48]
Not surprisingly, Bolton still regarded the law as an important safeguard
against the threat of the executive accountability to parliament.

[46] Gilbert (ed.), *Irish Confederation*, III, pp. 175–8.
[47] For a full list of the membership of all the Confederate negotiating committees throughout the 1640s, see Ó Siochrú, *Confederate Ireland*, p. 228 (table 6).
[48] Bolton claimed that the Irish parliament did not possess the right of judicature, and on
the specific issue of impeachment, that no precedent existed for 'any such proceedings
since Poynings' Act . . . and the explanation [of it] in 3 & 4 Philip and Mary, and
therefore . . . it trenches much upon his majesties prerogative', John McCafferty, ' "To
follow the late precedents of England": The Irish impeachment proceedings of 1641'
in D. S. Greer and N. M. Dawson (eds.), *Mysteries and Solutions in Irish Legal History*
(Dublin, 2001), pp. 63–6.

The talks, which finally began in September 1644 and continued for one month, witnessed rapid progress on a whole range of less contentious issues.[49] However, the two sides remained divided on a number of key points, including Poynings' Law. The Confederates demanded a suspension of the act, primarily to hasten the ratification process, but also in order to prevent the alteration of bills, which in normal circumstances would be transmitted to England.[50] On the royalist side, Bolton argued that the 1569 amendment to Poynings' Law meant that a suspension would delay ratification of the peace treaty by up to four months. The parliament would first have to assemble, prepare a suspension bill, transmit this to England, and wait for the approval of the king and council before proceeding with the articles of treaty.[51] The lord chancellor dismissed Confederate fears of possible alterations to bills if transmitted to England, as this would involve the breach of a legally binding treaty. Bolton's position was substantially correct, but only if the articles of treaty did not need to be explained or amended in any way. The subsequent peace settlement, agreed in March 1646, illustrates the scale of this potential problem. Article 21, for example, gave the Irish parliament the right to seek a redress of grievances not included in the peace treaty.[52] Legislation arising from this review would, without a suspension of Poynings' Law, need to be transmitted to England and a potentially hostile reception.

In reply to Bolton, Darcy insisted that 'they desired that it should only be suspended as unto the ratifying of the matters to be agreed on upon the treaty and to no other purpose'.[53] This attempt to accommodate the king's concerns for Irish Protestants expressed at Oxford, in fact represented a major concession by the Confederates. Anxious above all else to secure ratification of the peace terms, Darcy did not pursue earlier demands for a repeal of Poynings' Law. The wider issue of who possessed the legislative initiative in Ireland – parliament or the executive – disappeared completely from the agenda.[54] The moderation of Confederate

---

[49] Formal negotiations continued until the end of September, at which time they were suspended while Ormond waited for further instructions from the king, Dónal Cregan, 'The Confederation of Kilkenny: its organisation, personnel and history' (Ph.D. thesis, University College, Dublin, 1947), pp. 158, 164.

[50] Peace debates, September 1644, Gilbert (ed.), *Irish Confederation*, III, pp. 279–81.

[51] It is unclear whether Bolton believed that poor communications or royalist prevarication would have been responsible for such a long delay.

[52] Treaty articles, 28 March 1646, Bodl., Carte MSS 176, ff. 205–8.

[53] Gilbert (ed.), *Irish Confederation*, III, pp. 279–81.

[54] It is clear that Darcy fundamentally accepted Bolton's interpretation at this time, probably in deference to the lord chancellor's experience in constitutional matters, and the fact that he had access to all the relevant parliamentary and legal records in Dublin. The Irish House of Commons had noted in 1641 that 'the few ancient records which are left here were, and are as yet, at the command of the said Lord Chancellor and the Lord

demands came at a very opportune moment for Ormond. Following the crushing defeat of Prince Rupert at Marston Moor in July 1644, Lord Inchiquin and the Munster Protestants had defected to the English parliament, leaving the lord lieutenant with little room for political manoeuvre. Significant concessions to the Catholic Confederates at this sensitive time might well have resulted in the complete collapse of the royalist cause in Ireland.

On 16 September, the debate shifted to the constitutional status of the Irish parliament. The Confederate negotiators favoured a declaratory act of independence, while Bolton argued the case for a simple declaration by both houses. Although the lord chancellor explained (correctly) that the English parliament was not bound by an Irish act, an act of parliament nonetheless carried more weight than a declaration, principally because it required the king's consent. As Clarke has outlined, the administration adopted a pragmatic negotiating position, with officials stating that 'it was to be wished that there was such an act, but the time was not seasonable to desire it'. The Confederates, however, hoped to force the king to take sides in their dispute with Westminster and recognise the independence of the Irish parliament.[55] Darcy and his colleagues dismissed the notion of the king's constitutional neutrality as he 'was drawn to give the royal assent to the acts of subscription [Adventurers' Act]'. The Confederates repeated the demand for a declaratory act and insisted that, given the self-evident nature of Ireland's independence from the jurisdiction of Westminster, 'to draw this into any debate or question might prove of most dangerous consequence to this nation'.[56] Ormond postponed the talks shortly afterwards, primarily to await fresh instructions from the king, but also to assuage growing unease among the Protestant community in Ireland.

With renewed moves towards a peace settlement in England at the end of 1644, the king delayed for months before sending a reply to Ormond. The failure of talks with the English parliament in February 1645, however, forced Charles to consider granting major concessions to Irish Catholics. A few days after the collapse of the Uxbridge negotiations the king wrote to Ormond, desperate for military aid for the forthcoming campaigning season. He instructed the lord lieutenant 'to conclude

---

Justice [i.e. Gerard Lowther, lord chief justice of the Court of Common Pleas] who even since their impeachment had the custody of the parliament rolls in their private studies', McCafferty, 'The Irish impeachment proceedings of 1641', p. 65.

[55] Clarke, 'Colonial constitutional attitudes', p. 361; Peace debates, September 1644, Gilbert (ed.), *Irish Confederation*, III, pp. 286–7.

[56] Peace debates, 1644, Gilbert (ed.), *Irish Confederation*, III, pp. 294, 307–11, 313–19, quote at p. 311.

a peace with the Irish whatever it cost'. He would not 'think it a hard bargain' to repeal penal legislation and suspend Poynings' Law, in return for a settlement with the Confederates.[57] Ormond received this letter from Viscount Taaffe the following month, but decided not to inform the Confederates of its contents. On the constitutional issue, he believed that suspension was not necessary and reported to the king in May that 'After much discourse upon it, they [the Confederates] seem convinced that what your majesty intends them may as speedily and securely conveyed to them, without the suspension as with it.'[58] Ormond's stubbornness and Bolton's persuasiveness had apparently convinced the Confederates to concede the argument on Poynings' Law. In fact, throughout the summer of 1645 internal Confederate politics had begun increasingly to impact on the peace talks.

There was growing concern in Confederate circles, particularly among the clergy, about the limited nature of the concessions on offer in the treaty negotiations.[59] In May 1645 the Confederate General Assembly, meeting to discuss the proposed settlement with the royalists, witnessed the emergence for the first time of organised clerical opposition. The Confederate negotiators in Dublin felt sufficiently pressured in early June to resurrect a number of demands, including the suspension of Poynings' Law. Ormond, however, repeated his objections to any constitutional reform, and his tough stance appeared to pay immediate dividends. The Confederate leadership, eager to reach a settlement to forestall the growth of opposition in Kilkenny, engaged in an abrupt *volte-face* on the outstanding constitutional issues. Confederate agents in Dublin sought assurances from Ormond that if the treaty terms had to be transmitted to England,

---

[57] Carte, *Life of Ormond*, VI, pp. 257–8. The king's increasingly desperate letters to Ormond survive in the Clarendon papers, Bodl., Clarendon MSS 98, ff. 44–5, 55, 63–4, 77–8.

[58] Ormond to Charles I, 8 May 1645, Carte, *Life of Ormond*, VI, pp. 278–83; Armstrong, 'Protestant Ireland', p. 185.

[59] Ó Siochrú, *Confederate Ireland*, p. 80. At the time of the cessation agreement in September 1643 the papal representative in Ireland had argued the case for a total military victory throughout the kingdom. Opposition to the ruling faction in Kilkenny, however, lacked cohesion until late in 1644 Ormond introduced the question of church property into the peace talks. His mistake was not in insisting that Protestants retained churches, a policy fully supported by Charles, but in publicly raising the matter. As the Catholic hierarchy would never agree to returning property to Protestants, the Confederate leadership in Kilkenny had hoped simply to ignore the issue. This strategy proved impossible following Ormond's intervention, and provided the opposition in the Confederate ranks with a powerful pretext to reject peace terms without sufficient religious guarantees. The royalist earl of Clanricard warned in October 1644 that 'If the treaty be brought to this issue [religion], to break upon that point will certainly be very prejudicial to his majesty's service, and of so great an advantage to them [the Confederates] both home and abroad, that it had been better not to have consented to any such treaty.' Remembrances for Viscount Taaffe, 12 October 1644, John Lowe (ed.), *Clanricarde Letter-book, 1643–47* (IMC, Dublin, 1983), pp. 111–14.

they would 'receive no alteration or diminution there, and this to be expressed in the articles of the treaty'.[60] Concerning a declaratory act, they agreed to drop demands for an act of parliament and settle for a declaration of 'the independency of our parliament of the parliament of England'.[61] In his reply, Ormond, delighted at the removal of Poynings' Law from the agenda, willingly provided the necessary assurances that the articles of treaty would not be altered in England. Moreover, the lord lieutenant consented to any declaration made by both houses of parliament 'agreeable to the laws of the land . . . and therewith the persons formerly attending us from your party [the Confederates] declared they were satisfied'.[62]

The royalist disaster at Naseby in June 1645 threatened to undermine this cosy compromise. The parliamentarians published the king's correspondence, seized after the battle, including his letter of February that year, offering among other things a suspension of Poynings' Law. A copy reached Kilkenny in mid-August and caused uproar in the General Assembly, with members demanding to know why they had not been informed of this significant constitutional concession.[63] Fortunately for Ormond, at this very moment the earl of Glamorgan, recently arrived from England and claiming to represent the king, signed a treaty in Kilkenny which granted clerical demands on religious issues. Leaving to one side the controversy over Glamorgan's mission to Ireland, the subsequent euphoria over his treaty spared Ormond the embarrassment of having to justify withholding the king's offer on Poynings' Law.[64]

In November 1645 Ormond reported to Charles that the suspension of Poynings' Law 'was denied upon such important reasons of law and state as hath given that satisfaction therein, as their agents insist no further upon it'.[65] Despite growing clerical opposition within Confederate ranks – which intensified after the arrival of a papal nuncio, Giovanni

---

[60] Treaty negotiations, 1645, Gilbert (ed.), *Irish Confederation*, IV, pp. 289–351, quote at p. 293. See also Bodl., Carte MSS 15, ff. 86, 92, 102–5, 200, 211–12, 242, 251.

[61] Gilbert (ed.), *Irish Confederation*, IV, p. 294.

[62] *Ibid.*, p. 318. In fact, Ormond's consent (or the king's, for that matter) was not required for a declaration of parliament.

[63] According to Clanricard, the published letters arrived in Ireland from France. Clanricard to Ormond, 21 August 1645, Bodl., Carte MSS 15, ff. 478–9.

[64] This treaty was signed by the Catholic earl of Glamorgan on 25 August 1645, BL, Add MSS 25,277, f. 62. For the controversy over Glamorgan's mission see John Lowe, 'The Glamorgan mission to Ireland, 1645–6', *Studia Hibernica*, 4 (1964), pp. 155–96; John Lowe, 'The negotiations between Charles I and the confederation of Kilkenny, 1642–49' (Ph.D. thesis, University of London, 1960). Ormond, although not directly party to the Glamorgan treaty, was fully aware of its existence and probable content, Ó Siochrú, *Confederate Ireland*, pp. 93–5.

[65] Gilbert (ed.), *Irish Confederation*, V, p. 115.

Battista Rinuccini, archbishop of Fermo, in October 1645 – and the repudiation of Glamorgan by Charles in early 1646, nothing now seemed to stand in the way of a peace treaty.[66] The peace faction in Kilkenny proceeded to conclude a settlement with Ormond in March 1646, which contained no significant constitutional (or religious) concessions.[67] A new parliament would meet in November 1646 to ratify the articles of agreement, but only after transmission of bills to England 'according to the usual form'. The treaty did state, however, according to the compromise of the previous year 'that the said acts so to be agreed upon, and so to be passed, shall receive no alteration or diminution here or in England'.[68] Ormond never explained how exactly the bills should be transmitted, a striking omission, given that by the end of July 1646 (the date of publication of the treaty) the king was already a prisoner of the Scottish covenanting army in England. Article 11 of the treaty dealt with the issue of parliamentary independence and simply left 'both Houses of Parliament within this kingdom to make such declaration therin as shall be agreeable to the laws of the kingdom of Ireland'.[69]

The problem of transmission did not need to be addressed, as the treaty collapsed shortly afterwards. Accounts of clerical opposition to the peace deal have traditionally focused on the absence of religious terms in the agreement with Ormond, but the failure to gain any constitutional concessions also outraged opponents of the peace faction. The declaration of the ecclesiastical congregation at Waterford on 24 August, condemning the treaty, criticised Confederate commissioners for not obtaining a suspension of the Poynings' Law, despite the king's offer contained in his letter of February 1645.[70] The cleric Walter Enos went even further in his survey of the negotiations, accusing the commissioners of breaking the

---

[66] Charles was forced to repudiate Glamorgan after parliamentary forces found a copy of his treaty on the body of Malachy O'Queely, Catholic archbishop of Tuam, and publicised the terms to an outraged Protestant audience in England. *The Irish Cabinet or His Majesties Secret Papers . . . taken in the carriage of the archbishop of Tuam . . .* (London, 1645–46). The news of Glamorgan's 'secret' treaty appears to have reached Dublin at the end of December. Ormond ordered Glamorgan's immediate arrest, although he was released shortly afterwards, Bodl., Carte MSS 16, f. 339. News of yet another treaty, between Pope Innocent X and Sir Kenelm Digby (representing Queen Henrietta Maria), further complicated issues. The treaty articles, signed in November 1645, reached Kilkenny in February 1646. They contained significant concessions to Catholics, all of which were to be enacted in a free Irish parliament, independent of that of England, Giuseppe Aiazza, *The Embassy in Ireland of Monsignor G. B. Rinuccini, archbishop of Fermo, in the years 1645–49*, trans. Annie Hutton (Dublin, 1873), pp. 573–4.

[67] Treaty articles, 28 March 1646, Bodl., Carte MSS 176, ff. 205–8. See also Gilbert (ed.), *Irish Confederation*, V, pp. 286–310.

[68] Gilbert (ed.), *Irish Confederation*, V, p. 288.   [69] *Ibid.*, p. 294.

[70] Declaration of the ecclesiastical congregation, 24 August 1646, PRO, SP 261/51, ff. 207–10.

oath of association, having 'wilfully rejected the suspension of Poynings Act and resolved nothing for the repeal thereof'.[71] On the issue of parliamentary independence, Enos condemned the Confederate negotiators for failing to insist on a declaratory act, which he insisted had been a key Confederate demand since 1642.[72] The clerical opposition highlighted the weakness of the constitutional concessions contained within the treaty. With the king a prisoner of the Scots, and parliament victorious in the English Civil War, the threat of an English executive controlled by Westminster loomed large. In such circumstances, a suspension (or repeal) of Poynings' Law and a declaratory act were deemed vital to protect the gains made by Irish Catholics.

Negotiations took place between the two main Confederate factions in early September 1646 to avoid an open split over the treaty. Those who favoured the peace agreement appeared unwilling at this stage to accept the possible constitutional implications of the king's defeat in England. Although anxious to placate clerical opposition, Muskerry and his supporters feared the radicalisation of Irish Catholic opinion, which was already apparent within the General Assembly at Kilkenny. The peace faction willingly acceded to almost all of the clerical demands, except for a repeal of penal legislation and the suspension of Poynings' Law. Without some English involvement in Irish affairs, guaranteed by Poynings' Law, a new parliament might prove impossible to control. Muskerry insisted that 'it was upon public debate for saving of time unanimously agreed that the suspending of it should not be insisted upon' – an interpretation vehemently denied by the clerical faction.[73]

The compromise talks failed, and the treaty collapsed soon afterwards. The supporters of the clergy briefly took control in Kilkenny, to be followed by a more moderate regime, in which the lawyer Nicholas Plunkett emerged as the dominant figure. No substantive negotiations took place between the royalists and Confederates during 1647, as Ormond surrendered Dublin to the English parliament in June and departed for England shortly afterwards. The lord lieutenant blamed the 'perfidy of the Irish' for forcing him to deal with Westminster, and explained to the king that he preferred to surrender Dublin to the English parliament 'than to the

---

[71] Enos, 'Survey', Gilbert (ed.), *Irish Confederation*, VI, p. 422. Although the oath of association contained nothing specific on Poynings' Law, the Confederates did swear to uphold the liberties of the kingdom. Enos believed that this included a commitment to repeal or suspend Poynings' Law.

[72] *Ibid.*, pp. 409, 422.

[73] Gilbert (ed.), *Irish Confederation*, VI, pp. 132–4. The destruction of assembly records makes it difficult to verify the extent to which the assembly was kept informed of the treaty negotiations. See Ó Siochrú, *Confederate Ireland*, pp. 101–3 for the dispute between the various factions on this issue.

Irish rebels'.[74] The delivery of Charles I to the Westminster parliament by the Scots on 30 January 1647 had convinced the lord lieutenant of the need for a rapprochement with the victors in the English Civil War. Moreover, having recently suffered a humiliating setback at the hands of the clerical faction, Ormond was in no mood for further negotiations with Kilkenny.[75] For the Confederates, however, the constitutional implications of his actions were absolutely clear. In a crisis, even a chief governor who was one of their own – Ormond was, after all, a Kilkenny Butler, related to many of the leading Confederates – would support the English parliament at their expense. Therefore in any future peace talks there could be no compromise on the key constitutional issues.

In a year dominated by military developments, the Confederates suffered two major defeats (at Dungan's Hill in August and Knocknanuss in November) at the hands of forces loyal to the English parliament. The peace party gradually regained the initiative in Kilkenny, and in late 1647 the General Assembly decided to reestablish contact with the royalist court in exile. Viscount Muskerry led a Confederate delegation to Paris in an attempt to negotiate a settlement with Queen Henrietta Maria and unite their forces against Westminster. The agents stressed the difficulty in transmitting parliamentary bills in the existing political and military climate, and sought approval for an act in the next parliament confirming peace terms without any transmission.[76] Although such an arrangement would directly contravene the provisions of Poynings' Law, harsh political reality – the king's continuing imprisonment in England – necessitated drastic measures.

Yet nothing was agreed in Paris except that talks would begin again, with Ormond, who had fled from England to Paris, representing the king. The lord lieutenant returned to Ireland in late September 1648. He received a warm welcome from the peace faction, but his instructions from Queen Henrietta Maria merely authorised the concessions already agreed with the Confederates in earlier negotiations.[77] On constitutional matters, he pledged to defend the privileges of parliament and the liberty of subjects, but offered no indication of how this was to be achieved.[78]

[74] Ormond to Charles I, 17 March 1647, Bodl., Clarendon MSS 29, f. 153.
[75] Ormond ignored instructions from the English royal court, exiled in Paris, to negotiate a deal with the Confederates. He explained why in a detailed report presented to the king at Hampton Court, BL, Egerton MSS 2541, ff. 377–81. The instructions from Paris appear in the 'Memoirs of George Leyburn, 1722', *Clarendon Historical Society's Reprints* (2nd series, London, 1884–86), pp. 307–11.
[76] Propositions of Confederate commissioners in Paris, 2 April 1648, Bodl., Carte MSS 22, ff. 85–6.
[77] Instructions for Ormond [1648], Bodl., Carte MSS 63, f. 568.
[78] Declaration by Ormond, 6 October 1648, HMC, *Ormonde*, OS, II, p. 81. Ormond made this declaration to Inchiquin's Protestant troops in Cork, illustrating a convergence of

Confederate proposals called for a parliament within six months, or failing that a General Assembly within two years, for 'settling of the affairs of the kingdom, without any transmission into England, and that an act shall pass in the next parliament enacting, establishing and confirming the peace to be concluded, and all the articles thereof: and Poynings' Act to be repealed'.[79] With the king unlikely to emerge from the conflict in England with his powers intact, the Confederates sought to protect themselves from the possibility of an English executive controlled by parliament. In these changed circumstances, as the clerical faction had anticipated in 1646, Poynings' Law had to be repealed.

On the issue of the independence of the Irish parliament, however, the Confederates accepted the royalist argument that the demand for a declaratory act would prove of no immediate use to them. It might well delay the conclusion of the treaty unnecessarily and cause severe problems for Charles I in England. They simply requested (as in the 1646 treaty) that the king would 'leave both houses of parliament in this kingdom to make such a declaration therein as shall be agreeable to the laws of the kingdom of Ireland'.[80] Ormond readily agreed to a declaration, but despite the desperate plight of the king, he still refused to concede on the crucial issue of transmission. His obstinacy reflected the concerns of Irish Protestants, expressed at Oxford in 1644, that concessions on Poynings' Law would seriously weaken the constitutional link with England and leave them vulnerable to a Catholic political resurgence.

In December 1648, after two months of tortuous talks, Ormond informed the chairman of the General Assembly that he could not see how to confirm the treaty articles 'without the transmission into England, nor that Poynings' act can be suspended or repealed until a bill for the same be first agreed on in the same session of parliament to be held in this kingdom and then transmitted'.[81] Although strictly correct from a legal point of view, the political landscape had altered dramatically since negotiations first began in 1643–44. Moreover, Ormond's delaying tactics had contributed to the crisis in which Confederates and royalists now found themselves. On 24 December, he wrote to Inchiquin that the treaty negotiations had reached such a point that they 'must immediately

Catholic and Protestant interests on the issue of parliamentary privileges. Sir Richard Bolton had died in March 1648 depriving Ormond of his leading constitutional expert. I am grateful to Aidan Clarke for this information.

[79] Propositions from the Confederates, 17 November 1648, Gilbert (ed.), *Irish Confederation*, VII, pp. 134–6.

[80] *Ibid.*

[81] Ormond to Sir Richard Blake, 21 December 1648, Gilbert (ed.), *Irish Confederation*, VII, pp. 161–2.

determine in an agreement or rupture'.[82] Two days later, in an effort to break the impasse, the Confederates suggested that if parliament were to meet, it should be at liberty to consider whatever 'they shall think convenient for the repeal or suspension of Poynings' act, or any part thereof'. A final clause stated 'that his majesty shall consent to what both the said houses shall therein desire'.[83] The Irish parliament, not the king, would have the final word on the issue.

On 28 December, however, news of the king's impending trial outraged Confederate opinion. In a conspicuous display of loyalty, Sir Richard Blake informed Ormond that the General Assembly, 'upon consideration of his majesty's present condition', had unanimously accepted the terms on offer.[84] The peace treaty signed on 17 January 1649 contained a clause for the holding of a parliament within six months or an assembly within two years. The articles of treaty would be 'transmitted into England, according to the usual form', but would 'receive no disjunction or alteration here, or in England'. The formula appeared almost identical to that used in 1646, except for an amendment declaring 'that both houses of parliament may consider what they shall think convenient touching the repeal or suspension of the statute commonly called Poynings' Act'.[85] This final clause suggested the possibility of further concessions, but the king was not required to consent to parliament's demands on this issue.

With a declaratory act no longer on the agenda, the royalists (as in 1646) recognised the right of the Irish parliament to make any declaration regarding the independence of that parliament 'as shall be agreeable to the laws of the kingdom of Ireland'.[86] The 1649 treaty also retained the original residential and property clauses from 1646 for members of the Lords and Commons. Regarding the elections, the agreement stated that 'All impediments which may hinder the said Roman Catholics to sit or vote in the next parliament, or to choose, or be chosen knights and burgesses to sit or vote there, shall be removed, and that before the said parliament.'[87] However, these concessions would not guarantee an overall Catholic majority in parliament, and on the substantive

---

[82] Ormond to Inchiquin, 24 December 1648, Bodl., Carte MSS 23, f. 108.

[83] Gilbert (ed.), *Irish Confederation*, VII, pp. 168–9.

[84] Blake to Ormond, 28 December 1648, Bodl., Carte MSS 23, f. 123. News of the trial apparently first reached Cork. Inchiquin immediately disseminated news-sheets among the Confederate delegates in Kilkenny, with dramatic results. The shocking developments in England also silenced the complaints of Inchiquin's Protestant troops about the impending peace treaty. Carte, *Life of Ormond*, III, p. 407.

[85] 1649 peace treaty in Gilbert (ed.), *Irish Confederation*, VII, pp. 184–211, quotes at pp. 187–8.

[86] *Ibid.*, p. 194.   [87] *Ibid.* p. 189.

constitutional issues the Confederates had little to show for five years of tough negotiations.

V

While in 1641 Irish MPs may well have retained the mistaken belief that Poynings' Law still benefited parliament, the Confederates did not share any such illusions.[88] The outbreak of civil war in England and the threat of an English executive controlled by the Westminster parliament forced them to reexamine their position on this vital piece of legislation. Similarly, after the Adventurers' Act in March 1642 the predatory ambitions of Westminster in Ireland could no longer be ignored. Indeed, although Patrick Little has described Westminster's preferred stance on Irish constitutional affairs as 'studied indifference', the outcome of the English Civil Wars fundamentally altered the relationship between the two kingdoms.[89] In these changed circumstances, the Confederates believed that the independence of the Irish parliament needed to be firmly reasserted.

Throughout the peace negotiations with the royalists the Confederates insisted on the repeal or suspension of Poynings' Law, along with a declaration of the independence of the Irish parliament from its English counterpart. The fact that they ultimately accepted a compromise agreement does not imply a lack of principle. Rather, with the very survival of the monarchy under threat in late 1648, a continued argument over Poynings' Law was a luxury they could ill afford. But the constitutional issues, which had caused such controversy during the 1640s, were to arise again in the Jacobite parliament of 1689 and at various occasions throughout the eighteenth century until the final disappearance of the Irish colonial parliament in 1801. For the moment, however, the Cromwellian conquest of 1649–53, and subsequent abolition of the Irish parliament, rendered the constitutional debate redundant, at least until the restoration of Charles II in 1660.[90]

---

[88] Clarke, 'History of Poynings' Law', pp. 221–2.
[89] Little, 'The English parliament and the Irish constitution' in Ó Siochrú (ed.), *Kingdoms in Crisis*, p. 121.
[90] See chapter 16 below.

11 Protestant churchmen and the Confederate Wars

Robert Armstrong

In August 1646 eleven bishops of the Church of Ireland put their signatures to a remonstrance delivered to the lord lieutenant, James Butler, marquis of Ormond. Their present purpose was to record their approval of the 'most necessary peace' recently concluded between Ormond and the Confederate Catholics, 'the only meanes to continue the great blessings of Religion and Loyaltye amonge us: And to be the only hopefull way to reduce this Kingdome wholly to his Ma[jes]tys obedience'. But they also articulated their gratitude to the lord lieutenant for preserving, in Dublin and its out garrisons, 'free and full exercise of the trewe reformed Religion according to the Liturgie and Canons soe many years received in the Church . . . Which with sadd and bleedinge Harts we may say is more than we knowe to be in any part of the three Dominions.'[1] The Irish capital had become, however briefly, not merely an isolated religious outpost in Ireland, but the last bastion of a form of church order and worship within the Stuart realms.

The 1640s are the lost decade in the history of the Protestant church establishment in early modern Ireland, and not without good reason. Scholarly work over the last thirty years has transformed our understanding of the Church of Ireland in the years before the watershed event of the 1641 rising, as well as the fate of the Protestant establishment in the 1650s and beyond.[2] The 1640s witnessed a Protestant church presence leached away from much, if not most, of Ireland. Older histories depict a refugee church, fleeing the revanchist Catholic hordes, but entering more or less secure Protestant enclaves only to receive a pummelling from the forces of Anglo-Scottish Presbyterianism or fanaticism. The image is of a church

I would like to thank Dr Patrick Little for his characteristically insightful comments on this chapter, and Dr Tadhg Ó hAnnracháin and Professor Alan Ford for advice and useful references.

[1] Bodl., Carte MSS 18, f. 235, printed in John Rushworth, *Historical Collections of Private Passages of State* (4 vols. in 7 parts, London, 1659–1701), IV, part 1, p. 414 but without a list of signatures.

[2] James Murray *et al.*, 'The Church of Ireland: a critical bibliography 1536–1992', *IHS*, 28 (1992–3), pp. 345–84.

shrivelling before the storms, then flourishing anew in 1660.[3] But clearly the restored Church of Ireland could not simply turn back the clock. Aidan Clarke, surveying the Church of Ireland before the wars, observed that the church of the 1660s re-emerged from the 'catharsis of the 1640s and 1650s' having 'failed, not once, but twice'; the 'legal fiction that the church and community were co-extensive was silently abandoned', for not only had the Catholic population not been absorbed, but earlier decades had seen 'the slow development of a Dublin-centred core of authentic Protestantism', adequate to its miniature pastoral tasks, but so scaled down as to be incapable of integrating the Scots Protestants of Ulster.[4] The gap between 'national' claims and a reality of geographical confinement, now more starkly apparent, was to persist into the 1640s. Notions of a national church continued to be deployed in both an inclusive and an exclusive sense – a church embracing all the inhabitants of the island, but also a church free unto itself – perhaps particularly by those churchmen whose vision of doctrine, discipline and liturgy was that articulated in the 1646 remonstrance.[5] The threats which emerged and seemed likely to engulf the established church, and the responses of that influential body of churchmen and those lay authorities from whom they had sought shelter from the storm, will be the subject of this chapter.

I

The position of the established church of Ireland required it to interpret and defend its position in 'three-kingdom' terms. Not only was there the need for it to accommodate itself to the stance of its absentee supreme governor, it also faced threats emanating from within each of the insular kingdoms. The Catholic challenge meant wide-ranging demands and often harsh local realities. For all the subsequent exaggeration, the insurrection did see the established church sustain heavy losses

---

[3] For an often insightful look at the established church in the 1640s and 1650s, but one concentrating on 'sufferings', see St John D. Seymour, 'The church under persecution' in W. A. Phillips (ed.), *History of the Church of Ireland from the Earliest Times to the Present Day* (3 vols., Oxford, 1933–34), III, pp. 59–116, which complements Seymour, *The Puritans in Ireland 1647–1661* (Oxford, 1912).

[4] Aidan Clarke, 'Varieties of uniformity: the first century of the Church of Ireland' in W. J. Sheils and Diana Wood (eds.), *The Churches, Ireland and the Irish* (Studies in Church History 25, Oxford, 1989), pp. 105–22, at pp. 121–2. Cf. John McCafferty, ' "God bless your free Church of Ireland": Wentworth, Laud, Bramhall and the Irish convocation of 1634' in J. F. Merritt (ed.), *The Political World of Thomas Wentworth, Earl of Strafford, 1621–1641* (Cambridge, 1996), p. 206.

[5] Alan Ford, 'Dependent or independent: the Church of Ireland and its colonial context, 1536–1647', *The Seventeenth Century*, 10 (1995), pp. 163–87 for the development of these ideas.

through killings and, to an ever greater extent, through the expulsion of Protestant populations.[6] Small residues of Protestant churchmen were left behind as the tide of reformed religion receded after 1641. As late as September 1645, Henry Tilson, bishop of Elphin, testified to the presence of twenty Protestant clergymen who, like himself, had remained in their western diocese.[7] Their position was doubtless an unenviable one. The formidable bishop, who shared his cathedral town with a marauding Protestant garrison commanded by his son, berated Ormond as early as 1643 over non-payment of tithes within the quarters 'under the English commaunds and protection' where 'zealous and ravenous covetousness (the forerunner of the Scottish discipline)' led to all tithes being seized and his rents engrossed by local commanders.[8] Elsewhere, one clergyman from Tuam province later claimed that he had spent the decade ministering in Loughrea, deep behind Confederate lines, under the protection of the Catholic but royalist marquis of Clanricard, while Protestant worship appears to have been countenanced in Confederate-held Limerick as late as 1646.[9] Nonetheless, the practice of Protestantism generally retreated to heavily militarised and often self-contained zones in Ulster, in and around Dublin, and along the south Munster coast.

As early as 1642 the Confederate General Assembly committed itself to securing not merely the free exercise of Catholicism but the restoration to the Catholic church of church livings, lands and buildings, and ecclesiastical jurisdiction in areas then held or to be gained.[10] The demands put forward by Ormond on behalf of the Protestant clergy were a mirror image of the Catholic position: they should be 'restored to theire respective churches, jurisdiction, and possessions, both spiritual and temporall, and to the free exercise of their several and respective functions'.[11]

If the Confederates threatened the displacement of the church, as established by law, over most of Ireland, threats from beyond the island raised the prospect of its being dismantled. The full force of religious 'reform' as sponsored by the English parliamentarian camp was made manifest with the delivery of Dublin to the parliamentarians in 1647, but it had

---

[6] Seymour, 'Church under persecution', pp. 66–95.

[7] Bishop Tilson to Dean Margetson, Bodl., Carte MSS 15, f. 652.

[8] Tilson to Ormond, 8 November 1643, Bodl., Carte MSS 7, f. 387.

[9] Seymour, 'Church under persecution', pp. 89, 84.

[10] J. T. Gilbert (ed.), *History of the Irish Confederation and of the War in Ireland, 1641–53* (7 vols., Dublin, 1882–91), II, pp. 73–90, 210–12. For the importance of such issues to Catholic clergy see Tadhg Ó hAnnracháin, 'Rebels and Confederates: the stance of the Irish clergy in the 1640s' in John R. Young (ed.), *Celtic Dimensions of the British Civil Wars* (Edinburgh, 1997), pp. 96–115, at pp. 104–7.

[11] Gilbert (ed.), *Irish Confederation*, III, p. 321. Confederate negotiators simply refused to respond, beyond pointing Ormond to the relevant sections of their own propositions, *ibid.*, IV, pp. 243–4, 304.

been flagged for the past several years.[12] In 1641 the Antrim-based MP for Maldon, Sir John Clotworthy, had failed to have Ireland included within the terms of 'root and branch' legislation.[13] Two years later he proved more successful when he secured the insertion of the two words 'and Ireland' into the Solemn League and Covenant, thereby pledging Westminster and Edinburgh to secure 'reformation of religion . . . in doctrine, worship, discipline and government' in the third kingdom as in England.[14] Yet, as Toby Barnard has shown, Westminster signally failed to translate its ecclesiastical plans into legislation for Ireland.[15] Ordinances designed to replace the Book of Common Prayer with the Directory of Worship, to abolish episcopacy and erect presbyterian structures were quite clearly limited to England and Wales.[16] Not that that commitment was lost sight of altogether. The propositions delivered to the king at Uxbridge in 1645 explicitly called for royal recognition of the abolition of the hierarchy in Ireland as in England, a demand repeated in the propositions of Newcastle a year later.[17] Moreover, it was clear that there was never any intention of allowing an Irish church settlement out of line with the English one. Within a week of the ordinance against the Book of Common Prayer, parliament had approved instructions to accompany a commission to Murrough O'Brien, Lord Inchiquin, Protestant commander in Munster, as lord president of the province. He was mandated to 'conform yourself, and all others there under your Command, to such Form of Church Government and Discipline as shall be set forth by Authority of Parliament' and to make provision for 'Godly Ministers' conformable to such arrangements.[18] Such instructions were duplicated later in the year for Sir Charles Coote as lord president of Connacht, and for the

---

[12] Seymour, *Puritans in Ireland*, pp. 1–6.

[13] Conrad Russell, *The Causes of the English Civil War* (Oxford, 1990), p. 28.

[14] BL, Harleian MS 165, ff. 163–164 (journal of Sir Simonds D'Ewes); *Journals of the House of Commons, 1547–1714* (17 vols., London, 1742–), III, pp. 224, 230; S. R. Gardiner (ed.), *Constitutional Documents of the Puritan Revolution* (3rd edn, 1906, reprinted Oxford, 1979), pp. 267–71 at p. 268.

[15] T. C. Barnard, *Cromwellian Ireland: English government and reform in Ireland 1649–1660* (Oxford, 1975), pp. 95–7.

[16] The text of the August 1648 measure entitled 'An ordinance for the form of church government to be used in the Church of England and Ireland' only refers to England and Wales, C. H. Firth and R. S. Rait (eds.), *Acts and Ordinances of the Interregnum 1642–1660* (3 vols., London, 1911), I, pp. 1188–215; for earlier legislation, I, pp. 582–3, 749–54, 833–8, 879–83, 1062–3.

[17] Gardiner (ed.), *Constitutional Documents*, pp. 275, 291.

[18] *Journals of the House of Lords, 1578–1714* (19 vols., 1767–), VII, p. 138. Webster suggests at least one instance of Inchiquin's using his authority to settle clergy, that of Bernard Packington as 'pastor and minister of the rectory of St Peter's', Cork. The Cork chapter admitted him as *de facto* archdeacon in 1649, and he was subsequently collated as archdeacon in 1662, C. A. Webster, *The Diocese of Cork* (Cork, 1920), pp. 263–4.

three commissioners dispatched to take 'the Office and Charge of Chief Governors of Our said Province of *Ulster*'. In the last instance additional provisions were included, to remove scandalous ministers as well as ensure godly ones, to tender the 'National League and Covenant' and to collect profits from bishops', and deans' and chapters' lands.[19] In concrete situations on the ground, parliament was committing its regional nominees simply to keep in step with whatever it deemed fitting, a stance compatible with its constitutional attitude to Ireland, namely, a willingness to allow 'constitutional muddle', reliance on conservative justifications rather than fresh claims, and a tendency to have events run ahead of assertions on paper.[20] Of course, in England, reality both pre-empted legislative enactment in some areas and staggered to catch up in others.[21] The Ulster commissioners and Coote (whose authority in practice extended to north-west Ulster as well as Connacht) effectively delegated their ecclesiastical responsibilities to the emergent Presbyterian regime in the northern province to the satisfaction, for the moment, of all concerned.[22]

In form the Ulster presbytery was an outgrowth of the ecclesiastical structures of the Scottish army sent to the province in 1642; in essence it was the product of a spiritual imperative, sprung from popular religious demand, which bound the Kirk of Scotland and its 'little sister' in Ireland.[23] The post-plantation church in Ulster had witnessed 'the arrival of new patrons and the tapping of fresh sources of clergy [which] largely by-passed the existing patterns of influence and control', with established linkages to Scotland outweighing new connections to the 'Dublin-centred' Church of Ireland.[24] What appears to have been a manpower surplus within the Scottish Kirk could only have aided such developments.[25] The labours of some Scottish ministers have been associated

---

[19] *Journals of the House of Lords*, VII, pp. 349–50 (May 1645), 596–7 (September 1645).

[20] Patrick Little, 'The English parliament and the Irish constitution, 1641–9' in Micheál Ó Siochrú (ed.), *Kingdoms in Crisis: Ireland in the 1640s* (Dublin, 2001), pp. 106–121.

[21] John Morrill, *The Nature of the English Revolution* (London, 1993), pp. 152, 156–7, 161–2.

[22] Patrick Adair, *A True Narrative of the Rise and Progress of the Presbyterian Church*, ed. W. D. Killen (Belfast, 1866), pp. 127–9, 139. Adair, a participant in events, but writing after the Restoration, was adamant that the commissioners did not authorise, but merely 'encouraged and countenanced', the presbytery.

[23] Edward M. Furgol, 'The military and ministers as agents of Presbyterian imperialism in England and Ireland, 1640–1648' in John Dwyer, Roger A. Mason and Alexander Murray (eds.), *New Perspectives on the Politics and Culture of Early Modern Scotland* (Edinburgh, 1982), pp. 95–115; Robert Armstrong, 'Viscount Ards and the presbytery: politics and religion among the Scots of Ulster in the 1640s' in John R. Young (ed.), *Scotland and Ulster* (forthcoming).

[24] Clarke, 'Varieties of uniformity', p. 119.

[25] W. R. Foster, *The Church before the Covenants: the Church of Scotland 1596–1638* (Edinburgh, 1975), pp. 136–8.

with the emergence of 'popular Protestant religious enthusiasm' in 1620s Ulster, while their deprivation was to be linked to an angry petitioning campaign directed against the established church from within the Protestant community. It was a campaign connected to, but not solely motivated by, the contemporary covenanting revolution in Scotland.[26] As directed towards the English parliament by 1641, the campaign takes its place alongside corresponding developments in England. But neither the outcry against episcopal activities nor subsequent petitions to the Kirk of Scotland for the dispatch of ministers should be viewed solely as harbingers of the Presbyterian system. Pressure from within Ulster for pastoral assistance must surely be seen as directed towards a felt spiritual need, one manifestation of an oft-encountered pressure from below for the ministrations of clergy, preferably educated and diligent clergy, present across the religious spectrum of post-Reformation Europe.[27]

The Kirk, aware that it might be trading on jurisdictional toes, responded in a rather miserly manner in practical terms, but noted that though they were 'loath to usurp without their own bounds . . . they dare not be wanting to the enlargement of Christ's kingdom' when faced with 'so loud a cry, of so extreme necessity'.[28] In 1643, as the Solemn League and Covenant was being negotiated, the Scottish General Assembly pressed the English commissioners that ministers sent to Ireland might have 'liberty of adhering to the doctrine and discipline of this Kirk of Scotland, and not to be ejected for nonconformity, as heretofore they were'.[29] With the Covenant agreed, a greater confidence prevailed. The General Assembly urged 'that by authority of both Houses of the Parliament of England, the Covenant, Confession of Faith, Directory of Worship, Forme of Church Government and Catechisms may be setled in Ireland as well as in England, according to the first article of the Solemn League and Covenant'.[30]

The Church of Scotland recognised that the Irish church settlement belonged within Westminster's sphere of influence, but used the Covenant as a lever to exert pressure for reform. On the ground in Ulster, there was less caution in introducing changes. On 25 July 1644 the Scottish general, Robert Monro, referring to the 'neglect of Church discipline' and the resulting unpunished offences, ordered all soldiers together with

---

[26] Alan Ford, 'The origins of Irish dissent' in Kevin Herlihy (ed.), *The Religion of Irish Dissent, 1650–1800* (Dublin, 1995), pp. 24–9 (quotation at p. 29); J. S. Reid, *History of the Presbyterian Church in Ireland*, ed. W. D. Killen (3 vols., Belfast, 1867), I, pp. 282–91.

[27] I owe this point to conversations with Dr Tadhg Ó hAnnracháin.

[28] Reid, *History*, I, pp. 379–81.   [29] *Ibid.*, p. 397, note 20.

[30] A. F. Mitchell and J. Christie (eds.), *Records of the Commissioners of the General Assemblies of the Church of Scotland, 1646–52* (Scottish History Society, 3 vols., 1892–1909), I, p. 183.

the inhabitants of Counties Antrim and Down to 'give all obedience to the presbitrie' and to submit to its rulings, 'provideing alwayes that the sayd presbetrye proceed according to the discipline of the Church of Scotland'.[31] Ulster was caught up in the covenanting dynamic in a manner unparalleled in England. As with Catholicism, what churchmen feared in England became a reality in Ireland.

The Covenant was carried south. Administered in the precarious Protestant holds in Connacht and Munster, it prompted protests that it was endured rather than welcomed. Inchiquin claimed to 'earnestly desire' the maintenance of the pre-existing church government, but argued that 'Liberty of our Relligion' could only be secured through joining with the anti-episcopalians.[32] Inchiquin's claims, when addressing Westminster in 1647, that he was not committed to any form of church order save as decreed by parliament, may reflect an ingrained Erastianism that lay behind his twists and turns on matters ecclesiastical.[33] But in 1645 his correspondent George Synge, bishop of Cloyne, was not impressed by such a case. He insisted that 'to take armes in defence of Religion . . . against the Prince, or without him, I never said I would doe, being fully assured . . . that there is nothinge off Christ that doth direct or will Iustifie such Actions'.[34] From Dublin's perspective, the Covenant was the glue which would attach more and more of Protestant Ireland to an Anglo-Scottish coalition at odds with all that was sacred. A solvent must be found to dissolve it.

II

From royal headquarters in Oxford the response to the Covenant had been a brief proclamation, crisply forbidding reception of the treasonable bond.[35] Dublin contemplated a more considered response. On 18 December 1644 it declared against the Covenant, warning that it contained 'divers things . . . not only tending to a seditious combination against his Majesty but alsoe contrary to the municipall Lawes of this Kingdome of Ireland, and destructive to the Church Government established by Law in this Kingdom'.[36] In April 1644 what was

---

[31] Bodl., Carte MSS 11, f. 582.

[32] Inchiquin to bishop of Cloyne, 30 August 1645, Bodl., Carte MSS 15, f. 547.

[33] John A. Murphy, 'The politics of the Munster Protestants, 1641–49', *Journal of the Cork Historical and Archaeological Society*, 76 (1971), pp. 1–20 at p. 15.

[34] Unsigned and undated letters, Bodl., Carte MSS 13, ff. 156, 154, which appear to form a sequence with that from Inchiquin to Cloyne in note 32 above.

[35] J. F. Larkin (ed.), *Stuart Royal Proclamations*, vol. II: *Royal proclamations of King Charles I, 1625–46* (Oxford, 1983), pp. 956–7.

[36] Bodl., Carte MSS 8, f. 134, issued in the names of the lords justices (Borlase and Tichborne) and the council, Ormond having not been sworn in as lord lieutenant.

left of the parliament of Ireland conferred its blessing upon this proclamation, describing it as a product of 'great Wisdom and Reason', and
issued a supporting letter from the lord chancellor and the Speaker of
the Commons.[37] In the upper house the lord chancellor, Sir Richard
Bolton, mentioned the 'sending out some Declaration in Answer of the
Covenant, touching the illegality of it'. The matter, he revealed, had been
'in Agitation' at the council, and he was to 'make Answer, touching the
Illegality of it, for matter of Law; and, for the point of Divinity, Doctor
Parry and others were employed'.[38] Bolton's draft was duly read and
approved in the Lords and passed on to the Commons, where it seems that
the draft was referred to lawyer-MPs to consider.[39] Despite Ormond's
approval, the declaration does not appear to have been printed, but the
survival of a document in the form of at least a draft version may provide
some insight into council thinking.[40]

Framed as to be authorised by the lords justices and council, it sets
itself to provide a right understanding of the Covenant, building on the
statement of its unlawfulness in the October proclamation. It takes its
ground on the Covenant's being 'unlawfull and altogeather repugnant to
the municipall Lawes and Statutes of England and Ireland. And tending
to the subversion of the monarchicall and politique Governement and
due administration of iustice in both those kingdomes, as well in Causes
Ecclesiasticall, as Civill.' These themes are developed throughout the
text. Thus the royalist strategy of opening up a gap between England
and Ireland on the one hand, and Scotland on the other, is brought
to bear upon article 1, where the pledge to ensure 'preservation' of the
Church of Scotland lies alongside that to secure 'reformation' in the
other churches. Thereby the Covenant implicitly condemned the latter as
'erroneous; both in Doctrine, Worshipp, Discipline and Governement',
while portraying the Kirk as 'without blemish'; if in former times, the
papacy had sought to 'uniustly compell All other Churches' to conform
to its norms, that role was now taken by the Church of Scotland.[41]

Questions of law dominated most of the argument. Not only was
the present ecclesiastical system secured by statute, but the 'mutuall

---

[37] *Commons' Jnl, Ire,* I, pp. 324–5; *Lords Jnl, Ire,* I, p. 206; *The Copy of a Letter Written by Direction of the Lords Spirituall and Temporall, and Commons* . . . (Dublin, 1644).

[38] *Lords Jnl, Ire,* I, p. 207.

[39] It does seem to have re-emerged. *Lords Jnl, Ire,* I, pp. 207–10; *Commons' Jnl, Ire,* I, pp. 327–8. The Lords had earlier agreed to add their legal expertise to the discussion of the document and 'for the Part of Divinity, to lay a Charge on the Lords the Bishops, whereby it may be the better debated the next session', *Lords Jnl, Ire,* I, p. 210.

[40] Bodl., Carte MSS 8, ff. 390–405; Ormond to Digby, 27 April 1644, in Thomas Carte, *History of the Life of James, First Duke of Ormonde* (2nd edn, 6 vols., Oxford, 1851), VI, pp. 100–1.

[41] Bodl., Carte MSS 8, ff. 396–7.

sympathie and correspondensie' between church and civil government meant that 'the one cannot subsist w[i]thout the other'.[42] Legal texts from Magna Carta onwards, English and Irish, were rehearsed concerning the protection of the church and the buttressing of episcopal government. Much of the text is given over to the legal consequences of the suppression of episcopacy or of ecclesiastical courts: the implications for testamentary law, the impact of the lack of an authority to provide proof of marriage or legitimacy, even the thirty-eight common-law writs which would prove 'fruitlesse and to noe purpose' are listed.[43] The king would lose his right of nomination of bishops, lay patrons would lose the benefit of advowsons without bishops to induct candidates, and the clergy could not compel payment of tithe. The document moved towards the concern that the Covenant would 'subvert and overthrowe the whole frame of the civill Governement, and administratton of iustice' and 'annihillate all the said statutes, and principles of the comon lawe'.[44]

Other documents among Ormond's papers tackle the spiritual and ecclesiastical implications of the Covenant more directly. The threat to the king's position as 'Supreame Rightfull Authoritie in Causes Eccelsiasticall or Civill' is to the fore, the query being raised whether the Covenant did 'not deprive the king of those his Royall Prerogatives and Rightfull Authoritie Ecclesiasticall'.[45] To press the Covenant would be to cause the king to break his coronation oath to uphold the church and would intrude upon the consciences of fellow subjects. Again the different status accorded the churches of Scotland and of England and Ireland was taken up, if more subtly.[46] The removal of episcopacy was queried since it was alleged that it had been acknowledged as *jure divino* by all churches before Calvin, and scorn was reserved for the notion of placing episcopacy on a par with heresy or popery. To do so was to charge and condemn all churches since the Apostles. Moreover, who was to be the judge of 'Heresie, Superstition, Schisme'? According to this anonymous refutation of the Covenant,

---

[42] *Ibid.*, f. 398.   [43] *Ibid*, f. 401.   [44] *Ibid*, f. 403.

[45] *Ibid.*, ff. 384, 386–9. These drafts may have emerged from the attempt to answer the Covenant in terms of 'divinity' mentioned as having devolved upon 'Doctor Parry'. This was presumably Edward Parry, nominated (unsuccessfully) by Ormond for appointment to the see of Killala and, successfully, for Killaloe in 1646, Ormond to Digby 14 August 1645, Carte MSS 15, f. 416; TCD, MS 1120 (Bishop Reeves's annotated copy of Ware's 'Bishops of Ireland', published in vol. I of Ware, *Works Concerning Ireland*), note p. 596, from privy seal, 29 November 1646.

[46] The Covenant's compromise wording, to uphold the Church of Scotland but to reform England and Ireland by Scripture and the 'best reformed churches' was being exploited. Why promise to 'uphold' the Scottish church unless it was reformed by the Word of God without human addition? And if this was so, why should not all the churches of the world be made to conform to it?

If the Parliaments of England and Scotland, and the Assembly of Divines chosed by them, or the Churches representative of both kingdomes All, or any of them should be acknowledged to have Authoritie to determine what is Heresie etc And this determination should bee Imposed to binde other free churches not consulted with, whether This bee not a swearing and submitting to the same Tyranny over the Conscience, and blinde obedience, w[hi]ch wee haue Justly Condemned the papacy for, and an abiuration of True Christian Liberty.

Moreover, the use of the 'materiall sword' was questioned, in that the notion that it was 'Lawfull to settle Relligion or Reformation by force of Armes, or to sweare soe to doe' was seen as contradictory to the teaching of the Apostle Paul.[47]

An oath was framed, pledging loyalty to the king against 'all forreine Invasions and Domestick Rebellions, and Insurrections' and adjuring the Covenant.[48] The existence of several drafts testifies to the care taken in framing it.[49] The defenders of the established church are less associated with religious oaths than either the Covenanters or Confederates, yet they constantly returned to the existing, and legally warranted, oaths of allegiance and supremacy as binding and as the context within which an Irish establishment must be ordered.[50] The query was mooted whether the obligation to defend the king, especially if warranted by oath, did not outweigh any covenanted bond between man and man.[51] Though not exploited in print, such material suggests the presence of relatively sophisticated arguments directed against the covenanting project.[52] Emphasis was placed upon a holistic vision of church and society, a seamless web of order which must not be disrupted. The king's authority was an inextricable component. Threats were externalised, and though the rights of national churches were upheld, those of Ireland and England were regarded as validated through the same process of legal development. These same concepts were as pertinent in countering the Catholic threat to the ecclesiastical establishment.[53]

---

[47] Bodl., Carte MSS 8, ff. 384, 386–9.   [48] *Ibid.*, MSS 11, f. 40.

[49] *Ibid.*, MSS 8, ff. 374–5, 378; MSS 11, f. 42.

[50] For the notion of the 'et cetera' oath as 'in effect Charles's reply' to the 1638 Scottish National Covenant see Julian Davies, *The Caroline Captivity of the Church: Charles I and the Remoulding of Anglicanism, 1625–1641* (Oxford, 1992), p. 275.

[51] Bodl., Carte MSS 8, ff. 386–9, 398.

[52] The author(s) of the 'declaration' accepted that all churches should agree on doctrine, there being only one way to salvation, but did not open up the matter, using the argument only as a prelude to the claim that variation was acceptable on matters of discipline and government – he rounded off his point with a reference to Hooker (Bodl., Carte MSS 8, f. 397).

[53] Cf. Robert Armstrong, 'Ormond, the Confederate peace talks and Protestant royalism' in Ó Siochrú (ed.), *Kingdoms in Crisis*, pp. 122–40 at pp. 134–7.

In a context of renewable cessations, Charles I had mandated negotiation on Confederate grievances, allowing distinctively Catholic claims and requests to be aired. The onus fell upon Ormond to formulate a response or at least to divert debate into acceptable channels.[54] Though any argument based on presence or absence of surviving documentation is flimsy in the extreme, it may be worth noting that there is less evidence of his seeking advice from ecclesiastical than from legal sources, whose input was significant even on matters religious.[55] By 1645 Ormond believed he had conceded enough to allow 'quiett exercise of theire religion in teaching or instructing in Christiane doctrine' but not the 'transferring of the power to governe, or correct his subjects with which God had imediatley intrusted' to the king.[56] His primary concern with royal rights was one which matched exactly his monarch's own priorities. George Synge, bishop of Cloyne, appointed to the council on Ormond's recommendation, was asked by the lord lieutenant for his opinions on the possible 'inconveniences' of granting Catholics liberty from Protestant ecclesiastical jurisdiction.[57] He insisted that this would inescapably mean the 'bringing in of Papall power into the Church', since any alternative Catholic jurisdiction would lead back to Rome. In turn, granting the pope power to make bishops 'is to denude the King of his royall power, whoe by the lawes of the kingdome is the patron of all Bishopricks'. Moreover, it 'blemisheth all the lawes made to repress the Popish invasion upon the state ecclesiasticall, made long before the twentieth of Henry the Eighth'.[58] Ormond would insist upon a distinction between post-Reformation statutes with 'religious' implications, and medieval *praemunire* legislation 'not concearning any matter of religion'.[59] The question of royal authority was as bound up both with the state of the law and the need to exclude 'foreign' threats as it had been when considering the Covenant. Confederates could also press into service the notion of the church as entwined with the common law, as when the 1642 Confederate General Assembly sought to apply Magna Carta's defence of the rights

---

[54] Raymond Gillespie, 'The religion of the first Duke of Ormond' in Toby Barnard and Jane Fenlon (eds.), *The Dukes of Ormonde, 1610–1745* (Woodbridge, 2000), pp. 101–13 provides a useful assessment of Ormond's own religious position.

[55] See, for example, the legal opinion on the state of the law on penalties (or lack of same) 'for saying of Masse, or he whoe shall heare Masse', Gilbert (ed.), *Irish Confederation*, IV, pp. 325–7.

[56] Gilbert (ed.), *Irish Confederation*, IV, pp. 348–50.

[57] Ormond to Digby 4 February 1645, Digby to Ormond, 23 February 1645, Bodl., Carte MSS 14, ff. 22–4, 113.

[58] *Ibid.*, MSS 15, f. 164 (to which the date July 1645 has been added); Gilbert (ed.), *Irish Confederation*, IV, pp. 329–30.

[59] Gilbert (ed.), *Irish Confederation*, IV, pp. 334–5 (18 July 1645).

of the church for present-day Catholic benefit.[60] But their admission that medieval regulation of relations of church and state would have to be amended to take account of a non-Catholic king was regarded as puncturing the legislative fabric of the Irish Christian commonwealth, spun out over centuries.[61]

The established church had long lamented the failures of ecclesiastical jurisdiction, particularly the reliance upon secular authority which, in the hands of sheriffs with Catholic sympathies, could not be relied upon.[62] Immediately before the outbreak of the rebellion several bishops had reiterated these concerns, with the added complaint that their Catholic counterparts were not merely active pastorally, but exercising the kind of spiritual jurisdiction the established church could not match.[63] Their concern was not simply a matter of maintaining order. It had genuinely pastoral implications. As peace talks honed in on crucial religious issues in the summer of 1645 Ormond asked the assembled bishops how far questions of jurisdiction were matters of conscience. The reply, signed by eight bishops, was emphatic. On the question of absolution granted by 'that part of the Catholick Church that is established by law within this kingdom', they asserted that 'conscience cannot be satisfied if it be not demanded and received by every Christian, however distinguished by name of heresy or schism'. Though erroneous consciences might see sin in seeking absolution from them, yet 'we cannot with a good conscience forego the power of the keys which Christ hath committed unto us'. Here was an implicit commitment to the notion of an 'inclusive' national church, albeit inclusive by compulsion, not concession.[64]

Not that the bishops were unwilling to entertain Ormond's request that they suggest some expedient remedy for the problem. Their offer blended temporal remedies with a notable increase in the power of the courts ecclesiastical. If granted the power to fine or imprison on their own authority, they would need to resort to excommunication less frequently. The temporal impact of excommunication could be removed for Catholic offenders through their submission to punishment, but without the need

---

[60] *Ibid.*, II, p. 74. For the 'explosive nature' of the Catholic 'clerical programme' see Tadhg Ó hAnnracháin, 'Lost in Rinuccini's shadow: the Irish clergy, 1645–9' in Ó Siochrú (ed.), *Kingdoms in Crisis*, p. 177.

[61] Gilbert (ed.), *Irish Confederation*, IV, pp. 335–7 (18 July 1645).

[62] Alan Ford, *The Protestant Reformation in Ireland, 1590–1641* (2nd edn, Dublin 1997), pp. 117, 154.

[63] Reports on the state of their dioceses by bishops of Ferns and of Clonfert, *CSPI, 1647–60*, pp. 257–8.

[64] Gilbert (ed.), *Irish Confederation*, V, pp. 39–40 (2 August 1645 for reply). The signatories were Bulkeley of Dublin, Richardson of Ardagh, Sibthorp of Limerick, Leslie of Down and Connor, Williams of Ossory, Golborne of Kildare, Synge of Cloyne and Baily of Clonfert, several of whom had been present in Oxford since 1641.

for them to sully their conscience in seeking absolution. The price was the enhancement of the temporal power of church courts over all subjects. This sense that it was still possible to press for enhanced ecclesiastical powers had surfaced earlier, at Oxford. Submitting a petition to the king for protection against those who sought to 'disinherit the church', Robert Maxwell, bishop of Kilmore, included a request that the king recommend to the lord lieutenant and council means to settle a process to compel attendance at ecclesiastical courts (as for common law or equity courts).[65]

In fact the terms offered by Ormond to the Confederates involved a trimming of the branches of Protestant ecclesiastical jurisdiction, but no digging at the roots. The Court of High Commission could be removed and an act passed to deal with abuses in excommunication, excessive fees and the regulation of visitations. But there would be no exemptions from Protestant jurisdiction, and the king 'must' take churches into 'his owne disposall'.[66] The related questions of excommunication and absolution had been given added emphasis in recent years in both England and Ireland, particularly in the canons of 1634.[67] Ecclesiastical jurisdiction was no side issue for the established church. The edifice, understandable in English terms, of mutually entwined church and law, guiding and nurturing as well as disciplining a Christian people, was one which tallied with the aspirations of royalists promoting the notion of Ireland as a settled, common-law kingdom, if not with the realities of Irish life. Well beyond 1660 the distinction continued to be drawn between either Catholic or dissenting Protestant clergy who would practise their rites quietly and those who would dare to, and could not be allowed to, exercise any form of jurisdiction.[68]

III

If Ormond had obtained the opinion of a clutch of eight bishops on a matter of great moment to the affairs of state, this hardly matched the rise

---

[65] The petition was recommended to Dublin, but actions taken are unclear, Bodl., Carte MSS 13, ff. 240, 501.

[66] He refused to countenance a 'Comission derived from his Majestie' to oversee probate, matrimony, 'bastardy', and tithes. Gilbert (ed.), *Irish Confederation*, IV, p. 319, 339–40, 346–7.

[67] Davies, *Caroline Captivity*, pp. 54–5, 268–9; Anthony Milton, *Catholic and Reformed: The Roman and Protestant Churches in English Protestant Thought, 1600–1640* (Cambridge, 1995), pp. 472–3; McCafferty, ' "God bless your free Church of Ireland" ', pp. 201–2; F. R. Bolton, *The Caroline Tradition of the Church of Ireland* (London, 1958), pp. 130–7.

[68] Richard L. Greaves, ' "That's no good religion that disturbs government": the Church of Ireland and the nonconformist challenge, 1660–88' in Alan Ford, Kenneth Milne and James McGuire (eds.), *As by Law Established* (Dublin, 1995), pp. 120–35.

in the political power of the Catholic hierarchy.[69] But a fairer comparison perhaps lies with the bishops of the Church of England. Subject to their own difficulties in the war years, they scattered and, while maintaining the continuities of ordination and collation, offered little in the way of collective guidance to 'ordinary Anglicans as they struggled to find ways of being faithful to the Church'.[70] Irish bishops had almost invariably taken flight in the aftermath of insurrection, not merely from exposed sees to safe havens like Dublin, but often on to England or Scotland or, in the case of Archibald Hamilton of Cashel, to his kinsmen in Sweden.[71] Given that a majority of the episcopate were British-born, this is hardly surprising. A number of them, in their days of trial, simply went home, dying in or near their home town or county, or even in the parish of their birth.[72] Several of the bishops had resided, at least temporarily, in Oxford, the royalist hub for much of the decade. Indeed, when William Baily was consecrated for the see of Clonfert in the royalist capital on 2 May 1644, it was by three bishops of the Church of Ireland, Ussher of Armagh, and fellow Scots John Maxwell of Killala and Henry Leslie of Down and Connor.[73]

Bishops of the Irish church cast more than a mite in the treasury of royalist polemic. Bramhall of Derry, Williams of Ossory and Maxwell of Killala (later Tuam), the latter almost a professional anti-Covenanter, produced voluminous polemical tracts.[74] Henry Leslie chipped in with published sermons on the office of kingship, and even James Ussher preached and wrote, if he proved reluctant to publish, in the royal cause. If this appears like an abandonment of the fate of the Irish church to concentrate on what was perceived as the more important English, or Anglo-Scottish, struggle, this might be correct. But too rigid a demarcation should not be attempted. Arguments could be deployed on both sides of the Irish Sea. Maxwell dedicated his *Sacra-Sancta Regum Majestas* (1644) to Ormond. In April 1644 Sir James Montgomery, writing to the lord lieutenant from County Down, requested a copy of what would appear to be this very

---

[69] By 1646 the Catholic episcopal convocation had 'emerged as a direct partner in government', Ó hAnnracháin, 'Lost in Rinuccini's shadow', p. 186.

[70] Morrill, *Nature of the English Revolution*, pp. 158–60. See also P. King, 'The episcopate during the Civil War, 1642–1649', *EHR*, 83 (1968), pp. 526–48.

[71] *DNB* for 'Hamilton, Archibald'.

[72] For example, Synge of Cloyne died at Bridgenorth 'the Town of his Nativity' in 1652, Dawson of Clonfert died at Kendal 'the Place of his Birth' in 1643, J. Ware, *Sir James Ware, His Works Concerning Ireland* [ed. Walter Harris] (2 vols. in 3, Dublin, 1739–46), I, pp. 579, 643.

[73] Ware, *Works Concerning Ireland*, I, p. 643.

[74] All three are discussed in David L. Smith, *Constitutional Royalism and the Search for Settlement, c. 1640–1649* (Cambridge, 1994), chapter 7.

work, in the hope of deploying it against Presbyterian clergy there.[75] In March 1645 Archbishop John Williams of York told Ormond that his namesake, Griffith Williams of Ossory, was headed for Ireland 'to have one Bowte w[i]th the Parliamenteeres in that Meridian, as he hath hadd many, in print, w[i]th those kinde of people in ours'.[76] Even though such publications rarely touched on Ireland, they are nevertheless indicative of the kind of thinking which influenced the stance of the upper reaches of the Church of Ireland.[77]

The limitations of the polemical format are apparent: vigour and clarity were prized more than carefully qualified argument. Nor should too much novelty be sought in the publications of the bishops of Ireland. Themes and arguments deployed in the attack on the Solemn League and Covenant make their reappearance, not least in questions of churches and kings, and the rights and liberties of national churches.[78] Henry Leslie had already published on the 'two distinct powers', civil and ecclesiastical, and on the church's inability to extend its censures to rulers, when he had gone on the offensive against the intrusion of covenanting ideas into Ulster in the late 1630s.[79] With it went a distaste, as expressed by Scotsmen, for Presbyterianism. Maxwell gave vent to his anger at 'what enormous, extravagant sovereignty hath been acted by the Presbytery' in Scotland, adding: 'You will hardly find so much acted by all the Popes since *Hildebrand's* time, as by them in this short space.' He boosted the royal view that 'Popular reformations are neither warrantable, nor successful.'[80] Yet just such a popular reformation was arguably even than being enacted in Ulster. If *The burthen of Issachar* (1646) is Maxwell's work, then he was capable of a detailed attack on Scottish reformation history culminating in the view that 'I blesse and prayse God most heartily, that we were delivered from the Popes Tyrannie . . . but for the manner of proceeding, the way they tooke, I dare not, I will not approve it.'[81]

---

[75] Bodl., Carte MSS 10, f. 201. Montgomery only mentions a recent work by the bishop of Killala dedicated to Ormond. The ascription to Maxwell is sometimes disputed. The dedication is signed 'I. A.' which could stand for John, bishop of Achonry, the diocese united with Killala.

[76] Bodl., Carte MSS 14, f. 195.

[77] Moreover, Maxwell, Leslie and Williams had all returned to Dublin by 1646.

[78] For a political text, compare the article 'On the civill magistrate' of the 1615 Irish articles, printed in James Ussher, *The Whole Works of . . . James Ussher*, ed. C. R. Elrington and J. R. Todd (17 vols., Dublin, 1847–64), I, appendix iv, p. xliii.

[79] Henry Leslie, *A Treatise of the Authority of the Church* (Dublin, 1637), pp. 13–14, 94–5, 129; *A Full Confutation of the Covenant* . . . (London, 1639), p. 8.

[80] [Maxwell], *Sacro-Sancta*, pp. 73, 157. Maxwell did not address the Irish situation directly, though he did commend Ormond for his negotiation of 'that more than admirable piece of prudence', the cessation with the Confederates, Dedicatory Epistle to *Sacro-Sancta*.

[81] *The Burthen of Issachar* (1646), p. 28.

Leslie had earlier picked up on what he considered the excesses of Scottish Presbyterian self-confidence in 'matters of Discipline . . . matters of Order': they had 'ascribed unto themselves an absolute perfection, more than ever did the *Pharisees* in Christs dayes . . . or the Popes of late, since they established their own infallibility'.[82] He lamented the Scottish reformers' failures regarding church property – 'in a sacrilegious fury, they pulled downe so many goodly Churches: A fact so abominable, that it made their reformation stinke in the eyes of the whole world.'[83] Behind the muddled metaphor his repugnance was clear.

Griffith Williams echoed the other Irish bishops in their commitment to the royal role to defend and uphold the church in return for their commitment to the monarch. He shared their propensity to berate the parliamentarians, Puritans or Presbyterians as worse than papists.[84] His *The Discovery of Mysteries* (1643) recorded his arrival back in England to find 'a rebellion farre *greater* and more odious than either *Popish*, *Irish*, or any *Sect* or *Nation* of the world hath hitherto produced'.[85] Allowing for rhetorical hyperbole, it was expressive of the author's views of Catholics and Covenanters. The 'faction' were blamed for causing Irish Catholics to '*defend* themselves by a *plain Rebellion*' and 'shewed themselves worse Christians, lesse Subjects, and viler Traitors than all the Papists are' through justifying war against the king, 'whereas the Doctrine of the Church of *Rome* utterly denieth the same, and concludes them no Children of the Church that do it'.[86]

Williams's earlier pamphlet, *Vindiciae Regum* (1643), shows him addressing concerns in both England and Ireland, indeed sometimes conflating them, sometimes addressing one implicitly through the other. The prefatory material claims a composition in Ireland, based on 'notes, that about 25 yeares agone I had collected'. Williams clearly addressed English issues and tackled English parliamentarian writers, even while noting that 'The *Parliament* of *England* it is beyond my sphere, and I being a *transmarine* member of this Parliament of *Ireland*, I will onely direct my speech to that whereof I am a peere.'[87] In addressing the standard royalist argument that a parliament could not be valid without royal participation he overtly directed his comments not to Westminster but to the Confederate General Assemblies which '*meete*, as you doe now, in my Episcopall See at *Kilkenny*, and *continue* your Parliament there'.[88]

[82] Leslie, *A Full Confutation*, pp. 25–6.   [83] Leslie, *Treatise*, p. 154.
[84] Cf. Henry Leslie, *The Blessing of Judah* (Oxford, 1644), p. 23.
[85] Griffith Williams, *The Discovery of Mysteries: or, the plots and practices of a prevalent faction in this present parliament* (Oxford, 1643), p. 2.
[86] Williams, *The Discovery of Mysteries*, pp. 37, 72, 70, 102.
[87] Griffith Williams, *Vindiciae Regum; or, the Grand Rebellion* (Oxford, 1643), p. 63.
[88] *Ibid.*, pp. 66–7.

Of course, for the bishop, the well-worn royalist trope of papist-Puritan equivalence could stand in for the disparate threats to Charles I – king and bishops were 'pressed, opposed and abused betwixt two *rebellious* factions . . . *persecuted* and crucified betwixt two *hereticall* and *tyranicall* parties'.[89] Williams was making more explicit than most the royal claim to defend Protestantism from foes on two flanks, and using his Irish vantage-point to do so.

There is no need to insist upon any of these individuals as in any way typical of the established church. Maxwell had been newly placed in Ireland after being forced out of Scotland, though he had been there long enough to undergo severe treatment from the Connacht insurgents. Williams had moved from court preacher to Irish bishop even more recently and, by his own account, had barely touched down in Kilkenny (preaching only one sermon there) before being put to flight.[90] They articulated an outlook which could find room for negotiations with the Confederates at the expense of pan-Protestantism. Ultimately it was a stance which would not be saleable to most of their flock but which had its own constituency. The primate, Ussher, defended royal authority. But in 1646 he claimed that when he heard that Irish Catholic agents had gone to Oxford, he 'besought his Majesty not to make any concessions to the Irish on the subject of religion without consulting him'. Toleration was duly denied, while 'he, for his part, was ever opposed to it, as a thing most dangerous to the Protestant religion'.[91] As late as August 1647, when Charles I's options were rather limited, Ussher gave only a grudging acquiescence to the question of permitting alternative religious practices, and that in the context of intra-Protestant disputes. In extreme circumstances, 'they cannot say that in Conscience it is unlawfull but that A Christian Prince hath in such exigence a latitude alowed him, the bounding whereof is by God left to him'.[92] It would not take much imagination to picture the bounds of Charles's conscience as rather straitened. Perhaps significantly, it was of the other surviving Irish-born bishop, Anthony Martin of Meath, that it was recorded that he opposed peace with the Irish 'untill the Kings

---

[89] *Ibid.*, p. 97. For a like notion of the king, as Christ crucified between thieves, neither good, but this time Presbyterians and Independents, see Henry Leslie, *The Martyrdome of King Charles* (1649).

[90] Griffith Williams, *The Persecution and Oppression of John Bale . . . and of Gruffeth Williams* (London, 1664).

[91] He was replying to charges by Sir Charles Coote, one of the Protestant agents, that Ussher had acknowledged that the introduction of popery was 'the intention which he knew better than I did, and said, we must submit', C. R. Elrington, 'The life of James Ussher' in Ussher, *Whole Works*, I, pp. 248, 236–7. I owe this point to Professor Alan Ford.

[92] Quoted in John W. Packer, *The Transformation of Anglicanism, 1643–1660* (Manchester, 1969), p. 175.

honour was vindicated from their Aspersions, and more Safe, and Satisfactory Terms obtained for the Protestants'.[93] In the end, of course, the
Ormond Peace of 1646, praised by the assembled bishops in Dublin, did
not formally concede even toleration, shunting aside all religious issues
for later resolution. Consciences were not unduly prodded.

IV

Reactions to the threats of Confederates and Covenanters had been
expressed in terms of commitment to the notion of a 'national' church,
in terms both of autonomy and, geographically speaking, comprehen-
siveness. Clearly steps would have to be taken to maintain even a sem-
blance of reality for such claims. Of the twenty-five bishops of 1641,
seven had died between the outbreak of the rising and the surrender of
Dublin to parliament in 1647.[94] All were replaced, either by new consecrations or by promotions. The share-out of influence in new appointments between Ormond and the royal court at Oxford is unclear, though
both were involved. The process of placing bishops was easier to sustain
in the Irish church than in England; royal nomination in Ireland did not
require even a nominal capitular election, allowing consecrations to proceed in a church reduced to enclaves or exile. The final consecration, that
of Edward Parry to Killaloe, occurred in Dublin after negotiations had
begun for the surrender of the capital to parliament.[95]

Ormond showed some concern that clergy who could be considered
reliable should be supported until they could be restored to their livings.
With the 1646 treaty approaching the moment of promulgation, he sought
from the bishops resident in Dublin lists of clergymen who could be considered honest and well affected to the government of the church, the
king's service and the present peace.[96] Some of the resulting lists present
less than glowing pictures. Henry Leslie could only vouch for seven from
Down and Connor, including his own curate Hugh O'Heny [O'Henan],
four of whom had been ousted by the presbytery and were still 'lurking'
in the diocese.[97] Efforts had been made to sustain the uprooted clerics.

---

[93] Ware, *Works Concerning Ireland*, I, pp. 157–8.

[94] T. W. Moody, F. X. Martin and F. J. Byrne (eds.), *New History of Ireland*, IX: *Maps, genealogies, lists* (Oxford, 1984), pp. 392–438.

[95] Bolton, *Caroline Tradition*, p. 22. Consecrations were invariably conducted by bishops of the Irish church, even when they took place outside Ireland.

[96] Bodl., Carte MSS 18, ff. 208r, 385, 387, 398, 391. Bodl., Carte MSS 21, ff. 555–9 for what appears to be a conflation of these lists, for the provinces of Armagh, Dublin and Cashel, though the document is undated. Though a couple of clergy are located in Munster, almost all are currently placed in Dublin (the vast majority) or in Leinster garrisons under Ormond's control.

[97] Bodl., Carte MSS 18, f. 385; 21, f. 555.

Vacant city livings, including those attached to Dublin's two cathedrals, were awarded, and stipends were drawn in the corporate context.[98] However, the prospect of destitution must have been a real one in some quarters at least.[99] It is unclear what grounds existed for the claims of the papal nuncio that the 1646 Ormond Peace saw Protestant clergy sally forth to reclaim their livings in Catholic quarters.[100] But any incentives to do so must have included pressures greater than any ideological need to realise the nationwide claims of a church in internal exile.

The reality, of course, was that even the Dublin redoubt fell with Ormond's surrender of the city, his hopes of an accommodation with the Confederates having collapsed.[101] The prohibition of the Book of Common Prayer by the newly installed English parliamentary commissioners called forth two papers of protest which are among the better-known productions of the 1640s Church of Ireland.[102] The signatories' arguments appealed to both statute and canon law in defence of the established liturgy and to the king's right to determine forms of worship, as acknowledged in the oath of supremacy. The status of the Irish church as a 'free national church' was advanced both as an argument for the necessity of one liturgy for the entire kingdom and in an assertion of the right to determine its own mode of worship.[103] A recycling but also a redirection of the arguments of recent years had taken place, used now in defence of liturgy. The strategy of linking the two, national, English and Irish churches, through centuries of legislative measures, against Rome, or latterly Scotland, had now to be superseded to counter an overt threat from within England itself.[104]

The signatories numbered only one bishop, Parry of Killaloe, among their number, though some would survive to attain episcopal rank after 1660.[105] As befitted the assault on religious mores in Dublin, virtually all of them appear to have had a connection to one or other of the city's two

---

[98] *Ibid.*, MSS 13, f. 240 for stipends.

[99] A weekly bread allowance had been instituted for clergymen, Seymour, *Puritans in Ireland*, p. 6.

[100] Gilbert (ed.), *Irish Confederation*, VI, pp. 131–2.

[101] Patrick Little, 'The Marquess of Ormond and the English Parliament, 1645–1647' in Barnard and Fenlon (eds.), *Dukes of Ormonde*, pp. 83–99.

[102] Seymour, *Puritans in Ireland*, pp. 2–6; cf. Ford, 'Dependent or independent', p. 179; McCafferty, ' "God bless your free Church of Ireland" ', p. 190.

[103] Bodl., Carte MSS 21, ff. 241–2, 284–5; Charles McNeill (ed.), *The Tanner Letters* (IMC, Dublin, 1943), pp. 245–50.

[104] The petitioners defended the right of the Irish church to determine its liturgy and noted how the use of the Book of Common Prayer in both England and Ireland had been a bond of their communion (McNeill (ed.), *Tanner Letters*, p. 248).

[105] James Margetson, archbishop of Dublin, later of Armagh; Edward Synge, bishop of Limerick, later Cork; Henry Hall, bishop of Killala.

cathedrals.[106] The group had collectively taken stock of the impending threat in advance. Seventeen of the twenty individuals concerned had recently put their names to a call to the Irish House of Lords to defend their livings and their ministries should oaths emerge against their conscience. They also called for the Lords to uphold liturgy, doctrine and discipline, and 'to provide for the repressing of all factious preaching, schisms and heresies' that may arise.[107] Their brief campaign was at once the high point and the last hurrah of the intermittent struggle to preserve the Irish established church, as a church of bishops and prayerbooks, from being subsumed within English norms. 'Ussher's nightmare' of the fate of the free Church of Ireland fallen under English control would be rendered more terrifying by the mix of Erastianism, dubious legality and distasteful religious preferences in which it would appear.[108]

V

That was not quite the end of the story. Ormond, who had departed for England in 1647, made another foray to Ireland in late 1648, in a fresh attempt to forge a cross-religious royalist coalition. Once more he entered the morass of treaty negotiations. With each exchange of papers in 1648–49 he inched closer to short-term capitulation on questions of religion, while conceding nothing 'in perpetuity'.[109] In the end, reduced to approving Confederate drafts confirming the present position of the Catholic church save for the substitution of the single word 'functions' for 'jurisdiction', he conceded even this.[110] What he gave was all, and nothing. In terms of Protestant safeguards, the pragmatic Inchiquin had, a year earlier, cut the deal which the legalistic Ormond would effectively endorse, of leaving clergy of both allegiances to the enjoyment of what they held in zones carved up on the basis of military control.[111] Yet, having made his bed of nails, Ormond needed to lie on it. Generalities, however clearly stated, needed to be translated to interpret the messy realities of conflicting claims, and petitions were submitted to Ormond

---

[106] Nineteen individuals signed the 22 June statement, all but two of whom signed the 9 July remonstrance, with one addition (Seymour, *Puritans in Ireland*, pp. 2–4). Henry Cotton, *Fasti Ecclesiae Hibernicae* (5 vols., Dublin, 1847–60) provides information on the careers of most of these men.

[107] Bodl., Carte MSS 21, f. 165.

[108] The phrase is that of John McCafferty, '"God bless your free Church of Ireland"', p. 207.

[109] Gilbert (ed.), *Irish Confederation*, VII, pp. 155–6, 185–6.

[110] *Ibid.*, VII, pp. 157–8, 160–1, 164–5.

[111] *Ibid.*, VI, pp. 235–9 (though the word 'functions' was used, as Ormond noted, VII, pp. 164–5).

and his ex-Confederate associates demanding action. What, for example, was to become of Waterford cathedral, where the building itself lay in Catholic quarters but where capitular lands were in the zone assigned for support of the Protestant forces?[112] What of the complaint that Protestant clergy (in Protestant quarters) were demanding fees for christenings, marriages and burials from Catholics, although the functions were performed by Catholic priests?[113] Former Confederates pointed to Ormond's continued favouritism to the Protestant interest, despite its numerical negligibility.[114] Conversely, Bishop Synge of Cloyne, now removed from Dublin to the Protestant zone in County Cork, pointed to increased alienation among the Protestant Munster army and added that the concession of jurisdiction to Catholic clergy had seen them 'use that power to the invading of all civill rights'.[115] By 1648 competition in Limerick had even descended to the level of a struggle not merely for the soul, but the bodily remains, of the earl of Roscommon.[116] Ormond could only hope for the arrival in Ireland of the new king, Charles II. The calling of a new parliament with the king present as a 'free & powerfull umpire' would terminate all existing arrangments and, he hoped, provide a means by which the demands of the Catholic clergy could be resisted.[117]

In the summer of 1649 Ormond issued a declaration warning that 'any Ecclesiastical Person' who would 'exercise the People to Sedition or Disobedience' or 'intermeddle' in civil affairs would be treated 'as the Enemy shall deserve'.[118] In Protestant south Munster clergymen were instructed to avoid reflection on 'mysteries of Estate' but preach instead 'faith and good manners with obedience to the Civil Magistrate'.[119] After all, not only the Catholic clerical establishment but also the nascent Presbyterian system in Ulster would pronounce emphatically on 'civil' matters and expect to have their voice heard and heeded. 'Anglican' political theology, as understood in the mid-seventeenth-century Irish church, did not encourage such activity, any more than the king's lieutenant did. The noxiousness of rebellion and the notion of the king as capstone to the arch of order, with spiritual as well as temporal implications, was

---

[112] Seymour, 'Church under persecution', p. 109.
[113] Ormond ordered them to 'forbeare', Athenry *et al.* to Ormond, 8 August, 1649, Bodl., Carte MSS 25, ff. 185, 187.
[114] Muskerry to Ormond, 29 October 1649, Bodl., Carte MSS 26, ff. 45–6.
[115] Bishop Synge and Dean Boyle to Ormond (received 7 May 1649), Bodl., Carte MSS 24, f. 634.
[116] Bodl., Carte MSS 26, ff. 150, 183, 208, 217.
[117] Ormond to Charles II, 22 June 1649 (draft), *ibid.*, MSS 25, ff. 19–22.
[118] Edmund Borlase, *The History of the Execrable Irish Rebellion* (London, 1680), pp. 215–17.
[119] Carte MSS 65, fos. 445–6; Webster, *Cork*, p. 254.

close to the heart of the vision of Protestant royalism, lay and clerical, in England and Ireland. However far removed from the realities of the Irish situation, the concept of a reformed 'national' church continued to inform responses to both Confederate and Covenanter threats. Anglicanism of the Dublin variety was edging towards an equidistance of distaste as between those Restoration bugbears, papist and fanatic. John Leslie, bishop of Raphoe, confessed: 'I am no Papist, but I should be loath to find myself in New England when I come to Ireland. Protestant, or rather Catholic Christian I am, and Popery I know, but from this gallamafrye of so many new religions . . . good God deliver me.'[120]

In 1643 a prayer for the use of the king's army had been published under the name of Lancelot Bulkeley, archbishop of Dublin. It had included petitions for 'the advancement and establishment of the true ancient Catholike, Apostolike Protestant Faith, the rooting out of Popery, Idolatry, and superstition, the conversion of this rebellious seduced Nation unto Loyaltie and the obedience of thy Gospell'.[121] The assumption of historicity, the aspiration towards the assimilation of the populace, the equation of sedition and irreligion were all present, but in years to come the need to embrace royal policy would compromise such strident language about anti-christian popery. Yet many within the Protestant community would give voice to such sentiments. It made it easier to uncouple Protestant doctrine from commitment to prayer-book and bishops in what could be presented as the best interests of Protestantism and the English connection.[122] This is not to say that the three-pronged 'Anglican' programme could not win, and retain, support across the years of effective disestablishment. The churchmen around Ormond conceded very little. And in the end the Irish church produced enough 'sufferers' to man many of the more senior offices of the restored church of the 1660s, a number of them close associates of Ormond.[123] If the 1640s had seen them outmatched in political influence by other constellations of clerics, they had at least demonstrated their resilience and durability.

---

[120] HMC, *Egmont MSS*, I, p. 201 (23 February 1644).

[121] Bodl., Carte MSS 65, f. 30 (28 February 1643).

[122] Nor must it be forgotten that a number of established church clergymen conformed to the loose Irish establishment of the 1650s, undoubtedly not merely from self-interest but out of a sense of pastoral responsibility outweighing personal scruples, which has been demonstrated for similar figures in England, Seymour, *Puritans in Ireland*, pp. 206–24; John Spurr, *The Restoration Church of England, 1646–1689* (New Haven, 1991), chapter 1.

[123] James McGuire, 'Policy and patronage: the appointment of bishops, 1660–61' in Ford, Milne and McGuire (eds.), *As by Law Established*, pp. 112–19.

12 The crisis of the Spanish and the Stuart monarchies in the mid-seventeenth century: local problems or global problems?

Geoffrey Parker

Many people living in the early seventeenth century complained bitterly about the unprecedented harshness of their world. In 1623 an Italian preacher, Secondo Lancellotti, set out to refute these pessimists in a book entitled *L'hoggidì, overo il mondo non peggiore ne più calamitoso del passato* [*Nowadays, or how the world is not worse or more calamitous than it used to be*]. First he identified forty-nine *Inganni* ('fallacies') held by the *Hoggidiani* ('people nowadays', with the sense of 'whiners'). Then he laboriously gave examples in each of the forty-nine categories (the *Disinganni*) to prove the *Hoggidiani* wrong. Thus 'women nowadays are not more vain than those in the past'; 'princes nowadays are not more avarious or indifferent towards their subjects than they used to be'; and 'human life nowadays is not shorter, so that men do not live for less time now than they have done for thousands of years'. Lancellotti devoted eight of his last chapters, covering almost 200 pages, to natural phenomena: he reviewed recent accounts of severe earthquakes, floods, cold weather, famines and plague epidemics 'nowadays' and pointed out that similar events in the past had been far worse. According to Lancellotti, life had never been so good; but proving his case took over 700 pages![1]

Although *L'hoggidì* proved a publishing success – Philip IV owned a copy and a sequel soon appeared – evidence multiplied to support most of the 'fallacies' that Lancellotti denounced. 'Princes avarious and indifferent towards their subjects' provoked an avalanche of new taxes; human life became both shorter and harsher; above all famines, epidemics and natural disasters all increased markedly. The ranks of the *Hoggidiani* swelled until by 1643 even the count-duke of Olivares, Favourite and first minister of Philip IV, had joined them. According to the *Nicandro*, an apologetic tract composed shortly after his fall from power:

I thank Jane Ohlmeyer and Andrew Mitchell for helpful suggestions in writing this chapter, and Aidan Clarke for his inspiration and example in studying the Stuart monarchies.
[1] S. Lancellotti, *L'hoggidì, overo il mondo non peggiore ne più calamitoso del passato* (Venice, 1623).

Sometimes Providence punishes the world with universal and evident calamities, whose causes we cannot know. This seems to be one of the epochs in which every nation is turned upside down, leading some great minds to suspect that we are approaching the end of the world. We have seen all the north in commotion and rebellion, its rivers running with blood, its populous provinces deserted; England, Ireland and Scotland aflame with Civil War; the Ottoman Sultan dragged through the streets of Constantinople; the Turks, after fighting the Persians, at war with each other. China invaded by the Tartars, Ethiopia by the Turks, and the Indian kings who live scattered through the region between the Ganges and the Indus raging with rivalry. What area does not suffer, if not from war, then from earthquakes, plague and famine? How is Olivares to blame because the world suffers from these misfortunes?[2]

The authors of *Nicandro* were remarkably well informed, and the next few years provided yet more examples of 'universal and evident calamities'. In 1648, an irate Muscovite taxpayer warned that 'There is great shaking and the people are troubled'. They were indeed: a major uprising in Moscow triggered urban revolts all across Russia and even beyond the Urals. At the same time, the Cossacks of the Ukraine rebelled against their Polish overlords, starting a war that would last for two decades. In 1649 Robert Menteith, a Scottish exile in France, then also racked by civil war, declared that he and his contemporaries lived in an 'Iron Age' that would become 'famous for the great and strange revolutions that have happened in it . . . Revolts have been frequent in both East and West.'[3] Soon, these 'revolts' had become so widespread – especially in the Stuart and the Spanish monarchies – that two Italian writers published competing handbooks in the 1650s to keep readers abreast of developments. Between them, Giovanni Battista Avogadro of Genoa and Majolino Bisaccione of Venice described the major uprisings in Brazil, Catalonia, England, France, Ireland, Moscow, Naples, the Papal States, Poland, Portugal, Scotland, Sicily and the Ottoman empire. 'There have been so many popular revolts in my time', Bisaccione sighed, 'that they could reasonably be called earthquakes of state.'[4]

The only area of the world to suffer as many upheavals as Europe during the mid-seventeenth century was China. In 1636, a scholar-official noted ominously:

---

[2] J. H. Elliott and J. F. de la Peña, *Memoriales y cartas del Conde-Duque de Olivares* (2 vols., Madrid, 1978–81), II, p. 275.

[3] P. Avrich, *Russian Rebels* (London, 1972), p. 55; R. Mentet de Salmonet, *Histoire des troubles de la Grande Bretagne* (Paris, 1649), p. ii.

[4] M. Bisaccione, *Historia delle guerre civili di questi ultimi tempi* (1652; 4th edn, Venice, 1655), p. 2; and G. B. Birago Avogadro, *Delle historie memorabili che contiene le sollevationi di stato di nostri tempi* (Venice, 1653), reissued the following year as *Turbolenze di Europa dall'anno 1640 sino al 1650* (Venice, 1654).

The disaster caused by the bandits in the northwest has already spread to the central plain. Only the walled cities remain; no one knows how many villages, towns and markets have been burned to the ground. Today, people are killed by bandit mobs; tomorrow, they may die at the hands of government troops. No one can tell how many fields have been left fallow by farmers fleeing disaster or in how many fields already-planted crops wither under the sun.[5]

Eight years later, the last Ming emperor committed suicide when 'bandit mobs', having taken over most of China, seized his capital. This unleashed a far worse cataclysm. The bandits moved north against the Ming loyalist forces deployed along the Great Wall to prevent an invasion by China's northern neighbours, the Manchu. The Ming commander invited the Manchus to help him defeat the bandits, which they did; but they then entered Beijing and called upon all China to recognize their leaders as the lawful new imperial dynasty. Enforcing their authority over the whole country would take a generation and cause untold destruction and death. 'According to my prudent estimate', a Chinese scholar has written, during the 1640s and 1650s 'the cultivated area of land decreased by about one-third in comparison with the late Ming, and the demographic losses were nearly the same.'[6]

Few areas of the world seem to have survived the mid-seventeenth century unscathed. In Istanbul, in 1622 (as the *Nicandro* noted) rebels murdered the Ottoman sultan. In 1648 they did so again and a senior minister predicted that, without urgent preventive measures, 'it is certain that the curse of disobedience to the law and the burden of injustice and violence will ruin the Empire'.[7] In India, between 1627 and 1630, one of the worst droughts on record killed over a million people in Gujarat; more famines occurred in the subcontinent during the early 1640s; and for most of the 1650s a succession dispute in the Mughal empire produced a vicious civil war.

The widespread devastation caused by these human and natural forces led some contemporaries to fear that civilisation as they knew it might perish from the earth. In 1651 Thomas Hobbes, then a refugee from the English Civil War living in France, offered a particularly graphic refutation of Secondo Lancellotti's euphoric vision, a generation earlier:

[5] Pei-kai Cheng and Michael Lestz, with J. D. Spence, *The Search for Modern China: a documentary collection* (New York, 1999), pp. 4–5.

[6] Shi Zhihong in A. Hayami and Y. Tsubochi (eds.), *Economic and Demographic Developments in Rice-producing Societies: some aspects of East Asian history, 1500–1900* (Tokyo, 1989), p. 155.

[7] B. Lewis, 'Ottoman observers of Ottoman decline' in Lewis, *Islam in History: ideas, men and events in the Middle East* (London, 1973), p. 209.

There is no place for industry [Hobbes wrote], because the fruit thereof is uncertain, and consequently no culture of the earth; no navigation, nor use of the commodities that may be imported by sea; no commodious building; no instruments of moving and removing such things as require much force; no knowledge of the face of the earth; no account of Time; no arts; no letters; no society. And, which is worst of all, continual fear and danger of violent death; and the life of man, solitary, poor, nasty, brutish and short.[8]

I

What are we to make of these contradictory sources: do we accept Lancellotti's optimism and say 'Crisis? What crisis?'; do we subscribe to the view of the *Nicandro* that the problem was global and not limited to any one state; or do we believe (with Thomas Hobbes) that a 'system collapse' threatened? Simple coincidence cannot explain so many simultaneous eruptions of violence and revolution around the globe, so what were its common denominators and why did it affect some areas far more than others?

Let us look more closely at some of the 'fallacies' proposed by Lancellotti, with special reference to the Spanish and the Stuart monarchies, starting with the natural disasters that (he asserted) were *not* more numerous 'nowadays' – and that many historians consider the most likely cause of the mid-century crisis. This has always been the most difficult category to evaluate, because instrumental data for measuring the early modern climate did not exist; but historians and climatologists have recently recreated a convincing picture from 'proxy data' of a generally cooler climate, with more extreme variations, in the mid-seventeenth century. For example, a team of Spanish climatologists recently studied the weather patterns in Castile between 1634 and 1648 revealed by the correspondence of members of the Jesuit Order (who were instructed always to mention the weather in their letters). This source clearly showed winters characterised by excessive rains and frosts and colder temperatures than today, and summers with more droughts. The years 1640–41 and 1646–47, during which major revolts occurred, stood out as particularly harsh.[9] Other written records confirm this pattern. Thus, one morning in May 1641, the entire central government received an order to stop

---

[8] T. Hobbes, *Leviathan, or the Matter, Forme, and Power of a Common-wealth, Ecclesiasticall and Civill*, ed. R. Tuck (London, 1651; Cambridge, 1996), p. 89.

[9] F. S. Rodrigo *et al.*, 'On the use of the Jesuit private correspondence records in climate reconstructions: a case study from Castile (Spain) for 1634–1648', *Climatic change*, 40 (1998).

work and join the royal family in a procession that followed the body of St Isidro (patron saint of Madrid) around the streets of the capital to pray for rain.[10] During the winter of 1646–47, by contrast, rain fell on Castile almost without ceasing. According to a news-sheet:

> In Spain, and even they say in all Europe, the era of Noah's flood came again with a vengeance, because the rains that fell were so heavy and so continuous, and the rivers rose so excessively, that commerce and communication ceased between the cities, towns and villages. Many lives were at risk; many buildings collapsed.

In February 1647, according Don Juan de Chumacero, president of the council of Castile and therefore the official responsible for domestic law and order:

> The torrential and persistent rain has made it impossible to provision the Court from villages up to 100 kilometres away . . . because they are already out of flour and cannot get to the fields for firewood to heat the ovens. Few mill wheels are working, because of the floods . . . We have been forced to consume all the flour in the city granary.[11]

In the city's poorer parishes, births plunged and deaths soared. Although Chumacero and his colleagues bought grain from communities up to 300 kilometres away, when this still did not suffice they introduced bread rationing, since:

> This town [Madrid] is very volatile and every day becomes more insolent, which leads to fears of some violence . . . because hunger respects no one. So it is necessary to do all we can to help, and to avoid any decision whatever which people might regard – however wrongly – as a [new] burden.

He concluded wearily: 'There is no shortage of people who blame Your Majesty, and say that he does nothing, or that the council is to blame, as if we could control the weather.'[12]

This 'era of Noah's flood' also brought other parts of the Spanish monarchy to the edge of ruin. In Sicily, a fertile island that normally produced two crops of grain annually, it rained almost continuously from September 1645 to September 1646, destroying the winter crops and drastically reducing the yield of the summer harvest. In addition, the floods washed away houses and bridges, while gales destroyed the

---

[10] Biblioteca Nacional, Madrid [hereafter BNM], MS 8177/141–5, B. de Riquer i Permanyer (ed.), *Historia, politica, societat i cultura dels Paisos Catalans*, IV (Barcelona, 1997), p. 42.

[11] BNM *VE* Ca 68-94; Archivo del Ministerio de Asuntos Exteriores, Madrid [hereafter AMAEM], MS 42/7.

[12] AMAEM, MS 42/15–16v; C. Larquié, 'Les soulèvements populaires en Espagne au milieu du XVIIe siècle', *Revue d'histoire diplomatique*, 92 (1978), pp. 37–39.

olive trees and 'Mount Etna threw up large quantities of fire, doing notable damage to the neighbouring fields and towns.' Then, 'the following autumn, having ploughed and sowed the land, the peasants desired rain, but a great drought occurred, not only then but for almost the whole succeeding winter. The same drought continued into the spring of 1647', which seemed 'to threaten a universal catastrophe'. That winter was exceptionally cold. In Palermo, the capital, some churches became shelters, with fires to warm the homeless, but still people died every day and the hospitals were full.[13] In May 1647, rioters took control of the capital and violence promptly erupted in most other cities of the island: it took over a year to restore royal control. Two months later Naples followed suit, defying the king's authority for nine months.

The Stuart monarchy also saw both extreme weather and major rebellions in these years. In Scotland, in October 1637, the earl of Lothian complained to his father, then in London:

The earth has been iron in this land . . . and the heavens brass this summer, till now in the harvest there have been such inundations and floods and winds, as no man living remembers the like. This has shaken and rotted and carried away the little corn [that] came up, [so] that certainly they that are not blind may see a judgment come on this land. Besides there is no kind of coin in it, [so] that men that are in debt can not get their own to give their creditors, and the few that have money keep it for themselves for the[ir] great advantage in this penury and necessity. So that, for me, if your Lordship persuade not my Lord Treasurer to pay the arrears of your pension, I think I shall be forced this term to run away and let the creditors of the estate catch that catch may, for I cannot do impossibilities.[14]

Nevertheless, the earl did not 'run away'; instead, the combination of extreme weather conditions with Charles's religious and political innovations led Lord Lothian to join a rebellion that shook the entire monarchy to its foundations.

In Ireland, 1639 saw the first of three disastrous harvests, which reduced exports (almost all livestock and farm produce) by about one-third. According to a correspondent in Belfast, by May 1641 the poor 'are so much impoverished that they can no longer subsist'. The inhabitants of the town, he continued, 'have spent their whole year's provision and have not wherewith to furnish themselves with necessary victuals to maintain them and their families'. Many Ulster farms lacked sufficient manpower

[13] G. di Marzo (ed.), *Diari dell città di Palermo dal secolo XVI al XIX* (4 vols., Palermo, 1868–70), III, pp. 35–38; A. Pocili [pseudonym for Placido Reina], *Delle rivoluzioni della città di Palermo avvenute l'anno 1648* [*sic*] (Verona, 1649), p. 1; di Marzo, *Diari*, IV, pp. 201–2.
[14] D. Laing (ed.), *Correspondence of Sir Robert Kerr, first earl of Ancram, and his son William, third earl of Lothian* (2 vols., Edinburgh, 1875), I, pp. 93–8.

to bring in the poor harvest of 1641 – the third in a row – and land rents fell by half, creating great tension between the natives and newcomers in the province.[15] The following October, unusually early snow and frost killed hundreds – perhaps thousands – of half-naked English and Scots settlers as they fled the violent attacks of their Irish neighbours. The number of subsequent 'depositions' that mention the death of settlers through exposure and privation equals those that specify murder.[16]

In England, William Laud, archbishop of Canterbury, noted in his diary a remarkable number of climatic disasters in the 1630s: 'extreme dry and hot' in 1634, 1636 and 1637; 'the greatest tide that hath been seen' in 1635; 'the most extream wind that ever I heard' in 1636 and again in 1639. The following year, one observer noted that 'owing to an abundance of rains and cold winds, the spring is wonderfully late' while another complained about 'the extraordinary distemperature of the season in August 1640, when the land seemed to be threatened with the extraordinary violence of the winds and unaccustomed abundance of wet'.[17] The 'distemperature' complicated assembling the English army with which Charles I hoped to subdue the Scots because its commander, Thomas Wentworth, earl of Strafford, found 'the waters mightily risen and the ways as foul as Christmas'.[18] In January 1642, the worst frosts in living memory and unseasonable floods prevented about 200 members of parliament from reaching the capital after the holiday recess – encouraging Charles to exploit the situation by leading his 'gentlemen', armed with swords and pistols, to arrest five members accused of treason.[19]

The year 1648 also saw some of the worst weather ever recorded in England. Charles I, when a prisoner on the Isle of Wight, asked a local

---

[15] See the three path-breaking articles by R. Gillespie: 'Harvest crises in early seventeenth-century Ireland', *Irish Economic and Social History*, 11 (1984); 'The end of an era. Ulster and the outbreak of the 1641 rising' in C. Brady and R. Gillespie (eds.), *Natives and newcomers. Essays on the making of Irish colonial society* (Dublin, 1986); and 'Destabilizing Ulster' in B. MacCuarta (ed.), *Ulster 1641. Aspects of the Rising* (2nd edn, Belfast, 1997), quotation on p. 111.

[16] M. Perceval-Maxwell, *The Outbreak of the Irish Rebellion of 1641* (Dublin, 1994), p. 228: N. Canny, *Making Ireland British, 1580–1650* (Oxford, 2001), p. 476; A. Clarke, 'The 1641 depositions' in P. Fox (ed.), *Treasures of the Library: Trinity College Dublin* (Dublin, 1986), p. 113. The Stuart kingdoms still used the Julian calendar, ten days behind the Gregorian one, so that the Irish rebellion occurred on 1 November by current reckoning; nevertheless, heavy snow and frosts are virtually unknown in Ireland during the first week of November. I thank Aidan Clarke for illuminating discussions of the '1641 Depositions'.

[17] H. Wharton, *The History of the Troubles and Tryal of . . . William Laud* (London, 1695), pp. 51–7; *CSPD, 1640*, p. 118; George Naworth [Sir George Wharton], *A New Almanacke and Prognostication for the yeere of our Lord and Saviour Iesus Christ 1642* (London, 1642), sig C2.

[18] *CSPD, 1640*, p. 627.   [19] *CSPD, 1641–43*, pp. 240–2.

gentleman if 'that weather was usual in our island. I told him that in this forty years I never knew the like before', because

From Mayday till the 15th of September [1648], we had scarce three dry days together. Men made an ill shift with their wheat. When a dry day came, they would reap and carry it presently into the barns, although they mowed it wet. I believe most was mowed so wet that much of it will grow in the barn, and I am confident wheat and barley will bear such a price as was never known in England.

He was right. Even in London, normally the best-supplied region in England, the price of flour used by households as well as by bakers to make their daily bread reached a higher price than ever before in 1648 and 1649.[20] At least the king could watch the torrential rain from indoors. The troops fighting the Second English Civil War, by contrast, had to march along roads like quagmires and at the end of the day slept 'in the mire'. After their victory at Preston in 1648, Cromwell and his men 'lay that night in the field close by the enemy, being very dirty and weary, having marched twelve miles [over] such ground as I never rode in all my life, the day being very wet'. The New Model cavalry ended the campaign 'so exceedingly battered as I never saw them in all my life', while 'these ways and the weather have shattered [the infantry] all to pieces'.[21] Meanwhile, in Ireland, there was 'so great a dearth of corne, as Ireland hath not seene in our memorie, and so cruell a famine, which hath alreadie killed thousands of the poorer sort'. The Spanish agent in Kilkenny complained that the disastrous harvest had raised the cost of a loaf of bread fivefold.[22]

Throughout the northern hemisphere, unusual cold and drought in the 1640s produced three of the worst harvests recorded during the past six centuries. Modern reconstructions of the Alpine climate suggest an *average* temperature there one degree Celsius (and in March two degrees) lower in the 1640s than in the 1630s; while at the other end of Eurasia, studies of mountainous areas of China suggest a climate *on average* more than one degree colder in the west and more than two degrees colder in the north-west. It is important to stress 'average' because some individual years fell below – perhaps far below – the norm. The combination of these and other deleterious developments – advancing glaciers,

[20] F. Bamford (ed.), *A Royalist's Notebook. The Commonplace Book of Sir John Oglander* (London, 1936), pp. 119 and 120–1; J. Boulton, 'Food prices and the standard of living in London in the "Century of revolution", 1580–1700', *Economic History Review*, 53 (2000), pp. 468 and 481–2.

[21] W. C. Abbott, *The Writings and Speeches of Oliver Cromwell* (4 vols., Cambridge, 1937), I, pp. 636 and 641.

[22] J. T. Gilbert (ed.), *History of the Irish Confederation and War in Ireland* (7 vols., Dublin, 1882–91), VI, pp. 270–1. I thank Jane Ohlmeyer for this reference.

lower snow lines, more droughts, floods and other extreme weather events, combined with generally cooler, wetter summers and more severe winters – have led historians and climatologists to speak of the period as 'The Little Ice Age', reaching its greatest intensity between the 1620s and the 1660s.[23]

The Little Ice Age affected the human population via a simple but cruel calculus. First, population increases geometrically while agricultural output grows only arithmetically: rather like 'compound interest', a sustained demographic increase of 1 per cent per year over a century will cause population size not merely to double, but to triple. A 2 per cent increase, sustained over a century, will produce a sevenfold growth in overall population. Since crop yields do not normally increase in this way, eventually they become inadequate for the increased number of mouths to feed, starting in the areas where population has increased fastest. Second, any climatic change that reduces crop yields will lower the threshold at which the food supply becomes inadequate to support the existing population. Third, a series of major volcanic eruptions between 1638 and 1644 was followed by an unprecedented absence of sunspots; both reduced the amount of solar energy received on earth. Even though the solar cooling registered at the equator may have been only one degree, recent simulations of the global climate reveal that its effect over Europe and North America was between five and ten times larger, due to a shift in atmospheric winds and more frequent 'extreme climatic events'.[24] Furthermore, even slight solar cooling encourages the movement of warm bodies of water within the tropical Pacific Ocean, an effect known as El Niño, which creates marked anomalies in rainfall around the Pacific and far beyond. Indeed, El Niño forms one of the principal determinants of climate around the globe, and episodes occurred in 1640, 1641, 1647, 1650 and 1652 – all of them years of abnormal droughts and floods throughout the northern hemisphere.[25] Some regional climates are particularly El Niño sensitive. First, the climate around the Pacific Rim changes markedly during El Niño years, with torrential rains on the American side, carrying over to the Caribbean, and droughts along the Asian side, affecting Indonesia, Australia and southern China. Second,

---

[23] G. Parker, *The World Crisis of the Seventeenth Century* (London, 2005), chapter 1, will discuss the causes and impact of the Little Ice Age.

[24] D. T. Shindell *et al.*, 'Solar forcing of regional climate change during the Maunder Minimum', *Science*, 294 (7 Dec. 2001). I thank Martha Peach for this reference.

[25] Details in H. F. Diaz and V. Markgraf (eds.), *El Niño. Historical and paleoclimatic aspects of the Southern Oscillation* (Cambridge, 1993), pp. 122–3; P. D. Jones *et al.* (eds.), *Climatic Variations and Forcing Mechanisms of the Last Two Thousand Years* (Berlin, 1996), pp. 388–9; and R. J. McIntosh *et al.* (eds.), *The Way the Wind Blows: climate, history and human action* (New York, 2000), p. 58, table (c).

droughts in Ethiopia and north-west India associate strongly (although not exclusively) with El Niño events.[26]

II

Nevertheless, historians cannot 'blame El Niño' for everything. The global cooling of the 1640s affected three economic zones of the northern hemisphere above all: newly cultivated marginal lands; the cities; and economic regions geared to production for a distant market. All had prospered disproportionately during the economic boom – and generally benign climate – of the sixteenth century; all suffered disproportionately when the climate deteriorated.

In all epochs, those who till marginal lands soon become trapped in a high-risk, high-input, low-yield operation that requires constant attention; even had the climate of the seventeenth century remained warm, farmers would have been hard pressed to keep up yields after a few years of cultivating poor soils. But of course the climate did not remain warm. In southern Scotland, the new farms established in the Lammermuir hills in the sixteenth century were almost all abandoned in the seventeenth. In Sicily, where early modern farmers normally achieved yields of 7–10 grains for each grain of wheat sown, torrential rains between 1647 and 1650 drove yield ratios below 1:4 on estates in more fertile land and on marginal lands down to 1:3 and even 1:2 (the lowest recorded in the entire early modern period). At Leonforte, a new town in western Sicily with some 2,200 inhabitants in 1647, catastrophic weather the following year halved wheat production and the parish priest registered 426 burials but only 60 births.[27]

The Little Ice Age also hit cities with particular force. In the early seventeenth century over a million people lived in Beijing, the largest city in the world, and almost as many in Nanjing, with 500,000 or more in six other Chinese cities and over 100,000 living in a score more. Mughal India, the second most urbanised area in the world, boasted three cities

---

[26] The 'global footprint' is admirably discussed in R. H. Grove and J. Chappell (eds.), *El Niño: history and crisis* (London, 2000), chapter 1 and C. Caviades, *El Niño in History: storming across the centuries* (Gainesville, 2001), p. 198.

[27] On Scotland, see J. M. Grove, *The Little Ice Age* (London, 1988), pp. 407–12; and T. M. L. Wigley *et al.*, *Climate and History. Studies of past climates and their impact on man* (Cambridge, 1981), pp. 327–35. On yield ratios, see M. Aymard, 'Rendements et productivité agricole dans l'Italie moderne', *Annales: Économies, Sociétés, Civilisations*, 28 (1973), pp. 483–7, and 'Rese e profitti agricoli in Sicilia, 1640–1760', *Quaderni storici*, 14 (1970), p. 436. On Leonforte, see T. Davies, 'Changes in the structure of the wheat trade in seventeenth-century Sicily and the building of new villages', *Journal of European Economic History*, 12 (1983), pp. 393–7; and D. Ligresti, *Sicilia moderna: le città e gli uomini* (Naples, 1984), pp. 108, 156.

with 400,000 or more inhabitants and nine more with over 100,000. In Europe, Istanbul had 600,000 or more, Paris, Naples and London over 250,000, and ten more cities boasted over 100,000. By contrast, only Mexico City and Potosí in the Americas, and only Cairo in Africa, exceeded 100,000 inhabitants.

Xie Zhaozhe, author of a seventeenth-century Chinese encyclopaedia, graphically described the perils of city living, where the houses,

Are so closely crowded together that there is no spare space, and in the markets there is much excrement and filth. People from all directions live together in disorderly confusion, and there are many flies and gnats. Whenever it becomes hot, it is almost intolerable. A little steady rain has only to fall and there is trouble from flooding. Therefore malarial fevers, diarrhoea and epidemics follow each other without stopping.[28]

Examples of similar urban problems are legion, from both the Spanish and Stuart monarchies: all their leading cities consumed far more food than they could produce and so depended totally on a secure supply of food (especially grain) from their hinterland. When the bread supply failed, starvation – and therefore disorder – soon threatened. The 'wants' of the cloth workers of Colchester were said to be 'so great that they cannot be without worke one weeke' without starving; while in Madrid, 'if the provision of bread should fail for one day, Your Majesty would have the whole population in the square before the palace'.[29]

The most advanced economic zones (sometimes called 'macroregions') proved doubly vulnerable. Since water transportation offered the only realistic means of carrying bulk goods (like foodstuffs) before the coming of railways, macroregions developed mainly in coastal plains or along the banks of the major rivers, where most of the major resources could be found: the best arable land, the densest population, the hubs of communication and transport, the largest capital accumulations.[30] The tendency

---

[28] H. Dunstan, 'The late Ming epidemics: a preliminary survey', *Ch'ing-shih wen- t'i*, 3:3 (1975), p. 7.

[29] K. E. Wrightson, *Earthly Necessities. Economic lives in early modern Britain* (New Haven and London, 2000), p. 195; AMAEM, MS 42/11. On the perils of London, see E. A. Wrigley 'A simple model of London's importance in changing English society and economy', *Past and Present*, 37 (1967); on those of Madrid, see D. R. Ringrose, *Madrid and the Spanish Economy, 1500–1750* (Berkeley, 1983).

[30] This general framework is taken from the seminal (although much criticised) studies by G. W. Skinner, 'Marketing and social structure in rural China', *Journal of Asian Studies*, 24 (1964) and 25 (1965); and 'Cities and the hierarchy of local systems' in Skinner (ed.), *The City in Late Imperial China* (Stanford, 1977), 281–301. For a summary of the criticisms, see L. E. Eastman, *Families, Fields and Ancestors. Constancy and change in China's social and economic history, 1550–1949* (Oxford, 1988), p. 255 notes 21–23.

to specialise in preparing goods for export in the macroregions led to the neglect of other economic activities, creating not only dependence on imported foodstuffs but also vulnerability to the ebb and flow of international trade. Some, like the farmers of the Guadalquivir valley, concentrated on cereals; others, like those in Portuguese Macao or Spanish Manila, and their hinterlands, concentrated on entrepot trade. They therefore suffered not only from the disruption and dislocation caused by local wars, famines and other catastrophes in their own vicinity but also from similar events far away. Thus the prohibition of all trade with Catholics issued by the Japanese shogun in 1639 ruined Macao; while the Dutch blockade of Manila destroyed the prosperity of many of Philip IV's subjects in Mexico and Spain as well as in the Philippines. In London, the directors of the East India Company could not fill their outgoing ships with goods because not only has 'all trade and commerce in this kingdom' ceased, but also 'as the badness of trade and scarcity of money are here, so is all Europe in little better condition, but in a turmoil, either foreign or domestic war'.[31]

III

The macroregions and the cities also suffered more acutely during the crisis of the mid-seventeenth century because they experienced more directly and dramatically than other areas the increasing demands of the early modern state. Fulvio Testi, an Italian warrior and man of letters, claimed in 1641 that 'This is the century of the soldiers', while, in England, Thomas Hobbes argued in the same year that 'man's natural state, before they came together into society, was war: and not simply war, but the war of every man against every man'.[32] It is easy to see why both writers saw war rather than peace as the norm; armed conflicts in Europe became more common than ever before. In the sixty-one years between 1618 and 1678, Poland was at peace for only twenty-seven, the Dutch Republic for only fourteen, France for only eleven, Spain for only three – and many states fought several wars at the same time, both by land and by sea. Charles I fought Spain between 1625 and 1630, and France from 1627 to 1630; and he mobilised troops and ships against the Scots in 1639 and 1640. In between, although at peace, he spent heavily on the Royal Navy.

[31] E. B. Sainsbury (ed.), *A Calendar of the Court Minutes etc of the East India Company 1644–1649* (Oxford, 1912), p. i.
[32] M. L. Doglio (ed.), *Lettere di Fulvio Testi*, III (Bari, 1967), p. 204; T. Hobbes, *On the Citizen*, ed. R. Tuck and M. Silverthorne (*De cive*, 1641; Cambridge, 1998), p. 29.

Faced by deepening economic recession, taxpayers resisted with growing ingenuity, irritation and implacability the fiscal demands of their government to finance their wars. Throughout the 1620s, assemblies of taxpayers in both the Stuart and the Spanish monarchies did their best to stop or sabotage every attempt by the crown to increase revenues. Ministers in both states therefore turned to alternative means. Aidan Clarke has observed: 'It was the deliberate policy of Wentworth in the 1630s to abstract the state still further from society in Ireland by creating a government wholly unresponsive to its local environment.'[33] His insight applies equally to the policies pursued by the ministers of Charles I in Scotland and England, and to those pursued by the ministers of Philip IV throughout the Spanish monarchy. Thus Whitehall imposed the 'Revocation' on Scotland, and Monopolies, Forest Fines and Ship Money on England; while Madrid sought to introduce a universal stamp duty (*papel sellado*), the *media anata* (half of the first year's salary from every new office-holder, secular and ecclesiastical) and a salt monopoly. All these new taxes were 'regalian rights' which both monarchs could impose and increase at will; none required parliamentary approval. Some ministers worried about the dangers inherent in such innovations. 'This is a matter, Sire, on which we must embark with great caution', the president of the council of Castile warned Philip IV, 'because every novelty brings with it great inconveniences'; but the king pressed ahead regardless.[34]

Most of these regalian rights had not been levied for decades, and so to legitimize their resurrection the crown's apologists ransacked legal and historical works for justifications. This naturally led some taxpayers to search the sources themselves for precedents that restricted or (better yet) precluded each royal 'novelty'. Unfortunately for the crown, they (and their predecessors) had been at work on this project for a while. Thus the scholarly elite of Barcelona, many of them trained in the law, had since the 1590s produced books that stressed the distinctive character, heritage and language of Catalonia and emphasised the 'contractual' origins of the state after its 'liberation' from Islam by the Carolingian emperors. They published accounts of the laws and privileges which (they claimed) formed the 'fundamental laws' or 'constitutions' of the principality that no ruler – especially no ruler residing outside the principality – could violate. Similarly, scholars in Naples (jurists once more prominent among them) wrote books that condemned government by a viceroy in

---

[33] A. Clarke, 'Ireland and the General Crisis', *Past and Present*, 48 (1970), p. 91.

[34] J. E. Gelabert, *Castilla convulsa (1631–1652)* (Madrid, 2001), p. 20. Most historians have overlooked the novelty of simultaneously imposing the same taxes throughout the Spanish monarchy: see Parker, *The World Crisis*, chapter 8.

alliance with the nobles, contrasting it with the city's 'republican' past characterised by parity between the nobles and the 'people'.[35] Similarly, in the kingdoms ruled by Charles I, the 'Revocation' in Scotland, Ship Money in England, and 'Thorough' in Ireland all prompted scholars to ransack historical and legal sources for precedents that might strengthen their opposition to the government's 'novelties'.

Since these developments will be familiar to readers of this volume, let me suggest some common denominators between four major rebellions against Philip IV (Catalonia and Portugal after 1640; Sicily and Naples in 1647) and three against Charles I (Scotland after 1638; Ireland after 1641; and England after 1642).[36]

(1) Most obvious, yet most neglected, all seven occurred at a time of unparalleled climatic adversity, five in El Niño years: 1640, 1641 and 1647 (page 260 above).

(2) All centred on the capital cities, no doubt because they bore the full brunt of the 'novelties' decreed by the central government at a time of sharp economic recession.[37]

(3) All began in 'composite monarchies' made up of various states, most of which had surrendered their independence in return for guarantees concerning the continuance of their traditional institutions and customs. This promoted political instability in two ways. First, when central governments sought to impose innovations, local elites appealed to the 'ancient constitution' and 'traditional liberties' of their area in order to broaden support. The exasperation of Olivares at the Catalans' skill in using the principality's 'ancient constitution' to oppose his policies is highly revealing. 'By now I am at my wits end', he fumed, 'But I say, and I shall still be saying on my deathbed, that if the constitutions do not allow this, then the devil take the constitutions!' He never seems to have appreciated that riding roughshod over 'the constitutions' was the surest way of turning intransigence into revolt. A second tendency

---

[35] V. I. Comparato, 'Barcelona y Nápoles en la búsqueda de un modelo político: analogías, diferencias, contactos', *Pedralbes*, 18 (1998).

[36] C. Russell, *The Fall of the British Monarchies, 1637–1642* (Oxford: 1991), provides an excellent account of the collapse of Charles I's rule in Scotland, Ireland and England, and of the connections between them. A modern account that links the revolts of Catalonia, Portugal, Sicily and Naples against Philip IV is urgently needed; until one appears, see the vintage account of R. B. Merriman, *Six Contemporaneous Revolutions* (Oxford, 1938).

[37] Admittedly, in four of the capitals refugees played an important role. Men seeking temporary farm work (the *segadors*) led the attack on Viceroy Coloma and his judges in Barcelona, while the conspirators who tried to capture Dublin entered the city just before a fair in order to mingle with the crowds of outsiders. Likewise, in 1647, Palermo swarmed with thousands of refugees from the countryside, attracted by subsidised food; and *Palermitanos* were prominent in the crowds that stormed the viceregal palace in Naples.

towards political instability inherent in 'composite monarchies' lay in the obvious temptation for one peripheral area with grievances to exploit the opportunity offered by unrest or rebellion in another. Thus, according to one observer, Portugal 'would never have dared revolt [in December 1640] without the example of Catalonia, fearing that it would be rapidly overwhelmed if it joined in so dangerous a dance alone'.[38]

(4) In six cases, the 'novelties' that triggered rebellion arose from military demands: either a sudden increase in the burden of raising, feeding and quartering an army or the demand for new taxes to pay for troops serving elsewhere. The catalyst in Catalonia and Ulster was the burden of royal troops billeted on communities already facing economic disaster for climatic reasons; while Portugal rose against the requirement that the nobles recruit and lead their vassals to fight the Catalans. In Palermo, by contrast, the trouble began with a decision, on explicit orders from Madrid, to end a subsidy that kept down the price of bread, and in Naples with the imposition of an excise on fruit: in both cases, the measures arose directly from the need to raise and export funds to pay for the central government's wars in Spain and Italy. Charles I's English opponents, for their part, objected first to the proposal to raise taxes to pay the Scots army before redressing grievances, and then to the 'commissions of array' issued to raise a royal army ostensibly for use against the Irish rebels. Only Scotland followed a different course, provoked by the central government's insistence on imposing new forms of religious worship.

(5) Five rebellions began with popular rioting. Often it involved relatively few (a few hundred in Barcelona, fewer in Lisbon, fewer still in Edinburgh; more in Palermo and Naples), and soon local 'alienated intellectuals' (mostly secular but some clerical) exploited the temporary paralysis of the local authorities and the fear among the middle class (both created by the sudden popular violence) in order to secure a part at least of their political programme. Even the two exceptions involved violence. In Ireland, a group of alienated landowners planned to seize the leading Protestant strongholds and, when they failed to secure Dublin, popular violence swiftly overwhelmed their plans; and in England, the available

---

[38] J. H. Elliott, *The Revolt of the Catalans. A study in the decline of Spain* (Cambridge, 1963), p. 375; Archives du Ministère des Affaires Étrangères, Paris, *Correspondance Politique: Espagne* [hereafter AMAEP *CPE*] *Supplément* 3/240v–1. See also the quotation on p. 270 below. For the special vulnerability of composite monarchies to multiple revolts, see J. H. Elliott, 'A Europe of composite monarchies', *Past and Present*, 137 (1992); C. Russell, 'Composite monarchies in early modern Europe: the British and Irish example' and N. Canny, 'Irish, Scottish and Welsh responses to centralization, *c.* 1530–*c.* 1640: a comparative perspective' in A. Grant and K. Stringer (eds.), *Uniting the Kingdom? The making of British history* (London, 1995).

evidence suggests that parliamentary leaders manipulated the violence of the London crowd.

(6) The leadership of four revolts included clerics – Pau Claris in Barcelona; Giulio Genoino in Naples; Alexander Henderson and many other ministers in Scotland; most Catholic priests in Ireland – and the clergy throughout the Stuart kingdoms as well as in Catalonia and Portugal preached sermons and published propaganda in support of the rebel cause.[39] Many other leaders came from two prominent groups: lawyers and historians. Notable among the former in Scotland was Archibald Johnstone of Wariston, who drafted the National Covenant and rose to be lord advocate, clerk register and finally president of the Council of State of Great Britain; in Ireland, Patrick Darcy, Richard Bellings and Nicholas Plunkett (equivalent in office to lord chancellor, secretary of state and speaker of the Catholic Confederation); and in England the 306 original members of the House of Commons who had attended the Inns of Court. Lawyers prominent among the opponents of Philip IV included Francesco Arpaja, Vincenzo d'Andrea and Giovanni Antonio Summonte in Naples; and in Catalonia, Joan Pere Fontanella, his son Josep, and Francesc Martí i Viladamor. Historians and antiquarians who featured among the opponents of Charles I included William Prynne, Sir James Balfour of Denmylne and Conor O'Mahony (who wrote his provocative *Disputatio apologetica de jure regni Hiberniae* in the safety of Lisbon); while those who opposed Philip IV included Francesco Baronius in Sicily, Francesco de Petri in Naples and Joan Luis Montcada in Catalonia.

(7) In all cases, the rebels wanted to restore their 'Ancient Constitution': the charters granted by Charles V and equality of representation between nobles and '*popolo*' in Palermo and Naples; respect for the *fueros* in Catalonia; abolition of the stranglehold of Vasconcelos and Soares in Portugal; a return to parliamentary government in England; implementation of the 'Graces' in Ireland; and maintenance of traditional worship in Scotland.

(8) Remarkably similar language appeared in several different revolts. The Scots (followed by the English) opponents of Charles I condemned as 'incendiaries' those (like Laud and Strafford) whom they blamed for

---

[39] A. Simón i Tarres, *Els orígens de la revolució catalana de 1640* (Barcelona, 1999), chapter 5; L. Reis Torgal, *Ideologia política e teoria do estado na Restauração* (2 vols., Coimbra, 1981–82); J. F. Marques, *A parenética portuguesa e a Restauração* (2 vols., Porto, 1989); T. Ó hAnnracháin, 'Rebels and Confederates: the stance of the Irish clergy in the 1640s' in J. R. Young (ed.), *Celtic Dimensions of the British Civil Wars* (Edinburgh, 1997).

the breakdown of public peace; in Catalonia, Naples and Sicily, contemporaries used almost the same word – '*incenditori*' or '*incendiarij*' – to describe those accused of causing disorders. They were also denounced as 'enemies of the fatherland' in Catalonia, Naples and Sicily (and as 'enemies of the state' in England in 1647). In both England and Naples, scholars denounced the 'Norman Yoke' imposed by a foreign dynasty to subvert a previously free society.[40]

(9) Four groups of rebels entirely repudiated the authority of their sovereign. Portugal almost immediately proclaimed a rival (the duke of Braganza) as King João IV;[41] while Catalonia and Naples declared themselves independent republics after negotiations with Madrid failed. The leading English opponents of Charles I eventually put him on trial and, after his execution, declared themselves to be a republic and imposed their form of government (first a Commonwealth and then a Protectorate) on Scotland, Ireland and all other parts of the Stuart monarchy. In addition, although they remained nominally loyal to the person of the king, both the Scots and Irish insurgents radically restricted his role: the former by insisting that he subscribe to the National Covenant, the latter by drafting a new Constitution (chapter 10 above). (Except in Portugal, all these new constitutional experiments failed; the alternative ideology, whether Republican or theocratic, did not endure.)

(10) The rebel leaders in Scotland, Catalonia and Portugal immediately summoned the 'Estates of the Realm' to enact new policies and levy new taxes. In England, parliament was already in session and simply continued to sit after the king withdrew his consent. In Ireland, since the parliament remained loyal to the crown, the rebels created their own assembly (in fact, one that represented the kingdom far better, see chapter 10 above). In Naples, where the capital had no representation in the *Parlamento*, the leaders of the 'Serenissima Reale Repubblica' planned to convene an assembly of the twelve provinces of the kingdom, but the

---

[40] For the 'Norman Yoke' in Naples, see A. Calabria and J. A. Marino (eds.), *Good Government in Spanish Naples* (New York, 1990), pp. 291–2; for England, see the article with that title in C. Hill, *Puritanism and Revolution. Studies in interpretation of the English Revolution of the seventeenth century* (London, 1958). Naturally, Scots and Irish writers developed similar theories of foreign oppression; so, after 1640, did the Catalans and Portuguese.

[41] Schaub, *Le Portugal*, pp. 243–4, records a subsequent claim by Margaret of Mantua's majordomo that on the night of 1–2 December most of the nobles involved in murdering Secretary Vasconcelos would have returned to Philip IV's allegiance so long as he dismissed Diogo Soares, who handled Portuguese affairs at court. But, as Schaub notes, did this reflect a genuine possibility at that juncture or merely part of the campaign against Soares (who remained in office until 1643)?

revolt collapsed before it could be done.[42] Only Sicily did not conform to this pattern; the hostility to the revolt of the prelates, the nobles and the city of Messina ruled out a meeting of the kingdom's *Parlamento*.

(11) Six of the seven rebellions relied on foreign aid. The new republics of Catalonia and Naples soon placed themselves under French protection; Portugal immediately sought assistance not only from France but also from the Dutch Republic and later from Britain. The opponents of Charles I in England, Scotland and Ireland all asked sympathetic continental powers for support. The Covenanters called on 'all Protestant potentates and republics to enter or join in the same or similar Solemn Covenant with the kingdoms of Great Britain and so go on unanimously against the common enemy'. They therefore approached the Dutch Republic, Sweden and Denmark for a 'mutual league with Britain for the defence of religion'.[43] The Irish rebels received, almost immediately, subsidies and recognition from France, Spain and the papacy.[44]

(12) Revolt in one part of each composite monarchy facilitated uprisings elsewhere; in the words of the historian of the various revolts of the mid-century, Birago Avogadro: 'Popular uprisings are infectious diseases' that spread from one area to another, unhindered by time, distance, climate or custom. Thus, the defiance of the English parliament was inconceivable without the prior rebellion of Scotland, while the Irish Catholic leaders resolved 'to imitate the Scots who got a privilege by that course', vowing that just as 'the Scots had their wills by force of arms, so would they here in this kingdom'. One of the leading rebels remarked that 'the Scots have taught us our A. B. C.'.[45] As for the Spanish monarchy,

---

[42] B. de Rubí (ed.), *Les Corts Generals de Pau Claris. Dietari o procés de Corts de la Junta General de Braços del 10 de septembre de 1640 a mitjan març de 1641* (Barcelona, 1976); A. M. Hespanha, 'La "Restauração" portuguesa en los capítulos de las Cortes de Lisboa de 1641' in *1640: la Monarquía hispánica en crisis* (Barcelona, 1992); V. Conti, *Le leggi di una rivoluzione. I bandi della repubblica napoletana dall'ottubre 1647 all'Aprile 1648* (Naples, 1983), pp. 67–9 and 183–4.

[43] J. R. Young, 'The Scottish parliament and European diplomacy 1641–47: the Palatinate, the Dutch Republic and Sweden' in S. Murdoch (ed.), *Scotland and the Thirty Years' War, 1618–1648* (Leiden, 2001), pp. 92, 96.

[44] See J. H. Ohlmeyer, 'Ireland independent: Confederate foreign policy and international relations during the mid-seventeenth century' in Ohlmeyer (ed.), *Ireland from Independence to Occupation, 1641–1660* (Cambridge, 1995); and T. Ó hAnnracháin, 'Disrupted and disruptive: continental influence on the Confederate Catholics of Ireland' in A. I. Macinnes and J. H. Ohlmeyer (eds.), *The Stuart Kingdoms in the Seventeenth Century: awkward neighbours* (Dublin, 2002). Sicily was once again the 'odd man out', perhaps because of its remoteness.

[45] Birago Avogadro, *Turbolenze di Europa*, p. 369; Canny, *Making Ireland British*, pp. 471 and 536 (with more Scottish parallels quoted at pp. 489, 526 and 529); TCD, MS 832/145b, claim by Colonel Plunkett, one of the leading conspirators, to Reverend George Creighton.

as one of Philip IV's leading diplomats observed with resignation: 'In a monarchy that comprises many kingdoms, widely separated, the first one that rebels takes a great risk because the rest can easily suppress it; but the second takes much less risk and from then onwards any others can try it without fear.'[46] Perhaps he understated, because the 'Restoration' in Portugal destabilised three other areas. First, and most serious, there was a 'panic in the Indies', with Brazil declaring independence, a round-up of Portuguese settlers in all Spanish colonies, the arrest of the viceroy of Mexico (João IV's brother-in-law) and the emergence of Don Guillén Lombardo, an Irish adventurer who aspired to make himself king of Mexico (and, when he escaped, led a daring career that created the legend of 'Zorro').[47] Second, all Portugal's overseas dominions in Africa and Asia followed the example of Lisbon (and Brazil) and defied Philip IV. Third, two major nobles of Andalusia (the marquis of Ayamonte and the duke of Medina Sidonia) attempted to declare their independence of Madrid, with Dutch, French and Portuguese assistance.[48]

(13) Revolt in more than one place also led to links between them. João IV sent envoys to Barcelona to make common cause with the Catalan rebels and their arrival on the morning when Philip IV's troops launched a general attack on Barcelona greatly strengthened the resolve of the defenders.[49] He also sent his principal adviser, the Jesuit António Vieira, to Rome to arrange for his son to become king of Naples.[50] When revolution broke out in Naples, a pro-Spanish source noted that 'Some people from Palermo became involved . . . who incited them to demand

[46] *Colección de documentos in éditos para la historia de España* [hereafter *Co. Do. In.*] (112 vols., Madrid, 1842–98), LXXXIII, p. 313. See also the similar remark by Duplessis-Besançon on p. 266 above.

[47] S. B. Schwartz, 'Panic in the Indies: the Portuguese threat to the Spanish empire' in W. Thomas and B. de Groof (eds.), *Rebelión y resistencia de el mundo hispánico del siglo XVII* (Leuven, 1992); R. Valladares, 'El Brasil y las Indias españolas durante la sublevación de Portugal (1640–1668)', *Cuadernos de historia moderna*, 14 (1993); F. Troncarelli, *La spada e la croce. Guillén Lombardo e l'inquisizione in Messico* (Rome, 1999).

[48] A. Domínguez Ortiz, 'La conspiración del duque de Medina Sidonia y el marqués de Ayamonte' in Domínguez Ortiz, *Crisis y decadencia de la España de los Austrias* (Madrid, 1969).

[49] M. A. Pérez Samper, *Catalunya i Portugal el 1640* (Barcelona, 1992), pp. 265–79. Olivares also arrested and imprisoned the viceroy of Aragon, a Neapolitan nobleman, on suspicion of plotting with the Catalans: see J. H. Elliott, *The Count-Duke of Olivares. The statesman in an age of decline* (New Haven and London, 1987), pp. 615–16; E. Solano Camón, *Poder monárquico y estado pactista (1626–52): los aragoneses ante la Unión de Armas* (Zaragoza, 1987), pp. 51–61; and J. Sanabre, *La acción de Francia en Cataluña en la pugna por la hegemonía de Europa (1640–1659)* (Barcelona, 1956), p. 647.

[50] R. Valladares, 'Portugal desde Italia. Módena y la crisis de la Monarquía Hispánica (1629–59)', *Boletín de la Real Academia de la Historia*, 195 (1998), p. 261, and *La rebelión de Portugal. Guerra, conflicto y poderes en la Monarquía Hispánica (1640–1680)* (Valladolid, 1998), pp. 194–5.

everything, in the same way that had happened in Palermo.' One of these 'Palermitanos' was surely Giuseppe Alesi, the gold worker who had fled from Sicily to Naples after the first riots and then returned to lead the movement that secured the same concessions from Viceroy Los Vélez in August as those conceded the previous month by Viceroy Arcos in Naples.[51] The French government, for its part, sent the same minister (Bernard de Duplessis-Besançon) to persuade both the Catalans in 1640 and the Neapolitans in 1648 to accept its protection.[52]

The opponents of Charles I in one area also hastened to make contact with their fellows elsewhere. In 1639, some Scottish ministers in Ulster found Strafford's hostility so intolerable that they chartered a vessel to take them to Massachusetts (John Winthrop had visited Ulster the previous year), but storms drove them back to their native land. They saw this as a divine sign that they should 'find an America in Scotland' and, once arrived there, many joined the Covenanters' opposition to Charles I. Later, the Ulster planter Sir John Clotworthy, excluded by Strafford from the Dublin parliament, visited Edinburgh and from that vantage point worked to coordinate opposition to the king with colleagues in both Ireland and England.[53] Clotworthy, related by marriage to the English parliamentary leader John Pym, was one of several men with Irish interests whom the English Puritans sought to include in the Long Parliament – some, like him, in the House of Commons, others like Lords Cork and Clanricard, in the House of Lords.[54]

(14) Naturally, each group of insurgents also followed keenly the progress of rebellions in other parts of the monarchy. Although this has been widely noted among the opponents of Charles I, it has been largely overlooked in the Habsburg case. Nevertheless, the rebels in both Palermo and Naples were well aware of the course – and success – of the revolt of the Catalans through letters, pamphlets and books. When the marquis of Los Vélez, viceroy of Sicily, died in 1648, Vincenzo Auria (lawyer, poet and historian of Palermo) reconstructed in his *Diario* a full account of the marquis's earlier career as viceroy of Navarre and Catalonia and ambassador in Rome drawn from the history books in his own

---

[51] BNM, MS 2662/4v–5; di Marzo, *Diari*, IV, pp. 95–6, 103–4.
[52] AMAEP, *CPE: supplément* 4/96–9v and 111–13; J. Reinach (ed.), *Recueil des instructions données aux ambassadeurs et ministres de France. X. Naples et Parme* (Paris, 1893), pp. 15–19.
[53] R. S. Dunn, J. Savage and L. Yeandle (eds.), *The Journal of John Winthrop 1630–1649* (Cambridge, MA, 1996), p. 160: P. Donald, *An Uncounselled King* (Cambridge, 1990), pp. 191–6.
[54] See chapter 10 above. On the interlocking agendas of the Scottish, Irish and English opponents of Charles I during Strafford's trial, see M. Jansson (ed.), *Proceedings of the Long Parliament* (3 vols., Rochester, NY, 2002), III.

library.[55] As soon as news arrived in Naples that riots in Palermo against excise duties had secured their abolition, in the streets and marketplaces Neapolitans began to ask each other:

> What? Are we less than Palermo? Are not our people . . . if they unite, more formidable and warlike? Have we not more reason [by] far, being more burdened and oppressed? On, on to arms: time is precious. 'Tis no good to delay the enterprise etc.

They also began to put up 'pungent and bitter invectives' that 'incited people to create a revolution like Palermo'.[56] In October 1647, the news of Don Juan de Austria's bombardment of Naples undermined the modestly successful measures of Los Vélez to pacify Palermo: the rebels immediately reneged on their promise to lay down their arms.[57] Likewise, in Spain, Don Carlos de Padilla, linchpin of the 'conspiracy of the duke of Híjar' in 1648, looked to João IV of Portugal for support; and the name of Don Miguel de Iturbide, who had recently spearheaded successful opposition to royal policies in Navarre, was found among his papers.[58] Finally, in Valencia, where the central government had unilaterally changed the manner of electing city magistrates, broadsheets appeared in the streets that read:

> If you're looking for good government
> Naples, Messina and Palermo
> Have shown you the way.[59]

(15) Discontented vassals in other countries also took a close interest in foreign rebellions. The revolt of Naples, and particularly its first charismatic leader, awakened interest all over Europe. In life, artists captured Masaniello's likeness in paintings and wax statuettes (some made for

---

[55] Di Marzo, *Diari*, III, pp. 206–11 (citing books by Assarino, Birago Avogadro and Collurafi). R. Villari, *Elogio della dissimulazione. La lotta politica nell '600* (Rome, 1987), pp. 60–1, notes the publication of Alexandre de Ros's history of the Catalan revolt in Naples in 1646 – the year before the uprising.

[56] J. Howell, *An exact history of the late revolutions in Naples and of their monstruous successes not to be paralleled by any antient or modern history* (2nd edn, London, 1664: an English version of A. Giraffi, *Le revolutioni di Napoli*), pp. 4–8.

[57] Di Marzo, *Diari*, IV, pp. 174–80, and III, pp. 191–2.

[58] R. Ezquerra Abadía, *La conspiración del duque de Híjar (1648)* (Madrid, 1934); Valladares, *La rebellión de Portugal*, pp. 98–100; and J. Gallastegui Ucín, 'Don Miguel de Iturbide y Navarra en la crisis de la monarquía hispánica (1635–48)', *Cuadernos de historia moderna*, 11 (1991).

[59] X. Gil, '"Conservación" y "Defensa" como factores de estabilidad en tiempos de crisis: Aragón y Valencia en la década de 1640' in *1640: La Monarquía Hispánica en Crisis* (Barcelona, 1992), p. 88. See also J. G. Casey, 'La Crisi General del segle XVII a València 1646–48', *Boletín de la Sociedad Castellonense de Cultura*, 46:2 (1970); and D. de Lario, *El comte-duc d'Olivares i el regne de València* (Valencia, 1986).

export) and intellectuals composed epigrams extolling his achievements. After his death, commemorative medals were struck in Amsterdam and plays about him were published (and probably performed) in London and Amsterdam. In Paris, in January 1648, a crowd of several hundred angry taxpayers mobbed the judges of the Supreme Court and shouted menacingly 'Naples, Naples'.[60] In the 1650s, Oliver Cromwell sponsored efforts to export England's new republican form of government to France.[61]

(16) Charles I, Philip IV and their principal advisers initially responded to rebellion in similar ways. Thus, Charles twice used force to restore his authority in Scotland, and his attempt to do the same in Ireland accelerated the drift to war in England. Likewise, Philip's initial response to the revolt of the Catalans was to send an army, and seven years later he sent a powerful expeditionary force to crush the revolts of Naples and Sicily. Once he had subdued all three, his forces invaded Portugal. Few of these attempts at coercion succeeded. Charles I never regained control over any of his states; Portugal remains an independent nation to this day. In most of the other cases, the restoration of central control involved major concessions (pages 276–7 below) and little bloodshed: in England, only the regicides and a few others paid for rebellion with their lives; in Scotland, Naples, Sicily and Catalonia – all eventually subdued by force – even fewer perished at government hands. Only Ireland saw massive reprisals. The 'Act for the settling of Ireland' of 1652 named several hundred 'notorious rebels', who automatically forfeited both life and land; so did 'all and every Jesuit, priest and other person or persons who have received orders from the pope' and who had 'countenanced, aided, assisted or abetted . . . the rebellion or war in Ireland'. It also excepted all who had participated in any act of rebellion or killing in 1641–42. In addition, all, whether Protestant or Catholic, who had held a position of command 'in the war

---

[60] See F. Palermo, *Narrazioni e documenti sulla storia del Regno di Napoli dall'anno 1522 al 1667* (Florence, 1846: Archivio storico italiano, 9), p. 353, on the busts; BNM, MS 2662/32 is a sketch probably done for Viceroy Arcos. On the epigrams, see F. F. Blok, *Nikolaus Heinsius in Napels (april–juli 1647)* (Amsterdam, 1984), pp. 29–31. R. Villari, 'Masaniello: contemporary and recent interpretations', *Past and Present*, 108 (1985), pp. 126–31 reproduces and discusses the medals. The plays are 'T. B.', *The Rebellion of Naples, or the Tragedy of Massenello Commonly so called: But Rightly Tomaso Aniello di Malfa Generall of the Neopolitans, Written by a Gentleman who was an eye-witness where this was really acted upon that bloudy Stage, the streets of Naples* (London, 1649); and Thomas Asselijn, *Op- en ondergang van Masaniello* (Amsterdam, 1668). On the events in Paris, see A. Chéruel, *Histoire de France pendant la minorité de Louis XIV* (2 vols., Paris, 1879), II, p. 496.

[61] C. H. Firth, 'Thomas Scot's account of his activities as intelligencer during the Commonwealth', *EHR*, 12 (1897), 119; Gabriel Jules, count of Cosnac, *Souvenirs du règne de Louis XIV* (5 vols., Paris, 1876), V, pp. 256–77; and P. A. Knachel, *England and the Fronde. The impact of the English Civil War and revolution in France* (Ithaca, 1967), pp. 198–200 and 268.

of Ireland against the parliament of England, or their forces' would lose two-thirds of their estates, while any Irish Catholic who could not demonstrate 'constant good affection to the interest of the Commonwealth of England' throughout the period 1641–50 would forfeit one-third. Even those in the above categories who retained some land would not keep their original holdings: instead they would receive the equivalent 'assigned in such places in Ireland as the parliament, in order to the more effectual settlement of the peace of this nation, shall think fit to appoint for that purpose'. Finally, Irish Protestants who had not 'manifested their good affection to the interests of the parliament of England, having opportunity to do the same, shall forfeit one fifth part of their estates to the use of the said Commonwealth'.[62] No other European rebellion of the 1640s ended like that.

(17) In part, the similarity of government reactions stemmed from the fact that the same ministers shaped policy towards more than one group of insurgents. Once again, the Stuart example has attracted more notice. Most obviously, William Laud and the earl of Strafford helped to forge the policies that provoked opposition in Scotland and Ireland as well as in England, and framed the initial responses; while Oliver Cromwell and other members of the Council of State in London imposed their will throughout the Anglo-Atlantic world.[63] At a lower level, Randal MacDonnell, marquis of Antrim, and others with land and influence in more than one kingdom mobilised their resources in one area to help the king in another; while Cromwell used Roger Boyle, Baron Broghill, to head the regional administration first in Ireland and then in Scotland.[64] The interchange of royal ministers in beleaguered outposts of the Habsburg empire has attracted less notice. Nevertheless, apart from Los Vélez, whose disastrous decision to retreat from Barcelona in January 1641 did not prevent his appointment as viceroy of Sicily, Philip IV's illegitimate son Don Juan not only led the royal expeditionary force sent to regain control of Naples but, having done so, moved on to do the same in Sicily (September 1648), and remained there as viceroy for over a year

---

[62] S. R. Gardiner, *The Constitutional Documents of the Puritan Revolution, 1625–1660* (Oxford, 1906), pp. 394–9.

[63] C. Pestana, *The English Atlantic in an Age of Revolution, 1640–60* (Cambridge, MA, 2004).

[64] See J. H. Ohlmeyer, *Civil War and Restoration in the Three Stuart Kingdoms: The career of Randal MacDonnell, marquis of Antrim, 1609–1683* (Cambridge, 1993) for a brilliant reconstruction of Antrim's efforts in Ireland, Scotland, England, France and the Spanish Netherlands. On Broghill, see Patrick Little, 'The political career of Roger Boyle, Lord Broghill, 1636–1660' (Ph.D. thesis, Birkbeck College, University of London, 2000) and F. Dow, *Cromwellian Scotland, 1651–1660* (Edinburgh, 1979). Note also the Irish support for George Monck's march on London early in 1660, described by A. Clarke, *Prelude to Restoration in Ireland. The end of the Commonwealth, 1659–1660* (Cambridge, 1999).

until his recall to Spain to spearhead the successful siege of Barcelona in 1651–52. A decade later, he would also lead his father's armies (unsuccessfully) against the Portuguese.[65] In Madrid, the same ministerial team dealt with – and allocated scarce resources between – Catalonia and Portugal after 1640 (the *Junta de Ejecucion*) and Naples and Sicily in 1647–48 (the *consejo de Italia*); while the *consejo de Estado* evaluated reports from all overseas areas of interest to Spain on a daily basis.[66]

IV

These seventeen common denominators between the major rebellions against Philip IV and Charles I should not surprise us. On the one hand, both the Stuart and Spanish monarchies had striven to 'familiarise' (to use the term favoured at the time) their various realms one with another. For example, in 1625 Olivares unveiled his 'Union of Arms' scheme to create a 'rapid reaction' force of 140,000 men, allocated among the monarchy's various component parts; if any part came under enemy attack, a portion of the reserve army from the other states would immediately rally to its rescue. The following year, Charles I instructed his ministers to discuss a measure expressly modelled on this 'Union of Arms' which would 'unite his three kingdoms in a strict union and obligation each to [the] other for their mutual defence when any of them shall be assailed, every one with such a proportion of horse, foot or shipping as may be rateably thought fit'.[67] Some striking chronological parallels also linked unrest in the two monarchies. In 1637, the riots in Edinburgh that began the Scottish revolution broke out in the same month as a serious rebellion in Portugal, and Spain's chief minister recommended his treatment of the Portuguese as a model for Charles in dealing with the Scots. In 1640, news of the revolt of the Catalans arrived in Madrid on practically the same day as news of the dissolution of the Short Parliament followed by rioting in

---

[65] Likewise, the marquis of Oropesa provoked opposition as viceroy of Navarre and, when transferred to Valencia, soon did the same there! Many subordinate commanders served in more than one war. Apart from the officers and troops who sailed with Don Juan de Austria, Don Juan de Garay, whose troops had done much through their cruelty towards the Catalans to ignite the revolt there, later became commander on the Portuguese front.

[66] Because of the structure of the Spanish monarchy, the councils' role was mostly reactive – that is, they discussed incoming reports and letters – and so tended to deal with one problem at a time (Naples then Sicily etc.) rather than formulating an overall policy. That was the task of the *Junta de Ejecucion*, which could (for example) issue general orders to all its commanders such as 'let there be offensive warfare on the Catalan front and defensive on the Portuguese front' (Archivo General de Simancas [hereafter AGS] *Guerra Antigua libro* 187/22).

[67] No overview of the Union of Arms exists but Elliott, *Olivares*, pp. 244–77, provides an excellent overall discussion; on the Stuart 'proposal', see PRO, SP 16/527/104–6.

London by '10,000 or more apprentices' demanding the sacrifice of 'the king's favourite'.[68] The use of that term to describe Strafford serves as a reminder that Olivares, Philip IV of Spain's Favourite and chief minister, pursued similar policies to hold together the multiple monarchy over which he ruled, and even used similar language to justify them. In 1632, Strafford informed a colleague, 'Let the tempest be never so great, I will much rather put forth to sea, work forth the storm, or at least be found dead with the rudder in my hand' – an uncanny echo of Olivares's claim seven years earlier that 'As the minister with paramount obligations, it is for me to die unprotesting, chained to my oar, until not a fragment is left in my hands.' Although Olivares never gave his political programme a boastful name like 'Thorough', he conceived a political vision that was equally ambitious and pursued it with equal ruthlessness.[69]

As already noted, demands for money and men to defend *other* parts of the composite monarchies at a time of economic recession provoked six of the seven 'major' revolts. Since the central government was well aware of this dire situation, one might have expected the king and his advisers to conclude that they needed to change their policy. To be sure, on occasion this happened; as Don Juan de Chumacero had warned Philip IV: 'Hunger respects no one and so it is necessary to do all we can to help, and to avoid any decision whatever which people might regard – however wrongly – as a [new] burden.' Shortly afterwards, Philip issued a full pardon to those who had rebelled in the cities of Andalucía (including Granada, the provincial capital) and ordered the viceroys of Naples and Sicily to act with clemency because, as he observed to his confidante Sor María de Ágreda, 'In these stormy times it is better to utilize deception and tolerance rather than force.'[70] A few months later, according to an unsympathetic observer, Philip IV was so desperate for a settlement with the Dutch that 'To get [it] he would crucify Christ again if he had to'; and, indeed, in January 1648 the Spanish negotiators at Münster swore in the king's name to a peace that recognised the former Dutch rebels as a sovereign state.[71] Later that year, although he protested vehemently about some items, the king also approved the concessions made by his

---

[68] BNM, MS 9402/29; BNM, MS 8177/46v–48v; Elliott, *Revolt of the Catalans*, p. 489. See also the coincidence of dates in 1640–41 and 1647–48: pp. 255–9 above.

[69] J. H. Elliott, 'The year of the three ambassadors' in H. Lloyd Jones *et al.* (eds.), *History and Imagination. Essays in honour of H. R. Trevor-Roper* (London, 1981), p. 181. Elliott also notes the frequent but fruitless negotiations between the two 'favourites' in 1640–41.

[70] C. Seco Serrano, *Cartas de Sor María de Jesús* (Madrid, 1958), I, p. 118. On the troubles, see A. Domínguez Ortiz, *Alteraciones andaluzas* (Madrid, 1973), pp. 47–55. Chumacero quoted on p. 256 above.

[71] E. Prestage (ed.), *Correspondência diplomática de Francisco de Sousa Coutinho, durante a sua embaixada em Holanda, 1643–50* (Coimbra, 1926), II, p. 256.

agents in Naples to the leaders of the 'Serenissima Reale Repubblica' in order to end the rebellion.[72]

Nevertheless, such 'rational' behaviour remained rare. In 1647, just before he heard about the revolts of Sicily and Naples, one of Philip IV's diplomats wrote to a dispirited colleague:

> You believe that the war will last many years, but you are entirely mistaken . . . My lord, the vassals of both kings [France and Spain] find themselves so exhausted that asking them for more could lead either monarch to complete ruin . . . Whether we win or lose, we both must have peace.

News of the two Italian uprisings deepened this conviction yet further: 'The Naples rising has been widespread. For God's sake, Sir, we have to settle in some way.' Nevertheless news of a relatively minor Spanish success – the relief of Lleida in 1647 ('the most important and pleasing news I have ever had in my life') – convinced the same diplomat that God once again fought for Spain and so the king should now concentrate on exploiting the victory and negotiate later![73]

Charles I also steadfastly refused to make terms with his 'rebels' despite the fact that they kept defeating him. In 1638, when his Scottish subjects defied him, he declared: 'I will rather die than yield to these impertinent and damnable demands.' Four years later, just after civil war broke out in England, he stated: 'I have set up my rest upon the justice of my cause, being resolved that no extremity or misfortune shall make me yield, for I will either be a glorious king or a patient martyr.' And three years after that, following a string of military 'misfortunes', Charles refused a suggestion that he should seek the best terms possible from his adversaries because:

> If I had any other quarrel but the defence of my religion, crown, and friends, you had full reason for your advice; for I confess that, speaking either as a mere soldier or statesman, I must say that there is no probability but of my ruin. Yet as a Christian, I must tell you that God will not suffer rebels and traitors to prosper, or this cause to be overthrown . . . A composition with them at this time is nothing else but a submission, which, by the grace of God, I am resolved against, whatever it cost me; for I know my obligation to be, both in conscience and honour, neither to abandon God's cause, injure my successors, or forsake my friends.[74]

---

[72] For two examples, see AGS *Secretarías Provinciales* legajo 218/37 and *libro* 443/31–32v. Charles I also made concessions, but usually with even more 'deception' – as in his negotiations with the Irish parliamentary leaders in 1640–41 (chapters 8 and 9 above).

[73] *Co. Do. In.*, LXXXIV, pp. 312–13 and 371.

[74] Ohlmeyer, *Civil War and Restoration*, p. 77; G. Burnet, *Memoirs of the Dukes of Hamilton* (London, 1677), p. 203; and J. O. Halliwell, *Letters of the Kings of England* (2 vols., London, 1846), II, pp. 383–4.

He held to this policy steadfastly, rejecting all compromise, until his infuriated foes in January 1649 made him a 'patient [albeit profoundly irritating] martyr'.

V

In one sense, Secondo Lancellotti was right: the princes of Western Europe (at least) were 'not *more* avarious or indifferent towards their subjects than they used to be' in the first half of the seventeenth century than before. One can find similarly insensitive fiscal policies and inflexible statements to those of Philip IV and Charles I from many earlier monarchs (indeed Charles's grandmother, Mary queen of Scots, had also been executed because she would not compromise, while Philip IV's grandfather, Philip II, had lost the Netherlands for the same reason). On other issues, however, Lancellotti was wrong (perhaps any book that requires 700 pages to prove its case should be suspect?). Above all, the natural disasters and extreme climatic events to which he devoted so many pages became far more numerous 'nowadays' than before.

The prolonged deterioration in prevailing weather conditions, which vitally affected the agricultural sector in which 95 per cent of the population worked and on which 100 per cent of it depended, should surely have encouraged rational statesman to increase public assistance and reduce public expenditure. In Europe in the 1640s, however, it did not. The English Republic continued to deploy a vast army and navy – not only to preserve control over its constituent parts but also to impose its will abroad (in the Caribbean, in the Low Countries, in the North Sea, and in the Baltic) – despite continuing climatic adversity (the government decreed national prayers for rain in 1656), and despite mounting protests against the heavy taxation levied. Three years later, with the central government bankrupt, the English troops stationed in Scotland and Ireland both defied London's authority and, early in 1660, a 'Convention' hastily assembled in both England and Ireland that recalled Charles II (albeit by the narrowest of margins).

The Spanish monarchy, too, survived the crisis of the mid-seventeenth century; by 1653, the central government had recovered all areas in rebellion except Portugal and its overseas colonies. However, as the Venetian ambassador in Madrid noted tartly, this remarkable change of fortune stemmed principally from 'the present commotions of the kingdom of France, which has chosen to turn its victorious arms against its own breast, and exchanged a glorious war for a dreadful slaughter of the

French themselves'.[75] Paradoxically the Little Ice Age, which so undermined the Spanish monarchy, also helped to preserve it because the same adverse climatic conditions simultaneously undermined the power of its principal enemies. Philip IV, like Charles II, could consider himself fortunate that the crisis of the mid-seventeenth century was indeed a global and not merely a local problem.

[75] L. Firpi (ed.), *Relazioni di ambasciatori Veneti al Senato. X: Spagna (1635–1738)* (Turin, 1979), p. 198.

13 Settlement, transplantation and expulsion: a comparative study of the placement of peoples

Sarah Barber

Control over place, power and social status was vital in the efforts made during the sixteenth and seventeenth centuries to fix the boundaries of the state. Within wider geopolitical manifestations of state-formation was the parallel, related, but different drive to stabilise nation, nationality and territorial boundaries.[1] In this process, as in others, the victors constructed a narrative of their own. Accordingly, the growing consciousness of national identity and the corresponding evolution of the state were usually accompanied by the twin movements by which those cultural groups which were already dominant increased their control while, at the same time, manifesting a suspicion of those who lay on the margins of this process or who seemed to hamper its development. Trying to impose order on one's territories involved exploring the status and position of minority communities and intransigent peoples.

This chapter explores the identities imposed on the Irish and the Moriscos by the English and the Spanish during the first half of the seventeenth century. It uses the perception of delinquent behaviour, allied with the concept of place, in order to discuss the comparative marginalisation of peoples. Its method of procedure involves the detailed examination of

---

[1] The work on state formation was largely done by scholars within the Marxist tradition, following Norbert Elias's work in the 1930s and subsequently, by scholars within the field of Cultural Studies. In both cases, work on the early modern period, despite its importance in terms of state formation in Western Europe, has remained, in the words of Philip Corrigan, 'even more fragile' than other periods. A sample of the work available in state formation includes: Philip Corrigan, 'Towards a history of state formation in early modern England' in Philip Corrigan (ed.), *Capitalism, State Formation and Marxist Theory: historical investigations* (London, 1980), pp. 27–48, quote at p. 27; Norbert Elias, *The Civilizing Process* (trans. Edmund Jephcott, revised edn, ed. Eric Dunning, Johan Gouldsblom and Stephen Marshall, Oxford, 2000); Stephen Mennell, *Norbert Elias: civilization and the human self-image* (Oxford, 1989); Jeffrey C. Alexander, 'Citizen and enemy as symbolic classification: on the polarizing discourse of civil society' in Michèle Lamont and Marcel Fournier (eds.), *Cultivating Differences: symbolic boundaries and the making of inequality* (Chicago and London, 1992), pp. 289–308; Steve Pile and Nigel Thrift, 'Mapping the subject' in Steve Pile and Nigel Thrift (eds.), *Mapping the Subject: geographies of cultural transformation* (London, 1995), pp. 13–51.

a limited source base. It draws on part of the writing of Jaime de Bleda on the expulsion of the Moriscos between 1609 and 1614 and compares it with the exchanges between Vincent Gookin and Richard Lawrence over the proposed transplantation of much of the Gaelic Irish population in the mid-1650s, to suggest a way in which the cultural conquest of Ireland in the seventeenth century can be reconceptualised.[2]

In adopting such an approach, this chapter does not attempt to tackle the question of race,[3] choosing not to define either the Moriscos or the Irish in such terms.[4] Means to distinguish between peoples in the seventeenth century may have carried racial undertones; however, even if this is so, insufficient work has been done on the definition to be applied to the term 'race'.[5] Lawrence's and Bleda's discussions included considerations of the degree to which the behaviour of minorities was intrinsic or indigenous. Here, however, the focus is on the description of delinquency. While the scope of the present study allows for the comparison of limited sources, of differing natures, produced in different circumstances and timescales, both the cases under scrutiny offer a discourse on the relationship between minority delinquent populations, the land they inhabited and their potential for movement. An examination in these three areas reveals policies of assimilation which gave way to integration, marginalisation and dispersal, and finally more wholescale movements such as, in these cases, the expulsion of the Moriscos and the transplantation of the Catholic Irish.

I

During the late sixteenth and early seventeenth centuries members of the Spanish, especially Castilian, elite stepped up their debate about the position of the Moriscos within Spain's territories. The Moriscos, or 'little Moors', were those considered to be of Moorish descent who,

---

[2] For a discussion of Lawrence's career see chapter 14 below.

[3] There has been some recent work in this area, for example, Paul McGinnis and Arthur H. Williamson, 'Britain, race, and the Iberian world empire' in Allan I. Macinnes and Jane Ohlmeyer (eds.), *The Stuart Kingdoms in the Seventeenth Century: awkward neighbours* (Dublin, 2002), pp. 70–93.

[4] As McGinnis and Williamson sum up their argument, '[t]he preoccupation with the *limpieza* (purity) and the preoccupation with culture were ostensibly two conflicting and competing ways of looking at people and the world. "Blood" might well become highly activist, but the actions it enjoined were contained within the limits of nature. Culture was different in that its activism would inherently prove more conceptually far-reaching', McGinnis and Williamson, 'Britain, race, and the Iberian world empire', p. 92.

[5] A. Smedley, '"Race" and the construction of human identity', *American Anthropologist*, 100:3 (1998), pp. 690–702; S. Clark, 'International competition and the treatment of minorities: seventeenth-century cases and general propositions', *American Journal of Sociology*, 103:5 (1998), pp. 1267–308.

after a series of edicts, had been expected to convert to the (Catholic) Christian faith.[6] Territorially, the reconquest of Spain and the defeat of Islam were completed with the fall of the kingdom of Granada in 1492. A residual population of Moorish descent, however, was a reminder that, at some level in the Spanish psyche, Spain could not be entirely free of its Moorish past for as long as a minority population remained to remind them of an Islamic influence and presence. In 1502 the state took steps towards integration with legislation demanding Christian baptism.[7] There followed, through the sixteenth century, the revival of medieval measures to elucidate and clarify the relationship between Christian and Muslim Spaniards; their application varied in time, place, severity and consistency.[8] The interests of the kings were swayed by the papacy, the Inquisition, landowners who relied on Morisco labour, and the Moriscos themselves. The state reacted to particular crises in a largely *ad hoc* fashion.[9] In 1609 Philip III, under advice from the duke of Lerma, signed the order for the forcible transportation of approximately 300,000 Moriscos from the Spanish mainland to north Africa. The province of Valencia was among the areas hardest hit, losing around a third of its population following rebellion and riot by the Morisco population in the mountains.

Bringing peace and order to its territories in Ireland exercised the English state throughout these two centuries, and successive measures were introduced to find a 'solution' to the Irish 'problem'. The English government was generally reactive, anticipating allegiance and intervening whenever rebellion demonstrated the disappointment of their expectations. Its response was to assess and tax wealth and to escheat and

---

[6] There is an interesting, and possibly telling, semantic difference between the minority of Jews in Spain who were, after 1492, supposed to have converted to Christianity, and whose name, *conversos*, literally, the converted, reflects this, and the Moors, whose epithet, 'little Moors', implies that conversion was not enough to change their basic nature.

[7] The legislation of 1502 applied to Granada; similar legislation for Valencia and Aragon followed in 1526.

[8] The measures taken in Granada by Charles V, the Edict of Granada, in 1526, were not seriously enforced, and in a process of accommodation and exploitation similar to the granting of the Graces in Ireland, the full effect of the law was mitigated by financial payments. The Edict of 1525 was revived in the Pragmática of Philip II of 1 January 1567. One of the difficulties faced, when tracing Spanish policy towards the Moriscos, as in many things, is that Spanish policy differed throughout its quite distinct regions. There are therefore several regional studies of the Morisco question, Nicolás Cabrillana, *Almería Morisca* (Granada, 1989); Bernard Vincent, 'L'expulsión des morisques du Royaume de Granade et leur repartition en Castille', *Mélanges de la "Casa de Velázquez"*, 6 (1970), pp. 212–46; Antonio Dominguez Ortiz and Bernard Vincent, *Historia de los Moriscos y Christianos Viejos en Valencia* (Valencia, 1980); H. Lapeyre, *Géographie de l'Espagne Morisque* (Paris, 1959).

[9] For example, the different approaches suggested are described by Henry Charles Lea, *The Moriscos of Spain: their conversion and expulsion* (New York, 1901, reprinted 1966), pp. 151–3.

confiscate land, which was resettled by English and Scottish undertakers and planters. Rebels could be transported, either to service in foreign armies, particularly Spain, or to the English plantations in the West Indies and Americas.[10] After the Irish rebellion of 1641, the suppression of which had been funded by the investment of English 'adventurers', who demanded recompense and received Irish land, Ireland was settled by legislative treaty. Subsequently, Irish Catholics who could prove their innocence in the Irish rebellion and subsequent civil wars were ordered to move to the western province of Connacht and the county of Clare, an area delineated by the River Shannon. They had until 1 May 1654 (extended to 1 March 1655) to relocate. The process of transplanting was deemed complete by the summer of 1657, but it did not amount to the total movement of all Irish Catholics. A total of 1,130 landowners moved, receiving 700,000 acres. The scale of the intended transplantation is not known, and is further complicated by the speed with which exceptions were made, orders amended and the impracticality of the policy became evident.[11]

There was a wide spectrum of opinion and a considerable war of words about both the Irish and the Morisco question. Only three authors will be studied here and they may not be representative of majority opinion. However, Richard Lawrence claimed to be writing at the behest of particular interests, and the accounts of the Moriscos published by the Dominican inquisitor, Fray Jaime de Bleda, were widely renowned. Bleda's *Coronica de los Moros de España* appeared in Valencia in 1618, four years after the Morisco expulsion he sought to justify and explain had been completed.[12] Vincent Gookin, an Irish member sitting in the British parliament in London, and Richard Lawrence, an Oxford-educated English planter in Ireland, debated the proposal that the Irish be transplanted to Connacht. Their exchanges were published in London during the first six months of 1655.[13]

---

[10] John P. Prendergast, *The Cromwellian Settlement of Ireland* (London, 1996), pp. 237–40; Aubrey Gwynne (ed.), 'Documents relating to the Irish in the West Indies', *Annalecta Hibernica* 4 (1932), pp. 139–286.

[11] Prendergast had access to the most complete set of documentation but does not hazard a figure, Prendergast, *Cromwellian Settlement*, pp. 26–34.

[12] Bleda was also the author of the shorter attack on the newly converted Moors, *Defensio fidei in causa neophytorum siue Morischorum Regni Valentiae totiusque Hispaniae* (1610).

[13] Fray Iayme Bleda, *Coronica de los Moros de España, dividida en ocho Libros* (Valencia, 1618). I am grateful to the Biblioteca Nacional, Madrid and Lancaster University Library for making these materials available; [Vincent Gookin], *The Great Case of Transplantation in Ireland Discussed* (London, [3 January] 1655); Richard Lawrence, *The Interest of England in the Irish Transplantation, Stated* (London, [9 March] 1655); Vincent Gookin, *The Author and Case of Transplanting the Irish into Connaught Vindicated* (London, [12 May] 1655).

While the search for cultural attitudes within these texts will follow the same path, this analysis will not seek to minimise the differences between them; one is not comparing like with like. First, Bleda was a single author expressing his own, albeit popular, view (together with numerous letters of support from worthy backers), whereas Gookin and Lawrence were engaged in an exchange in which they represented conflicting interests. Lawrence was famously pushed into responding to Gookin's (anonymous) first blast, 'at the request of several persons in eminent place in *Ireland*'.[14] Second, making a direct comparison between Bleda on expulsion and Lawrence on transplantation overemphasises the difference in length between the two pieces, already significant even if Lawrence and Gookin are taken together. Bleda described Moorish influence in Spain in over a thousand dense pages; Lawrence's and Gookin's endeavours together amount to ninety.

Furthermore, the pieces were designed to fulfil different functions. Bleda justified the expulsion *ex post facto*. It was, as its title indicated, a chronicle: a 'history of the false prophet, Mohammad, and of the kings, or Caliphs, that succeeded him, up to the year of our Lord 1613, when his destruction began in Spain'.[15] Bleda's tone derived from the comfort of describing policy already implemented, although it did not follow the path he had originally advocated. Nevertheless, he represented one extreme of the views of the Moriscos exhibited by his contemporaries.[16] This is to read the Moriscos' expulsion as an end point – a climactic measure. Lawrence and Gookin were fighting over the direction of a policy which, depending on one's reading of the two, was either in the midst of debate or in the process of being implemented. Theirs were didactic pieces, designed to sway opinion while there was still opportunity to affect the outcome. It was not intended that transplantation should be read as the end of the history of the Irish. Indeed, even in Spain, the history of the Moriscos was not ended by expulsion, nor did Islamic or north

---

[14] Lawrence, *Interest*, frontispiece. There was no dedication or introduction to Lawrence's piece.

[15] 'Historia del falso profeta Mahoma, y de los Reyes, o Halifas, que le sucedieron, hasta el año de Señor sietcientos y treze, en que comencò la destruycion de España', Bleda, *Coronica*, book 1, p. 1.

[16] Bleda's astonishing advocacy of genocide as a more fitting vengeance punishment for heretics is described by Lea, whose century-old study remains the most complete account of the Spanish Moriscos in English, Lea, *The Moriscos of Spain*, pp. 297–8. Henry Kamen has discussed the wide spectrum of ideas generated by the debates about Moriscos and especially *conversos*, and highlights Bleda's extremism, in 'Una crisis de conciencia en la Edad de Oro en España: Inquisición contra "Limpieza de Sangre"', *Bulletin Hispanique*, 88 (Bordeaux, 1986), reprinted in revised form as 'A crisis of conscience in Golden Age Spain: the Inquisition against "Limpieza de Sangre"' in Henry Kamen, *Crisis and Change in Early Modern Spain* (Aldershot, 1993), pp. 1–19.

African influence within Spanish territory cease.[17] In the aftermath of the expulsion, an economic and cultural discourse debating the contribution of the Moriscos was more vital than before.[18] The degree to which an underpopulated territory had been further depleted of vital economic interests was reflected in a more positive cultural image of the Morisco, now that he no longer posed a threat.

In some ways, Bleda bears more direct comparison with Sir John Davies, whose *A Discoverie of the True Causes Why Ireland Was Never Entirely Subdued* was almost directly contemporaneous with the expulsion of the Moriscos – a point not lost on Davies himself.[19] Like Bleda's chronicle, it took the form of a continuous history. These narratives are teleological, presenting policy as a continuous struggle, the climax of which would be the triumph of the measures taken in the reign of the incumbent monarch. Davies, the attorney general of Ireland, dedicated his work to James I, under whose 'happie Raigne' he predicted Ireland would be subdued, because James's government would learn from the mistakes of the past. Davies, in a passage that was to prove of enormous significance to Lawrence and particularly to Gookin, discussed how a sense of place had historically influenced English policy towards the Irish. The ideal social solution was, according to Davies, to create mixed settlements, but within a topographical context which would enable each of the communities to identify clearly the place of the other:

His Majesty did not utterly exclude the Natives out of this plantation, with a purpose to roote them out, as the Irish wer excluded out of the first *English* Colonies; but made a mixt plantation of *Brittish* & *Irish*, that they might grow up together in one Nation: Only, the Irish were in some places transplanted from the Woods & Mountaines, into the Plaines & open Countries, that being removed (like wild fruit trees) they might grow the milder, and beare better & sweeter fruit. And this truly, is the Maisterpiece, and most excellent part of the worke of Reformation, and is worthy indeed of his Majesties royall paines.[20]

This was to promote what were seen as the advantages of integration by the policy of dispersal.

---

[17] See, for example, the cases cited in Manuel Barrios (ed.), *El Tribunal de la Inquisición en Andalucía* (Seville, n.d.).

[18] Jacques Lezra, *Unspeakable Subjects: the genealogy of the event in early modern Europe* (Stanford, 1997).

[19] Sir John Davies, *A Discoverie of the Trve Cavses why Ireland was neuer entirely Subdued, nor brought vnder Obedience of the Crowne of England* (London, 1612), (and with an introduction by John Barry, Shannon, 1969).

[20] Davies, *Discoverie*, pp. 281–2; Gookin, *Author and Case*, p. 40; Lawrence, *Interest*, pp. 15–16.

Gookin and Lawrence did not intend their didactic pieces as histories, but the past nevertheless provided an expository tool. Karl Bottigheimer's account of the 'evolution of "plantation" in Irish history' implies that transplantation should be seen as a culmination of – though, he is at pains to stress, not the inevitable result of – a continuous policy of plantation. The supposed failure of the 'colony' of Ireland could, therefore, be measured, unlike the 'successful' colonisation of the Americas, by the failure of the English to extirpate the Irish.[21] Lawrence related the measures by which transplantation had been authorised, digressing at length with an account of the 1641 rebellion.[22] In his riposte, Gookin differentiated between history – detachable recollections of an autonomous past – and policy, which should not necessarily be shaped by self-contained narratives. History was 'telling a story what was acted in *Ireland*', and should be discounted, 'being a tale, and not reason'.[23]

The force of history, for Lawrence and Bleda, lay in its discursive technique: by tracing the course of events towards an (inevitable) end, it pre-empted those who might question its veracity. Bleda dedicated the chronicle to Lerma, the man whose advice was important in persuading Phillip III that only mass expulsion could rescue Spain from the Moriscos' malign influence. Bleda held himself responsible for much of the persuasive force that changed Spanish policy, and indeed for influencing Lerma.[24] The *Coronica* was an epic account of the growth of Islam and the influence of Muslims in Spain. Bleda and others portrayed the Moriscos' exile from Spain, enacted between 1609 and 1614, as the culmination of a series of policies. The strategy was already implemented, freeing him to argue that Philip III was not obliged to explain or justify his actions. Although the debate about the Moriscos was of long duration, Bleda believed it could be simply defined. The policy of expulsion having been implemented, those who had argued against it were the defeated 'politicians'. Bleda referred to those with politic motives who had sought some form of utilitarian or pragmatic rationale for retaining the Moriscos within Spanish society. Within the triumphant party, Bleda wished to establish himself as the spokesman for those who had recognised that it was the redemptive destiny of Spain to reclaim its territory for Christianity, and this could only be accomplished by the expulsion of the Moriscos.[25]

---

[21] Karl S. Bottigheimer, *English Money and Irish Land: the 'Adventurers' in the Cromwellian settlement of Ireland* (Oxford, 1971), pp. 1–29.
[22] Lawrence, *Interest*, pp. 2, 11–13.   [23] Gookin, *Case*, pp. 5, 22.
[24] Bleda, *Coronica*, pp. 940, 942–4; Lea, *The Moriscos*, pp. 309–10, n. 2.
[25] '[Y] arrancar de toda España la condenada secta Mahometana': Bleda, *Coronica*, p. 871.

As Bleda had portrayed Castilian–Morisco relations, so Lawrence presented the transplantation of sections of the Irish population to Connacht as a *fait accompli*. It would be the natural culmination of all that had gone before.[26] Lawrence argued that since a wise parliament 'first contrived and agreed the business of transplantation', so it was not for Gookin to question it. It 'lies not upon the Authority there', he asserted, 'to shew any farther reason for what they do therein'.[27] In response, Gookin's republican sympathy for the Commonwealth government forced him to agree that the 1652 Act of Settlement was a wise measure, but denied that subsequent policies carried parliamentary authority, because they had been introduced by the Council of State and only subsequently ratified by Barebones' Parliament.[28] There was no unbreakable historical chain, as far as Gookin was concerned, between the English victory in Ireland, the Act of Settlement and an ultimate, inevitable transplantation.

Gookin, like Davies before him, was the politician in the Irish case, pragmatically rationalising why it remained in the English interest to have settlers mixed among a native Irish population. His section 'Concerning Publick Good' included arguments for retaining the status quo. For example, although the wealth of Ireland lay in corn, conditions in Ireland required that the crop should be constantly manured and tended, vital functions which would be lost in the hiatus between the native Irish leaving and new tenants arriving. Should the corn crop fail, the consequence would be a significant reduction in the Irish revenue. Therefore, with English plantations continuing to establish themselves in Ireland, native people would be better employed providing a workforce skilled in the production of woollen and linen cloth.[29] Both the politic Gookin and the Spanish *politicos* stressed the economic benefits to be derived from the labour of Irish and Morisco communities on the land.

The technique by which the supporters of more drastic replacements of minorities overcame such pragmatism was to repeat and to stress levels of antisocial behaviour which were sufficient to override any possible benefits to be drawn from the two communities' presence. This was manifested in two kinds of conduct. The first struck at the dominant community's cultural self-presentation as a civilised polity; the second at political

---

[26] Lawrence, *Interest*, pp. 2, 5–9.

[27] Bleda, *Coronica*, p. 938; Lawrence, *Interest*, pp. 4, 9.

[28] Gookin, *Author and Case*, p. 18. Gookin referred to the short-lived legislative body which sat for six months before relinquishing its power to Cromwell in December 1653. Disparaging of its authority, he referred to it as the 'Little Parliament'.

[29] [Gookin], *Case*, pp. 15–20. The Moriscos were known for their skill in silk production.

moves which indicated that the minority would undermine or overturn the structure of the state.[30]

The first presented alien behaviour as natural, and those who were discriminated against for this reason could never hope to blend into the mainstream. In sixteenth-century Spain the dynamo behind integration was the requirement to be baptised, but Bleda's review of the previous century made little attempt to distinguish between Muslim *Moros* and (unsuccessfully) converted *Moriscos*.[31] The terms were used interchangeably, both reflecting equally uncivilised behaviour, as, for example, in Bleda's description of his subjects as 'wild barbarians'.[32] Their universal apostasy made and confirmed them so. Moriscos, as presented by Bleda, either made no attempt to disguise their continuing adherence to Islam, or made a mockery of Christian festivals and symbols. They were a bad, condemned sect, an incorrigible and depraved nation, and villainous people.[33]

Lawrence used the language of violent barbarism to invoke a fearful memory of the Irish rebellion of 1641. As with Bleda, the implication was that any concessionary, sympathetic treatment was pointless in the face of people who would not respond as anticipated. By stressing how peaceful Ireland had been during the 1630s, Lawrence employed retrospective syllogism to show that the Irish had not been provoked by heavy taxation or oppressive legislation:[34]

---

[30] See below for the economic parallel to this political dichotomy.

[31] Lea points out that this refusal extended to those Christians who were martyred for their refusal to abjure the Christian faith once they arrived in North Africa, Lea, *Moriscos*, p. 363 n. 2; Bleda, *Coronica*, p. 1042. Discussions of the true piety of Morisco converts and the crisis of conscience their expulsion provoked formed a trope in Spanish picaresque literature. There have been a number of studies which examine the same phenomenon amongst the *converso* communities, Nina Cox Davis, 'Confidence and the Corullero: Guzmán de Alfarache' in Peter William Evans (ed.), *Conflicts of Discourse: Spanish literature in the Golden Age* (Manchester, 1990), pp. 48–68; Marcel Bataillón, 'Les nouveaux chrétiens dans l'essau du roman picaresque', *Neophilogus*, 4 (1964), pp. 238–98; Edward Nagy, 'El anhelo de Guzmán de Alfarache de "conocer su sangre", una posibilidad interpretiva', *Kentucky Romance Quarterly*, 16 (1970), pp. 75–95; Victorio Aqüera, 'Salvación del christiano nueva el Guzmán de Alfarache', *Hispania*, 57 (1974), pp. 23–30; Richard Bjornson, *The Picaresque Hero in European Fiction* (Madison, 1977).

[32] Bleda, *Coronica*, p. 869, 'barbaros feroces'. The same lack of distinction, perhaps reflecting the fact that as a people in rebellion, the Moriscos had revealed their 'true colours', was made by the four painters employed to portray the expulsion of the Moriscos of Valencia, Manuel Ardit and Jesús Villamanzo Cameno, *La Expulsión de los Moricscos del Reino de Valencia* (Fundación Bancaja, 1997).

[33] Bleda, *Coronica*, pp. 870, 871; p. 896, 'Era tan incorrigible esta peruersa nacion'; p. 901, 'vil gente'.

[34] It may be the case, but if so, it was implied, that Lawrence, in citing taxation and oppressive legislation as justifications for rebellion was drawing a comparison between the (justified) English revolution of 1642 and the (unjustified) Irish rebellion of 1641.

when the bloudy Rebells in 1641 committed that inhumane Massacre upon a company of poor, unarmed, peaceable, harmless people . . . wherein neither Age nor Sex were spared, but from the old man stooping for age to the Babe of a span long were their cruelties extended, nay the Infants in the womb were not secure from their merciless butchery, but even the women with childe were ript up, Virgins deflowred, and Wives ravished in the sight of their Parents and Husbands, and then all destroyed together by the most inhuman cruelties that could be devised.[35]

The emotive language reinforced his espousal that the rebellion had been a universal 'National Quarel' committed by a 'bloudy generation'.[36] Pressure to transplant the Irish came from those who had been horrified by the tales of Irish brutality and cruelty recounted in the abstracts of the depositions, read first to the Irish commissioners and then to the Westminster parliament.[37]

II

The extent to which policies of expulsion or transplantation could be invoked was therefore dependent on demonstrating degrees of culpability. Bleda was on secure ground in that he could both castigate a people whose presence was no longer an outstanding issue, and bask in the implementation of a policy that had justified his claims. Lawrence's argument proved more problematic. It was vital to both Lawrence and Gookin that they be seen to support government policy; the possibility that Gookin's objections to transplantation might evidence disloyalty provided a key platform for Lawrence's attack. Meanwhile, because Gookin emphasised the degree of discrimination which the English authorities had exercised towards the guilt or innocence of particular Irish people and their subsequent treatment, Lawrence was compelled to be equally scrupulous about the concepts of guilt, innocence and 'punishment'. Gookin believed the Irish had been forced into war, because there were those whom he denounced for 'reckon[ing] an Irish man and a Rebell tantamount'.[38] Thus Lawrence's descriptions of the events of 1641 demonstrated the need to transplant the Irish; and the supposed brutality of the rebels, symptomatic of universal crimes for which transplantation was consequently to be regarded as a punishment for past crimes rather than as a plank of policy in itself. This revealed the nature of the tension

---

[35] Lawrence, *Interest*, pp. 11, 12.   [36] *Ibid.*, pp. 12, 13.
[37] Richard Bagwell, *Ireland under the Stuarts* (3 vols., 1909–16, Frome, reprint 1963), II, pp. 315–16.
[38] [Gookin], *Case*, pp. 7, 9.

between himself and Gookin.[39] For example, Lawrence's tirade against the excesses of the rebellion followed immediately on the statement that general transplantation was not intended nor designed as vengeance for blood-guilt.[40] However, now denying that transplantation was punishment, he went on to admit that it was 'in some degree to be done upon the account of punishment' because of 'the most horrid causeless Rebellion, and bloudy Massacre that hath been heard of in these late Ages of the world, and the Offenders not particular persons or parties of the *Irish* Nation . . . but the whole *Irish* Nation it self . . . all engaged as on[e] Nation in this Quarell'. Gookin accused Lawrence of desiring a general transplantation, with successive acts and orders resulting in a huge movement of people, but nowhere did Lawrence admit that the entirety of the Irish should be transplanted.

The second form of anti-social behaviour involved deliberative action, designed to express enmity towards the state. Since the state defined authority, and hence illegal action, these were 'crimes', referred to explicitly by Bleda[41] and implicitly by Lawrence. The exchanges between Lawrence and Gookin were more particularly about punishment for counter-allegiance and acts of barbarism than for acts against the law.[42] Bleda's position was shaped by his experience as a preacher amongst the Morisco community and member of the Inquisition in Valencia, but his colleagues throughout the nation furnished him with further specific examples. In the community of Argel, perched on the highest outcrop of the Sierra de Alcaraz, there were 200 'Moors' who turned the act of kneeling before the priest into a joke, refused to carry a rosary, or to invoke the name of Christ.[43] Although the Christian villagers customarily kept a pig each year, there were some who would not participate in its rearing or eat its meat.[44] The archbishop of Valencia could provide a story from Corvera, south of Murcia, where in 1585 the Moriscos had made a mockery of the Eucharist.[45] South-east of Mérida, in the fortified town of Hornachos, the Moriscos formed alliances with African Moors, murdering those Christians who discovered their plots.[46] In Valencia, the

---

[39] Gookin argued that the brutality of the 'Papists' in 1641 had persuaded some Catholics away from their faith, [Gookin], *Case*, p. 2.

[40] Lawrence, *Interest*, pp. 10, 11.   [41] *Delitos*: [orig.] *delictos*.

[42] There may well be an important distinction to be drawn, although not within the space of this piece, between social and political treasons.

[43] Argel probably referred to the highest mountain in the range, where the Moriscos would have been cave-dwellers in territory perched above Manchegan villages. Argel is in south-eastern Spain, close to the border between La Mancha and Andalusia.

[44] Bleda, *Coronica*, p. 903.

[45] *Ibid.*, p. 938. Corvera is a community in the depth of the Murcian desert, beneath a mountain range.

[46] *Ibid.*, p. 921. Hornachos is east of Villafranca de los Barrios, in the present-day province of Extremadura.

Moriscos celebrated holy festivals on a Friday and, with the help of the Ottomans, were raising an armada to send to the 'heretic' king of France, Henry IV.[47]

The provinciality which furnished Bleda's anecdotal style was a consequence of the sixteenth-century policy of *repartimiento*, the movement of population, by which, after previous uprisings, the Moriscos had been distributed more sparsely around a wider area of Spain. This was an attempt to weaken their ability to act as a coherent force, which would, in turn, stimulate integration. However, if, like Bleda, one was convinced that the Moriscos would never truly convert, or that conversion was impossible, *repartimiento* merely subdivided one great border between Christianity and Islam into a number of internal borders throughout Spain. Morisco communities thus formed minority enclaves within even the smallest villages.[48] In urban areas, Moriscos lived in segregated neighbourhoods, *Morerías*, created by the legislation of Ferdinand and Isabella.[49] Thus, Bleda argued, although the Moriscos had been geographically scattered, their faith kept them united among themselves and separate from their Christian neighbours. This resulted in pockets of criminality that undermined the fabric of Spanish society on a much more extensive geographical scale.

Bleda, a pious if not fanatical Catholic, analysed the Morisco problem and its solution in religious terms. His world-view was one which established everything within a set, Christian place; the rituals of, and conformity to, Catholic worship, the materialisation of divine order. For him, the Moriscos represented the inversion of God's plan; they could be associated with disorder at every level. In places in which Catholicism was practised, Moriscos openly mocked it. And yet, along with such antagonism, they derided Catholicism surreptitiously, since, while appearing to comply with Catholic worship, they maintained an outward adherence without true faith, substituting their own religious practice within the security of their sequestered communities.[50]

In all spheres, therefore, from the personal to the global, and from the humble to the profound, the presence of Moriscos within Spain created internal borders. At the base (and to Bleda, most important) level, if conversion were impossible, then each Morisco had wilfully set up a border through which the Word of God could not pass. At the level beyond

---

[47] *Ibid.*, pp. 924–6.
[48] *Ibid.*, p. 905, 'De los Granadinos, que se repartieron por los lugares despues de la rebelion de Granada, se tenia mas siniestra opinion' [One has more suspicions of the people of Granada who returned to their places after the rebellion there].
[49] Which, of itself, built on medieval legislation, Lea, *Moriscos*, p. 11.
[50] Bleda, *Coronica*, p. 938: for example, 'vi que aquellos infieles *en lugar de* adorar la Sacratissima Hostia, y Caliz a la hora de la eleuacion hazian todos escarnio, y burla de la sacrosanta Eucharistia' (my emphasis).

the individual, a Morisco dwelling constituted a place which defiled its environment. The *Pragmática* of 1567 ordered Moriscos to leave open the doors of their houses, allowing Old Christians to view inside and to reassure themselves of what they saw of the domestic practices of their neighbours. It was a response to the suspicion that Moriscos passed, by public display, as Christians, while within the private space of their houses they maintained Islamic ritual.[51] Bleda followed St Ambrose, who had held that if someone were granted an easy pardon, it merely offered a greater incentive to stray. This made the desecration committed by the Moriscos all the more blatant: 'The treacherous Moriscos scoffed at and mocked the Sacred Sacrament, as has been said, every Sunday, and at festivals, when they heard mass they insulted all the crosses at the waysides, and on leaving their places.'[52]

Lawrence invoked the same fears about the Irish living in the midst of the English. He focused on security, concerned that Irish people remaining within a settlement of English planters would resent their masters whose newly acquired wealth had once been theirs. Allowing the Irish to live with the victorious English would breed such resentment that 'the posterity of that *Irish* Proprietor shall hardly ever pass by the *English* man's dwelling, without cursing him and his Successors'.[53]

Pockets of intransigent, unassimilated people living in the midst of the 'law-abiding' provoked the crime of incursion. The Moriscos of Andalusia were described as thieves and highwaymen.[54] The Irish equivalent was the much-feared tories. Both Gookin and Lawrence utilised the fear instilled by the thought of tory raiders to justify their point of view. Gookin was convinced that the oppressive extremity with which the settlement was being interpreted was destroying the Irish economy. There were so few who were not liable to penalty that 'Necessitie makes them turn Theeves and *Tories*.'[55] According to Gookin, transplantation would augment their ranks, recruiting among the servants of those Irish gentlemen forced to scale down their domestic economies. The terrain of Connacht would prove their perfect nursery:

[T]he range of *Tories* will be so great, and advantages thereby of securing themselves and cattel so much, that untill the whole Land be otherwise planted, it will not be probable that our Armies should either have intelligence of their places of

[51] Lea, *Moriscos*, p. 228. For a response to the *Pragmática*, see the petition of Francisco Núñez Muley, trans. D. Goodman, in David Englander *et al.*, *Culture and Belief in Europe, 1450–1600* (Oxford, 1990), pp. 301–3.
[52] 'Hazian los perfidos Moriscos mofa, y escarnio del Santissimo Sacrame[n]to, como se ha dicho, todos los Domingos, y fiestas, oyedo Missa injuriauã todas las Cruzes de los caminos, y de las salidas de sus lugares', Bleda, *Coronica*, pp. 917, 904.
[53] Lawrence, *Interest*, p. 24.   [54] *Ibid.*, p. 906.   [55] [Gookin], *Case*, p. 13.

abode in their fastnesses, or be enabled to find them, those who are acquainted with the service of *Tory*-hunting, know much of this difficulty. And impossible it is, that those parts of the Land which adjoyn to those Fastnesses, should be planted in many ages, if *Tories* (secured in them) make incursions on such as shall plant.[56]

In other words, the combination of massing the Irish together, while confining them to a remote and desolate place, would provide them with the means and the purpose to endanger English planters.

A situation which Gookin believed the English would create was one which Lawrence thought 'natural' to the Irish: 'In the work of surprizings and unexpected assaults and inroads upon the *English*, the *Irish* have been usually more expert and vigilant, for the *Irish* are naturally a timorous, suspicious, watchfull People . . . the *English* are confident, credulous, careless People.'[57] Lawrence admitted, as had Gookin, that the English army was more afraid of the tories than it was of the regular Irish forces, and too timid to venture into the woods and bogs which constituted their fastnesses. What better solution, therefore, than to group together in a single place all of the Irish with 'rebellious Principles and active spirits'? Their position would be known and a watch could be applied.[58]

In the cases of Bleda and Lawrence, though more explicitly in the writing of the latter, the Moriscos and the Irish were charged with wasting the economy and creating pockets of poverty, effectively undermining the prosperity of the whole.[59] While Moriscos toiled to benefit their own economies, Bleda maintained that they undercut Old Christian labourers and sent their earnings to Africa. Perhaps surprisingly, Bleda did not seek to decry Africa's conditions or cultures, his point being that by working at cheaper rates than Christians, Moriscos made money for themselves, rather than for the Spanish economy as a whole, keeping their income behind the borders of the Morisco community. That money was then exported from the Spanish economy. His gaze was first internal – that the Moriscos corralled their wealth, and then externalised – that it was employed to undermine the state.

Lawrence described the Irish creation of their own 'waste Wilderness', which necessitated the presence of English military order. By implication, the Irish had forfeited their right to the land, but the order imposed by the English army would, as a natural consequence, build prosperity.[60] He made no allowance for the harsh terrain to be found in the west: 'For one hundred pound *per annum* in *Connaught* is as good as a hundred *per*

---

[56] *Ibid.*, p. 21.   [57] Lawrence, *Interest*, p. 16.   [58] *Ibid.*, p. 18.
[59] Was this the economic version of the faith and political borders created by the minorities?
[60] Lawrence, *Interest*, pp. 23–13.

annum in *Lemster* [*sic*] . . . Without doubt they may and shall live as comfortably and plentifull in *Connaught*, as elsewhere in *Ireland*, after they are settled.'[61] Gookin, however, stressed the 'wast and uncultivated Lands of *Connaught*' to which the transplanted would be sent.[62] Gookin and Lawrence reversed the priorities of the order of place: Lawrence would transplant the Irish from a wilderness of their own making to new opportunities on fresh land, whereas Gookin argued that the Irish should be seen as a useful labour force which would be underutilised if transplanted to a wilderness.

Bleda used an emotive Biblical metaphor or parallel for the wilderness (although there is surprisingly little Christian imagery in the work of either Gookin or Lawrence). The Old Christians of Spain were identified as the Israelites and the Moors as the direct descendants of the Saracens and Ishmaelites, whose conquest is the subject of numerous references in the Books of Genesis and Psalms.[63] The implication that Christianity was the faith of the light of God meant that,

in a great miracle, God our Father divided these kingdoms of Israel and differentiated them from Egypt: where Israel was established, it knew cities, towns and places where the faithful Christians lived, there all was light: the least and the greatest took confession, and reverenced Jesus Christ our Lord. Where the Egyptians lived, were the treacherous Moriscos, there was horrible, tangible darkness: no way through, so that they [the godly] would not stumble, and purposely err in the faith, and in the rules of the Christian law.[64]

The story of Hagar and Ishmael provided the evidence of the rigour that should rightly be exercised towards heretics. The Catholic monarchs Ferdinand and Isabella represented Abraham and Sarah, who threw out their slave Hagar and her son Ishmael to wander in the wilderness 'on the lonely coast of Africa'.[65] Bleda thus introduced a specifically Christian 'origin'

[61] *Ibid.*, p. 19.   [62] [Gookin], *Case*, p. 15.

[63] Bleda, *Coronica*, p. 871, Psalm 79 recounts the desolation of Jerusalem, 80 is a prayer for its deliverance, including 80:8, 'Thou hast brought a vine out of Egypt: thou hast cast out the heathen and planted it', and the particularly cited Psalm 82 is a call for the judgement of God: 'Arise, O God, judge the earth: for thou shalt inherit all nations.'

[64] Bleda, *Coronica*, p. 903, 'Porque Dios nuestro Señor con grande milagro diuidio en estos Reynos a Israel, y le diferencio de Egypto: donde estaua Israel, es a saber en las ciudades, villas, y lugares donde viuian los fieles Christianos, alli todo era luz: todos del menor al mayor confessauan, y reuereciauan a Iesu Christo nuestro Señor. Donde habitauan los Egypcios, esto es los perfidos Moriscos, alli auia horrendas tinieblas, y palpables: no dauan passo, que no tropeçassen, y errassen adrede en la Fe, y en las reglas de la ley Christiana.'

[65] Bleda, *Coronica*, pp. 906–8. Ishmael married an Egyptian, and fathered twelve sons. He is considered a prophet within Islam, and his descendants are the Arabs, thus distinguishing them from the twelve tribes of the Israelites, who were descended from Isaac, Ishmael's half-brother.

myth, while implicitly referring to the providential theory of Spanish redemptive reconquest, by which Spain would be purified by returning to the unsullied Gothic origins of its people in the era preceding the Muslim invasion of 711.[66] It was the duty of Christian monarchs to promote peace and to leave the church unmolested.[67]

III

Between them, Gookin and Lawrence were rehearsing a debate about the relative merits of concentrating or scattering an intransigent and antagonistic people that had been taking place within Spain for over a century. Gookin favoured continuing what had effectively been the result of successive plantations in the past: that the Irish be divided among themselves by separating the leaders of society from their followers.[68] This would effectively lessen their ability to obtain assistance from foreign powers.[69] The policy of keeping the pre-plantation Irish communities intact was considered counter-productive, bolstering their profession of Catholicism 'or making them turn Atheists, the knitting again like Worms their divided septs and amities which are now cut in sunder, the entailing barbarousness upon them by such a consociation for ever, the giving them power to rebel again by crouding them all together'.[70]

Conversely, Lawrence concluded that it had been the weakness of the English interest in Ireland to have its own people scattered throughout the country. The 1641 rebellion, he argued, had been able to take hold of Ireland because the English 'were not imbodied . . . not cohabiting together . . . scattered up and down the whole Nation'. They were 'neither in a capacity to resist nor fly, being in the midst of their Enemies, and

---

[66] This held that the Muslim conquest of 711 was a providential punishment for Don Rodrigo's sexual abuse of La Cava Rumía, and political abuse of the state by inviting in the Moors to help him in a dynastic dispute, E. Michael Gerli, *Refiguring Authority: reading, writing and rewriting in Cervantes* (Lexington, KY, 1995), see especially chapter 3, 'Rewriting myth and history: discourses of race, unoriginality, and resistance in the *Captive's Tale (Don Quijote,* I, 37–42)'; Miguel de Luna, *Historia verdadera del Rey Don Rodrigo: en la qual se trata la causa principal de la pèrdida de España* (6th edn, 1676); Biblioteca Nacional, Madrid, MSS 10336, Ambrosio de Morales, Compendio de la III parte de la Chronica de España. Libros XIII–XVII de Ambrosio de Morales; con muchas correcciones y adiciones por F[rancisco] C[erdá] R[ico], p. viii.

[67] Bleda, *Coronica*, p. 918, as Frederick, duke of Saxony, had done by exiling Martin Luther from his territories. The treatment of the Jews also demonstrated a history of expulsion. Lawrence likens the Irish to heathens and Jews, Lawrence, *Interest*, p. 23.

[68] The voluntary exile of the Irish lords, represented by the Flight of the Earls in 1607, which facilitated the Ulster Plantation, had been foreshadowed by the voluntary departure for North Africa and the Middle East of the leaders of Muslim society in Spain, who refused to stay and accept conversion and baptism.

[69] [Gookin], *Case*, p. 23.   [70] *Ibid.*, p. 26.

far from Friends'.[71] It was requisite that the English be 'entire Colonies of themselves'.[72] In order to create ideal, integral settlements, in which, according to Lawrence's calculations, the English must outnumber the native Irish by at least five to one, those Irish who would inevitably be surplus population must be transplanted elsewhere.[73] To leave them scattered was to encourage them in the practice of toryism. This involved 'sculking', by which the Irish would be controlling the interaction with the English according to their own rules:

> We play our game in *Irish* with them (wherein lies their excellency and skill) but bringing them into a body, confining them into small Circuits together, (that if they will be Torying they may be Torying upon one another, or otherwise if they have a minde to try their strength, they may be forced to imbody) you are in *English* with them.[74]

Where Lawrence took events he described as universal crimes to explain a specific policy, Bleda's analysis started with an account of particular circumstances from which he extrapolated general assumptions about the place of Moriscos within Spanish society. He was explicit, referring to place as a generic term and also using its specific Spanish meaning of residence, such as town or village (*lugar*). The Moriscos offered small models of resistance: individual crimes were evidence of communal guilt. The guilt of all justified the punishment of 'general expulsion'. Once universal faithlessness or apostasy was accepted, all the places allocated to Moriscos became violated. There was no point in trying to assign places to the Moriscos if they would always transgress them; there was no place for them in Spain.

The previous policy of *repartimiento* offered the key to an analysis of place and expulsion. As A. W. Lovett has put it, 'the deportation of one community in 1570 ended with the expulsion of all the communities in 1609'.[75] The link between the provincial *repartimientos* of the late sixteenth century and the general expulsion of 1609 was taken much further in Bleda's work. Bleda established a huge chain of spatial relationships in order to demonstrate that the Moriscos had violated them all. *Repartimiento*, involving moving peoples around the Spanish provinces, implied that a thin distribution of disloyal people would be less troublesome than a concentration of them, but failed to recognise the post-conquest dynamic behind a united Spain. A concentration of Moriscos may have been moved from Andalusia, but, if they were still seen as comprising a hostile element, they continued to exercise a destabilising influence within Spain,

---

[71] Lawrence, *Interest*, pp. 13, 15.   [72] *Ibid.*, p. 14.
[73] *Ibid.*, pp. 15–16.   [74] *Ibid.*, p. 19.
[75] A. W. Lovett, *Early Hapsburg Spain, 1517–1598* (Oxford, 1986), pp. 268–9.

no matter how thinly dispersed. *Repartimiento* implied a series of borders throughout Spain, rather than a single country reunited as a result of a redemptive conquest. Bleda's work implied that the Morisco presence in Spain was part of a spatial network – a series of places. At one end was the most humble and domestic – the private space of the house in which the cross was mocked. At the other were transgressions of borders on a national scale – the traitorous activities of Moriscos in providing aid to France, the Barbary pirates or the Ottomans. The presence of Moriscos desecrated them all. Within a Catholic analysis, all non-Catholic profession was heresy, and, as far as Bleda was concerned, heresy was a given state, from which there was no escape, and which guaranteed malignity towards Catholics. Spain with a Morisco minority could never be united.

The British government faced a question of unity after the conquest of Ireland. For several hundred years the English state had laid claim to the whole of Ireland, unable to make its authority a reality, but the military achievements of the 1650s offered an opportunity to secure Ireland unified and at peace. That was the aim behind Vincent Gookin's campaign against transplantation. According to his analysis, if the Irish were allowed to continue to live amongst the English settlers, they would be more likely to convert to Protestantism, living under English law and providing a workforce for English planters. Gookin saw the situation in Ireland as a conflict within Christianity, which should consequently be managed according to Christian rules, among which was 'that [the] separation of persons [was] . . . onely Lawfull when necessary, and then onely necessary when the malignity of the person is greater then the vertue of the Antidote'.[76] Gookin's vision of Ireland's future peace and prosperity was forward-looking and optimistic. Lawrence, in contrast, was the pessimist, whose analysis looked back to Ireland's troubled past. Furthermore, in contrast to Bleda's interpretation, his analysis was remarkably devoid of Christian metaphor, but was based on the implication that the Irish people were unlikely to convert or be integrated, at least in the medium term. Expedient concerns over security compelled him to plead that the English live close together, as should the Irish, enabling the English to place their enemies – to know where they were. His interpretation, however, stressed the importance of provincial boundaries in Ireland: the Irish being 'safer' in the province of Connacht, where the land would be as good as any in the country. Lawrence wanted to establish an internal boundary, banishing the intransigent Irish to the periphery.[77]

---

[76] [Gookin], *Case*, p. 2.
[77] Michael Hechter, *Internal Colonialism, the Celtic Fringe in British National Development* (London, 1975); Hans-Heinrich Nolte, 'Internal peripheries, from Andalucia to Tatarstan', *Review* (Fernand Braudel Center), 18.2 (1995), pp. 261–80.

By implication, the English state was still not in a position to govern all of Ireland under civil authority. The country would be subdivided into the two-thirds in which allegiance could be guaranteed and that third in the west where it could not. Bleda's interpretation reinforced an absolute Spanish national boundary between Christianity and Islam, which, having been pushed further south throughout the medieval period, would now be marked by the Mediterranean.

Neither Bleda nor Lawrence was convinced by the ability of the Moriscos or the Irish to assimilate within the dominant tradition. In Bleda's case this was because the Moriscos would never be genuine converts to Christianity. Lawrence believed the Irish would retain their enmity towards the physical presence of English people in Ireland and the imposition of English law and custom. They offered diverse solutions, however, which reflected their attitudes towards place. Bleda rejected the politics of *repartimiento*, because intransigence could not be countenanced, no matter how sparsely the intransigent communities were dispersed. Intransigence could only be expelled. Lawrence proposed an expulsion, but within Ireland's boundaries. Both cited security. Bleda had to ensure that any opposition to Spain came from outside Spain. Lawrence controlled opposition by delimiting its place at the margins of the islands.

14   Interests in Ireland: the 'fanatic zeal and irregular ambition' of Richard Lawrence

Toby Barnard

Richard Lawrence is chiefly remembered as the pamphleteer who entered the lists against Vincent Gookin in 1655.[1] His role in defending the scheme to transplant many of the defeated Irish west of the River Shannon is well known.[2] Rather than revisit one controversial episode, it is his entire career in Ireland which will be considered, and particularly Lawrence's reflections on it. Lawrence, having arrived with the Cromwellian army in 1649, stayed until he died in 1684. During those thirty-five years he shifted from championing the English to advancing the locals' interest in Ireland. So much was proclaimed in the titles of his books. The brace from the Interregnum were entitled *The Interest of England*[3] and *England's Great Interest in the Well Planting of Ireland*.[4] In contrast, the compendium which was published in 1682 was *The Interest of Ireland in its Trade and Wealth Stated*.[5] This was a personal journey made by numerous other settlers from England, Wales and Scotland in the sixteenth and seventeenth centuries. Apart from its intrinsic interest, Lawrence's altered perspective shows something of the rapid physical and cultural transformations around him, especially in Dublin from the mid-1650s.

The value of Lawrence lay less in his originality than as a conductor of what was in the air. Anxieties which he voiced often had long histories. In several cases – dislike of luxury and absenteeism – they would concern commentators well into the eighteenth century. A few later reformers, such as Francis Hutchinson, the indefatigable bishop of Down and Connor, in the 1720s and 1730s referred explicitly to

---

[1] HMC, *Report on the manuscripts of the duke of Ormonde*, NS (8 vols., London, 1902–20), VII, p. 54; see chapter 13 above.

[2] On the project, see S. R. Gardiner, 'The transplantation to Connaught', *EHR*, 14 (1899), pp. 700–34; T. C. Barnard, 'Crises of identity among Irish Protestants, 1641–1685', *Past and Present*, 127 (1990), pp. 58–68.

[3] R. Lawrence, *The Interest of England in the Irish Transplantation, stated . . .* (London, 1655).

[4] [R. Lawrence], *England's Great Interest in the Well Planting of Ireland with English People Discussed* (Dublin, 1656).

[5] R. Lawrence, *The Interest of Ireland in its Trade and Wealth Stated*, 2 parts (Dublin, 1682).

Lawrence's writings.[6] More generally, organisations such as the Dublin
Society and the Physico-Historical Society continued to press a programme which, both in ideological underpinning and detailed agenda,
recalled Lawrence's.[7] Recently it has been argued that approaches to
social reforms of the kind wanted by Lawrence changed in the mid-
seventeenth century. These shifts were associated especially with the
Hartlib group and its leading adherent in Cromwellian Ireland, William
Petty. A new methodology which reduced hitherto intractable problems
to 'number, weight and measure' gave pioneering political arithmeticians the confidence to address poverty and underdevelopment more
constructively. Traditional belief in an unbreakable cycle of degeneration
and renewal gave way to a linear conception of improvement. At much
the same time, during the 1650s, the notion that improvements could
be achieved through collective action led to the foundation of voluntary
associations dedicated to such ends.[8] These developments touched the
Ireland of Lawrence's time. Several of Hartlib's followers laboured in
Ireland. Petty, most notably, directed his talents into analysing and alle-
viating Ireland's troubles.[9] Lawrence knew Petty, sat with him on the
Council of Trade in Dublin after 1664 and latterly debated with him
how best to reform the Irish coinage.[10] Lawrence might, therefore, have
been expected to fall under the spell of the novel approach. Superficially,
indeed, it looked as if Lawrence was bewitched. He used quantification to
back his contentions: as, for example, over how much specie was drained
annually from the island by absentee landowners and office-holders.[11]
However, he did not repudiate an essentially religious conception of what
was wrong with Ireland and how it could be remedied. This outlook might

---

[6] [F. Hutchinson], *A Second Letter to a Member of Parliament Recommending the Improvement of the Irish Fishery* (Dublin, 1729), pp. 4–5.

[7] *The Dublin Society's Weekly Observations* (Dublin, 1739), pp. 18–19, 27–8, 41, 146–7, 342; Richard Barton, *Lectures in Natural Philosophy* (Dublin, 1751), pp. v–vi, 111–13; Richard Barton, *A Dialogue, Concerning Some Things of Importance to Ireland* (Dublin, 1751), pp. 21–2; W. Henry, *An Appeal to the People of Ireland. Occasioned by the insinuations and misrepresentations of the author of a weekly paper, entitled 'The Censor'* (Dublin, 1747); W. Henry, *Religion and Virtue: the foundation of courage and victory* (Dublin, 1744).

[8] P. Slack, *From Reformation to Improvement* (Oxford, 1999), pp. 81–3; P. Clark, *British Clubs and Societies, 1580–1800* (Oxford, 2000), pp. 49–50, 85.

[9] T. C. Barnard, 'The Hartlib circle and Ireland', *IHS*, 19 (1974), pp. 56–71; T. C. Barnard, 'Sir William Petty, Irish landowner' in H. Lloyd-Jones, V. Pearl and B. Worden (eds.), *History and Imagination* (London, 1981), pp. 201–17; L. Sharp, 'Sir William Petty and some aspects of seventeenth-century natural philosophy' (D.Phil. thesis, Oxford University, 1976).

[10] W. Petty, *The History of the Survey of Ireland Commonly Called the Down Survey*, ed. T. A. Larcom (Dublin, 1851), pp. 12, 30, 267, 269, 277, 279; HMC, *Ormonde*, NS, VII, p. 14.

[11] Lawrence, *Interest of Ireland*, I, pp. 80–9.

make him seem old-fashioned by some standards. Yet it persisted among
many active in the work of the Dublin Society and the Physico-Historical
Society after 1731. Lawrence borrowed heavily from contemporaries,
including those whose vision appeared more secular and rational – Petty,
William Temple and Francis Brewster – but still used explanatory and
expository frameworks which invoked hidden and supernatural powers.[12]

In so far as Lawrence set his account of Ireland in a providential cos-
mography, his mentality can be linked with what is known of his biography.[13] He arrived in Ireland as an officer of the Cromwellian army.
He was soon identified with the party of radical republicans favoured by
the lord deputy, Charles Fleetwood. This alignment was strengthened
when Lawrence emerged as public proponent of the enforced removal of
much of the indigenous population to Connacht and Clare.[14] He subscribed wholeheartedly to the anti-Catholic and anti-Irish sentiments
prevalent in England and among the English soldiers and administrators around Fleetwood. After Charles II's return in 1660 Lawrence may
briefly have contemplated exile in the Low Countries. However, he had
no need to skip overseas. He had not been a regicide, and soon agilely
accommodated himself to the restored monarchy. When James Butler,
duke of Ormond, arrived in Dublin as lord lieutenant in 1662, Lawrence
placed himself under the duke's protection. By 1668 Lawrence gallantly
declared his intention henceforward to 'trust God's providence and my
Lord's [Ormond's] nobleness for a livelihood'.[15] Before this, Ormond
had appointed him to the Council of Trade, made him manager of
the prestigious textile works at Chapelizod outside Dublin, and even
restored him to an army command during the invasion alert of 1666.
Later Ormond read *The Interest of Ireland* in manuscript and encouraged
Lawrence to publish it.[16] Deferentially, Lawrence would dedicate the
volume to Ormond's grandson and heir, Lord Ossory.

[12] F. Brewster, *Essays on Trade and Navigation* (London, 1695); W. Petty, *The Political Anatomy of Ireland* (London, 1691); W. Temple, 'An essay on the advancement of trade in Ireland (written to Lord Essex), 22 July 1673' in W. Temple, *Miscellanea* (London, 1680), pp. 97–145. Cf. D. Armitage, 'The political economy of Britain and Ireland after the Glorious Revolution' in Jane Ohlmeyer (ed.), *Political Thought in Seventeenth-century Ireland* (Cambridge, 2000), pp. 227–8.
[13] The fullest account remains C. H. Firth and G. Davies, *A Regimental History of Cromwell's Army* (2 vols., Oxford, 1940), I, pp. 356–9. His activities in 1659–60 can be traced in A. Clarke, *Prelude to Restoration in Ireland* (Cambridge, 1999). The life in R. L. Greaves and R. Zaller (eds.), *A Biographical Dictionary of Seventeenth-century English Radicals* (3 vols., Hassocks, 1982–4) adds little.
[14] T. C. Barnard, 'Planters and policies in Cromwellian Ireland', *Past and Present*, 61 (1973), pp. 31–69.
[15] R. Lawrence to Sir G. Lane, recd. 20 May 1668, Bodl., Carte MSS 36, f. 330.
[16] HMC, *Ormonde*, NS, VII, p. 27. Cf. *ibid.*, IV, pp. 38–40.

Against this political flexibility has to be set Lawrence's steadfastness as a Baptist. Unusually among survivors from the Interregnum in Ireland, he continued in the Dublin congregation. As such, he was the city's most prominent Baptist. This affiliation brought him under suspicion: first, in 1663 during the alarm lest Dublin Castle be seized, and then in 1683 at the time of the Rye House Plot in England.[17] In the event, he did nothing seriously to disturb the authorities. Indeed, rather the reverse: he kept the Dublin administration informed of thinking in the dissenting communities.[18] Little in his public stance after 1660 could be traced to the specific doctrines of the Baptists. Yet his experiences as a nonconformist subject to legal disabilities help to explain two emphases in his writings. Lawrence insisted on the fundamental loyalty of the Irish Protestant dissenters both to the crown and to English rule over Ireland. He contrasted this outlook with the political subversiveness of the Irish Catholics. Lawrence stressed the good affection of his nonconformist colleagues in the hope that their condition would be eased. The government was unmoved by his pleas. In the absence of any official relaxation of statutory penalties, Lawrence urged a second strategy. Convinced of the vitality of the Catholic menace, he reiterated the importance of Protestant unity. The ideal way to achieve it would be for the state to comprehend all the more theologically orthodox Protestant sects. Hopes that this might happen rose and fell between the early 1660s and 1680s, but came to naught. In default, Lawrence, residing in an Ireland where the Protestant minority seemed beleaguered by aggressive Catholics, was prepared to rally to the Episcopalian Church of Ireland. A 'national religion', he believed, would guard against atheism, 'popery and confusion' and promote godliness.[19] In an increasingly edgy atmosphere, as the accession of a Catholic monarch impended, Lawrence may have obeyed his own published advice. His last-born son was baptised according to Church of Ireland rites in 1682.[20]

I

Reformation and improvement exercised Lawrence. In 1655 Ireland was, like 'a white paper' or 'clay on the potter's wheel', awaiting a distinctive impress.[21] Lawrence, like many before him, designed a blueprint

---

[17] Bodl., Carte MSS 45, f. 437; HMC, *Ormonde*, NS, VII, pp. 54, 63, 65, 70–1.

[18] R. Lawrence to Sir G. Lane, received 20 May 1668, Bodl., Carte MSS 36, f. 330.

[19] Lawrence, *Interest of Ireland*, II, pp. 269–70.

[20] J. Mills (ed.), *The Register of the Parish of S. Peter and S. Kevin, Dublin, 1669–1761* (Dublin, 1911), p. 234; K. Herlihy, 'The Irish Baptists, 1650–1780' (Ph.D. thesis, Trinity College Dublin, 1992), p. 98.

[21] T. C. Barnard, *Cromwellian Ireland: English government and reform in Ireland, 1649–1660* (Oxford, 1995), p. 14.

for the pacification, anglicisation and enrichment of the island. By 1682 a disillusioned Lawrence admitted that the materials had proved more stubborn than he had predicted. His disappointment, it can be argued, was as much personal as at the collective failures of the Irish Protestants. Lawrence, having stayed on in Restoration Ireland, struggled for a living and a standing commensurate with what he had enjoyed under the Cromwellian regime. After 1660 he was styled variously as 'merchant', 'esquire' and 'colonel'.[22] Movement between the different designations accurately reflected his assorted stratagems and somewhat precarious situation. He dabbled in commercial and proto-industrial ventures, of which the textile factory at Chapelizod was merely the most celebrated. He had acquired large estates in the 1650s, partly as payment of his arrears of salary and also in the speculative market. Some of these spoils had to be disgorged in the 1660s. More were lost thanks, apparently, to those who purported to help, notably Roger Boyle, earl of Orrery, who was later alleged to have cheated Lawrence of £1,000 per annum in lands.[23]

Through marriage Lawrence compensated for the loss of the recently gained estates in Counties Dublin and Limerick with holdings in County Down. These arrived with his wife. Others oversaw them on his behalf, so giving him some insight into the predicament of internal absentees.[24] Rents alone could not keep Lawrence in the manner to which he had become accustomed. He may have sunk as much as £2,000 of his own into the cloth factory, which, in the event, brought a sorry return.[25] To supplement his income, he engaged in trade. This business – in wool, hides, tallow and butter – emboldened him to lecture his contemporaries.[26] By 1679 all had gone awry. At this low ebb he confided: 'My whole dependence is upon my rents and if I must wait three or four months after they are due, I must run upon ticket for my family and supply, which goeth against the grain.'[27]

---

[22] Petition of 20 Oct. 1664, Bodl., Carte MSS 154, f. 40; HMC, *Ormonde*, NS, VII, p. 97.

[23] Surrey CRO, 84/49/1–4; paper why R. Lawrence should not lose his lands, Petworth House, West Sussex, Orrery MSS, general series, 13; J. Hall to Orrery, 14 November 1671, 18 May 1672, *ibid.*, 28; E. MacLysaght (ed.), *Calendar of Orrery Papers* (IMC, Dublin, 1941), pp. 59–60, 77, 84–5; *A Memoir of Mistress Ann Fowkes (Née Geale)* . . . *with some recollections of her family* (Dublin, 1892), pp. 25–6.

[24] Indenture of 3 May 1674 between R. and Agnes Lawrence and Francis Hall, esq. of Laggan, County Down; Agnes Lawrence to W. Waring, 30 December 1698, private collection, County Down.

[25] Bodl., Carte MSS 160, f. 36v; *CSPI, 1669–70*, p. 635; HMC, *Ormonde*, NS, V, pp. 450–1.

[26] Account book of David Johnson, MSS of earl of Rosse, Birr Castle, MS A/16; HMC, *Ormonde*, NS, III, pp. 332–7, 346–51; Lawrence, *Interest of Ireland*, II, pp. 31–2.

[27] R. Lawrence to R. Trueman, 30 December 1679, private collection, County Down.

The fragility of Lawrence's finances was remembered by his descendants. The family preserved a tradition in which he had apportioned blame for his setbacks among tricksters and impersonal forces.[28] Despite these rubs, Lawrence contrived to live in a style which befitted his position. Towards the end of his life he was able to move into the new housing development north of the River Liffey in Smithfield.[29] Disappointments in his money-making projects encouraged him to generalise about institutional and structural deficiencies. Ireland, he concluded, suffered from retarded development because the state had failed adequately to back promising enterprises such as his at Chapelizod, and because most in government and the propertied elite were openly contemptuous of trade. Furthermore, inadequate credit facilities and unsound coin hampered commerce. All cried out for reform.[30]

Less than diplomatic was the way in which Lawrence widened his criticism of the government for neglecting promising initiatives into critiques of English policy towards Ireland and of absenteeism. Lawrence contended that the council of trade, on which he sat, made excellent recommendations. These were then ignored by the Irish council. Indeed, the Irish council became a sepulchre in which promising plans were interred.[31] Much of the fault could be traced to the ignorance of and prejudice against trade among the councillors. More blame attached to the lord lieutenant. Lawrence contrasted the zest with which Ormond had sponsored improving ventures with the sorry performance of his successors. The duke had persuaded the government to assist the works at Chapelizod. Meanwhile, on his own estates at Carrick-on-Suir and Callan he introduced foreign textile workers. Those who succeeded Ormond – Robartes, Berkeley and Essex – lacked his enthusiasm. Evidently it suited Lawrence to shift responsibility for his own losses at Chapelizod on to others. Accordingly, he berated the administration in Dublin for its meagre backing after 1669. Although the works had diversified to cater for the growing market for furnishing fabrics, making tapestry and turkeywork, their staple was to clothe the Irish army.[32] However, the promised contracts never materialised. Lawrence explained the failure by the fact that Robartes, Berkeley and Essex were all English. With no stake in

[28] *Memoir of Ann Fowkes*, pp. 25–6.
[29] *Ibid.*, p. 27. For the previous residences on Cork Hill and in Kevin Street: 'Rental of landgable rents, city of Dublin, 1665', *The Fifty-seventh Report of the Deputy Keeper of the Public Records . . . in Ireland* (Dublin, 1936), p. 557; Bodl, Rawlinson MSS B 508, f. 40.
[30] Lawrence, *Interest of Ireland*.   [31] *Ibid.*, I, sig. †7.
[32] *Memoir of Ann Fowkes*, pp. 26–7; R. Lawrence to Ormond, received 30 October 1668, Bodl, Carte MSS 36, f. 521; W. Penn, *My Irish Journal, 1669–1670*, ed. I. Grubb (London, 1952), p. 22; HMC, *Ormonde*, NS, VII, p. 27. Cf. *ibid.*, IV, pp. 38–40.

Ireland, they obediently peddled the English line. By the 1670s this was to subordinate the Irish economy firmly to the English economy and to stifle any enterprises which might compete against English industries.[33]

An analysis which emphasised personal and institutional opposition allowed Lawrence to suggest why most of the fourteen manufactures started in the 1660s had failed by 1682.[34] In stressing such factors, he overlooked structural problems which later analysts have invoked.[35] His criticism developed into an indictment of others who apparently harmed Irish interests. Chief among the culprits were England and the English government. Not only were unsympathetic strangers sent to rule the kingdom, the English, Welsh and (more rarely) Scots gained much of the property and many of the profitable offices in Ireland. The majority of these beneficiaries were absentees, so that specie was drained from Ireland and the country denied potential leaders.[36] To reverse the trend, Lawrence pleaded that Ireland should always be governed by one of its own. This surprising volte-face from his attitude in the 1650s, when even Protestants of Irish birth were not to be trusted, arose from more than sycophancy towards his patrons, the Butlers. The damage inflicted by absenteeism was beginning to trouble other of Lawrence's contemporaries, notably Petty and the elder Sir Richard Cox.[37] But, along with matters such as the inadequate coinage and credit, it featured most conspicuously on the 'patriot' agenda of the 1720s and 1750s.[38] In identifying these problems Lawrence stood near – if not at – the start of a tradition of proto-'patriotism' among Irish Protestants.[39] It was a surprising relocation for the upholder of English interests in the 1650s.

Lawrence's premonitory diagnosis of the causes of Irish economic weakness coexisted alongside traditional explanations, more in keeping

[33] Lawrence, *Interest of Ireland*, II, pp. 102–5. [34] *Ibid.*, I, sig. *4; II, pp. 104, 189.

[35] L. M. Cullen, *An Economic History of Ireland since 1660* (London, 1972), pp. 26–49; D. Dickson, *New Foundations: Ireland, 1660–1800* (Dublin, 2000), pp. 109–41.

[36] For this trend see T. C. Barnard, 'Scotland and Ireland in the later Stewart monarchy' in S. G. Ellis and S. Barber (eds.), *Conquest and Union: fashioning a British state, 1485–1725* (Harlow, 1995), pp. 252–8, 265–70.

[37] *The Economic Writings of Sir William Petty*, ed. C. H. Hull (2 vols., Cambridge, 1899), I, pp. 46, 185, 193; R. Cox, 'Regnum Corcagiense; or a description of the kingdom of Cork' ed. R. Day, *Journal of the Cork Historical and Archaeological Society*, 2nd series, 8 (1902), pp. 70–1.

[38] T. Prior, *A List of the Absentees of Ireland* (Dublin, 1729); A. P. W. Malcomson, 'Absenteeism in eighteenth-century Ireland', *Irish Economic and Social History*, 1 (1974), pp. 15–35.

[39] P. H. Kelly, 'The politics of political economy in mid-eighteenth-century Ireland' in S. J. Connolly (ed.), *Political Ideas in Eighteenth-century Ireland* (Dublin, 2000), pp. 105–29; S. Rashid, 'The Irish school of economic development, 1720–1750', *The Manchester School of Economic and Social Studies*, 54 (1988), pp. 345–69; J. G. McCoy, 'Local political culture in the Hanoverian empire: the case of Ireland, 1714–1760' (D.Phil. thesis, Oxford University, 1994), pp. 131–58.

perhaps with what was to be expected of a Cromwellian sectary. Certain attitudes hampered Ireland's improvement. The obvious leaders of local society were not only uninterested in commerce but set bad examples. Lawrence's religion did not make him argue that an elite based on spiritual worth should be substituted for the existing carnal one. Rather, he was dismayed that those who had acquired high responsibilities when inheriting property failed to fulfil them. He stated baldly that 'Nobles' titles void of nobles' estates and noble qualities renders nobility contemptible, and not only the reproach but the pest of a country.'[40] Lawrence pilloried those among the peerage who engaged in less obviously useful pastimes. He may have had Orrery, his personal adversary after the débâcle over Lawrence's lands, in his sights when he lampooned playwrights as 'no more useful in a commonwealth than fiddlers in a country parish, to incite to idleness and debauchery'.[41]

Lawrence was particularly hard on those who, by virtue of possessions and standing, should have guided Protestant Ireland. Individuals were adjudged wanting. But he reserved more fire for collectives. He followed convention in expecting leadership from the peerage. Indeed, he devoted considerable space to this order. If the peers, in their patronage of entrepreneurial schemes, had so far done too little, in one respect he was heartened by them. With a flurry of statistics, Lawrence demonstrated how, between the 1630s and 1680s, the Irish parliamentary peerage had shifted decisively towards Protestantism.[42] This change encouraged Lawrence to hope that other influential groups in Irish society would move in the same direction. He recognised, however, that the government had to assist the process. In an entirely traditional fashion, he advocated a mixture of coercion and cajolery.

As he scrutinised Catholic and Protestant communities in turn, he observed much that was amiss. His anti-Catholicism was profoundly conventional. Often it was interwoven with an antipathy towards the Irish. This diminished as he dealt more frequently with the indigenes, but there survived traces of a determinism which assumed that the Irish were by nature incapable of coexisting amicably alongside the English.[43] Yet Lawrence was never altogether consistent in his arguments. Even in the same book, let alone over the interval between 1655 and 1682, he veered from optimism to pessimism. In the 1650s he endorsed the complaints of Spenser and Davies, that the intermingling of ethnic and

---

[40] Lawrence, *Interest of Ireland*, I, p. 12.   [41] *Ibid.*, I, sig. *6v–*7v.

[42] *Ibid.*, I, p. 69; T. C. Barnard, 'Introduction' in T. Barnard and J. Fenlon (eds.), *The Dukes of Ormonde, 1610–1745* (Woodbridge, 2000), pp. 12–13, 48–53.

[43] Lawrence, *The Interest of England*, pp. 13–16, 24–6; Lawrence, *England's Great Interest*, pp. 6–9, 12–13.

confessional populations had led to the dangerous acculturation of the weaker English Protestant communities. To avoid such 'degeneration' in the future, he supported the project to corral the Irish west of the River Shannon. Elsewhere, he approved the likely gains if the peoples lived together. Strict prohibitions against characteristic Irish language, dress, settlement and husbandry, when coupled with the examples of English industry and prosperity and a stronger Protestant presence, would induce the majority to adopt 'civil deportments'.[44] In 1682 Lawrence detected numerous signs that Ireland was undergoing social and cultural transformation to become 'West England'.[45] He had still to concede that progress was frustratingly slow. Both in the 1650s and the 1680s he expected the state to act to speed change. By 1682 the failure of the government to do so had become an important element in his strictures. Also included were the failings of both Catholics and Protestants. Tactfully he distinguished the respectable from the restless. He made the conventional nod towards 'the more serious and better principled papists', who had not perpetrated the alleged atrocities of the 1640s and who lived as loyal subjects of their English king. Only adherents of 'bloody savage Tridentine principles' and of the Jesuits were relentlessly attacked.[46] But it was difficult to know how many followed these inflammatory teachings. Again, Lawrence repeated a common belief that the priesthood had been addicted to these doctrines, and so had caused much of the recent trouble.[47] Yet these principles were not confined to the clergy. They reached deeper into Irish Catholic society; how far, it was often impossible to ascertain.[48]

Lawrence, writing early in the 1680s, when a Catholic resurgence loomed, alternated between strident warnings and emollience. In the second mode, he insisted: 'It is not the religion of the Church of Rome . . . but the policies of the state of Rome that render them so incompatible with civil order and society.' Accordingly, and in anticipation of Protestant protests throughout the eighteenth century, he denied any wish to stop the Catholics from practising their religion.[49] But once more he was not consistent. Erroneous doctrines did more than delude the Catholics. The tenacity with which they stuck to and defended misguided opinions, he believed, increased their propensity to sin. Through this reasoning, he traced much of the behaviour which stunted the economy in Ireland back

---

[44] Lawrence, *England's Great Interest*, pp. 37–9.
[45] Lawrence, *Interest of Ireland*, I, p. 51.
[46] *Ibid.*, I, ††2v–††3v; ii, pp. 222, 239; T. C. Barnard, '"Parlour entertainment for an evening": histories of the 1640s' in M. Ó Siochrú (ed.), *Kingdoms in Crisis: Ireland in the 1640s* (Dublin, 2001), pp. 31, 40.
[47] Lawrence, *Interest of Ireland*, II, pp. 89, 258–71.
[48] Lawrence, *Interest of England*, p. 11; Lawrence, *England's Great Interest*, p. 16.
[49] Lawrence, *Interest of Ireland*, II, p. 93.

to the prevalence of Catholicism there.[50] These social ills added to the more general unsuitability of Catholicism as a civil religion on which a stable society could be erected. Catholicism, Lawrence regretted, was inimical to 'civil order and society'. This uncannily foreshadowed a declaration from Dublin in 1725 that popery constituted 'the grand enemy to our religious and civil liberties'. Its tenets – according to Lawrence – obstructed 'neighbourly society and civil converse betwixt private persons'.[51] Lack of trust made trade difficult: not least because Catholics, with their notorious willingness to enter mental reservations, would not necessarily honour oaths and contracts. Lawrence glumly prophesied that, so long as Catholicism flourished in Ireland, there 'can be no true friendship, nor comfortable neighbourhood'.[52] At times Lawrence accused ardent Catholics of reducing civil society to something akin to a Hobbesian state of nature. Their principles were worse than 'little peccadilloes only inconvenient to neighbourly society and civil converse between private persons'. They threatened to bring humanity to a condition 'worse than brutish'.[53] Such objections, not new when Lawrence aired them, would be repeated frequently. In 1698 Bishop Foy of Waterford thought that the unsocial or anti-social habits of the Irish Catholics were worsened by their living in scattered and makeshift settlements. The bishop would herd them into nucleated villages centred on church and manor, on the model of lowland England.[54] By the mid-eighteenth century sociability was identified as a vital badge of civility and civic responsibility. It led Irish Catholics to be impugned for 'dissociability'.[55] As such, they unsettled society, and could justifiably be excluded from full citizenship.[56]

A sense of impending danger from the assertive Irish Catholics pulsed through *The Interest of Ireland*. When, in 1682, Lawrence wrote: 'While God blesses us with an English Protestant king and parliament, Ireland can never degenerate from an English Protestant interest', it hardly amounted to a resounding affirmation of confidence in the future.[57] Within three years the Catholic James II had ascended the throne, but

---

[50] *Ibid.*, I, p. 70.

[51] *Ibid.*, II, pp. 194–5; 'Dublin, St. Andrew's Vestry' [December 1725], Marsh's Library Dublin, MS Z1.1 13, item 97.

[52] Lawrence, *Interest of Ireland*, II, p. 271.   [53] *Ibid.*, II, pp. 194–5, 199, 225.

[54] N. Foy, *A Sermon Preached in Christ's-Church, Dublin; on the 23d of October, 1698* (Dublin, 1698), pp. 27–8; H. Maule, *A Sermon Preached in Christ-Church, Dublin . . . on Tuesday, the twenty-third day of October, 1733* (Dublin, 1733), p. 21.

[55] John Brett, *A Friendly Call to the People of the Roman Catholick Religion in Ireland* (Dublin, 1757), p. 12.

[56] For some general discussion: T. C. Barnard, 'The languages of politeness and sociability in eighteenth-century Ireland' in D. G. Boyce and R. Eccleshall (eds.), *Political Discourse in Seventeenth- and Eighteenth-century Ireland* (London, 2001), pp. 193–21.

[57] Lawrence, *Interest of Ireland*, II, p. 58.

by then Lawrence was dead. Despite the ingenuity with which Lawrence connected economic malaise to Catholic theories and practices, his preoccupation was in danger of unbalancing an otherwise measured survey.[58] A second departure from the seemingly objective analysis favoured by the political arithmeticians was Lawrence's invective against his fellow Protestants. He accepted the widely held interpretation that Irish Protestants' negligence and sins had provoked divine wrath in 1641 and might do so again if not quickly corrected.[59] In parallel, he wanted material betterment and spiritual reformation. He focused most sharply on four 'wealth-wasting' and 'God-provoking sins': swearing, gambling, adultery and drunkenness. He argued that 'these evils not only hazard the eternal safety of immortal souls, but also are superlatively destructive to the trade and wealth of this nation'.[60] In this view, a commonly held one, the material and immaterial worlds were inseparable. It had long prevailed among Protestant activists in England. There, since the reign of Elizabeth I, it had inspired a sequence of designs to reform conduct and to relieve the poor, from Colchester, Coventry and Leicester to Dorchester, Gloucester, Plymouth and Salisbury.[61] It would underpin the campaigns of the 1690s, in England, Wales and Ireland, to reform manners.[62] In Ireland it persisted throughout the eighteenth century, evident in the hospitals founded in Dublin, the charter schools, the Dublin Society, the Physico-Historical Society and (at the end of the century) the Society for Discountenancing Vice.[63] Lawrence's direct influence on those later undertakings can occasionally be detected, as in Bishop Hutchinson's explicit references to *The Interest of Ireland* when he recommended support of the Irish fisheries to the Irish parliament and the Dublin Society.[64]

---

[58] Bibliographical evidence, with the pagination of pp. 96–113 of the second part of the *Interest of Ireland* duplicated, suggests that this section – on the imperative for Protestant unity – was inserted while it was in the press. Also, the final section, a partisan Protestant history of Catholic conspiracies, has the appearance of being tacked on.

[59] Lawrence, *Interest of Ireland*, I, sig. ††1v; T. C. Barnard, 'The uses of 23 October 1641 and Irish Protestant celebrations', *EHR*, 106 (1991), pp. 889–920.

[60] Lawrence, *Interest of Ireland*, I, pp. 37, 51, 57.

[61] Slack, *From Reformation to Improvement*, pp. 29–52.

[62] T. C. Barnard, 'Reforming Irish manners: the religious societies in Dublin during the 1690s', *Historical Journal*, 35 (1992), pp. 805–38.

[63] T. C. Barnard, 'The Hartlib circle and the cult and culture of improvement in Ireland' in M. Greengrass, M. Leslie and T. Raylor (eds.), *Samuel Hartlib and Universal Reformation* (Cambridge, 1994), pp. 281–97; J. Liechty, 'Irish evangelicalism, Trinity College, Dublin and the mission of the Church of Ireland at the end of the eighteenth century' (Ph.D. thesis, St Patrick's College, Maynooth, 1987); K. Milne, *The Charter Schools* (Dublin, 1997).

[64] Hutchinson, *A Second Letter*, pp. 4–5. Lawrence's *Interest of Ireland* is found in the libraries of Charles Willoughby and Claudius Gilbert, both of which later passed to Trinity College, Dublin. TCD, MS 10, f. 104; 11, f. 119. A copy in Marsh's Library,

Indirectly, the godly milieu of Dublin in which Lawrence was prominent can be reconstructed. Lawrence's granddaughter recalled him saying that 'he was fond of employing the poor and giving them bread'. In *The Interest of Ireland* he adverted to the plight of the destitute in Dublin; in his will he bequeathed them money.[65] The early 1680s seem to have been the moment when the municipality and the parishes first tackled systematically the visible threat of the poor.[66] The two whom Lawrence chose to execute his testament, the Reverend Daniel Williams and James Knight, carried the ethos and projects of Restoration Dublin into the schemes of the 1690s and beyond. Williams, a dissenting minister in Dublin, quit the city for England in 1688. Nevertheless, he then put his weight (and purse) behind the Irish moral reformers of the 1690s.[67] Knight's connection with Lawrence may have originated with his father, a Baptist pastor in Cromwellian Ireland. The younger Knight translated his humanitarian concerns into endowing parochial schools and charities.[68] What in Lawrence's day had been largely unsystematic was gradually developed into a concerted response to endemic and episodic poverty, especially in the capital.[69]

Dublin had belonged to Peter Wybrants, probably the lawyer son of the Dublin alderman of the same name. From Wybrants it may have passed to John Stearne, bishop of Clogher and ardent preserver of anti-Catholic traditions. G. D. Burtchaell and T. U. Sadleir, *Alumni Dublinenses* (2nd edn, Dublin, 1935), p. 899; T. C. Barnard, 'A bishop and his books', forthcoming.

[65] Proposal for Chapelizod, *c.* 1668, Bodl., Carte MSS 36, f. 523; will of R. Lawrence, 26 June 1684, private collection, County Down; *Memoir of Ann Fowkes*, p. 26; Lawrence, *Interest of Ireland*, I, pp. 45–6.

[66] R. Dudley, 'Dublin's parishes, 1660–1729: the Church of Ireland parishes and their role in the civic administration of the city' (Ph.D. thesis, 2 vols., Trinity College, Dublin, 1995), I, pp. 167, 205–6; Accounts, 1680–81, Vestry Book, St Catherine's Dublin, 1657–92, RCB, P. 117/5/1.1; J. T. Gilbert and R. M. Gilbert (eds.), *Calendar of the Ancient Records of Dublin* (19 vols., Dublin, 1899–1944), V, pp. 586–7.

[67] J. Richardson to Society for Promotion of Christian Knowledge, 18 July 1718, Abstract letter book, 8, no. 5289; D. Williams, *A Sermon Preach'd before the Societies for Reformation of Manners, in Dublin: July the 18th 1700* (Dublin, 1700); R. L. Greaves, *God's Other Children: Protestant nonconformists and the emergence of denominational churches in Ireland, 1660–1700* (Stanford, 1997), p. 260.

[68] St J. D. Seymour, *The Puritans in Ireland, 1647–1661* (Oxford, 1921), pp. 155, 215; indenture of 12 April 1698, NAI, M. 6252; Jane Bulkeley(?) to J. Bonnell, [1720], NLI, PC 435/11: H. Maule to R. Stearne, 10 January 1717[18], SPCK, Abstract letter book, no. 5502; H. Newman to Knight, 14 April 1718, *ibid.*, CS 2/7, ff. 17v–18; *Faulkner's Dublin Journal*, 15 November 1726; Monck Mason collections relating to Dublin, Gilbert MSS 67, p. 726, Pearse St. Library, Dublin; will of James Knight of Dublin, gent., 21 February 1725[6], PRONI, D 3168/2/7.

[69] Barnard, 'Reforming Irish manners', pp. 805–38; Dudley, 'Dublin's parishes, 1660–1729', I, pp. 164–209; D. W. Hayton, 'Did Protestantism fail in early eighteenth-century Ireland? Charity schools and the enterprise of religious and social reformation, *c.*1690–1730' in A. Ford, J. McGuire and K. Milne (eds.), *As by Law Established: the Church of Ireland since the Reformation* (Dublin, 1995), pp. 166–86.

Lawrence shared with observers in England a sense that the poor constituted an unrealised resource. He allowed that some, owing to their stage in the cycle of life, had been reduced to indigence and were fitting objects of Christian charity. The able-bodied, in contrast, needed employment. Increasingly the cultivation of flax and hemp and the making of linen were seen as best providing it. Not the least of Ormond's merits, in Lawrence's account, was his support of these ventures. Lawrence himself, in his work for the council of trade, prepared directions for the planting of hemp and flax.[70] The Irish council ordered that they be printed, but no copy has survived. Such practical guides again prefigure what was done in the first half of the eighteenth century under the auspices of the Linen Board and the Dublin Society.[71] Chapelizod itself disappointed Lawrence's perhaps extravagant hopes. Incidentally, his failure to turn it into a profitable enterprise blasted his reputation with some contemporaries.[72] The experiment, always conceived as a showpiece akin to the Mortlake tapestry factory or the Gobelins works, was revived. As Lawrence had hoped, it became the focus of patriotic endeavour, though not in his own lifetime.[73] One unwelcome result of this proto-industry had been to crowd unruly workers onto a single site. Other pioneering entrepreneurs discovered that labour did not always conduce to discipline, but could be a source of unrest.[74]

Lawrence was also linked with the embryonic linen industry of Ulster. Through his wife he gained lands in County Down, which were managed by a local resident, William Waring. The latter keenly promoted the cultivation and spinning of flax. The extent to which experience at Chapelizod informed ventures elsewhere in Ireland remains elusive. Notable among Lawrence's achievements was the dispatch of an auxiliary, Alexander van Fornenbergh, probably a Protestant refugee, to observe and evaluate techniques in England and the Low Countries. Fornenbergh's reports, together with the presence in Ireland of foreign artificers, may gradually

---

[70] Lawrence, *Interest of Ireland*, I, sig. †7.

[71] Royal Dublin Society, *A Bibliography of the Publications of the Royal Dublin Society from its foundation in the year 1731* . . . (2nd edn, Dublin, 1953), items 3, 8, 18; H. D. Gribbon, 'The Irish Linen Board, 1711–1828' in L. M. Cullen and T. C. Smout (eds.), *Comparative Aspects of Scottish and Irish Economic and Social History, 1600–1900* (Edinburgh, 1977), p. 81.

[72] HMC, *Ormonde*, NS, IV, p. 156.

[73] *CSPD, 1691–2*, pp. 321–2; A. Longfield, 'History of tapestry-making in Ireland in the seventeenth and eighteenth centuries', *Journal of the Royal Society of Antiquaries of Ireland*, 68 (1938), pp. 92–9; A. Longfield, 'Some tapestry makers in Ireland', *Burlington Magazine*, 85 (1944), p. 250.

[74] T. C. Barnard, 'An Anglo-Irish industrial enterprise: iron-making at Enniscorthy, County Wexford, 1657–92', *Proceedings of the Royal Irish Academy*, 85, section C (1985), p. 141; Barnard, 'Sir William Petty as Kerry ironmaster', *ibid.*, 82, section C (1982), p. 26.

have disseminated better methods.[75] The Warings intermarried with the Lawrences.[76] Even so, the former, innovators in the Ulster industry, had sources other than Lawrence and Chapelizod from which to gain knowledge of continental methods. In the 1680s the heir to the Waring estate toured the Low Countries, the Rhineland and Italy.[77] Lawrence himself subscribed to the prevalent axiom that the exertions of individuals bettered not only themselves but also the commonwealth. Later analysts have tended to be more sceptical of what could be done by particular proprietors, no matter how energetic and civic-minded. Notwithstanding the favourable publicity which at first surrounded Chapelizod or the value of the printed manuals such as Lawrence's, structural and ecological factors did most to implant linen-making in late seventeenth- and early eighteenth-century Ireland.[78]

Other barriers to the economic development of Ireland, notably the lack of a bank and the shortage and corruption of the circulating coin, continued to worry pamphleteers. High interest rates (often 10 per cent) deterred investors and improvers. Lawrence proposed that a joint-stock company be formed. This solution was recommended by others, and would be tried in the 1690s as a means to nourish the puny linen industry.[79] Soon enough it was replaced by a state subsidy. Fresh efforts were made in the 1720s to found an Irish equivalent of the Bank of England, but failed.[80] Similarly, successive administrations wrestled with the defects of the coinage. The problems of bimetallism, and the habit of consistently overvaluing the main medium of Irish exchange – silver – inhibited trade. Not enough low value coins circulated. This lack was to some extent overcome by urban traders issuing tokens. But the situation was thought to discourage trade and slow modernisation by necessitating barter. Additionally, matters were confused by large quantities of foreign

---

[75] R. Lawrence to Sir G. Lane, received 20 May 1668, received 30 October 1668, 16 December 1668, Bodl., Carte MSS 36, ff. 330, 521, 609; instructions from Lawrence to A. van Fornenbergh, recd. 20 May 1668, *ibid.*, ff. 332–3; van Fornenbergh's reports, received 26 May and September 1668, *ibid.*, ff. 347–8, 497–8.

[76] Agnes Lawrence to W. Waring, 30 December 1698, private collection, County Down; *Memoir of Ann Fowkes*, p. 26.

[77] T. C. Barnard, 'What became of Waring? The making of an Ulster squire' in V. Carey and U. Lötz-Heumann (eds.), *Taking Sides? Colonial and confessional mentalités in early modern Ireland* (Dublin, 2003), pp. 185–212.

[78] W. H. Crawford, 'The origins of the linen industry in North Armagh and the Lagan valley', *Ulster Folklife*, 17 (1971), pp. 42–51 and 'The evolution of the linen trade in Ulster before industrialisation', *Irish Economic and Social History*, 15 (1988), pp. 32–53.

[79] W. R. Scott, 'The king's and queen's corporations for the linen manufacture in Ireland', *Journal of the Royal Society of Antiquaries of Ireland*, 31 (1901), pp. 371–7.

[80] L. M. Cullen, 'Landlords, bankers and merchants: the early Irish banking world, 1700–1820', *Hermathena*, 135 (1983), pp. 25–41; M. Ryder, 'The Bank of Ireland, 1721: land, credit and dependency', *Historical Journal*, 25 (1982), pp. 557–80.

specie, particularly (it would seem) from Spain and Portugal. Lawrence, like others, pressed the council of trade to tackle these questions, but his suggestions were too contentious to be introduced. In 1683 Lawrence and Petty wrangled before the Irish council over revaluing the coinage, 'but with little edification to the hearers'.[81] Lawrence hoped to turn his expertise in monetary matters to personal profit. In 1676 he offered unsuccessfully to manage the inland revenues of Ireland. With equal lack of success he sought the post of accountant general.[82]

Projectors had long bombarded the makers of policy for Ireland with ideas: some utopian, others severely practical. Many resembled what had been attempted in Tudor and early Stuart England.[83] Governments, although eager for a placid and prosperous Ireland, seldom looked beyond instant gains. This was notoriously the case under Charles II. Not just Lawrence with his ragbag of prejudices and pretensions, but also the seemingly more objective Petty, failed to persuade the administration to apply their palliatives to Ireland.[84] Instead it was to the well-connected and unashamedly venal, like Lord Ranelagh, that Charles II and his ministers harkened.[85] Much that the hopeful Lawrence suggested was ignored. Yet he expressed thoughts important to future policies for Ireland. There was no novelty in learning lessons from the economic miracle which had so enriched the Low Countries. Sir William Temple, Dr Benjamin Worsley, Sir Francis Brewster and Petty applied Dutch lessons to Ireland. Furthermore, within Ireland itself several grandees – Ormond, Orrery and Lane – knew the Low Countries at first hand either through exile or travel. After 1660 they turned thither for artisans and ideas. Possibly Lawrence was also in direct contact, through either his Baptist kinsman, Henry Lawrence, or the sectarian *internationale*.[86] Another craze of the moment enslaved Lawrence. Whether as novice political arithmetician or failed businessman, he constantly totted up costs. Sometimes these efforts at quantification were more ingenious than persuasive. He berated notables in Restoration Ireland for importing mistresses along with other non-Irish goods. Lawrence reckoned that between £300 and £400 were

[81] HMC, *Ormonde*, NS, VII, p. 14.

[82] HMC, *Ormonde*, NS, V, pp. 434, 451; VI, p. 39.

[83] J. Thirsk, *Economic Policy and Projects* (Oxford, 1978).

[84] T. C. Barnard, 'Sir William Petty, Irish landowner' in H. Lloyd-Jones, V. Pearl and B. Worden (eds.), *History and Imagination* (London, 1981), pp. 201–17; F. Harris, 'Ireland as a laboratory: the archive of Sir William Petty' in M. C. W. Hunter (ed.), *Archives of the Scientific Revolution: the formation and exchange of ideas in seventeenth-century Europe* (Woodbridge, 1998), pp. 73–90.

[85] S. Egan, 'Finance and the government of Ireland, 1660–1685' (Ph.D. thesis, Trinity College Dublin, 2 vols., 1983).

[86] I am grateful to Professor John Morrill for telling me of Henry Lawrence's links with Arnhem.

annually spent on each.[87] Fiscal losses were compounded by other harmful consequences. Effeminacy set in, turning the once 'courageous lion' into 'the lascivious goat'. From the era of Sardanapalus and the fall of the Assyrian empire, such activities enfeebled states.[88]

Lawrence was not the first analyst of social and economic maladies in Ireland to posit sin – collective and individual – as the prime cause. More innovative was his attack on the evils which arose from prosperity as well as from poverty. In print he expatiated on the consumerism which was gripping Dublin. It endangered alike the physical well-being and immortal souls of Dubliners. There were ironies in his diatribe. The success of the Chapelizod works depended on the fashion for more sumptuous furnishings. The venture sought both to stimulate and satisfy the demand. Moreover, in his own house, Lawrence adopted these same comforts.[89] As yet, only isolated voices – the bishop and archdeacon of Cork and ascetic Quakers – joined Lawrence's.[90] By the eighteenth century the volume of complaint against luxury had risen to a crescendo. Later pamphleteers united anger at the financial waste with anxiety over the spiritual damage. As with other aspects of the manifesto of the eighteenth-century 'patriots', a strong moral dimension survived behind the statistics and more impersonal language.[91] Many of the matters which obsessed Lawrence in the 1680s – Catholic error and malevolence, Protestant sin, English misgovernment and incomprehension of Ireland – continued to bother public-spirited commentators. Into the 1750s and beyond, the interest of Ireland still called for the public and private measures which he had championed. For this reason, he expressed better the characteristic outlook of Protestants in Ireland than his more brilliant contemporary, Petty.

---

[87] Lawrence, *Interest of Ireland*, I, pp. 45–6.   [88] *Ibid.*, I, pp. 48–9.

[89] *Memoir of Ann Fowkes*, p. 26; proposal for Chapelizod, *c.* 1668, Bodl, Carte MSS 36, f. 523; Lawrence, *Interest of Ireland*, I, pp. 45–6; will of R. Lawrence, 26 June 1684, private collection, County Down.

[90] E. Wetenhall, *A Sermon Preached Octob. 23. 1692* (Dublin, 1692), p. 18; R. Synge, sermon of 30 March 1684, Synge MSS, private collection, Greenwich; *A Narrative of the Christian Experiences of George Bewley* (Dublin, 1750), pp. 11, 15, 33, 43; *Some Account of the Life of Joseph Pike of Cork* (London, 1837), pp. 59–61, 64–6; R. L. Greaves, *Dublin's Merchant-Quaker: Anthony Sharp and the Community of Friends, 1643–1707* (Stanford, 1998), pp. 201–10.

[91] T. C. Barnard, 'Integration or separation? Hospitality and display in Protestant Ireland, 1660–1800' in L. Brockliss and D. Eastwood (eds.), *A Union of Multiple Identities: the British Isles, c.1750–1850* (Manchester, 1997), pp. 127–46; T. C. Barnard, 'Public and private uses of wealth in Ireland, *c.*1660–1760' in J. R. Hill and C. Lennon (eds.), *Luxury and Austerity: Historical Studies XXI* (Dublin, 1999), pp. 66–83; P. H. Kelly, '"Industry and virtue versus luxury and corruption": Berkeley, Walpole and the South Sea Bubble crisis', *Eighteenth-Century Ireland*, 7 (1992), pp. 57–74.

15 Temple's fate: reading *The Irish Rebellion* in late seventeenth-century Ireland

Raymond Gillespie

In the late 1670s the Bristol ship *Diligence* made regular trips to north-west Ireland. It was only one of a small flotilla of ships from Bristol which forayed in the late seventeenth century to the apparently isolated ports of Killybegs and Sligo. These ships carried a range of goods essential to the survival of those who lived at the edge of Europe. The hold of the *Diligence* contained bottles, window glass, gunpowder, lead, leather, sugar, hops, drinking glasses and wool cards. Other ships bound for Sligo and Killybegs in the 1670s had molasses, oil seed, tobacco, madder, logwood, figs, tobacco pipes, bellows, shot and brass manufactures. The contents of the holds of these ships contained a wide range of materials, but the cargo which most had in common was books, ranging in quantity from 14 lb to a hundredweight.[1] This brief glimpse of the trade of some of the remote parts of north-west Ireland is a reminder that in the late seventeenth century the inhabitants of even the more distant areas of Ireland found themselves drawn into a world in which the printed word was a commonplace.[2] Fed initially by imports from Chester and Bristol, the demand for books by the end of the century was more frequently met by the output of a reinvigorated Dublin press. As contemporaries became more confident in handling this great outpouring of print, their attitudes to their world were increasingly moulded by it, and in turn they shaped the texts with which they came into contact by reading them in a variety of ways. Some even took to exposing their own ideas in printed form to what one contemporary writer described as 'the sharpest censure of an uncharitable world'.[3] By the end of the seventeenth century the mind of Protestant Ireland had become dominated by a triptych of printed works: William King's *State of the Protestants of Ireland* (London, 1691), William Molyneux's *The Case of Ireland . . . Stated* (Dublin, 1698) and Sir John

---

[1] PRO, E190/1138/1, f. 116v; E190/1140/3, ff. 19v, 40; E190/1139/3, ff. 15v, 30v.

[2] Raymond Gillespie, 'The circulation of print in seventeenth-century Ireland', *Studia Hibernica*, 29 (1995–7), pp. 31–58.

[3] John Sterne, *A Sermon on the Prayer of Moses* (Dublin, 1695), sig. A4.

Temple's *The Irish Rebellion* (London, 1646, 1679; reissued in Dublin in 1698).[4]

The first two of these works reflected on the relationship of Irish Protestants with their king and parliament respectively, but the older work of Temple tackled a wider canvas, the relationship of Irish Protestants with their native Irish neighbours. The original context for the publication of the work seems fairly clear. It was intended to stir up support in England for the dispatch of a military force under the command of the son of Temple's patron, Lord Lisle, as part of a reconquest of Ireland.[5] By the later seventeenth century this context had been forgotten, but Temple's work retained an enduring fascination for English and Irish readers. For English readers it remained an important source of information about the untrustworthiness of the Catholic Irish which could be recirculated at times of crisis in England. At one level, the godly Samuel Clarke drew heavily, though without acknowledgement, on Temple's work for his *A General Martyrology*, which first appeared in 1651 and was reprinted twice in the 1670s.[6] English pamphleteers of the 1660s and 1670s in turn drew on Clarke's book and hence indirectly made Temple's ideas available to a wider audience.[7] Clarke's work was, for instance, pillaged without acknowledgement by the Quaker George Fox for his anti-Catholic polemic of 1669 which included massacre stories taken from the depositions 'taken before the commissioners appointed for that purpose'.[8] Even at this remove, Temple's massacre stories could have a profound impact, since when Fox came to Ireland in 1669, he noted on arriving at Dublin 'the earth and the very air, smelt with the corruption of the nation, and gave another smell than England to me, with the corruption and the blood, and the massacres, and the foulness that ascended'.[9] At

---

[4] The interdependence of at least some of these is suggested by the fact that the Dublin bookseller and printer Patrick Campbell issued a volume containing the work of both King and Temple in 1713. See chapter 16 below.

[5] Karl Bottigheimer, *English Money and Irish Land* (Oxford, 1971), pp. 101, 104–5; John Adamson, 'Strafford's ghost: the British context of Viscount Lisle's lieutenancy of Ireland' in Jane Ohlmeyer (ed.), *Ireland from Independence to Occupation, 1641–60* (Cambridge, 1995), pp. 131, 139–40.

[6] Samuel Clarke, *A General Martyrology* (London, 1651), pp. 347–63. The debt to Temple is clear from the fact that the massacre stories in Clarke appear in the same order as in Temple's work and in almost identical words.

[7] For example, the Irish material in Clarke's work appears almost verbatim in *A Looking Glass for England Being an Abstract of the Bloody Massacres in Ireland* (London, 1667) reprinted as *An Accompt of the Bloody Massacre in Ireland* (London, 1678).

[8] George Fox, *The Arraignment of Popery* ([London], 1669), pp. 84–95. The debt to Clarke is clear from the language and the ordering of the information.

[9] George Fox, *The Journal*, ed. Nigel Smith (Harmondsworth, 1998), pp. 443–4. At Portadown he also noted, 'I passed over the water, where so many was drowned in the massacre' (p. 450). The story of the Portadown drownings appears in Clarke.

a lower social level the material on the Irish rising in the chapbooks of Nathaniel Crouch (written under the pseudonym of Richard Burton) was drawn almost exclusively from Temple's book.[10] Again in 1673 when an anonymous description of Ireland, *The Present State of Ireland*, was published in London, most of the section on the 1640s was drawn from Temple without acknowledgement.[11] It was this later work, rather than *The Irish Rebellion*, which informed the participants in the late 1660s English debate on Catholic loyalty to the crown between William Lloyd, later bishop of St Asaph, and Roger Palmer, earl of Castlemaine. Lloyd introduced the issue of the alleged Irish massacres based not on Temple but on the writings of Roger Boyle, earl of Orrery. Castlemaine in reply relied on *The Present State of Ireland* for his information on the massacres with little knowledge of the origins of the ideas he was dealing with. Thus Temple's estimate of the number killed was described by Castlemaine as the 'usual computation' or arrived at by 'common calculation'.[12] Even as a massacre narrative in an English context, Temple's work was usually a heavily mediated text which was usually edited to convey a specific message, usually a massacre narrative.

In Ireland the book received plaudits for other reasons. At one end of the social and religious spectrum, Edmund Borlase, a son of one of the lords justices in Ireland in the 1640s, declared Temple's historical work to be

a piece of integrity that few can equal. He having (as a privy councillor) opportunity to view and consider all despatches rarely obvious to others and being singular entire and ingenious adventured into the list when some dared scarce to think on the attempt. A consideration (in reference to what he suffered) very considerable though more in that to this day (whatever hath been barked against other accounts of the rebellion) never any thing was objected against his.[13]

The admiration was mutual, according to Temple's son.[14] At the other end of the spectrum, the Baptist Richard Lawrence echoed similar sentiments, but for different reasons, in 1682 declaring Temple to be

---

[10] Nathaniel Crouch, *The Wars in England, Scotland and Ireland* (first published London, 1681) (5th edn, London, 1684), p. 70 has a few phrases from Temple. Nathaniel Crouch, *The History of the Kingdom of Ireland* (first published London, 1693) (8th edn, Dublin, 1737), pp. 35–52 is drawn almost exclusively from Temple with the addition of the prophecy of the rising by Archbishop Ussher (p. 45) which circulated widely in broadsheet form.

[11] *The Present State of Ireland* (London, 1673), pp. 21–44 is largely drawn from Temple.

[12] [William Lloyd], *The Late Apology in Behalf of the Papists Reprinted and Answered in behalf of the Royalists* (London, 1667), p. 42; Roger Palmer, earl of Castlemaine, *The Catholique Apology with a Reply to the Answer* ([London], 1674), pp. 52–8.

[13] Edmund Borlase, *A History of the Execrable Irish Rebellion* (London, 1680), pp. 7, 19.

[14] BL, Sloane MSS 1008, f. 253.

a person so universally applauded for his prudence, gravity and integrity that the truth of history never was or ever will be questioned by any but those whose works of darkness hate the light. A book worth chaining to every church's desk and reading over once a year by every family.[15]

The position of Temple's *Irish Rebellion* as a paradigm of Protestant thought seemed assured in 1689 when the Jacobite parliament proposed to burn the work together with a copy of the Acts of Settlement and Explanation. Temple's work seems to have been reprieved because the statutes were deemed to be expressions of royal will, and burning them could have been seen as rebellious.[16]

Acting on hints such as this, historians have used Temple's work as a guide to how Protestants in Ireland thought in the seventeenth and eighteenth centuries. It 'assumed the status of an official interpretation [of the 1640s] from the moment of its publication. It soon became the standard Protestant interpretation.'[17] Such a generalised approach to Temple's work is characterised by the assumption that Irish Protestants were passive figures, mere recipients of the unchanging, fixed reading of the text. Traditions and the social memory, however, are rarely static and are constantly being transformed, reinterpreted or reconstructed, and the reading of texts is reshaped by their changing contexts. What may be more fruitful in understanding the influence of *The Irish Rebellion* is to consider how individuals received and used the ideas which Temple had to offer – in other words, to consider how Temple's work was read within the context of the burgeoning world of print in late seventeenth-century Ireland. This chapter will try to elucidate some of those readings.

I

Perhaps the simplest form of reading Temple was that of an individual who owned or borrowed a copy of the text and opened it in the hope of finding something useful in it. What was useful varied a good deal from individual to individual. Scholarly readings of the text concentrated on Temple's work as narrative history supported by extensive quotation from

---

[15] Richard Lawrence, *The Interest of Ireland in its Trade and Wealth State* (Dublin, 1682), part 2, p. 84. The suggestion is reminiscent of the role played by John Fox's *Acts and monuments* . . . and in 1838 an edition of this work appeared edited by Reverend M. Hobart Seymour which included an abridged version of Temple's *Irish Rebellion* as appendix IV.

[16] BL, Egerton MSS 917, f. 108. For Lawrence, see chapter 14 above.

[17] Nicholas Canny, 'What really happened in Ireland 1641' in Ohlmeyer (ed.), *Ireland from Independence to Occupation*, p. 25; T. C. Barnard, 'Crises of identity among Irish Protestants, 1641–85', *Past and Present*, 127 (1990), pp. 51–6; Thomas Bartlett, *The Fall and Rise of the Irish Nation* (Dublin, 1992), pp. 7–9, 70–1.

contemporary sources. This is certainly how the work was presented. The preface, in which Temple set out his methodology, was underpinned with quotations from classical historical works such as those by the Roman historian Cicero and the Greek Polybius.[18] The text was written in an apparently objective way, and Temple's own memories are not presented as an isolated source. Indeed, when Temple appears in the text, he does not refer to himself in the first person but as the 'master of the rolls' and in the preface disparaged those who are lovers of their own actions, since this produced imperfect history.[19] Again in the preface he declared the work to be one of history 'departing from my own interests' and added that in taking up the task, 'I took up with it a resolution most clearly to declare the truth.'[20] The proof of this was to be found in the fact that the work was founded on primary sources, especially the 'very originals or authentic copies of the voluminous examinations' taken after the rising of 1641.[21] These were arguments which impressed some contemporary readers and were combined with the fact that Temple, as a member of the privy council, had access to material which others did not. Scholars such as Edmund Borlase when writing his own account of the 1640s plundered Temple's work remorselessly for copies of official documents. This was clearly a highly selective reading. Borlase, for instance, did not use any of Temple's deposition evidence for massacre, preferring to select material for that part of his narrative from Henry Jones's less spectacular *Remonstrance* of 1642.[22] Scholars read not only selectively but also critically. Some of that critical reading came from comparing a range of texts on the same subject and identifying contradiction and confusion. One reader of Temple's *Irish Rebellion*, probably a Henry Echlin, in the late seventeenth century annotated his copy: '2 Nalson page 8 of introduction suspistion [i.e. suspicion] of our authors partiality'.[23] Others might look for internal contradictions within the text or with their own experience of such recent history. The earl of Castlehaven in the 1680s, while not denying the existence of a massacre in 1641, had severe doubts about Temple's handling of the evidence, declaring 'I am certain in Sir John Temple's muster rolls, of whom the subsequent scribblers borrowed all their catalogues there are not 50,000 persons to be found, though 'tis manifest that in divers places he repeats the same people with

---

[18] John Temple, *The Irish Rebellion: or the History of the Beginning and First Progress of the General Rebellion Raised Within the Kingdom of Ireland, Upon the Three and Twentieth Day of October, 1641* (London, 1646), sigs. a3, b2.
[19] *Ibid.*, sig. a2v.   [20] *Ibid.*, sig. a3v.   [21] *Ibid.*, sig. a4.
[22] Borlase, *History*, sig. A4v; pp. 51–2.
[23] Copy of Temple now TCD, RR 11 64. The reference is to the second volume of John Nalson, *An Impartial Collection of the Great Affairs of State from the Beginning of the Scotch Rebellion in the year 1639 to the Murder of King Charles I.*

the same circumstances twice or thrice over and mentions hundreds as then murdered that lived many years after, nay some even to this day.'[24] Such scepticism was of importance in the confessional battles in which Temple's work became embroiled in the late seventeenth century. Thus Hugh Reily in his 1695 Jacobite history of Ireland paraphrased Castlehaven's comments, recited the English peer Castlemaine's assessment of the numbers killed in 1641, and drew the conclusion that Temple's work was no more than a 'Romantick legend'.[25] Many contemporaries did not accept Temple's narrative at face value, but its apparatus as a work of history certainly proved useful.

Scholars were not the only readers of Temple's text, and it was read in search of things other than a historical narrative. One man in Chester reading the work in May 1646, shortly after it had been published, declared it to be a piece of massacre literature, Sir John being 'largest' on 'cruelties'.[26] Reading a piece of massacre literature was rather different from scholarly reading of history. It was not subjected to the same critical appraisal, nor was it confined to Protestants. In 1652 Brian Kavanagh of Carlow deposed to Cromwellian commissioners that about four years earlier he had met James Butler of Tinnahinch in County Carlow, who told him

that he had seen the copy of a printed book setting forth some murders acted in Ireland in which book the murder of the English at Graige is charged on him the said James by the Lady Butler . . . but he the said James denied that he was guilty thereof and hoped to find all those who gave orders for it.[27]

From the description the work must be Temple's *Irish Rebellion*, yet it was being read for its stories of murder by a Catholic and probably one involved in those murders. This reflects another reading of Temple. The appeal of the murder stories to a Catholic reader may have stemmed from their capacity to shock and titillate, and some of the later short abstracts of the depositions published without commentary may have been aimed at this popular market.[28] Temple's commentary on stories of ripped-up bellies, live burials, knocked-out brains and hangings is immediate and violent, dwelling lovingly on the details of the murders. The excitement could be prolonged by reading not just the text but the extracts from the depositions themselves conveniently printed as part of

[24] *The Earl of Castlehaven's Review or his Memoirs* (London, 1684), pp. 28–9.
[25] Hugh Reily, *The Impartial History of Ireland* (London, 1742), pp. 20–1.
[26] HMC, *Report on the Manuscripts of the Earl of Egmont* (2 vols., 1905–9), I, p. 292.
[27] TCD, MS 812, f. 118v.
[28] For example *An Abstract of Some of Those Barbarous Cruel Massacres of the Protestants and English in Some Parts of Ireland* (London, 1662).

the text yet separated from it. Moreover, the stories of social inversion by which servants attacked their masters and 'Irish tenants and servants [made] a sacrifice of their English landlords' may well have appealed to an anarchic streak in some readers.[29]

Apart from this straightforward narration of murders and maimings there were other ways of approaching this sort of writing. The stories of numbers killed could provide evidence in a confessional struggle. Some certainly read such massacre literature in this way. One copy of a 1662 work by R. S. which documented murders by English soldiers during the 1640s as a way of replying to the anti-Catholic massacre literature was carefully annotated in the margin by its reader with the numbers killed in each encounter.[30] Even this does not exhaust the possibilities of reading the sort of material Temple presented. One manuscript copy of abstracts of depositions made in Dublin by Edward Gibbon in the 1660s before being taken to Salisbury is marked in the margin by at least three readers, one of whom read the text in Ireland.[31] One of these readers, John Gibbon, had enough education to annotate in both Latin and English. Most of the comments concentrate on one section of the depositions and much of the interest centred on the spectacular wonders recorded in the text. On the first appearance of ghosts in the testimonies, the early annotator provided an index to where other references to ghosts and spectres might be found, and this index was repeated on subsequent references to spirits.[32] Most heavily annotated is the deposition of Robert Maxwell, the marginal notes including 'a fiery pillar in the air', 'silence and dumbness of dogs and cocks', 'slain bodies not corrupted' and 'marks of blood not washed off'.[33] Such wonders were clearly of considerable significance to contemporaries. Indeed, most of the depositions which Temple printed as typical, having 'made choice, for the most part of them, of such as have been put in by persons of good quality of known integrity and credit', contain such wonder stories.[34] The stories of ghosts appearing in the River Bann after a massacre appear in a number, in another there is the desertion of the river at Sligo by fish after a massacre (which occasioned an exorcism of the river), and miraculous thunderstorms at the moment

---

[29] Temple, *Irish Rebellion*, part 1, p. 40.

[30] *A Collection of some of the Murthers and Massacres Committed on the Irish in Ireland since the 23rd of October* . . . (London, 1662), copy now in NLI, LO P136.

[31] RIA, MS I iv 1. The manuscript was taken from Ireland in 1663 by Edward Gibbon and given to John Gibbon. On the basis of the sequence of notes on pp. ix, xi and xii of the manuscript the earliest hand, which made many of the notes discussed below, appears before that of Edward and the manuscript may be presumed to be in Ireland when the first hand annotated it.

[32] RIA, MS I iv 1, pp. 152, 162, 189.   [33] RIA, MS I iv 1, pp. 190, 191, 196.

[34] Temple, *Irish Rebellion*, part 1, p. 111.

of a murder as 'a sign of God's anger' appear in a third.[35] Such a selection was clearly intended to make a point. In a less spectacular way, Temple's language did something similar. His reference to the rising itself as 'this monstrous birth', for example, echoes the European tradition of monstrous births and other wonders as portents of judgement.[36]

Contemporaries were clearly attracted to unusual occurrences that were part of the literature of massacre, but for many they had a wider meaning. When in 1643 a number of Irish commissioners prepared a manuscript abstract of the depositions taken in the wake of the rising, they declared that the wonders which had been seen during the early months of the rising were 'manifest evidence to the rebels (confessing them) of God's displeasure toward them and acts of divine interposition which ought to be taken notice of'.[37] Some years later, in 1650, the Cromwellian Thomas Waring prepared his selection from the depositions for popular consumption and he urged his readers to consider

what those hideous cries of revenge against their [the insurgents'] murders and other fatal meteors, signs, wonders in the firmament, the water, earth and fire (which have been seen and known to succeed their bloody cruelties) do portend and thereby be the more terrified to expect God's heavy judgement laying their iniquities on their heads.[38]

Such an understanding of the wonders which Temple included in his text opens the way to yet another possible reading of the text, as a godly providential narrative. This is precisely the sort of reading which Temple seems to have expected his readers to exploit. For Temple, the providential narrative of judgement and deliverance was set in a wider historical context. The social fracturing which the 1640s had brought about was nothing less than a judgement of God for the sins of the settlers, though in turn divine retribution would be directed against the Irish for having taken vengeance 'with a deceitful heart'.[39] By the end of the book there are signs of the deliverance following judgement, as there was 'so strange a turn, such a remarkable declination of their [Irish] power, their hearts

---

[35] *Ibid.*, part 1, pp. 113, 121, 126, 133–6.

[36] *Ibid.*, part 1, p. 65; R. W. Scribner, *For the Sake of Simple Folk: popular propaganda for the German Reformation* (Oxford, 1994), pp. 127–32; Katherine Park and Lorraine J. Daston, 'Unnatural conceptions: the study of monsters in sixteenth and seventeenth-century France and England', *Past and Present*, 92 (1981), pp. 25–35.

[37] BL, Harley MSS 5999, ff. 33–4v. For the context, Aidan Clarke, 'The 1641 Rebellion and anti-Popery in Ireland' in Brian MacCuarta (ed.), *Ulster, 1641* (Belfast, 1993), pp. 150–7.

[38] T[homas] W[aring], *A Brief Narration of the Plotting, Beginning and Carrying on of the Execrable Rebellion and Butcherie in Ireland* (London, 1650), p. 27. For a detailed examination of the role of wonders and providential judgement, Raymond Gillespie, *Devoted People: belief and religion in early modern Ireland* (Manchester, 1997), chapters 3 and 6.

[39] Temple, *Irish Rebellion*, part 1, p. 64, part 2, p. 53.

failing them for fear, their councils infatuated, their designs blasted . . . as we needs must give glory to our maker, and acknowledge that God hath most wonderfully wrought for this deliverance of the poor small remnant of his people'.[40] Such a providential narrative held together the historical past in the face of social fracture. The precedents were clear: the Book of Ezekiel, from which Temple drew most of his scriptural allusions, and in the first part of the work a story drawn from Giraldus Cambrensis which attributed a judgement on Ireland for 'the sins of the people'.[41]

Some certainly read such massacre literature in this way. When Thomas Waring revealed in his work that the judgement of God on the Irish was the parliamentary campaign of 1649–50, one contemporary reader noted in margin of the work: 'Blessed be the Lord.'[42] Later in the century the Baptist Richard Lawrence urged families to read Temple not as an example of the untrustworthiness of the Irish but rather to prevent themselves falling into sin by compromising with the Irish and 'swallow down full cups of their superstition and close in with that religion'.[43] Such providential narratives based on judgement could be adjusted as required to identify new sources of sin. In 1679 during the Popish Plot, for instance, an abstract of murders from the Irish rising was published in London which warned of the danger of another judgement. This time it was the judgement which arose from the division within Protestantism and the need to tolerate dissenters to 'avert those judgements which press so near upon us'.[44] The providential ideas of Temple were infinitely malleable to suit many situations.

This sort of godly providential theme may well explain something of the publishing history of Temple's book. Its first London publisher was the bookseller Samuel Gellibrand, who specialised in such godly works. Between 1641 and 1646, when he published Temple's work, almost a third of his sixty-seven titles were supplied by four authors, all godly preachers of a Presbyterian providentialist cast of mind: Francis Cheynell, Stephen Marshall, Obadiah Sedgwick and the Scottish Presbyterian Robert Baillie.[45] Seen in this context, the importance of the history as a providential work increases.

Temple's *Irish Rebellion*, therefore, was not a simple text amenable to just one reading or to an 'official' interpretation. It could be read in a

---

[40] *Ibid.*, part 2, p. 54.   [41] *Ibid.*, part 1, p. 64.
[42] W[aring], *A Brief Narration*, sig. a3–3v., copy now, NLI, LOP 39.
[43] Lawrence, *Interest*, part 2, p. 84.
[44] *A Collection of Certain Horrid Murders in the Several Counties of Ireland* (London, 1679), sigs. A3–3v.
[45] Gellibrand's publishing activities have been reconstructed using the indices in D. G. Wing *et al.*, *Short Title Catalogue of Books Printed in England, Scotland, Ireland, Wales and British America . . . 1641–1700* (4 vols., New York, 1982–97).

number of different ways for very different purposes. Those in search of titillation, scholarly enlightenment or godly providential reassurance could all turn to *The Irish Rebellion* for something to instruct, entertain or improve. These various readings were not mutually exclusive, since few individuals read with a single motive in mind. The text therefore needs to be considered in the context of the very different communities who read it for their diverse reasons.

II

Given the diversity of possible ways of reading Temple's work, it is necessary to make some assessment of which individuals actually read it, and in what contexts. Unfortunately there are no booksellers' records which might indicate how widely the text spread in Ireland; however, one proxy, the appearance of the work in lists of the libraries of Irish Protestants in the late seventeenth century, might help to clarify its popularity. Such lists are, of course, a biased sample. They represent the collecting habits of bishops, gentlemen and institutions, rather than the lower end of the social spectrum. Fifteen library lists between 1660 and 1695 reveal that Temple's *Irish Rebellion* appeared in only one collection, that of Trinity College, Dublin.[46] This copy was presented by Temple to his former college, where it was retained and lent out to four readers in twenty years.[47] There is other, more fragmentary, evidence that Temple's work did not capture the imagination of the upper levels of Irish society that bought books. Roger Boyle, earl of Orrery, who had read Spenser in the 1660s, had clearly not read Temple. It was not in his library, and in 1662, when replying to a tract by the Franciscan Peter Walsh, he estimated the number killed in the rebellion as 'increasing to that above two hundred thousand

---

[46] Representative Church Body Library, Dublin, MS 25, ff. 99–100 (Henry Jones, bishop of Meath, 1661); TCD, MS 10 (Library catalogue, TCD); T. W. Moody, J. G. Simms (eds.), *The Bishopric of Derry and the Irish Society of London* (2 vols., IMC, Dublin, 1968–83), I, pp. 417–19 (Charles Vaughan's donation to Derry diocesan library, 1668); *Irish Book Lover*, 30 (1946–8), pp. 31–2 (Mr Taylor, Munster, 1672); TCD, MUN/LIB/1/15 (Jerome Alexander, 1670s); West Sussex Record Office, Petworth House Papers, Orrery MS G. S. 14 (earl of Orrery, 1670s); TCD, MS 865, ff. 295v–86v (Michael Ward, bishop of Raphoe, 1680); BL, Add MS 47024, ff. 81–3v (Philip Perceval, Cork, 1684); HMC, *Report on the Manuscripts of the Marquis of Ormonde*, NS (8 vols., London, 1902–20), VII, pp. 513–27 (James Butler, duke of Ormond, 1685); TCD, MS 1490 (William King, rector of St Werburgh's, 1688); Marsh's Library, Dublin, Z4.5.14, ff. 274–4v (Dudley Loftus, 1689); NLI, MS 11048/144 (two lists, one anon. but of a medical doctor, 1691, and second of Coronet Wilkinson, Kilkenny, 1691); *A Catalogue of the Books of the Most Rev. Father in God Samuel Foley* (Dublin, 1695) (Samuel Foley, bishop of Down and Connor, 1695); TCD, MS 10 (Charles Willoughby, 1685–95).

[47] The copy, with its inscription, is now TCD, P k 12. The borrowing register is TCD, MS 2087.

in the first two years'. This was a long way short of Temple's estimate of 300,000 killed, a fact Walsh happily pointed out.[48] The bishop of Meath, Henry Jones, was guilty of a similar lapse in 1676 when he estimated that the numbers of Protestants killed in the rising was only 100,000.[49] This does not mean that such Protestants lacked interest in the issues that Temple tackled. Jones, for instance, had a copy of Thomas Waring's work on the depositions and three others had copies of Borlase's work.[50]

Two reasons might be advanced for the lack of interest in Temple's specific interpretation of the events of the 1640s by a certain class of Irish Protestant in the late seventeenth century. The first lies in the nature of the text itself. *The Irish Rebellion* is not an easy book to read as a continuous narrative. It was not so much written in late 1645 or early 1646 as thrown together from available fragments. The book itself is in three parts, the final part of which is paginated separately and therefore probably printed later than the rest of the text. The oldest part of the text seems to be the second part, or the massacre section, beginning in the first edition on page 65 of the first pagination and with its own headpiece. Temple must have had access to the originals of the depositions in compiling this middle section of the work. There were certainly other works in circulation from which Temple could have drawn his deposition material, but he seems not to have used them. Of the ninety depositions that Temple printed, all or part of only fourteen occur in Henry Jones's 1642 *Remonstrance*. Thirty-seven of Temple's depositions occur in the 1643 abstract, which Temple may well have seen in Dublin Castle, and in many cases there are significant differences between Temple's text and that of the abstract. It seems clear that Temple was working with the original depositions, and so the work must have existed in some form before November 1644, when he left Dublin for London.[51] It may have been compiled during late 1643 and 1644, when Temple was imprisoned in Dublin Castle, where the material was held. Indeed, an early draft of this section may be what Temple referred to in January 1644, when he asked to go to England to justify his actions to the king and to give him 'such a true relation of the

---

[48] [Roger Boyle], *The Irish Colours Displayed* (London, 1662), p. 3. The same figure appears in Roger Boyle, *An Answer to a Scandalous Letter Lately Printed and Subscribed by Peter Walsh* (London, 1662), p. 29; Peter Walsh, *The Irish Colours Folded* (London, 1662), p. 3.

[49] Henry Jones, *A Sermon of Antichrist Preached at Christ Church, Dublin November 12 1676* (Dublin, 1677), p. 22. The same figure reappears in the London reissue of 1679 (p. 23).

[50] Representative Church Body Library, MS 25, f. 100; NLI, MS 11048/141; TCD, MS 1490, f. 3v; TCD, MS 10, f. 15v.

[51] *Calendar of the Proceedings of the Committee for Compounding, 1643–60* (London, 1890), p. 1511.

state of his affairs here [Ireland] as would make him see how extremely
he is misinformed of the condition of his kingdom'.[52]

The second oldest part of the work seems to be the opening section,
which must have been written or revised after November 1644, to judge
from a reference to a deposition of that date quoted in the text.[53] It also
seems to have been written in London where Temple had access to records
of the Westminster parliament that he used in the text.[54] The final part of
the work, which is separately paginated and probably slightly later than the
other two sections, was clearly written quickly and is unfinished. Temple
declared that he had been 'unexpectedly called away' about the business
of 'restoring of this kingdom and the resettlement of our affairs'.[55] It
may be that this was connected with the beginnings of Viscount Lisle's
attempt to redefine the parliamentary war aims in Ireland towards the
end of 1645.

The result of this complex textual history is that Temple's work is
not a straightforward narrative. It is repetitive. The general comments
made about massacre in the first part are taken up again in the second.
The providential argument, which features strongly in the first part, is
not developed in the second, but returns in the third. Within this rather
disjointed framework, the text is sometimes inconsistent and sometimes
contradictory. At the beginning of the third part, for instance, Temple
declares that he does not propose to print Robert Maxwell's deposition
'because it is of great length', but seems unaware that he had already
done so at the end of part two.[56] Again at the beginning of Part II Temple
declares that he knows nothing of the 'first contrivers' of the rebellion or
where it was planned, oblivious to the declaration at the beginning of
Part I of the full details of the plotters and their planning in Tyrone and
Fermanagh on the basis of Sir William Cole's correspondence.[57] All this
points to the fact that the text was hastily thrown together, some parts
having been sent to the printer while other parts were still being written,
and this may explain some of the internal confusion. At any rate, it was
not a clearly constructed or well-developed narrative.

The second reason why Temple's work may not have attracted the
attention of the book-buying public lies in Temple's own career in the
1640s. His support for the Independent party in the late 1640s through
his patron Robert Sidney, earl of Leicester, has left textual traces. His
allusion to the Greek historian Polybius suggests something of his intellectual baggage since this work was the *locus classicus* of English republican

---

[52] Bodl., Carte MS 65, ff. 40–1.   [53] Temple, *Irish Rebellion*, part 1, p. 17.
[54] For example, *ibid.*, part 1, pp. 47–51.   [55] *Ibid.*, part 2, p. 53.
[56] *Ibid.*, part 2, p. 2 compared with part 1, pp. 123–7.
[57] *Ibid.*, part 1, pp. 65–6 compared with part 1, pp. 16–21.

thought in the 1650s.[58] Certainly Temple's links with the Sidney family resulted in him moving in dangerous circles, and he was also in touch with the republican Algernon Sidney in the early 1660s, albeit as a family friend.[59] Moreover, Temple's activities in the 1640s would not have endeared him to Restoration grandees. In 1643 he had been imprisoned in Dublin Castle, accused of writing 'two traitorous letters against your majesty . . . and use made of them to cast false aspersions upon your majesty as fomenting and favouring the rebels in Ireland'.[60] Moreover, in the 1640s he had been associated with a Dublin circle of radical preachers including Faithful Teate and Stephen Jerome, as well as John Harding, the chancellor and sub-dean of Christ Church, Dublin. Harding arranged for the pulpit of Christ Church to be available to these radicals, and at least one, Stephen Jerome, was imprisoned for a traitorous sermon preached there. Harding organised the 1643 Dublin reprint of a radical sermon by the English godly preacher John Geree, for which he was stripped of the chancellorship of Christ Church and his Trinity College degrees, as well as being degraded from the priesthood, after which he became a Baptist. He had dedicated the reprint of the 1643 tract to Sir John Temple.[61]

Little of this had been forgotten at the Restoration. It seems likely that Temple was restored as master of the rolls because, as he pointed out when the position was under threat in 1673, he had been appointed for life in 1640.[62] The return of others of Temple's circle to Ireland was not welcomed. John Parker, bishop of Elphin, recorded in 1661 that 'It is very ill taken by the bishops at court and much worse by the lord lieutenant that Mr Teate is again permitted to preach in Dublin.'[63] Temple himself was anxious to disassociate himself from his 1646 work. When in 1674 another issue of the work was planned in London, Temple denied that he had supported the move.[64] Part of the reason for the ill-feeling generated by the work was certainly that it destabilised relations between Catholics and Protestants at a sensitive time. However, it posed a threat to the internal workings of Protestant Ireland also. Lord Coventry in England reported that many no longer believed the massacre stories in *The Irish*

[58] *Ibid.*, sig. b2; Barnard, 'Crises of Protestant identity', p. 54; Nigel Smith, *Literature and Revolution in England, 1640–1660* (London, 1994), pp. 151, 337–8.
[59] R. W. Blencowe (ed.), *Sydney Papers* (London, 1825), p. 181; Arthur Collins, *Letters and Memorials of State* (2 vols., London, 1746), II, pp. 709, 718, 721.
[60] Thomas Carte, *The Life of James, Duke of Ormond* (6 vols., Oxford, 1851), V, p. 521.
[61] TCD, MS 6404, f. 136v. For the details of these events, Raymond Gillespie, 'The crisis of reform, 1625–60' in Kenneth Milne (ed.), *Christ Church Cathedral, Dublin: A History* (Dublin, 2000), pp. 203–5.
[62] *CSPD, 1672–3*, p. 435.
[63] HMC, *Report on the Manuscripts of R. R. Hastings* (4 vols., London, 1928–47), IV, p. 123.
[64] BL, Stowe MS 206, ff. 240, 312; *Letters Written by Arthur Capel, Earl of Essex* (London, 1770), pp. 2–3.

Rebellion and equally many 'had hardly faith enough to believe all the apparitions and legend like stories in it'.[65] The wonders that had been a central part of the providential interpretation on the 1640s now seemed, in a new theological climate in England and Ireland, to be positively dangerous. The experience of the 1640s had demonstrated that allowing the idea of independent readings of providential events was highly dangerous because it could be used to justify all manner of actions. One reading of Temple was thus positively discouraged after 1660. For many of the book-buying public, Temple's work was better avoided than acquired except in rather specific circumstances, such as historical research.

III

Sir John Temple's *Irish Rebellion* would seem to provide an example of a book whose reputation outstripped the desire of at least one type of reader to own, read and think about the text and its message. This does not mean that the work was without influence. The godly who still held to the importance of a providential reading of history, such as Richard Lawrence, did read it and recommend it to others. However, the large number of genres which the work straddled, from scholarly history through massacre story to providential narrative, together with its episodic structure, made it a work that was easy to read selectively. Such selective reading within an agreed interpretative framework could serve to neutralise some of the more undesirable elements of Temple's work. Thus contemporaries constructing new narratives of the history of Ireland selected carefully from Temple to present a new face of the work. In 1673, for instance, the anonymous tract *The Present State of Ireland* drew heavily from Temple's work in its retelling of the story of the rising of 1641. Fragments from Temple's text were extracted and cobbled together to provide a narrative of the 1640s.[66] What is significant in this process is what was omitted from the text. All trace of the providential strain in *The Irish Rebellion* was removed and much of the detail of the massacre literature was ignored. The resulting narrative is an almost entirely secular explanation of the rising as betrayal of the settlers by the Irish and a breaking of the social obligations forged before 1641.

Such readings need not have been private ones, and indeed on most occasions they were not. One such occasion for a public controlled reading of Temple's text was the religious sermon preached on 23 October, the day of thanksgiving appointed for deliverance from the hands of the

---

[65] BL, Stowe MSS 206, f. 312.   [66] *The Present State of Ireland,* see above n. 11.

insurrectionists. How frequently Temple was used on these occasions it is difficult to say, since very few of the 23 October sermons made their way into print before the 1690s. This was not because they were actively censored, but because the preachers lacked the patronage, parliamentary or otherwise, which was needed to have such sermons published. It is likely that works such as Temple were used, since preachers wanted to 'make the narrative of the Irish conspiracy more authentic', as one listener put it in 1679.[67] William King, rector of St Werburgh's, Dublin, preaching the 23 October sermon before the lords justices in 1685, for instance, drew on Temple and Borlase for copies of depositions and other documents to spice up his sermon. He did not adopt their narrative section, preferring to use Sir John Davies and Richard Bellings as sources from which to quote opinions.[68] Another preacher in Christ Church on 23 October 1661 was certainly aware of Temple's work, and while he did not use it in the sermon as preached, he certainly made use of it in the published version. William Lightburne, who had himself been robbed of over £3,000 in the early 1640s in Kildare,[69] drew attention to the ghostly apparitions on the River Bann after the drownings at the bridge of Portadown, not as a wonder to illustrate God's active providence in the world, but rather as an indicator of how terrible the massacre had been. The response to this story was not for the individual to puzzle about what this wonder might mean, with possibly heterodox conclusions, but rather to give thanks for deliverance from this terrible event. Thus the story from Temple was to be read in the context that 'our danger was great, our deliverance was great and therefore we should endeavour to render to the Lord according to the great blessings we have received. This is the sum and substance of the following sermon.'[70] The sermon clearly enjoyed some success, and rather than becoming a piece of printed ephemera, was still on sale by Dublin booksellers two years later.[71]

The liturgy constructed for the 23 October commemoration and the 1662 act that authorised it, which was read on 23 October in parish churches, provided another context for the reading of Temple's work. In particular, it resolved ambiguities in Temple's interpretation of the events of the 1640s. While *The Irish Rebellion* was explicit that the rising was a punishment for sin, he did not specify the nature of that sin although

---

[67] BL, Sloane MSS 1008, f. 226.

[68] TCD, MS 865, ff. 190v–182 (foliation reversed).   [69] TCD, MS 813, f. 225.

[70] W[illiam] L[ightburne], *A Thanksgiving Sermon Preached at Christ Church Before the Lords Justice and Council upon 23 Oct. 1661* (Dublin, 1661), sigs. A3–4.

[71] It was advertised by Samuel Dancer in Jeremy Taylor, *A Discourse of Confirmation for the Use of the Clergy and Instruction of the People of Ireland* (Dublin, 1663), p. 91.

it was strongly implied that the sin was the toleration of Catholicism. In such a context, the king, as an agent of toleration, was guilty, and some of the Christ Church preachers made precisely this point in the 1640s. Similar sentiments may have led to the accusations of treason against Temple in 1643. However, the liturgy shifted the emphasis in this interpretation by defining the sin not as one of the state but a multitude of personal sins. According to the liturgy, the judgement of God was brought on Ireland by 'our neglect and contempt of thy sacred ordinances, our vain and false swearing . . . our unchristian charitableness and shameful intemperance, our sacrilege and covetousness, hypocrisy, slandering and deep security in the midst of all our sins and dangers'. Such an explanation allowed a reading of Temple that emphasised corporate repentance for personal sin. This allowed the message to be controlled and the text read in a particular way. For this reason, many of the sermons preached on 23 October came to have almost a ritualistic quality, emphasising the same framework for understanding massacre and deliverance.[72] In such ways might large audiences become acquainted with an approved version of the ideas presented in Temple's *Irish Rebellion*.

In the 1690s interest in Temple underwent something of a revival, as evidenced by the appearance of the first Dublin edition of *The Irish Rebellion* in 1698, which was bought by a number of Dubliners.[73] However, this reprinting does not seem to accord with an upsurge of anti-Catholic sentiment as was the pattern with later reprintings. Most of this interest can be accounted for by the success of the moral reading of the text outlined above. In the wake of the Jacobite attempt to control Ireland, Protestant theologians considered what had happened in 1688 and 1689 as a judgement of God upon Protestant Ireland, in the same way that Temple had interpreted the 1640s. A range of measures was resorted to, including the formation of Societies for the Reformation of Manners.[74] When preaching before these societies, clergy reiterated the need for moral reform so as to avert a further national judgement. That such preaching reached its peak the year Temple's work was reprinted was hardly a coincidence. Only one preacher, Alexander Sinclare, drew the message which Temple seemed to be implying, that judgement came from tolerating Catholics, the others preferring the sort of moral reading

---

[72] T. C. Barnard, 'The uses of 23 October 1641 and Irish Protestant celebrations', *EHR*, 106 (1991), pp. 889–920.

[73] For example Charles Willoughby's library list which contains titles to *c.* 1695 does not contain a copy of Temple (TCD, MS 10) yet a copy was later said to be missing from the library (TCD, MS 2087, under 'Mr Foley') which suggests that it may have been the 1698 Dublin printing.

[74] T. C. Barnard, 'Reforming Irish manners: the religious societies in Dublin during the 1690s', *Historical Journal*, 35 (1992), pp. 805–38.

associated with the liturgy for 23 October.[75] Preachers on 23 October warmed to the same theme. John Travers, for instance, preaching before the House of Commons on 23 October 1698, not only drew on the well-known stories of the ghostly apparitions on the River Bann, citing Temple as his source, but urged moral reform, without which there would be earthquakes, fire, pestilence or 'another Irish rebellion'.[76] The triumph of Temple's work in the 1690s provides a clear example of how it was reconstructed to meet the needs of a later generation of Irish Protestants.

IV

What Sir John Temple called for in the preface to *The Irish Rebellion* was the creation of a memory of what had happened in the 1640s. It was no coincidence that the order for the celebration of 23 October as a day of remembering the Irish plot was made in November 1642 while Temple was a member of the privy council.[77] The 1643 abstract of the depositions, discussed above, similarly emphasised the importance of recalling events of the early 1640s; in particular, the depositions served as 'a perpetual testimony of our suffering and their wickedness' which was 'never to be forgotten', so that Protestant Ireland would remain alert to Catholic plotting.[78] Temple also laid stress on the importance of the evidence of the depositions, and he claimed the Irish impugned the deposition evidence since it would 'perpetuate the memory of them to their eternal infamy'.[79] With a lawyer's concern for written proof, he was determined that the evidence should be remembered. The insurgents had wanted to destroy the records of the Dublin administration – even though, as Temple reminded his readers, 'to raze, to corrupt a record is a crime of a very high nature' – yet Catholic opinion wanted the indictments against them 'taken

---

[75] Thomas Pollard, *A Sermon Preached Before the Religious Societies in St Michael's Church, Dublin September the 25th 1698* (Dublin, 1698), p. 11; Peter Brown, *A Sermon Preached at St Bride's Church, Dublin, April 17 1698* (Dublin, 1698), pp. 25–9; Thomas Emlyn, *A Sermon Preached Before the Societies for the Reformation of Manners in Dublin: October the 4th 1698* (Dublin, 1698), p. 21; Joseph Boyse, *A Sermon Preach't Before the Societies for the Reformation of Manners in Dublin: Jan. 6 1697/8* (Dublin, 1698), pp. 7–9; Nathaniel Weld, *A Sermon Before the Societies for the Reformation of Manners in Dublin: Preached in New Row April the 26th 1698* (Dublin, 1698), pp. 16–17; Alexander Sinclare, *A Sermon Preach'd Before the Societies for the Reformation of Manners in Dublin, April the 11th 1699* (Dublin, 1699), pp. 9–17.

[76] John Travers, *A Sermon Preached in St Andrew's Church Dublin Before the Honourable House of Commons the Twenty Third of October 1698* (Dublin, 1698), pp. 7–9, 11–13.

[77] John Hennig, 'The Anglican Church in Ireland: prayers against the rebels', *Irish Ecclesiastical Record*, 5th ser. 64 (July–December 1944), pp. 247–8; HMC, *Ormonde MSS*, NS, II, p. 217.

[78] BL, Harley MSS 5999, f. 36.   [79] Temple, *Irish Rebellion*, sig. b1.

off the file and cancelled'.[80] Preserving records, and therefore memory, was of paramount importance, so that in the early weeks of the rising when Dublin Castle had become 'a common repository of all things of value' one of the valuables of Protestant Ireland, 'the rolls were by special order removed thither, the records of several other offices were likewise brought in'.[81] In this concern for the preservation of records, Temple was not unique. Four years later, Thomas Waring demanded that the events of 1641 in Ulster 'be known not only to this age but to the children that are yet to be born it is held fit that such discoveries as have been brought to them [the Cromwellian commissioners] should clearly and freely be brought to light that all men might bear witness against those savages against whom the blood of so many innocents cries beneath the altar'.[82] Waring's response was to publish his 1650 tract, which was intended as a 'forerunner' of 'a large volume' of the depositions themselves.[83]

This venture into print by both Temple and Waring marked a new departure in an Irish context, although it was accepted practice in England. Writing, and particularly print, preserved memory. As the Dublin Presbyterian minister, Robert Chambers, expressed it in 1680, 'Writing is of singular use to keep things on record which else would be forgotten and to extend the use to many even to such as are yet unborn.'[84] The desire of the emerging Anglo-Irish in the years after 1660 to remember their own history, both recent and more remote, may well have been one of the impetuses behind the wave of print which engulfed the country in ships from Bristol and Chester. However, the world of print was not as simple as men such as Temple and Waring might have thought. There were many different memories of what had happened in the 1640s and some of these were contested. Printed texts constructed around one of those memories, such as that of massacre, had a relatively short shelf life. Temple's work, however, was so constructed that it could be read in many different ways by diverse groups of people. Thus, it had a longer existence, not for what it said but rather because of the flexibility with which it could be used in reconstructing memories of the past. Its repeated crossing of genre boundaries, between history, massacre literature and a providential narrative variously interpreted, made it an ideal work for use by scholars, preachers and polemicists to express their own reading of

---

[80] *Ibid.*, sigs. a3, b1–b1v.
[81] *Ibid.*, part 1, p. 63. The records of Christ Church were moved to the castle at the same time, Gillespie, 'Crisis of reform', p. 205.
[82] W[aring], *A Brief Narration*, sig. A3v.
[83] Aidan Clarke, 'The 1641 depositions' in Peter Fox (ed.), *Treasures of the Library, Trinity College, Dublin* (Dublin, 1996), pp. 113–14.
[84] Union Theological College, Belfast, MS, 'Explication of the Shorter Catechism' by Mr Robert Chambre, 1680, f. A2.

the text. While for most of the book-buying public the text was, in an unexpurgated form, problematic, when read in the context of a liturgy or political narrative it became safe and was appropriated by a 'textual community' which understood the book within its own set of presuppositions. In this way, Temple's story is not a window into the unchanging Protestant mind or an official history of the 1640s, but rather a provider of the raw material from which Protestant memories were shaped and reshaped over generations.

16   Conquest *versus* consent as the basis of the English title to Ireland in William Molyneux's *Case of Ireland . . . Stated* (1698)

Patrick Kelly

William Molyneux's *The Case of Ireland's being bound by Acts of Parliament in England, Stated* (1698) is generally regarded as the key text in discrediting the claim that English rights over Ireland rested on the conquest carried out by Henry II in 1171–72, a presumption then widely current, not only in England but also amongst those whom for reasons of convenience (if perhaps not strict accuracy) we may term the Anglo-Irish.[1] In its place Molyneux argued that the submission of the Irish kings to Henry had been entirely voluntary and that in return Henry had conferred upon them the benefits of English laws and customs, including the right of holding parliaments. Moreover, by terming the agreement between Henry and the Irish the 'Original Compact' of the English government in Ireland, Molyneux assimilated his narrative to the language of Revolution principles which carried such weight in both England and Ireland after 1688.[2] Finally, he sought to ground Ireland's status as a possession of the English crown, but independent of the English parliament, on the universal, natural right to consent to government, thereby

A brief version of this chapter was presented at the Trinity College, Dublin, conference, 24 March 2000, and an extended draft at a seminar at the Keough Institute for Irish Studies, University of Notre Dame, Indiana, 25 June 2001. I am grateful to the participants in the ensuing discussion, particularly Professor Christopher B. Fox (director) and Professor Jim Smyth, for making me aware of the need for clarification of various points.

[1] Molyneux was by no means the first Irish writer to deny that Henry's title to Ireland had been based on conquest. The notion that the Irish were a free, i.e. unconquered people, had been prevalent amongst both Catholics and Protestants in the early 1640s; Michael Perceval-Maxwell, *The Outbreak of the Irish Rebellion of 1641* (Dublin, 1994), pp. 164–76. Later English thinkers tended to remain unconvinced by Molyneux's arguments, and a classic formulation of the title through conquest is provided in William Blackstone, *Commentaries on the Laws of England* [1765–69] (17th edn, 4 vols., London, 1830), I, pp. 99–101. Even some Irish writers still adhered to conquest theory, e.g. the Regius Professor of Laws at Trinity College, Dublin, Francis Stoughton Sullivan, *An Historical Treatise on the Feudal Law, and the Constitution and Laws of England* (London, 1777), p. 239.

[2] William Molyneux, *The Case of Ireland's Being Bound by Acts of Parliament in England, Stated* (Dublin, 1698), pp. 37–8. In text page references for citations from *The Case* are henceforth given in parentheses, e.g. '(p. 29)'.

making Ireland's case not just a local issue but an assertion of what he termed 'the Inherent Right of *all Mankind*' (p. 3). However, closer examination shows Molyneux's arguments to be considerably less transparent than they might at first seem. For all his seeming rejection of conquest as the basis of England's title to Ireland, Molyneux was forced to readmit conquest and arguments deriving from conquest theory at a crucial point in his account of the establishment of English power in Ireland, namely to fit the Anglo-Irish themselves into his story. But, having done so, he was able to justify the subsequent deprivation of the Catholic Irish of their property on a far more incontrovertible basis than a title based on conquest could provide, thus establishing the Irish Protestants as the true inheritors of the constitution granted by Henry II in 1171–72.

I

Before examining the debate as to whether the English title to Ireland rested on conquest or on consent, something must be said about the theoretical basis of how the seventeenth century understood states or rulers could legitimately acquire new territories. The most important legal tradition for English and Anglo-Irish thinkers was that of the common law, in which the primary means of acquiring territory was either by *inheritance* or by *conquest*. The consequent assumption that everything that had not been acquired by inheritance must have been acquired by conquest reflected the origins of the common-law theory of acquisition as an extrapolation of principles dealing with private real property to the actions of states. The result was that conquest was a wide-ranging category extending from full military subjection at one end of the spectrum to straightforward purchase at the other, with the latter being undoubtedly the more common meaning. By contrast, in the tradition represented by Roman law and its increasingly important offshoot the *jus gentium*, or law of nations, conquest as a title to new territory was largely (though never exclusively) thought of in terms of military subjection. Such a conqueror acquired rights over the persons and property of the conquered, together with the right to impose new laws on the conquered.[3]

[3] See further, Barbara Black, 'The constitution of empire: the case for the colonists', *University of Pennsylvania Law Review*, 124 (1976), pp. 1177–91; Hans Pawlisch, *Sir John Davies and the Conquest of Ireland* (Cambridge, 1985), pp. 8–11; Sharon Korman, *The Right of Conquest: the acquisition of territory by force in international law and practice* (Oxford, 1996), chapters 1–2, and Richard Tuck, *The Rights of War and Peace: political thought and the international order from Grotius to Kant* (Oxford, 1999). Sir Matthew Hale, *The Prerogatives of the King*, ed. D. E. C. Yale (Selden Society, London, 1976), pp. 3–5, offers a useful mid-seventeenth-century overview of the Common-Law theory of acquisition, followed by specific consideration of Ireland, pp. 32–5.

In the common-law tradition the categories of inheritance and conquest further admitted the important subcategories of donation in the case of inheritance, and consent or compact for conquest.[4] While the relationship between donation and inheritance is fairly unproblematic, one gift being *inter vivos* and the other on decease, the link between conquest and compact may seem at first sight rather puzzling. Under the influence of the liberal tradition, we tend to think of the concepts of consent and conquest as wholly opposed to each other. For us, consent enjoys moral credibility as a basis for title, while conquest is regarded as questionable, if not indefensible, despite its recognised status in international law until the early twentieth century.[5] For the seventeenth century, however, the answer to the conundrum lay in what was regarded as the essential element in conquest from which the right to possession or dominion derived. To many thinkers (including Thomas Hobbes), the right of conquest derived not from the subjugation of the conquered but from their submission, which, though in practice scarcely voluntary, was held to be tantamount to a form of consent.[6] From this perspective, transferring the right to rule over a people through voluntary consent or compact could therefore be understood as a subcategory of conquest. The status of such consent remained, however, rather equivocal, as can be seen from Hugo Grotius's comment that 'a Surrender doth but voluntarily yield up, what would otherwise be taken away by force';[7] while John Locke – and following him Molyneux – would challenge the attempt to capitalise on the equation of submission with consent as a confidence trick.[8]

Moreover, for (military) conquest to constitute a valid basis for title to territory, certain subsidiary conditions had also to be fulfilled. The most important was that the conqueror had to have some prior right to the territory in question in order to make the conquest a just one, rather than an act of mere aggression.[9] Such rights corresponded to the causes of waging a just war, though opinions as to what constituted a just

---

[4] Cf. Hale, *Prerogatives of the King*, pp. 3–4. He also acknowledges an intrinsic title based on compact or consent, but what is of relevance here are what Hale specifies as extrinsic titles.

[5] Cf. Korman, *Right of Conquest*, pp. 7–8.

[6] Thomas Hobbes, *Leviathan*, ed. C. B. MacPherson (Harmondsworth, 1968), pp. 255–6; Hale, *Prerogatives of the King*, pp. 3–4.

[7] Hugo Grotius, *De Jure Belli ac Pacis, Libri Tres* [London, 1625], book III, chapter 8, section 1, trans. John Morris *et al.* (3 vols., London, 1715), III, p. 142.

[8] John Locke, *Two Treatises of Government*, ed. Peter Laslett (Cambridge, 1960); *Second Treatise*, section 186. Henceforth cited in the form '*Treatises*, II, 186'; Molyneux, *Case*, pp. 25–6. See further pp. 349–50 below.

[9] Cf. Locke, *Two Treatises*, II, p. 176: 'he that *Conquers in an unjust War can thereby have no Title to the Subjection and Obedience of the Conquered*'.

right in this context varied considerably. Grotius, for example, held that a just conqueror could acquire territory through (*inter alia*) punishing a third party's violation of the laws of nature.[10] Others, such as Samuel Pufendorf, held that the conquered had actually to have wronged the conqueror himself rather than a third party; while, by contrast, less exigent commentators went so far as to admit pre-emptive action or even the pursuit of glory among justifiable causes for war.[11] Other conditions arose from the nature of conquest itself. In order to constitute a valid title to territory, it was generally thought necessary that the conquest should be complete and thoroughgoing, and followed through by the imposition of actual control over the conquered territory.[12]

When we turn to how these concepts were applied to the understanding of England's title to rule over the Irish, it is clear that since the English title did not derive from inheritance it must therefore be seen in the common-law context to derive from conquest. The alternative interpretation of Henry's right to Ireland in virtue of the papal donation of 1155 (deriving from the pope's supposed ownership of the world's islands) was scarcely likely to appeal to either English or Anglo-Irish Protestants, and references to it are sparse.[13] But when English thinkers applied the category of conquest to Ireland, they almost invariably did so in terms of a hostile military conquest – that is, in the *jus gentium* sense of conferring on Henry II the right to the lives and property of the Irish, together with the right to impose whatever laws he saw fit. Moreover, this pejorative interpretation of Henry's rights as a conqueror was asserted even by those who were prepared to concede that Henry had not actually fought the Irish, much less defeated them, and that the rulers of Ireland had submitted to him

---

[10] Grotius, *De Jure Belli ac Pacis*, book II, chapter 1, sections 2–3 (trans. 1715, II, pp. 56–7); chapter 20, esp. sections 27–8 (*ibid.*, pp. 502–30).

[11] Samuel Pufendorf, *De Iure Naturæ et Gentium* [Lund, 1672], book 8, chapter 6, section 3, trans. Basil Kennet (2nd edn, London, 1717), p. 88; Tuck, *Rights of War and Peace*, pp. 28–31, 158–61.

[12] Cf. Sir John Davies, *A Discoverie of True Causes why Ireland was Never Entirely Subdued* (London, 1612), pp. 6–8; Hale, *Prerogatives of the King*, p. 4. The problem of an incomplete Norman conquest of Ireland is also raised in Giraldus Cambrensis, *Expugnatio Hibernica: The Conquest of Ireland*, ed. A. B. Scott and F. X. Martin (RIA, Dublin, 1978), pp. 231–3, 249.

[13] The papal grant is mentioned straightforwardly in [Sir Richard Bolton], 'A Declaration setting forth how, and by what Means, the Laws and Statutes of England, from Time to Time, came to be of force in Ireland', *Hibernica*, ed. Walter Harris, part II (Dublin, 1750), p. 18. William Atwood, *The History, and Reasons of the Dependency of Ireland upon the Imperial Crown of the Kingdom of England* (London, 1698), pp. 11–12, 38–9, gets around its ideological unpalatableness by equating papal authority with 'the then general consent of Nations'. Hale, *Prerogatives of the King*, pp. 33–4, refers to the bull *Laudabiliter* of 1155 and the papal confirmation of Henry's grant to John in 1177 but denies their relevance to England's title to Ireland.

on a voluntary basis. Apart from the obvious temptations of expediency, it is by no means clear why this should have been the case for thinkers operating in the common-law tradition.[14] The *jus gentium*, however, held that 'voluntary' submission in the face of overwhelming military threat was fully equivalent to military subjugation in battle, and the army which had accompanied Henry in 1171–72 had indeed been a substantial one.[15] However, a number of those who thought in terms of an initial conquest of Ireland by Henry II went on to claim that the Irish princes' voluntary acceptance of English law on their submission to Henry established a secondary title to Ireland through consent as well as conquest.[16]

The crucial precedent for establishing Ireland's status as a conquered territory in English law in the seventeenth century was Sir Edward Coke's judgement in Calvin's Case (as recorded in his *Seventh Report*) in 1608: 'Albeit Ireland was a distinct Dominion [from England], yet the title thereof being by conquest, the same by judgement of law might by express words be bound by the parliaments of England.'[17] Its definitive standing in the Restoration era can be seen in Chief Justice Vaughan's judgement in *Crawe vs. Ramsey* in 1672 that 'That [Ireland] is a Conquered Kingdom is not doubted, but is admitted in Calvin's Case several times.'[18] Coke's judgement is also of importance in distinguishing between Ireland's position as a consequence of Henry II's conquest and that of territories occupied at the expense of native peoples in the New World. In Ireland, as the conquest of a Christian kingdom, the existing laws were held to remain in force until the conqueror imposed new ones. Once this had been done, the conqueror was not at liberty to vary these new laws without the consent of the conquered.[19] In the case of a

---

[14] Cf. paper listing objections to the English Lords' *coram non judice* verdict in the bishop of Derry's appeal, *c.* May 1698, item 5: 'Because a Conqueror by the Laws of England and of nations having power to introduce what laws he will in the Conquered Country . . .'; TCD, MS 1180, ff. 7–9.

[15] Grotius, *De Jure Belli*, book III, chapter 8, section 1 (as n. 7 above). Cf. Hale, *Prerogatives of the King*, pp. 33–4, on submission in the face of overwhelming force as equivalent to conquest.

[16] See citation from Cox, *Aphorisms*, p. 339 below. Hale, *Prerogatives of the King*, p. 5, considers a 'mixed acquisition' of this kind as a particularly compelling form of title, 'though it be the consequence of force on the one side, and fear on the other'.

[17] Coke, *La Sept Part des Reports de Sir Edw. Coke Chivalier, chiefe Iustice del Common Bank* (London, 1608), p. 17b. A number of Irish statutes referred to Ireland's having been conquered by the current ruler's ancestors – notably the 1569 Act of Attainder of Shane O'Neill, 11 Eliz. Sess. 3, c. 1 (see further p. 343 below), and the 1613 Act of Repeale of diverse Statutes concerning the Natives of this Kingdom (11, 12 & 13 Jas. I, c. 5).

[18] Sir John Vaughan, *The Reports and Arguments of the Learned Judge, Sir John Vaughan, Kt* (2nd edn, London, 1714), p. 292. Cf. Coke, *The Fourth Part of the Institutes of the Laws of England* (1644), p. 349.

[19] The implications of this doctrine for Ireland are considered in Molyneux, *Case*, p. 122, in relation to John's grant of English law in 1210.

heathen kingdom, however, the laws were forthwith voided following a just conquest, as offensive to God and natural law.[20]

Belief that the English title to Ireland rested on conquest was not, of course, confined to Englishmen, but held attractions for the Anglo-Irish as well. Numerous well-known examples can be cited throughout the seventeenth century from Archbishop Ussher in the 1610s to William Petty in the 1680s.[21] Fresh impetus to the discussion of the basis of the English title to Ireland was provided by the Revolution of 1688. While the country remained under a government different from that of England, Irish Protestant anxiety to regain control of their polity and their property encouraged resort to the doctrine of conquest. This form of title both provided a convenient imperative for reconquest and identified their cause with England's strategic interest, while at the same time differentiating the colonists' position from that of the native Irish – a distinction not always as self-evident to Englishmen as the Anglo-Irish would have wished. England's original acquisition of Ireland through the conquest effected by Henry II in 1172 was therefore a standard trope of the prolific literature produced by colonist exiles in Britain. The most sophisticated presentation of the conquest theory was in Sir Richard Cox's two-volume history, *Hibernia Anglicana* (1689–90), whose arguments were conveniently summarised in his *Aphorisms Relating to the Kingdom of Ireland* (1689). The latter spoke of a title 'by a lawful Conquest in a just War, and by the [subsequent] repeated Oaths and voluntary Submissions of the *Irish* Potentates and Gentry in all Ages, and by several Statutes of Recognition, and Acts of Parliament in that Kingdom, and by above Five Hundred Years Prescription'.[22]

Once the war was over, the disadvantages of conceding an original conquest came to outweigh the short-term utility of the title through conquest for the Anglo-Irish. It became apparent that for some Englishmen the hidden subtext of the imposition of English government in Ireland through a hostile conquest in 1171–72 was that the form of government

---

[20] Coke, *Seventh Report*, 17b; see further Robert A. Williams Jr, *The American Indian in Western Legal Thought: the discourse of conquest* (New York and Oxford, 1990), pp. 202–4.

[21] Cf. James Ussher, 'Of the first establishment of English laws and parliaments in the Kingdom of Ireland, October 11th 1611' in *Collectanea Curiosa . . .* , ed. John Gutch (2 vols., 1781), I, p. 24; Sir John Temple, *The Irish Rebellion* (London, 1646), pp. 3–5; Edmund Borlase, *The Reduction of Ireland to the Crown of England* (London, 1675), Intro., A2v; Sir William Petty, 'The state of the case between England and Ireland (?1686)' in *The Petty Papers*, ed. marquis of Lansdowne (2 vols., London, 1927; reprint New York, 1967), I, p. 57.

[22] Richard Cox, *Hibernia Anglicana* (London, 1689), Epistle Dedicatory; Cox, *Aphorisms Relating to the Kingdom of Ireland* (London, 1689), p. 1; Edward Whetenhall, *The Case of the Irish Protestants . . .* (London, 1691), p. 6; William King, *The State of the Protestants in Ireland under the late King James's Government* (London, 1691), pp. 21–2, 88, 108–9.

in Ireland could be legitimately altered following the reconquest of 1690–91 to make it more directly dependent on England like the other colonies and plantations. Likewise, the claim that the English parliament was a partner with the crown in the conquest of 1171–72 was seen to entitle it to share in the disposal of the forfeited estates of the Jacobites after the war. Such views were voiced in debates on Ireland in both houses of the English parliament in the spring of 1693, but the indecisive conclusion had allowed William to dispose of these estates without further consultation.[23] Yet with the ending of the war against the French in 1697 the issue of forfeited Jacobite estates in Ireland resurfaced and the Anglo-Irish who had acquired *bona fide* interests through their disposal were deeply anxious over the prospect of resumption by an English act of parliament. This concern surfaces in *The Case* through the strident repudiation of the notion that the English parliament had somehow or other 'purchased' Ireland by paying for the suppression of the recent rebellion of the 'Irish Papists' (pp. 142–5).

II

Since Molyneux considered that the basis of the English parliament's claim to legislate for Ireland derived primarily from what he termed 'the *Imaginary Title of Conquest*' (p. 4), the issue of conquest was of central significance to *The Case of Ireland, Stated*. It is scarcely surprising, therefore, that his strategy should have been to restrict the meaning of conquest to military subjugation and to refuse to acknowledge at any point in his treatise that Henry's acquisition of Ireland could be termed a conquest.[24] This he set out to do by defining conquest as '*an Acquisition of a Kingdom by Force of Arms, to which Force likewise has been Opposed*', going on to say: 'If we are to understand Conquest in any other Sense, I see not of what Use it can be made against *Irelands* being a Free Country. I know *Conquestus* signifies a Peaceable Acquisition, as well as an Hostile Subjugating of an Enemy. *Vid. Spelman's Glos.*' (pp. 12–13).[25] Interpreting the acquisition of Ireland as a hostile conquest was, moreover, as Molyneux pointed out, in striking contrast to the way in which most Englishmen

---

[23] Narcissus Luttrell, *The Parliamentary Diary of Narcissus Luttrell, 1691–1693*, ed. Henry Horwitz (Oxford, 1972), pp. 438–43.

[24] For the one surreptitious but crucial exception, see pp. 350–1 below.

[25] It is not surprising that this attempt to restrict the definition of conquest should have been among the thirty-two extracts from *The Case* singled out for censure by the English Commons in June 1698: *Commons Journals [England]*, XII, pp. 325–6. Cf. Henry Spelman, *Glossarium Archaiologicum* (London, 1687), s.v. *Conquestus*: 'William I is called the Conqueror because he conquered England, i.e. acquired . . . it, not because he subdued it.'

understood William of Normandy's acquisition of the English throne in 1066, holding it not to have entailed a conquest – regardless of the battle of Hastings. Englishmen's reasons for denying that a conquest of England took place in 1066 turned on the right of a conqueror to substitute his own laws for those of the conquered. If there had been a hostile Norman conquest, continuity between post-conquest England and the laws of the free Saxon past would have been broken, and the immemorial common law of England reduced to the whim of a conqueror. The question was therefore of considerable ideological importance, and in its most recent manifestation in the Brady controversy of the early 1680s, the debate over what happened in 1066 had seen the proponents of the conquest inter-pretation such as Robert Brady denounced as champions of monarchical absolutism.[26]

To counter the claim that the English title to Ireland rested on Henry II's conquest of 1172, Molyneux set out to use the evidence of contempo-rary historians, Giraldus Cambrensis, Roger Hoveden, John Brompton and Matthew Paris, to show that, far from being a military conquest, Henry had acquired 'this Kingdom . . . without the least Hostile Stroke on any side' (p. 13). The source on which Molyneux chiefly relies, Giral-dus Cambrensis's *Expugnatio Hibernica*, is not only the fullest contem-porary account of the Norman invasion of Ireland available, but also the one which most consistently depicts the submission of the Irish rulers to Henry II as voluntary.[27] However, when we compare Molyneux's relation of Giraldus with the actual text of the *Expugnatio*, we find a highly selec-tive reading which has filtered out all remaining references that might suggest that the Irish submission to the English king was other than total or less than entirely voluntary. Moreover, Molyneux exaggerates the value of Giraldus as a witness by claiming that he had accompanied Henry's

---

[26] See J. G. A. Pocock, *Fundamental Law* (2nd edn, Cambridge, 1987), pp. 393–409. One of the more sophisticated attempts to avoid the consequences of a conquest in 1066, while acknowledging the inescapable fact of the battle of Hastings, was the distinction between a conquest *in regem* and a conquest *in populum* made in Hale, *Prerogatives of the King*, pp. 4–5, 62–3. In the former instance since war had been made only against the ruler, the existing laws, institutions and property rights remained intact. Hale's opportunism, however, is exposed by his assertion (p. 32) that Henry II's conquest of Ireland in 1172 was a conquest *in populum*.

[27] The history of the text of the *Expugnatio* is extremely complex, see Scott's introduction to the 1978 edition (see n. 12 above), pp. xl–lxxv. The 1603 edition of William Camden, in *Anglica, Normannica, Hibernica, Cambrica, a Veteribus Scripta* (Frankfurt, 1603), which Molyneux used (cf. *Case*, p. 16), contains significant additions by Giraldus that do not figure in the early version which Scott has chosen as his copy-text (though they are recorded in the *apparatus criticus*). For comparison of Giraldus with other contempo-rary histories of the invasion, see Marie-Therese Flanagan, *Irish Society, Anglo-Norman Settlers, Angevin Kingship: interactions in Ireland in the late twelfth century* (Oxford, 1989), pp. 170–4, 199–201.

expedition to Ireland in 1172 as the king's 'Historiographer' (p. 7). In point of fact, while many of the earliest Normans to reach Ireland were Giraldus's close kinfolk, he himself did not actually go to Ireland till 1184, nor did he enter regular royal employment till the late 1180s, though he had accompanied Prince John's expedition of 1185–6.[28]

Most notably, Molyneux represents Giraldus as recounting that the Irish rulers submitted to Henry II in the most binding fashion, and in particular that the high-king, Rory O'Connor (Ruaidrí Ua Conchobair), did homage in person to Henry at Dublin, thereby symbolising the submission of the entire nation to the English king. In actual fact, Giraldus not only relates something more akin to a treaty with O'Connor, negotiated through envoys on the banks of the Shannon (though he does emphasise that O'Connor's submission symbolised the submission of the nation as a whole), but also expressly states that the rulers of Ulster did not join in the general submission to the English king.[29] When we investigate further, this revised version of Giraldus's account of Henry's dealings with the Irish in *The Case* interestingly turns out not to have originated with Molyneux, nor even with his father-in-law, Sir William Domville, from whose paper, 'A Disquisition touching that Great Question Whether an Act of Parliament made in England shall binde the Kingdome, and people of Ireland without theire Allowance and Acceptance of such Act in the Kingdome of Ireland' (1660), Molyneux had copied most of this material. Instead it draws, in places verbatim, on the account of Henry's conquest of Ireland retailed in the Elizabethan statute for the attainder of Shane O'Neill (11 Eliz., sess. 3, c. 1) – as Domville, though not Molyneux, acknowledged.[30] Added importance is given to this parallel by the fact that at the time O'Neill's attainder was passed in 1569 no printed version of Giraldus's *Expugnatio* had yet appeared (either in translation or the original Latin).[31] The lengthy 1569 act included a recital of Elizabeth's various titles to the sovereignty of Ireland, the fourth of which was stated

[28] Scott's introduction to *Expugnatio*, 1978 edn, pp. xii–xx. N. B. Giraldus and his contemporaries date Henry's expedition to 1172–73 rather than 1171–72.

[29] Molyneux, *Case*, pp. 7–12. Cf. *Expugnatio*, 1978 edn, chapter 33 (pp. 94–6 and *apparatus criticus*).

[30] Domville, 'Disquisition' (TCD, MS 890, ff. 45r–59r), p. 8, which cites (*inter alia*) a clause from the act: 'for the Chronicles make no mention of any Warr or Chivalry don by King H.2. All that Time he was in Ireland . . . Saith the Act of Parliament 11⁰ Elizabethæ Cap. 1⁰.'

[31] An English precis of the *Expugnatio* is found in the 1577 edition of Holingshed's *Chronicle* (which differs considerably from the version in the 1569 act), and a complete translation of the work in the 1587 edn. The first Latin text was printed in the 1602 edition of Camden's *Anglica, Normannica, Hibernica . . .* (reprinted the following year). See Scott, introduction to *Expugnatio*, 1978 edition, pp. xl–lxxiii, which also refers to manuscript translations and abbreviations.

to have been derived from Giraldus' account of the Irish submission to Henry II, later going on to refer to having obtained its knowledge of Giraldus from 'a short collection of this his historie'.[32] Significantly, the list of kings which Molyneux provides as having submitted to Henry at Dublin ('*Macshaglin* King of *Ophaly, O Carrol* King of *Uriel . . . O Rourk* King of *Meath*, [and] *Rotherick O Connor* King of *Connaught*, and *Monarch* as it were of the whole Island' (p. 9)) agrees with the shortened list of names given in the 1569 act as submitting at Dublin (with the exception of Macshaglin, whose submission the act places at Cashel).[33] However, though what Molyneux and Domville retail is identical to the claims in the Elizabethan act, the various passages quoted by them are in Latin, while the act itself is entirely in English. The most important and extensive of the Latin passages is that referring to Rory O'Connor's submission to Henry as symbolising in his person the submission of the whole of Ireland: 'in singulari Rotherico Conactiæ Principe tamquam Insulæ Monarchâ subditi redduntur universi, nec alicujus fere in Insula vel nominis vel ominis erat qui Regiæ Majestati & Debitam Domino Reverentiam, non exhiberet' (pp. 9–10). This particular extract does not correspond at all closely to the English of the 1569 act, but seemingly comes from the full text of the *Expugnatio*, which Molyneux subsequently claims to cite from William Camden's edition of 1603. On closer investigation, however, the passage differs from Camden's text in significant respects, notably in leaving out the reference to the omission of the Ulster rulers and in not describing Rory as 'chief of the Irish' (*Hibernensium capite*), as well as in other less important details.[34]

This selective reading of Giraldus is followed by supposedly corroborating extracts from the contemporary and near-contemporary historians:

---

[32] *The Statutes of Ireland, beginning the 3rd yeare of k. Edward III . . . untill the 13th yeare of k. James I*, ed. Sir Richard Bolton (Dublin, 1621), pp. 316–17.

[33] *Case*, p. 9 (italics in original). Since Macshaglin's was the last name mentioned in the act prior to those listed for Dublin, its inclusion more probably reflects hasty reading rather than reliance on a different source. The full list of rulers who submitted to Henry provided in the *Expugnatio* is the most extensive contemporary account; see Flanagan, *Irish Society, Anglo-Norman Settlers, Angevin Kingship*, appendix 2. Edmund Campion, *A History of Ireland* (London, 1633), p. 61, names the same four kings as submitting at Dublin and also asserts O'Connor came to Dublin to submit to Henry 'for himselfe, and the whole Island'. For Campion's role in the drafting of the 1569 act, see chapter 2 above.

[34] Molyneux, *Case*, pp. 9–10. Cf. *Expugnatio*, ed. Camden, 1603, p. 750: 'Qui . . . firmissimis de fidelitatis et subiectionis vinculis innodarunt. Sic itaque praeter solos Ultonienses, subditi per se singuli. Sic et in singulari, Rotherico scilicet Connactiæ Principe, et tamquam Hibernensium capite et insulæ Monarcha: subditi redduntur universi. Nec alicuius fere in Insula vel nominis erat vel ominis, qui Regiæ Maiestati, vel sui presentiam, vel debitam Domino Reverentiam, non exhiberet.' The phrase reading 'Rotherico . . . Monarcha', represents material added by Giraldus to the later versions of the *Expugnatio*; see 1978 edn, p. 96, *app. crit.*

Roger Hoveden, John Brompton and Matthew Paris. Some of these too turn out to omit similar qualifications as to the total submission of the Irish to Henry, such as Hoveden's important exception of Rory O'Connor (*praeter Roger de Conacto*) among those who submitted to Henry, and his statement that the ecclesiastics who submitted at Waterford had come at the king's command (*ad mandatum regis*).[35] Furthermore, Molyneux's account of Henry's settling the state of the Irish church at the synod of Cashel fails to mention the moral and doctrinal shortcomings which Giraldus details as establishing the necessity of the English king's reforms.[36] Molyneux presumably omitted this material because any reference to the need for reform or to the barbarity of the Irish (as found for example in Stanihurst's *De Rebus in Hibernia Gestis*) would have been seen as underwriting the notion of a conquest rather than a free and voluntary submission by the Irish.[37] The papal bull *Laudabiliter* of 1155 had earlier cited the need to reform the Irish church as justification for England's forcible appropriation of Ireland.[38]

A major difficulty for the interpretation of Henry II's dealings with the Irish in terms of a voluntary submission to the English king, followed by his grant to them of English laws and customs, was the lack of documentation in the form of charters or grants confirming Henry's concession. This objection had been raised earlier in the seventeenth century by Serjeant Samuel Mayart, who (in a manuscript seemingly unknown to Molyneux) asserted that the only accounts of Henry's grant came from 'histories written by *Monks*, or other men, who understand not the laws'.[39] Molyneux's solution to this lacuna serves both to provide what he regards as authentic confirmation of Henry's grant to the Irish and to emphasise the principle of consent underlying the Irish constitution, in

---

[35] Molyneux, *Case*, pp. 10–11. Roger Hoveden, or Howden, was a royal clerk who presumably obtained information directly from those who had accompanied Henry to Ireland. All contemporary accounts other than Giraldus recount Rory O'Connor's submission to Henry as taking place through envoys and away from Dublin, a version of affairs seemingly confirmed by the events of the Treaty of Windsor. See Flanagan, *Irish Society, Anglo-Norman Settlers, Angevin Kingship*, pp. 230–4. Another instance of Domville/Molyneux's tampering with the sources is found in the citation from Matthew Paris, *Historia Maior* (1640 edn), p. 126, where the bishops and archbishops of Ireland are said 'to have received Henry as king and lord [of Ireland], and sworn fealty and homage to him' (original citation in *Case* (1698), p. 11, in Latin; trans. from 1776 edn), though the phrase reading '& *Homagium*' is not found in Paris's text.

[36] Cf. *Expugnatio*, 1978 edn, pp. 97–9.

[37] Richard Stanihurst, *De Rebus in Hibernia Gestis. Libri Quattuor* (Antwerp, 1584), pp. 128–9.

[38] Text in Giraldus, *Expugnatio*, 1978 edn, pp. 144–6. See further, Flanagan, *Irish Society, Anglo-Norman Settlers, Angevin Kingship*, pp. 52–4.

[39] Samuel Mayart, 'Serjeant Mayart's Answer to a Book Intitled, A Declaration . . . by Sir Richard Bolton' in *Hibernica*, ed. Harris, II, p. 24.

terms of what he subsequently calls 'the Great *Law of Parliaments* . . . By [which] I mean that Law whereby all Laws receive their Sanction, [from] *The Free Debates and Consent of the People, by Themselves or their Chosen Representatives*' (p. 56).[40] The evidence is the Irish *Modus Tenendi Parliamenta*, which Molyneux, despite the diplomatic criticism of Selden and Prynne, accepts as the authentic product of Henry II, adapted from the original *Modus* which Edward the Confessor produced for England in Saxon times. The Irish *Modus*, rediscovered by the antiquary William Hakewill in the early seventeenth century, was, however, accepted as genuine by Coke in his *Fourth Institute* and was published in 1692 by Molyneux's brother-in-law, Anthony Dopping, bishop of Meath.[41] Together with two further documents, King John's famous (but long missing) charter granting English law to the Irish on his second visit to the country in 1210, and the Irish Magna Carta of 1216 (known through its reissue in 1227), the Irish *Modus* constitutes for Molyneux the core of an Irish version of the 'ancient constitution' myth so cherished by the those of broadly Whig ideology in the seventeenth century.[42]

In terms of selling his argument for Ireland's legislative independence to what Molyneux evidently regarded as the potentially sympathetic constituency of English Whigs, this Irish ancient constitution ironically turned out to be a severe liability. As the combined voices of his three earliest critics, John Cary, William Atwood and Simon Clement, make abundantly clear, far from fitting in with English Whig ideology, Molyneux's Irish ancient constitution was seen as undermining the status of the English ancient constitution, in that Molyneux claimed the Irish version had been granted by Henry II independently of the English parliament.[43] This claim, which so cavalierly ignored the pretensions of the English parliament of their own time, led to Molyneux's being denounced as an advocate of royal absolutism, 'another Brady' as Atwood expressed

---

[40] Cf. the extract describing the right to consent to law as a 'Universal *Law of Nature*' from *Case* by William Molyneux, p. 48, cited on p. 346 below. This right is subsequently equated with the consent that establishes political societies, on which 'depends the *Obligation* of all *Humane Laws*; insomuch that without it, by the Unanimous Opinion of all *Jurists*, no Sanctions are of any *Force*'; *ibid.*, pp. 150–1.

[41] *Case*, pp. 29–36. Anthony Dopping (ed.), *Modus Tenendi Parliamenta et Concilia in Hibernia* (Dublin, 1692), preface. See further, Nicholas Pronay and John Taylor (eds.), *Parliamentary Texts of the Later Middle Ages* (Oxford, 1980), pp. 107–23.

[42] Molyneux, *Case*, pp. 44–9, 54–5. An interesting conspectus of the English ancient constitution in terms of fundamental laws is found in *ibid.*, 58–63.

[43] John Cary, *A Vindication of the Parliament of England, in Answer to a Book Written by Molyneux, of Dublin, Esquire* . . . (Bristol, 1698); Atwood, *History of the Dependency* (1698), and [Simon Clement], *An Answer to Mr Molyneux his Case of Ireland's Being Bound* . . . (1698); the same point is made in the (generally overlooked) response to Molyneux in Charles Davenant, *An Essay upon the Probable Methods of Making the People Gainers in the Balance of Trade* (London, 1699), pp. 106–20.

it.[44] What Molyneux had failed to appreciate was that English Whigs saw their ancient constitution as the ancient constitution not merely of England alone but of all the dominions of the English crown. They conceived the Angevin monarchy not as a disparate agglomeration of territories in France, Ireland, Scotland and Wales, owing allegiance to the English ruler, but as an 'English Empire' (to use the term employed in Simon Clement's *Answer to Mr Molyneux*) ruling over all the dependencies of the crown much as the English parliament aspired to rule over them in the late seventeenth century.[45] To have mobilised sympathy for Ireland's cause, Molyneux's image of the Irish ancient constitution would have needed to have complemented the English Whig perception of the ancient constitution rather than challenged it. The discrepancy between the two positions was further increased by Molyneux's insistence that from the very beginning Henry had intended to maintain Ireland as a separate and distinct polity, which would serve as an inheritance for his youngest son, John. This, he asserts, was given effect in Henry's donation of Ireland in 1177 in a parliament at Oxford to Prince John with the title of Lord of Ireland. On Henry's death, his heir in England, Richard I, had, so Molyneux asserted, no suzerain rights over Ireland, which but for the accident of Richard's childlessness would have continued separate and distinct from the kingdom of England.[46]

Molyneux's demonstration 'from our best Historians' (p. 5) that the foundation of the English polity in Ireland rested on consent, not conquest, serves two major purposes. First, it constitutes 'an Original Compact' (p. 37) of government which renders the previous relations between England and Ireland irrelevant for the future. This means that all the quasi-mythical pre-Henrician claims to domination over Ireland, from Gurmundus, son of Belin, through Arthur, King Edgar and the alleged suzerainty of William the Conqueror, are written out of the story, together with the parallel claims of Canterbury to primacy over the Irish church.[47] Second, it establishes the universal right to consent to the laws by which one is governed, 'that Universal *Law of Nature,* that ought to prevail throughout the whole World, *of being Govern'd only by such Laws to which they give their own Consent by their Representatives in Parliament*' (p. 48), instanced by Henry's granting the Irish the right to hold parliaments as provided for in the Irish *Modus Tenendi Parliamenta*. In developing this

[44] Atwood, *History of the Dependency*, preface.
[45] [Clement], *Answer to Mr Molyneux*, pp. 24, 61, 110.   [46] *Case*, pp. 44–9, 54–5.
[47] Cf. 1569 Act of Attainder of Shane O'Neill; Coke, *Fourth Institute*, p. 359; Atwood, *History of the Dependency*, pp. 13–26. Even Domville, 'Disquisition', pp. 3–4, had thought it necessary to discuss these claims.

argument later in *The Case*, and drawing on extracts from Hooker's *Laws of Ecclesiastical Polity*, Molyneux exploits the principle of consent to government to enunciate the novel and important claim that no one nation has the right to dominate another, a claim that in the eighteenth century would be seen as highly relevant to England's relations with its other colonial possessions.[48] The final advantage of basing the Irish polity on consent rather than conquest is that it does away with the problem of the latter title requiring a complete military subjugation of the territory in question, not just a partial or incomplete one.[49]

Yet for all these advantages, basing the English title to Ireland on consent left Molyneux with a seemingly insuperable problem which did not arise for those who opted for a 'conquest' approach, namely how to account for the legitimate presence of the English as landowners in Ireland given the original voluntary submission of the native population to Henry II. How Molyneux solved this problem can be seen by examining the critique of the rights conferred by conquest which follows his account of Henry II's expedition to Ireland.[50]

III

As his contemporary English critics Cary and Clement found so embarrassing, Molyneux's discussion of conquest is explicitly founded on the sixteenth chapter of Locke's *Second Treatise of Government*.[51] Though the extent of these borrowings has been established in detail in the notes to Peter Laslett's critical edition of *Two Treatises* of 1960, it is also, as we shall see, illuminating to consider some of Molyneux's more significant departures from Locke's theory of conquest.[52] Molyneux's avowed purpose in

---

[48] *Case*, pp. 3, 151–3(italics in original); extracts cited by Locke, *Treatises*, II, 5n, 134.

[49] Cf. p. 337 above.

[50] To turn from Molyneux's 'history' of the foundation of English government in Ireland to his extended discussion of the rights acquired through conquest is to be reminded of the formal structure of the pamphlet as indicated by its title *The Case of Ireland . . . Stated*. The contemporary term, 'The State of the Case', referred to the printed pleadings produced preliminary to certain hearings in court, in which litigants set out their various arguments in domino fashion. That is, the first legal point is argued, and when that is exhausted the next argument, and so on successively. In his pamphlet Molyneux first presents the case against there having been a hostile conquest of Ireland by Henry II. Then, as if forced to concede on this point, he proceeds to demonstrate how limited are the rights which conquest confers over the conquered. Finally, he argues that even these limited rights have been extinguished by subsequent English concessions to the Irish, starting with John's grant of English law in 1210.

[51] *Case*, pp. 26–7. Cf. Cary, *Vindication of the Parliament of England*, p. 103; [Clement], *Answer to Mr Molyneux*, p. 30.

[52] Cf. Laslett's notes to *Treatises*, II, 4, 134 and 176–86.

discussing conquest is to demonstrate how limited are the rights which even a just conqueror acquires under natural law, and thus indirectly to suggest how unsatisfactory a title conquest affords for annexing the lands of the Irish. Just conquerors are shown to obtain rights only over those who have directly and unjustly resisted them, for which the resisters forfeit their lives, and as such may as an alternative be subjected to slavery. Dismissing unjust conquerors, or aggressors, as acquiring no rights whatsoever over the lives or properties of the conquered, Locke states that those they conquer 'may *appeal*, as *Jephtha* did, *to Heaven*, and repeat their *Appeal*, till they have recovered the native Right of their Ancestors, which was to have such a Legislative over them, as the Majority should approve, and freely acquiesce in'.[53] Molyneux subsequently makes clear, however, that the circumstances of the voluntary submission of the Irish to Henry II were such that their seventeenth-century descendants are in no position to avail themselves of this inextinguishable right of appeal.

Surprisingly, despite the crucial importance which he attaches to the distinction, Locke had devoted little attention to what distinguishes just conquerors from aggressors. His ambiguous reference to William of Normandy's invasion of England ('if it were true . . . that *William* had a Right to make War on this Island') suggests that a just conqueror must have some prior right or claim denied by those who forcefully resist him.[54] Beyond this, Locke, unlike continental jurists such as Grotius or Pufendorf, does not concern himself with what constitutes a just occasion for war, not even citing the right to punish breaches of the law of nature and protect the subjects of another ruler from such violations that some contemporary apologists advanced to justify William of Orange's expedition to England in 1688. Although Molyneux, when condemning war as a means of dealing with commercial rivals later in *The Case*, states: '*War* is only Justifiable for *Injustice* done, or *Violence* offer'd, or *Rights* detain'd' (p. 146), his main discussion of conquest adopts as casual an approach as Locke had done.[55] Ignoring the question of what factors distinguish the just conqueror, all Molyneux offers is the passing comment: 'supposing King *William* the First had *Right* to Invade *England* . . . In like manner supposing *Hen*. II. had *Right* to Invade this Island, and that he had been opposed therein by the Inhabitants . . .' (p. 19).

Despite this initial vagueness, the limitations which Molyneux derives from Locke as to the rights of the just conqueror are extensive. Not only

---

[53] *Treatises*, II, 176.   [54] *Ibid.*, 177.

[55] Though this formulation sounds like an established dictum, I have not been able to identify the source. The reasons listed correspond to those in Pufendorf, *De Iure Naturæ et Gentium*, book 8, chapter 6, section 3 (trans. 1717), p. 88 (italics in original), though their order differs.

does he acquire no rights over the wives and posterity of the conquered, who did not join 'in the *Forcible Opposition* of the Conquerours *Just* Arms', since 'any Man should be punished but for his own fault . . . and as it would be highly Unjust to Hang up the Father for the Sons Offence, so the Converse is equally Unjust, that the Son shou'd suffer any Inconvenience for the Fathers Crime' (p. 22); but for the same reason the just conqueror acquires only very limited rights over the property of the conquered. 'The *Father* by his Miscarriages and Violence can forfeit but his own Life, he involves not his *Children* in his Guilt or Destruction. His *Goods*, which *Nature* (that willeth the Preservation of all *Mankind* as far as possible) hath made to belong to his *Children* to sustain them, do still continue to belong to his *Children*' (p. 24). All that the just conqueror is entitled to, therefore, is recompense for the damage which he has incurred from the unjust resistance of the conquered. This, Locke had implied, would only be small in relation to the value of the land: 'For the Damages of War can scarce amount to the value of any considerable *Tract of Land*, in any part of the World, where all the Land is possessed, and none lies waste.'[56] The residue of the possessions then 'belongs to the *Wife* and *Children* of the Subdued' (p. 24). Such a claim was fairly startling in the light of earlier seventeenth-century conquest theories such as Grotius's.[57] Like Locke, Molyneux concedes that such narrow limitations on the rights of the just conqueror may well appear 'a strange Doctrine' and goes on to admit that 'It must be confess'd that the Practice of the World is otherwise.' What is at issue for Molyneux, however, are the fundamental principles involved: 'we Enquire not now, what is the *Practice*, but what *Right there is to do so*' (pp. 24–5). A further target of Molyneux, as also of Locke in his criticism of the title to rule by conquest, is the claim that the conqueror's right is somehow made retrospectively acceptable by the submission of the conquered. This is principally rejected on the ground that such submission is tantamount to a promise extracted by force, a violation of the law of nature which cannot thus be binding. Such a claim is further shown to rest on faulty reasoning; a conqueror who relies on the submission of the conquered for his title implicitly concedes the need for the consent of the conquered: 'If it be said the Conquered submit by their own *Consent*: Then this allows *Consent* necessary to give the Conqueror a Title to Rule over them' (p. 25). Rejection of this equivocal equation of conquest and the free consent of the conquered

---

[56] Molyneux, *Case*, p. 24. Cf. Locke, *Treatises*, II, 184.

[57] Locke's argument represents a transitional position between Grotius's view that everything and everybody in the conquered territory was at the disposal of the just conqueror, and the later eighteenth-century view of Vattel that the rights of private citizens were in no way affected by conquest. See further Korman, *The Right of Conquest*, pp. 18–25.

was particularly relevant to the Irish situation, since, as we have seen, some proponents of England's title by conquest advanced a secondary, corroborating, title through consent based on the Irish princes' 'voluntary' submission to Henry II in accepting the grant of English law at Lismore.[58]

Having seen how Molyneux follows Locke in relation to the limitations on the just conqueror's acquisition of rights over the conquered, we must now turn to aspects of Locke's theory of conquest that Molyneux fails to adopt. The first and most obvious difference is that while Locke completely rules out the possibility of founding legitimate government on any form of conquest, Molyneux is rather more ambiguous. For Locke, conquest and consent are so contrary in their natures – being said to be as different as demolishing a house and building one – that conquest can be of no relevance to establishing legitimate government.[59] For all his anxiety to deny that Henry II conquered Ireland, Molyneux is by no means as explicit in dismissing conquest as a foundation of government. The requirements of his argument merely commit him to showing that conquest did not happen to have been the foundation of English government in Ireland. But while insisting that Ireland was not conquered by Henry, Molyneux is driven back on exploiting Locke's demonstration that conquest has no effect on the status of the members of the conqueror's army, as a means of bringing the Anglo-Irish back into the story. His problem is that the straightforward account of the origin of the kingdom of Ireland based on the agreement between Henry and the Irish leaves no place in the narrative for the English who accompanied the king to Ireland. Following Locke virtually word for word, Molyneux claims that the conqueror 'gets by his Conquest no Power over those who *Conquered with him*; they that fought on his side, whether as private Soldiers or Commanders, cannot suffer by the Conquest, but must at least be as much Freemen, as they were before' (p. 19).[60] Molyneux then reinforces this general proposition by a comparison between the events of William of Normandy's conquest of England (as retailed by Locke) and Henry II's invasion of Ireland: 'In like manner supposing *Hen. II.* had *Right* to Invade this Island . . . the *English* and *Britains*, that came over and Conquered with him, retain'd all the Freedoms and Immunities of *Free-Born* Subjects; they nor their Descendants could not in reason lose these, for being Successful and Victorious' (p. 19). Thus not only does the identification of the Anglo-Irish as 'the Assisters in the Conquest' (to use the term employed in the marginal heading on p. 19) account for their continuing presence in Ireland, but it also serves to authenticate the post-Revolution Anglo-Irish

---

[58] See p. 336 above.   [59] Locke, *Treatises*, II, 175.   [60] Cf. *ibid.*, 177.

perception of themselves as Englishmen overseas entitled to the same birthright of legal freedoms as Englishmen at home.[61]

So obsessed have recent commentators been with the assertion in the same paragraph that descendants of the 'Ancient *Irish*' (p. 20) scarcely amount to one in a thousand of the population, that the astonishing nature of Molyneux's claim that the English in Ireland represent the descendants of those who conquered Ireland together with Henry II has altogether escaped attention.[62] To put the matter at its most basic: how can Molyneux speak of 'the *English* and *Britains* that came over and conquered with [Henry II]' when he has already so emphatically told us that Henry did not conquer Ireland in 1171–2? It is perhaps not so surprising that Molyneux's contemporary critics, particularly the three English Whigs, John Cary, William Atwood and Simon Clement, each of whom subjected *The Case of Ireland* to detailed page-by-page analysis, failed to pick up on this anomaly, since they were firmly committed to the notion that Henry II had conquered the Irish.[63] But it is startling that subsequent commentators should also have ignored this astonishing discrepancy. It almost seems as if accepting the presence of the Anglo-Irish as conquerors is so self-evident for both the settler and native traditions, that even Molyneux, for all his resolute denial of a conquest by Henry II, cannot conceive the Anglo-Irish in any other guise.

Although prepared to reintroduce conquest to account (by sleight of hand) for the presence and rights of the co-conquerors, Molyneux is equally ready in other parts of his discussion of conquest to reaffirm the

---

[61] Molyneux goes on to show that everybody in Ireland is entitled to claim the birthright of English freedoms, since descendants of the conquered and the co-conquerors become (as Locke states) so inextricably mingled that nobody is in a position to challenge any particular individual's descent; *Case*, pp. 19–20. On the colonists' birthright of English liberties, cf. Hale, *Prerogatives of the King*, p. 34.

[62] Cf. J. G. Simms, *William Molyneux of Dublin* (London, 1982), pp. 105–6; Jacqueline Hill, 'Ireland with Union: Molyneux and his legacy' in John Robertson (ed.), *A Union for Empire: political thought and the British Union of 1707* (Cambridge, 1995), pp. 280–1; Anthony Carty, *Was Ireland Conquered? International law and the Irish question* (London and Chicago, 1996), pp. 68–9. An honourable exception is Jim Smyth, '"Like amphibious animals": Irish Protestants, Ancient Britons, 1691–1707', *Historical Journal*, 36 (1993), pp. 789–90.

[63] It might be objected that Locke is similarly inconsistent in denying a Norman conquest of England, while speaking of 'The *Normans* that came with him, and helped to Conquer, and all descended from them are Freemen and no Subjects by Conquest; let that give what Dominion it will' (*Treatises*, II, 177). However, while Locke's reference to the Norman invasion merely illustrates his theoretical argument, acknowledgement of a conquest of Ireland by Henry II is contrary to the whole thrust of Molyneux's book. Furthermore, Locke, in striking contrast to Molyneux, saw little place for precedent in political discourse: 'at best an Argument from what has been, to what should of right be, has no great force . . .' (*Treatises*, II, 103).

superiority of arguments based on consent. This can be clearly seen in his next significant divergence from Locke, namely his discussion of the consequences of rebellion in relation to conquest, an issue not considered by Locke. Indeed, it may at first sight seem strange that Molyneux himself should find it necessary to introduce this topic, since immediately before his discussion of conquest he had claimed that suppression of rebellion could not be regarded as a conquest: 'If every Suppression of a Rebellion may be call'd a *Conquest*, I know not what Country will be excepted' (p. 17). Despite this apparent inconsistency, the connection between conquest and rebellion turns out to be of enormous importance in allowing Molyneux to account for the Irish losing their property as a punishment for rebellion, while doing away with the limitations on confiscation attaching to rights deriving from conquest. If the suppression of rebellion was to be regarded as a fresh conquest, then, in the light of what Molyneux had already argued, the conqueror would only be entitled to the small proportion of the conquered's property necessary to compensate for the costs of defeating him.[64] Under common law, however (which the Irish have already been shown to have freely accepted from Henry II), forfeiture for rebellion would involve the complete loss of the rebel's property for his posterity as well as himself.

Molyneux raises the topic of rebellion in the context of discussing a son's responsibility for the actions of his father when the latter has resisted a just conqueror. Answering the question firmly in the negative as far as the life and liberty are concerned, since the father has no 'power over the Life and Liberty of his Child' (p. 23), and having already shown that the just conqueror has rights only over those who have personally resisted him and not over the share of their estates to which their innocent wives and children are entitled, Molyneux finally goes on to bring in the apparently unconnected question of the consequences for family property of rebellion within a state:

And tho we find in the Municipal Laws of particular Kingdoms, that the Son loses the Fathers Estate for the Rebellion or other Demerit of the Father, yet this is Consented and Agreed to, for the Publick Safety, and for deterring the Subjects from certain Enormous Crimes that would be highly prejudicial to the Commonwealth. And to such Constitutions the Subjects are bound to submit, having consented to them . . .[65]

---

[64] See p. 349 above.

[65] *The Case*, p. 23: the manuscripts show that Molyneux only added the phrase 'having consented to them' at a later stage. The seemingly redundant remainder of the passage, 'tho' it may be unreasonable to put the like in Execution between *Nation* and *Nation* in the *State of Nature*' (especially when contrasted with p. 22) brings out the hasty and unfinished condition of the book, about which Molyneux wrote to Locke, 19 April 1698; E. S. de Beer (ed.), *The Correspondence of John Locke* (Oxford, 1976–), VI, 376.

Consideration of the consequences of rebellion thus enables Molyneux to achieve the seemingly impossible feat of legitimately transferring the property of the Irish kings and magnates, whose ownership was in no way compromised by their voluntary submission to Henry II, to the present-day Anglo-Irish. The Irish have lost their property not as the result of the initial conquest (or any subsequent conquest putting down rebellion). Rather, they have forfeited it in the course of history on terms to which they themselves had originally consented in receiving English laws and customs from Henry II, under which the penalty for future rebellion was to be forfeiture.[66] Under the terms of the original compact with Henry II, the Irish have therefore already become complicit in their own future dispossession should they, or their descendants, be so unwise as to rebel against the English government. Moreover, given the way in which the meaning of the term 'property' had broadened by the later seventeenth century to include political rights as well as goods and land, the descendants of those who submitted voluntarily to Henry II must be understood to have also forfeited their constitutional rights.[67] Such rights represent the post-Revolution manifestation of the liberties and immunities of Englishmen, granted to their ancestors by Henry II and John, as well as the right to be represented in parliament. Above all, the Irish have incurred these losses in such a way that it is not open to them to claim the rights of peoples who have been forcibly deprived of their property against their consent, rights which Locke elsewhere in the chapter on conquest makes clear persist however long a time has elapsed since the original conquest:

The *Inhabitants* of any Countrey, who are descended, and derive a Title to their Estates from those, who are subdued, and had a Government forced upon them against their free consents, *retain a Right to the Possessions of their Ancestors* . . . Who doubts but the Grecian Christians descendants of the ancient possessors of that Country may justly cast off the Turkish yoke . . . when ever they have a power to do it? For no Government can have a right to obedience from a people who have not freely consent to it . . .[68]

---

[66] The importance of this material for Molyneux is highlighted by the rather laboured changes to the manuscript at this point. Not only did he add the 'having consented to them' referred to in the previous note, but also a reinforcing sentence at the end of the paragraph reading 'For in Settled Governments, Property in Estates is Regulated, Bounded and Determined by the Laws of the Commonwealth, consented to by the People, so that in these, 'tis no Injustice for the Son to lose his Patrimony for his Fathers Rebellion or other Demerit.'

[67] Cf. Howard Nenner, 'Liberty, law and property' in J. R. Jones (ed.), *Liberty Secured? Britain before and after 1688* (Stanford, CA, 1992), pp. 95–8. The reference in *Case*, p. 18 to 'my *Natural Estate*, and Birth-right, of being govern'd only by Laws to which I give my *Consent*' seemingly confirms that Molyneux understood property in the broad sense as including political rights.

[68] Locke, *Treatises*, II, 192.

In contrast to the Greek Christians who had never consented to domination by the Turks, the dispossessed native Irish Catholics are ineluctably bound to obedience to the English government in Ireland because their ancestors had freely submitted to Henry II.

A further reason for Molyneux's rejecting the English title through conquest may have been an awareness of the inherent vulnerability of the concept of the 'just conquest'. While pro-English historians claimed that Henry had invaded Ireland in 1171–72 in furtherance of his existing rights, Irish writers such as Conor O'Mahony in *Disputatio de Iure Regni Hibernicæ* (1645) could just as easily assert that Henry II had no such right and that his 1172 expedition had been an act of unwarranted aggression.[69] This ambiguity as regards just rights in war has obvious parallels with the refutation of the claim that orthodoxy has the right to suppress heresy in Locke's *Letter Concerning Toleration*. Once it is realised that every church is orthodox in its own eyes, the seemingly self-evident rights of orthodoxy over error become impossible to sustain.[70] Similarly, the title to a territory based on conquest is always vulnerable to the belief of the descendants of the conquered that right had been on their side rather than on that of the conquerors. Moreover, certain humanist-educated exponents of Roman law in the Renaissance had rejected the scholastic view that there could be only one just party in a two-sided conflict, arguing that in accordance with natural law anyone who was attacked had a right to defend themselves and their property. The view that both sides in a conflict could equally claim to be in the right was forcefully reasserted by Alberico Gentili in *De Iure Belli* (1612). Since Gentili was professor of civil law at Oxford, and a widely regarded jurist, Molyneux may well have been familiar with his opinion that neither side in a conflict could necessarily be characterised as unjust, if not with Gentili's actual text.[71]

Molyneux's founding the polity on an original act of consent under which the Irish freely accepted English law and custom as granted to them by Henry II has turned out, therefore, to provide a far more secure basis for English property in Ireland than conquest could ever have aspired

---

[69] Conor O'Mahony, *Disputatio apologetica de Iure Regni Hiberniæ pro Catholicis Hibernis, adversus Hereticos Anglos* (Lisbon, 1645), cited by Tadhg Ó hAnnracháin, 'Political ideology and Catholicism in Ireland' in Jane H. Ohlmeyer (ed.), *Political Thought in Seventeenth-century Ireland* (Cambridge, 2000), pp. 159–61. Tadhg Ó hAnnracháin points out that other Catholic writers such as John Lynch, *Cambrensis Eversus* (1662), arguing from an Old English perspective (as opposed to an Old Irish one), accepted the legitimacy of the twelfth-century Henrician conquest.

[70] [John Locke], *A Letter Concerning Toleration* [1689], ed. James Tully (Indianapolis, 1985), p. 32.

[71] Tuck, *The Rights of War and Peace*, pp. 31–3. Cf. Gentili, *De Iure Belli Libri Tres* [1612], trans. J. C. Rolfe (Oxford, 1931), p. 31.

to. Under the title based on consent, the Irish who sought to repudiate the original compact and rebel against English government had become complicit in their future forfeiture for rebellion. By accepting English laws and customs they (or their ancestors) had already bound themselves to accept such a penalty for rebellion. Contrary to what might at first seem the case, therefore, free consent, binding people to its consequences – both foreseen and unforeseen – is ultimately far more coercive than military conquest. Finally, it is tempting to think that Molyneux may also have drawn this Machiavellian insight from Locke. A similarly ambiguous exploitation of the moral status of consent is found in Locke's key move in the transition from the original state of nature to political society in *Treatises*, II, chapter 5. An initial free consent to the adoption of money is shown to lead to a situation in which some people have considerable amounts of land and others none at all.[72] So disadvantageous is this unforeseen outcome for those left without property, that it is as hard to conceive of them freely 'consenting' to it as it is to believe that the Irish who submitted to Henry II would in any meaningful sense have 'consented' to the subsequent dispossession of their descendants for treason.

IV

By this skilful manipulation of the themes of conquest and consent Molyneux has justified both the presence of the Anglo-Irish in Ireland and the deprivation of the Irish and their descendants of their territory and constitution as punishment for rebellion. He has thus solved the apparently baffling conundrum of how the present-day Anglo-Irish could legitimately claim to be the heirs to the 500-year-old polity of the kingdom of Ireland, though differing in race and religion from the original beneficiaries of the agreement with Henry II. A judicious combination of arguments based on conquest and consent has reduced their descendants from the status of the 'People of Ireland' – the moral community which Molyneux invokes as the authenticating source of law and custom – to the nugatory category of 'Irish Papists', guilty of rebellion against both king and Irish Protestants on two separate occasions in the seventeenth century.[73] In their place the Irish Protestants now constitute the 'People of Ireland' (p. 172) and enjoy the moral and political standing which the designation entails. In accusing Molyneux of having failed to realise who were the rightful heirs of the constitution instituted by 'the three first Kings of *Ireland* of the *Norman Race*' (p. 54), his contemporary critic Simon Clement revealed not, as he claimed, Molyneux's ignorance of

[72] See especially *Treatises*, II, 37–50.   [73] Molyneux, *The Case*, pp. 38, 54, 106, 143.

the realities of Irish history, but his own.[74] Far from being the mutually contradictory titles for the foundation of English government in Ireland that on first sight Molyneux may appear to present them as, conquest and consent have turned out to be closely complementary categories in his theory of origins of the kingdom of Ireland, 'as close', indeed, to quote Louis MacNeice, 'as the Irish to the Anglo-Irish'.[75]

---

[74] [Clement], *Answer to Mr Molyneux*, Epistle Dedicatory (A3v–A5r), pp. 4, 163.
[75] Louis McNeice, 'The closing album' in E. R. Dodds (ed.), *Collected Poems* (London, 1963), p. 164.

Principal publications of Aidan Clarke

BOOKS

The Old English in Ireland, 1625–42 (London and Ithaca, 1966; paperback edn, Dublin, 2000)
The Graces, 1625–41 (Dundalk, 1968)
Prelude to Restoration in Ireland: the end of the Commonwealth, 1659–1660 (Cambridge, 1999)

ARTICLES AND CHAPTERS

'November 1634: a detail of Strafford's administration', *Journal of the Royal Society of Antiquaries of Ireland*, 93 (1963)
'The earl of Antrim and the first Bishops' War', *The Irish Sword*, 6 (1963)
'The army and politics in Ireland, 1625–30', *Studia Hibernica*, 4 (1964)
'The policies of the Old English in parliament, 1640–1' in J. L. McCracken (ed.), *Historical Studies V* (London, 1965)
'A note on the parliament of 1634', *Journal of the Royal Society of Antiquaries of Ireland*, 97 (1967)
'The colonization of Ulster and the rebellion of 1641 (1603–60)' in T. W. Moody and F. X. Martin (eds.), *The Course of Irish History* (Cork, 1967; revised and enlarged editions, 1984 and 1994)
'A discourse between two councillors of state, the one of England and the other of Ireland' [BL Egerton MS 917], *Analecta Hibernica*, 26 (1970)
'Ireland and the General Crisis', *Past and Present*, 48 (1970)
'Historical revision: the history of Poynings' Law, 1615–41', *IHS*, 70 (1972)
'The Irish economy, 1600–60'; 'Pacification, plantation and the catholic question, 1603–23'; 'Selling royal favours, 1624–32'; 'The government of Wentworth, 1633–40'; 'The breakdown of authority, 1640–1'. Chapters 6–10, in T. W. Moody, F. X. Martin and F. J. Byrne (eds.), *A New History of Ireland, III: Early Modern Ireland, 1534–1691* (Oxford, 1976)
'Colonial identity in early seventeenth century Ireland' in T. W. Moody (ed.), *Nationality and the Pursuit of National Independence: Historical Studies XI* (Belfast, 1978)
'The Atherton file', *Decies: Journal of the Old Waterford Society*, 9 (1979)
'Hell or Connacht?' in R. Fitzpatrick (ed.), *Milestones or Millstones? Watersheds in Irish history* (Belfast, 1980)

'The genesis of the Ulster rising of 1641' in P. Roebuck (ed.), *Plantation to Partition: essays in Ulster history in honour of J. L. McCracken* (Belfast, 1981)

'Ireland, 1534–1660' in Joseph Lee (ed.), *Irish Historiography, 1970–9* (Cork, 1981)

'Recent work (1977–1982) on early modern British history' (with Patrick Collinson, John Morrill and Geoffrey Parker), *Tijdschrift voor Geschiedenis*, 97 (1984)

'The 1641 depositions' in Peter Fox (ed.), *Treasures of the Library: Trinity College, Dublin* (Dublin, 1986)

'The plantations of Ulster' in Liam de Paor (ed.), *Milestones in Irish History* (Cork, 1986)

'The English' in Patrick Loughrey (ed.), *The People of Ireland* (Belfast, 1988)

'Sir Piers Crosby (1590–1646): Wentworth's "tawney ribbon"', *IHS*, 102 (1988).

'Varieties of uniformity: the first century of the Church of Ireland' in W. J. Shiels and Diana Wood (eds.), *The Churches, Ireland and the Irish*, Studies in Church History, XXV (Oxford 1989)

'Bishop William Bedell (1571–1642) and the Irish reformation' in Ciaran Brady (ed.), *Worsted in the Game: losers in Irish history* (Dublin, 1989)

'Colonial constitutional attitudes in Ireland, 1640–1660', *Proceedings of the Royal Irish Academy*, 90, section c, 11 (1990)

'Bibliographical supplement: introduction, part I' in Moody, Martin and Byrne (eds.), *A New History of Ireland, III: Early Modern Ireland, 1534–1691* (3rd edn, Oxford, 1991)

'A commentary on John Lukacs's "Polite letters"' in Ciaran Brady (ed.), *Ideology and the Historians: Historical Studies XVII* (Dublin, 1991)

'Alternative allegiances in early modern Ireland', *Journal of Historical Sociology*, 5:3 (1992)

'The 1641 rebellion and anti-popery in Ireland' in Brian McCuarta (ed.), *Ulster 1641: Aspects of the rising* (Belfast, 1993)

'1659 and the road to Restoration' in Jane H. Ohlmeyer (ed.), *Ireland: from independence to occupation, 1641–1660* (Cambridge, 1995)

'Patrick Darcy and the constitutional relationship between Ireland and Britain' in Jane H. Ohlmeyer (ed.), *Political Thought in Seventeenth-century Ireland* (Cambridge, 2000)

'Donal Cregan, historian' in M. Ó Siochrú (ed.), *Kingdoms in Crisis: Ireland in the 1640s* (Dublin, 2001)

'A woeful sinner: John Atherton' in V. Carey and U. Lotz-Heumann (eds.), *Taking Sides? Colonial and confessional mentalités in early modern Ireland* (Dublin, 2003)

Index